Financial Assets, Debt and Liquidity Crises

The macroeconomic development of most major industrial economies is characterised by boom-bust cycles. Normally such boom-bust cycles are driven by specific sectors of the economy. In the financial meltdown of the years 2007–9 it was the credit sector and the real-estate sector that were the main driving forces. This book takes on the challenge of interpreting and modelling this meltdown. In doing so it revives the traditional Keynesian approach to the financial–real economy interaction and the business cycle, extending it in several important ways. In particular, it adopts the Keynesian view of a hierarchy of markets and introduces a detailed financial sector into the traditional Keynesian framework. The approach of the book goes beyond the currently dominant paradigm based on the representative agent, market clearing and rational economic agents. Instead it proposes an economy populated with heterogeneous, rationally bounded agents attempting to cope with disequilibria in various markets.

MATTHIEU CHARPE works as an economist for the International Institute for Labour Studies at the International Labour Organization in Geneva.

CARL CHIARELLA is Emeritus Professor and Professor of Quantitative Finance in the School of Finance and Economics at the University of Technology, Sydney.

PETER FLASCHEL is Emeritus Professor in the Faculty of Economics at Bielefeld University.

WILLI SEMMLER is Professor of Economics at The New School for Social Research, New York.

Financial Assets, Debt and Liquidity Crises: A Keynesian Approach

Matthieu Charpe

Carl Chiarella

Peter Flaschel

Willi Semmler

CAMBRIDGE
UNIVERSITY PRESS

CAMBRIDGE UNIVERSITY PRESS
Cambridge, New York, Melbourne, Madrid, Cape Town,
Singapore, São Paulo, Delhi, Mexico City

Cambridge University Press
The Edinburgh Building, Cambridge CB2 8RU, UK

Published in the United States of America by Cambridge University Press, New York

www.cambridge.org
Information on this title: www.cambridge.org/9781107004931

First published 2011
3rd printing 2012

Printed at MPG Books Group, UK

A catalogue record for this publication is available from the British Library

Library of Congress Cataloging in Publication data
Financial assets, debt, and liquidity crises : a Keynesian approach / Matthieu Charpe... [et al.].
p. cm.
Includes bibliographical references and index.
ISBN 978-1-107-00493-1
1. Macroeconomics. 2. Business cycles. 3. Financial crises.
4. Keynesian economics. I. Charpe, Matthieu.
HB172.5.F516 2011
330.9′0511–dc22 2011011256

ISBN 978-1-107-00493-1 Hardback

Contents

Figures

Tables

Notation

Steady state or trend values are indicated by a sub- or superscript 'o'. When no confusion arises, letters F, G, H may also define certain functional expressions in a specific context. A dot over a variable $x = x(t)$ denotes the time derivative, a caret its growth rate; $\dot{x} = dx/dt$, $\hat{x} = \dot{x}/x$. In the numerical simulations, flow variables are measured at annual rates.

As far as possible, the notation tries to follow the logic of using capital letters for level variables and lower case letters for variables in intensive form, or for constant (steady state) ratios. Greek letters are most often constant coefficients in behavioural equations (with, however, the notable exceptions being π, ω).

The following list of symbols corresponds to the notation used in Parts I and II and Chs. 8 and 11 of the book and it contains only domestic variables and parameters (Chs. 9 and 10 contain some notation that is specific to them). Foreign magnitudes are defined analogously and are indicated by an asterisk ($*$). To ease verbal descriptions we shall consider in the following the 'Australian dollar' (or the Norwegian Krona, in Ch. 2) as the domestic currency (A$) and the 'US dollar' ($) as a representation of the foreign currency (currencies).

A. Statically or dynamically endogenous variables

Y	Output of the domestic good
Y^d	Aggregate demand for the domestic good
Y^p	Potential output of the domestic good
Y^e	Expected sales for the domestic good
Y_w^{Dn}, Y_c^{Dn}	Nominal disposable income of workers and asset holders
$u = Y/Y^p$	Rate of capacity utilisation of firms
Y_f	Income of firms
L_1	Population aged 16–65
L_2	Population aged over 65
L_0	Population aged 0–15
L^d	Total employment of the employed
L_f^d	Total employment of the workforce of firms

$L_g^d = L_g^w$	Total government employment (= public workforce)
L_f^w	Workforce of firms
L^w	Total active workforce
u_f^w $(\bar{u}_f^w)$	(Normal) Employment rate of those employed in the private sector
α_l	Participation rate of the potential workforce
$e = L^d/L$	Rate of employment ($\bar{e}$ the employment complement of the Non-Accelerating Inflation Rate of Unemployment or NAIRU)
$C_w(C_w^o)$	Real (equilibrium) goods consumption of workers
$C_c(C_c^o)$	Real (equilibrium) goods consumption of asset owners
$C = C_w + C_c$	Total goods consumption
C_h^s	Supply of dwelling services
C_h^d	Demand for dwelling services
I	Gross business fixed investment
I_h	Gross fixed housing investment
$\Lambda_f, \Lambda_w, \Lambda_g$	Debt of firms, workers, government
$I^a(I^{na})$	Gross (net) actual total investment
$\mathcal{I}$	Planned inventory investment
N	Actual inventories
N^d	Desired inventories
i	Nominal short-term rate of interest (price of bonds $p_b = 1$)
i_l	Nominal long-term rate of interest (price of bonds $p_b = 1/i^l$)
$\pi_b = \hat{p}_b^e$	Expected appreciation in the price of long-term domestic bonds
i^r	Required rate of interest
p_e	Price of equities
$\pi_e = \hat{p}_e^e$	Expected appreciation in the price of equities
$S^n = S_p^n + S_f^n + S_g^n$	Total nominal savings
$S_p^n = S_w^n + S_c^n$	Nominal savings of households
S_f^n	Nominal savings of firms (= $p_y Y_f$, the income of firms)
S_g^n	Government nominal savings
$T^n(T)$	Nominal (real) taxes
G	Real government expenditure
r^e	Expected short-run rate of profit of firms
r^a	Actual short-run rate of profit of firms
r^l	Expected long-run rate of profit of firms
r_h	Actual rate of return for housing services
r_h^l	Expected rate of return for housing services
K	Capital stock
K_h	Capital stock in the housing sector

w^b	Nominal wages including payroll tax
w	Nominal wages before taxes
$\omega = w/p$	Real wages
w^u	Unemployment benefit per unemployed
w^r	Pension rate
w^e, l^e	Wage and labour intensity in efficiency units
p_v	Price level of domestic goods including value-added tax
p_y	Price level of domestic goods net of value-added tax
p_x	Price level of export goods in domestic currency
p_m	Price level of import goods in domestic currency including taxation
p_h	Rent per unit of dwelling
p	Price level (in the one good case)
$\pi^c = \hat{p}_v^e$	Expected rate of inflation or inflation climate
s	Exchange rate (units of domestic currency per unit of foreign currency: A$/$)
$\epsilon_s = \hat{s}^e$	Expected rate of change of the exchange rate
$\sigma = sp^*/p$	Real exchange rate
L	Labour supply
l^e	Labour supply in efficiency units per unit of capital
B	Stock of domestic short-term bonds (index d: stock demand)
B_w	Short-term debt held by workers
B_c	Short-term debt held by asset owners
B^l	Stock of domestic long-term bonds, of which B_1^l are held by domestic asset holders (index d: demand) and B_1^{l*} by foreigners (index d: demand)
B_2^l	Foreign bonds held by domestic asset holders (index d: demand)
E	Equities (index d: demand)
W^n, W	Nominal and real domestic wealth
n	Natural growth rate of the labour force (adjustment towards $\widetilde{n}$)
$z = Y/L^d$	Labour productivity
$\hat{z}$	Rate of Harrod neutral technical change
X	Exports
J^d	Imports
$NX^n = p_x X - sp_m^* J^d$	Net exports in terms of the domestic currency
NFX^n	Net nominal factor export payments (in A$)
NCX^n	Net nominal capital exports (in A$)
τ_w	Tax rate on wages, pensions and unemployment benefits
τ_m	Tax rates on imported commodities

t^n	Total taxes per value unit of capital
g_k^d, g_k	Desired and actual rate of growth of the capital stock K
g_h^d, g_h	Desired and actual rate of growth of the housing capital stock K_h
$\lambda_f, \lambda_w, \lambda_g$	Actual debt to capital ratios of times, workers and government respectively

B. Parameters of the model

The parameters of the non-linear extensions of the model are described when such functions are introduced in the text.

δ_k	Depreciation rate of the capital stock of firms
δ_h	Depreciation rate in the housing sector
α_i^j	All α-expressions (behavioural or other parameters)
β_x	All β-expressions (adjustment speeds)
γ	Steady growth rate in the rest of the world
$\bar{e}$	NAIRU employment rate (NAIRE)
$\bar{u}$	Normal rate of capacity utilisation of firms
$\bar{u}_h$	Normal rate of capacity utilisation in housing
κ_w, κ_p	Weights of short- and long-run inflation ($\kappa_w \kappa_p \neq 1$)
κ	$= (1 - \kappa_w \kappa_p)^{-1}$
y^p	Output-capital ratio
x_y	Export-output ratio
l_y	Labour-output ratio
j_y	Import-output ratio
p_m^*	World market price of import commodities
p_x^*	World market price of export commodities
$\bar{d}$	Desired public or firm debt/output ratio
ξ	Risk and liquidity premium of long-term over short-term debt
ξ_e	Risk premium of long-term foreign debt over long-term domestic debt
τ_c	Tax rates on profit, rent and interest
τ_v	Value-added tax rate
τ_p	Payroll tax
c_y	Propensity to consume goods (out of wages)
c_h	Propensity to consume housing services (out of wages)

C. Further notation

$\dot{x}$	Time derivative of a variable x
$\hat{x}$	Growth rate of x

r_o, *etc.*	Steady state values
$y = Y/K$, *etc.*	Real variables in intensive form
$m = M/(p_v K)$, *etc.*	Nominal variables in intensive form
GBR	Government Budget Restraint

D. Commonly used abbreviations

AD	Aggregate Demand
ADF	Augmented Dickey-Fuller
AS	Aggregate Supply
BOJ	Bank of Japan
CAO	Central Application Office
CB	Central Bank
CDO	Collateralised Debt Obligation
CES	Constant Elasticity of Substitution
DSGE	Dynamic Stochastic General Equilibrium
ECB	European Central Bank
FED	Federal Reserve Board
GBR	Government Budget Restraint
GDP	Gross Domestic Product
GMM	Generalised Method of Moments
GNP	Gross National Product
IMF	International Monetary Fund
KMG	Keynes–Metzler–Goodwin
MBS	Mortgage Backed Security
METI	Ministry of Economy, Trade and Industry
MFT	Mundell–Fleming–Tobin
NAIRE	Non-Accelerating Inflation Rate of Employment
NAIRU	Non-Accelerating Inflation Rate of Unemployment
MOF	Ministry Of Finance
NDP	Net Domestic Product
NDP-F	Net Domestic Product at Factor costs
NNP	Net National Product
ODE	Ordinary Differential Equation
OECD	Organisation for Economic Co-operation and Development
OLG	OverLapping Generations
PC	Phillips Curve
PPP	Purchasing Power Parity
RBC	Real Business Cycle
RMBS	Residential Mortgage Backed Security
WB	World Bank

Preface

When the capital development of a country becomes a by-product of the activities of a casino, the job is likely to be ill-done.

(John Maynard Keynes, *The General Theory of Employment, Interest and Money*, 1936, p.159)

Deflation is also harder to fight than inflation. Over the past two decades central bankers have gained plenty of experience in how to conquer excessive price increases. Japan's ongoing inability to prevent prices falling suggests the opposite task is rather less well understood. Although it is true that heavily indebted governments might be tempted to erode their debts through higher inflation, there are few signs that political support for low inflation is waning.

(*The Economist*, 'The deflation dilemma', 3 June 2010)

The current macroeconomic development of the USA as well as of most major industrial economies is characterised by boom-bust cycles. Such boom-bust cycles start with overconfidence, expectations of high returns and overleveraging. Often an asset price boom goes hand in hand with a credit boom and rising prices. When a downturn is triggered, often initiated by a sudden bankruptcy or similar event, frequently entailing long-term protracted periods of low growth and low employment, prices may fall and periods of debt deflation are experienced. Normally such boom-bust cycles are driven by specific sectors in the economy. In the most recent boom-bust cycle, the credit sector and the real estate sector were the main driving forces.

To study such phenomena, this book takes a macroeconomic perspective. It uses a dynamic framework that builds on the theoretical tradition of non-clearing markets. The modelling philosophy behind most of the chapters of this book is of a Keynesian nature, representing an attempt to revive this theoretical approach on the working of the interaction of the financial market and macroeconomy from a fundamental perspective that also takes account of very recent developments. In its empirical application it refers to the various financial crisis episodes that the new century has already experienced.

The macroeconomic research approach that we employ differs in significant ways from the mainstream literature that uses the Dynamic Stochastic General Equilibrium (DSGE) approach as the basic modelling device. The key difference is that our approach represents an out-of-equilibrium approach which assumes that macrofoundations have to precede microfoundations. Most importantly, we dispense with the well-informed agents that are a key assumption of the rational expectations school. The main features of the DSGE approach are – by contrast – the assumptions of intertemporally optimising agents, rational expectations, competitive markets and price mediated market clearing through sufficiently flexible prices and wages. Credit markets and financial markets have no particular role in this framework since all shocks are real shocks, coming from the real side of the economy. The New Keynesian approach to macroeconomics has, in the last decade or so, to a large extent, also adopted the DSGE framework, building on the intertemporally optimising agents and market clearing paradigm, but favouring more the concept of monopolistic competition, sticky wages and prices and nominal as well as real rigidities. An excellent description of this line of research is Eggertsson and Woodford (2003).

The focus of our approach in this book is to revive the Keynesian business cycle perspective on macrodynamics by giving a central role to the financial sector, as it was already formulated by Keynes (1936). It is well known that the intertemporal approach of smoothly optimising agents and fast adjustments in order to establish temporal or intertemporal marginal conditions in the product, labour and capital markets has not been very successful in matching certain stylised facts on those markets. A further deficiency of the intertemporal decision models is that macroeconomic feedback effects, in particular the ones that come from the financial sector – as well as their stabilising or destabilising impact on the macroeconomy – are rarely considered. Yet such feedback mechanisms, which are indeed relevant for the interaction of all three markets, have been central to the theoretical and empirical explorations by Keynesian authors since the 1930s. The emphasis of the topics here lies in the study of the relative strength and interaction of these feedback mechanisms as well as the transmission channels with respect to all three markets, those for labour, goods and financial assets. We are, in particular, interested in their impact on the stability of the economy once their working is considered in the context of a fully developed dynamical system approach.

We do not deny that forward-looking behaviour and (the attempt at) intertemporal optimisation by economic agents might be relevant for the dynamics of the economy, but in our view the exclusive focus on these issues in the present academic literature leaves completely to one side too many interesting, important and relevant issues. In particular, in the interaction of all three markets there may be non-linear feedback mechanisms at work which do not necessarily give rise to market clearing, nor necessarily to convergence towards a (unique) steady state growth path. Also, as recent research has shown, there is heterogeneity of agents and beliefs present in modern economies, as well as a large variety of informational, structural and financial frictions in the real world. We believe that this leaves many questions open so that the true understanding of the economy might better be pursued by a variety of frameworks. Often it is said with respect to the DSGE models that one needs to use an intertemporal optimising and rational expectations framework, otherwise one would leave 'too much money on the sidewalk'. But one might also add, that by doing so, there is a danger that one might also leave too many problems in macroeconomics on the sidewalk.

Central points in our book on Keynesian macrodynamic theory, and its application to the study of the financial market and boom-bust cycles, are the mechanisms generating non-cleared markets and the phenomenon of disequilibrium recurrently present in certain markets such as the labour or goods markets. In contrast to the tradition that stresses the clearing of all markets at each instant of time,[1] in our modelling approach, as it will be stressed at several occasions throughout this book, disequilibrium situations are the main driving forces of wage and price inflation dynamics. Moreover, disequilibrium in financial markets is often generated by overleveraging in the real sector, the household sector as well as the financial sector of the economy. Some of the markets may act as either stabilising or destabilising forces through a variety of different macroeconomic channels such as the real wage feedback channel, product market, financial market as well as debt devaluation channels, showing that there are indeed different (and also valid) possibilities to specify and analyse the dynamics of the macroeconomy in a different way from that of the DSGE framework.

Due to the fact that in our modelling approach the stability of the analysed dynamical system is not imposed *ab initio* by the assumption of rational expectations (which requires that the economy always 'jumps' to some stable path and therefore always converges to the steady state after any type of shock), its stability properties (and its analysis) are based on the relative strength of the interacting macroeconomic and financial feedback channels. Such stability analysis, despite its importance for the understanding of the dynamics of an economy, does not seem to be relevant for the literature based on the rational expectations market clearing tradition and divergent paths (apart from anomalies) do not appear to be an issue there. However, the ongoing occurrence of 'bubbles' and 'herding' in financial markets worldwide, as well as the large macroeconomic imbalances present nowadays in the global economy through overleveraging indicate that such divergent paths can indeed take place in significant and sometimes long-lasting ways.

In our framework we finally dispense with another prominent assumption of mainstream economics, namely the assumption of a single representative household. In a capitalist economy there are – almost by definition – always at least two representative households to be considered, workers and asset holders. Of course, there exist more household types in actual economies and also hybrid configurations of them, but certainly not a single type as far as utility formation and budget constraints are concerned, as the current subprime and credit crises make obvious. Macroeconomic theory with only 'Robinson Cruse', and not also 'Man Friday', not only ignores the conflict over income distribution and labour and employment issues, but also neglects the impact of financial and real boom-bust cycles on the labour market and job creation and destruction. The labour market will thus play an important part in our modelling strategy.

A number of professional colleagues, too numerous to name here, have contributed to the present project through stimulating discussions on various aspects of the subject

[1] This is really an heroic assumption in a continuous-time modelling framework.

matter of this book as well as on related research projects. We are also grateful for comments and criticisms we have received from numerous participants at presentations of aspects of the material of this book at numerous international conferences and research seminars. Of course, we alone are responsible for the remaining errors in this work. We are indebted to two anonymous referees who read the original version of the manuscript and offered many, even detailed, suggestions for its improvement. We also wish to thank Stephanie Ji-Won Ough of the University of Technology, Sydney 'UTS' for her excellent editorial work. Finally we would like to thank Chris Harrison of Cambridge University Press for all he has done to make the publication process go as smoothly as it has.

1 Financial crises and the macroeconomy

Success breeds disregard of the possibility of failures. The absence of serious financial difficulties over a substantial period leads ... to a euphoric economy in which short-term financing of long-term positions becomes the normal way of life. As the previous financial crisis recedes in time, it is quite natural for central bankers, government officials, bankers, businessmen and even economists to believe that a new era has arrived.

(Hyman P. Minsky, *'Can "It" Happen Again?' Essays on Instability and Finance*, 1982, p. 213).

As the above citation from Hyman Minsky shows, one may think of modern macroeconomic development as a sequence of boom-bust cycles. Boom-bust cycles occur not only for specific sectors, but also for the entire macroeconomy. Macroeconomic boom periods are usually characterised by overvaluation of assets, overconfidence, expectations of high returns and undervaluation of risk, and by overleveraging. Bust periods reverse confidence and expectations. The current macroeconomic developments in the USA as well as in other regions of the world have features of a typical bust period that is characteristic of boom-bust cycles. In the boom period not only do prices increase but there is often also an asset price boom and credit boom. High asset prices serve as collateral for new borrowing. When a downturn starts, often initiated by a sudden bust, and frequently entailing long-term protracted periods of low growth and low employment, prices may fall and periods of debt deflation are often experienced. Normally such boom-bust cycles are driven by specific sectors in the economy. In the recent boom-bust cycle in the USA, the real estate and credit sectors were the main driving forces. Open economies may magnify those boom-bust scenarios.

Much theoretical and empirical work on the impact of the financial sector on the macroeconomy has been undertaken by different schools of economic thought. One currently prominent school builds on the theory of perfect capital markets, which are mostly assumed in intertemporal general equilibrium theory, which deals with stochastic growth and develops into Real Business Cycle (RBC) theory. Yet it is rare to find in the literature from this school explicit modelling of the interaction of credit, asset prices and real economic activity. In the context of that class of models it is in particular difficult to explain credit crunches and the rising default premia at the onset of the bust periods. Default or risk premia are explained on the basis of consumption-based asset pricing models, which have great difficulty in matching actual risk premia.

In contrast, many theoretical and empirical studies have applied the theory of imperfect capital markets. Moreover, there are other traditions, for instance, the Keynesian tradition as revived by Minsky (1975, 1986), Mishkin (1998), Kindleberger (2000) and Tobin (1975) that have been very influential in studying the interaction between financial markets and economic activity. This approach puts stress on how the instability of credit has a strongly magnifying effect on macroeconomic activity. Another important perspective on this interaction is that of Shiller (1991, 2001), which also explicitly deals with the overconfidence and overreaction in financial markets.

Our own thinking on these issues is heavily influenced by the Keynesian tradition. Yet one can also draw upon recent developments in information economics, as it has been developed by Stiglitz and others, wherein systematic attempts have been made to describe how actual financial markets operate. Many studies of financial markets, and this is Stiglitz's view, claim that a crucial impediment to the functioning of the financial system is asymmetric information. In this situation, one party to a financial contract has much less information than the other. Borrowers, for example, usually have much better information about the potential returns of their investment projects and the associated risks than do the potential lenders. Asymmetric information leads to two other basic problems: adverse selection and moral hazard. Adverse selection occurs when those borrowers with the greatest potential for default actively seek out loans. Moral hazard takes place after a transaction has taken place. Here, lenders are subject to hazards since the borrower has incentive to engage in activities that are undesirable from the lenders' point of view.

The Keynesian view as well as the information-based view of the financial markets explains why there is an important role for the government in the regulation and supervision of the financial marketplace. To be useful, proper financial architecture, regulation and supervisory mechanisms must aim towards the maximisation of access to information, while minimising overconfidence and underestimation of risk. This requires transparency and the creation of information through proper accounting, screening and monitoring. Firms and banks need to be required to adhere to standards of accounting and to make known publicly information about their sales, assets and earnings. Additionally, safety nets for institutions as well as for individuals are necessary to avoid the risks from a rapid liberalisation of financial markets. Before starting our formal analysis it is worthwhile for us to describe three types of typical financial crises that macroeconomies have experienced repeatedly over many decades.

1.1 Open economies, foreign debt and currency crises

The first type of crisis that we want to discuss is the financial crisis triggered by currency crises. In open economies the boom period is often accompanied by a consumption boom, huge consumption imports and current account deficits. Capital market liberalisation became popular during the 1980s and 1990s. Financial liberalisation has actively been advocated by such organisations as the International Monetary Fund (IMF) and the World Bank (WB) and has been pursued by many governments since the 1980s.

Liberalisation of capital markets was thought to generate a long period of expansion of the world economy due to the establishment of global markets for products and financial services.

Yet as others have warned the rapid liberalisation and enlargement of the financial markets may lead to more financial instability which, in turn, could be devastating, see for example Stiglitz *et al.* (2006). The Mexican (1994), Asian (1997/8) and Russian (1998) financial crises demonstrated the degree to which a too-rapid market liberalisation could lead to a currency crisis wherein a sudden reversal of capital flows is followed by financial instability and a consequent decline in economic activity. It is interesting to note that this very volatility and lack of trust, especially when combined with the increasing globalisation of markets, had also led to new financial products, spread across the world, and to heightened activity in these same markets. Usually the operations were undertaken with little or unchecked collateral on the borrowers' side.

In contrast to the foregoing view, the liberalisation of financial markets has been more positively evaluated by other schools of thought. An emphasis on the benefits of financial globalisation in general can be found within the American business and financial community, citing mainly the possible benefits of free capital mobility such as:

- reduced trading costs, and in particular low costs of financial transactions;
- an increase in investment returns;
- a lowering of the cost of capital when firms invest;
- an increase in liquidity in the financial market;
- an increase in economic growth and positive employment effects.

Certainly, capital market liberalisation has benefits. Yet, as mentioned earlier, there are also costs if it is done too quickly and imprudently, in particular with inappropriate sequencing.[1] Often the theory of perfect capital markets has been used in order to justify rapid and radical market liberalisation, in particular product and capital market liberalisation. Whereas some parts of the academic profession broadly continue to see the benefits of market liberalisation outweighing the costs, others see increasing problems, so that the strategy of rapid capital market liberalisation has recently come under scrutiny. Too rapidly liberalised capital markets, with a wrong sequencing, can trigger financial instability, contagion effects and strong negative external effects on the real side of the economy.

The negative externalities that can arise from rapid capital market liberalisation (CML) have been laid out in the recent book by Stiglitz *et al.* (2006). This book gives a fair account of the pros and cons of rapid CML. The major argument of the authors is that too rapid a CML leads to financial instability and to boom and bust cycles, hampering economic growth in the long run. Taking the view that capital markets are basically imperfect, they argue that free capital markets have significantly different

[1] Meaning for instance liberalisation occurs before appropriate regulations are put into place.

effects than free trade. CML might not produce the promised benefits but rather, as Stiglitz *et al.* (2006, Chs. 10 and 11) summarise:

- National fiscal and monetary policies become difficult to pursue, since national governments have to respond exclusively to the signals of the capital market, when pursuing policy objectives.
- Boom and bust cycles, rather than steady development, may come about. Booms in the housing sector, in land prices and equity prices as well as consumer purchases of imported goods lead to distortions of balanced growth, and are usually corrected by periods of bust.
- Financial instability and credit crises, leading to a general contraction of credit and higher risk premia for loans, can hamper economic development.
- There are strong contagion effects of financial busts, since capital movements – the inflow and outflow of capital – are fast in comparison with the changes in trade flows.
- The low income segment of the population as well as small businesses cannot insure and protect themselves against the risks that arise when bubbles burst and recessionary periods occur (or are prolonged). Indeed, those groups are very much affected.

Thus the proponents of (fast) CML frequently overlook the imperfect working of capital markets and attribute too much to their self-correcting mechanism. Frequently there is also mention of insufficient regulatory or supervisory institutions for the banking system, the stock market or the real estate market such that there are no stabilising forces or safety nets for certain countries – this in particular holds, as recent history of financial events has shown, for emerging markets and developing economies. Yet, even advanced countries with a long tradition of regulatory institutions such as for the banking sector and stock markets are also not protected from such events and the negative externalities of financial crashes and busts – as recent history, after the introduction of the new wave of financial innovations, has shown.

Already in the 1990s much critical work on the issue of open economy financial market liberalisation and currency and financial crises was published. Mishkin (1998), for example, posited an explanation of the Asian financial crisis of 1997/8 using the above information-theoretic ideas. A similar theory by Krugman (1999, 2000) pointed to the deteriorating balance sheets of banks and firms in the process of currency and capital market liberalisation. Miller and Stiglitz (1999) employed a multiple-equilibria model to explain financial crises in general.

Whereas these theories point to the perils of too rapid a liberalisation of financial markets and to the role of government bank supervision and guarantees, Burnside *et al.* (2001) view government guarantees as actual causes of financial crises. These authors argue that the lack of private hedging of exchange rate risk by firms and banks led to financial crises in Asia. Other authors, following the bank run model of Diamond and Dybvig (1983), argue that financial crises occur if there is a lack of short-term liquidity. Further modelling of financial crises triggered by exchange rate shocks can be found in Schneider and Tornell (2004), Edwards (1999) and Rogoff (1999), with Rogoff discussing the role of the IMF as the lender of last resort. A recent book elaborating on the sequence of events in many types of financial crisis is that of Reinhart and Rogoff (2009).

Recent work on the roles of currency in financial crises can be found in Corsetti *et al.* (1998), Aghion *et al.* (2004), Kato and Semmler (2005), Flaschel and Semmler (2006), Proaño *et al.* (2007) and Röthig *et al.* (2007). Röthig *et al.* pursue a macroeconomic approach to model currency and financial crises and consider also the role of currency hedging in mitigating financial crises.[2] A further review of the stylised facts and literature on the interrelation of currency crisis, financial crisis and output loss is given in Chapter 2, where a proper modelling of this type of crisis is presented.

1.2 Household borrowing, debt default and banking crises

Another type of financial market instability and crisis arose from the interplay of household borrowing, a housing boom and new financial engineering tools developed and applied by the financial market. Although the financial market should play the essential role of channelling funds to households and firms that have potentially good buying or investment opportunities, and financial markets should permit economic agents to borrow against future income, this has not always been properly done.

Financial deepening is often accompanied by waves of financial innovations. Recent new financial innovations are hedge funds and all kinds of options and derivative instruments. Collateralised debt obligations (CDOs) and collateralised loan obligations (CLOs) are financial instruments where the loans of households and companies are turned into tradable securities (the so-called process of securitisation). These are relatively new financial instruments that have helped to diversify risk for the issuer of household mortgages or commercial credits. The number of such innovative financial products has grown rapidly, in fact credit derivatives in the form of credit default swaps, mortgage-backed securities or loan-backed securities have expanded exponentially, but so too have financial markets for them, which have also grown enormously. Yet in the USA as well as in many other countries, this interplay of new financial instruments and real estate boom has helped to build up an enormous bubble in real estate as well in the financial sector.

It is worth focusing more in detail on the housing and financial sector bubble. In the USA this triggered what has become known as the subprime crisis. How did it evolve, and why did it lead to a financial market meltdown, creating contagion effects and externalities not only to other sectors in the USA but had worldwide repercussions? Both the Federal Reserve Board (FED) and the European Central Bank (ECB) had few means to deal with this sudden meltdown and bust. Let us first survey briefly what led to the financial market meltdown from the middle of 2007.

As recent events have shown, reflected also in recent academic debates, there are large externalities and contagion effects arising from financial instabilities – either

[2] For further details on the early literature on currency and financial crises, see Reinhart and Rogoff (2009) and Semmler (2011).

arising from the stock market (as in the 1990s) or from the credit market, for example as now triggered by the subprime crisis. The evolution of the subprime crisis and its effect on the financial sector in the USA is described by the following trends:[3]

- the current financial market crisis is likely to have originated in low interest rates, rapidly rising household debt and a bubble in the housing market (high housing prices compared with fundamentals);
- the bubble phase has undergone an acceleration due to the outsourcing of risk because of the securitisation of mortgages (that were packaged and sliced into risky securities of different types, in particular CDOs);
- expectation of returns from investment in real estate and CDOs were rising, due to low interest rates, low default rates and high recovery rates;
- liquidity in the housing sector (and financial market) was pumped up by capital inflows, partly from abroad;
- the burst of the bubble was triggered by the failure of hedge funds (for example by the hedge funds of Bear Stearns), triggering a credit crunch in the banking sector;
- default risk and risk premia suddenly shooting up and a credit crunch occurring (as at the beginning of all downturns);
- the feedback to the real sector causing the growth rate of GDP to fall, with further feedback effects expected from the real to the financial side, that is, insolvency of financial institutions.

Indeed, as we have recently experienced, besides the open economy and currency crisis mechanism, an important financial market instability is likely to arise from the interplay of the real estate boom and the financial market boom. In the USA the financial market crisis of 2007/8 originated in the interaction of the housing market and the banking sector. Often one can also observe other scenarios; see Kindleberger (2000). For instance a stock market crash, together with the instability of credit, can trigger a downturn. Yet, this time in the USA it was not the stock market that triggered the bust. The stock market reaction came later. When the investors in subprime mortgages felt the first fallout, the holders of those securities experienced a massive credit crunch.

The real estate and banking crisis in the USA and UK has all the hallmarks of a boom-bust cycle. Although there was a regular business cycle from 2001 to 2007/8 the real estate boom-bust cycle had already started in the middle of the 1990s, during the information technology and stock market boom, the latter lasting from the beginning of the 1990s to 2000/1.

There are many views as to why the boom-bust cycle in real estate continued beyond the regular economic expansion, ending with the contraction of 2001. Some researchers attribute the boom-bust cycle in the real estate market and the run-up of the housing prices to the Greenspan low interest rate policy. In contrast, one might say that interest rates had already come down earlier (from the middle of the 1980s) with the decline of the inflation rate, but the housing boom started much later. There is also some truth

[3] For details see Semmler and Bernard (2009).

in the view that Greenspan nowadays has expressed: the FED can lower the short-term interest rate, but it has no power over the long-term interest rate, and thus the yield curve. Indeed, the yield curve over a long time period, in fact until quite recently, was rather flat or even downward sloping. The USA had become a magnet of capital inflow and attracted savings from the rest of the world and this has kept the interest rate at the long end rather low.

A further explanation, proposed by Piazzesi and Schneider (2009) and Piazzesi *et al.* (2005), uses a portfolio approach and argues that the fraction of housing assets in household portfolios went down in the 1980s, whereas the fraction of equity held in the portfolios rose rapidly in the 1990s. Then, the trend reversed starting in 2000/1 with a rapid increase of housing assets in portfolios and a decline in the equity fraction. They attribute this to the shift in expected returns from three types of asset: from nominal assets (bonds), from equity and from real estate assets. Piazzesi *et al.* (2005) also argued that this large change in asset allocation has something to do with the inflation rate since the 1980s. Housing assets and equity assets show a negative co-movement which seems to arise from their different sensitivity to inflation rates. Yet, still the question remains as to why the equity prices and returns relatively declined as compared with housing prices and returns. Why did the housing asset boom take over from the equity boom starting at the end of the 1990s?

One could realistically attribute the housing price boom, as Shiller (2000) does, to some overshooting mechanism and excess volatility, namely first in the equity market and then in the real estate sector. Shiller also stresses the mechanism of overvaluation, overconfidence and overleveraging as causes of the housing and banking boom.

As above mentioned, another explanation refers to the recent development of new financial instruments, in particular credit derivatives, which have been rapidly and widely employed in the financial market. This has led, as many researchers have pointed out, to the outsourcing and diversification of risk. The main instruments in the real estate sector were mortgage-backed securities (MBS) and CDOs.

Yet, most of the literature seems to explain only the expansion period of the boom-bust cycle in the real estate market. The subsequent issue is thus how the bust was triggered. One might need a theory that explains both the excessive run-up in asset prices as well as the surprisingly fast decline and bust in the real estate sector.

For those asset pricing theories that adopt an intertemporal approach the occurrence of sudden busts is also a problem. According to the intertemporal view, the asset price represents the discounted expected future income stream, and these expectations drive the asset prices. Yet, usually it is hard to explain boom-bust cycles of the magnitude observed by an intertemporal model, since temporary blips or temporary strong deviations of pay-offs from the trend usually get smoothed out in intertemporal models, and boom-bust cycles are rarely observable in such models. Even strong technology shocks are not able to deliver such results.

The way, however, such boom-bust cycles have been constructed is to allow for expectation dynamics – for some time periods – that get revised after some time.

When agents realise that they have followed incorrect expectation dynamics this might then trigger at some point some sudden revision of expectations. Models of this type can be found in Beaudry and Portier (2004), Christiano *et al.* (2006, 2008) and also Lansing (2008), all of which work with the above mentioned mechanism of expectation dynamics.

Yet, in most literature based on the Dynamic Stochastic General Equilibrium (DSGE) model, the expectation dynamics concern technology shocks, which are capable of explaining only a small part of the boom-bust cycle in asset markets. Another source of expectation dynamics would be related to the expected pay-offs which themselves could be ill-founded, at least in the long run. In this approach we also can allow expected pay-offs to be discounted in order to arrive at some asset price dynamics. This looks like a realistic approach where one can assume that there is some expectation (as erroneous and ill-founded as it might be) that will be self-justifying. But then certain events may trigger the collapse of this self-justifying mechanism.[4] Since the real estate sector has the feature of being mostly credit financed, an important component of this mechanism is the build-up of debt. Yet, the expansion and then the contraction of credit, has something to do with the instability of credit as mentioned in Kindleberger (2000) to be relevant for the Great Depression. We thus need to explain the rapid build-up and contraction of credit, and thus the triggering of a collapse in asset prices. A detailed modelling of some of these issues in the context of this type of financial crisis is undertaken in Chapter 3.

1.3 Overleveraging, debt and debt deflation

Overborrowing is not only typical for households but also for commercial banks, investment banks, firms, states and even entire countries. If there is general overleveraging and unsustainable debt, triggering a credit crisis there may not be only a downturn, but also a deflation, in commodity prices as well as in asset prices. In recent public debate on problems of the world economy, indeed 'deflation' or more specifically 'debt deflation,' has again become an important topic. The possible role of the credit crisis and debt deflation in triggering the Great Depression of the 1930s has come back into academic studies as well into the writings of economic and financial journalists. It has been observed that there are similarities between recent global trends and the 1930s, namely the joint occurrence of high levels of debt and falling prices. But with prices falling the real value of debt will rise. Debt deflation thus concerns the interaction of high nominal debt of banks, firms, households and countries and shrinking economic activity due to falling output prices and increasing real debt.

There is often another mechanism accompanying the one above, focusing on how a large amount of debt may exert an impact on macroeconomic activity by working through the asset market. Asset price inflation during economic expansions normally

[4] For details of such a model, see Semmler and Bernard (2009).

gives rise to generous credit extension and lending booms. Assets with inflated prices serve as collateral for borrowing by firms, households or countries. On the other hand, when asset prices fall the borrowing capacity of economic agents shrinks, financial failures may set in, macroeconomic activity decreases and consequently large output losses may occur.

Countries that have gone through such booms and busts are some Asian countries (in particular Japan), Russia and Brazil in 1998 and 1999. In all of those countries as well as during the financial crisis in Mexico in 1994 asset price inflation and lending booms entailed subsequent debt crisis and asset price deflation. Thus, usually the mechanism of debt deflation due to falling output prices has been accompanied by the asset price deflation mechanism. Some academic commentators have recently also criticised the single-minded preoccupation of certain central banks and the IMF with inflation, and the word reflation has been coined in order to stress the fact that providing some room for inflation should be of help in preventing global financial crises. The viewpoint of the FED and of the government in the USA has of course received particular attention in this respect. When Alan Greenspan was chair of the FED, he was widely regarded as a person taking wise monetary policy decisions by lowering interest rates in 1998 and 1999 as a pre-emptive strike against a global debt deflation process.

Moreover, global growth strategies, and the elements they should contain, continue to be discussed in academic and policy circles. The need for a fundamental restructuring of the IMF and World Bank and a new financial architecture is currently stressed in such discussions, based on the judgement that in 2007/8 the world faced its biggest financial challenge since the 1930s. Debt deflation and its destabilising potential therefore appears to be an important threat that the world economy is still facing.

Modern macroeconomic theory, as it has evolved since the Second World War, has paid scant attention to the above described mechanism of debt deflation. No doubt this is due to the fact that during that period the major economies in the world experienced a long period of growth followed by a long period of inflation from which we have only recently emerged. The classic study of debt deflation remains Fisher (1933), although Minsky (1975, 1982) in his writings on the financial instability hypothesis continued to warn of the dangers of another great depression. There is therefore an urgent need for economists to model the process of debt deflation in its interaction with monetary and fiscal policies that may stop the process of rising debt, falling output and asset prices and a collapse into depression.

In Chapter 4 we embed the process of debt accumulation and debt deflation via a sequence of partial models of debt accumulation and price deflation into fully integrated macroeconomic models of closed and open economies that are consistent with respect to budget constraints. At the core of the model will be firms that finance fixed investment as well as involuntary inventory investment not from retained earnings, but by loans from the credit market. In that chapter we neglect equity finance. Our model will thus focus mainly on the first mechanism of the debt deflation process, the destabilising role of flexible wages and prices in economies with high nominal debt. The destabilising role of asset prices will be by and large neglected.[5]

Our macroeconomic model contains a sufficient number of agents and markets to capture the essential dynamic features of modern macroeconomies, and stresses the dynamic interaction between the main feedback loops of capital accumulation, debt accumulation, price and wage inflation/deflation, exchange rate appreciation/depreciation, inventory accumulation and government monetary and fiscal policies. Our modelling framework relies on previous work by the authors and contributions by other co-authors.[6] The essential difference is that here we focus on debt-financed investment of firms in place of pure equity financing considered in the earlier works. We will thus add a further important feedback loop missing in our earlier approach to macro modelling, namely, from a partial point of view, the destabilising Fisher debt effect of deflationary (or inflationary) phases of capital accumulation arising from the creditor–debtor relationship between asset-owning households, banks and firms.

Keen (2000) has investigated the Fisher debt effect, between firms and financial intermediaries, in the context of an augmented classical growth cycle model of Goodwin (1967) type. He has found that it may imply local asymptotic stability for the overshooting mechanism of the growth cycle, but the overshooting can lead to instability, for high debt outside a corridor around the steady state of the model. In addition he provides an interesting discussion of Fisher's vision of the interaction of over-indebtedness and deflation and of Minsky's financial instability hypothesis. Keen extends the proposed model of the interaction of indebted firms and income distribution to also include a study of the role of government policies in such an environment. He focuses on nominal adjustment processes in the place of the real ones of the classical growth cycle model.

We will start our analysis in Chapter 4 from Keen's 3D model of the debt accumulation process, expand it by flexible prices (to obtain a 4D model), include inflationary expectations and an interest rate policy rule (so getting to an 8D model) and will finally provide general 16D dynamics with a complete representation of stock-flow interactions, adjusting prices and quantities, asset market behaviour, issues of open economies and fiscal and monetary policy rules. We discuss briefly subjects of importance in the development of market crises (and domestic or foreign policy intervention) on this general level. These issues have to be integrated and investigated, however, in much more detailed ways in order to allow a full treatment of the dangers of the joint occurrence of debt and deflation in certain areas of the world economy or on a worldwide scale.

1.4 Plan of the book

In Part I we provide an introduction to our modelling philosophy of financial and real interactions. We provide a basic model of the three types of financial crisis phenomena

[5] For work on the credit market, economic activity and the destabilising role of asset price inflation and deflation, see Minsky (1975) and Mishkin (1998).

[6] See Chiarella and Flaschel (2000), Chiarella *et al.* (2000) and Chiarella and Flaschel (1999b,c,d).

as discussed above and as observed in the last few decades. We model (1) the currency and financial crises in open economies with a large amount of foreign debt, (2) the US current mortgage and real estate crisis and its spillover as a credit crisis for the whole banking sector, and (3) we deal with the effect of general overleveraging and the consequent threat of the emergence of the process of debt deflation. All of these types of financial crises are fundamentally overleveraging crises that first appear as liquidity crises and then as solvency crises. The liquidity crises may be associated with what Keynes had called the liquidity trap.

In Part II we discuss a general framework for Keynesian macroeconometric model building from the out-of-equilibrium perspective, in the form of a structural macroeconometric model of the interaction of financial and real markets. It derives the intensive form of this type of model and thus (for econometric application) the stationary variables of the model, since the existence of a (uniquely determined) steady state in these variables can be shown for this matured type of Keynesian model. We use various techniques to discuss the feedback channels of this general approach to macrodynamics, first in isolation and then in their interaction.

In Part III finally we apply the framework developed to issues of the interaction of firms' investment decisions with the emergence of overleveraging and then debt deflation spirals. We here refer to the relationship of firms and commercial banks on the market for loans, on the one hand, and to the feedbacks between households' housing demand decisions and the mortgage supply by asset holders on the other hand. We also elaborate the processes of debt default and bankruptcies that may follow, if the liquidity problem turns into a solvency problem for households, banks or firms. In a further chapter we investigate the performance of the Japanese economy in the light of such a crisis scenario. In contrast to the related models of Part I we use more complete approaches here to study such phenomena.

Part I

The non-linear dynamics of credit and debt default

2 Currency crisis, credit crunches and large output loss

2.1 The emergence of currency crises

With the end of the Bretton Woods system in the 1970s and the financial market liberalisation in the 1980s and 1990s, the international economy has experienced several financial crises in certain countries or regions entailing, in most cases, declines in economic activity and large output losses. This has occurred regardless of whether the exchange rates were pegged or flexible. There appear to be destabilising mechanisms at work from which even a flexible exchange rate regime cannot escape. In this chapter we review some of the stylised facts that appear to be common to such financial crises and develop a Mundell–Fleming–Tobin (MFT) type model based on Rødseth (2000, Ch. 6). Our approach builds on Miller and Stiglitz (1999) and takes up Krugman's (1999a, 1999b, 1999c and 2001) suggestions in order to study the real and financial crises generated by large exchange rate swings.

With respect to exchange rate shocks due to currency runs triggering financial and real crises, there are three views, in fact three generations of models, that have been presented in the literature. The first view maintains that news on macroeconomic fundamentals (such as differences in economic growth rates, productivity differences and differences in price levels, in short-term interest rates as well as in monetary policy actions) may cause currency runs. The second view maintains that speculative forces drive exchange rates where there can be self-fulfilling expectations at work, destabilising exchange rates without deterioration of fundamentals. Third, following the theory of imperfect capital markets, it has recently been maintained that the dynamics of self-fulfilling expectations depend on some fundamentals, for example, the strength and weakness of the balance sheets of the economic units such as households, firms, banks and governments. From the third point of view we can properly study the connection between the deterioration of fundamentals, exchange rate volatility, financial instability and declining economic activity. Although recently diverse microeconomic as well as macroeconomic theories have been proposed to explain currency runs, financial crises and recessions, we think that particularly relevant are those types of models that show how currency crises may entail destabilising mechanisms, leading possibly through non-linearities and multiple equilibria, to large output losses.

Such a model type can be found in Miller and Stiglitz (1999), who base their model on the work by Kiyotaki and Moore (1995) and various papers by Krugman (1999, 2000). For a detailed survey of the literature on exchange rate volatility, financial crisis and large output loss, see Semmler (2011, Ch. 12). The work by Krugman is most closely related to this chapter. It, however, contains a different motivation as to how the destabilising mechanism, triggered through currency crises, actually takes its course. Our model is narrower than the framework discussed in Krugman and thus concentrates on a few but essential elements of the currency crises. This is due to the fact that many behavioural equations of the MFT type model that is employed remain stable despite large currency depreciation, implied large declines in investment and large output losses.

The remainder of the chapter is organised as follows.[1] Section 2.2 introduces some stylised facts. Section 2.3 presents the basic model. Section 2.4 then adds the budget restrictions and considers the accounting relationships that characterise the model in order to provide a clear picture of the scope of the model. Section 2.5 studies the dynamics under flexible exchange rates and Section 2.6 under the breakdown of a fixed exchange rate system. In Section 2.7, we significantly extend the model towards a treatment of international capital flows and show that this gives further momentum to the crises scenarios we have developed earlier, for the case of only domestic trade in foreign assets. Section 2.8 concludes the chapter.

2.2 Some stylised facts

In recent times there have been major episodes of international financial crises in certain regions or countries entailing a large output loss. The balance sheets of firms, households, banks and governments were central in this context. Weak balance sheets of these economic units mean that liabilities are not covered by assets. In particular heavy external debt denominated in foreign currency, for example dollars, can cause a sudden reversal of capital flows and a currency crisis. Credit risk and a sudden reversal of capital flows is often built up by a preceding increase in foreign debt. The deterioration of balance sheets of households, firms and banks has often come about by a preceding lending boom, increased risk taking and an asset price boom. Subsequently a currency crisis is likely to occur, entailing a rise in the interest rate, a stock market crash and a banking crisis and large output loss. Yet, financial and exchange rate volatility do not always lead to an interest rate increase and a stock market crash. It is thus not necessary that financial instability will be propagated. The major issue is in fact what the assets of the economic units represent. If economic units borrow against future income streams they may have to use net worth as collateral. The wealth of the economic units (or of a country) are the discounted future income streams. Sufficient net wealth makes

[1] This chapter is based on the MFT baseline exchange rate model of Krugman type outlined in Flaschel and Semmler (2006). It generalises their treatment of financially driven exchange rate crises towards an inclusion of international capital flows in the balance of payments of the domestic economy.

the agents solvent otherwise they are threatened by insolvency which is equivalent to saying that the liabilities outweigh the assets. The question is only what are good proxies to measure insolvency, that is what is sustainable debt. Of course, exchange rate volatility and currency crises are relevant factors as well and thus the question arises as to what are the causes for large exchange rate shocks.

There are typical stylised facts to be observed before and after the financial crises which have been studied in numerous papers (see for example Mishkin (1998), Milesi-Ferretti and Razin (1996, 1998), Kamin (1999)). The empirical literature on financial crisis episodes may be summarised in the following stylised facts:

- there is a deterioration of balance sheets of economic units (households, firms, banks, the government and the country);
- before the crisis the current account deficit to GDP ratio rises;
- preceding the currency crisis the external debt to reserve ratio rises, after the crisis the current account recovers;
- there is a sudden reversal of capital flows and unexpected depreciation of the currency;
- the foreign debt denominated in foreign currency of the economic agents suddenly rises due to a drastic depreciation of the currency;
- domestic interest rates jump up, partly initiated by CB policy;
- subsequently stock prices fall;
- a banking crisis occurs with large loan losses by banks and subsequent contraction of credit (sometimes moderated by a bailout of failing banks by the government);
- the financial crisis entails a large output loss due to large scale investment declines and bankruptcies of firms and financial institutions.

Recent financial crises, such as the Asian crisis 1997–8, were indeed triggered by a sudden reversal of capital flows and an unexpected strong depreciation of the currency. In the next section we will build up a model which attempts to explain some of the stylised facts, in which we will stress in particular the impact of large currency depreciations on the breakdown of investment decisions and the resulting large output loss. This can occur despite significant improvements in the trade balance. We will use a standard portfolio approach to describe the financial sector of the economy and concentrate on the balance sheets of firms, their investment behaviour and the multiplier dynamics that derive from it in order to show how ongoing reallocation of assets into foreign bonds can imply a currency crisis, a breakdown of investment and a large output loss.

2.3 The Krugman model: an MFT representation

Krugman (2000, p. 83) states that 'a fully fledged model of balance-sheet driven crisis is necessarily fairly complex'. That paper, however, shows that Krugman's ideas can indeed be represented in a coherent way even on the textbook level if his type of investment function is assumed and if imperfect substitution between financial assets is modelled as in Tobin. Here we build on a simplified and modified version of the MFT model developed by Rødseth (2000, Ch. 6.2). We aim at a fully fledged model of a balance-sheet driven crisis considered in Krugman (1999, 2000). With respect to consumption and investment behaviour, the model only contains the necessary variables to make Krugman's point and thus does not use wealth and interest rate effects in consumption and investment behaviour. Instead, we make use of the following simple representation of consumption, investment and goods market equilibrium:

$$Y = C(Y - \delta\bar{K} - \bar{T}) + I(s) + \delta\bar{K} + \bar{G} + NX(Y, \bar{Y}^*, s). \tag{2.1}$$

Here s is the exchange rate measured in units of domestic currency per unit of foreign currency.[2] We assume behind equation (2.1) given price levels $\bar{p}, \bar{p}^*$ at home and abroad, given foreign output $\bar{Y}^*$ and a given world interest rate $\bar{i}^*$ as is often done in Mundell–Fleming models of small open economies. We normalise the price levels to 'one' for reasons of simplicity which allows us to identify quantities and value terms in national accounts. We finally assume as usual $C' + NX_Y < 1$, $NX_s > 0$ and, as already stated, neglect the influence of the domestic rate of interest on consumption and investment. Since we presume that there is no inflation at home and abroad we also do not need to consider real interest and real exchange rates. The assumed type of investment behaviour is described in detail below. Note finally that the above equation implicitly assumes that all investment demand concerns domestic goods in order to get strong multiplier effects on the economy in the case of strong currency depreciation.

Private households consume and save out of their disposable income $Y - \delta\bar{K} - \bar{T}$. We assume that capital stock $\bar{K}$ is given, as is the rate of depreciation δ, and $\bar{T}$ is an assumed lump-sum tax.[3] Feedbacks from the flow of savings into the asset holdings of households are still ignored, but could be added as in Rødseth (2000, Ch. 6.6) via the government budget constraint, which would however add further laws of motion to the model (see the next section for the discussion of the flow conditions that characterise asset markets as time evolves). Here, however, we only consider explicitly the stock constraint of private households and their portfolio demand functions as first proposed in Tobin (1969) and as modelled in Rødseth (2000) on various levels of generality:[4]

$$W_p = M_o + B_o + sF_{po} \tag{2.2}$$

$$M = m(Y, i) \tag{2.3}$$

$$sF_p = f(\varepsilon, W_p), \quad \varepsilon = \bar{i}^* + \hat{s}^e - i \tag{2.4}$$

$$B = W_p - m(Y, i) - f(\varepsilon, W_p). \tag{2.5}$$

[2] Since the domestic economy is assumed to be a small open economy it will be convenient to think of it as Norway (as in Rødseth (2000)) and so denote the domestic currency as Krona. The exchange rate s is measured on this basis in units of Krona per US dollar (simply denoted dollar hereafter).

[3] Lump-sum taxes are here calculated net of interest, see Rødseth (2000, Ch. 6) for a similar assumption.

[4] We present the portfolio model using the gross substitute assumption in the way that asset demands always depend positively on their own rate of return and negatively on the other ones. We therefore define the risk premium on foreign bonds as the negative of the one considered in Rødseth (2000) in order to get a positive dependence of the demand for foreign bonds on the risk premium in the place of the negative one in his book.

Note again that we have normalised the price level to be equal to 1. In equation (2.2) we consider the reallocation of money holdings, M_o, fixed-price domestic bond holdings, B_o, and foreign fixed-price bond holdings of domestic households, F_{po}, between money M, dollar-dominated (private) foreign bonds F_p and domestic bonds B (the prices of these bonds are also assumed to be equal to one in terms of their currency, again for reasons of simplicity).

We do not yet consider any specific exchange rate regime of Mundell–Fleming type and thus do not yet state in detail which of the quantities M, B, F_p, F_c the foreign bond holdings of the CB are to be considered as exogenously determined. We should point out that, under the assumption that domestic bonds are not or cannot be traded internationally, a fixed exchange rate regime would imply that $F_p + F_c$ can be considered as fixed, while in a flexible exchange rate regime we would have that F_p can be considered as fixed, since the CB then need not intervene in the foreign exchange market. Equation (2.2) provides the definition of private wealth currently held in the household sector, when the nominal exchange rate is s. In equation (2.3) money demand equals money supply and we assume $m_y > 0, m_i < 0$ as in the usual LM Approach. In equation (2.4) demand for dollar-denominated bonds sF_p, expressed in domestic currency, is assumed to depend on private wealth W_p and the risk premium ε, which is defined by the difference of foreign and domestic interest rates augmented by expected capital gains or losses $\hat{s}^e$, with $\hat{s}^e$ as the expected rate of depreciation or appreciation. We assume $f_\varepsilon > 0$ and $F_{W_p} \in (0, 1)$. Demand for domestic bonds B is then determined residually in equation (2.5) by Walras' Law of Stocks. With respect to expected depreciation $\hat{s}^e$ we assume

$$\hat{s}^e = \hat{s}^e(s), \quad (\hat{s}^e)' \leq 0, \quad \hat{s}^e(s_o) = 0 \quad \text{at the given steady state value of } s. \tag{2.6}$$

Equation (2.6) is a general formulation of regressive expectations, see Rødseth (2000, Ch. 1.4) for details.[5] Note here already, however, that we assume that economic agents have perfect knowledge of the relevant steady state value of s of the model (denoted by s_o) and that they are therefore forward looking in their behaviour. It is thus expected that the actual exchange rate adjusts with possibly varying speed to this steady state value. Such an expectational scheme may also be characterised as asymptotically rational behaviour and represents a very fundamental and tranquil type of expected exchange rate adjustment scheme. This assumption ensures that expectations are therefore not central in the explanation of the currency crises considered in this chapter.

As the above portfolio demand approach is formulated, we have substitution between money and domestic bonds on the one hand and between domestic and foreign bonds on the other hand. The first is determined in reference to the nominal rate of interest i and the second in reference to the risk premium ε between domestic and foreign bonds. Furthermore, all domestic money and bonds are held by domestic residents. There is thus no international trade in domestic bonds. There is nothing extraordinary

[5] A specific formulation could be $\hat{s}^e = \beta_{\hat{s}^e}(s_o/s - 1)$, where s_o denotes the steady state value to which the economy is converging.

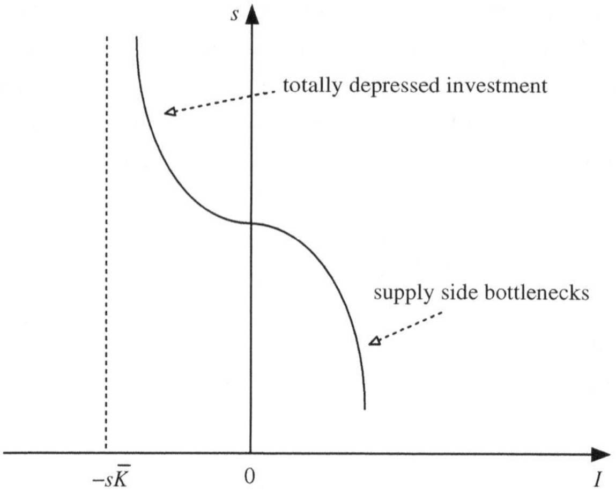

Figure 2.1 A Krugman (2000) type of investment function

involved in our description of the sector of private households which is characterised by a simple consumption and savings function and a standard portfolio approach to imperfect capital mobility.

The sector of firms, here so far only represented by its net investment function $I(s)$, is however quite different from what is usually used to characterise investment behaviour. Investment is here made dependent solely on the nominal exchange rate s, in the way shown in Figure 2.1.

We assume that investment depends negatively on the exchange rate s, and strongly so in an intermediate range of the exchange rate s. The story behind this assumption is that depreciation worsens the balance sheet of firms (see the next section), due to the fact that their past investment decisions were financed by foreign bonds (firm bonds denominated in foreign/dollar currency). Depreciation thus increases the debt of firms when measured in domestic currency and lowers the credit rating and the credit-worthiness of the firms and their ability to finance current investment. Investment is therefore reduced when depreciation of the domestic currency occurs and, by the assumption made below, in the considered middle range for the exchange rate is reduced to such a degree that dominates the positive (normal) reaction of net exports NX with respect to exchange rate changes, that is

$$-I'(s) > NX_s > 0.$$

In this range we therefore have for the aggregate demand function $Y^d(Y, s)$ that

$$Y^d_Y \in (0, 1) \text{ and } Y^d_s < 0.$$

The latter partial derivative represents a striking difference to the usual assumptions on aggregate demand in models of the Mundell–Fleming type.

For very high and very low exchange rates we however assume that investment is not very sensitive to further exchange rate changes for two reasons: on the one hand, there are supply bottlenecks for very high investment demand and on the other hand, there are some investment projects that must and can be continued – despite severe credit rationing of firms – even for very high levels of the exchange rate. For extreme values of the exchange rate we therefore have the usual positive dependence of goods market equilibrium on the level of the exchange rate.

We have already stated that the implications of the government deficit with respect to changes in the supply of money and domestic bonds are still ignored in the current short-term analysis of a small open economy. With respect to the CB, we assume that it can change not only the supply of money and domestic bond holdings instantaneously through standard open market operations, but also the amount of the dollar-denominated bonds if it desires to do so. Following Rødseth (2000, Ch. 6) we however assume that the following constraint must hold true:

$$F_p + F_c = \bar{F}^*,$$

with F_c the foreign bond holdings of the CB and $\bar{F}^*$ the total amount of dollar-denominated bonds held in the domestic economy (treated separately from the credit given to firms). This assumption can be justified by considering regimes where money can only be exchanged against foreign currency in the domestic economy (through the monetary authority) and by assuming that domestic bonds cannot be traded internationally which may be a realistic assumption for the type of economy considered here. This completes the short-run equilibrium description of the considered small open economy. We stress again that we even get a fixed F_p-value if the monetary authority need not intervene in the foreign exchange market.

Finally we note again that the above feature of investment behaviour has been chosen so that in its middle range the investment function is characterised as being very elastic with respect to the exchange rate s. For very high and very low exchange rates, however, investment becomes very inelastic in this regard. If the currency is strong (low s), investment runs into a bottleneck and is limited by supply side conditions, be they actual or only perceived ones. If the currency is very weak, net investment is reduced to its floor level (which may even be negative). In sum, we have an investment behaviour formally similar to the one considered in the Kaldor (1940) trade cycle model, but here based on net worth effects resulting from exchange rate changes, instead of an influence of economic activity Y on the net investment of firms.

As in Kaldor (1940) (see also Blanchard and Fischer (1989, p. 532)), we consider the following goods market adjustment process off the IS or goods market equilibrium curve:[6]

$$\begin{aligned}\dot{Y} &= \beta_y(Y^d - Y)\\ &= \beta_y(C(Y - \delta\bar{K} - \bar{T}) + I(s) + \delta\bar{K} + \bar{G} + NX(Y, \bar{Y}^*, s) - Y). \qquad (2.7)\end{aligned}$$

This dynamic multiplier process is a stable one for any given level of s, since $Y^d_Y - 1 < 0$ is assumed to hold true.

[6] Note that this is a simplification of a more general goods market adjustment process where also inventories are adjusted by firms.

Next, we derive two equilibrium curves, for the goods and asset market equilibria respectively, situated in the Y, s phase space and surrounded by the multiplier dynamics just introduced. First we consider the IS curve, defined by the equation (2.1), and get by the implicit function theorem for the slope of this curve, with Y the dependent and s the independent variable,

$$Y'(s) = -\frac{I' + NX_s}{C' + NX_Y - 1} \gtreqless 0,$$

where the difference in signs is due to the ambiguity in the sign of the numerator, since the denominator is unambiguously negative. In the mid-range of s-values, discussed above, we have $Y'(s) < 0$ and so a backward bending IS curve, since I' dominates NX_s in this range, while we have a positive slope for this curve outside of this range, since $| I' |$ becomes close to zero there.

For the IS curve we thus get a scenario as shown in Figure 2.2, where we have also added the output adjustment of firms when economic activity departs from the IS curve. This shows that the IS curve is a global attractor with respect to output adjustment whenever the economy is displaced from it by a shock. Note also that the IS curve should become very steep for very large and very small values of the exchange rate s, since investment and net exports may be very insensitive to further exchange rate changes then. Note also that this curve should cut the horizontal axis at a positive value of output Y, since $\dot{Y}$ is positive at $Y = 0$ by assumption.

Let us next consider the asset market equilibrium as described by equations (2.2)–(2.6). From equation (2.3) we have, for any given M, a positive dependence of i on Y and a negative one with respect to M as is generally the case in such simple LM

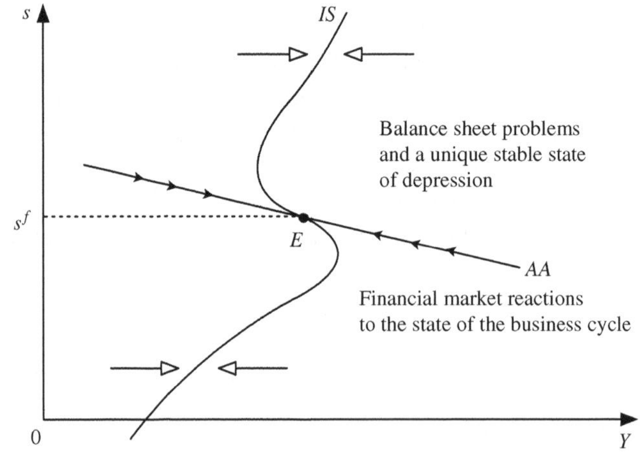

Figure 2.2 IS equilibrium and output adjustment along the AA curve in the case of an output and asset market determined exchange rate

approaches to the money market, thus we denote this dependence as $i(Y, M)$ and have

$$i_Y > 0, \ i_M < 0. \tag{2.8}$$

Inserting this reduced form equation and equation (2.6) into equation (2.4) gives rise to[7]

$$sF_p = f(\bar{i}^* + \hat{s}^e(s) - i(Y, M), \ M_o + B_o + sF_{po}), \quad M \quad \text{given.} \tag{2.9}$$

This condensed representation of full asset markets equilibrium will give rise (for flexible exchange rates and thus given F_p) to a strictly negatively sloped equilibrium curve AA (representing the influence of the business cycle on exchange rate determination). This curve cuts the vertical axis by assumption and for reasons of simplicity will be always drawn as a straight line in the following.[8] Under Walras' Law of Stocks we thus have a well-defined single curve for the characterisation of equilibrium in the financial markets of the economy for any given level of money supply M.[9] Summarising we thus have in the present modelling framework a new and extended type of IS–LM diagram, where LM equilibrium is combined with an FF-equilibrium for dollar-denominated[10] bonds to provide a strictly decreasing function in the Y, s phase space in place of the usual output-interest rate phase space, the AA asset market equilibrium curve. Furthermore, the IS or goods market equilibrium curve is now situated in the same phase space where it usually assumed strictly positive slope is only valid for very high as well as very low values of the exchange rate s. We thus have to deal with new slopes of IS–LM curves in a newly defined economic phase space in the following analysis.

2.4 Sectoral budget equations and national accounts

In this section we consider explicitly the dynamic adjustment of foreign reserves (or bonds) in the domestic economy (as well as flows into domestic money and bond holdings) that occur due to the investment decision of firms, the saving decision of households, the decisions of the government and of the CB, also taking into account the net exports of our model economy. We want to show that all the foreign account flows balance each other in the balance of payments (under certain consistency assumptions on new domestic money and bond supply) so that there is no need – beyond what happens

7 Note that the use made of this equation and the restriction that F is fixed in this chapter assumes that domestic bonds are non-tradable, which implies that the tradable amount of foreign bonds is fixed to the domestic holdings of such bonds at each moment of time. In the case of a flexible exchange rate this simply reduces to a given F_p due to the non-intervention of the domestic CB in this case.

8 Although it may only approach the horizontal axis for exchange rates approaching zero.

9 This distinguishes our approach to the AA curve from the one suggested in Krugman (2000), where a leaning against the wind strategy seems to be part of the AA curve. Leaning against the wind in our model means shifting the AA curve to the left by means of restrictive monetary policy (reduced money supply). This is indeed also stated in Krugman and Obstfeld (2003) where, however, the interest rate parity condition is used for the derivation of the AA curve in the place of our explicit (imperfect substitute) portfolio representation of the asset markets.

10 Note that we assume in this chapter that dollar-denominated bonds held by domestic households can only be traded on the domestic financial markets; see Rødseth (2000) for more details.

in the stock markets – for the CB to intervene in order for the foreign exchange market to be in equilibrium. We will in particular describe here the changes in foreign bond holdings of households and the CB and the change in the foreign debt of firms.

First of all, we assume now explicitly that all income generated by firms is transferred into the household sector, however we formally deduct depreciation in order to arrive at net magnitudes. Since we allow for negative net investment, the amount representing depreciation need not be kept back by, and invested within, firms. We thus assume here that there is a positive floor to gross investment I^g and that enough foreign credit is available in order to finance at least a minimum amount of investment projects that are not scrapped during a currency crisis. This gives rise to the following budget equations of firms:[11]

$$Y - \delta\bar{K} - s\bar{i}^* F_f = wL^d + \Pi_p, \quad I = s\dot{F}_f, \tag{2.10}$$

Equation (2.10) states that firms have to pay interest on their foreign debt and transfer all remaining proceeds into the households sector as wages wL^d and profits Π_p. Their investments I (if positive) thus have to be financed completely by new foreign debt, since we assume that investment goods are completely purchased on the international goods markets. They thus represent foreign goods, here however – in the investment demand function – already measured in terms of the domestic currency. This means that the quantity demanded on the world market must depend on the exchange rate with an elasticity that is smaller than -1 in order to give rise to an investment schedule in the domestic currency with the assumed property $I'(s) < 0$. This investment behaviour may be due to credit constraints, but also simply due to the fact that such investment is not profitable at the currently prevailing exchange rate.

For the household sector we next obtain a flow budget constraint, in view of what has been stated for firms,

$$Y - \delta\bar{K} - s\bar{i}^* F_f + s\bar{i}^* F_p - \bar{T} - C = \dot{M} + \dot{B} + s\dot{F}_p. \tag{2.11}$$

Note that lump-sum taxes are here calculated net of domestic interest payments by the government, similar to the procedures applied in Rødseth (2000, Ch. 6). The government budget constraint here simply reads

$$\bar{G} - \bar{T} = \dot{M} + \dot{B}, \qquad \bar{T} = T - iB.$$

We assume with respect to CB behaviour that all interest income on government bonds that are held by the CB (due to past open market operations) is transferred back to the government sector and thus does not appear in the government budget constraint as a separate item. We therefore represent explicitly only privately held government bonds, as is usually done in the literature. The budget equation (2.11) of households says that household savings on its left-hand side is spent on new money and new domestic bonds as they are supplied by the government; the remainder goes into new foreign bonds. This in fact represents a flow consistency assumption that guarantees that the balance

[11] In the case of negative net investment we thus get that firms are paying back part of their foreign debt.

of payments[12] will always be balanced in the present framework. Note again that all prices (goods and assets) – apart from the exchange rate – are set equal to one in the present form of the model.

With respect to CB behaviour we finally assume that its (remaining) income (equal to its savings) is spent on the acquisition of foreign reserves in the form of foreign bonds, so that we have

$$s\bar{i}^* F_c = s\dot{F}_c.$$

Aggregating all (dis-)savings of households, government and the CB gives the equation

$$Y - \delta\bar{K} - C - \bar{G} + s\bar{i}^*(F_p + F_c) - s\bar{i}^* F_f = s(\dot{F}_p + \dot{F}_c),$$

which in turn implies due to the assumed goods market equilibrium condition:[13]

$$CA + I = NX + s\bar{i}^*(F_p + F_c) - s\bar{i}^* F_f + I = s(\dot{F}_p + \dot{F}_c) = S = S_p + S_g + S_c.$$

Inserting the foreign bonds that finance firms' investment then gives rise to the equality between the current account deficit (or surplus) and the surplus (or deficit) in the capital account as shown in the equation

$$NX + s\bar{i}^*(F_p + F_c) - s\bar{i}^* F_f = s(\dot{F}_p + \dot{F}_c) - s\dot{F}_f.$$

We thus have that the balance of payments is always balanced, although we stress that this is under the assumption that households absorb the new money and the new domestic bonds shown in the government budget constraint. All flows that need foreign currency thus will obtain it and the stock markets are, as assumed, always in equilibrium. Net exports and net interest payments on foreign bonds are always equal in sum to net capital exports or net foreign bond imports, with households and the CB as creditors and firms as debtors in the interest and foreign bond flows. Note that although we have this balance in the balance of payments we have nevertheless included the possibility of credit rationing of firms, subsumed in the assumed shape of the investment function, that is, investment and its financing does not reflect demand side aspects solely. The investment function is therefore based to some extent on factual outcomes.

We note again that domestic money can only be exchanged against foreign currency in the domestic economy. Combined with the assumption that domestic bonds are not traded internationally, this is sufficient to provide the constraint $F_p = F_{po}$ for asset reallocations in the case of a flexible exchange rate. In the case of a fixed exchange rate system, this gives an endogenous F_p determination, served by the domestic CB. These two alternatives will find application in the next two sections. Note that the case of an exchange rate that is fixed by the domestic CB will exhibit the inequality $F_p \leq F_{po} + F_c$ as a feasibility constraint on the reallocation of foreign bonds between households and

12 Note that we show planned magnitudes solely.

13 This condition states that the current account surplus (or deficit) CA plus net investment must be equal to aggregate savings.

Table 2.1. *The balance sheet of firms (current values)*

Tangible Assets	Liabilities
pK	sF_f Net worth (measuring credit-worthiness)

the CB. This therefore characterises the range within which the CB is capable of fixing the domestic exchange rate.

Note finally that the balance sheet effect for firms, here debts in foreign bonds solely, with no retained earnings and with no equity financing, reads simply as in Table 2.1.[14]

The actual change in this balance sheet, through investment/disinvestment, is here simply represented by the assumption

$$I(s) = s\dot{F}_f(s), \quad I'(s) < 0,$$

implying that there holds

$$\frac{d\dot{F}_f}{\dot{F}_f} \Big/ \frac{ds}{s} < -1,$$

an assumption which is not explained in detail here as far as the credit rationing process or voluntary investment reduction underlying this investment schedule are concerned.

Firms, which are run by domestic households, thus combine labour L^d and capital K, financed solely by foreign financial capital, to produce the output Y and the accounting net worth $pK - sF_f$. Portfolio markets determine the interest rate i and the exchange rate s (if flexible) for any given output level. The goods market determines the output level Y of firms for any given exchange rate separately in a fixed exchange rate system (where asset markets determine i and F_p) and jointly with the asset markets in the case of a flexible exchange rate. Financial flows caused by the savings and investment decisions of the considered sectors of the economy do not matter in this interaction, but have been considered here in addition for consistency reasons. Financial crisis in the proper sense of the word is here only present in the assumed investment behaviour and its financing condition, up to the consideration of the capital flight parameter α later on, since consumption behaviour and asset demands remain stable otherwise (or are here not explicitly considered with respect to critical behavioural non-linearities). There is also no explicit consideration of bankruptcies.

In the remaining part of this section we finally summarise our model economy from the perspective of national accounts, based on the budget restrictions just discussed.

[14] This balance sheet is thus based on the historical (current) value of the capital stock and does not take into account any discounted cash flows in the formulation of the net worth of firms (equities are also not yet present in the model; their value may be measured by such discounted cash flows). We thus ignore any interest rate effect on the measure of the net worth of firms, on the basis of which credit rationing will then be decided.

Due to these restrictions, and to the assumption that the type of financing of the government deficit (the inflow of new money and domestic bonds) is always accepted by the private sector of the economy, we will again find that the balance of payments, representing the real and financial flows planned by the various sectors, is always balanced and thus of no importance for the determination of the exchange rate. This rate is in fact determined by a stock or portfolio approach solely, on the basis of the stocks the economy inherited from the past (disregarding the given foreign debt or credit to firms).

We start by introducing some notation not used so far in this chapter:

- FD_f: Financial deficit of firms;
- FD_g: Financial deficit of the government;
- FD_p: Financial surplus of the private sector;
- FD_c: Financial surplus of the CB;
- I^g: Gross investment ($I^g = I + \delta \bar{K}$);
- J, X: Imports and exports of commodities.

We assume again that the given domestic as well as the foreign price level are both set equal to one by appropriate normalisation so that we can use just the nominal exchange rate only to express all quantities in terms of the domestic commodity. We have five sectors in the economy: households, firms, the government, the CB and the world economy or the foreign account. We distinguish four accounts for the first four sectors: production, income, wealth accumulation and financial account. Our model is based on the assumptions that households and the fiscal authority have no production account and firms no income account (all profits are transferred to the household sector). Of course all accounts only show items that exist in the model of this paper and thus exclude many factual items of the System of National Accounts.

Note, furthermore, that imports are explicitly represented in terms of the foreign commodity, while their consumption by households, firms and the government is left implicit and expressed in terms of the domestic commodity solely. We here follow the usual practice of summarising the role of imports in the net export function which therefore represents the influence of the exchange rate on domestic consumption and investment. We stress again that taxes in our model are calculated net of interest paid to the household sector, so that $\bar{T} = T - iB$, while the interest received by the CB on government bonds is transferred back into the government sector. Taxes are thus endogenous in the present model, but held constant after interest payments have been deducted. Interest on foreign bonds received by the CB is counted as income in this sector and used for the further accumulation of foreign bonds by the CB. Note also that money financing of the government deficit is assumed to take place via corresponding open market operations of the CB which are however not represented in this sector, but simply stated as a final outcome in the government sector.

Table 2.2 summarises production/income accounts, the change of wealth accounts and the flow of funds accounts of firms, households and the government. Table 2.3 gives the income, change of wealth and flow of funds accounts of the CB.

Table 2.2. *The production, change of wealth and flow of funds accounts of firms, households and the government*

Firms					
Production Account		Change of Wealth Account		Flow of Funds Account	
Debits	Credits	Debits	Credits	Debits	Credits
δK		I^g	δK	FD_f	$s\dot{F}_f$
$s\bar{i}^* F_f$	I^g		FD_f		
wL^d	G				
Π_p	C				
$s\ J$	X				
Households					
Income Account		Change of Wealth Account		Flow of Funds Account	
Debits	Credits	Debits	Credits	Debits	Credits
T	wL^d	FS_p	S_p	$\dot{M}$	FS_p
C	iB			$\dot{B}$	
S_p	$s\bar{i}^* F_p$			$s\dot{F}_p$	
	Π_p				
The Government					
Income Account		Change of Wealth Account		Flow of Funds Account	
Debits	Credits	Debits	Credits	Debits	Credits
G	$\bar{T} = T - iB$		S_g	FD_g	$\dot{M}$
S_g			FD_g		$\dot{B}$

Table 2.3. *The income, change of wealth and flow of funds accounts of the CB*

The CB					
Income Account		Change of Wealth Account		Flow of Funds Account	
Debits	Credits	Debits	Credits	Debits	Credits
S_c	$s\bar{i}^* F_c$	FS_c	S_c	$s\dot{F}_c$	FS_c

There is finally the balance of payments, shown in Table 2.4, which records the items that concern the current and the capital account, the latter also including the reserve changes of the CB. As mentioned above, the balance of payments is always balanced due to our treatment of the budget equations of the four sectors of the economy and

Table 2.4. *The balance of payments account*

Balance of Payments (measured in domestic currency) Debits ——— Credits	
Trade Account:	
Imports	Exports
$s \cdot J$	X
Interest Income Account:	
Interest payments of firms to the foreign economies	Interest payments from the foreign economies
$s\bar{i}^* F_f$	$s\bar{i}^* F_p + s\bar{i}^* F_c$
Capital Account:	
$s\dot{F}_p = 0$	$\dot{B}_p^{d*} = 0$
Official Reserve Transactions of the CB:	
$X - sJ + s\bar{i}^* F_p + s\dot{F}_c - s\bar{i}^* F_f$	

thus does not represent a further restriction (besides the stock portfolio equilibrium equations) to the working of the economy. Note that since domestic bonds have been assumed non-tradable internationally (an assumption that we will relax in a final section of this chapter) we must have $\dot{F}_p = 0$ in the capital account (if interest payments are made in the domestic currency).[15] Table 2.4 displays the balance of payments account.

This concludes our presentation of the flow conditions that characterise the small open economy under consideration. We stress that in view of the above considerations, the situation considered here is still a fairly ordered one in the case of a crisis. Capital accumulation has been financed by foreign credit throughout and all interest payments are always met at the world rate of interest. However, new credit will become rationed as expressed by the investment function if the balance sheet of firms worsens through depreciation. This credit rationing being given, the crisis considered in this chapter is then a purely macroeconomic one: a Keynesian effective demand depression with large loss in domestic output and income due to a large reduction in investment demand, but still with flow consistency in particular in the balance of payments. The crisis scenario we investigate in this chapter is thus still a partial one with credit rationed firms and a capital flight parameter (to be introduced in the next section), but otherwise stable portfolio demand equations, a stable expectations scheme, stable behavioural equations on the goods market and given wages and prices.

2.5 Flexible exchange rates: output and exchange rate dynamics

We consider here exclusively the case of flexible exchange rates and thus the case where the CB in general does not need to intervene in the market for foreign exchange and

[15] The term $\dot{F}_c$ is neglected in the following treatment since $F_p + F_c = \bar{F}^*$ is assumed to hold.

conduct trade in foreign bonds. The equilibrium in the foreign exchange market can therefore be described by

$$F_{po} = F_p = const \quad \text{at all time,}$$

that is the amount of dollar-denominated (foreign) bonds that can be traded in this market is simply given by the amount of such bonds already held by private households. That is so because we continue to assume that domestic bonds cannot be traded internationally and that M (or i) is kept fixed by open market operations (concerning domestic bonds) by the monetary authority. The case of a flexible exchange rate will be used in Section 2.6 to describe the consequences of a breakdown of a fixed exchange rate regime.

Since there is no change in the supply of foreign currency by means of changes in the reserves F_c of the CB we can now determine an asset market equilibrium curve $s(Y)$ from the reduced form asset market representation provided by equation (2.9) at the end of Section 2.3. For any given output level, the equation (2.9) determines the exchange rate s that clears the asset markets, the interest rate i being determined by equation (2.8) that came from the LM curve of the model. According to the implicit function theorem the slope of the curves $s(Y)$ is given by

$$s'(Y) = -\frac{-f_\varepsilon i_Y}{-F_{po} + f_\varepsilon(\hat{s}^e)' + f_{W_p} F_{po}}. \tag{2.12}$$

We have $(f_{W_p} - 1)F_{po} < 0$ and $f_\varepsilon(\hat{s}^e)' \leq 0$, since $f_{W_p} < 1$ and $(\hat{s}^e)' \leq 0$ has been assumed. Furthermore, the numerator of equation (2.12) is always positive, so we can assert that $s'(Y) < 0$ holds. Hence the asset markets equilibrium curve AA is always negatively sloped, as shown in Figure 2.2 (there as a straight line). We note that the AA curve becomes steeper as the capital mobility (as measured by f_ε) becomes higher, the interest rate elasticity of money demand becomes lower, the more dominant is the demand for dollar bonds is in the portfolio of asset holders and the more sluggishly regressive expectations adjust.

Next, we investigate the implications of a steep AA curve that under otherwise normal conditions gives rise to a situation as shown in Figure 2.3, which now exhibits three IS-AA equilibria. As Figure 2.3 immediately reveals, however, only two of the equilibria are stable when exchange rates are flexible and when output adjusts sluggishly through the dynamic multiplier process.

Below E_2, at a point on the AA curve (which is always binding if the exchange rate is perfectly flexible) we have expanding output according to the IS curve and thus convergence to E_1, while the opposite holds true for points above E_2 on the AA curve. We stress that the AA-equilibrium must here prevail by assumption (when s is treated as a statically endogenous variable), while the economy may temporarily be off the IS curve. As shown, this implies that E_1 and E_3 are attractors, while E_2 is a repeller.

Assume now that – for some reason – the AA curve shifts to the right to AA (see again Figure 2.3) so that only the upper stationary equilibrium remains in existence.

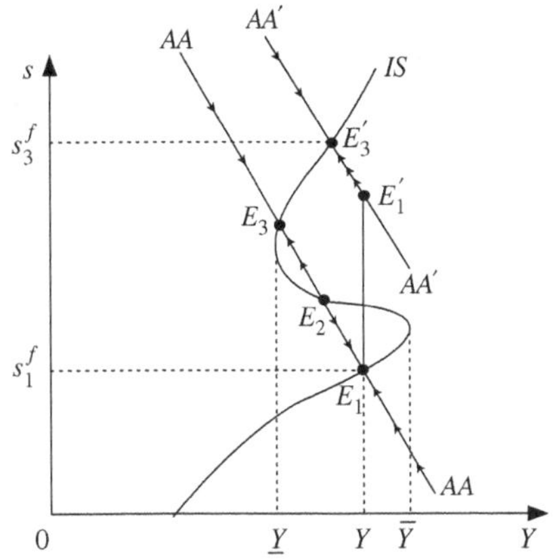

Figure 2.3 Dynamic multiplier analysis under perfectly flexible exchange rates. Here the dynamics undergo a fold catastrophe

Assume further that the economy was initially at E_1. Since output Y cannot react instantaneously, the economy must jump to the new asset market equilibrium E_1' and will thus undergo an instantaneous process of strong currency depreciation.[16] Yet, despite such strong depreciation, the economy will not expand its activity level thereafter via the exchange rate effect on net exports, but will instead start to contract until the new stationary equilibrium E_3' has been reached, a process which is accompanied by further depreciation of the currency as Figure 2.3 shows.

The effects of the considered shift in the asset market equilibrium curve are therefore a sudden first and then a continuous further depreciation of the currency, a radical first and then a continuous improvement in the trade balance (due to rising s and falling Y), a strong first and then a continuous decrease in domestic investment near to its floor and as a result of this dominant change in aggregate demand, declining economic activity and declining domestic interest rates.

The question now is what the reasons for such a rightward shift in the AA curve (to AA′) could be. To provide the grounds for one possible explanation we expand the functional dependence of the asset demand curve f so that it reads:

$$sF_p = f(\bar{i}^* + \hat{s}^e(s) - i(Y, M), W_p, \alpha), \quad f_\alpha > 0. \tag{2.13}$$

In equation (2.13) we use the new parameter α to express the risk of investing in domestic bonds, from the international perspective of domestic asset holders. Since a devaluation of the domestic currency deteriorates the international position of asset holders, we assume here that dollars represent the preferred currency and that *dollar-denominated bonds* are thus the preferred assets in the household sector. If there is a potential threat of depreciation of the domestic currency, asset holders may gradually

[16] In the language of the theory of dynamical systems this type of sudden change is known as a fold catastrophe. See Rosser (2000).

decide (as expressed by an increase of the parameter α) to reallocate their asset holdings into dollar-denominated bonds. This process may be considered as capital flight from the domestic currency into the foreign one. An increasing parameter α, expressing increasing dollar-liquidity preference,[17] therefore induces an attempt as reallocation into foreign bonds. Even though these reallocations cannot take place here since $F_{po} = F_p$ is fixed in a regime of flexible exchange rates, these attempts nevertheless move E_1 since an increasing parameter α shifts the AA curve to the right. This may even be the case to the extent that this lower equilibrium completely disappears and gives way to the sole equilibrium E_3' shown in Figure 2.3. An increasing parameter α thus indeed produces currency depreciations (but also output expansions as long as the lower equilibrium E_1 remains in existence) and may thus induce further increases in the shift parameter.

What can be done by the CB to stop this tendency towards small and (if E_1 disappears) even large depreciations of the domestic currency? One such possibility is to increase the domestic rate of interest to counteract such capital flight, by way of a contractionary monetary policy. Reducing money balances through internal open market operations shifts the AA curve to the left and thus may prevent the AA curve – under the assumed capital flight conditions – shifting so much to the right that the lower equilibrium E_1 disappears. There is then only some depreciation (if E_1 remains in existence), which still expands output (if α is strong enough to overcome the contractionary impact of the restrictive monetary policy), yet which nevertheless moves the economy closer to the output level where the strong currency equilibrium E_1 (the normal equilibrium in Krugman's (2000) words) may disappear. This leaning against the wind strategy thus may be of help if α increases, at least to some extent or for some time.

Note again that output expands if α dominates the monetary strategy, but not to such an extent that the lower equilibrium E_1 disappears.

If, however, the economy gets trapped in E_3', the monetary authority can nevertheless attempt to bring the economy back to the lower stable part of the IS curve. Contractionary monetary policy moves the economy towards E_3, and if continued, eventually to a situation where the upper equilibrium disappears. Exchange rate appreciation will then lead the economy vertically down until the asset market equilibrium curve is reached again. From there on we have a continuously rising exchange rate and rising output until a new stationary point of type E_1 is reached. It is however a questionable assumption that the capital flight parameter α would stay in place[18] in the early phase of such economic contraction (caused by restrictive monetary policy), even though this policy tends to increase the domestic nominal rate of interest (which in turn is counteracted, but not fully offset, by the output contraction to which it leads).

17 This is to be contrasted with f_ε which measures capital mobility for a given state of dollar-liquidity preference.
18 In particular, if the rapid depreciation (accompanied by restrictive monetary policy) leads to a significant degree of bankruptcy of firms.

Note that monetary policy can be made more direct if the interest rate is directly set by the monetary authority, while M is then adjusted to money demand $M(Y,i)$ through appropriate technical instruments of the CB. The expression $i(Y,M)$ in the asset market equilibrium equation is then replaced by an exogenously given i, which is called an interest rate peg. This obviously changes the qualitative results so far discussed considerably, since the AA curve then becomes horizontal with only one unique intersection with the IS curve under all circumstances.[19] Note also that an extended investment function of type

$$\dot{K} = I = I(s(Y), K), \quad I_K < 0$$

would now introduce the Kaldor (1940) trade cycle analysis into the present framework. Note finally that, for given α and an equilibrium position E_1, expansionary monetary policy may lead to a contraction if the economy, via the AA curve, is shifted so much to the right that the equilibrium E_1 disappears. As long as the economy is on the lower branch, lowering i leads to mild depreciation and to goods market improvements, since the net export effect dominates the investment effect. Yet, beyond $\bar{Y}$ we reach the region where depreciation accelerates and output contracts (since investment then dominates net export effect) until stationarity is reached again in a situation where output and investment are at very low levels, in a stable state of depression.

In order to investigate exchange rate dynamics in more detail and in less perfect situations, we consider the excess demand function on the market for foreign bonds, which we denote by the function $X(s)$ that is given by[20]

$$X(s) = f(\bar{i}^* + \hat{s}^e(s) - i(Y,M),\ M_o + B_o + sF_{po}) - sF_{po}. \tag{2.14}$$

The slope of this function is given by

$$X'(s) = f_\varepsilon(\hat{s}^e)'(s) + f_{W_p}F_{po} - F_{po} < 0,$$

the sign following from our earlier assumptions that $(\hat{s}^e)'(s) < 0$ $(f_{W_p} < 1)$. Excess demand for foreign bonds basically means excess supply of domestic bonds and thus domestic demand for foreign currency. It is therefore natural to assume that

$$\hat{s} = \beta_s X(s)/(sF_{po}), \quad \beta_s > 0 \tag{2.15}$$

Equation (2.15) describes (here in a linear fashion) the reaction of the exchange rate with respect to the excess demand function (2.14). This implies a stable adjustment process for the exchange rate to its equilibrium value s_o[21] so far only considered – as shown in Figure 2.4.

[19] The AA curve is again negatively sloped in the case of a Taylor rule which uses the output gap on its right-hand side where therefore the interest rate responds again to the state of the business cycle. This implies that it may be wise in certain situations to avoid automatic interest rate movements and thus the possibility of multiple and in particular bad equilibrium selections.

[20] Here we assume that $i(Y,M)$ given or that the CB simply sets $i = \bar{i}$.

[21] The equilibrium exchange rate is defined by $X(s_o) = 0$.

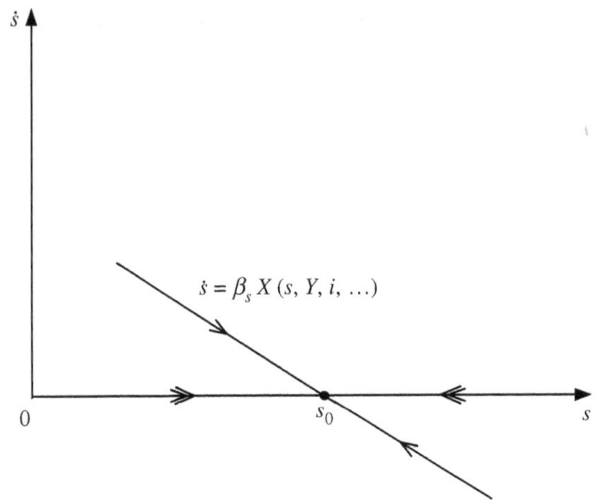

Figure 2.4 The market for foreign bonds and exchange rate adjustments

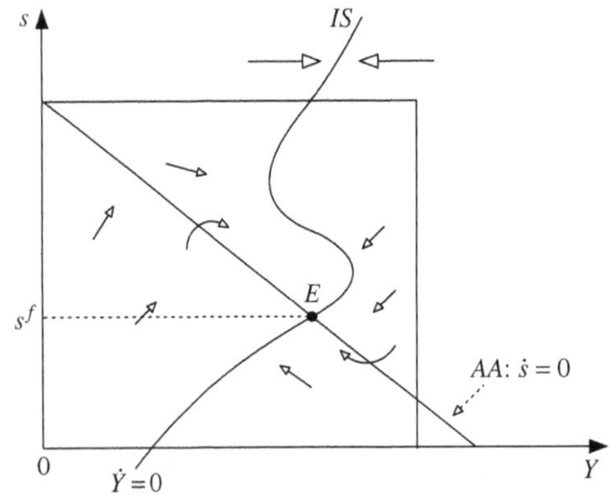

Figure 2.5 The Krugman dynamics extended to the whole Y, s phase space

Using the additional law of motion (2.15) together with those for Y given by equation (2.7), the dynamics along the asset market equilibrium curve AA can in fact now be extended to the whole (Y, s) phase space, as shown in Figure 2.5 (where we have returned for the moment to the consideration of a single stationary point E_1, but we remind the reader of the possibility of multiple equilibria as shown in Figure 2.3). Note that the AA line is now crossed horizontally by the (Y, s) trajectories and the dynamics not characterised by the motion shown along the AA-line as in Figure 2.3 since now s does not adjust instantaneously.

The situation depicted in Figure 2.3 in fact characterises the limit case of infinitely fast exchange rate dynamics, $\beta_s = \infty$, which instantaneously places the exchange s on the AA curve, along which output still has to adjust. It thus represents a different dynamical system, as compared with the somewhat sluggish adjustment of the exchange rate that is now considered (the case $\beta_s = \infty$ is approached in a continuous fashion as β_s

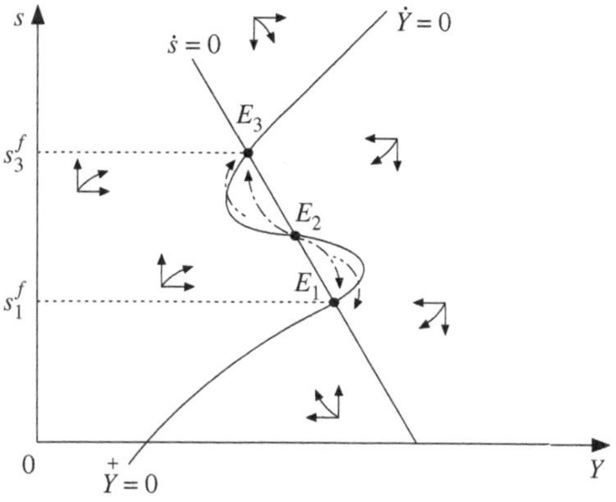

Figure 2.6 The extended dynamics in the Y, s phase space with three equilibria. The equilibria E_1 and E_3 are stable while E_2 is a saddle point

approaches ∞, as indicated by the thick double arrows in Figure 2.5). Note furthermore that the positive orthant is an invariant set of the dynamics, it cannot be left since the change in output (in the exchange rate) is always positive sufficiently close to the axis $Y = 0$ $(s = 0)$.[22]

We conjecture with respect to Figure 2.5 that the sole equilibrium, shown there, is globally asymptotically stable in the positive orthant of $\Re^2$, but do not prove this here (via an appropriate application of Olech's theorem on global asymptotic stability, see Flaschel (1984) for similar applications). Since the dynamics cannot leave the box shown in Figure 2.5, the occurrence of *semi-stable or stable* limit cycles cannot be excluded, unless the adjustment speed of the exchange rate is close to ∞ where the dynamics are then close to those of the limit case we considered in Figures 2.2 and 2.3.

We return to the situation of Figure 2.3 with its multiple equilibria, but now embedded into the dynamics for Y and s given by equations (2.7) and (2.15). This situation is illustrated in Figure 2.6 where we again see two locally asymptotically stable equilibria and one unstable. These stability results can easily be shown by calculating the trace and determinant of the corresponding Jacobians. The process thus exhibits the equilibria E_1 and E_3 as (sole) stable equilibria under the now interacting dynamics of output Y and the exchange rate s.

Note also that Figure 2.6 suggests, and analysis of the corresponding Jacobians reveals, that the dynamics around E_2 are of saddle point type, with unstable arms leading to E_1 and E_3 respectively. It is more difficult to determine analytically the basins of attractions of the two attracting equilibria (indeed this may not be possible) and so determine what may happen elsewhere in the phase space. Numerical investigations need to be used to determine these basins explicitly. Here we shall simply assume that the dynamics are generally convergent to one of the two equilibria E_1 and E_3 after

[22] The latter always holds if the non-linearity of the AA curve for small values of the exchange rate s is taken into account, since excess demand on the foreign exchange market must become positive then.

any shocks or disturbances. We justify this with the limit case $\beta_s = \infty$ where global convergence along the AA curve to either one or the other equilibrium is obvious (with the exception of the situation where the economy sits exactly in the unstable equilibrium E_2 between the two other ones).

We observe finally that, in the case of flexible exchange rates, the assumption of regressive expectations has to be interpreted and applied with care. If the economy converges to either E_1 or E_3 we know that the exchange rate will again become stationary, while the assumed type of regressive expectations $\hat{s}^e = \hat{s}^e(s)$, in particular with $(\hat{s}^e)'(s) < 0$, would imply that the expected rate of depreciation $\hat{s}^e$ can only be zero in at most one of the three considered equilibria. This behaviour however is implausible in an environment where exchange rates can settle down at multiple stationary values. This situation can be remedied as follows.

Assume that the shock shown in Figure 2.3 has hit the economy, eventually leading it to the point $E_3^{'}$. Imbedded into the new AA curve shown here is a second shock, namely a revision of the long-run reference value s_o, to which regressive expectations are implicitly referring. This long-run reference value is here supposed to be always determined from the AA-situation, where in the defining equation we have set $\hat{s}^e$ identically equal to zero. It is therefore the value of the exchange rate at which stationarity can be assured. Thus we assume here that expectations formation immediately switches to this new long-run value once the α-shock has occurred, for example by way of the explicit formula

$$\hat{s}^e(s) = \beta_{\hat{s}^e}(s_o/s - 1),$$

with s_o now the relevant long-run value of the exchange rate s. Regressive expectations are therefore always forward looking with respect to the long-run situation and thus change their schedule when an α-shock occurs. This means that the AA curve is subject to changes, the first caused by the parameter α (from which s_o can then be determined) and the second due to the shift in the $\hat{s}^e$ schedule by means of s_o, which makes the AA curve steeper and guarantees that at $E_3^{'}$ we arrive at s_o with $\hat{s}^e = 0$.

2.6 Fixed exchange rates and the emergence of currency crises

In this section we consider the case of a fixed exchange rate system, where $\hat{s}^e(s)$ can be assumed to be zero and where the amount of depreciation that takes place in the event of a currency crisis is not foreseen by the economic agents. The discussed dynamics of s therefore can then even be considered with $\hat{s}^e(s) \equiv 0$ and be viewed as being only implicitly present until the currency crisis in fact occurs (and modifies the expectations mechanism as discussed at the end of the previous section).

Flexible exchange rates do not represent the only exchange rate regime to which this model of large exchange rate swings and real crisis can be applied. We now turn to the fixed exchange rate case in order to see, for a normal situation of a seemingly fairly strong currency and high economic activity, how the discussed tendency to capital flight may gradually give rise to situations where the economy becomes trapped in a depressed stationary equilibrium of type E_3 in Figure 2.3. It exhibits there a weak currency and low economic activity, but a significant reversal of net exports from a trade deficit to a trade surplus, despite the crisis state to which the economy has jumped and then continually made more severe in the direction of large output loss after the initial depreciation shock. In the fixed exchange rate regime we consider again the cases of fixed money supply. Now however the quantity F_p (foreign bonds demand realised by households) can depart from the level households already own and indeed rise beyond this level until the foreign reserves F_c of the CB become exhausted.

In order to investigate the possibility of an exchange rate crisis for the fixed exchange rate regime by means of the modelling framework of this paper, let us first introduce as reference curve a balanced trade line in its relationship to the IS or goods market equilibrium curve of Figure 2.3. Obviously, the equation

$$0 = NX(Y, s), \ NX_Y < 0, \ NX_s > 0$$

defines an upward sloping curve, representing balanced trade in the Y, s phase space. We have positive net exports on the upper part of the IS curve and negative net exports on its lower part. We assume for this curve that the situations depicted in Figure 2.7 hold true.

Figure 2.7 shows that output is completely fixed by the exchange rate in our model when a given exchange rate (say $\bar{s}$) is assumed. In the depicted situation we have a high level of economic activity, a trade deficit due to a strong currency and based on this high level of activity a capital market curve AA that would imply slight currency depreciation and even higher economic activity (with a lower trade deficit in addition) in the case of perfect exchange rate flexibility. Note here that the AA curve is however only implicitly present; it determines in the background of Figure 2.7 the stock of foreign bonds demanded by the public (excess demand being met out of the stocks held by

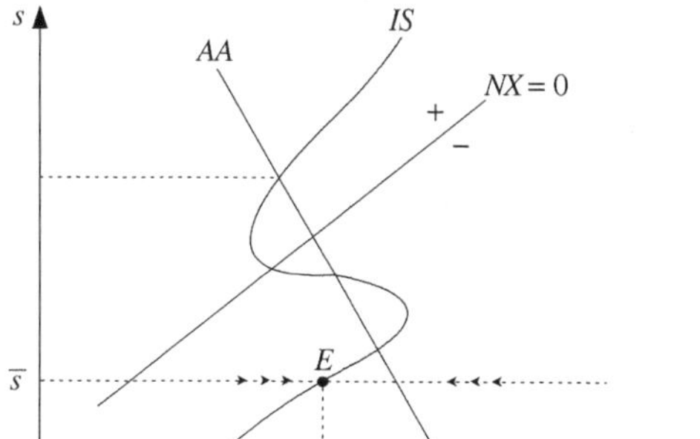

Figure 2.7 Balanced trade line and a normal equilibrium in a fixed exchange rate regime, with 'excess demand' for the foreign asset

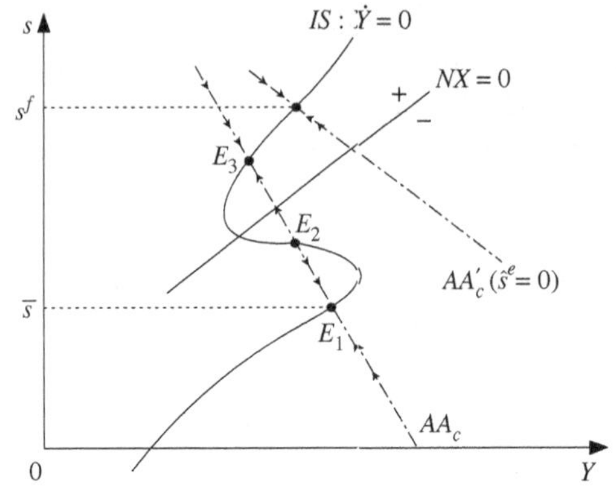

Figure 2.8 The normal real equilibrium, limited intervention range and the shadow dynamics in a fixed exchange rate regime

the CB) and that this curve is based on the assumption of $\hat{s}^e = 0$ in the fixed exchange rate case. The equilibrium Y may be called a normal equilibrium as in Krugman (2000).

The dynamics shown in Figure 2.8 (for the case $\beta_s = \infty$ in equation (2.15)) are therefore only shadow dynamics that would come into existence if the fixed exchange rate regime were to be abandoned by the CB. As long as this is not the case we always have that excess demand for foreign bonds $F_p - F_{po}$ of the private sector, determined by

$$\bar{s}F_p = f(\bar{i}^* - i(Y, M), M_o + B_o + \bar{s}F_{po}, \alpha),$$

is always serviced by the CB out of its foreign bond reserves F_c. Current foreign bond reserves are assumed to be sufficiently large to allow for this balancing of the market for foreign currency. This indeed then allows for the fixed exchange rate regime and implies that in the course of time (when the capital flight parameter α starts to increase in a continuous fashion) that private households hold more and more foreign bonds in their portfolio without a change in the total value of this portfolio, W_p, and thus their nominal wealth position, since the exchange rate is fixed.

We thus assume now that the expression F_p is slowly increasing through the influence (and solely through the influence) of the parameter α, since output is fixed by the given exchange rate. However only the IS curve matters for the domestic equilibrium on the real markets, while the AA curve only determines the position F_p of the stock of foreign bonds currently held in the private sector. Note here again that the expectations mechanism $\hat{s}^e(s)$ is not present in a fixed exchange rate regime, as long as people do not speculate about an exchange rate crisis in terms of exchange rates, which may nevertheless be approaching because of increases in the capital flight parameter α.

Besides the $NX = 0$ curve we also show in Figure 2.8 the critical line AA_c where $\alpha = \alpha_c$ has become so large that $\bar{F}^* = F_p$ (and so $F_c = 0$) holds, a situation in which the CB no longer has any reserves of the foreign currency. At this critical value of α, or indeed even before this value has been reached, the fixed exchange rate system will

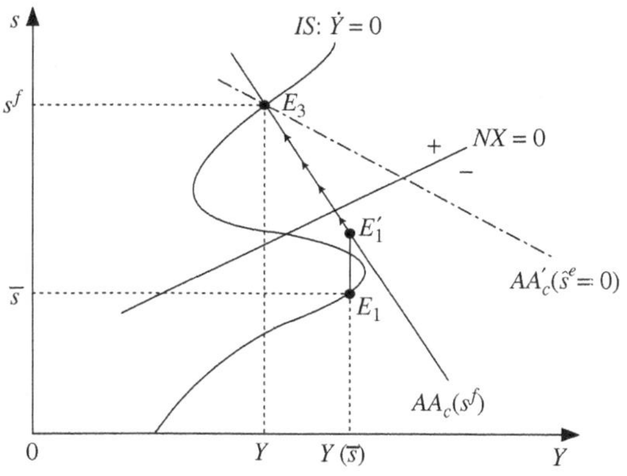

Figure 2.9 The breakdown of the fixed exchange rate regime: currency crisis, investment collapse and large output loss

break down and by assumption be replaced by the regime of perfectly flexible exchange rates considered in the preceding section. We thus assume now that the ongoing process of a financial capital restructuring of private households, via further increases in the capital flight parameter α, has progressed to such a point that the foreign exchange reserves of the CB are basically exhausted as represented by the line AA_c (where $\hat{s}^e = 0$ still holds). We have already indicated in Figure 2.8 the dynamics that would then come about if the exchange rate were to become flexible and be determined by the asset markets. This would however then also re-establish the regressive expectations mechanism, based on the now sole equilibrium E_3 and would thus in addition rotate the line AA_c in a clockwise fashion around this equilibrium to the position $AA_c^{'}$, as explained in the preceding section and shown in Figure 2.9. In Figure 2.9 we go from the potential situation shown in Figure 2.8 to what would actually happen if the exchange rate were again subject to market forces with an adjustment speed $\beta_s = \infty$ in equation (2.15).

When this situation is reached, the exchange rate – by assumption – becomes completely flexible and the shadow dynamics of Figure 2.8 switch on, leading the economy in the way described in the preceding section to the bad equilibrium E_3 along the AA'_c curve. The latter is steeper than the intervention limit curve AA_c shown, but also runs through the single equilibrium point E_3. In addition, the regressive expectations mechanism for the exchange rate dynamics becomes active with a long-run reference value for the exchange rate that is determined through E_3.[23]

The result of such a currency crisis will be (if Figure 2.9 applies) a large initial devaluation of the domestic currency, and based on this a larger and larger loss in output

[23] We thus in fact consider here some sort of asymptotically rational expectations which always know the long-run value of the exchange rate to which the economy will converge. This presumes knowledge of the IS curve and the AA curve for $\hat{s}^e = 0$ at least for the ranges where investment is very unresponsive to the exchange rate. Under this assumption along with the assumption that exchange rate dynamics must again come to a rest, the intersection of these two curves provides the agents with the long-run values of s that enter into their regressive expectations scheme.

as the currency continues to depreciate towards the value s_o (due to the dominance of the investment crisis). In the course of this process there will be a radical improvement in the trade balance (but this will still be too weak to overcome the loss of investment demand). Against this background recall that the domestic CB has lost (nearly) all of its currency reserves due to the flight from domestic bonds into foreign bonds. The economy thus tumbles into a real crisis with large output loss, based on a breakdown of investment, only partly counteracted by net exports due to the strong currency depreciation, with a CB that has become powerless with respect to any further intervention in the foreign exchange market.

Next we consider in addition to the above (again for the case of a fixed exchange rate $\bar{s}$) a law of motion for the capital flight parameter α that by assumption shifts the AA curve to the right if it increases. In the case of fixed exchange rates we again have Figure 2.8 in place of Figure 2.9. It shows the AA curve as the dotted line, an attracting curve that could lead the economy to either E_1 or E_3 if exchange rates were completely flexible (still for $\hat{s}^e = 0$). Note that there is excess demand for foreign bonds below the AA curve and excess supply above it. We have assumed that flexible exchange rates will come about when AA_c- and immediately thereafter AA_c applies in a situation where there is no longer a normal equilibrium point of type E_1.

We have assumed that the demand function f for foreign bonds depends positively on the capital flight parameter α, since an increasing tendency to capital flight means that residents attempt to substitute domestic bonds by foreign bonds. Excess demand (calculated before CB intervention) increasing with α may in fact give rise to a law of motion for α of the following type (presented in discrete time here solely),

$$\alpha_{t+h} = \alpha_t + \beta_\alpha(f(\bar{i}^* - i(Y, M), W_p, \alpha_t) - f(\bar{i}^* - i(Y, M), W_p, \alpha_{t-h})),$$

where $\bar{i}^*$, $i(Y, M)$, $W_p = M_o + B_{0,t} + \bar{s} F_{po,t}$ are all taken as given magnitudes despite the change in the composition of the bond holdings of the public. Note that we have inserted here $\bar{s} F_{p0,t} = f(\bar{i}^* - i(Y, M), W_p, \alpha_{t-h})$ as the result of the past foreign market intervention of the CB at each point in time, in order to express excess demand by the change in demand that has happened from $t - h$ to t. Demand for foreign bonds and their actual holdings are changing in this manner through time (without any change in total private wealth). An initial increase in this demand may therefore set in motion a continuous increase in the parameter α, by way of contagion, for instance. This may lead to an explosive movement of α if $\bar{s}$ and $\alpha(0)$ are such that there is a positive excess demand at these initial values.

Again assume that some shock (for example coming from a neighbouring country) shifts the AA curve to the right to another curve AA$'$. At E_1 we now have excess demand for foreign bonds and thus an increasing α that continues to shift the AA curve to the right until AA_c is again reached. The normal equilibrium of the economy with flexible exchange rate shifts during this process towards higher output and exchange rate levels, until it finally disappears. During this process excess demand for foreign bonds may be increasing in an accelerating fashion, so far always met by the central bank. When α continues to increase there may again arise the situation that the reserves of the CB become exhausted, so that $F_c = \bar{F}^* - F_p \approx 0$.

The fixed exchange rate regime by the CB will then break down and give rise to the exchange rate adjustments already discussed, leading the economy through a sudden depreciation to point E_1'. Here output will start to decrease and the exchange rate will continue to increase until the new stationary point E_3 is reached. The economy is now trapped in a bad equilibrium E_3 as discussed in Krugman (1999, 2000), but with a significant reversal from trade deficits to a trade surplus.

We stress that this outcome may depend to some extent on the way Figure 2.9 has been drawn and therefore only represents the one typical situation when the reserves of the CB are so large and its intervention lasts so long that the AA_c curve, where it ceases its intervention, exhibits only the upper bad equilibrium for the economy with a flexible exchange rate. An alternative situation that may arise in the case of shorter intervention is illustrated in Figure 2.10, which shows an overshooting exchange rate depreciation and in fact an increase in economic activity as the currency starts to appreciate after the initial devaluation shock.

Still another possibility is indicated in Figure 2.11, where there is again no loss in output, since the induced devaluation of the exchange rate is such that its subsequent appreciation leads to increasing output levels via the net export channel. Whichever situation prevails the likelihood of exchange rate crisis coupled with a major collapse in investment behaviour and thus large output loss will lead to a return to flexible exchange rates, due to the lack of reserves to persevere with the fixed exchange rate regime, and re-establish the importance of the AA_c curve as a global attractor and the output movement along it (not always to the left if the bad equilibrium applies) until a new stationary point has been reached. Since AA_c again restricts the positions of the economy we return to $X = 0$ and thus possibly also to a stationary value for the capital flight parameter α.

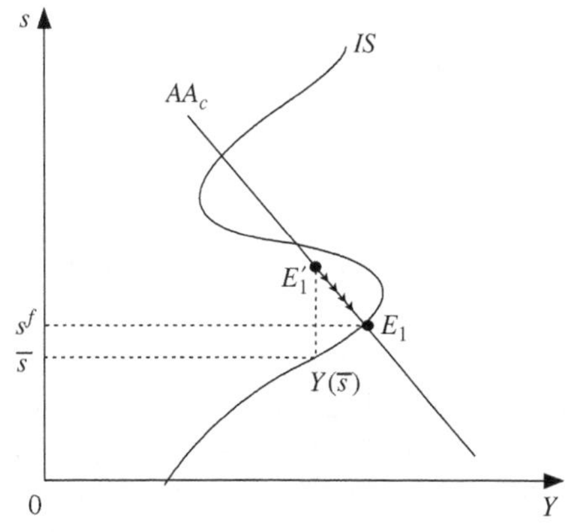

Figure 2.10 No currency crisis and output expansion in the case of a quick return to a flexible exchange rate regime

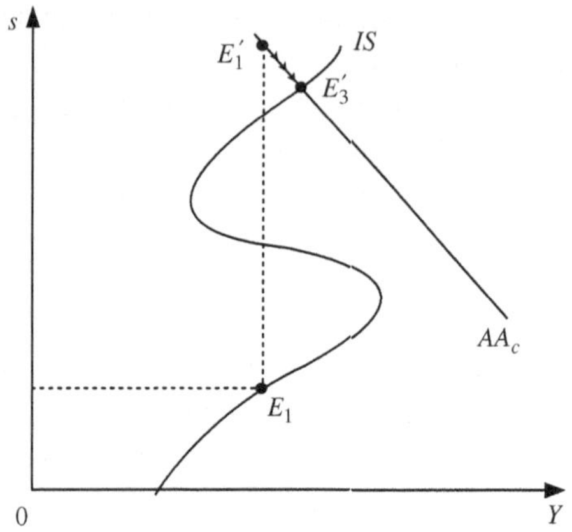

Figure 2.11 Overshooting exchange rate crisis and output improvements due to net export dominance

To sum up, the final consequence of the increasing propensity for capital flight is, if the situations Figure 2.10 and Figure 2.11 do not apply, that the exchange rate depreciates radically and that a severe economic depression will be induced, resulting from the balance sheet effect on investment, coupled with a pronounced reversal from a trade deficit to a trade surplus.

A leaning against the wind strategy of the CB, that is an increase in domestic interest rates in order to stem the capital flight, may, due to the consequent shift of the AA curves to the left, prevent the breakdown of the exchange rate system for some time, but will eventually fail due to the continuous increase in the parameter α as discussed above. This will then make the subsequent recession even more severe, since sooner or later the AA curve will apply, at the point where $\bar{F}^* = F_p$ (and so $F_c = 0$) has been reached.

2.7 International capital flows: adding capital account dynamics

We now extend the model, which has so far followed the assumptions made in Rødseth (2000, Ch. 6), by allowing for international trade in domestic bonds. In order to motivate this we again consider first the balance of payments of the domestic economy.

We now have two new entries (in the capital account) and in the following analysis will consider only equilibrium positions on the international market for domestic bonds so that the remaining part is to be interpreted as in the earlier sections of this chapter. As further simplification we assume that the impact of official reserve transactions on the domestic supply of money can be ignored in the goods market dynamics for the time being. We stress here that the current extension of the MFT model is an important one (though not from the purely mathematical perspective), since the financial markets of the economy are now no longer closed with respect to foreign capital movements,

Table 2.5. *Balance of Payments (in foreign currency)*

Debits	Credits
Trade Account:	
Imports	Exports
sJ	X
Interest Income Account:	
Interest payments of firms to the foreign economies	Interest payments from the foreign economies
$s\bar{i}^* F_f$	$s\bar{i}^* F_p + s\bar{i}^* F_c$
Capital Account:	
$s\dot{F}_p^d$	$\dot{B}^{d*}$
Official Reserve Transactions of the CB:	
$X - sJ + s\bar{i}^* F_p + s\dot{F}_c - s\bar{i}^* F_f$	

but are subject to foreign asset demands and thus now also vulnerable to speculative attacks from abroad.

There is however one further change to be made to the model which is suggested by our continuous-time model as well as the need to input flows $\dot{F}_p^d (= \dot{B}^{d*}/s)$ and not desired stock changes $f(\varepsilon, W_p)/s - F_p$ into the (flow) balance of payments. From the continuous-time perspective it is not very plausible to have full stock equilibrium at all moments in time. Moreover, since agents are facing some adjustment costs, it is therefore plausible to assume that only a portion γ of their desired stock changes $f(\varepsilon, W_p) - sF_p$ appears at the current moment of time as flow demand, here for foreign bonds, $f^d = \gamma(f(\varepsilon, W_p)/s - F_p)$, where γ as in the related (less fast) capital stock adjustment principle has a time dimension (not yet present in the excess stock demand function).

The behaviour of domestic agents on the international capital markets for domestic and foreign bonds assumed above is, as shown, closely related to the stock portfolio approach of this chapter. We assume that money market equilibrium is already ensured and consider the demand function

$$s\dot{F}_p^d = \gamma(f(\varepsilon, W_p) - sF_p)$$

as derived above from the stock demand for foreign bonds $f(\cdot, \cdot)$. The domestic flow demand for domestic bonds is then characterised residually by

$$\begin{aligned}\dot{B}_p^d &= \gamma[\{(M + B + sF_p) - M - f(\varepsilon, W_p)\} - B] \\ &= \gamma[sF_p - f(\varepsilon, W_p)] = -s\dot{F}_p^d = s\dot{F}_p^s.\end{aligned}$$

and thus need not be considered explicitly in the following if it matches with the foreign demand for domestic goods as is assumed below. It is thus obvious that these induced flows add up to zero and thus transform the initial form of a Walras' Law of Stocks into a Walras' Law of Flows on the asset markets.

We thus have to consider in the following only the two flow demand functions (which have to be interpreted as supply functions in their negative domain):

$$s\dot{F}_p^d = \gamma[f(\bar{i}^* + \hat{s}^e(s) - i(Y, M), M + B + sF_p) - sF_p] = f(s, \cdot), \ f_s < 0 \tag{2.16}$$

$$\dot{F}^{d*} = -\frac{\dot{B}^{d*}}{s} = \gamma^*[f^*(\bar{i}^* + \hat{s}^{e*}(s) - i(Y, M), M^* + F^* + \frac{B^*}{s}) - F^*]$$
$$= f^*(s, \cdot), \ f_s^* < 0 \tag{2.17}$$

As in earlier sections of the chapter we have again that f is a strictly decreasing function of the exchange rate s and get now in addition that this also holds true for the demand for foreign bonds by foreigners. The supply of foreign bonds by foreigners $s\dot{F}_p^{s*} = \dot{B}^{d*}$ is therefore an increasing function of the exchange rate. The market for foreign bonds concerning the domestic economy clears if $s\dot{F}_p^d = s\dot{F}_p^{s*}$ holds true, which holds if and only if the market for domestic bonds is cleared. We thus get a situation on the international capital market for domestic bonds as shown in Figure 2.12, describing through the intersection of the two curves shown the equilibrium in the trade between international and domestic bonds and the level of the exchange rate that achieves this result.

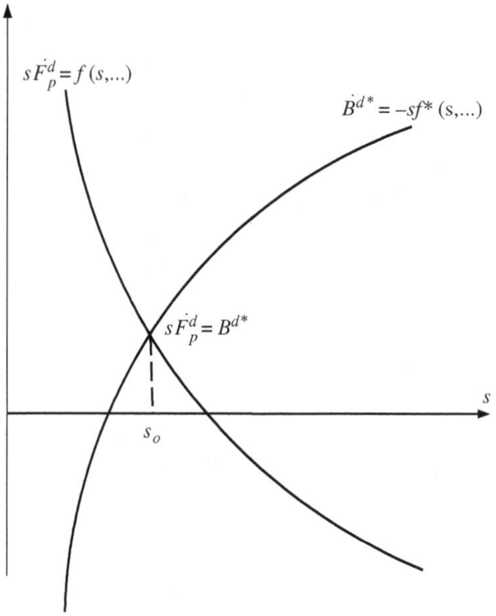

Figure 2.12 Equilibrium on the international market for domestic bonds

Summarising the above MFT extension towards the integration of international capital flows, we can state that the model assumes that cash management comes first and is always characterised by stock money market equilibrium $M/p = m^d(Y, i)$. Against this background domestic agents then plan to reallocate their interest-bearing assets according to the behavioural relationship $f(\varepsilon, W_p)$.

Figure 2.12 shows the level of the exchange rate s_o where the domestic demand curve for foreign bonds (the supply curve for domestic bonds) and the foreign demand curve for domestic bonds (the supply curve for foreign bonds) intersect and where therefore capital flow equilibrium is established. The equilibrium exchange rate now also depends on foreign characteristics in contrast to the case considered earlier in this chapter, where domestic bonds were considered as non-traded goods and where therefore the supply of such bonds (in the case of a flexible exchange rate regime) was just given by F_p. In this case the equilibrium in the domestic market for foreign bonds would be determined by the intersection of the f curve with the horizontal axis and would thus be independent of foreign asset demand. This is definitely a situation that is too simple to characterise today's international financial system. Note that the $-sf^*$ curve is a supply curve of foreign bonds, while in the form sf^* it would represent a demand curve for foreign bonds. In the case where the latter is identical to the f curve shown, the intersection of the f, $-sf^*$ must lie on the horizontal axis, so that the equilibrium exchange rate implies in this special case that there is no international capital flow.

We consider now the alternative situation of a fixed exchange rate regime ($s = \bar{s}$), where $\hat{s}^e = 0$ holds under normal conditions. Figure 2.13 depicts such a situation and shows that the CB is forced, in the depicted case of a domestic excess demand for foreign bonds, to supply the amount $\dot{F}_c$ to the market for foreign bonds in order to defend its particular choice of exchange rate level. Such a situation can be very vulnerable however in a small open economy, since the reserves of the country may have become small in the course of time and thus provoke a currency crisis.

Foreigners (and also domestic residents) might for example correctly regard a situation in the considered economy, where $\dot{F}^d_p = \dot{F}^{s*}_p + \dot{F}^s_c$, $\dot{F}^s_c > 0$ holds as not being sustainable and expect that the domestic CB must give in sooner or later and allow the exchange to float freely due to a lack of reserves. In the given excess demand situation they therefore expect a devaluation of the domestic currency and thus start to move out of domestic bonds into foreign bonds or, as Figure 2.14 in fact shows, reduce their demand for domestic bonds. If such a move is sufficiently strong, this may quickly undermine the possibility of the CB of defending the fixed exchange rate system and thus indeed produce the result of a flexible exchange rate regime s_o that was already expected.

Another possibility for the occurrence of such a situation may be given by a speculative borrowing of domestic currency (bonds). These funds are then used to buy foreign bonds on the international capital market. If this move into foreign currency is again sufficiently strong this can also cause the CB to switch towards a flexible exchange rate regime and allow thereby for a devaluation of the domestic currency. The initial

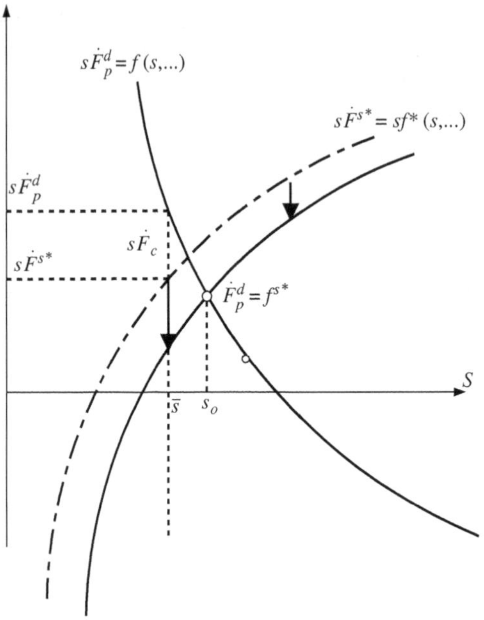

Figure 2.13 Fixed exchange rate regime and a speculative attack on the domestic currency

borrowers of the domestic currency can then make significant profits by going back into domestic bonds and paying back the credit with which they started their initial financial transactions.

Fixed exchange rate systems thus appear as vulnerable institutional configurations in countries where firms have high foreign debt, since an exchange rate crisis and a subsequent devaluation of the domestic currency can significantly affect the net worth of firms, their credit-worthiness and their investment financing. The resulting investment credit crunch then leads, via the Keynesian multiplier process, to large output losses. This was already demonstrated for the financially closed economy. The emergence of such credit crunch situations however becomes much more likely if there is international trade in domestic and foreign bonds, since capital movements can become much more pronounced in such a case.

We therefore now consider again a flexible exchange rate system in order to see what problems may arise in such a context. As flow demand functions on the international bond markets we have the equilibrium expression which determines now the equilibrium exchange rate at each moment in time. This may be written

$$s\dot{F}_p^d = \gamma[f(\bar{i}^* + \hat{s}^e(s) - i, M + B + sF_p) - sF_p], \quad \text{or equivalently} \tag{2.18}$$

$$\dot{B}^{d*}/s = -\gamma^*[f^*(\bar{i}^* + \hat{s}^{e*}(s) - i, M^* + F^* + B^*/s) - F^*] \tag{2.19}$$

Solving one of these equations for the equilibrium exchange rate by means of the implicit function theorem gives the general expression

$$s = s(i(Y, \bar{M}), \bar{i}^*, \bar{M}, \bar{M}^*, B, B^*, F_p, F^*). \tag{2.20}$$

This function generalises the original Dornbusch (1976) approach which assumed the uncovered interest rate parity condition $i = i^* + \hat{s}^e(s)$ and it implies (as in Dornbusch) that s depends positively on i^* and negatively on i, but here also with explicit influences from the stocks of financial assets that now impact the determination of the exchange rate s. On this basis we can write the laws of motion in the domestic economy as

$$\dot{Y} = \beta_y(C(Y - \delta\bar{K} - \bar{T}) + I(s) + \delta\bar{K} + \bar{G} + NX(Y, \bar{Y}^*, s) - Y) \tag{2.21}$$

$$\dot{F}_p = \gamma[f(\bar{i}^* + \hat{s}^e(s) - i(Y, M), M + B + sF_p)/s - F_p]. \tag{2.22}$$

In the background of the model we have now however also changes in the stocks of domestic and foreign bonds, due to the firms' and the government's budget constraints which implies that the above laws of motion do not constitute an autonomous system of differential equations.

We have however as in the case of a closed domestic capital market that the dependence of the exchange rate s on output Y is a negative one (with all stocks of financial assets considered as given magnitudes for the time being) and thus in this case again we have the AA curve depicted earlier. But this curve (and the resulting equilibrium exchange rate), shown in Figure 2.14, is now moving in time in ways not easy to

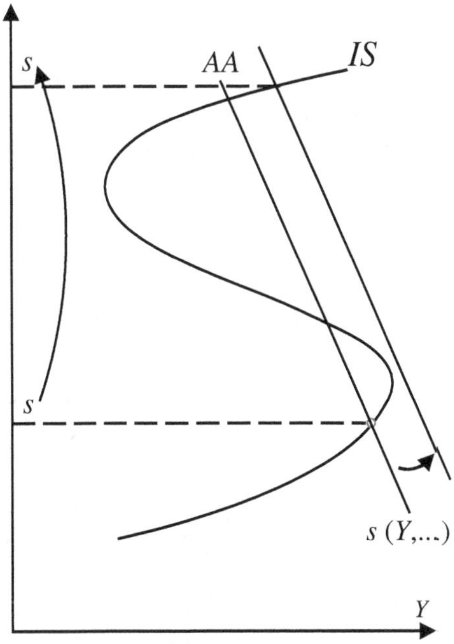

Figure 2.14 Flexible exchange rate and the endogenous change from booms to busts

determine and thus may in particular lead to situations where the boom equilibrium shown in Figure 2.14, exhibiting high investment, high output levels and a strong domestic currency, gets lost. This will then lead again to a radical depreciation of the domestic currency, and from there to severely depressed levels of investment and thus high output losses. The economy therefore remains vulnerable also in the case of a flexible exchange rate regime, due to its high dependence on foreign credit in the financing decision of domestic firms.

Economic policy should therefore aim to steer the economy away from the (not really known) right-hand output maximum of the IS curve in order to not allow for a situation that is easily vulnerable in the way just discussed. This means that investment should not be pushed up to its supply rationed level where such a regime switch to a currency crisis becomes likely. Finally, in a flexible exchange rate regime, the domestic economy is heavily dependent on foreign investment strategies and therefore of course not at all as safe as in the case with no international capital flows that we considered earlier.

2.8 Conclusions

We have introduced in this chapter an open economy portfolio model that has allowed us to study the channels that cause, and the feedback effects that arise from, large currency swings. We have demonstrated that large currency swings under flexible exchange rates as well as slowly progressing and then sudden capital flights under fixed exchange rates may lead to strong repercussions on the financial market when a large fraction of the domestic debt of firms is denominated in foreign currency. There are also strong repercussions under fixed exchange rates when there are capital flights that develop slowly at first and then become abrupt. These repercussions may in turn entail a low level equilibria and large output losses for the economy. Following a model suggested by Krugman (1999, 2000) we showed rigorously in a dynamic model with multiple equilibria that there are mechanisms at work that can indeed give rise to such phenomena. Our results point to the dangers that may be brought about for a country if financial and capital market liberalisation without safety nets and sufficient financial market regulations are pursued too quickly, and we have shown that a flexible exchange rate does not exclude such dangers.

We have considered the small and sometimes very large effects of increasing dollar-liquidity preference in a set-up where the exchange rate, if flexible, was moving counter-cyclically and where leaning against the wind policies were present via restrictive monetary policy. These policies attempt to shift the financial markets equilibrium curve to the left where there is reduced output but stronger currency values that partially neutralise the increasing dollar-oriented liquidity preference. Such policies may also be supported by the IMF as a lender of last resort. Those efforts may prevent the outbreak of the considered crisis and may be a more appropriate way to cope with the increased vulnerability of small open economies exhibiting a high level of foreign debt.

The model was completely explicit with respect to budget conditions, the accounts of the four sectors of the economy and the balance of payments, showing clearly however the narrow foundations on which this type of crisis model still rests. We have flow consistency and the fulfilment of all plans of the agents of the economy – up to firms which may be credit or supply rationed in their pursuit of new investment goods. We still have fixed-price bonds. Expectations thus solely concern changes in the exchange rate, depreciation or appreciation, and were assumed to be of the asymptotically rational (regressive) type. Assuming fixed-price bonds means that asset holders can indeed enforce a currency crisis (in a fixed exchange rate system) if they initially hold enough domestic bonds compared with the dollar-denominated bonds held by the CB. Speculation on the degree of success of currency attacks is thus quite possible in this framework.

Concerning expectations one might ask why we did not assume rational expectations (based on myopic perfect foresight) in this chapter. However, this would turn the two equilibria that were stable under regressive expectations into saddlepoint dynamics. Furthermore, the unstable equilibrium in the middle would then become a stable equilibrium, if the dynamic multiplier process is supposed to work with sufficient speed. We would therefore obtain a situation that is not easily handled by means of the conventional jump variable technique.

Rather than pursuing this type of extension one might approach goods market behaviour with more advanced behavioural functions as in Rødseth (2000, Ch. 6) or extend the asset market approach towards flex-price bonds and also add equity issuance of firms. A stock-flow interaction may then be added to the model.

Finally, in the place of a fixed money supply or its discretionary changes, we could consider interest rate policy rules (Taylor type rules) and also Phillips curve (PC) driven price dynamics. The latter could in particular help to elaborate the issue of debt deflation, since firms are already formulated here as being highly indebted and thus also very vulnerable with respect to output price deflation, in particular if wages and foreign interest rates remain given magnitudes; see Chapter 4 for a treatment of debt deflation in the context of a closed economy.

3 Mortgage loans, debt default and the emergence of banking crises

3.1 Mortgage and banking crises

The current financial crisis in the USA can be characterised by a fast expansion of mortgage loans to households in order to purchase real estate. A difference to the traditional Minskyan crisis and the previous type of financial crisis is that borrowers are not firms but households. The Japanese crisis was characterised by firms and banks borrowing to invest in real estate, and the East Asian crisis was characterised by firms and banks borrowing foreign-denominated debt. In the current worldwide crisis, financial fragility that has led borrowers from hedge to speculative and even Ponzi positions involves the dynamics of household income and interest payments.

There are three main reasons explaining the large increase in mortgage credit: competition between financial institutions; the interaction between real estate prices and credit constraints; financial innovations. These three elements have induced banks to relax screening and monitoring of borrowers and to increase the quantity of credit supplied to households. First, in the aftermath of the crash of the dotcom bubble in 2000 and in an environment characterised by low interest rates, banks, under the pressure of financial intermediaries such as hedge funds, found in mortgage debt a highly profitable business. Second, increasing real estate prices contributed to the relaxation of credit rationing. The increasing value of collateral has reduced default risk and has led banks to increase credit, in line with the financial accelerator model. Third, financial engineering is central to understanding why banks have reduced the screening and monitoring of borrowers.

Securitisation has been the major financial innovation. In 2006, securitisation concerned 87 per cent of prime mortgages and 75 per cent of subprime mortgages (Ashcraft and Schuermann, 2007). Securitisation aims at transforming loans into liquid assets in order to transfer the credit risk to the market. Mortgages with different qualities are bundled together and the resulting financial products are usually sold to the market through special purpose vehicles (SPVs) in the form of collateralised debt obligations (CDOs) or residential mortgage-backed securities (RMBSs). The belief was that credit risk was transferred to the market-led banks to expand the supply of credit, leading to a worsening of the average quality of loans. In addition, securitisation reduced the need of banks to increase their own funds following credit expansion. In a traditional banking sector, banks are exposed to credit risk and must provision reserves to cover the risk accordingly. As risks were transferred to the market, banks were not forced to provision for them. Although securitisation was supposed to reduce the exposure of banks to risk, it in fact induced banks to take on more risk.

As a result, low income households were able to access credit, the so-called subprime mortgages. While subprime borrowers accounted for 9 per cent of borrowers in 2000, this proportion had increased to 20 per cent by 2006 (Dell Ariccia *et al.* (2008)). This large increase in mortgage debt produced a deterioration of household incomes and soaring debt defaults.

However, the mortgage crisis led to a banking crisis because securitisation failed to protect banks against credit risk. SPVs turned out not to be independent of banks, as banks were funding these companies and were guaranteeing the emission of mortgage-backed securities. More importantly, banks bought asset-backed and mortgage-backed securities, so that banks were still exposed to default risk but had not built reserves accordingly.

In this chapter, we study the very first elements of the crisis: the macroeconomic effects of household debt. We leave aside for the moment the role played by real estate prices, financial innovations and debt default on credit rationing. We are mainly concerned with understanding the dynamics between household debt, interest payments, wages and aggregate demand. The starting framework is a Goodwinian cycle, in which household consumption and debt as well as independent investment behaviour is introduced in order to assess whether it adds stability or instability to the baseline dynamics.

We make use of an approach originally formulated in supply side terms only and introduce Keynesian elements into it. The central features of this approach to Keynesian macrodynamic theory, and its application to the study of the financial market and boom-bust cycles, are the mechanisms generating non-cleared markets and the phenomenon of disequilibrium that is recurrently present in certain markets such as the labour or goods markets. In contrast to the mainstream which generally stresses the clearing of all markets at each instant of time,[1] in our modelling approach, as it will be stressed on several occasions, disequilibrium situations are the main driving force of wage/price inflation dynamics. Moreover, disequilibrium effects in financial markets are often generated by overleveraging in the real sector, in the household sector as well as in the financial sector of the economy. Some of the markets may act as either stabilising or destabilising forces through a variety of different macroeconomic channels such as the real wage feedback channel, the product market, the financial market as well as debt devaluation channels. Thus we demonstrate that there are indeed different (and also quite valid) possibilities to specify and analyse the dynamics of the macroeconomy than just in the currently fashionable Dynamic Stochastic General Equilibrium (DSGE) framework.

[1] In our view an heroic assumption in a continuous-time modelling framework.

Due to the fact that in our modelling approach the stability of the analysed dynamical system is not imposed *ab initio* by assumptions of rational expectations, which require that the economy always 'jumps' to some stable manifold and therefore always converges to the steady state after any type of shock, its stability properties (and its analysis) are based on the relative strength of the interacting macroeconomic and financial feedback channels. The ongoing occurrence of 'bubbles' and 'herding' in the financial markets across the world, as well as the large macroeconomic imbalances present nowadays in the global economy through overleveraging, show that such divergent paths do indeed take place in significant and sometimes long-lasting ways.

In this chapter we add to the crisis analysis of the preceding chapter by considering a sequence of models (a sequence of parameter scenarios for a single three-dimensional dynamical model in fact) that run from situations of stable excessive overconsumption of worker households, to their weakly excessive overconsumption and a certain degree of instability, and from there to the situation of a strict credit rationing of worker households. In the fourth model type we then consider actions that rescue the economy from this last instability scenario and imply a path back to economic stability that is based on investment stimuli and monetary policy regarding the loan and the default rate on the credit market.

In the latter type of economy, the loan rate will again fall to a low value and workers' debt will reduce in time through their now positive savings. In the limit, this economy could even converge to a situation where workers are lending to asset holders, since they have a positive savings rate in the steady state. Yet, we view this phase as representing only a transient phase where the economy recovers to a certain degree from too high mortgage debt to its normal functioning, maybe subsequently followed again by the emergence of some behaviour that leads the macroeconomy back to the stable overconsumption situation from which we started. The sequence of events analysed in this chapter may play itself out in actual historical events.

In light of the quotation from Minsky at the beginning of Chapter 1 it may well be, if the transient phase is long enough, that the first type of excessive overconsumption reappears and that the whole process starts again, although possibly in a different historical garb. It is our view that certain features of Minsky's financial instability hypothesis[2] have indeed reoccurred in the present financial crisis.

3.2 A Keynes–Goodwin model with mortgage loans and debt default

We consider a Keynesian model where income distribution matters and where workers purchase goods and houses with a marginal propensity to consume significantly larger than one.[3] The worker households therefore need credit, supplied by asset holders (acting as commercial banks), and have to pay interest on their outstanding debt.

[2] See Minsky (1992).

[3] This chapter is based on the baseline model of a mortgage crises developed in Charpe *et al.* (2009). There the authors investigate overconsumption of worker households, their credit rationing and bailout monetary policy. Here we generalise this treatment of overconsumption driven mortgage crises towards an inclusion of commercial banks as lending and depositary institutions.

In this initial situation, the steady state is attracting, due to the fact that goods market equilibrium is profit-led (although aggregate demand is wage-led), since economic activity here depends, as an exception, positively on workers' debt. A marginal propensity somewhat closer to one however makes the steady state repelling, since economic activity then becomes wage-led as well. The stable excessive overconsumption case is thus a fragile one that can easily turn from a stable boom to explosiveness and from there through induced processes of credit rationing into a devastating bust. In such a situation the public authorities may prevent the worst by specifically stimulating investment, discouraging consumption of indebted workers to a certain degree and by acting as a creditor of last resort, purchasing loans where otherwise debt default (and bankruptcy regarding house ownership) would occur. This bailout policy, accompanied by supporting decreases in the loan rate on debt, re-establishes stability for the economy and reduces the loss of homes of worker households.

The model of this section consists of two household types: workers and asset holders, and firms that are owned by the asset holders (through their real investment contributions). Workers have wage income which they totally spend on goods consumption and the purchase of houses (part of which is financed through loans from the asset holders). Their combined marginal propensity to consume, $c_w = c_g^w + c_h^w$, is therefore assumed to be larger than one. Workers' real wage income, Y_w, is however reduced through the interest they have to pay on their actual real loans, Λ_w^a, and the excess of their spending over this income determines the amount of new loans $\dot{\Lambda}_w$, they need for their intended purchase of new houses. Since the model allows for debt default this rate of change is however not the rate of change of actual loans. In equations this all reads as

Workers:

$$Y_w = vY - i\Lambda_w^a, \quad v = \frac{\omega L^d}{Y} = \frac{\omega}{z} \quad \text{the wage share} \tag{3.1}$$

$$C_w = (c_g^w + c_h^w)Y_w, \quad c_w = c_g^w + c_h^w > 1 \tag{3.2}$$

$$\dot{\Lambda}_w = (c_w - 1)Y_w = -S_w \tag{3.3}$$

$$\dot{K}_w = c_h^w Y_w - \varphi_b K_w, \quad \varphi_b K_w = \varphi_d \Lambda_w^a \tag{3.4}$$

$$\hat{L} = n = const \tag{3.5}$$

In these equations we denote the real wage by ω (and the given state of labour productivity by $z = Y/L^d$). Labour supply L is subject to natural growth and employment L^d is determined in the sector of firms (see below). The symbol i denotes the loan rate on workers' real debt Λ_w^a and the demand of workers for new loans is here not subject to credit rationing (by asset holders), although there is debt default of amount $\varphi_d \Lambda_w^a$ that depends on the loan rate and that translates itself into bankruptcy (decay of the stock of houses) of the amount of houses $\varphi_b K_w$ (from which the owners are removed and which becomes useless as has been seen in the mortgage crisis in the US economy). This loss of housing capital reduces of course the rate of change of the housing stock of workers as shown in equation (3.4). Note finally that the consumption function of workers is the only behavioural assumption that is made in this module of the model.

Asset Holders:

$$Y_c = rK + i\Lambda_w^a, \quad r = \frac{Y - \delta K - vY}{K} \tag{3.6}$$

$$C_c = 0 \quad [S_c = Y_c] \tag{3.7}$$

$$\dot{\Lambda}_w^a = \dot{\Lambda}_w - \varphi_d \Lambda_w^a \tag{3.8}$$

$$W = R + K + \Lambda_w^a \tag{3.9}$$

$$\dot{R} = Y_c - \dot{\Lambda}_w - I = S_c + S_w - I = S - I \tag{3.10}$$

Asset holders, who play the role of commercial banks in this chapter, do not consume and spend their real profit income rK (with r the rate of profit of firms) and their interest income, through their savings, on new debt given to workers $\dot{\Lambda}_w$, on the new capital goods given to firms and on new reserve holdings $\dot{R}$.[4] They do not ration worker households' purchases with respect to their financing decisions and are also completely passive with respect to their demand for new reserves. In this formulation they are therefore fairly passive suppliers of funds. They do however set the loan rate for the credit market which by and large is a given magnitude in this chapter (see however Section 3.6 for an exception). Note here finally that the chapter still ignores a resale market for houses and thus cannot say anything on the occurrence of booms and busts in such a market (as they preceded the subprime crisis in the US economy).

The sector of firms is also still formulated in a very simple manner. Firms produce output according to effective demand Y (by means of a fixed proportions technology with y^p the potential output-capital ratio and $z = Y/L^d$ their employment function with a given labour productivity z) and are choosing their rate of net investment I[5] by the excess of their rate of profit over its steady state value. Moreover, the trend term in their investment behaviour is simply given by the natural rate of growth in order to avoid any discussion about how natural growth and capital stock growth adjust to each other.[6]

Firms:

$$u = Y/Y^p \quad \text{the rate of capacity utilisation} \tag{3.11}$$

$$y^p = Y^p/K = const \quad \text{the potential output capital ratio} \tag{3.12}$$

[4] In the subsequent analysis we will assume goods market equilibrium ($S = S_c + S_w = I + \delta K$) and can then show that the change in R is always zero. We therefore ignore the variable R altogether by setting it equal to zero in the following.

[5] Depreciation δK is retained by firms as replacement for worn-out capital goods.

[6] We will ignore in this chapter all effects that can result from changes in the rate of capacity utilisation of firms. This would demand the integration of a wage-price spiral as considered in Flaschel and Krolzig (2006) from the theoretical as well as from an empirical point of view. Such a wage-price spiral is also needed when the steady state assumption $y_o = y^p$, see below, is to be derived as an implied condition.

$$z = Y/L^d = const \quad \text{labour productivity} \tag{3.13}$$

$$I/K = i_f(r - r_o) + n, \quad r = \frac{(1-v)Y}{K} - \delta. \tag{3.14}$$

The present chapter concentrates on the interaction between indebted workers and credit supplying asset holders (playing the role of commercial banks). The sector of firms is therefore considered as fairly tranquil and not subject to volatile investment behaviour. There is in particular no debt financing of investment. Instead it is assumed throughout the chapter that asset holders directly invest part of their income into real capital stock formation and this at a rate that is smaller than one as far as the comparison with excess profitability (or loss) is concerned. Note here however that this gives rise in the real growth dynamics to a Goodwin (1967) type profit squeeze mechanism that can be either wage-led or profit-led. The debt feedback chain of the economy is therefore integrated with such a growth cycle model in this chapter and investigated with respect to the consequences it has in such a framework.

The final law of motion of this model of fluctuating growth and indebtedness in the housing sector concerns the real wage dynamic that drives the real part of the economy in the form of a real wage Phillips curve (PC) (a conventional textbook PC with myopic perfect foresight regarding price inflation)

Real Wage Adjustment:

$$\hat{\omega} = \beta_{we}(e - \bar{e}). \tag{3.15}$$

The variable $e = \frac{L^d}{L}$ denotes the rate of employment, with Y the demand driven output level of firms. Real wages are driven by excess demand pressure $e - \bar{e}$ on the labour market (with $\bar{e}$ the normal rate of employment). Such real wage dynamics are obtained from a conventional wage PC if myopic perfect foresight is assumed for its accelerator term.

3.3 Excessive overconsumption and an attracting steady state

The 3D dynamics implied by the model of the preceding section to be investigated in this section in a special case, is based on a PC distributive cycle mechanism interacting with a Goodwin (1967) type growth dynamics and a law of motion for the debt to capital ratio of workers. The system, in terms of the state variables, can be written as[7]

$$\hat{v} = \beta_{we}(y/l - \bar{e}), \quad v = \frac{\omega}{z}, \tag{3.16}$$

$$\hat{l} = -i_f(r - r_o), \quad r = (1-v)y - \delta, \quad l = \frac{zL}{K}. \tag{3.17}$$

[7] The differential equations for v and l follow easily from their ratio definitions. The differential equation for λ_w^a is obtained by taking the logarithm of the ratio defining it and then time-differentiating it and substituting in the extensive form equations.

$$\dot{\lambda}_w^a = (c_w - 1)(vy - i\lambda_w^a) - (i_f(r - r_o) + n + \varphi_d)\lambda_w^a, \quad \lambda_w^a = \frac{\Lambda_w^a}{K}, \tag{3.18}$$

with the goods market equilibrium or IS expression for the output capital ratio

$$y = \frac{c_w i\lambda_w^a + i_f(\delta + r_o) - n - \delta}{(c_w - i_f)v + i_f - 1}. \tag{3.19}$$

This IS curve is easily obtained from the goods market equilibrium equation

$$Y = c_w(vY - i\Lambda_w^a) + (i_f(r - r_o) + n + \delta)K. \tag{3.20}$$

by transforming it into intensive form and by solving it for the output-capital ratio y. Note that the budget equations of the two households of the model imply $\dot{R} = 0$ if IS equilibrium is assumed.[8]

We assume in this section that

$$c_w > 1 + (1 - i_f)(1 - v_o)/v_o > 1 > i_f \quad \text{iff} \quad c_w > 1 > i_f > \frac{1 - c_w v_o}{1 - v_o}$$

holds true. In this case the Goodwin subcycle is characterised by stability and the marginal propensity of workers to consume is very large, and may be empirically beyond all reasonable values. We therefore consider this starting case to be an extreme situation of excessive overconsumption backed up by unrestricted loans. We have in this case that the denominator of the IS curve in (3.19) is positive and we will show below that the numerator of equation (3.19) is also positive when evaluated at the steady state value of λ_w^a. This assumption implies that goods demand is extremely 'wage-led', which is a natural assumption in the case where the marginal propensity to consume is larger than one. However this extreme case implies that the ratio y depends negatively on the wage share v (which one would not expect it to be true in a wage-led economy), since the denominator in the IS curve in equation (3.19) is positive, and it moreover implies a positive dependence of y on the debt to capital ratio λ_w^a (around the steady state of the model, to be discussed below).

The law of motion (3.17) for the labour-capital ratio l is easily obtained by means of the standard rules for growth rate calculations. The law of motion (3.18) for the wage share v is a simple consequence of our real wage PC when labour productivity is assumed to be constant.

We also have a further law of motion, for the ratio $k_w = K_w/K$, which however does not feed back into the above dynamics and which reads

$$\hat{k}_w = c_h^w(vy - i\lambda_w^a)/k_w - [i_f(r - r_o) + n] - \varphi_d\lambda_w^a/k_w. \tag{3.21}$$

Equation (3.21) shows how bankruptcy of worker households accompanies their debt default concerning credit they have obtained from the asset holders. Of course these

[8] On this basis we have

$$\dot{R} = rK + i\Lambda_w^a - \dot{\Lambda}_w - I = rK + i\Lambda_w^a - (c_w - 1)(vY - i\Lambda_w^a) - I = Y - \delta K - C - I = 0.$$

two laws of motion should feed back into the baseline dynamics (3.16), (3.17) and (3.18) in future extensions of the model. Note also that there is no resale market for houses in the present formulation of the model so that houses can be treated as consumption goods and need not be classified as investment goods, as is done in the system of national accounts. By assumption part of the housing stock has been financed by mortgages, and may therefore be subject to bankruptcy if debt default occurs on such loans.

Proposition 3.1 (The reference balanced growth path)
Assume that the risk premium r_o is given in an appropriate way (to be determined below). There is then in general a locally uniquely determined interior steady state of the dynamics (3.16)–(3.18) which is given by[9]

$$y_o = y^p, \tag{3.22}$$

$$e_o = \bar{e}, \quad l_o = y_o/\bar{e}, \tag{3.23}$$

$$y_{wo} = \frac{y_o - \delta - n}{c_w}, \tag{3.24}$$

$$\lambda^a_{wo} = \frac{c_w - 1}{n + \varphi_d} y_{wo}, \tag{3.25}$$

$$v_o = \frac{y_{wo} + i\lambda^a_{wo}}{y_o} = \frac{y_{wo}}{y_o}\left(1 + i\frac{c_w - 1}{n + \varphi_d}\right), \tag{3.26}$$

$$r_o = (1 - v_o)y_o - \delta. \tag{3.27}$$

Proof: The first two steady state values (3.22) and (3.23) have been set from the outside (and are determined in this way if the law of motion for the inflationary climate is added to the model). The goods market equilibrium then gives the equation for workers' income (3.24), which in turn can be used to determine the steady state debt ratio (3.25) by setting $\dot{\lambda}^a_w = 0$. The steady wage share (3.26) is then obtained from the definition of workers' income. Finally. the target rate of profit r_o in (3.27) is determined in such a way that the wage share allows for $\dot{l} = 0$. □

If one assumes the special case $i = n + \varphi_d$ one gets in particular that

$$y_o = y^p, \tag{3.28}$$

$$e_o = \bar{e}, \; l_o = y_o/\bar{e}, \tag{3.29}$$

$$y_{wo} = \frac{y_o - \delta - n}{c_w}, \tag{3.30}$$

$$\lambda^a_{wo} = (c_w - 1)y_{wo}/i, \tag{3.31}$$

[9] The condition $y_o = y^p$ is an assumption that can only be proved to be valid if a more complete framework is used that allows the integration of inflation and anti-inflationary monetary policy. The condition on r_o is therefore used here as a substitute for the introduction of that broader theoretical framework.

$$v_o = \frac{y_{wo} + i\lambda^a_{wo}}{y_o} = \frac{c_w y_{wo}}{y_o} = \frac{y_o - \delta - n}{y_o} > 0, \tag{3.32}$$

$$r_o = (1 - v_o)y_o - \delta = n, \tag{3.33}$$

which ensures that $v_o \in (0, 1)$ holds true and $r_o = n$, the so-called Cambridge equation (for the case $s_c = 1$). Note that this situation implies that the steady state rate of profit r_o is then equal to the rate of return on loans $(i\lambda^a_w - \varphi_d\lambda^a_w)/\lambda^a_w$. The analysis that follows will investigate, with the exception of cases where the loan rate is assumed to be close to zero (see also Section 3.6 on monetary policy), cases that are close to this special situation.

Remark 3.1 (1) It is obvious from the above that the steady state values are of meaningful size. They are also meaningful in the border case $i = 0$ (keeping $n + \varphi_d$ fixed). Note that the value of r_o has been adjusted in such a way that the assumption $i_f(\cdot) = 0$ is fulfilled at the steady state values.

(2) Assuming as in Goodwin (1967) a parameter value $c_w = 1$ gives as a special case $\lambda^a_w = 0$, to be considered later on. Note however that the investment function (through its interest rate dependence) still preserves the Keynesian IS curve and thus preserves the situation of a Goodwin growth cycle model that is demand driven on its market for goods. Considering the IS curve in this case in more detail gives

$$y = \frac{i_f(\delta + r_o) - n - \delta}{(i_f - 1)(1 - v)},$$

which exhibits a negative denominator in the case of $i_f < 1$.

We consider in the following however the case of a strongly wage-led goods demand characterised by

$$c_w > 1 + (1 - i_f)(1 - v_o)/v_o > 1 > i_f, \tag{3.34}$$

already briefly mentioned above. In this case we have a positive denominator in the expression for the IS curve of the model given by

$$y = \frac{c_w i\lambda^a_w + i_f(\delta + r_o) - n - \delta}{(c_w - i_f)v + i_f - 1}. \tag{3.35}$$

Under condition (3.34) the numerator and denominator of (3.35) are both positive at the steady state. For the partial derivatives of the functions y, vy, r with respect to v we find that[10]

$$\frac{\partial y}{\partial v} = -y\frac{c_w - i_f}{D} < 0, \quad \frac{\partial (vy)}{\partial v} = y\frac{i_f - 1}{D} < 0, \quad \frac{\partial r}{\partial v} = -y\frac{c_w - 1}{D} < 0. \tag{3.36}$$

[10] Note that in the subsequent analysis it is convenient to introduce a specific symbol for the denominator of (3.35) at the steady state, namely

$$D = (c_w - i_f)v_o + i_f - 1.$$

For the derivative $\frac{\partial y}{\partial \lambda_w^a}$ we in addition always have

$$\frac{\partial y}{\partial \lambda_w^a} = \frac{c_w i}{D} > 0, \qquad \frac{\partial r}{\partial \lambda_w^a} = \frac{c_w i}{D}(1-v) > 0$$

which transforms itself directly into corresponding derivatives for vy, $r = (1-v)y-\delta$. The partial derivatives with respect to the state variable v in equation (3.36) show in particular that these derivatives do not depend at the steady state on the interest rate i so that the influence of i on the Jacobian of the dynamics only comes in to play when the partial derivative $\frac{\partial y}{\partial \lambda_w^a} = c_w i/D$ is involved. Note that we will use for brevity y_v in place of $\frac{\partial y}{\partial v}$, etc. in the following discussion.

The sign of the derivative $y_v < 0$ shows the somewhat striking result that the goods market dynamics appear to be profit-led, although aggregate demand per unit of capital is clearly wage-led, because of $y_v^d = (c_w - i_f)y > 0$. This indicates that empirical findings on the role of income distribution on the market for goods (where we in fact can only observe empirically the interactions of demand and supply) which state that the goods market behaviour is profit-led (decreases with increases in the wage share) can be completely in line with the unobservable fact that planned goods demand depends positively on the wage share (so that it is wage-led). We note also that in the extreme case here considered we have a positive effect of increases in the loan rate on the state of the goods market. This is a further astonishing characteristic of the very excessive consumption case being considered here.

The Jacobian of the dynamic (3.16)–(3.18) reads in the special case being considered (note that we use the abbreviation $k = \beta_{we}/l_o$)[11]

$$J = \begin{pmatrix} k y_v v_o & -k\bar{e} v_o & k y_{\lambda_w^a} v_o \\ -i_f r_v l_o & 0 & -i_f r_{\lambda_w^a} l_o \\ (c_w - 1)(vy)_v - i_f r_v \lambda_{wo}^a & 0 & (c_w - 2)i - i_f r_{\lambda_w^a} \lambda_{wo}^a \end{pmatrix}. \quad (3.37)$$

To determine the sign of the determinant of this Jacobian we therefore have to investigate the sign of the determinant

$$\begin{vmatrix} y_v & -\bar{e} & y_{\lambda_w^a} \\ -r_v & 0 & -r_{\lambda_w^a} \\ (c_w - 1)(vy)_v - i_f r_v \lambda_{wo}^a & 0 & (c_w - 2)i - i_f r_{\lambda_w^a} \lambda_{wo}^a \end{vmatrix}$$

$$= \begin{vmatrix} -y\frac{c_w - i_f}{D} & -\bar{e} & \frac{c_w i}{D} \\ y\frac{c_w - 1}{D} & 0 & -(1-v_o)\frac{c_w i}{D} \\ (c_w - 1)y\frac{i_f - 1}{D} + i_f y \frac{c_w - 1}{D}\lambda_{wo}^a & 0 & (c_w - 2)i - i_f(1-v_o)\frac{c_w i}{D}\lambda_{wo}^a \end{vmatrix}$$

[11] In the special case being considered here we have $i = n + \varphi_d$, and hence the $(c_w - 2)$ term in the Jacobian J due to this assumption.

$$= \frac{yi}{D} \begin{vmatrix} -(c_w - i_f) & -\bar{e} & \frac{c_w}{D} \\ c_w - 1 & 0 & -(1-v_o)\frac{c_w}{D} \\ (c_w-1)(i_f-1) + i_f(c_w-1)\lambda^a_{wo} & 0 & (c_w-2) - i_f(1-v_o)\frac{c_w}{D}\lambda^a_{wo} \end{vmatrix}.$$

The sign of this determinant is therefore equal to the sign of its sub-determinant

$$\begin{vmatrix} 1 & -(1-v_o)\frac{c_w}{D} \\ i_f - 1 + i_f\lambda^a_{wo} & (c_w-2) - i_f(1-v_o)\frac{c_w}{D}\lambda^a_{wo} \end{vmatrix}.$$

The sign of the latter determinant depends upon the expression

$$c_w - 2 - i_f(1-v_o)\frac{c_w}{D}\lambda^a_{wo} + (1-v_o)\frac{c_w}{D}(i_f - 1 + i_f\lambda^a_{wo})$$

which finally simplifies to

$$c_w - 2 + (1-v_o)\frac{c_w}{D}(i_f - 1). \tag{3.38}$$

The expression in (3.38) is negative if there holds $i_f \leq 1$ and if c_w is not too large (an assumption which can be justified from the empirical point of view). In the case $i_f > 1$ we calculate from $D = (c_w - i_f)v_o + i_f - 1 > i_f - 1 > 0$ that

$$c_w - 2 + (1-v_o)\frac{c_w}{D}(i_f - 1) < c_w - 2 + (1-v_o)c_w < 1.5c_w - 2 < 0$$

for all $i_f < c_w$ if $c_w < 4/3$, and $v_o > 0.5$ holds true. Thus we get a negative determinant $|J|(\equiv -a_3)$ for all empirically plausible parameter values $c_w > 1$ and $v_o = (y_o - \delta - n)/y_o$.

The assumption on the size of c_w implies that the trace of $J(\equiv -a_1)$ is negative as well. For the sum of the principal minors of order two we have

$$a_2 \equiv \frac{ky_o v_o(c_w - 1)}{D} i_f y_o + \begin{vmatrix} J_{11} & J_{13} \\ J_{31} & J_{33} \end{vmatrix}.$$

From the above calculations we have

$$J_2 = \begin{vmatrix} J_{11} & J_{13} \\ J_{31} & J_{33} \end{vmatrix}$$

$$= kv_o \begin{vmatrix} y_v & y_{\lambda^a_w} \\ (c_w-1)(vy)_v - i_f r_v \lambda^a_{wo} & (c_w-2)i - i_f r_{\lambda^a_w}\lambda^a_{wo} \end{vmatrix}$$

$$= kv_o \begin{vmatrix} -y_o\frac{c_w - i_f}{D} & \frac{c_w i}{D} \\ (c_w-1)y_o\frac{i_f-1}{D} + i_f y_o \frac{c_w-1}{D}\lambda^a_{wo} & (c_w-2)i - i_f(1-v_o)\frac{c_w i}{D}\lambda^a_{wo} \end{vmatrix}$$

$$= \frac{kv_o y_o i}{D^2} \begin{vmatrix} -(c_w - i_f) & c_w \\ (c_w-1)(i_f-1) + i_f(c_w-1)\lambda^a_{wo} & D(c_w-2) - i_f(1-v_o)c_w\lambda^a_{wo} \end{vmatrix}$$

$$= \frac{ky_o v_o(c_w-1)}{D}\frac{i}{D} \begin{vmatrix} -(c_w - i_f)/(c_w-1) & c_w \\ i_f(1+\lambda^a_{wo}) - 1 & D(c_w-2) - i_f c_w(1-v_o)\lambda^a_{wo} \end{vmatrix}$$

A sufficient assumption to obtain $a_2 > 0$ is to assume that the loan rate i is chosen sufficiently small, such that, should the considered determinant be negative, it is dominated by the first principal minor $\frac{k y_o v_o (1-c_w)}{D} i_f y_o$.

The remaining Routh–Hurwitz condition for local asymptotic stability is

$$a_1 a_2 - a_3 > 0 \quad \text{where} \quad a_1 = -\text{ trace } J, a_3 = -|J|.$$

The determinant of J is however dominated by the remaining terms in $a_1 a_2$, if the adjustment speed of money wages β_{we} is chosen sufficiently large, since it enters a_1, a_2, a_3 linearly with a positive slope and thus in $a_1 a_2$ through a positively sloped quadratic term.

Therefore to summarise we have

$$a_1 > 0, a_2 > 0, a_3 > 0, a_1 a_2 - a_3 > 0$$

for the coefficients of the characteristic polynomial of the matrix J (the Routh–Hurwitz conditions) and have thus shown the local asymptotic stability of the steady state of the model. This gives us the proposition:[12]

Proposition 3.2 (Stability for a 'normal' range of parameter values)
Assume that i is sufficiently small and β_{we} sufficiently large. Then the steady state of the dynamical system (3.16)–(3.18) is locally attracting for all empirically relevant parameter sizes of the model.

This result is perhaps not as surprising as one may at first think in a significantly debt driven economy. Default so far only appears as if it were a gift from asset holders to worker households, since bankruptcy (the loss of a house) does not yet feed back into the considered dynamics. Moreover, the Goodwin part of the model (the interaction of the state variables v and l) is here of a convergent type, while the only destabilising feedback loop is the one between the state variables v and λ_w^a through their positive interaction as shown through the entries J_{13} and J_{31}. Debt has a positive effect on the growth rate of the wage share and the latter may have a positive effect on the time rate of change of the debt to capital ratio. But this accelerating mechanism is not really dominant in the overall interaction of the three state variables that are considered here.

There is however an element in the considered situation that can lead the investigated dynamics into a situation where the steady state becomes unstable and where the assumed degree of wage flexibility will lead the economy towards explosive fluctuations. This case comes about when it is assumed that the considered excessive overconsumption stimulates asset holders to invest in real capital at a rate i_f that is larger than c_w. In this case we get $y_v > 0$ and thus a wage-led goods market behaviour. Since the stability proof of this section required for a degree of wage flexibility β_{we} that is sufficiently high, it is then very likely that the trace of J, given by

$$\beta_{we} y_v v_o - (c_w - 1)i - i_f r_{\lambda_w^a} \lambda_w^a - (n + \varphi_d),$$

[12] This proposition also holds true for all $c_w > 1 \geq i_f$.

becomes positive and the steady state becomes repelling. We will investigate such a situation in more detail in Section 3.5.

3.4 Weakly excessive overconsumption and a repelling steady state

We consider now the only mildly excessive wage-led case

$$i_f < 1 < c_w < 1 + (1 - i_f)(1 - v_o)/v_o. \tag{3.39}$$

In this situation the propensity to consume of workers c_w is still greater than 1 but is bounded above as shown in equation (3.39). This case we shall dub as weakly excessive consumption.

On the basis of the assumption (3.39) we now have a significantly changed situation in the expression (3.35) for the goods market equilibrium expression at the steady state since the sign of the denominator D changes sign. For the partial derivatives of the functions y, vy, r with respect to v we therefore now have

$$y_v = -y\frac{c_w - i_f}{D} > 0,\ (vy)_v = y\frac{i_f - 1}{D} > 0,\ y_v = -y\frac{c_w - 1}{D} > 0. \tag{3.40}$$

In addition for the derivative $(vy)_{\lambda_w^a}$ we continue to have

$$(vy)_{\lambda_w^a} = \frac{c_w i}{D} < 0$$

which transforms itself directly into corresponding derivatives for $vy, r = (1 - v)y - \delta$. Note that all partial derivatives now have the opposite sign as compared with the overconsumption case considered in the previous section. The sign of the derivative $y_v > 0$ now shows the normal result that the goods market dynamics appear to be wage-led when aggregate goods demand per unit of capital is wage-led, that is $y_v^d = (c_w - i_f)y > 0$. Moreover interest rate effects, via rising loan rates, are now contractionary since $y_i < 0$ (instead of increasing activity) as one would intuitively expect in a debt driven economy.

Under the above assumption we have for the determinant of the Jacobian the result

$$|J| = \begin{vmatrix} 0 & -k\frac{y_o}{l_o}v_o & 0 \\ -i_f r_v l_o & 0 & -i_f r_{\lambda_w^a} l_o \\ (c_w - 1)(vy)_v & 0 & (c_w - 1)i - (n + \varphi_d) \end{vmatrix} \approx \begin{vmatrix} 0 & - & 0 \\ - & 0 & + \\ - & 0 & -n - \varphi_d \end{vmatrix}.$$

and thus can assume that this determinant is always positive for values of $c_w - 1$ and i that are of empirical relevance (under a relatively normal working of the economy). This assumption also no longer implies that the trace of J is negative. For the sum of the principal minors of order two we have from the above considerations that

$$a_2 = \begin{vmatrix} k y_v v_o & -k\frac{y_o}{l_o}v_o \\ -i_f r_v l_o & 0 \end{vmatrix} + \begin{vmatrix} k y_v v_o & k y_{\lambda_w^a} v_o \\ (c_w - 1)(vy)_v - i_f r_v \lambda_w^a & (c_w - 1)i - i_f r_{\lambda_w^a}\lambda_w^a - (n + \varphi_d) \end{vmatrix}.$$

Using the expressions and signs for the partial derivatives in (3.40) we see that a_2 has the same sign as the expression

$$\begin{vmatrix} - & -k\frac{y_o}{l_o}v_o \\ i_f\frac{y_o(c_w-1)}{D}l_o & 0 \end{vmatrix} + \frac{ky_o v_o c_w i}{D^2}\begin{vmatrix} -(c_w-i_f) & 1 \\ (c_w-1)[i_f(1+\lambda^a_{wo})-1] & -i_f(1-v_o)\lambda^a_{wo}-\frac{n+\varphi_d}{c_w i D} \end{vmatrix}.$$

We conjecture that the second determinant of this expression is very likely to be negative. The validity of the conditions

$$a_1>0, a_2>0, a_3>0, a_1a_2-a_3>0$$

on the coefficients of the characteristic polynomial of the matrix J (the Routh–Hurwitz conditions) is therefore in general not likely to hold from various perspectives, implying the proposition:

Proposition 3.3 (Instability of the weakly excessive consumption case)
Assume $i_f < 1 < c_w < 1+(1-i_f)(1-v_o)/v_o$. The steady state of the dynamical system (3.16)–(3.18) is locally repelling for empirically plausible choices of the parameter values of the model.

The case of weakly excessive overconsumption in the sector of worker households therefore does not represent a viable situation, in particular since the previously stable dynamics of the Goodwin substructure with its state variables v, l have now become totally unstable. This is further exemplified by the following proposition which states that even very low loan rates i cannot be of help in the considered case.

Proposition 3.4 (Instability for small values of the loan rate)
Assume that $i = 0 < n + \varphi_d$. Then the steady state of the dynamical system (3.16)–(3.18) is locally repelling. This result also holds for all loan rates chosen sufficiently small.

Proof: It is easily shown that the sign structure of the Jacobian in the case $i = 0$ is of the qualitative form

$$J = \begin{pmatrix} ky_v v_o & -k\bar{e}v_o & ky_{\lambda^a_w}v_o \\ -i_f r_v l_o & 0 & -i_f r_{\lambda^a_w} l_o \\ (c_w-1)(vy)_v - i_f r_v \lambda^a_{wo} & 0 & (c_w-2)i - i_f r_{\lambda^a_w}\lambda^a_{wo} \end{pmatrix}$$
$$= \begin{pmatrix} + & - & 0 \\ - & 0 & 0 \\ ? & 0 & - \end{pmatrix}.$$

This immediately implies the instability of the (wage-led) Goodwin part of the model (capturing the interaction of v and l), since the subsystem corresponding to the state variables v and l does not depend on the third state variable λ^a_w. The real parts of the

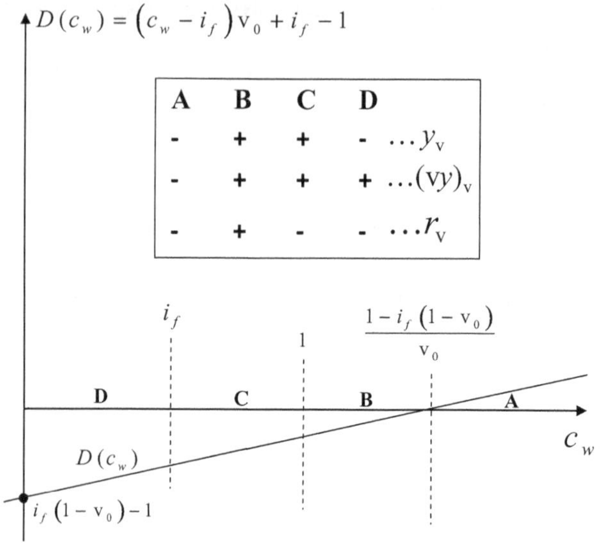

Figure 3.1 A summary of the stability scenarios for a varying parameter c_w. The table in the figure gives the signs of y_v, $(vy)_v$ and r_v in the various scenarios – A, B, C, D

eigenvalues are therefore not all negative, a fact that extends to all sufficiently small i, since the eigenvalues depend continuously on the parameters of the model. □

So far we have investigated the parameter situations denoted by A and B in Figure 3.1. We have found out that case A (see Section 3.3) represents by and large a stable, although exceptional performance of the economy (since a wage-led aggregate demand is here represented by a profit-led IS curve, due to a high debt to capital ratio), while case B (this section) does not result in a viable situation. A further conclusion here is that if case B prevails, investment should be stimulated to the extent such that $i_f > \frac{1-c_w v_o}{1-v_o}$ holds true. For example through a loan rate policy that lowers the loan rate to a sufficient degree such that this inequality can be assured (assuming that the parameter i_f depends negatively on the loan rate i). Stimulating investment in this way shifts the $D(c_w)$ line of Figure 3.1 upwards until the point is reached where the value of c_w, which currently characterises the economy, has been moved into the stable region A.

However it may not be possible to stimulate investment decisions to such a degree (such that situation A becomes established) starting from the situation B considered in this section. Credit rationing, to be considered in the next section, may then need to be enforced – leading eventually to the situation C as shown in Figure 3.1. In situation C the entry J_{31} in the matrix J has become unambiguously negative which increases the destabilising elements in the Routh–Hurwitz coefficient a_2. The overall situation is clear in this case, it represents an unstable situation, since we still have a positive entry J_{11} that will destabilise the economy if wages are sufficiently flexible with respect to demand pressure on the market for labour. Since the stability proof of Section 3.3 required a degree of wage flexibility β_{we} that is sufficiently high it is thus very likely in this case that the trace of J, given by

$$\beta_{we} y_v v_o - (c_w - 1)i - i_f r_{\lambda_w^a} \lambda_w^a - (n + \varphi_d),$$

is then positive and the steady state becomes repelling. We will investigate this situation in the next section.

If there is no possibility of a return to the (fragile) situation A, because the debt to capital ratios involved may be considered as too exceptional, policy can therefore only attempt to establish a situation as represented by case D (to be considered in Section 3.6) where a profit-led regime is re-established on a non-exceptional basis, meaning that both aggregate demand as well as the IS curve are depending negatively on the share of wages in national income, which will be the content of Proposition 3.6.

3.5 Credit rationing, reduced consumption and the emergence of mortgage crises

We start from the case of excessive overconsumption and assume now that asset holders stop lending to worker households due to the just observed tendency of the economy to become an unstable one or simply due to a change in their risk perception concerning worker households' debt. One may for example assume that the loan rate i (and with it the default rate φ_d, see the next section for more details on this) has been increasing in a stepwise fashion until a level has been reached that persuades asset holders to stop their lending to worker households. The immediate consequence is that the propensity to consume is forced to the value 1 (or close to 1 if some lending still goes on, the case we considered in the preceding section). In the following analysis we therefore consider the stability features for the case $c_w \leq 1$.

When $c_w \leq 1$ (or sufficiently close to 1) as in the preceding section we have that $D < 0$, but now in addition also $\lambda_{wo}^a < 0$. The assumed shock to worker households' propensity to consume has an immediate effect on the goods market equilibrium, which we recall from equation (3.19) may be written

$$y = \frac{c_w i \lambda_w^a + i_f(\delta + r_o) - n - \delta}{(c_w - i_f)v + i_f - 1},$$

but now with $(c_w - i_f)v + i_f - 1 < 0$. The change in IS equilibrium resulting from the change in the parameter c_w is obtained by taking the total differential of the IS equation, so that

$$dc_w vy + [(c_w - i_f)v + i_f - 1]dy = dc_w i \lambda_w^a = 0$$

Rearranging this equation appropriately yields

$$\frac{dy}{dc_w} = \frac{vy - i\lambda_w^a}{(1 - i_f)(1 - v)}$$

Viewed from the situation $c_w = 1$ we thus have the result that a positive shock to c_w increases economic activity (since the steady state value of λ_w^a is zero at this position), that is, in reversed terms, the jump to a marginal propensity to consume of unity in the above considered crisis situation is contractionary and would lead the economy into the deflationary region if it were at its steady state position initially. This would induce a process of debt deflation and thus an increasing debt and interest burden for the worker households.

The steady state position is now given by

$$y_o = y^p\ l_o = y_o/\bar{e},\ y_{wo} = y_o - \delta - n,\ \lambda^a_{wo} = 0,\ v_o = y_{wo},$$

and for the employed partial derivatives we have in this case (since the denominator in the IS curve is now negative)

$$y_v = -y\frac{1-i_f}{D} > 0, \quad (vy)_v = y\frac{i_f - 1}{D} > 0, \quad y_v = 0.$$

For the derivative $(vy)_{\lambda^a_w}$ we find that $(vy)_{\lambda^a_w} = \frac{c_w i}{D} < 0$.

Proposition 3.5 (Full credit rationing implies a repelling steady state)
Assume $c_w = 1$. Then: The steady state of the dynamical system (3.16)–(3.18) is surrounded by explosive forces. This then also holds for all marginal propensities c_w chosen sufficiently close to 1.

Proof: The Jacobian of the dynamics at the steady state now reads as

$$J = \begin{pmatrix} ky_v v_o & -k\bar{e}v_o & ky_{\lambda^a_w} v_o \\ -i_f r_v l_o & 0 & -i_f r_{\lambda^a_w} l_o \\ (c_w - 1)(vy)_v - i_f r_v \lambda^a_{wo} & 0 & (c_w - 2)i - i_f r_{\lambda^a_w} \lambda^a_{wo} \end{pmatrix}$$

$$= \begin{pmatrix} ky_v v_o & -k\frac{y_o}{l_o} v_o & ky_{\lambda^a_w} v_o \\ 0 & 0 & -i_f r_{\lambda^a_w} l_o \\ 0 & 0 & -(n + \varphi_d) \end{pmatrix}.$$

This gives the qualitative sign structure

$$J = \begin{pmatrix} + & - & - \\ 0 & 0 & + \\ 0 & 0 & - \end{pmatrix}.$$

This immediately implies the instability of the dynamics, since two of the principal minors of order 2 are zero while the third one is negative, since we can calculate that $a_2 < 0$. □

Note that the determinant of the Jacobian J is zero in the situation $c_w = 1$, and non-zero (positive or negative) for $c_w < 1$. There will be one eigenvector direction where the dynamics move very slowly, and there is in addition always one unstable (and one stable[13]) root, where the former drives the system away from the steady state.

13 Since $a_2 > 0$ holds.

In the case of an arbitrary $c_w \in (i_f, 1)$ we get for the Jacobian the qualitative structure

$$J = \begin{pmatrix} + & - & - \\ + & 0 & + \\ - & 0 & - \end{pmatrix},$$

since there holds

$$J_{31} = (c_w - 1)y\frac{i_f - 1}{D} - i_f(-y)\frac{c_w - 1}{D}\lambda^a_{wo} = (c_w - 1)y\frac{1 - i_f}{|D|} + i_f y\frac{1 - c_w}{|D|}\lambda^a_{wo} < 0$$

due to $\lambda^a_{wo} < 0$. We therefore get as sufficient condition for instability:

$$a_2 < 0 \quad \text{iff} \quad -J_{12}J_{21} < -J_{11}J_{33} + J_{13}J_{31}.$$

The last condition states that the stability created by the profit-led Goodwin (1967) subcycle of the model is overcome by the feedback chain between the wage share v and the debt to capital ratio λ^a_w. Of course further instability scenarios may come about through the trace of J if wages are sufficiently flexible with respect to the labour market gap and through the determinant of J if $-J_{23}J_{31}$ becomes dominant. The case where workers save in order to reduce their prevailing level of debt therefore does not at all represent a situation where recovery and convergence towards the steady state of the economy can be expected.

3.6 Monetary policy in a mortgage crisis

In order to determine what monetary policy should do in the situation we have investigated in the preceding section we now consider the rise in the loan rate i that triggered the crisis in more detail. We consider for this purpose the situation shown in Figure 3.2.

The basic assumption in Figure 3.2 is that the default rate φ_d is an increasing convex function of the loan rate i. We add to this function the term $r_o = n$ and obtain an expression (as a function of the loan rate i) that shows the minimum loan rate needed to obtain as rate of return on loans the profit rate of the sector of firms. We next assume that the actual loan rate tends, under normal conditions, to the minimum loan rate as shown in the situation A. Such an adjustment leads in the limit to the loan rate i_o and thus to a fairly tranquil situation where the loan rate as well as the default rate is small, a situation that is attracting smaller as well as larger loan rates in an asymptotically stable way. Yet as Figure 3.2 shows, the basin of attraction of the loan rate i_o is limited to the right by the loan rate i_1, since the considered stable adjustment process becomes an unstable one to the right of i_1.

Consider now the case B in Figure 3.2. We here assume that external events have led to this increase in the loan rate (maybe in a stepwise fashion) where asset holders now insist on a loan rate that leads to a higher rate of return on their loans than the one in the sector of firms. Assume that the increase in the loan rate eventually leads to a loan rate that is higher than i_1, then the financial market of the economy will be pushed into the unstable region where the loan rate gives rise to an upward spiralling process C. We

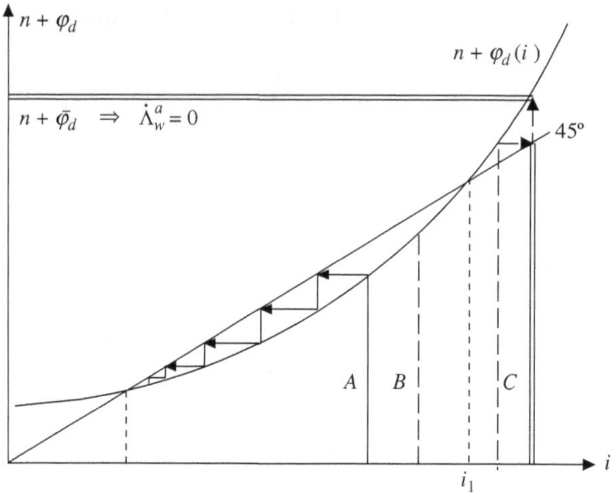

Figure 3.2 Loan rate adjustment dynamics

next assume that this process comes to an end at the value determined by the double line, since asset holders then stop giving credit to worker households as discussed in the preceding section (due to the high default rate that accompanies the then existing loan rate). The economy is then trapped into a situation where the loan rate as well as the default rate is very high and where the propensity to consume houses is zero and the overall propensity to consume therefore is less than one.

In this still very basic scenario (as far as mortgage crises are concerned) the policy to be adopted by the central bank (which is now assumed to enter the stage) is still a simple one. The first step in the solution to the credit crisis is simply to buy an amount of bad loans φ_c that allows for a loan rate i smaller than i_1 for the bad loans $\bar{\varphi}_d(i) - \varphi_c$ that then remain in the sector of asset holders. This increases the reserves of asset holders and must be conditioned on their acceptance of the minimum loan rate that is consistent with the debt default situation they are then facing. If this acceptance is followed in all subsequent steps we may then expect that the process leading back to the loan rate i_o may again become effective, now in the situation where the overall propensity of worker households to consume is less than 1 (and where debt of worker households is reduced in each point in time through their now positive savings rate). The question then becomes how the private sector of the economy (the real part of the economy and debt decumulation) behaves in such a situation.

The downward correction of the loan rate just considered is however not yet sufficient in order to stabilise the economy, since the Jacobian we considered at the end of the preceding section is plagued by a wage-led situation as far as the entry J_{11} is concerned and exhibits a destabilising feedback mechanism through the entries J_{13} and J_{31} which are both negative and thus endanger the positivity of a_2. In order to obtain a situation where the stability of the private sector can be assured we consider again the sign of the determinant of J as given by the expression (3.38). We continue to investigate the case $c_w < 1, i_f < 1$, that is the situation where $D < 0$ holds true. We assume now the situation where $1 > i_f > c_w > 0$ has been established, e.g. through forced savings of worker households, based on their debt that the central bank is now holding.

Simple empirical estimates as they were considered with regard to equation (3.38), or just the assumption that i_f is sufficiently close to 1, then ensure that the determinant of the matrix J is negative. Moreover we have in this case $y_v < 0$, $(vy)_v > 0$, $r_v < 0$, $y_{\lambda_w^a} < 0$, $r_{\lambda_w^a} < 0$ and thus get in this case the sign distribution

$$J = \begin{pmatrix} k y_v v_o & -k\bar{e} v_o & k y_{\lambda_w^a} v_o \\ -i_f r_v l_o & 0 & -i_f r_{\lambda_w^a} l_o \\ (c_w - 1)(vy)_v - i_f r_v \lambda_{wo}^a & 0 & (c_w - 2)i - i_f r_{\lambda_w^a} \lambda_{wo}^a \end{pmatrix}$$

$$= \begin{pmatrix} - & - & - \\ + & 0 & + \\ - & 0 & - \end{pmatrix}.$$

This immediately implies the stability of the Goodwin part of the model.

Proposition 3.6 (Stability for small values of i and flexible wage adjustment) *Assume $c_w < i_f$, and that the parameter k is sufficiently large and $i = n + \varphi_d(i)$ is sufficiently small. Then the steady state of the dynamical system (3.16)–(3.18) is locally attracting.*

Proof: We have already that $a_1 = -\text{trace } J > 0$ and $a_3 > 0$. Choosing k sufficiently large also gives $a_2 > 0$ if the entries in the last column of J are made sufficiently small, and this can be done by choosing a low value of the loan rate i. The latter situation also ensures $a_1 a_2 - a_3 > 0$, since a_3 can be made small relative to $a_1 a_2$ in this way. □

In view of what we have shown with respect to Figure 3.1, see also Figure 3.3, the first objective of the central bank thus should be to support the maintenance of the loan rate at sufficiently low level. In a next step consumption should be discouraged or/and investment encouraged. One may for example assume that the value of i_f depends negatively on the loan rate i. Improving the investment climate to a sufficient degree may therefore be one policy option of the central bank. Moving i_f upwards increases not only the domain A and thus makes the excessive case more robust, but it also increases the domain D and thus allows the economy to settle down in an enlarged region D (after credit rationing and the reduction of c_w to a value smaller than 1 have occurred) where the steady state is again attracting and where current mortgage debt is decreasing over time.

The central bank starts by buying a fraction α of the volume of defaults, the bad loans $\varphi_d \lambda_w^a$. This increases the disposable income of asset holders[14] and leads to an

[14] Note that we here assume that the disposable income of asset holders is given by:

$$Y_c = rK + i\Lambda_w^a + \alpha\varphi_d(i)\Lambda_w^a.$$

This however does not alter the steady state of the model, since aggregate defaults remain the same (implying no change in the law of motion for λ_w^a), although part of them is now held by the central bank.

increase of either their reserve holding R (which we have ignored so far) or their investment, leading to an adjustment of the parameter i_f that may become permanent even if the central bank stops buying bad loans. In the case it continues to do so we have the situation that bad loans no longer lead to bankruptcy (loss of homes) of the corresponding worker households. One may assume in addition that the central bank starts demanding some low interest payment from them, but we do not consider this here explicitly.

Since asset holders now face less bad loans, in fact $(1-\alpha)\varphi_d\lambda_w^a$ due to the bailout exercised by the central bank, we have moreover assumed that the loan rate falls, as was intended by the central bank. This induces a further reduction in the amount of bad loans and thus (taken together) improves not only investment in real capital formation, but also the credit situation worker households are facing. There is less default and less bankruptcy (which was accompanied by the destruction of workers' homes) and cheaper credit for worker households and, as we have argued, increased robustness in the stability scenario of the private sector that this policy implies.

We summarise the stability analysis of this chapter by Figure 3.3 which provides another representation of what we have already considered in Figure 3.1. In Figure 3.3 we show this from the perspective of the borderline case that separates a positive denominator in the IS curve from a negative one (where debt increases are contractionary). We have that all marginal propensities c_w above this borderline represent the case of excessive consumption where the debt to capital ratio (in the steady state) is so high that it implies a profit-led IS curve despite a wage-led aggregate demand function. The cases B and C are again the unstable ones and case D represents a stable situation, since

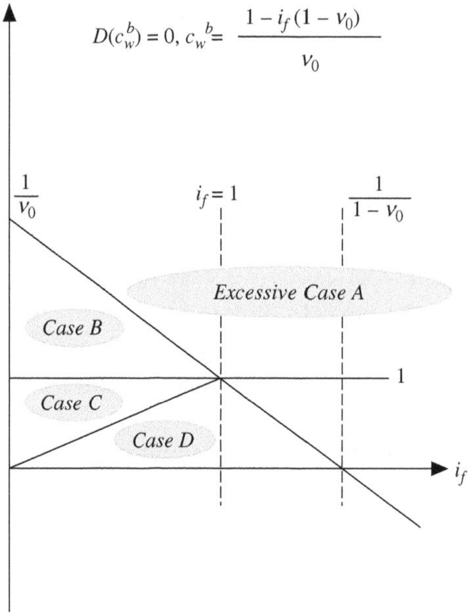

Figure 3.3 A alternative summary of the stability scenarios for a varying parameter c_w

demand as well as goods market equilibrium are profit-led so that flexible wages are then stabilising the economy.

The domains A and D are therefore the ones where the economy may be able to reproduce itself in the long run. The central bank should then only take care to keep the investment climate in an appropriate range and the loan rate on workers' debt reasonably low. Nevertheless it is still possible to conceive cases where there is a latent tendency towards instability (approached through investment weaknesses or investment booms), since in particular the regime of overconsumption may not be the best of all accumulation regimes.

3.7 Adding commercial banking

In this section we extend the model by allowing now for commercial banks as lending and depositary institutions in place of the lending activities of asset holders we have so far assumed as the basis for the mortgage loans to worker households. We thus no longer have to consider the reserve holdings R of asset holders which in fact could be, and indeed was, assumed to be zero due to the IS equilibrium assumption on the market for goods. Besides serving the investment plans of firms, asset holders now hold their remaining wealth as saving deposits at the commercial banks which now lend these saving deposits to a certain extent to the workers and in addition hold reserves in view of the deposits they have received from the asset holders. In a first step we will assume that reserves are adjusted towards a level of desired reserves at each moment in time, and that the remainder is given to worker households as a given mortgage loan rate. The worker households accept this supply of credit and invest it in residential space. This channels the savings of asset holders into consumption demand of workers and thus gives rise to the validity of Say's Law whereby the Keynesian regime is removed from the model (since reserves are also goods demand in this real model of capital and mortgage accumulation). We then investigate the ways in which Keynesian goods market rationing can again be introduced into this modelling framework and the business cycle implications to which it gives rise.

As before we have the sector of workers given by

Workers:

$$Y_w = vY - i_c \Lambda_w^a, \tag{3.41}$$

$$C_w = Y_w + \dot{\Lambda}_w, \tag{3.42}$$

$$\dot{K}_w = \dot{\Lambda}_w - \varphi_b K_w, \quad \varphi_b K_w = \varphi_d \Lambda_w^a, \tag{3.43}$$

$$\hat{L} = n = const. \tag{3.44}$$

Note however that the consumption of residential space by worker households is now dependent on the credit supply of banks and thus 'rationed' through the commercial banking sector (at the given loan rate i_c). All supplied credit (and only credit) is now assumed to be invested by worker households in residential space.

Asset holders no longer supply credit, but put all income that is not invested into their stock of real capital as saving deposits in the commercial banking sector (at a given interest rate i_d on these saving deposits):

Asset Holders:

$$Y_a = rK + i_d D, \quad r = y(1 - v) - \delta, \tag{3.45}$$

$$C_a = 0, \quad [S_a = Y_a], \tag{3.46}$$

$$\dot{D} = Y_a - I, \tag{3.47}$$

$$W_a = K + D, \tag{3.48}$$

$$\dot{K} = I = i_f(r - r_o)K + nK. \tag{3.49}$$

The new sector is that of commercial banks, which use the new saving deposits $\dot{D}$ of asset holders to provide new credit $\dot{\Lambda}_w$ to worker households at a given level of actual reserve changes $\dot{R}$ at each moment of time. There is a given loan rate–deposit rate spread in this banking sector, implying that there are profits Y_c accruing to commercial banks, which are used to supply further credit to the sector of worker households. The net worth of commercial banks is given by W_c. Thus we have:

Commercial Banks (CBs):

$$Y_c = i_c \Lambda_w^a - i_d D, \tag{3.50}$$

$$C_c = 0 \quad [S_c = Y_c], \tag{3.51}$$

$$\dot{\Lambda}_w^a = \dot{D} + Y_c - \dot{R} - \varphi_d \Lambda_w^a, \tag{3.52}$$

$$\dot{\Lambda}_w = \dot{D} + Y_c - \dot{R}, \tag{3.53}$$

$$W_c = \Lambda_w^a + R - D. \tag{3.54}$$

Reserves are adjusted with some delay towards desired reserves, which provides a rule that allows us to determine residually the volume of loans supplied to workers:

$$\dot{R} = \beta_r(\psi^* - \psi)D = \beta_r(\psi^* D - R), \quad \psi = R/D, \tag{3.55}$$

$$i_c = (1 + \mu)i_d. \tag{3.56}$$

We assume that the loan rate on mortgages i_c is given by a markup on the interest rate paid on the saving deposits of asset holders. For completeness we also introduce a very simple central bank sector into this extension of the baseline model of this chapter, which holds the reserves R of commercial banks and which sets the interest rate on saving deposits (by legislation), but which does not yet supply any high-powered money.

The Central Bank (CB):

$$R = R, \tag{3.57}$$

$$i_d = i. \tag{3.58}$$

The central bank therefore has just one instrument to influence the working of the economy (the rate of interest on asset holders' deposits). Otherwise it just controls the reserves held by the commercial banks, by setting the desired reserve ratio ψ^*, eventually enforcing higher minimum reserves if it decrees that the commercial banking sector is not working properly.

The next set of equations check that income matches expenditure in our set-up of a credit-financed economy:

$$\begin{aligned}
Y_w + Y_a + Y_c &= (vY - i_c\Lambda^a_w) + (Y(1-v) - \delta K + i_d D) + (i_c\Lambda^a_w - i_d D) = Y - \delta K,\\
C_w + I_f + I_c &= (vY - i_c\Lambda^a_w + \dot{\Lambda}_w) + I + \dot{R}\\
&= (vY - i_c\Lambda^a_w + \dot{\Lambda}_w) + (rK + i_d D - \dot{D}) + (i_c\Lambda^a_w - i_d D + \dot{D} - \dot{\Lambda}_w)\\
&= Y - \delta K.
\end{aligned}$$

Note that we consider only real goods (in a one-sector framework) which implies that also reserves of commercial banks represent real commodity inventories. The activities in the real sector therefore concern consumption proper and housing demand of worker households, net investment of firms and reserve holdings of commercial banks, describe a consumption function of worker households, an investment function of firms and the reserve adjustment of commercial banks. All remaining activities are residual ones.

The above extension of the baseline model of this chapter gives as new laws of motion:

$$\begin{aligned}
\hat{D} &= \frac{\dot{D}}{K}\frac{K}{D} = [r + i_d d - (i_f(r - r_o) + n)]/d, \quad r = y(1-v) - \delta,\\
\hat{R} &= \frac{\dot{R}}{K}\frac{K}{R} = \beta_r(\psi^* d - \rho)/\rho, \quad \psi^* = const, \rho = R/K,\\
\hat{\Lambda}^a_w &= \frac{\dot{\Lambda}^a_w}{K}\frac{K}{\Lambda^a_w}\\
&= [r + i_d d - (i_f(r - r_o) + n) + i_c\lambda^a_w - i_d d - \beta_r(\psi^* d - \rho) - \varphi_d\lambda^a_w]/\lambda^a_w\\
&= [r - (i_f(r - r_o) + n) + i_c\lambda^a_w - \beta_r(\psi^* d - \rho) - \varphi_d\lambda^a_w]/\lambda^a_w.
\end{aligned}$$

This in turn gives the intensive form representation of the model as

$$\begin{aligned}
\dot{d} &= y(1-v) - \delta + i_d d - (i_f(y(1-v) - \delta - r_o) + n) - (i_f(y(1-v) - \delta - r_o) + n)d,\\
\dot{\rho} &= \beta_r(\psi^* d - \rho) - (i_f(y(1-v) - \delta - r_o) + n)\rho,\\
\dot{\lambda}^a_w &= y(1-v) - \delta - (i_f(y(1-v) - \delta - r_o) + n) + i_c\lambda^a_w - \beta_r(\psi^* d - \rho)\\
&\quad - (i_f(y(1-v) - \delta - r_o) + n + \varphi_d)\lambda^a_w,
\end{aligned}$$

which is quite a different situation compared to with the original one (where asset holders supplied the credit to the worker households) and where only a single law of motion was needed to describe the dynamics of credit financing, namely (see equation (3.18))

$$\dot{\lambda}_w^a = (c_w - 1)(vy - i\lambda_w^a) - (i_f(r - r_o) + n + \varphi_d)\lambda_w^a, \quad \lambda_w^a = \frac{\Lambda_w^a}{K}.$$

The goods market equilibrium is now determined by

$$\begin{aligned} Y &= C_w + I_f + I_c + \delta K \\ &= (vY - i_c\Lambda_w^a + \dot{\Lambda}_w) + (rK + i_d D - \dot{D}) + (i_c\Lambda_w^a - i_d D + \dot{D} - \dot{\Lambda}_w) + \delta K, \end{aligned}$$

which in intensive form gives rise to

$$\begin{aligned} y &= (vy - i_c\lambda_w^a + \dot{\Lambda}_w/K) + (r + i_d d - \dot{D}/K) + (i_c\lambda_w^a - i_d d + \dot{D}/K - \dot{\Lambda}_w/K) + \delta \\ &= vy - i_c\lambda_w^a + r + i_d d + i_c\lambda_w^a - i_d d + \delta = y. \end{aligned}$$

We thus get that Say's Law is valid in such an economy, that is the goods market is in equilibrium at all levels of output Y, quite in contrast to the cases we have investigated earlier in this chapter. This holds since consumption is now endogenously determined by workers' disposable income and the credit that is supplied out of the saving deposits of asset holders by the commercial banks to them. Summing up the full dynamics of this extended case is given by the five laws of motion

$$\hat{v} = \beta_{we}(y^p/(zl) - \bar{e}), \tag{3.59}$$

$$\hat{l} = -i_f(y^p(1 - v) - r_o), \tag{3.60}$$

$$\dot{d} = y^p(1 - v) - \delta + i_d d - [i_f(y^p(1 - v) - \delta - r_o) + n](1 + d), \tag{3.61}$$

$$\dot{\rho} = \beta_r(\psi^* d - \rho) - (i_f(y^p(1 - v) - \delta - r_o) + n)\rho, \tag{3.62}$$

$$\begin{aligned} \dot{\lambda}_w^a &= y^p(1 - v) - \delta + i_c\lambda_w^a - \beta_r(\psi^* d - \rho) \\ &\quad - [i_f(y^p(1 - v) - \delta - r_o) + n](1 + \lambda_w^a) - \varphi_d\lambda_w^a. \end{aligned} \tag{3.63}$$

The first two differential equations (3.59) and (3.60) provide the conventional Goodwin (1967) closed orbits growth cycle dynamics, but these are now appended with laws of motion for deposits d, actual debt λ_w^a and reserves ρ, all measured per unit of capital.

It is easily shown that the appended dynamics are asymptotically stable if the interest rates i_d, i_c are chosen sufficiently small, since the Jacobian at the steady state of the dynamical system (3.59)–(3.63) is characterised by

$$J = \begin{pmatrix} - & 0 & 0 \\ + & - & 0 \\ - & + & - \end{pmatrix}.$$

The interior steady state itself is given by

$$l_o = \frac{y^p}{z\bar{e}}, \quad v_o = \frac{y^p - r_o}{y^p}, \quad d_o = \frac{r_o - n}{n - i_d}, \quad \rho_o = \frac{\psi^* d_o}{1 + n/\beta_r}, \quad \lambda_{wo}^a = \frac{r_o - n(1 + \rho_o)}{\varphi_d + n - i_c}.$$

This implies that r_o must be sufficiently large and i_d, i_c sufficiently small in order to provide a meaningful set of steady state conditions.

The end result of the extension of the baseline model of this chapter is that we have returned to a Goodwin type supply driven model of the distributive cycle, augmented by stable dynamics of deposits of asset holders, reserves of commercial banks and mortgage debt of workers (all per unit of capital). This is a classical growth cycle model where asset holders not only accumulate real capital and where workers not only consume their real wages, but also buy residential space through the credit that is supplied to them by the commercial banks. We consider this as an interesting extension of the original Goodwin (1967) model, but one that has lost the Keynes component through the specific formulation of credit supply driven housing consumption of workers.

In order to show in a simple way how effective demand problems can be re-introduced into the extension of the baseline model of this chapter (which in fact is more a modification, since the consumption function of workers has been changed in this section) we now add the existence of high-powered money to the model, supplied by the central bank in line with the demand for this asset by asset holders in order to fix the interest rate on savings deposits, which we have already assumed above. We assume that asset holders want to add to their high-powered money holdings (or reduce it) according to a function $\dot{M} = \dot{M}(Y, r, i)$ with partial derivatives $\dot{M}_1 < 0$, $\dot{M}_2 < 0$, $\dot{M}_3 < 0$. Hence this function assumes that new money hoardings by asset holders decrease with economic activity (are negative in the boom and positive in the bust), decrease with declining profitability of firms (for a given state of economic activity) and decrease when the interest rate on the saving deposits of asset holders is increasing.

We assume moreover that the interest rate i is set by the central bank as a decreasing function of the rate of profit r with the value of i we have so far considered given by $i(r_o)$. We finally assume that there is a unique level of economic activity Y_o where $\dot{M}(Y_o, r_o, i(r_o))$ is zero.[15] This level of economic activity therefore now prevails in the steady state of the economy which is given as before, since $\dot{M}$ is zero there and the flow conditions of the model being of the same type as the previous ones. The central bank activities are now characterised by the expressions:

Central Bank (CB):

$$\begin{aligned} R + M &= R + M, \\ i_d &= i(r), \\ \dot{M} &= \dot{M}(Y, r, i). \end{aligned}$$

These equations summarise the balance sheet of the central bank, its interest rate policy and its new supply of high-powered money. Money supply is here still of a helicopter type, since there are no other financial assets in the present formulation of the model that can be subject to open market operations of the central bank. This is a provisional

[15] This assumes that the condition $\dot{M}_2 + \dot{M}_3 i'(r) \neq 0$ is fulfilled.

assumption for the time being which will be removed in the more advanced model types considered in this book. It serves to illustrate in the simplest way possible how hoarding can lead to Keynesian effective demand problems in an otherwise classical framework.

For the consumption demand of workers we now have the expressions

$$\begin{aligned} C_w &= vY - i_c\Lambda_w^a + Y_a - I - \dot{M} + Y_c - \dot{R} \\ &= vY - i_c\Lambda_w^a + rK + i_dD - I - \dot{M} + i_c\Lambda_w^a - i_dD - \dot{R} \\ &= vY + rK - I - \dot{M} - \dot{R} \\ &= Y - \delta K - I - \dot{M} - \dot{R}. \end{aligned}$$

From the last expression we have for total demand $Y^d = C_w + I + \delta K + \dot{R}$ the simple representation

$$Y^d = Y - \dot{M}.$$

IS equilibrium then implies, as in the case of the baseline model, that such a change in asset holdings must be zero. It follows that $\dot{M}(Y, r, i(r)) = 0$, from which by means of the implicit function theorem we obtain $Y = Y(r)$, the derivative of which is given by

$$Y'(r) = -\frac{\dot{M}_2 + \dot{M}_3 i'(r)}{\dot{M}_1}. \tag{3.64}$$

We thus now have that economic activity is a decreasing or increasing function of the wage share v (since we have assumed that $\dot{M}_2 + \dot{M}_3 i'(r) \neq 0$) and this in a way that is completely different from the one we have used in the baseline model of this chapter. The real dynamics of the model of this section therefore now become, due to what we have here assumed for workers' consumption and the money demand of asset holders:

$$\hat{v} = \beta_{we}(y(v)/(zl) - \bar{e}), \tag{3.65}$$

$$\hat{l} = -i_f(y(v)(1-v) - r_o) = -i_f(r(v) - r_o). \tag{3.66}$$

We consider in the following analysis only situations where the rate of profit remains a negative function of the wage share, so that the effect of the wage share on Y is not that positive that it makes the overall effect of the wage share on the rate of profit a positive one. In this case the Jacobian of the real dynamics of the model is characterised at the steady state by

$$J = \begin{pmatrix} \beta_{we} y'(v_o)/(zl_o)v_o & - \\ + & 0 \end{pmatrix}. \tag{3.67}$$

In order to get the result that the steady state of the real dynamics is asymptotically stable we must therefore postulate that the monetary policy of the central bank is conducted in such a way that the condition

$$Y'(r) = -\frac{\dot{M}_2 + \dot{M}_3 i'(r)}{\dot{M}_1} > 0$$

holds true. This is exactly the case when the condition

$$\frac{dY(r(v))}{dv} = \frac{\dot{M}_2 r'(v) + \dot{M}_3 i'(r(v))r'(v)}{|\dot{M}_1|} < 0, \quad \text{that is,} \quad |i'(r)| > \frac{|\dot{M}_2|}{|\dot{M}_3|}$$

is fulfilled.

We thus get the result that the goods market appears, due to the money demand of asset holders, as if economic activity were wage-led. The interaction of the result on the market for goods with the law of motion of the wage share is thus an unstable one if an active interest rate policy of the central bank is absent, while an interest rate policy that is exercised with sufficient strength can remove this type of instability from the considered dynamics. We thus have the end result that credit rationing of a certain type can make the economy unstable and so there is a need for monetary policy in order to make it sustainable. This section therefore indicates in conjunction with the earlier sections how the baseline model of this chapter may be augmented in order to arrive at a Keynes–Goodwin growth cycle model where a variety of stability scenarios can be explored. In the next chapter we will by contrast focus on the debt financing behaviour of firms and the instability problems to which this gives rise.

3.8 Conclusions and outlook

In this chapter we have investigated a second type of crisis scenario, now within a closed economy and concerning worker households and their indebtedness. Adding to the crisis scenarios of Charpe *et al.* (2009), we have considered here a sequence of models (a sequence of parameter scenarios for a single three-dimensional dynamic model in fact) which run from situations of stable excessive overconsumption of worker households, to weakly excessive overconsumption and a certain degree of instability, and from there to the situation of a strict credit rationing of worker households. In the fourth model type, we considered actions that can rescue the economy from this last instability scenario and that imply a solution that leads the economy back to economic stability, with mortgage debt shrinking in time. The return to stability is based on investment stimuli (or alternatively, and not so attractive, further reductions in workers' marginal propensity to consume), coupled with a monetary policy that aims at a decrease in the loan rate and the default rate on the credit market.

In this latter type of economy, the loan rate will fall to a low value again and workers' debt will reduce in time through their now positive savings. In the limit, this economy would even converge to a situation where workers are lending to asset holders, since they have a positive savings rate in the steady state. Yet, in our view this would only be a transient phase in which the economy recovers to a certain degree from too high mortgage debt back to its normal functioning, perhaps subsequently followed again by the emergence of some behavioural parameter changes which lead the macroeconomy back to the stable overconsumption situation from which we started. The sequence of events analysed in this chapter thus may repeat itself in historical time.

In the next chapter we go on from workers' indebtedness to firms' debt accumulation and from there to processes of debt deflation as another important feedback channel that can endanger the viability of the entire economy in a downward direction. Compared with the considered exchange rate crises in Chapter 2 and the mortgage crises of the present chapter, the Fisher (1933) process of accelerating debt deflation in the private sector may be one that is very difficult to attenuate or even reverse by economic policy.

3.9 Appendix: some simulation studies of the baseline model

We consider in this appendix the system (3.16)–(3.18) in its various configurations from the numerical point of view.

Excessive overconsumption ($c_w > 1 + (1 - i_f)(1 - v_o)/v_o > 1 > i_f$)
The first set of simulations illustrates the case of a profit-led economy. The propensity to consume is set at 1.2, which corresponds clearly to an excessive overconsumption case. In addition, $c_w < 4/3$, implies that the goods market dynamics are profit-led, even though aggregate demand is wage-led. The value of i_f is fixed at 0.02 and is smaller than c_w also implying that the impact of the wage share on output is negative.

The dynamics of the economy following a 1 per cent debt shock are displayed in Figure 3.4. The steady state is attracting even though convergence takes place at a slow pace. Convergence takes place as a result of the stable interaction between the wage share and the output to capital ratio, and despite the cumulative channel between debt and the wage share. As shown by the maximum real part of eigenvalues in Figure 3.4(d), increasing wage flexibility increases the stability of the system. Similarly, reducing β_w to 0.01 increases shock-dependence and economic fluctuations as we see from Figure 3.5.

Weakly excessive consumption ($i_f < 1 < c_w < 1 + (1 - i_f)(1 - v_o)/v_o$)
We now consider the case of weakly excessive overconsumption by way of Figure 3.6:

Figure 3.6(a) represents the wage-led case, where the value of c_w has been lowered from 1.2 to 1.05 such that the condition $1 < c_w < (1 + (1 - i_f)(1 - v_0)/v_0)$ holds. In the wage-led case, the unstable interaction between the wage share and the output to capital ratio is strongly unstable. The dynamics of the wage share and the output are cumulative. Any increase in the wage share fosters output, which feeds back positively on the wage share as employment increases. In the wage-led case, the Goodwin part of the model is strongly unstable. As stated in Proposition 3.4, the system loses stability even in the case $i = 0$ which turns off the impact of debt on the system. Forcing β_w to zero allows the unstable dynamic interaction between the wage share and output to be turned off. In such a case, the economy is stable as shown in Figure 3.6(b).

The overall impact of the propensity to consume on the stability of the system is summarised by the maximum real part of eigenvalues represented in Figure 3.6(c) and 3.6(d). In Figure 3.6(c), the propensity to consume lies between 1 and 1.1. At

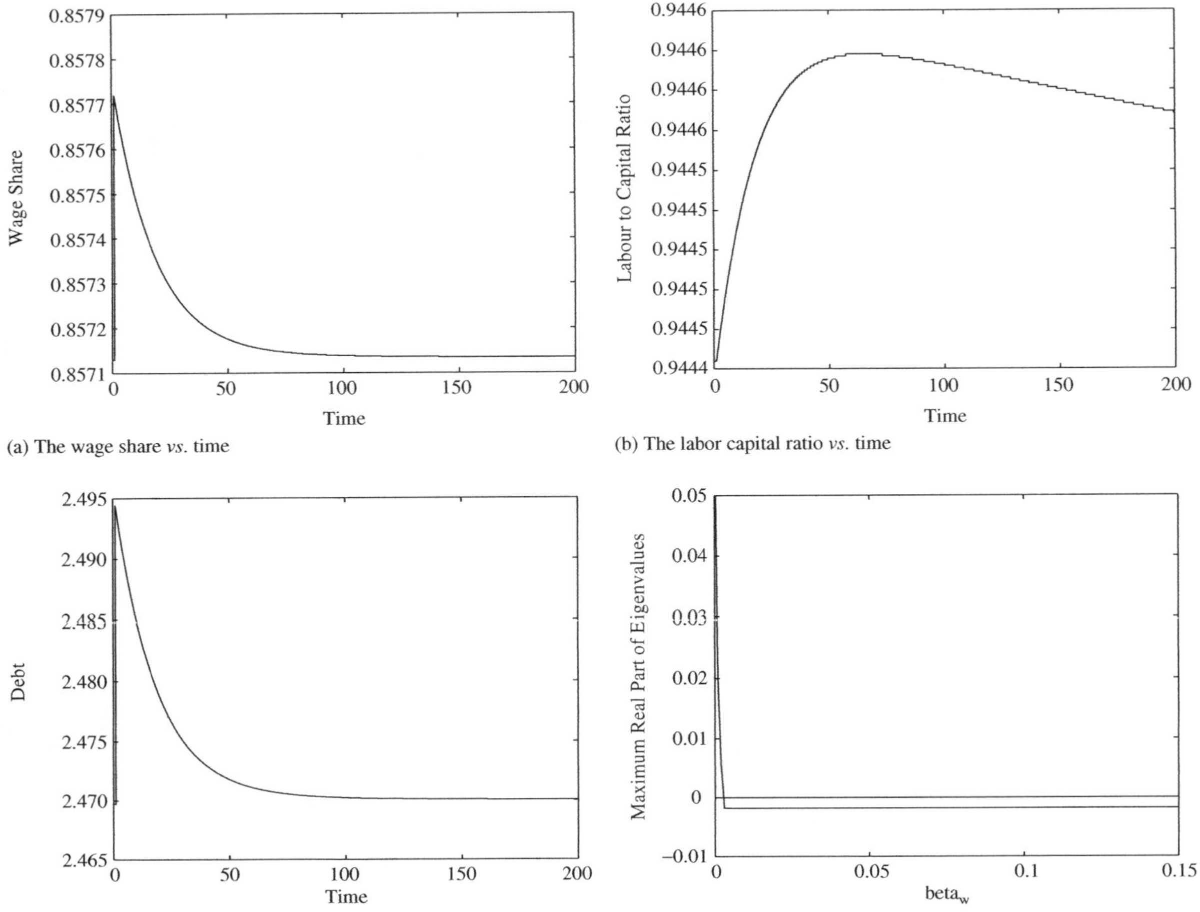

(a) The wage share *vs.* time

(b) The labor capital ratio *vs.* time

(c) The debt level *vs.* time

(d) The max. real part of eigen-values *vs.* β_w

Figure 3.4 The dynamics of the economy following a 1 per cent debt shock – the profit-led case

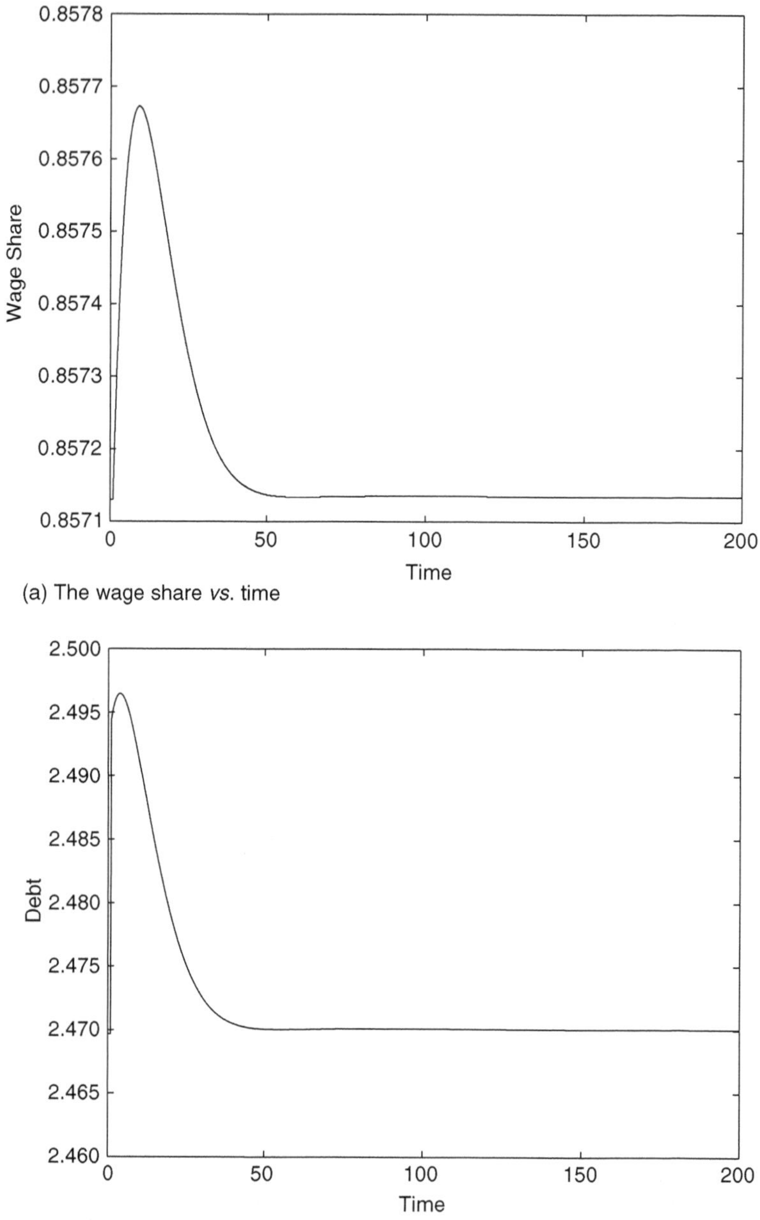

(a) The wage share *vs.* time

(b) The debt level *vs.* time

Figure 3.5 The dynamics of wage share and debt. The case of weak wage adjustment

$c_w = 1$, households can be seen as credit constrained. Households consume all their income as they do not have access to debt financed consumption. Full credit rationing implies a repelling steady state as proved in Proposition 3.5. Eigenvalues are positive and quickly increasing with respect to c_w. The economy is wage-led and unstable

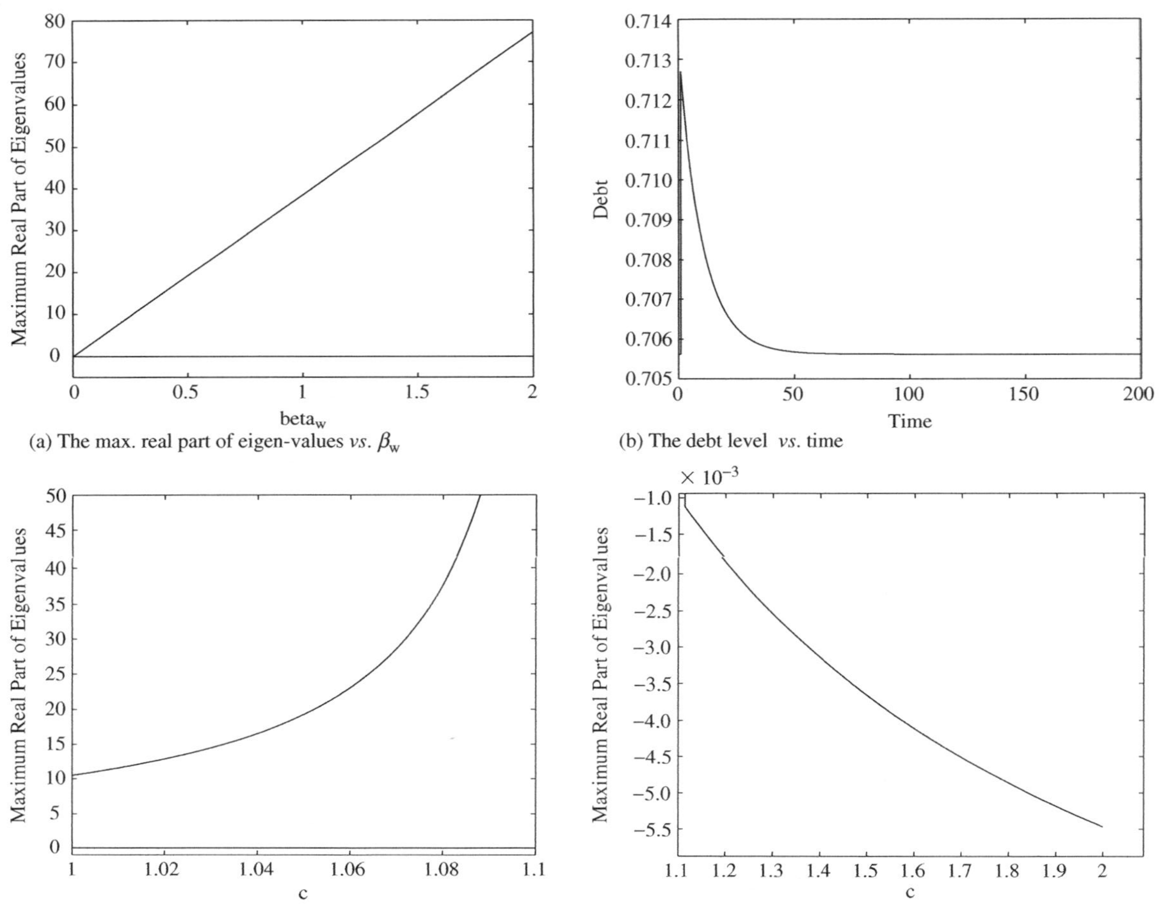

(a) The max. real part of eigen-values *vs.* β_w

(b) The debt level *vs.* time

(c) The max. real part of eigen-values *vs.* c_w with $1 < c_w < 1.1$

(d) The max. real part of eigen-values *vs.* c_w with $1.1 < c_w < 2$

Figure 3.6 Eigenvalues and debt in the wage-led case

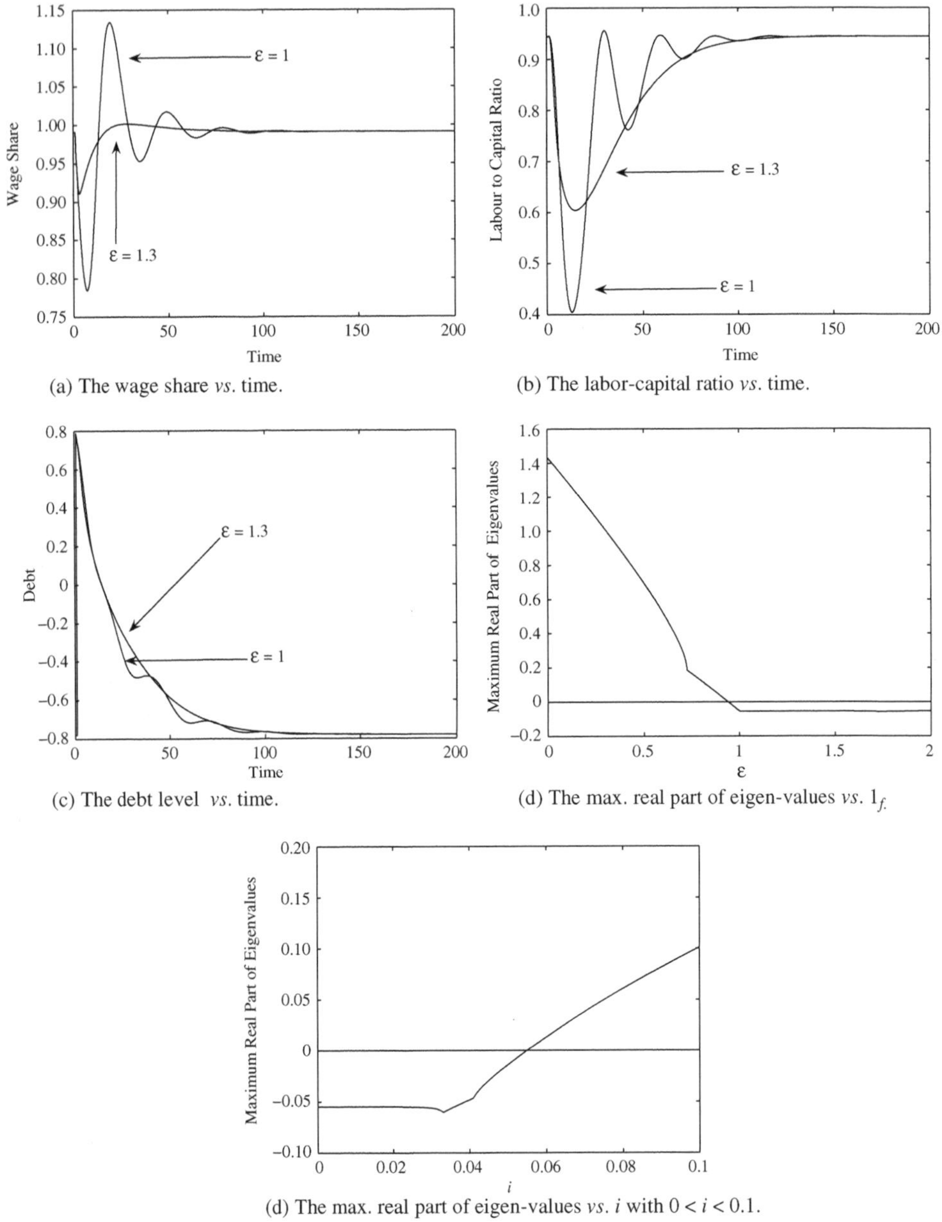

(a) The wage share *vs*. time.

(b) The labor-capital ratio *vs*. time.

(c) The debt level *vs*. time.

(d) The max. real part of eigen-values *vs*. 1_f.

(d) The max. real part of eigen-values *vs*. i with $0 < i < 0.1$.

Figure 3.7 Stabilising the investment climate in the case when $i_f > 1$ and $c_w < 1$

given the output, wage share interaction. Up to $c_w = 1.1$, the economy is wage-led and unstable. In Figure 3.6(d), the propensity to consume lies between 1.1 and 2, where the economy is profit-led. Now eigenvalues are negative and decreasing in c_w. The system converges given the stability of the wage, output interaction.

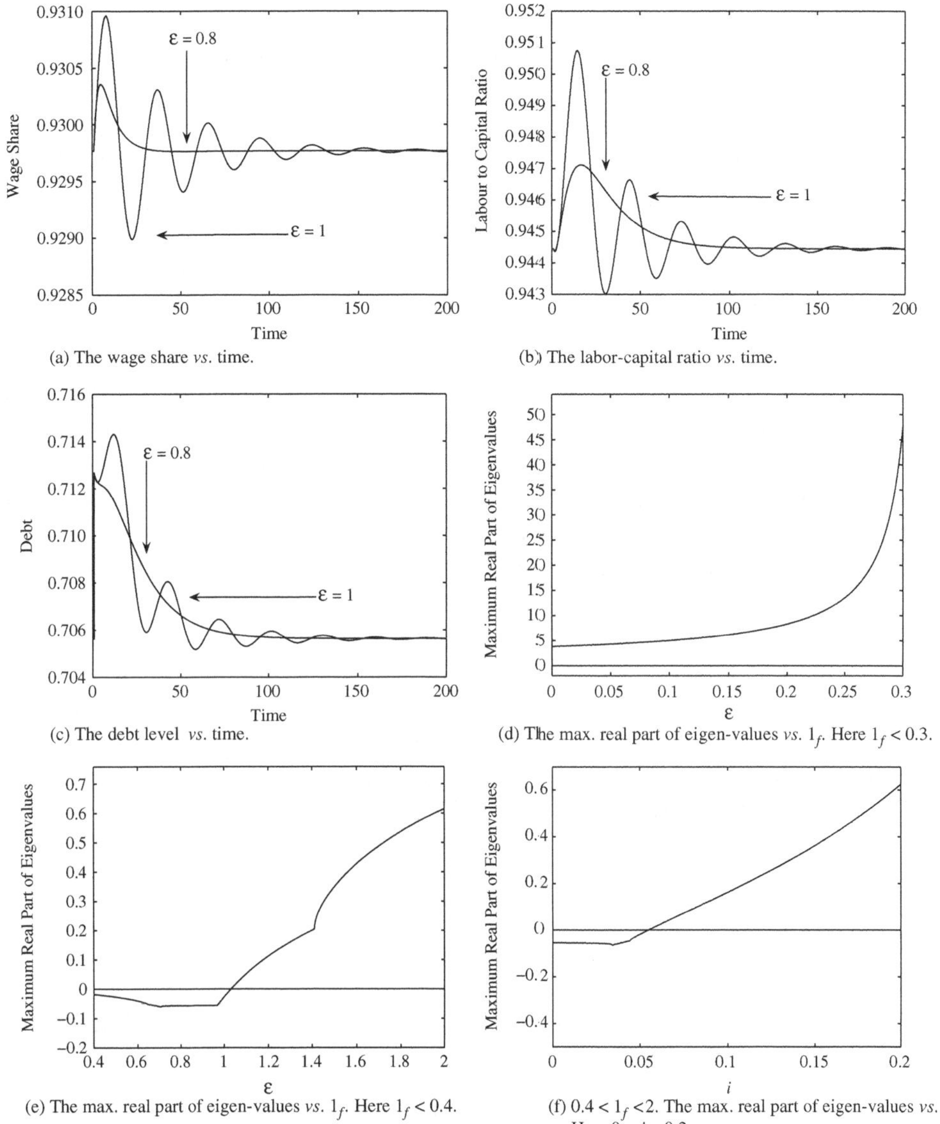

(a) The wage share *vs.* time.

(b) The labor-capital ratio *vs.* time.

(c) The debt level *vs.* time.

(d) The max. real part of eigen-values *vs.* 1_f. Here $1_f < 0.3$.

(e) The max. real part of eigen-values *vs.* 1_f. Here $1_f < 0.4$.

(f) $0.4 < 1_f < 2$. The max. real part of eigen-values *vs.* i. Here $0 < i < 0.2$.

Figure 3.8 Stabilising the investment climate in the case $i_f > 1$ and $c_w > 1$

Transition from crisis to 'pre-crisis' level ($i_f \geq 1$ ***and*** $c_w < 1$)

Figure 3.7 illustrates the role of monetary policy in stabilising consumer debt dynamics. The interest rate is kept low at 2 per cent, the investment climate variable i_f is larger than the propensity to consume c_w, which at $c_w = 0.95$ is lower than 1. A propensity to consume lower than 1 implies a negative debt ratio at the steady state. The aim of the simulations is to understand whether monetary policy can stabilise the economy after a shock that increases the debt ratio to positive values. In other words, the simulations aim at understanding whether monetary policy can restore a 'pre crisis' situation in which households are not getting mortgage debt, but are either rationed or have net savings. As shown by the two eigenvalues diagrams, Figures 3.7(d) and 3.7(e), a relatively significant interest rate ($i > 10$ per cent) and a good investment climate ($i_f > c_w$) are associated with stability, as eigenvalues are negative. Households reduce their mortgages until they reach a situation in which they are net savers. Increasing i_f from 1 to 1.3 improves the investment climate and stabilises the economy (Note that here i_f is here equal to $i + \epsilon$).

Weakly excessive overconsumption and monetary policy ($i_f > 1$ and $c_w > 1$)
With respect to the previous simulations, they enquire as to whether monetary policy can stabilise the economy when it is characterised by weakly excessive overconsumption and strong instability. In Figure 3.8, the economy is still characterised by a small interest rate, $i = 2$ per cent, and a rather good investment climate, $\imath_f = 0.8$. The main change is that the propensity to consume is now equal to 1.05, which implies that the economy is in the unstable case illustrated in Figure 3.6. The main result is that monetary policy can restore stability if it manages to keep interest rates low and there is a high propensity to invest profits. However, contrary to the previous case, the investment climate must belong to a corridor. Negative expectations as well as euphoric expectations are likely to make the economy unstable. Eigenvalues are negative for interest rates lower than 6 per cent, as shown in Figure 3.8(f). In addition, eigenvalues are still negative for i_f lying between 0.4 and 1. Increasing i_f from 0.8 to 1 increases business cycle fluctuations and slows down convergence.

4 Debt deflation and the descent into economic depression

4.1 The debt deflation debate

In the recent public debate on problems of the world economy, 'deflation', or more specifically 'debt deflation', has again become an important topic. The possible role of debt deflation in triggering the Great Depression of the 1930s has come back into academic studies as well as into the writings of economic and financial journalists. It has been observed that there are similarities between recent global trends and the 1930s, namely the joint occurrence of high levels of debt and falling prices, the dangerous downside of cheaper cars and TVs when debt is high. Debt deflation thus concerns the interaction of high nominal debt of firms, households and countries and shrinking economic activity due to falling output prices and increasing real debt.

There is often another mechanism accompanying the one just mentioned. That other mechanism involves how large debt may exert an impact on macroeconomic activity and works through the asset market. Asset price inflation during economic expansions normally gives rise to generous credit expansion and lending booms. Assets with inflated prices serve as collateral for borrowing by firms, households or countries. In contrast when asset prices fall the borrowing capacity of economic agents shrinks, financial failures may set in, macroeconomic activity decreases and consequently large output losses may occur.

Countries that have gone through such booms and busts are some Asian countries (in particular Japan), Russia and Brazil in 1998 and 1999. In all of those countries asset price inflation and lending booms entailed a subsequent debt crisis and asset price deflation. Thus, the usual mechanism of debt deflation due to falling output prices has been accompanied by the asset price deflation mechanism.[1]

Some academic commentators have also criticised the single-minded preoccupation of certain central banks and the IMF with inflation, and have suggested that providing some room for inflation should be of help in preventing a global financial crisis. Moreover, global growth strategies, and the elements they could contain, continue to be

[1] For a recent detailed study employing a different approach, namely asymmetric information theory, see Mishkin (1998).

discussed in academic and policy circles. The need for a fundamental restructuring of the IMF and World Bank and a new financial architecture is continuously stressed based on the judgement that the world has, in the last decade, faced several severe financial challenges, with the latest being the biggest since the 1930s. Debt dynamics can be, as Reinhart and Rogoff (2009) have argued, a very destabilising force and therefore appear to be an important problem that the world economy may be facing.

This issue was visibly exemplified in the recent financial market meltdown in 2007–9. It began with the very large indebtedness in the US subprime (mortgage) market in 2007, evolved as a credit crisis through the US banking system in 2008/9, and subsequently spread worldwide, causing a worldwide financial panic, and staggering declines in global growth rates. This time, the usual boom-bust mechanism with the risen asset prices and a credit boom was reinforced by new financial innovations; specifically, the development of new financial intermediations through complex securities, such as mortgage-backed securities (MBS), CDO and credit default swaps (CDS). The complex securities, which were supposed to outsource and diversify idiosyncratic risk, have, jointly with the changes in the macroeconomic environment, actually accelerated risk taking and the boom, but also the bust. First through high asset prices and high leveraging and then, second, on the downside through the instability of credit via a credit crunch. These innovations provided the underlying financial intermediation mechanism through which the asset price boom and busts were fuelled. Although the actual way in which boom-bust cycles in asset prices and borrowing and lending evolve may change over time the mechanisms at work are very similar; for further details we refer the reader to Bernard and Semmler (2009).

Modern macroeconomic theory, as it has evolved since the Second World War, has paid scant attention to the above described mechanism of debt deflation. No doubt this is due to the fact that during that time the major economies in the world experienced a long period of growth followed by a long period of inflation from which we have only recently emerged. The classic study of debt deflation remains that of Fisher (1933), although Minsky (1975, 1982) in his writings on the financial instability hypothesis continued to warn of the dangers of another great depression. More recently Keen (2000) has focused attention on the Fisher debt effect and Minsky's financial instability hypothesis. There is therefore an urgent need for economists to model the process of debt deflation in its interaction with monetary and fiscal policies that may stop the process of rising debt, falling output and asset prices, and a collapse into depression.

In this chapter[2] we embed the process of debt accumulation and debt deflation via a sequence of partial models of debt accumulation and price deflation into fully integrated and consistent (with respect to budget constraints) macroeconomic models of closed and open economies. At the core of the model will be firms that finance fixed investment as well as involuntary inventory investment not from retained earnings, but by loans

[2] This chapter represents a reformulation and extension of the original contribution on debt deflation by Chiarella *et al.* (2001a), where the Fisher (1933) approach to debt deflation was embedded into a theory driven structural macroeconometric framework of the KMG variety.

from the credit market. In the current chapter we neglect equity finance. Our model will thus focus mainly on the first mechanism of the debt deflation process, the destabilising role of flexible wages and prices in economies with high nominal debt. The destabilising role of asset prices will be by and large neglected.[3]

Our macroeconomic model contains a sufficient number of agents and markets to capture the essential dynamic features of modern macroeconomies, and stresses the dynamic interaction between the main feedback loops of capital accumulation, debt accumulation, price and wage inflation (deflation), exchange rate appreciation (depreciation), inventory accumulation and government monetary and fiscal policies. Our modelling framework relies on previous work by the authors and contributions by other co-authors.[4] The essential difference is that here we focus on debt-financed investment of firms in place of pure equity financing considered in the earlier papers. We will thus add a further important feedback loop missing in our earlier approach to macro modelling, namely, from a partial point of view, the destabilising Fisher debt effect of deflationary (or inflationary) phases of capital accumulation arising from the creditor–debtor relationship between asset-owning households, banks and firms.

Keen (2000) has investigated the Fisher debt effect, between firms and financial intermediaries, in the context of an augmented classical growth cycle model of Goodwin (1967) type. He has found that it may imply local asymptotic stability for the overshooting mechanism of the growth cycle, but the overshooting can lead to instability, for high debt outside a corridor around the steady state of the model. In addition Keen provides an interesting discussion of Fisher's vision of the interaction of over-indebtedness and deflation and of Minsky's financial instability hypothesis. He extends the proposed model of the interaction of indebted firms and income distribution to also include a study of the role of government policies in such an environment. He focuses on nominal adjustment processes in place of the real ones of the classical growth cycle model.

We will start from Keen's 3D model of this process, expand it by flexible prices (to obtain a 4D model), by a Metzlerian quantity adjustment process, inflationary expectations and an interest rate policy rule and will finally provide a general 10D dynamical system exhibiting a complete representation of stock-flow interactions, adjusting prices and quantities, asset market dynamics and fiscal and monetary policy rules. While we concentrate on debt accumulation and its real implications in the lower dimensional versions we will nevertheless have a full set of stock-flow interactions,[5] but not yet alternative financing instruments of firms (equity, debt and retained profits) in the general 10D version of the dynamics that we consider.

[3] For work on credit market, economic activity and the destabilising role of asset price inflation and deflation, see Minsky (1975) and Mishkin (1998).

[4] See Chiarella and Flaschel (2000).

[5] Such interactions were still totally excluded in the basic 6D Keynesian price/quantity dynamics derived from the models of Keynesian monetary growth in Chiarella and Flaschel (2000); see the following for a brief representation of this KMG disequilibrium approach to AS-AD growth.

In the general framework we develop on the basis of the final model of this chapter in Part II and III we will discuss important further issues in the development of debt deflation, such as credit rationing, bankruptcy, bank and foreign exchange market crisis and domestic or foreign policy intervention. These issues need to be investigated, however, in much more detailed ways in future research in order to allow a full treatment of the dangers of the joint occurrence of debt and deflation in certain areas of the world economy or on a worldwide scale.

4.2 3D debt accumulation

In this chapter we develop the core Keynes—Metzler—Goodwin (KMG) dynamics with pure debt financing (and retained earnings) in place of pure equity financing; see Chiarella and Flaschel (2000) for their original formulation and Chiarella *et al.* (2005) for the further development of this type of analysis. We proceed in a stepwise fashion by starting from a simple 3D supply side dynamics as in Goodwin (1967), but now with debt in addition to pure profits as a means of financing the investment projects of firms. At the next step we introduce a law of motion for the price level and can therefore then start to consider deflationary processes in addition to the debt accumulation dynamics of the 3D case. This 4D extension also makes use, in a preliminary way, of a demand side restriction for the output decision of firms and thus departs from full capacity growth (where deflationary processes concerning the price level are hard to justify) towards fluctuating capacity utilisation of firms.

Yet, the above approach to aggregate demand and the role it plays in debt accumulation and deflationary processes still represents a simplifying approximation of a complete and consistently formulated delayed adjustment process of the output decision of firms towards fluctuating aggregate demand, as it is part of the 6D KMG approach to economic growth as developed in Chiarella and Flaschel (2000, Ch. 6).

In a third step we therefore add the delayed Metzlerian output-inventory adjustment mechanism to the considered 4D dynamics and arrive thereby at a 7D dynamical system of the KMG variety, with the law of motion for the debt to capital ratio as a new differential equation and the sole representation of the stock-flow interaction of actual economies. We furthermore also add a law of motion for the rate of interest which increases the dimension again by one. In contrast to the KMG growth model considered by Chiarella and Flaschel (2000, Ch. 6), see here Section 4.4, we now have two further laws of motion, since this earlier approach determined the rate of interest by an equilibrium condition and since the evolution of equity quantities and prices did not yet feed back into the price-quantity-growth dynamics of this basic prototype model of the dynamics of Keynesian monetary growth.

We started in Chiarella and Flaschel (1999c) and Chiarella *et al.* (2001a, 2001b) the analysis of the macrodynamics of debt deflation with a very general 20D model (of applied type) and then approached the understanding of the role of debt and deflation in such a framework from an extended 3D supply side growth cycle dynamics of Goodwin (1967) type, as formulated and investigated in Keen (2000), which included loans to firms and thus debt financing of (part of) their investment expenditures in a very fundamental way. In the present chapter we will pursue an opposite approach by starting from the basic 3D framework of the Keen (2000) model and by developing it into 4D and 8D models which make it more and more complete and also consistent in its feedback structure between prices, quantities, expectations and rates of interest in particular.

Taken together, and based on the linear behavioural assumptions still used in our earlier approaches to debt and deflation, the equations of the Keen (2000) model can be represented as a 3D dynamical system in the state variables $v = wL^d/pY^p$ the wage share, $e = L^d/L$ the rate of employment, and $\lambda = \Lambda/pK$ the debt to capital ratio of the firms, as shown below. We note that the price level p is kept fixed in this core version of the Keen model[6] (and set equal to one for notational simplicity) and that the rate of interest $\bar{i}$ is also a given magnitude in this model, just as the reference (minimum) target rate of profit $\bar{r}$ which is compared with the actual pure rate of profit $r = y^p(1-v) - \delta - \bar{i}\lambda$ by firms in their investment decision.

In contrast to the macrodynamics developed in Chiarella and Flaschel (2000) we give budget equations a role to play in the price-quantity-growth dynamics of their KMG prototype model. However, only the budget equation of firms will really be of importance in the models of debt and deflation in this section, since the dynamics of the government budget constraint and interest payments of the government are still suppressed in the 7D model by way of appropriate assumptions and thus left for future research.

The 3D dynamics which are to be investigated in this section, and which are based on a Phillips curve (PC) mechanism, debt and profit driven investment behaviour and the budget restriction of firms, read (note that we still have $p = 1$):

$$\hat{v} = \beta_w(e - \bar{e}) - n_l, \quad e = L^d/L, \tag{4.1}$$

$$\hat{e} = g_k - (n + n_l), \quad g_k = I/K = \alpha_r^k(r - \bar{r}), \tag{4.2}$$

$$\dot{\lambda} = g_k(1 - \lambda) - r, \quad \lambda = \Lambda/K, \tag{4.3}$$

with the following definitions and supplementary algebraic equations[7]

$$\begin{aligned}
e &= L^d/L, && L^d = Y/z, \hat{z} = n_l = \text{ const.}, \hat{L} = n = \text{ const.},\\
C_w &= wL^d && \text{(budget equation: workers)},\\
C_b &= \bar{i}\Lambda - \dot{\Lambda} && \text{(budget equation: financial capitalists)},\\
I &= rK + \dot{\Lambda} && \text{(budget equation: industrial capitalists)},
\end{aligned}$$

6 Assuming that price inflation follows wage inflation via instantaneous or delayed markup pricing would introduce deflationary forces originating in the labour market into this framework which however will be introduced only later on in the 4D demand side reformulation of the model.

7 We use the term 'financial capitalist' for the suppliers of credit, for instance through commercial banks, and the term 'industrial capitalist' to denote the owners of firms that are also partly financed through retained earnings in their investment behaviour.

$$r = y^p(1 - v) - \delta - \bar{i}\lambda \qquad \text{(pure rate of profit)},$$

$$v = wL^d/Y \qquad \text{(wage share)},$$

$$y = y^p = y^p K, \quad y^p = \text{const.} \qquad \text{(potential output)},$$

with $\bar{e} \in (0, 1)$ a benchmark (yet not the NAIRU) rate of employment, $\bar{r} > 0$ the required rate of profit and $\bar{i} > 0$ the given rate of interest.

Given the way the model is constructed we have to assume that $C_b \geq 0, I \geq -\delta K$ hold true, which suggests (via later steady state considerations and on the intensive form level)

$$\bar{i} \geq \hat{\Lambda} \quad \text{(always)} \quad \Rightarrow \hat{\Lambda} = \hat{K} = n + n_l \text{ (in the steady state)},$$

$$r \geq \bar{r} - \delta/\alpha_1^k \text{ (always)}.$$

We note that the budget equations imply $C_w + C_b + I = Y - \delta K$, which is Say's Law in its simplest form in an economy with investment expenditures. There is thus no reason for deflation from the side of goods market behaviour in this model type (but there may of course be deflationary forces in labour market dynamics). Implicitly contained in the above equations also is the fact that the loans demanded by industrial capitalists are always supplied by financial capitalists, up to the point where $C_b = 0$ becomes binding. The credit supply is thus limited by interest income of financial capitalists in a very narrow way. Financial capitalists cannot supply new money in this 3D approach (in fact money M is totally neglected in the above formulation of the model) and thus cannot extend the above financing constraint via the mechanism $i\Lambda + \dot{M} = \dot{\Lambda} + C_b$. Could they do so, they would introduce money into the system and would then also allow aggregate demand for goods to deviate from aggregate supply, which at one and the same time would invalidate Say's Law and establish a Keynesian demand driven system in place of the above classical 3D supply side dynamics.

Equation (4.1) is based on a linear real-wage PC $\hat{\omega} = \widehat{w/p} = \beta_w(e - \bar{e})$ from which the growth rate n_l of labour productivity z has to be deducted in order to arrive at the growth law for the wage share $v = wL^d/pY = \omega/z$. Equation (4.2) says that capital stock growth has to be diminished by labour force growth n and productivity growth n_l in order to arrive at the growth law for the rate of employment (in our set-up of a fixed proportions technology z, y^p with Harrod neutral technical progress of the given rate $n_l = \hat{z}$). Equation (4.3), finally, is the new and difficult one of this extension of a Goodwin (1967) type growth model towards the inclusion of debt-financed investment. It is derived as follows:

$$\hat{\lambda} = \hat{\Lambda} - \hat{K} = \frac{\dot{\Lambda}}{K}/\lambda - \frac{I}{K} = \left(\frac{I}{K} - r\right)/\lambda - \frac{I}{K}.$$

This implies the differential equation (4.3) for the debt to capital ratio λ.

This closes the discussion of our partly debt-financed model of capital accumulation and cyclical growth. It is obvious from equation (4.3) that the dynamics of debt accumulation as they derive from the budget constraints of firms introduce a severe non-linearity into the simple Goodwin (1967) type real growth dynamics.

Proposition 4.1 (The balanced growth path of the model)
Assume $\alpha_r^k > 1$. There is a unique interior steady state of the dynamical system (4.1)–(4.3) given by

$$e_o = \bar{e} + n_l/\beta_w > \bar{e},$$

$$\lambda_o = 1 - \frac{r_o}{n + n_l} < 1, \quad r_o = \bar{r} + (n + n_l)/\alpha_r^k > \bar{r},$$

$$v_o = \frac{y^p - \delta - r_o - \bar{i}\lambda_o}{y^p}.$$

Proof: The value for e_o follows immediately from setting equation (4.1) equal to zero ($v \neq 0$). Next, the value of r_o can be calculated from equation (4.2) for $e_o \neq 0$ by setting the right-hand side equal to zero, and solving for r_o. Furthermore, inserting the resulting value for r_o into equation (4.3), setting $g_k = n + n_l$ and solving for λ_o immediately implies the steady state value for λ, which must be smaller than 1, due to $r_o > \bar{r} > 0$. The steady state value for v_o finally follows from the definition of the pure rate of profit $r = y_p(1 - v_o) - \delta - \bar{i}\lambda_o$. □

Remark 4.1 We assume that the parameters of the model are such that the inequalities $\lambda_o, v_o > 0$ hold true. Just as in Goodwin's (1967) growth cycle model there is in addition a border steady state that is given by $v_o = e_o = 0$, and λ_o the solution of

$$\alpha_r^k(y^p - \delta - \bar{i}\lambda - \bar{r})(1 - \lambda) - (y^p - \delta - \bar{i}\lambda) = 0.$$

Remark 4.2 In order to get a positive steady state debt to capital ratio it is necessary and sufficient that $r_o < n + n_l$ holds, so that the steady growth rate $n + n_l$ exceeds the growth rate that could be generated by investing pure profits solely. The condition $r_o < n + n_l$ in turn is equivalent to $\alpha_r^k > \frac{n+n_l}{n+n_l-\bar{r}}$, that is the propensity to invest must be chosen sufficiently large for this purpose, and the larger it is the closer the minimum rate of profit $\bar{r}$ will be to the natural rate of growth $n + n_l$. Note furthermore that the steady state level of the wage share is determined after the determination of r_o, λ_o and thus residually after income distribution for industrial and financial capital has been determined. An increase in the interest rate $\bar{i}$ only reduces the wage share and is thus of no concern for the pure rate of profit in the steady state. Note finally that an increase in $\bar{r}$ reduces both interest income and wage income per unit of capital.

Proposition 4.2 (The positive contribution of debt financing)[8]
Assume $\alpha_r^k > 1$. The steady state of the dynamics (4.1)–(4.3) is always locally asymptotically stable.

[8] Note that the Goodwin (1967) growth cycle model can be obtained by assuming $\alpha_1^k = 1, \bar{r} = 0$.

Proof: Evaluating the Jacobian J of system (4.1)–(4.3) at the steady state gives for its third row the expression

$$(\alpha_r^k(1-\lambda_o)-1)(r_u, 0, r_\lambda)-(0,0,n+n_l)$$

and for its second row $\alpha_r^k(r_u, 0, r_\lambda)$. Since $1-\lambda_o = 1/\alpha_r^k + \bar{r}/(n+n_l)$ we know that $\alpha_r^k(1-\lambda_o)-1$ must be positive. The sign structure of the Jacobian is therefore given by[9]

$$J = \begin{pmatrix} 0 & + & 0 \\ - & 0 & - \\ - & 0 & - \end{pmatrix}.$$

According to the Routh–Hurwitz theorem (see e.g. Gantmacher (1959)), we have to show that

$$a_1 = -\text{trace } J > 0, \quad a_2 = J_1 + J_2 + J_3 > 0, \quad a_3 = -\det J > 0, \quad a_1 a_2 - a_3 > 0,$$

holds, where J_1, J_2, J_3 are the three principal minors of order two with the index of J indicating the row and column that is ignored in the principal minor concerned.

Obviously, trace $J = -\gamma - (\alpha_1^k - 1)\bar{i} < 0 \quad (a_1 > 0)$ holds. Furthermore, when calculating the determinant of J, the third row term

$$(\alpha_r^k(1-\lambda_o)-1)(r_u, 0, r_\lambda)$$

can be removed without change in this determinant, giving rise to

$$\det J = \begin{vmatrix} 0 & + & 0 \\ - & 0 & - \\ 0 & 0 & -(n+n_l) \end{vmatrix} < 0 \quad (a_3 > 0).$$

Next, we immediately obtain

$$J_1 = \begin{vmatrix} 0 & - \\ 0 & - \end{vmatrix} = 0, \; J_2 = \begin{vmatrix} 0 & 0 \\ - & - \end{vmatrix} = 0, \; J_3 = \begin{vmatrix} 0 & + \\ - & 0 \end{vmatrix} > 0,$$

and thus $a_2 > 0$ holds true as well. Finally, $a_1 a_2 - a_3 = -(\alpha_1^k(1-\lambda_o)-1)r_\lambda > 0$ since $r_\lambda = -\bar{i} < 0$ and since $J_{33} = -(\alpha_1^k(1-\lambda_o)-1)\bar{i} - (n-n_l)$ dominates the element $-(n+n_l)$ that appears in the above calculation of det J $(\lambda_o < 1!)$. □

Remark 4.3 1. Adding partial debt financing of the investment of firms therefore always turns the centre type dynamics of the Goodwin (1967) growth cycle model into convergent dynamics. Note here again that the two constraints $C_b \geq 0, I \geq -\delta K$ imply for the pure rate of profit r that it must stay in the interval $[\bar{r}-\delta, (\bar{i}\lambda + \alpha_1^k\bar{r})/(\alpha_1^k - 1)]$ which establishes a corridor for this rate that must be ensured by appropriate non-linearities when its boundary is approached. We suggest here however that the lower and upper bound on the pure rate of profit will rarely become binding.

[9] This sign structure shows that debt evolution interacts in a very specific way with the cross-dual dynamical structure of the first two laws of motion.

2. Introducing credit into the Goodwin (1967) growth cycle thus makes their dynamics convergent, and this for all $\bar{i}, \bar{r}, n + n_l > 0$, so that interest, profit and growth are needed here (if $C_b \geq 0, \lambda_o > 0$ is not imposed).

3. We assert, but do not prove this here, that the addition of a term like

$$\alpha_i^k(\bar{\lambda} - \lambda),$$

where $\bar{\lambda}$ is a target debt to capital ratio makes the determination of steady state values r_o, λ_o more involved, but does not alter the stability properties of the dynamics. Adding to the pure budget *constraint* dynamics (4.3) a direct impact of the debt to capital ratio on investment *behaviour* therefore enhances the convergence of the system back to the steady state (with a debt to capital ratio $\lambda_o \neq \bar{\lambda}$ in general).

4. Ignoring the credit constraint $\bar{i} \geq n + n_l \quad (C_b \geq 0)$ requires the interpretation that $-C_b$ commodities have to be supplied by financial capitalists in order to ensure Say's Law on the market for goods. In the present simple supply side form of the model we therefore face the difficulty of justifying the case where the interest rate $\bar{i}$ is below the steady growth rate $n + n_l$ of output and the capital stock, a case that is often stressed in its importance if the dynamics of the government budget constraint are introduced and investigated.

5. In order to avoid credit rationing of the type $\dot{\Lambda} = \bar{i}\Lambda - C_b, C_b \geq 0$ one may introduce a flexible interest rate, for example by way of the law of motion

$$\dot{i} = \beta_r(\bar{\lambda} - \lambda), \tag{4.4}$$

according to which financial capitalists attempt to steer the economy to a desired debt to capital ratio $\bar{\lambda}$. Checking the steady state conditions, however, reveals that $\bar{\lambda}$ cannot be chosen arbitrarily, but has to be determined (as before) by

$$\bar{\lambda} = 1 - \left(\frac{\bar{r}}{n + n_l} + \frac{1}{\alpha_r^k}\right).$$

Making this choice furthermore implies that the steady state rate of interest cannot be determined in a unique fashion from the remaining steady state conditions, but can in effect be arbitrarily given (only subject to certain economic boundary conditions). For the Jacobian J of the 4D dynamics (4.1)–(4.4) one furthermore gets $\det J = 0$ which confirms the indeterminacy of interest rate from another angle. The Routh–Hurwitz conditions in the 4D case read

$$a_1, a_2, a_3, a_4 > 0, b_o = a_1 a_2 - a_3 > 0, b_1 = a_3 b_o - a_1^2 a_4 > 0,$$

where a_2, a_3 consist of the sum of minors of orders 2 and 3 respectively. It is easy to show that these conditions are all fulfilled in the extension of (4.1)–(4.3) by (4.4), up to $a_4 = \det J$ which is zero here. We therefore find that the dynamics are again convergent, up to the levels of i and v which are here dependent on historical conditions and exogenous shocks as the system evolves. Let us add here also that the system

(4.1)–(4.4) is characterised by two cross-dual adjustment mechanisms of Goodwin (1967) type, one (the conventional one) for the real part of the economy

$$e \overset{+}{\longmapsto} \hat{v}, \quad v \overset{-}{\longmapsto} \hat{e},$$

and one for its financial part

$$\lambda \overset{+}{\longmapsto} \dot{i}, \quad i \overset{-}{\longmapsto} \dot{\lambda},$$

which are here coupled with each other by the definition of the pure rate of profit, namely $r = y^p(1-v) - \delta - i\lambda$. However, due to the zero-root hysteresis in the financial part of the economy these two adjustment mechanisms differ considerably in their working.

6. We stress finally that the system so far investigated is characterised by $p = 1$, $e^c = Y/Y^p = 1$, assumptions that will be successively relaxed in the following sections of the chapter.

Proposition 4.3 (The negative contribution of debt financing)[10]
We consider the situation of Proposition 4.2, but in addition that $\beta_w = 0, n_l = 0$ holds, so that there is no adjustment in the wage share occurring when the other two state variables of (4.1)–(4.3) are changing. Then for each level of the wage share v satisfying $y^p(1-v) - \delta > \bar{r}$, (which allows for minimum profitability) there exists a threshold value $\tilde{\lambda} \geq 0$ of the debt to capital ratio λ above which this ratio will increase beyond any bound according to the then isolated dynamics (4.3).

Proof: If the state variable v is stationary by assumption, we get that the third law of motion of the dynamics represents an autonomous differential equation in the variable λ and is then given by

$$\dot{\lambda} = \alpha_1^k \bar{i}\lambda^2 - [(\alpha_1^k - 1)\bar{i} + \alpha_1^k r^c]\lambda + (\alpha_1^k - 1)r^c - \bar{r},$$

with r^c being defined by $y^p(1-v) - \delta - \bar{r}$, which we can assume to be positive under normal conditions of the working of the economy. The right-hand side of this equation represents a polynomial of degree 2, $p(\lambda) = c_o\lambda^2 + c_y\lambda + c_h$ with $c_o > 0, c_y < 0$. The unique minimum of this quadratic function is at $\lambda = -c_y/(2c_o) > 0$ and it exhibits of course only positive values after the larger of its two roots has been passed (if this root is real, otherwise all values of $p(\lambda)$ are positive for all $\lambda > 0$). Initial values of the debt to capital ratio λ which lie to the right of this root (if real, and to the right of zero if not) therefore imply a purely explosive behaviour of this ratio, since $\dot{\lambda}$ is and remains positive. □

We have pointed out above that, as a minimum requirement, the side condition $r \geq \bar{r} - \delta/\alpha_1^k$ should always be fulfilled in order to allow for economically meaningful trajectories (along which gross investment should always stay non-negative). Of course, negative rates of profit r may also be excluded from consideration by economic

10 Note that the case that is considered here can and must be approached as a limit case by reducing both n_l, β_w in size simultaneously.

reasoning. The threshold for an explosive evolution of the debt to capital ratio found to exist in Proposition 4.3 may however still be so large that explosiveness can only occur in a domain where the system is not economically viable in the above sense. In this case the proposition simply states that the dynamics will not always be globally asymptotically stable from the purely mathematical point of view, but does not yet prove that critical developments in the debt to capital ratio may also come about at initial situations to which there corresponds an economically meaningful environment. To show that such situations will indeed exist is the aim of the following Proposition 4.4.

Proposition 4.4 (Threshold values for monotonic divergence)
We consider the situation of Proposition 4.2. We assume again that $\beta_w = 0, n_l = 0$ is given and in addition that $n > \bar{i}$ holds. Then, for the steady state value of the wage share, v_o, the threshold value $\widetilde{\lambda} \geq 0$ of the debt to capital ratio λ of Proposition 4.3 implies a rate of profit $r \in (0, \bar{r})$. The considered dynamics (4.1)–(4.3) therefore become divergent (e monotonically decreasing and λ monotonically increasing) for values of λ that lie in an economically meaningful part of the state space.

Proof: First, we show that the threshold value $\widetilde{\lambda} > 0$ (after which $\dot{\lambda}$ is positive in the considered situation) must be larger than one if $n > \bar{i}$ holds true. To see this it suffices to show that the polynomial considered in Proposition 4.3 is still negative at $\lambda = 1$. At $\lambda = 1$ we have $\dot{\lambda} = -r = y^p(1 - v_o) - \delta - \bar{i}$. This gives $\dot{\lambda} = -[r_o + (\bar{i}\lambda^o - \bar{i})]$. Inserting the steady state values for r_o, λ_o from Proposition 4.1 into this expression then implies:

$$\dot{\lambda} = -\left[\bar{r} + \frac{n}{\alpha_1^k} + \bar{i}\left(\frac{\alpha_1^k - 1}{\alpha_1^k} - \frac{\bar{r}}{n} - 1\right)\right],$$

which upon rearrangement becomes

$$\dot{\lambda} = -[\bar{r}(1 - \frac{\bar{i}}{n}) + \frac{1}{\alpha_1^k}(n - \bar{i})] < 0,$$

where the inequality is due to the assumption $n > \bar{i}$. From this result there follows immediately that the second real root of the considered polynomial, $\widetilde{\lambda}$, must be larger than one (while the first coincides with the steady state due to our assumption $v = v_o$).[11]

Let us now calculate the rate of profit $\widetilde{r}$ at this threshold value $\widetilde{\lambda}$. Since we have $\dot{\lambda} = 0$ at this value, we get for $\widetilde{r} = y^p(1 - v_o) - \delta - \bar{i}\widetilde{\lambda}$ the expression:

$$0 = \alpha_1^k(\widetilde{r} - \bar{r})(1 - \widetilde{\lambda}) - \widetilde{r},$$

which in turn gives

$$\widetilde{r} = \frac{\alpha_1^k \bar{r}(1 - \widetilde{\lambda})}{\alpha_1^k(1 - \widetilde{\lambda}) - 1} = \frac{\bar{r}}{1 - 1/(\alpha_1^k(1 - \widetilde{\lambda}))},$$

[11] Note that the smaller root can be negative, meaning that firms are creditors not debtors in the steady state, if $\bar{r} > 0$ and if the parameter α_1^k is sufficiently close to one.

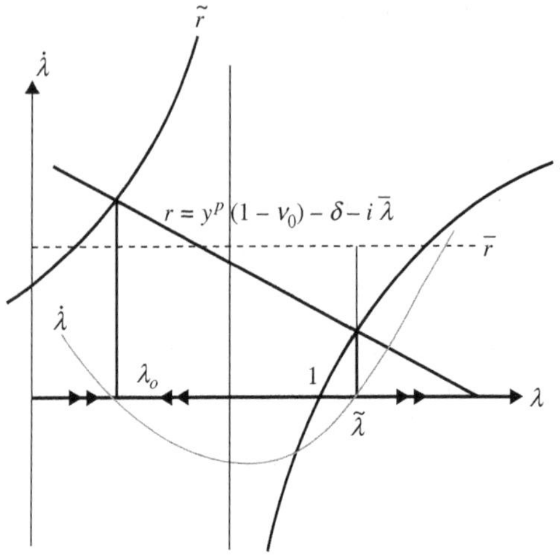

Figure 4.1 Debt dynamics around the steady state share of wages

from which we calculate that

$$\tilde{r}'(\tilde{\lambda}) > 0, \lambda \neq 1 - 1/\alpha_1^k.$$

Due to the above considerations we know however that the denominator of this expression is larger than one which implies that $\tilde{r}$ must lie in the open interval $(0, \bar{r})$ at the point $\tilde{\lambda}$. □

Note that the polynomial considered always has two positive real roots in the situation considered in Proposition 4.4, since its left one must exist and be equal to λ_o, the steady state value of the debt to capital ratio λ. Note also that the slope of the polynomial is negative there, in line with the stability result we obtained in Proposition 4.2.

The situation considered in Proposition 4.4 and its proof can be represented graphically as shown in Figure 4.1. The actual pure rate of profit r, for each value of the debt to capital ratio λ, is shown as a straight line in this figure. It cuts the $\tilde{r}$ function at $r_o(\lambda_o), \tilde{r}(\tilde{\lambda})$ where we have given either the steady state solution or the threshold after which $\dot{\lambda}$ becomes purely explosive. We stress that the figure in this form only applies to situations where $\bar{i} < n$ holds true. In the opposite case we have $\dot{\lambda} > 0$ at $\lambda = 1$ and thus for $\tilde{r}$ where $\dot{\lambda} = 0$ holds a value smaller than 1. Since the $\tilde{r}$ function does not depend in its position on the size of $\bar{i}$ we thus get that r must be negative at the second root of the given quadratic equation. The case $\bar{i} > n$ therefore implies a smaller basin of attraction for the state variable λ, but also a more rapid decline of r for increasing λ.

Should a shock throw the economy out of the steady state to a value of λ slightly above the threshold value $\tilde{\lambda}$ it will be caught in a situation where λ is monotonically increasing accompanied by a falling rate of employment e until trajectories leave the domain of economically meaningful values for these two state variables. We stress that this result is obtained on the basis of a wage share that remains fixed at its steady state value and which therefore neither improves nor worsens the considered situation through its movements in time. This result will also hold true for all adjustments in the wage share that are sufficiently slow. At present it is however not clear whether a strongly falling wage share (based on a high value of the parameter β_w), which significantly improves the profitability of indebted firms, can lead us back to the steady state. This may depend on the size of the implied change in gross investment and its consequences for the change of the debt of firms.

For sufficiently small parameter values β_w we however know that the dynamics will produce explosiveness of the debt to capital ratio λ and impulsiveness for the rate of employment e beyond threshold values $\tilde{\lambda}, \tilde{r}$. For sufficiently high debt, measured relative to the level of the capital stock, we thus find that debt accumulation feeds itself via its impact on the budget of firms and will lead to larger and larger debt to capital ratios if there is not sufficient support for the pure rate of profit from downward changes in the wage share. Yet, as there is no price deflation, there cannot be a 'perverse' adjustment (a rise) of the wage share in such a situation of depressed profitability and high debt accumulation. Such a problematic situation comes about when there is sluggish or no downward adjustment in the level of nominal wages, but – due to insufficient goods demand, which is not yet a possibility in the considered dynamics – downward adjustment in the price level causing increases in the real wage and the wage share. This scenario will be investigated by a suitable 4D extension in the next section.

Summing up we thus have that debt financing of investment, on the one hand, turns the global centre type dynamics of the Goodwin (1967) growth cycle model into damped cycles, but this, on the other hand, only in a limited domain, outside of which the dynamics become explosive.

Figure 4.2 shows simulation runs of the 3D dynamics for small and large shocks of the debt to capital ratio. The upper figure shows the type of cycle that is implied by this debt-financed extension of the Goodwin (1967) growth cycle model and confirms what is asserted in Proposition 4.2 (for a 100 per cent shock of the steady debt to capital ratio). The lower figure adds the evolution of the ratio λ to the (v, e) phase portrait and does so for multiplicative shocks of order 4 and 5. We can see that the multiplication of the ratio λ_o by 4 still leads to convergence and thus does not yet suffice to bring the dynamics onto an explosive path, which however does come about if the factor 5 is applied in the place of only 4. Note that the wage adjustment speed is low (= 0.1), but not zero as assumed in Proposition 4.4. Note also that the other assumptions of this proposition are fulfilled in the chosen numerical example.

The parameter set for Figure 4.2 is given in Table 4.1.[12]

This basic model of debt accumulation is augmented in later sections by Rose effects in the wage-price interaction (which reveal that either wage or price flexibility must be destabilising with respect to the implied real wage adjustments), by Keynes

[12] This parameter set implies for the interior steady state of the dynamics: $e_o = 0.9, r_o = 0.055; \lambda_o = 0.45, v_o \approx 0.61$.

Table 4.1. *The parameters of the simulation of the 3D dynamics*

$y^p = 0.5$; $\delta = 0.05$; $\bar{e} = 0.9$; $n = 0.1$; $n_l = 0$
$\bar{r} = 0.03$; $\bar{i} = 0.04$; $\beta_w = 0.1$; $\alpha_1^k = 4$

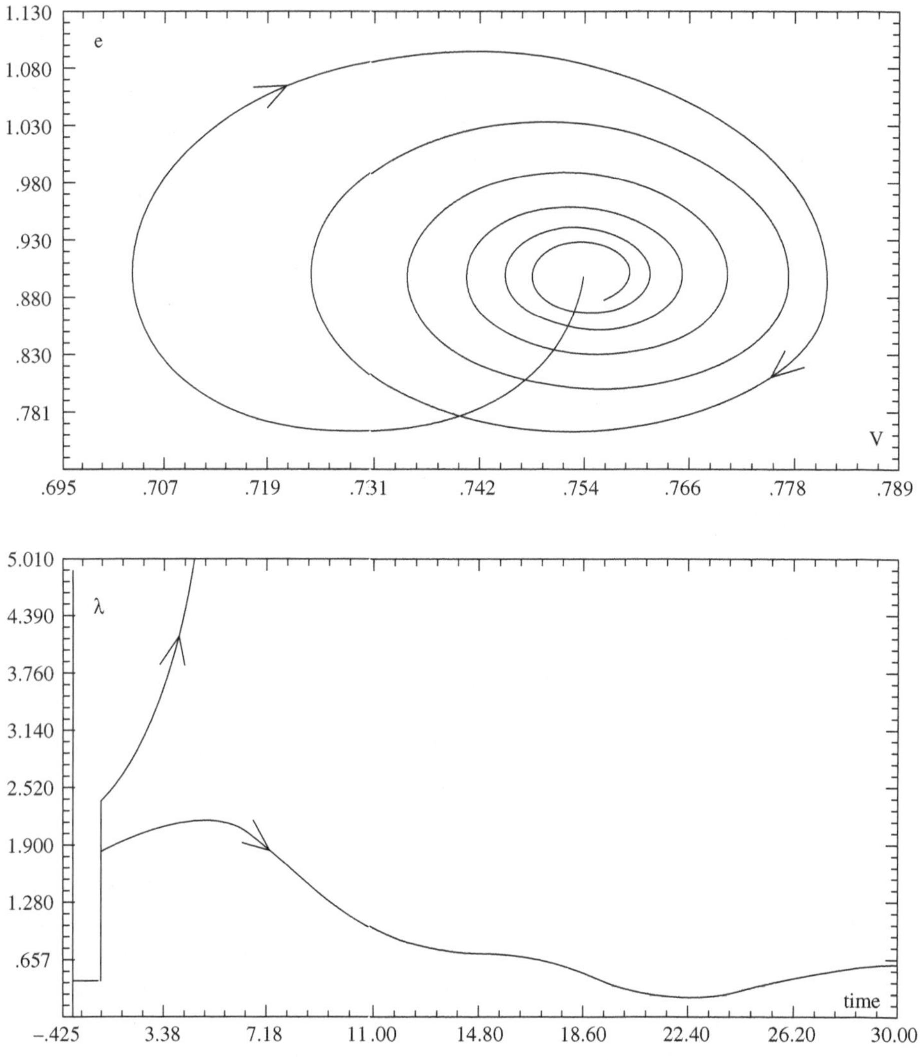

Figure 4.2 Convergence for small shocks and divergence for large shocks to λ

effects (which here are more direct than is usually the case due to the monetary policy rule assumed), by Mundell effects (which state that the interaction between price inflation and expected price deflation must be destabilising if the adaptive component of these expectations is operating with sufficient speed), by Metzler effects (which imply accelerator type instability of the inventory adjustment mechanism when it operates with sufficient speed) and by cumulative (destabilising) effects in financial markets (if adjustments are sufficiently fast) due to positive feedback loops between expected changes and resulting actual changes of financial variables in our delayed adjustment processes towards overall interest rate parity (uniform rates of return). All these effects are of course partial in nature and must be studied in their interaction in a complete analysis of the full 16D model, which is the most general model of debt deflation that will be considered in this chapter.

We have seen in this section that the (very narrow) financing constraint $C_b \geq 0$ requires that the interest rate $\bar{i}$ is larger than the natural rate of growth $n + n_l$, while the occurrence of explosive debt accumulation for a positive rate of profit happens only when the opposite holds true. In addition to what is exemplified in Figure 4.2 we therefore conjecture (also on the basis of further numerical studies) that the considered dynamics are convergent for most initial conditions that are economically meaningful. From the economic perspective, the interior steady state of the 3D model (with only debt accumulation and its sole feedback via the budget equation of firms), is therefore asymptotically stable from a fairly global point of view. Further mechanisms are thus needed, for example a direct effect of debt on the investment behaviour of firms or a credit multiplier, in order to generate stability problems for debt financed economic growth.

Adding, as in the remark 2 on the Proposition 4.2 a term like $\alpha_i^k(\bar{\lambda} - \lambda)$, ($\bar{\lambda} = \lambda_o$ the target debt to capital ratio) to the investment function, which thus directly responds to the state of indebtedness and (not only indirectly via its consequences for the budget equation of firms) adds the expression $\alpha_i^k(\lambda_o - \lambda)(1 - \lambda)$ to the law of motion 3) for the debt to capital ratio, without modifying its interior steady state solution. Such an addition would move the $\widetilde{\lambda}$ expression in Figure 4.1 into the domain where $\dot{\lambda}$ is positive and will also increase $\dot{\lambda}$ if α_i^k is increased. The probability of an explosive evolution of the ratio λ is thereby considerably increased. However we will show in the next section that demand side additions may even be more important for the detection of important sources of cumulative instability, then mainly from a local perspective.

Summing up, we have considered in this section a limited, but useful starting point for the analysis of debt deflation where deflationary forces may be added via markup pricing,[13] where demand pressure on the market for goods is however still missing and where there is a very narrow restriction on the amount of new loans available at each moment in time, given by the interest income of financial capitalists, due to the neglect of money (creation) and to the corresponding validity of Say's Law. This

[13] The addition of these forces would make the entry J_{32} in the Jacobian J of the dynamics at the steady state negative and thus introduce a negative term into the principal minors of order 2 of this Jacobian which is clearly destabilising. A downward floor to falling wages, in particular the institutional assumption that the general level of nominal wages may rise, but never falls in a noticeable way, would however remove this instability from the dynamics. Such a floor is not so obviously present in the case of price deflation to be considered in the next section.

starting point does not yet show that there may be severe consequences from high debt accumulation.

4.3 4D debt deflation

Let us thus now extend and modify the model (4.1)–(4.3) in order to include into it in a minimal, but empirically relevant, way the possibility for persistent price level deflation and thus the possibility for the occurrence of accelerating debt deflation. By the latter term we mean high levels of debt combined with declining profitability due to falling output prices, caused in turn by insufficient aggregate demand for goods. We thus have to introduce into the model on the one hand a law of motion for the price level and on the other hand a discrepancy between normal output of firms and the aggregate demand for their goods on which the required theory of price inflation is to be based. This process will turn the supply side dynamics into demand driven dynamics and thus removes the simple form of Say's Law used in the preceding section in favour of a Keynesian theory of effective demand or goods market equilibrium.

However we still assume that inflationary expectations remain fixed at their steady state level (which is zero here). On this basis we make use of the wage-price dynamics discussed in Chapter 6 of Chiarella and Flaschel (2000) and thus considerably extend the simple law of motion for nominal wages used in Section 4.2. Furthermore, we now make use of the extended investment function[14]

$$I/K = \alpha_1^k(r - \bar{i}) + \alpha_2^k(\lambda_o - \lambda) + \alpha_3^k(y/y^p - \bar{u}) + \gamma + \delta, \quad \alpha_i^k > 0, i = 1, 2, 3$$

which integrates the remarks of Section 4.2 and also introduces fluctuation of excess capacity as a further argument into investment behaviour as in the KMG growth dynamics of Section 4.4. Note that we now assume that trend investment γ is exogenously given and in fact determined by natural growth $n + n_l = \hat{L} + \hat{z}$. This gives the reason why there is no trend term in the law of motion for l^e which is to be calculated from $\hat{l}^e = \hat{L} + \hat{z} - \hat{K}$. We therefore now integrate the PC mechanisms with the growth law of the full employment labour intensity in efficiency units and the law of motion of the debt to capital ratio which as usual is given by $g_k(1-\lambda) - r$ but now with an additional term $-\hat{p}\lambda$ due to the inflationary dynamics that are now present and the definition of the debt to capital ratio by $\lambda = \Lambda/(pK)$.

This gives rise to the following type of nominal dynamics for wages w^e, prices p (adopted from the KMG growth dynamics introduced in Chiarella and Flaschel (2000) with inflationary expectations still fixed at zero) and debt λ coupled with an

[14] Investment behaviour is subject to modification in various (more or less significant) ways in this chapter, which gives rise to subtle differences with respect to steady state determination. It surely represents a behavioural equation where scope for alternative specifications is given. Note in particular here that this section introduces a target debt to capital ratio in the investment behaviour of firms that must be set equal to its steady state value in order to get consistency with respect to steady state solutions. Note also that $\bar{r}$ is given by $\bar{i}$ now. Note finally that we do not yet consider credit rationing explicitly, but in fact assume that in this respect a soft budget constraint of firms is in fact subject to such forces via the debt term in the investment equation which represents the working credit limitations through the behaviour adopted voluntarily by firms themselves.

investment driven growth path, now represented by the dynamics of full employment labour intensity l^e.[15] The intensive form of the dynamics can be written as

$$\hat{w}^e = \kappa[\beta_w(y/l^e - \bar{e}) + \kappa_w\beta_p(y/y^p - \bar{u})], \tag{4.5}$$
$$\hat{p} = \kappa[\beta_p(y/y^p - \bar{u}) + \kappa_p\beta_w(y/l^e - \bar{e})], \tag{4.6}$$
$$\hat{l}^e = -[\alpha_1^k(r - \bar{i}) + \alpha_2^k(\lambda_o - \lambda) + \alpha_3^k(y/y^p - \bar{u})], \tag{4.7}$$
$$\dot{\lambda} = [\alpha_1^k(r - \bar{i}) + \alpha_2^k(\lambda_o - \lambda) + \alpha_3^k(y/y^p - \bar{u}) + \gamma](1 - \lambda) - r - \hat{p}\lambda, \tag{4.8}$$

where the Metzlerian feedback mechanism from actually observed aggregate demand to expected demand to planned output and income and back to aggregate demand, namely

$$y^d = c_y\frac{w^e}{p}y + \alpha_1^k(r - \bar{i}) + \alpha_3^k(y/y^p - \bar{u}) + \gamma + \delta \to y^e \to y \to y^d,$$

will be simplified and specialised to the static (and again linearised[16]) relationship

$$y^d = y^e = y = y(\frac{w^e}{p}, \lambda) = \bar{u}y^p + d_1(\frac{w^e}{p} - (\frac{w^e}{p})_o) + d_2(\lambda - \lambda^o), \qquad d_w, d_\lambda \leq 0. \tag{4.9}$$

Equation (4.9) will be used in the following as a shortcut for the delayed feedback chain of the general case (and its richer concept of aggregate demand) in order to integrate the effects of price inflation and deflation into the Keen (2000) model as presented and analysed in the preceding section.[17] Note that the budget equations of the credit-giving institution (here the pure asset holders) are no longer subject to the problem we observed for the banks of the 3D Keen model, that is there may be a credit multiplier at work which always produces the amount of loans demanded by firms (and there is no need to consider the consumption demand of this sector). Note furthermore, that Goodwin type dynamics are obtained when $\bar{i}, \lambda(0), d_w, d_\lambda$ are all zero, while the more general pure Rose (1967) type of real wage dynamics requires $\bar{i}, d_\lambda = 0$ (with wage flexibility as a stabilising factor and price flexibility destabilising if $d_w < 0$ holds). Finally, the pure Fisher debt mechanism is obtained (due to $d_\lambda < 0$) by setting $\beta_w, \kappa_w, d_w = 0$. The above goods market representation therefore allows for Rose real wage effects of traditional type (where price flexibility is destabilising giving rise to adverse real wage adjustments) and for Fisher debt effects (where price flexibility is also destabilising, giving rise to unbounded increases of the real debt to capital ratio),

15 Here $\bar{e}, \bar{u}$ are the NAIRU utilisation rates of the labour force and the capital stock, w^e, l^e measured in efficiency units as in Section 4.4 and Section 4.5 below.

16 Linearised, that is, around the interior steady state solution.

17 Note that this shortcut of the originally delayed quantity adjustment process of Metzlerian type requires that the steady state value of this function y must be equal to $y^p\bar{u}$ in order to get a steady state solution for this 4D simplification and modification of the KMG dynamics.

but it excludes Mundell effects for example (that would require at the least the inclusion of inflationary expectations into the above model).[18]

Thus we here assume (implicitly) that the propensity to invest dominates the propensity to consume with respect to the impact of real wages w^e/p on consumption and investment (the orthodox point of view) and take also from the Metzlerian feedback chain and its shown shortcut the assumption that output depends negatively on the debt to capital ratio λ. The partial derivatives of the function $y(\frac{w^e}{p}, \lambda)$ in equation (4.9) are therefore both assumed to be negative in the following (that is $d_1, d_2 < 0$, representing two channels for destabilising price flexibility, or zero when certain limit cases are considered). Since employment l^{de} per unit of capital and in efficiency units is identical to output y, due to the measurement conventions of Section 4.4 and Section 4.5 and the fixed proportions technology assumed, we have that the employment rate exhibits the same type of dependence on the real wage and the debt to capital ratio as output y. Finally we of course again have $r = y - \delta - \frac{w^e}{p}y - \bar{i}\lambda$ for the rate of pure profits r.

The above represents the simplest way to integrate from the perspective of the KMG growth dynamics of Section 4.1 the dynamics of the price level into our representation of the Keen (2000) model by abstracting from Metzlerian delayed output adjustment, from inflationary expectations, a fiscal and monetary authority, and from endogenous determination of the interest rate.

The 4D dynamics (4.5)–(4.8) can be reduced to 3D dynamics, as shown in Section 4.5, giving rise to

$$\hat{v} = \kappa[(1-\kappa_p)\beta_w(y/l^e - \bar{e}) - (1-\kappa_w)\beta_p(y/y^p - \bar{u})], \quad v = wL^d/(pY) = w^e/p, \tag{4.10}$$

$$\hat{l}^e = -[\alpha_1^k(r-\bar{i}) + \alpha_2^k(\lambda_o - \lambda) + \alpha_3^k(y/y^p - \bar{u})], \quad l^e = zL/K, \tag{4.11}$$

$$\dot{\lambda} = [\alpha_1^k(r-\bar{i}) + \alpha_2^k(\lambda_o - \lambda) + \alpha_3^k(y/y^p - \bar{u}) + \gamma](1-\lambda) - r - \hat{p}\lambda, \quad \lambda = \frac{\Lambda}{pK}, \tag{4.12}$$

supplemented by the algebraic equations

$$y = y(v,\lambda) = \bar{u}y^p + d_1(v - v_o) + d_2(\lambda - \lambda^o), \qquad d_w, d_\lambda \leq 0,$$

$$r = y(v,\lambda)(1-v) - \delta - \bar{i}\lambda,$$

with an appended law for the price level dynamics

$$\hat{p} = \kappa[\kappa_p(\beta_w(y/l^e - \bar{e}) + \beta_p(y/y^p - \bar{u})]. \tag{4.13}$$

Due to the lack of changing inflationary expectations the Ordinary Differential Equation (ODE) for p does not feed back into the rest of the dynamics.[19] Our stability

[18] There is also no Keynes effect in the present formulation of the dynamics, since the nominal rate of interest is kept constant.

[19] Note however that this law has to be inserted into the law of motion for the debt to capital ratio (as shown), implying that deflationary forces are now present, based on demand pressure in the goods market and demand

analysis will be concentrated on the above 3D core dynamics (4.10)–(4.12), the stability features of which will also determine those of the price level dynamics.

Let us first calculate the interior steady state of the dynamics (4.5)–(4.8), which partly already assume knowledge of this steady state solution. This steady state is uniquely determined up to the steady level of prices p and is characterised by[20]

$$\lambda_f^o = 1 - \bar{i}/\gamma, \tag{4.14}$$

$$y_o = y^p \bar{u}, \tag{4.15}$$

$$l_o^e = y_o/\bar{e}, \tag{4.16}$$

$$r_o = \bar{i}, \tag{4.17}$$

$$v_o = \frac{y_o - r_o - \delta - \bar{i}\lambda^o}{y_o}, \tag{4.18}$$

$$p_o = \text{ determined by initial conditions}, \tag{4.19}$$

$$w_o^e = p_o(\frac{w^e}{p})_o = p_o v_o. \tag{4.20}$$

The steady state value for the debt to capital ratio is a direct consequence of equations (4.7) and (4.8) once it is shown that $r_o = \bar{i}$ must hold true, see below, since $\hat{p} = 0$ in the steady state. Equations (4.5) and (4.6) set equal to zero together imply furthermore that the two measures of demand pressure (on the market for goods and for labour) must be zero in the steady state, which determines the steady state values of y and l^e as shown. Due to the new form of the investment function[21] underlying equation (4.7), namely

$$I/K = \alpha_1^k(r - \bar{i}) + \alpha_2^k(\lambda_o - \lambda) + \alpha_3^k(y/y^p - \bar{u}) + \gamma + \delta,$$

we now have a different steady debt to capital ratio which is solely determined by trend growth γ in its deviation from the given rate of interest $\bar{i}$ on loans. Note here that the natural growth trend term $\gamma = n + n_l$ in the investment function enforces $\bar{i} = r$, in the steady state (since $y = y^p\bar{u}$ holds in the steady state, $r = \gamma(1 - \lambda)$ by equation (4.12) and $\lambda_o = \bar{i}/\gamma$ by assumption). Natural growth is thus responsible for the difference to the steady state solution we have obtained for the 3D dynamics of Section 4.4 where no such trend term was present. We assume throughout that $\gamma - \bar{i} > 0$ holds in order to have a positive steady state ratio λ.

Again, the wage share v_o is determined residually, once profit and interest per unit of capital have been determined. The two demand pressure benchmarks on the labour and the goods market, $\bar{e}$ and $\bar{u}$, are the NAIRU rates of capacity utilisation on these two markets. The steady state ratios for actual and full employment labour intensity (in efficiency units), $l^{de} = y$ and l^e are thus purely supply side determined, while the

pressure in the labour market (to the extent κ_p by which wages influence prices by way of cost pressure considerations).

20 We use $l_y^e = 1/z$ to express employment per unit of output measured in efficiency units (l_y^e a given magnitude).

21 Which (as gross investment function) must be non-negative along the relevant trajectories of the dynamics.

demand side expression (d_w, d_λ and the α_i^k's) only enter the analysis when the stability of the steady state solution is investigated. The determination of the rate of profit through the rate of interest on loans implies a well defined level of real wages measured in efficiency units, $v = (\frac{w^e}{p})_o$, which is positive if y^p is chosen sufficiently high relative to γ, δ, $\bar{i}$ and $\bar{u}$. This real wage level then determines the nominal wage level on the basis of a given price level which is determined through historical conditions and thus not uniquely determined. This is due to the fact that the price dynamics are not needed for the dynamic analysis of the evolution of the wage share, the full employment labour intensity and the debt ratio, and itself only dependent on these three state variables which implies that the determinant of the Jacobian of the 4D dynamics must be zero under all circumstances. Note in this respect that the price dynamics are needed as an equation in the determination of the interior steady state of the dynamics, but can be removed from explicit consideration in the dynamics surrounding this steady state solution.

Proposition 4.5 (Stabilising normal Rose effects)
Assume $0 < \bar{i} < \gamma, d_2 = 0$ and $\beta_p, \kappa_p = 0$,[22] so that the price level is a given magnitude. Assume furthermore a wage adjustment speed that is sufficiently high. Then the steady state (4.14)–(4.20) of the dynamical system (4.10)–(4.12) is locally asymptotically stable for all other admissible parameter values.

Proof: Note first of all that the dynamics are now truly of dimension three by assumption, since there is no longer an appended law of motion for the price level dynamics. Concerning the calculation of the determinant of the Jacobian of these reduced dynamics (4.10)–(4.12), at the steady state, we can first of all state that its third row can be reduced to $(-r_v, 0, \bar{i} - \gamma)$ by the addition of an appropriate multiple of the second row without changing its sign. This implies that this determinant can be characterised by the sign structure

$$\det J = \begin{vmatrix} - & - & 0 \\ + & 0 & + \\ + & 0 & \bar{i} - \gamma \end{vmatrix}$$

and is thus always negative if $\bar{i} < \gamma$ holds, which provides one of the Routh–Hurwitz conditions for local asymptotic stability. With respect to the sum a_2 of the principal minors of order 2, namely J_1, J_2, J_3, one furthermore gets from the full sign structure of the Jacobian matrix J in the case $d_2 = 0$ that

$$J = \begin{pmatrix} - & - & 0 \\ + & 0 & + \\ \pm & 0 & - \end{pmatrix}.$$

[22] This implies $\kappa = 1$. Note also that the assumption $\bar{i} < \gamma$ is much stronger than what is actually needed to imply $\det J > 0$.

We see that the calculation of det J involves two positive and one zero determinant and thus is unambiguously positive. Note furthermore that the entry

$$J_{33} = \bar{i} - \gamma - (\alpha_r^k \bar{i} + \alpha_i^k)(1 - \lambda_o)$$

in the Jacobian matrix J is negative and larger in absolute value than $\bar{i} - \gamma$. The trace of J is therefore indeed negative, too, since $\bar{i} < \gamma$ by assumption and since $\lambda^o < 1$ holds. The coefficients $a_1 = -\text{trace } J, a_2, a_3 = -\det J$ of the Routh–Hurwitz polynomial are therefore all positive and thus all support the local asymptotic stability claimed in the above proposition. Finally, we also have $a_1 a_2 - a_3 > 0$, since one of the expressions that forms det J is part of the all positive expressions contained in $a_1 a_2$ and thus cannot make the expression $a_1 a_2 - a_3$ less than or equal to zero, and since the other one depends linearly on the parameter β_w, while the component $J_{11} J_2$ of $a_1 a_2$ is a quadratic function of this parameter (with all coefficients being positive) that must dominate the value of the linear function if the parameter β_w is made sufficiently large. □

We thus have that the interior steady state (with $\lambda_o < 1, \bar{i} < \gamma$) of the reduced dynamics (4.10) – (4.12), where there is only *sluggish adjustment of prices* caused by demand pressure on the market for goods, that is where β_p, κ_p are both sufficiently small, is locally asymptotically stable if the influence of the debt to capital ratio λ on the level of output and employment, both in intensive form, is also sufficiently weak and if nominal wages adjust with sufficient speed. This outcome is due to the fact that the eigenvalues of the Jacobian of the dynamics are continuous functions of the parameters of the model, and thus cannot change sign of their real parts if the parameters that characterise price and output adjustment are chosen sufficiently small. Making the stabilising Rose effect or real wage adjustment sufficiently strong and the Fisher debt effect in the goods market and price inflation sufficiently weak thus produces stability (as was to be expected) in a world where only Rose and Fisher debt effects interact and where there is a positive amount of debt of firms in the steady state. We note that stability can get lost only in a cyclical fashion, by way of a *Hopf bifurcation* and the limit cycles they generate, when the parameter β_w is decreased, since such a change does not alter the negative sign of the determinant of the Jacobian at the steady state. This however need not hold true for the parameter β_p as we shall see below.

Proposition 4.6 (Two channels for destabilising price flexibility)[23]
Assume that $d_2 < 0$ holds. Then the steady state (4.14)–(4.20) of the dynamical system (4.10)–(4.12) loses its local asymptotic stability if the price adjustment speed β_p is sufficiently large.

[23] Assuming $d_w > 0$ and thus stabilising price flexibility from the viewpoint of the Rose effect, it can be shown that the destabilising forces of the Fisher debt effect will dominate the stabilising Rose effect, if price flexibility becomes sufficiently large.

Proof: Collecting the terms in the trace of the Jacobian J of the dynamics (4.10)–(4.12) at the steady state that depend on the parameter β_p one obtains[24]

$$-v_o\kappa(1-\kappa_w)d_w/y^p\beta_p - \kappa d_\lambda/y^p\beta_p$$

which involves positive expressions solely (up to the possibility that κ_w can be equal to one and either d_w or d_λ equal to zero). The first expression shows the strength of the destabilising Rose price flexibility effect and the second is the Fisher debt effect. Therefore the trace of J can always be made positive by choosing the parameter β_p sufficiently large. □

The local stability result for the 3D Keen model is therefore overthrown in the case where goods demand is negatively dependent on the debt to capital ratio (and the real wage) and where the price level adjusts with respect to demand pressure on the market for goods with sufficient speed. Local stability therefore gets lost for flexible price levels either through Fisher type debt deflation or through adverse Rose effects or through the joint working of these two adverse consequences of an adjustment of the price level that is sufficiently fast (and a given wage adjustment speed). In such a case, we conjecture and will test this assertion numerically, that a process of deflation will continue without end accompanied in particular by higher and higher debt ratios of firms which eventually will lead to negative profits and bankruptcy.

Proposition 4.7 (Convergent dynamics: limited basins of attraction)
We again allow $d_2 < 0$, $\beta_p > 0$ and assume in addition, as in Proposition 4.3, that nominal wages are completely fixed ($\beta_w = \kappa_w = 0$). Then the dynamical system (4.10)–(4.12) is monotonically explosive, implying higher and higher wage shares and debt to capital ratios, for initial debt to capital ratios chosen sufficiently high (in particular larger than 1), all wage shares above their steady state value and all positive adjustment speeds of the price level p.

Proof: The system (4.10)–(4.12) in the assumed situation can be reduced to

$$\hat{v} = -\beta_p(y/y^p - \bar{u}), \tag{4.21}$$

$$\dot{\lambda}_f = [\alpha_1^k(r-\bar{i}) + \alpha_2^k(\lambda_o - \lambda) + \alpha_3^k(y/y^p - \bar{u}) + \gamma](1-\lambda) - r - \beta_p(y/y^p - \bar{u})\lambda, \tag{4.22}$$

since l^e no longer feeds back onto the state variables of these dynamics. Since both v and λ are assumed to be larger than their steady state values, we get from the first law of motion that v must be rising further (due to falling price levels caused by $y < y^p\bar{u}$). Furthermore, since also $r - \bar{i} < 0$ and $1 - \lambda < 0$ hold, we get that $\dot{\lambda}$ must be larger than

$$\gamma(1-\lambda) - \bar{i} - \beta_p(y/y^p - \bar{u})\lambda > -\gamma\lambda - \beta_p(y/y^p - \bar{u})\lambda.$$

24 In the later 8D or 16D extensions of these dynamics the destabilising influence of price flexibility is no longer so obviously situated in the trace of the Jacobian J, but hidden in certain principal minors of J then.

If therefore $-\beta_p(y/y^p - \bar{u}) > \gamma$ has come about by choosing λ sufficiently high then $\dot{\lambda} > 0$ must be true, so that both v and λ must be rising which further strengthens the conditions for their monotonic increase. □

We thus get the same result as in Proposition 4.3, but now in an easier and more pronounced way (through the occurrence of price deflation), that there will indeed occur situations of debt *deflation* where profitability falls monotonically and where the debt of firms is increasing beyond any limit, leading to economic collapse sooner or later. Note that the above is only a first and crude estimate of such a possibility.

Proposition 4.8 (Conditions for convergence)
Assume that $\beta_p = 0, \kappa_p = 1$ holds, so that the price level is determined by cost-push considerations solely and hence by a conventional markup equation of the type

$$p = (1+a)\frac{wL^d}{Y} = (1+a)wl_y = (1+a)w^e l_y^e.$$

Assume furthermore that the given markup a is such that the implied wage share v is equal to its steady state level v_o. Assume next a given level of nominal wages (measured in efficiency units), that is $\beta_w = 0, \kappa_w = 0$.[25] *Assume finally that the investment parameters $\alpha_{1,3}^k$ are chosen such that the inequalities $\alpha_1^k > 1, \alpha_u^k > y^p(1-v)\frac{\gamma - \bar{i}}{\bar{i}}$ hold true.*[26] *Then the steady state (4.14)–(4.20) of the dynamics (4.10)–(4.12), which can then be basically reduced to adjustments of the debt to capital ratio, is locally asymptotically stable for all values of the parameter $d_\lambda < 0$.*

Proof: In the assumed situation we have $\hat{p} = 0$ due to the given level of nominal wages and thus get for the debt to capital ratio λ the single independent law of motion

$$\dot{\lambda} = [\alpha_1^k(r(\lambda) - \bar{i}) + \alpha_2^k(\lambda_o - \lambda) + \alpha_3^k(y(\lambda)/y^p - \bar{u}) + \gamma](1-\lambda) - r(\lambda).$$

We have to show that the derivative of the right-hand side of this equation is negative at λ_o for all d_λ. Note first that $r'(\lambda_o) = y'(\lambda_o)(1 - v_o) - \bar{i} = d_\lambda(1 - v_o) - \bar{i}$ holds. The derivative of the $\dot{\lambda}$ equation with respect to λ evaluated at the steady state reads[27]

$$-\gamma + [\alpha_1^k r'(\lambda_o) - \alpha_2^k + \alpha_3^k y'(\lambda_o)/y^p](1-\lambda_o) - r'(\lambda_o).$$

This expression can be rearranged to

$$-\gamma + (\alpha_1^k - 1)r'(\lambda_o)(1-\lambda_o) - \alpha_2^k(1-\lambda_o) + \alpha_3^k d_\lambda/y^p(1-\lambda_o) - r'(\lambda_o)\lambda_o.$$

From this expression we get through further rearrangement

$$-(\gamma - \bar{i}\lambda_o) + (\alpha_1^k - 1)r'(\lambda_o)(1-\lambda_o) - \alpha_2^k(1-\lambda_o) - d_\lambda[-\alpha_3^k/y^p(1-\lambda_o) + (1-v_o)\lambda_o]$$

25 The nominal wage is therefore then growing in line with labour productivity.
26 This inequality is equivalent to the inequality

$$\alpha_u^k > [(\gamma - \bar{i})^2 + 2(\gamma - \bar{i}) + \delta(\gamma/\bar{i} - 1)]/\bar{u}.$$

27 $\alpha_1^k(1-\lambda_o) > 1$ is already sufficient here.

with $\lambda_o = 1 - \bar{i}/\gamma, 1 - \lambda_o = \bar{i}/\gamma$. This expression must be negative, since $\bar{i} < \gamma$, $\lambda_o < 1, d_\lambda < 0, \alpha_r^k > 1, r'(\lambda_o) < 0$ and since

$$\alpha_3^k > y^p(1 - v_o)\lambda_o/(1 - \lambda_o) = y^p(1 - v_o)\frac{\gamma - \bar{i}}{\bar{i}}.$$

□

In a similar way it can also be shown that the above derivative is negative for all $\lambda \in (0, \lambda^o)$, so that there is convergence to the steady state for all positive debt to capital ratios below the steady state ratio. It is however not possible to provide an easy expression for the upper limit of the basin of attraction of the steady state (which may be less than 1). The situation that we have investigated here is indeed similar to the one considered in Figure 4.1, since the right-hand side of the above $\dot{\lambda}$ equation is again a quadratic function in λ with a positive coefficient in front of the λ^2 term and a global minimum at a positive value λ_{min} above the steady state value $\lambda_o < 1$, which of course is again one of the roots of this polynomial. The other one to the right of λ_{min} is then the limit for the basin of attraction shown to exist by Proposition 4.8.

We have formulated Proposition 4.8 in view of an intended policy application that, however, can only be sketched here. Consider the case where the debt to capital ratio λ is so large that there are cumulative forces at work (as in Proposition 4.7) that would lead to higher and higher debt and lower and lower profitability. In the case considered in Proposition 4.8 there are three possible ways to break this catastrophic tendency in the evolution of the economy:

- an increase in nominal wages w that, under the assumptions of Proposition 4.8, causes an immediate increase in the price level p and thus an immediate decrease in the ratio λ, which (if strong enough) may lead the economy back to the basin of attraction of its steady state;
- a decrease in the rate of interest $\bar{i}$ on loans, which moves the steady state of the economy to a higher sustainable debt to capital ratio;
- a decrease in the sensitivity of output y (through appropriate fiscal policies) with respect to λ, that is a parameter d_λ that is smaller in amount (which may enlarge the basin of attraction of the steady state).

There is therefore scope for economic policy to move the economy out of regions of developing debt deflation into regions where it converges back to the steady state. The details of such possibilities must however be left for future research.

What we have shown in this section is that there can be asymptotic stability under certain conditions as in the 3D dynamics considered in the preceding section. Moreover, this stability is destroyed once Fisher debt effects are present in the goods market reaction function and price level flexibility becomes sufficiently pronounced. Finally, even sluggish price levels give rise to instability outside certain corridors. It follows that certain wage-price regimes and properties of the investment function may generate

Table 4.2. *The parameters of the simulated 4D dynamics*

$\beta_w = 0.5$;	$\delta = 0.05$;	$\alpha_1^k = 0.5$;	$\alpha_2^k = 0$;	$\alpha_3^k = 0.5$;		
$\bar{i} = \bar{r} = 0.05$;	$\beta_p = 1$;	$\kappa_p = 0$;	$\kappa_w = 0$;	$p(0) = 1$;	$\gamma = 0.1$;	
$l_y^e = 1$;	$d_w = -0.4$;	$d_\lambda = -0.4$;	$\bar{u} = \bar{e} = 1$;	$y^p = 0.4$;		

regions of stability even for very high sensitivity of goods market positions with respect to the level of the debt to capital ratio.

We close this section by eigenvalue calculations which exemplify the stabilising and destabilising effects we have investigated for the considered 4D dynamics. To this end we perform some simulations using the parameter set in Table 4.2.

In Figure 4.3 we see first of all that wage flexibility is stabilising while price flexibility is not. Note that here again one eigenvalue of the 4D dynamics must always be zero so that stability is represented in this and the other eigenvalue diagrams by the horizontal line. We then set the parameter $\beta_w = 2$ in order to get convergent dynamics for the further evaluation of the feedback mechanisms of the dynamics by means of eigenvalue diagrams shown in the bottom six panels of Figure 4.3. In the second row of panels in Figure 4.3 we show on the left-hand side the 2D projection onto the (l^e, λ) space of a convergent trajectory of the dynamics generated by a shock of the debt to capital ratio of 10 per cent. To the right of this phase plot we then recalculate the eigenvalue diagram with respect to the parameter β_p for the now convergent dynamics and see that instability sets in much later than was the case at the parameter value $\beta_w = 0.5$.

The third row of panels shows eigenvalue diagrams that consider the role played by the Rose real wage and the Fisher debt effects. Note here the parameters d_w, d_λ are negative which means that stronger Rose and Fisher debt effects are obtained by moving to the left in the considered eigenvalue diagrams. We see that stronger Rose effects are stabilising in the considered situation (since wages are more flexible than prices), while the opposite holds for the Fisher debt effect.

In the lowest two panels of Figure 4.3, we display on the left-hand side the eigenvalue diagram for the parameter κ_p, the strength of the wage cost-push term in the price level PC. Wage flexibility is then transferred into price flexibility and thus becomes destabilising via the Fisher debt effect, overcoming the stabilising potential of wage flexibility through the Rose real wage effect. Finally, in the right-hand panel we observe that a rate of interest that is chosen sufficiently high destabilises the economy, since this increases the power of the destabilising Fisher debt effect. The opposite holds true if the parameter κ_p is increased (which is not shown here), since the stabilising Rose effect of wage flexibility is then strengthened.

We close this section with the observation that the dynamics considered in this section have been designed to display Fisher debt deflation as well as Rose real wage effects in their simplest form. This was done however in a way that is not fully consistent with the demand underlying the goods market equilibrium structure that has been employed. In the next section we represent aggregate demand and goods market adjustment processes

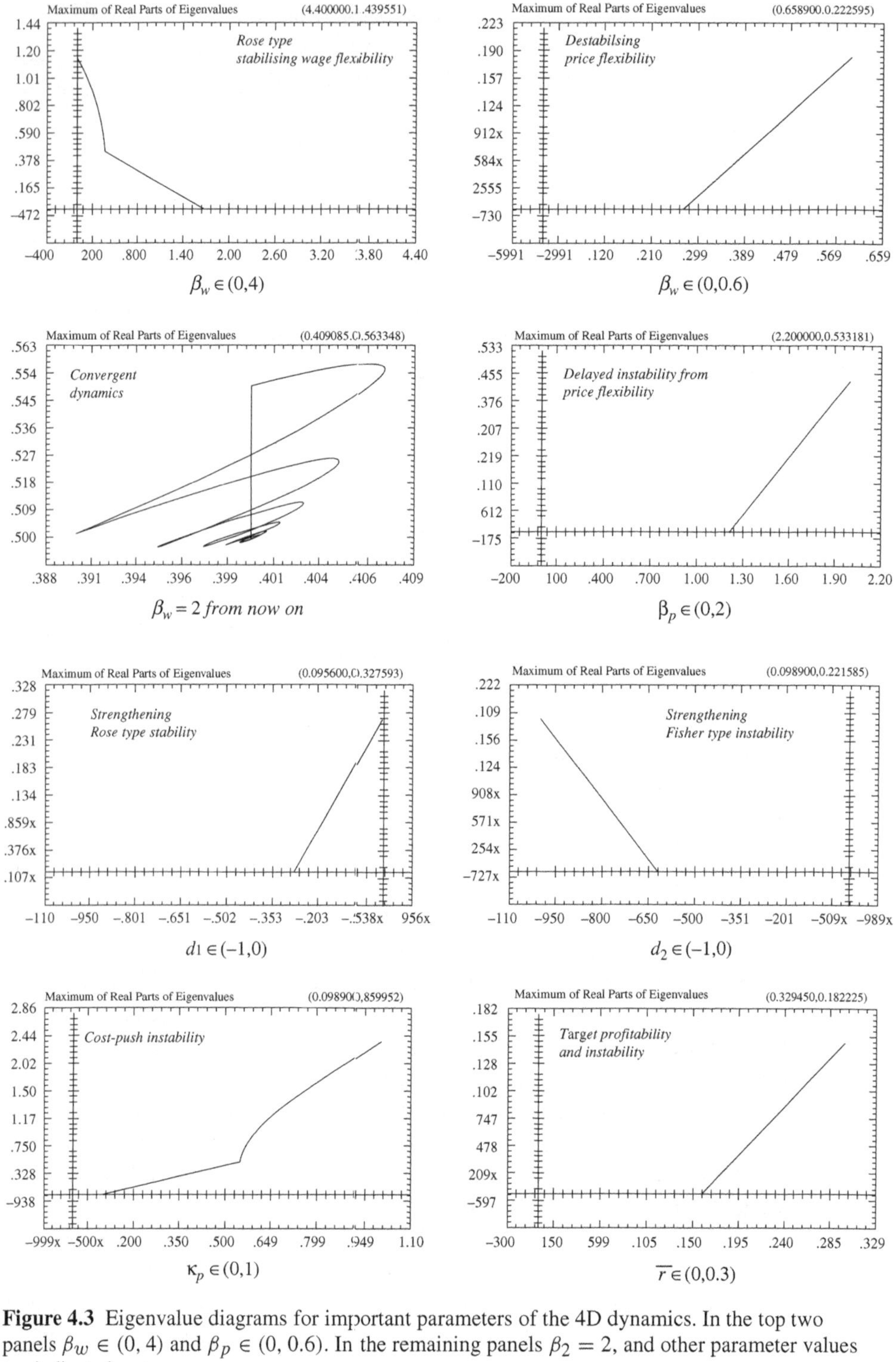

Figure 4.3 Eigenvalue diagrams for important parameters of the 4D dynamics. In the top two panels $\beta_w \in (0, 4)$ and $\beta_p \in (0, 0.6)$. In the remaining panels $\beta_2 = 2$, and other parameter values are indicated

explicitly in order to remove this inconsistency of the 4D approach and also complicated goods market equilibrium considerations. Instead, we have two further laws of motion for sales expectations and inventory adjustments as in KMG growth models. We also consider inflationary expectations and an interest rate policy rule of the monetary authority, which adds four further laws of motion to the dynamics of this section and thus increases considerably the analysis of interacting feedback chains of Keynesian disequilibrium growth.[28]

4.4 KMG real business fluctuations: the point of departure

In this section we introduce what is in our view the basic complete and coherently formulated Keynesian out-of-equilibrium macrodynamic model of the real sector of capitalist economies. The model combines on the markets for goods and labour both gradual quantity adjustment processes together with gradual price and wage adjustment. While gradual wage adjustment was always present in the old Keynesian AD-AS models of inflation and growth and while gradual price adjustment is characteristic for the New Keynesian baseline models of DSGE type, the joint consideration of both gradual wage and price adjustment processes is rarely done, not even in the old Keynesian literature. In this section we provide an introduction to the basic building blocks of the KMG model of business fluctuations and growth. We do this from an informal point of view in order to show the reader the philosophy behind this disequilibrium approach to conventional AS as well as AD analysis, which may therefore also be briefly characterised as a DAS-DAD modelling approach. Since the first publication of this model type in Chiarella and Flaschel (2000, Ch. 6) the model has been extended in numerous ways towards the treatment of the relevance of non-Keynesian regimes with supply side bottlenecks, the extension towards open economies, the calibration of this model type for the US economy, the issue of monetary policy and the inclusion of endogenous growth, to mention the most significant.

There exists in the New Keynesian approach to macrodynamics the consideration of both staggered wage and price setting, however the analysis of the resulting four dimensional dynamical system is missing in the literature.[29] Such a remark is even more applicable to the quantity side of these Keynesian approaches, both old and new, where the consideration of goods market equilibrium is the standard procedure to modelling the demand side of Keynesian AD analysis, in place of the interaction of firms' sales expectations with their inventory adjustment rules.

In view of the situation just described we shall build on the modelling philosophy of Chiarella and Flaschel (2000) and Chiarella *et al.* (2005) and their detailed investigation of models of so-called KMG type. We use continuous-time to model the data generating process of actual economies (which by and large is a daily one). In continuous-time we

[28] There are two further laws of motion for stocks, deriving from the budget equations of the model, which are now all present, but (by assumption) do not all exhibit feedback effects into the dynamics of the private sector.

[29] See however Flaschel *et al.* (2008) for a determinacy analysis of continuous-time limits of this type of model.

have on the quantity side sales expectations of firms on which they base their production decision (including planned inventory changes). The firms then experience actual demand for their goods which they service on the basis of their actual inventories, a process which leads to definite changes in their inventories.[30] We use reformulations of Okun's Law to relate the production decision of firms to the employment decision within firms and on the labour market.

On the price side, building on the work of Chiarella and Flaschel (1996) we have formulated a crossover wage-price spiral mechanism based on various gap measures for the labour as well as the goods market (in particular the employment rate and various utilisation rates). We have also used Blanchard and Katz (1999) type error correction mechanisms based on a wage share gap; see Chiarella *et al.* (2005) for a detailed discussion. These wage-price adjustment processes formally seem very similar to the equations used in the New Keynesian staggered-wages staggered-prices approach, however they differ significantly in their microeconomic details as well in their implications for the dynamics of the real wage. The significant outcome of this approach to the adjustment of real wages is that basically all mentioned gaps on the labour market and the goods market influence not only the law of motion of real wages, but also the formulation of a reduced form price PC (in theoretical as well as in applied inflation rate studies). This stands in stark contrast to current practice, particularly in empirical work.

4.4.1 The basic framework

We consider a closed three sector economy consisting of households (workers and asset holders), firms and the government. There exist five distinct markets: labour, goods, money, bonds and equities (which are perfect substitutes of bonds).

Our model is briefly summarised in Table 4.3, where real and nominal magnitudes are represented. The index d on a symbol refers to demand and the same symbol with no index represents supply, while the superscript index e is used to denote expectations. Table 4.3 shows the basic structure and the interaction of the sectors and the markets; the rows represent the sectors and the columns the markets. The links between the markets and sectors shown, the behavioural relationships and the dynamic adjustment processes that fill this structure have all been established in Flaschel *et al.* (1997) and in Chiarella and Flaschel (2000). They represent significant extensions of the Chiarella *et al.* (2000) baseline models in various ways. We extend this framework further by a discussion of the role of monetary policy rules and we also investigate the stability implications of kinked money-wage PCs already asserted to exist in fact by Keynes (1936).

The structure of the model is complete in the sense that it includes all major markets and sectors of a closed economy and all financing conditions and budget restrictions

[30] This scenario needs to be reformulated somewhat in the case of services, which however does not put into question the general idea of a gradual adjustment of quantities due to the observation of actual demand on the market for goods.

Table 4.3. *Sectors and markets of the economy*

	Labour market	Goods market	Money market	Bond market	Equity market
Households	L	$C = C_w + C_c$	M^d	B^d	E^d
Firms	L^d	$Y, Y^d, I + \delta K$	–	–	E
Government	–	G	M	B	–
Prices	w	p	1	1	p_e
Expectations	–	$Y^e, \pi^e = \hat{p}^e$	–	–	–

of households, firms and the government, as in Sargent (1987). However in contrast to Sargent (1987) we distinguish between workers and asset holders in the household sector, in a Kaldorian fashion. The really major difference from Sargent is however the extent of disequilibrium allowed for and the dynamical processes that follow from these disequilibria. Concerning the extent of these disequilibrium adjustment processes, firms have desired capacity utilisation rates and desired ratios of inventory to expected sales. Temporary deviations from those benchmarks are caused by unexpected changes in aggregate goods demand. We stress that a distinguishing feature of Keynesian models, in contrast in particular to equilibrium macromodels of the Sargent (1987) type, is that under- or over-utilised capital as well as an under- or over-utilised labour force are important driving factors of the economic dynamics.

The next section provides the building blocks of our KMG macrodynamics from the perspective of their fundamental adjustment mechanisms and the feedback structures that are implied. We motivate the structure of the model without presenting the many details which underlie its extensive form representation – for all of these structural details we refer the reader to Chiarella and Flaschel (2000, Ch. 6). The stability properties of the interaction of those feedback structures will be studied analytically and numerically using estimated parameters.

4.4.2 The 3D Rose type wage-price dynamics

The full dynamics, which are presented in ratio or intensive form directly, are best introduced and motivated by starting from a very basic, yet unfamiliar, wage-price module. In our first specification we follow Rose (1967, 1990) and assume two PCs in place of only one, thus providing wage and price dynamics separately, both based on measures of demand pressure $e - \bar{e}$ and $u - \bar{u}$, in the market for labour and for goods, respectively. These demand pressure influences on wage and price dynamics, or on the formation of wage and price inflation, $\hat{w}$ and $\hat{p}$, are both augmented by a weighted average of cost-pressure terms based on forward-looking myopic perfect foresight and a backward-looking measure of the prevailing inflationary climate, symbolised by π^c. Cost pressure perceived by workers is thus a weighted average of the currently evolving price inflation $\hat{p}$ and some longer-run concept of price inflation, π^c, based on past observations. Similarly, cost pressure perceived by firms is given as a weighted average of the currently evolving (perfectly foreseen) wage inflation rate, $\hat{w}$, and again the measure of the inflationary climate in which the economy is operating. Taken together we thus arrive at the following two PCs for wage and price inflation, which in this core version of the model are formulated in a fairly symmetrical way.[31]

The structural form of the wage-price dynamics is:

$$\hat{w} = \beta_w(e - \bar{e}) + \kappa_w \hat{p} + (1 - \kappa_w)\pi^c, \tag{4.23}$$

$$\hat{p} = \beta_p(u - \bar{u}) + \kappa_p \hat{w} + (1 - \kappa_p)\pi^c. \tag{4.24}$$

In the empirical application of the model we also have to take into account labour productivity growth $n_x = \hat{x}$, which from the theoretical perspective augments the cost pressure terms in the wage PC by the addition of n_x, while it reduces the wage cost pressure term $\hat{w}$ in the price PC by the same amount, as shown in calculations below.

Inflationary expectations over the medium run, π^c (the *inflationary climate* in which current inflation is operating), may be adaptively following the actual rate of inflation (for instance using an exponential weighting scheme), may be based on a rolling sample (hump-shaped weighting schemes), or may be based on other possible schemes for updating such expectations. We shall in fact simply make use of the conventional adaptive expectations mechanism in the presentation of the full model below. Besides demand pressure we thus use (as cost pressure expressions) in the two PCs weighted averages of the inflationary climate and the (foreseen) relevant cost pressure term for wage setting and price setting. In this way we get two PCs with very analogous building blocks, which despite their traditional outlook will have interesting and novel implications. In the later part of this chapter we will introduce in addition a non-linearity into the money wage PC.

Note that in the current version, the inflationary climate variable does not matter for the evolution of the real wage $\omega = w/p$. In fact nor does it matter for the wage share $v = \omega/x$ (due to the addition of productivity growth), the law of motion of which is given by

$$\hat{v} = \hat{\omega} - n_x = \kappa[(1 - \kappa_p)\beta_w(e - \bar{e}) - (1 - \kappa_w)\beta_p(u - \bar{u})].$$

[31] The use of two in place of only one PC – an unquestioned procedure during the rise of structural macroeconometric model building – see Chiarella *et al.* (2000) for a discussion of this on various levels of generality – is gathering force again, as indicated for example by the topics investigated in Cohen and Farhi (2001) and Mehra (2000). There are indeed numerous such questions that can be addressed from a closer look at the wage-price spiral in the place of the single reduced form PC of mainstream Keynesian theory, whether old or new.

The dynamics of ω follow easily from the obviously equivalent representation of the above two PCs, namely

$$\hat{w} - \pi^c - n_x = \beta_w(e - \bar{e}) + \kappa_w(\hat{p} - \pi^c),$$
$$\hat{p} - \pi^c = \beta_p(u - \bar{u}) + \kappa_p(\hat{w} - \pi^c),$$

by solving for the variables $\hat{w} - \pi^c - n_x$ and $\hat{p} - \pi^c$. The last two equations imply that the two cross-markets or *reduced form PCs* are given by:

$$\hat{p} = \kappa[\beta_p(u - \bar{u}) + \kappa_p\beta_w(e - \bar{e})] + \pi^c, \tag{4.25}$$
$$\hat{w} = \kappa[\beta_w(e - \bar{e}) + \kappa_w\beta_p(u - \bar{u})] + \pi^c + n_x. \tag{4.26}$$

Equations (4.25)–(4.26) represent *a considerable improvement* over the conventional view of a single-market price PC with only one measure of demand pressure, the one in the labour market. The traditional expectations-augmented PC formally resembles the above reduced form $\hat{p}$-equation given by (4.25) if Okun's Law holds in the sense of a strict positive correlation between $u - \bar{u}$ and $e - \bar{e}$, our measures of demand pressures on the market for goods and for labour. Yet, the coefficient in front of the traditional PC would even in this situation be a mixture of all of the $\beta's$ and $\kappa's$ of the two originally given PCs and thus represent a composition of goods and labour market characteristics (which moreover now hides the fact that myopic perfect foresight is indeed underlying these apparently only backward looking reduced form PCs). The currently prominent New Keynesian PC, see for example Gali (2000), is based on the reduced form representation for $\hat{p}$ shown above, but generally with $\beta_p = 0, \kappa_p = 1, \kappa_w = 0$ and π^c a one-period ahead forecast of the rate of price inflation. Under perfect foresight this basically implies in a continuous-time set-up a price PC of the type

$$d\hat{p}/dt = \beta_w(e - \bar{e}),$$

which provides an interesting alternative to our reduced form price PC. In the last equation the medium-run climate expression for price inflation plays no role, reducing in this way inflation dynamics to short-term expressions solely, which in our view provides one of the reasons why the New Keynesian PC behaves strangely from an empirical perspective.[32]

[32] The New Keynesian approach to the business cycle theory and in particular monetary policy is considered and evaluated in detail in King (2000). We do not go into such a discussion – on the New IS–LM model – in the present book which in this chapter in our view provides a significant alternative to the New Keynesian approach for the closed economy. A comparison with the New Keynesian IS–LM theory with its stress on microfounded, intertemporal and forward-looking behaviour is provided in Asada *et al.* (2010) where the potential and limitations of both approaches are discussed and evaluated.

Taken together our above structural approach to wage and price PCs gives rise to *three independent laws of motion* that we can write as

$$\hat{v} = \kappa[(1 - \kappa_p)\beta_w(e - \bar{e}) - (1 - \kappa_w)\beta_p(u - \bar{u})], \tag{4.27}$$

$$\hat{m} = \bar{\mu} - \hat{K} - \hat{p} \quad (\bar{\mu} = const.), \tag{4.28}$$

$$\dot{\pi}^c = \beta_{\pi^c}(\hat{p} - \pi^c) = \beta_{\pi^c}\kappa[\beta_p(u - \bar{u}) + \kappa_p\beta_w(e - \bar{e})]. \tag{4.29}$$

Equations (4.27), (4.28) and (4.29) are the first three differential equations of the full 6D Keynesian dynamics to be summarised in Section 4.5 below. The essential elements in these three laws of motion are the three adjustment speeds β_w, β_p and β_{π^c} for wages, prices and the inflationary climate which strongly influence their stability properties. Note that the law of motion for the capital stock K has not yet been provided, but will be introduced when the full 6D dynamics are presented.

4.4.3 *The 2D Metzlerian quantity dynamics and capital stock growth*

Next, we consider the quantity dynamics of the Keynesian macromodel, where we consider goods market adjustment dynamics and capital stock growth. The resulting 3D dynamics, which provide the quantity side of our Keynesian macrodynamic model, are given by[33]

$$\begin{aligned}
Y^d &= C + I + \delta K + G, \\
\dot{Y}^e &= \beta_{y^e}(Y^d - Y^e) + (n_l + n_x)Y^e, \\
N^d &= \alpha_{n^d} Y^e, \\
\mathcal{I} &= \beta_n(N^d - N) + (n_l + n_x)N^d, \\
Y &= Y^e + \mathcal{I}, \\
\dot{N} &= Y - Y^d, \\
\hat{K} &= I/K.
\end{aligned}$$

These equations represent a simple, yet consistently formulated, output and inventory adjustment process. The first equation defines aggregate demand Y^d as the sum of consumption, investment and government demand and the second equation states that expected sales Y^e follow aggregate demand in an adaptive fashion. In the third equation desired inventories N^d are then assumed to be determined as a constant fraction of expected sales, while in the fourth equation intended inventory adjustment $\mathcal{I}$ is based on the inventory adjustment process $\beta_n(N^d - N)$, with N the actual inventory holdings and β_n the speed with which the gap between desired and actual inventory holdings is closed, augmented by a term that accounts for trend growth (n_l the natural rate of growth of the labour force, $n = n_l + n_x$). In the fifth equation actual production Y must

[33] These quantity dynamics have been studied in isolation, with a non-linearity in the inventory adjustment process, in Franke and Lux (1993) and with capital stock growth in Franke (1996).

then of course be defined by the sum of expected sales and intended inventory changes, while actual inventory changes $\dot{N}$ are finally given by definition as the discrepancy between actual production and actual sales. Again, the crucial parameters in these adjustment equations are the adjustment speeds, β_{y^e} and β_n, of sales expectations and of intended inventory changes respectively. It is obvious from the above presentation of the Metzlerian inventory adjustment process that it will add two further laws of motion to those of the wage-price dynamics; these are the first two equations in the presentation of the full dynamics (4.36)–(4.41) below.

The growth dynamics of the model are based on the net investment demand of firms, as indicated in the last equation of the above quantity dynamics. We point out in addition that aggregate demand is based, on the one hand, on differentiated saving habits as far as the two groups of households of the model, workers and asset holders and their consumption functions, are concerned. On the other hand, the other part of aggregate demand, investment, is determined by the excess of the expected profit rate over the real rate of interest, on excess capacity and natural growth (including productivity growth). Moreover, there are given fiscal policy parameters for government behaviour in the intensive form of the model. We thereby in particular obtain the result that aggregate demand depends on income distribution and the wage share v, positively if consumption dominates investment and negatively if the opposite holds true. We add finally that the nominal interest rate is determined either by a conventional LM curve or by the Taylor interest rate policy rule, to be introduced below.

We already observe here that the short-run quantity dynamics are difficult to estimate; see the next section for some first results in this regard. This is partly due to the need to distinguish between output, demand and sales expectations on the one hand and between desired and actual inventory changes on the other hand. In subsequent developments of the model it would be desirable to take into account more modern cost-minimising inventory adjustment procedures on the goods market. Yet, at the present stage of development of the model a procedure that is a consistent extension of the familiar dynamic multiplier process is all that we need in order to make the model an internally coherent one.

4.4.4 Putting things together: the KMG growth dynamics

Let us finally make explicit the sixth law of motion, namely the one for economic growth, before we collect all laws of motion that are presented below. As already stated, in a Keynesian context, capital stock growth is given by net investment per unit of capital and is thus based on the assumption of an investment function of firms. This function is postulated to read

$$I/K = i_1(r^e - (i - \pi^c)) + i_2(u - \bar{u}) + n, \quad u = y/y^p, \tag{4.30}$$

with the expected rate of profit defined by

$$r^e = y^e - \delta - vy, \quad y^e = Y^e/K, \quad y = Y/K, \tag{4.31}$$

and the nominal rate of interest given by the reduced form LM equation

$$i = i_o + \frac{h_1 y - m}{h_2}. \tag{4.32}$$

Due to the assumed Metzlerian quantity adjustment process, the output to capital ratio is determined by

$$y = (1 + (n_l + n_x)\alpha_{n^d})y^e + \beta_n(\alpha_{n^d} y^e - \nu), \ y^e = Y^e/K, \ \nu = N/K. \tag{4.33}$$

The investment equation ensures that net investment depends on excess profitability with respect to the expected real rate of interest, on capacity utilisation in its deviation from desired capital utilisation and on a trend term which here has been set equal to the natural rate (including the rate of labour productivity growth) for reasons of simplicity.

The sixth state variable of our model is l, the full employment labour intensity, which in the context of Harrod-neutral technical change, with $x = Y/L^d, \hat{x} = n_x$, and $y^p = Y^p/K = const.$, is best represented by $l = xL/K$, where L denotes labour supply (which grows at the given natural rate of growth $n = \hat{L}$). Due to the assumed trend growth term in the investment equation shown above we find that the evolution of this state variable is given by

$$\hat{l} = -i_1(r^e - (i - \pi^c)) - i_2(u - \bar{u}).$$

We add as the final (algebraic) equation of the model the equation for aggregate demand per unit of capital that is given by

$$\begin{aligned} y^d &= (1 - s_w)\upsilon y + (1 - s_c)r^e + \gamma + I/K + \delta \\ &= (1 - s_c)y^e + (s_c - s_w)\upsilon y + \gamma + I/K + s_c\delta, \end{aligned} \tag{4.34}$$

and the defining equations for the rate of employment and the rate of capacity utilisation which we recall are

$$e = y/l \quad (= L^d/L = xL^d/xL), \quad u = y/y^p. \tag{4.35}$$

Due to our assumption of Kaldorian saving habits with $0 \leq s_w < s_c \leq 1$, we have that aggregate demand depends positively on the wage share υ through consumption and negatively on the wage share through the investment component in aggregate demand. There is wage taxation and property income taxation which are assumed to be constant per unit of capital, net of interest as in Sargent (1987) and Rødseth (2000). These fiscal policy parameters as well as government expenditures per unit of capital, also assumed to be constant, are collected in the parameter γ of the aggregate demand function shown above.

We are now in a position to present the full macrodynamic model, here for brevity immediately in intensive or state variable form. We recall that the dynamic model is based on five markets: labour, goods, money, bonds and equities; and three sectors: households (workers and asset holders, with Kaldorian differentiated saving habits), firms and the government (the fiscal and monetary authority). We stress again that all budget equations are fully specified on the extensive form level, so that all stock-flow interactions are present, although not yet fully interacting in the current version of the model.[34]

The resulting integrated six laws of motion of the dynamics to be investigated include the state variables: sales expectations $y^e = Y^e/K$; inventories $\nu = N/K$ per unit of capital; real balances per unit of capital $m = M/(pK)$; the inflationary climate π^c; the wage share $v = \omega/x$; labour intensity $l = L/K$. The laws of motion read:

$$\dot{y}^e = \beta_{y^e}(y^d - y^e) + \hat{l}y^e, \tag{4.36}$$

(the law of motion for sales expectations),

$$\dot{\nu} = y - y^d + (\hat{l} - (n_l + n_x))\nu, \tag{4.37}$$

(the law of motion for inventories),

$$\hat{m} = \bar{\mu} - \pi^c - (n_l + n_x) + \hat{l} - \kappa[\beta_p(u - \bar{u}) + \kappa_p\beta_w(e - \bar{e})], \tag{4.38}$$

(the growth law of real balances),

$$\dot{\pi}^e = \beta_{\pi^c}\kappa[\beta_p(u - \bar{u}) + \kappa_p\beta_w(e - \bar{e})], \tag{4.39}$$

(the evolution of the inflationary climate),

$$\hat{v} = \kappa[(1 - \kappa_p)\beta_w(e - \bar{e}) - (1 - \kappa_w)\beta_p(u - \bar{u})], \tag{4.40}$$

(the growth law of the wage share),

$$\hat{l} = -i_1(r^e - (i - \pi^c)) - i_2(u - \bar{u}), \tag{4.41}$$

(the growth law for labour intensity).

These equations can be easily understood from what has been stated about wage-price, quantity and investment dynamics if note is taken of the fact that everything is now expressed (with the exception of the wage share) in per unit of capital form. Inserting the algebraic equations (4.30)–(4.35) into these laws of motion one obtains a non-linear autonomous 6D system of differential equations that we will investigate with respect to the stability properties of its unique interior steady state in the remainder of the chapter.

4.5 Feedback-motivated stability analysis

As the model is formulated we can distinguish four important feedback chains which we now describe in isolation from each other. Of course these interact with each other in the full 6D dynamics and one or the other can become dominant depending on the model parameters chosen. These feedback channels are shown in bold in Figure 4.4, where also other feedback channels have been added: the Dornbusch exchange rate dynamics and other (primarily destabilising) feedback chains. Integrating these feedback channels

[34] See Chiarella and Flaschel (2000) for the details of this Keynesian working model, including the specification of all budget and behavioural equations on the extensive form level, and Chiarella *et al.* (2000) for various extensions of this model type.

into a coherently formulated Keynesian macrodynamic set-up is one of the main tasks of this book and of our future research agenda.

1. The Keynes effect: We assume IS–LM equilibrium in order to explain this well-known effect in simple terms. According to IS–LM equilibrium, the nominal rate of interest i depends positively on the price level p. Aggregate demand and thus output and the rate of capacity utilisation therefore depend negatively on the price level, implying a negative dependence of the inflation rate on the level of prices through this channel. A high sensitivity of the nominal rate of interest with respect to the price level (a low parameter h_2, the opposite of the liquidity trap) thus should exercise a strong stabilising influence on the dynamics of the price level and on the economy as a whole, which is further strengthened if price and wage flexibility increase.[35]

2. The Mundell effect: We again assume IS–LM equilibrium in order to explain this less well-known (indeed often neglected) effect. Since net investment depends (as is usually assumed) positively on the expected rate of inflation π^c, via the expected real rate of interest, aggregate demand and thus output and the rate of capacity utilisation depend positively on this expected inflation rate. This implies a positive dependence of $\hat{p} - \pi^c$ on π^c and thus a positive feedback from the expected rate of inflation on its time rate of change. Faster adjustment speeds of inflationary expectations will therefore destabilise the economy through this channel. The two effects just discussed work with further delays if Metzlerian quantity adjustment processes are allowed for.

3. The Metzler effect: In the Metzlerian quantity adjustment process, output y depends positively on expected sales y^e and this effect is stronger, the higher the speed of adjustment β_n of planned inventories. The time rate of change of expected sales therefore depends positively on the level of expected sales when the parameter β_n is chosen sufficiently large. Flexible adjustment of inventories coupled with a high speed of adjustment of sales expectations thus leads to a loss of economic stability. There will, of course, exist other situations where an increase in the latter speed of adjustment may increase the stability of the dynamics.

4. The Rose effect: In order to explain this effect we again assume for the time being IS–LM equilibrium. We know from our formulation of aggregate goods demand that output and in the same way the rate of employment and the rate of capacity utilisation may depend positively or negatively on real wages, due to their opposite effects on consumption and investment shown in equation (4.34). According to the law of motion for real wages (4.36) we thus get a positive or negative feedback channel of real wages on their rate of change, depending on the relative adjustment speed of nominal wages and prices. Either price or wage flexibility will therefore always be destabilising, depending on investment and saving propensities, i_1, s_c and s_w, with respect to the expected rate of profit and the wage share. The destabilising Rose effect (of whatever type) will be weak if both wage and price adjustment speeds β_w and β_p are low.

The effects just discussed are shown in their interaction in Figure 4.4. This figure is centred around the hypothesis that there is a downward hierarchy in the structure

35 The same argument applies to wealth effects which, however, are not yet included here.

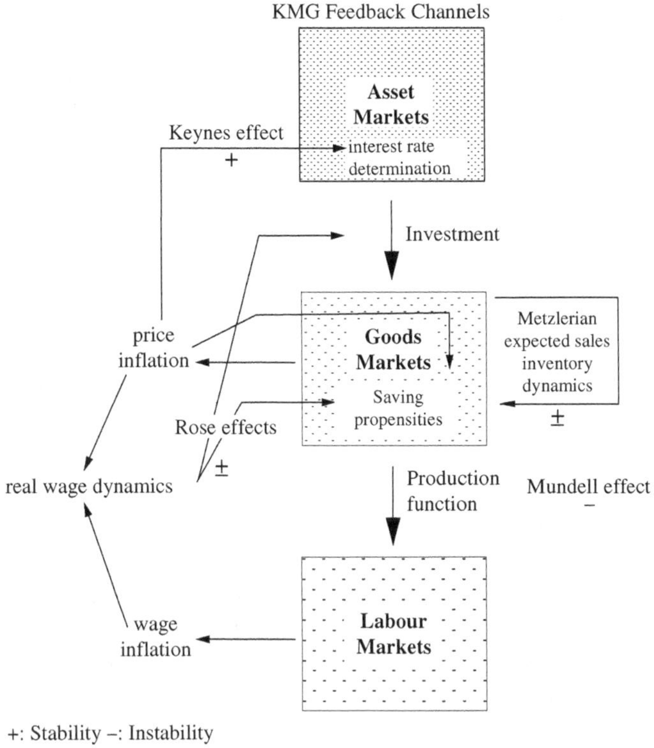

Figure 4.4 The feedback channels of the KMG modelling approach and their stabilising/destabilising tendencies

of market economies, with financial markets at the top of this hierarchy, with goods market dependence on the outcome on financial markets arising through investment behaviour and finally labour market dependence on the goods market outcome coming through the production function. However, this point of departure for macroeconomic theorising is modified in significant ways if repercussions from hierarchically lower markets are taken into account, the most prominent one being the Keynes effect, which is much favoured due to its stabilising role both with respect to wage-price increases and wage-price decreases through the change in nominal interest it implies. The Mundell inflationary expectations effect comes next in popularity, since it is generally present in Keynesian macrodynamics, whether old (through investment behaviour) or new (via the household's Euler equations) or of other contemporary type. Metzlerian inventory adjustment is generally neglected due to the consideration of IS equilibria in macroeconomics, as are other quantity adjustment processes such as the dynamic multiplier or the multiplier-accelerator process. Rose effects and the role of income distribution are rarely considered in Keynesian macrodynamics, although of course their existence is hardly surprising or difficult to grasp.

These more or less traditional feedback channels, the nominal-interest rate Keynes effect, the inflationary expectations Mundell effect, the Metzler inventory accelerator and the real-wage Rose effect, are here combined and determine in their interaction the stability of the interior steady state position of the model. If inventories are adjusted too quickly instability may arise despite the presence of a stable dynamic multiplier process, due to the fact that production is then too responsive to expected demand changes via the planned inventories channel. The Mundell effect is potentially destabilising, since inflation feeds into expected inflation, which in turn lowers the real rate of interest and further increases economic activity and thus the rate of inflation. The Rose effect can be destabilising in two ways, if aggregate demand depends positively on the real wage and the wage share in the case where wage flexibility exceeds price flexibility or in the opposite case of depressing effects of real wage increases if price flexibility exceeds wage flexibility.[36]

The only unambiguously stabilising effect is the Keynes effect whereby increasing prices and wages decrease real liquidity and thus raise nominal rates of interest which not only stops further wage-price increases, but in fact brings wages and prices back to their 'full' employment levels.

Based on the insights gained from these partial feedback chains we are now in a position to formulate Proposition 4.10 on local stability, instability and limit cycle behaviour. Our approach is based on what we term feedback-guided β-stability analysis. This methodology for the stability analysis of the high-dimensional dynamic models to which our approach leads is explained in detail in Asada *et al.* (2003).[37] This stability analysis methodology has also been applied to a variety of other situations, see in particular Asada *et al.* (2010). Here the β-stability analysis nicely confirms, for our integrated Keynesian dynamics, what has long been known (in principle) for its constituent parts.

Proposition 4.9 (KMG dynamics: basic stability results)
Assume that $0 \leq s_w < s_c \leq 1$ holds, so that the savings rate of workers is lower than that of asset holders. The following statements then hold with respect to the 6D dynamical system (4.36)–(4.41), under some further secondary assumptions on the parameters of the model:

1. *There exists a unique interior steady state of the model basically of supply side type.*
2. *The determinant of the 6D Jacobian of the dynamics at this steady state is always positive.*
3. *Assume that the parameters $\beta_w, \beta_p, \beta_{\pi^c}, \beta_n$ are chosen sufficiently small and the parameter β_{y^e} sufficiently large and assume that the Keynes effect works with sufficient strength (so that h_2 is small).*

Then, the steady state of the 6D dynamical system is locally asymptotically stable.

36 A more detailed explanation of such adverse Rose effects has to pay attention to the κ-weights in the cost-pressure terms as well.

37 See also Chiarella and Flaschel (2000, Ch. 6) and see also Köper (2000) for the first detailed presentations of such a stability investigation by means of varying adjustment speeds β_j where $j = n, \pi^c, w$.

4. *On the other hand, if any one of β_w (or β_p), β_{π^c}, β_n become sufficiently large (the latter for β_{y^e} sufficiently large), then the equilibrium is locally repelling and the system undergoes a Hopf bifurcation at an intermediate value of the relevant β parameter. In general stable or unstable limit cycles are generated close to the bifurcation value.*

Sketch of proof (the β-stability methodology). Based on our partial knowledge of the working of the four feedback channels of the considered 6D dynamics, we choose an independent 3D subsystem of the 6D Keynesian dynamics, by setting the parameters $\beta_n, \beta_{\pi^c}, \beta_w$ all equal to zero:

$$\dot{y}^e = \beta_{y^e}(y^d - y^e) + (n_l + n_x - I/K)y^e,$$

(the stable dynamic multiplier),

$$\hat{m} = \bar{\mu} - \kappa\beta_p(u - \bar{u}) - \pi_o^c - i,$$

(the stabilising Keynes effect),

$$\hat{v} = -\kappa(\kappa_w - 1)\beta_p(u - \bar{u}),$$

(sluggish price adjustment).

In this 3D system, the Keynes effect (h_2 small) and the dynamic multiplier (β_{y^e} large) dominate the outcome and imply the Routh–Hurwitz conditions for local asymptotic stability are satisfied if they operate with sufficient strength and if β_p is sufficiently small (which avoids stability problems arising from any type of Rose effect).

We then add step-by-step the further laws of motion by assuming that the adjustment speeds initially assumed to be zero are made slightly positive:

$$4D : \beta_w > 0 : \hat{l} = -i_1(r^e - (i - \pi^c)) - i_2(u - \bar{u}),$$

(labour intensity feeds back into the 3D dynamics via $e = y/l$),

$$5D : \beta_n > 0 : \dot{\nu} = y - y^d + ...,$$

(inventory accumulation feeds back into the 4D dynamics via y),

$$6D : \beta_{\pi^c} > 0 : \dot{\pi}^e = \beta_{\pi^c}[c_y\beta_p(u - \bar{u}) + c_h\beta_w(e - \bar{e})],$$

(inflationary climate starts moving and influencing the 5D dynamics).

Since the determinants of the Jacobian at the steady state of the sequentially enlarged dynamics always have the correct sign, as required by the Routh–Hurwitz stability conditions, we know that the eigenvalue that is departing from zero (as a result of a certain adjustment speed becoming slightly positive) must always do so through negative values. In this way, a system with at most one pair of complex eigenvalues (with negative real parts) and at least four real and negative ones is established, which proves the local asymptotic stability asserted in the proposition.[38] Since the determinant of the

[38] In numerical simulations we have frequently observed monotone convergence for very small positive values of the relevant adjustment speed, indicating that the complex eigenvalues occur at higher (positive) values.

full Jacobian is always non-zero, loss of stability can only occur by way of (in general non-degenerate) Hopf bifurcations, at which eigenvalues cross the imaginary axis with positive speed.

Although intrinsically non-linear, the above 6D Keynesian growth dynamics are generally, however, too weakly non-linear in order to guarantee the boundedness of trajectories when the adjustment speeds referred to in Proposition 4.9 are chosen such that local instability comes about. Extrinsic or behavioural non-linearities thus have to be added subsequently in order to ensure boundedness for the trajectories of the dynamics.

This closes the introduction into the KMG baseline model which however is extended in the next section through the introduction of debt deflation into this baseline framework.

4.6 Debt deflation in the KMG framework

The KMG growth model of the preceding sections represents the workhorse model for the remainder of the book to which we want to add now briefly the processes of debt accumulation and debt deflation already discussed, in order to indicate how its features change through the addition of such forces. We thus modify the KMG model and include debt financing of investment in place of equity financing. Furthermore we will replace the original set-up with a money supply rule (with the resulting interest rate determination) by an interest rate Taylor policy rule for the banking sector. This will allow control of what here remains of the Keynes effect in a more direct way in the attempt to stabilise the economy in the case of debt deflation.

Investment decisions are now solely based on a term $-\alpha_3^k\lambda$ in place of $\alpha_3^k(\lambda_o - \lambda) + \gamma + \delta$ of the 4D dynamics and therefore no longer refer to steady state values of the debt to capital ratio. This modifies the interior steady state solution to some extent, but does not influence the dynamics of the model significantly.[39]

Due to the Taylor rule and the implied endogeneity of the money supply we have again that price inflation, but not inflationary expectations, can be removed from explicit consideration in the stability analysis that follows. Furthermore, since public debt is now financed through the banking system (and not through the household sector) it also has no feedback on the private sector of the economy, so that government bond accumulation is still irrelevant for the dynamics of this sector. Finally, we can of course derive a law of motion for the evolution of real balances per unit of capital, to be obtained from the budget equation of the banking system, but there is now no feedback effect from this state variable on to the other ones.

This establishes a 7D system of interdependent laws of motion to be given below, by adding the dynamics of sales expectations, inventories, inflationary expectations and

[39] We now also use the normal rate of profit in place of the actual one in the investment function which makes the profitability term independent of the state of the business cycle and thus removes some correlations between the terms employed in the investment function.

the rate of interest to the core 3D dynamics considered in the preceding sections. The resulting dynamical system is thus still fairly close to the one of the preceding section and can also be investigated from the same perspective, although it is now complete and coherent in its description of goods market dynamics and the budget equations of workers, the government and the banking system, in addition to the one of firms already studied in the preceding sections from a supply side and a demand side perspective.

The complexity that the KMG approach seems to imply for the investigation of debt deflation can thus be reduced considerably by appropriate assumptions. The introduction of interdependence between money balances, government bond accumulation, and real and nominal magnitudes will be treated in Part III. The focus of interest here remains income distribution and capital accumulation, supplemented now by a Metzlerian quantity adjustment process plus the new element, the dynamics of the debt to capital ratio and the dynamics of the rate of interest on loans. In this way we obtain a 7D dynamical system that is coherent in its modelling of goods market adjustment process and is minimally complete in its treatment of the issue of debt deflation in a Keynesian set-up with sluggishly adjusting wages, prices, quantities and expectations. At the centre of the system's dynamics are the Rose effects and the Fisher debt effect of the preceding sections, now coupled with multiplier stability or instability and weak forms of stabilising Keynes and destabilising Mundell effects which here both work solely through the law of motion for the debt to capital ratio.

4.6.1 Integrating debt financing of firms

Let us first discuss the budget equations of the four sectors that interact in this extension of the KMG approach. First we consider wage earners who spend what they get (after wage taxation at rate τ_w) and who therefore do not lend, thereby contributing to the debt deflation mechanism, but exhibit the simplest type of behaviour that is possible in such a framework:

$$pC_w = (1 - \tau_w)wL^d, \quad T_w^n = \tau_w wL^d \tag{4.42}$$

Next there is the sector of industrial capital which always invests its pure profits (after taxation) and takes loans (corporate debt) in addition to realising its intended investment plans. We do not discuss processes of credit rationing in this section and thus assume that loans demanded are always supplied by the banking system. Up to taxation and the fact that pure profits are now based on actual sales we have no change in this description of partially debt financed investment of firms:

$$pI = (1 - \tau_c)rpK + \dot{\Lambda}, \quad rpK = pY^d - \delta pK - wL^d - i\Lambda, \quad T_c^n = \tau_c rpK. \tag{4.43}$$

Third there is the financial sector which gives loans to firms and the government (as demanded by these two sectors) and which creates or absorbs money to the extent that its interest income is different from the loans demanded by firms and the government, which therefore exhibits the soft budget constraint

$$\dot{\Lambda} + \dot{B} = i(\Lambda + B) + \dot{M}. \tag{4.44}$$

Finally, there is the government sector which finances its expenditures (goods purchases and interest payments) by means of the taxes it receives and by making loans (public debt) if necessary:

$$pG + iB = \quad T_w^n + \quad T_c^n + \dot{B}. \tag{4.45}$$

These budget equations show that there is no credit rationing by the banking system, apart from interest rate changes, so that financial capitalists accept the new issue of government bonds and also supply just the amount of new loans that is demanded by firms, through the creation or destruction of money if necessary. Money is fully endogenous in the present model and has of course inflationary consequences to the extent it feeds aggregate goods demand and thus creates demand pressure on the market for goods and for labour. Of course, due to this fact Say's Law no longer holds as in the 3D supply dynamics considered earlier.

To complete this description of budgets and spending we assume, as already discussed, that net investment of firms is determined as in the 4D case considered in this section, so that the investment function

$$I/K = [\alpha_1^k(r^n - \bar{r}) + \alpha_2^k(\frac{y}{y^p} - \bar{u})] - \alpha_3^k\lambda + \gamma \tag{4.46}$$

is now augmented by a third term and no longer makes use of a target debt to capital ratio of firms. For the final component in the aggregate demand function, government expenditure, we assume for reasons of simplicity in what follows that it is kept constant per unit of capital, in order to focus on investment and its debt financing. Government policy is thus basically characterised by a simple expenditure rule and two given tax rates and is thus kept fairly simple.

Yet, in an important respect we will depart from the representation of economic policy by given magnitudes throughout, namely with respect to monetary policy. We now assume that the monetary authority directly controls the (change in the) nominal rate of interest according to the rule

$$\dot{i} = -\beta_{i_i}(i - i_o) + \beta_{i_p}(\hat{p} - 0). \tag{4.47}$$

It therefore attempts to steer the economy to the steady state rate of interest, but deviates from this target when inflation deviates from zero inflation in an attempt to stop inflation by raising the interest rate, or stop deflation by lowering it (unless the floor of a zero rate of interest is reached). This provides a simple, but coherent description of the behaviour of the financial sector of the economy and posits implicitly that the interests of the owners of firms are more complex than just looking for the highest rate of return for the capital that they own.

4.6.2 Enterprise debt dynamics in the KMG framework

Putting together all the foregoing changes and adding them into the baseline KMG model of this chapter, gives rise to the following 10D (6D+4D) dynamical system in the state variables $w^e = w/z$, p, π^c, $l^e = zL/K$, $\lambda = \Lambda/(pK)$, $y^e = Y^e/K$, $\nu = N/K$, i, $b = B/(pK)$, and $m = M/(pK)$ as in the KMG model, but now with loans in place of equity financing and an interest rate policy rule in place of a money supply rule:

$$\hat{w}^e = \kappa[\beta_w(\frac{y}{l^e} - \bar{e}) + \kappa_w\beta_p(\frac{y}{y^p} - \bar{u})] + \pi^c \tag{4.48}$$

$$\hat{p} = \kappa[\beta_p(\frac{y}{y^p} - \bar{u}) + \kappa_p\beta_w(\frac{y}{l^e} - \bar{e})] + \pi^c \tag{4.49}$$

$$\dot{\pi}^c = \beta_{\pi^c}(\hat{p} - \pi^c) \tag{4.50}$$

$$\hat{l}^e = -(g_k - \delta - \gamma) \tag{4.51}$$

$$\dot{\lambda} = (g_k - \delta)(1 - \lambda) - (1 - \tau_c)r - \hat{p}\lambda \tag{4.52}$$

$$\dot{y}^e = \beta_{y^e}(y^d - y^e) - (g_k - \delta - \gamma)y^e \tag{4.53}$$

$$\dot{\nu} = y - y^d - (g_k - \delta)\nu \tag{4.54}$$

$$\dot{i} = -\beta_{i_i}(i - i_o) + \beta_{i_p}\hat{p} \tag{4.55}$$

$$\dot{b} = g + ib - (\tau_w(w^e/p)y + \tau_c r) - (\hat{p} + g_k - \delta)b \tag{4.56}$$

$$\dot{m} = g_k - \delta - (y^d - \delta - (1 - \tau_w)(w^e/p)y) - (\hat{p} + g_k - \delta)m \tag{4.57}$$

with the following algebraic equations supplementing these ten laws of motion ($\gamma = n + n_l$ the natural rate of growth always as trend term):[40]

$$y = \beta_n(\beta_{n^d}y^e - \nu) + (1 + \gamma\beta_{n^d})y^e,$$

$$y^d = (1 - \tau_w)(w^e/p)y + g_k + g,$$

$$r = y^d - \delta - (w^e/p)y - i\lambda,$$

$$r^n = y^d_o - \delta - (w^e/p)y_o - i\lambda,$$

$$g_k = \alpha^k_1(r^n - \bar{r}) + \alpha^k_2(\frac{y}{y^p} - \bar{u}) - \alpha^k_3\lambda + \gamma + \delta.$$

The laws of motion for wages in efficiency units w^e and the price level p are as before, but now augmented by inflationary expectations π^c in the form of the across market

[40] Note that we now make use of a normal rate of profit in place of the actual one (which is needed in the debt accumulation dynamics) in the investment function g_k. This has the advantage – compared with the one chosen for the 4D dynamics – that the state of the business cycle is eliminated from the α^k_1 expression and thus appears only once, in the α^k_2 expression. Note also that the α^k_3 expression no longer refers to a benchmark debt to capital ratio (which was set equal to the steady state debt to capital ratio in the 4D dynamics). The steady state debt to capital ratio is therefore now calculated in a different way than in the case of the 4D dynamics.

PCs derived in Section 4.5. Inflationary expectations are of the adaptive variety here for reasons of simplicity, and will not matter in the following analysis. Capital accumulation is represented by the full employment capital ratio (in efficiency units) driven as usual by investment demand in this Keynesian approach to economic growth. The evolution of the debt to capital ratio λ is as before and is represented by the budget equation of firms in intensive form. The Metzlerian quantity adjustment process on the market for goods, represented by sales expectations y^e and inventories ν per unit of capital, remains as in the baseline KMG growth dynamics. The Taylor rule for interest on loans i has already been explained. Finally, the laws of motion for government bonds b and money m per unit of capital have been obtained from the budget restrictions of the government and the monetary authority (here still viewed as a financial capital centre) by appropriate reformulation on the intensive form level. Output y per unit of capital in the algebraic equations is based on Metzlerian quantity adjustment as in the KMG growth dynamics of Section 4.4 and Section 4.5. Aggregate demand y^d is simply the summation of wages after taxes, gross investment and government expenditures per unit of capital. The actual pure rate of profit r is defined as before, as is investment.

4.6.3 *Analysis of the model*

The dynamical system (4.48)–(4.57) can be reduced to the following core dynamics which represent their interdependent part

$$\hat{v} = \kappa[(1-\kappa_p)\beta_w(\frac{y}{l^e} - \bar{e}) - (1-\kappa_w)\beta_p(\frac{y}{y^p} - \bar{u})], \quad v = w^e/p, \tag{4.58}$$

$$\hat{l}^e = -(g_k - \delta - \gamma), \tag{4.59}$$

$$\dot{\lambda} = (g_k - \delta)(1-\lambda) - (1-\tau_c)r - [\kappa[\beta_p(\frac{y}{y^p} - \bar{u}) + \kappa_p\beta_w(\frac{y}{l^e} - \bar{e})] + \pi^c]\lambda, \tag{4.60}$$

$$\dot{\pi}^c = \beta_{\pi^c}\kappa[\beta_p(\frac{y}{y^p} - \bar{u}) + \kappa_p\beta_w(\frac{y}{l^e} - \bar{e})], \tag{4.61}$$

$$\dot{y}^e = \beta_{y^e}(y^d - y^e) - (g_k - \delta - \gamma)y^e, \tag{4.62}$$

$$\dot{\nu} = y - y^d - (g_k - \delta)\nu, \tag{4.63}$$

$$\dot{i} = -\beta_{i_i}(i - i_o) + \beta_{i_p}[\kappa[\beta_p(\frac{y}{y^p} - \bar{u}) + \kappa_p\beta_w(\frac{y}{l^e} - \bar{e})] + \pi^c], \tag{4.64}$$

with the defining expressions

$$y = \beta_n(\beta_{n^d}y^e - \nu) + (1 + \gamma\beta_{n^d})y^e,$$

$$y^d = (1-\tau_w)vy + g_k + g,$$

$$r = y^d - \delta - vy - i\lambda,$$

$$r^n = y_o^d - \delta - vy_o - i\lambda,$$

$$g_k = \alpha_1^k(r^n - \bar{r}) + \alpha_2^k(\frac{y}{y^p} - \bar{u}) - \alpha_3^k\lambda + \gamma + \delta.$$

Note we have inserted the equation for the price level dynamics in whatever equations they appear. Due to the relation $\hat{v} = \hat{w}^e - \hat{p}$ this implies that the system could be reduced to a 7D system with the wage share v in place of w^e. The price level dynamics can therefore be removed from explicit consideration. This also implies that the 8D system with price level dynamics included must exhibit zero root hysteresis (one eigenvalue must always be zero), since the price level does not feed back into the 7D dynamics where w^e has been replaced by v. We thus obtain the result that nominal values, w^e, p, are determined by historical conditions and thus do not return to initial steady state levels as in the case of a money supply rule, $\hat{M} = \gamma$, which was considered in the original formulation of the KMG growth dynamics. This is due to the fact that money does not restrict the economy in the present extension of the KMG dynamics.

Proposition 4.10 (Existence of balanced growth)
Assume $\bar{r} < \gamma$. There exists a uniquely determined interior steady state *of the dynamics (4.48)–(4.57) (where w_o^e, l_o^e, $p_o \neq 0$ holds) which is given by*

$$y_o = l_o^{de} = \bar{u}y^p,$$

$$y_o^e = y_o^d = y_o/(1 + \gamma\beta_{n^d}), \qquad \nu_o = \beta_{n^d} y_o^e,$$

$$l_o^e = l_o^{de}/\bar{e} = y_o/\bar{e},$$

$$v_o = \frac{y_o^e - \delta - \gamma - g}{(1 - \tau_w)y_o} \in (0, 1) \quad \textit{by assumption},$$

$$\lambda_o = \frac{\alpha_1^k(\gamma - (1 - \tau_c)\bar{r})}{\alpha_1^k\gamma + \alpha_3^k(1 - \tau_c)} < 1,$$

$$r_o = \gamma\frac{1 - \lambda_o}{1 - \tau_c} \geq \bar{r},$$

$$i_o = (y_o^e - \delta - v_o y_o)/\lambda_o,$$

$$\pi_o^c = 0 \ (= \hat{p}_o = \hat{w}_o - n_l = \hat{w}_o^e),$$

$$p_o = \textit{arbitrary}, \quad w_o^e = p_o v_o,$$

$$b_o = \frac{g - (\tau_w v_o y_o + \tau_c r_o)}{\gamma - i_o},$$

$$m_o = \frac{\gamma - (y_o^d - \delta - (1 - \tau_w)v_o y_o}{\gamma}.$$

Note that the steady state value of i has to be inserted into the Taylor interest rate policy rule in order to guarantee that this policy rule is consistent with what happens in the private sector. Note also that the steady state wage share is determined via goods market equilibrium (and thus is demand determined), while the rate of profit and the capital to debt ratio have to be calculated from the two equations $\dot{\lambda} = 0$ and $g_k - \delta = \gamma$, the budget equation and the gross investment function of firms. The determination of the steady state wage share and of the steady rate of profit is thus independent of each other, while the rate of interest is determined residually on the basis of these two elements of income distribution. Output and employment by contrast are purely supply side determined and thus reflect monetarist propositions to some extent.

Setting to zero the right-hand sides of equations (4.58) and (4.61) implies that demand pressure in the market for labour and for goods must be zero, which provides the supply side expressions for y_o, l_o^e and from there, via the inventory adjustment mechanism, also the values for y_o^e, ν_o. Goods market equilibrium then gives v_o, and from there λ_o, r_o as already described above. The remaining steady state values then follow easily from what has already been determined.

Proposition 4.11 (Cyclical loss of stability)

1. *The determinant of the Jacobian J of the dynamical system (4.58) – (4.64) at the steady state is always negative.*
2. *Local asymptotic stability can only be lost by way of a Hopf bifurcation (if the speed condition on the crossing eigenvalues of the Hopf bifurcation theorem is fulfilled).*
3. *Local asymptotic stability becomes lost if the parameter β_p becomes sufficiently large, (even) if the speeds of adjustment $\beta_w, \beta_{\pi^c}, \beta_n$ are sufficiently low, the rate of interest is fixed at i_o, a stable dynamic multiplier process is given ($y^d_{y^e} < 1$) and a normal price level Rose effect prevails ($y^d_v > 0$) according to which price flexibility should be stabilising.*

Proof: 1. Similar to the proof of Proposition 4.9, since only the assumption $\beta_{i_i} = 0$ has to be made in order to perform the steps that helped to reduce the determinants to manageable expressions in that proof.
2. A direct consequence of det $J \neq 0$, since eigenvalues can then only cross the imaginary axis with real parts not equal to zero.
3. The dynamics that remain to be investigated are again of dimension 3 (representing one principal minor of order three in the very complicated set of Routh–Hurwitz conditions of the full 7D dynamics) and read

$$\hat{v} = -\kappa(1 - \kappa_w)\beta_p(u - \bar{u}),$$

$$\dot{y}^e = \beta_{y^e}(y^d(v, y^e, \lambda) - y^e), \quad y^d_v > 0, \, y^d_{y^e} < 1, \, y^d_\lambda < 0,$$

$$\dot{\lambda} = I/K(1 - \lambda) - (1 - \tau_c)r - \kappa\beta_p(u - \bar{u})\lambda.$$

We know in addition that $(u)_{y^e} > 0$ where $u = y/y^p$ holds true since output is strictly proportional to expected sales and only depends on this variable in the present situation.

The Jacobian of these dynamics at the steady state is characterised by

$$J = \begin{pmatrix} 0 & -\beta_p \text{ (Stable Rose Effect)} & 0 \\ + & -\beta_{y^e} \text{ (Stable Multiplier)} & - \\ - & -\beta_p \text{ (Unstable Fisher Debt Effect)} & - \end{pmatrix}.$$

We here only show the signs of the entries of the Jacobian and the parameter speeds that are present in it in order to indicate which adjustment processes are favourable for local asymptotic stability and which are not. This form of J implies for the Routh–Hurwitz conditions:

$$a_1 = -\text{trace } J > 0, \quad \text{(Basically due to the Stable Dynamic Multiplier Process)}$$

$$a_3 = -\det J - \begin{vmatrix} 0 & -\beta_p \text{ (Stable Rose Effect)} & 0 \\ + & 0 & - \\ - & 0 & - \end{vmatrix} > 0,$$

(Due to the Stabilising Rose or Real Wage Effect)

$$a_2 = J_1 + J_2 + J_3 \gtreqless 0: \quad \text{(Stabilising Rose vs. Destabilising Fisher Debt Effects)}$$

and

$$a_1a_2 - a_3 = b(-\beta_p), \ b' = const < 0.$$

The latter relationship holds, since the Rose effect appears (with the same expressions) in both a_1a_2 and a_3 and thus cancels when the term $b = a_1a_2 - a_3$ is formed, implying that only the Fisher debt effect remains present in $b = a_1a_2 - a_3$ as far as terms that depend on the parameter β_p are concerned. This effect however produces a negative and linear dependence of $b = a_1a_2 - a_3$ on the parameter β_p implying that b must become negative when the parameter β_p is chosen sufficiently large. We thus see that the destabilising Fisher debt effect must eventually overcome the stabilising Rose effect, if not in the Routh–Hurwitz condition a_2, then in the condition b where the stabilising role of price flexibility due to the real wage or Rose effect is not present. □

The isolated Fisher Debt Deflation Feedback Chain that we characterise as

> Debt Ratio $\lambda \uparrow \to$ Aggregate Demand $Y^d \downarrow \to$ Output $Y \downarrow \to$ Capacity Utilisation $u \downarrow \to$ Deflationary Impulse $\hat{p} \downarrow \to \lambda\uparrow\uparrow$.

must eventually become the dominant one if instability due to large parameters $\beta_w, \beta_{\pi^c}, \beta_n$ is excluded, if interest rates do not react to the state of the economy, even if multiplier and Rose effects are favourable for stability. It is however not easy to show that this result also holds for the full 7D dynamics, since the instability result of debt deflation is now not reflected in the trace of the Jacobian J, but is in fact present in one of the numerous products of principal minors that the 7D Jacobian implies for the calculation of the Routh–Hurwitz conditions on local asymptotic stability.

We have that local stability obtains if the system is in particular sufficiently sluggish in its adjustment behaviour (up to the speed of adjustment of sales expectations). Loss of stability will occur if either β_w or β_p is made sufficiently large, β_n sufficiently large and also when β_{π^c} is sufficiently large. We note however that the full 7D system is basically shaped by destabilising Fisher debt deflation effects ($\beta_p \uparrow$), destabilising Rose real wage effects (β_p or $\beta_w \uparrow$), destabilising Metzlerian accelerator effects ($\beta_n \uparrow$), but not by destabilising real rate of interest or Mundell effects ($\beta_{\pi^c} \uparrow$). This latter mechanism represents in the present model only an accelerator effect in the Fisher debt deflation mechanism. Furthermore, the Keynes nominal rate of interest rate effect (here present in the form of an interest rate policy rule) may be only a weak stabiliser in the considered 7D dynamics, since the dynamics of real balances do not feed back into the 7D dynamics under consideration and thus do not cause stabilising shifts of LM curve type. Instead, interest rate effects only work here through the term $i\lambda$ in the definition of the pure rate of profits r. We would therefore expect that the 7D dynamics are more often characterised by local instability than by local stability.

4.7 Conclusions and outlook

In this chapter we have introduced two basic models of debt dynamics and debt deflation and have investigated not only the issue of debt accumulation in the context of a growing economy, but also the dangers of price deflation in such a framework where there is high debt inherited from the past, in particular in the sector of firms. We have then integrated these processes into the more general KMG model of Chiarella and Flaschel (2000) and Chiarella *et al.* (2005) and shown how the tendencies discussed in the basic 3D and 4D models reappear in this more general and more coherently formulated approach to Keynesian monetary growth. Issues such as debt default, firm bankruptcies and credit rationing have been touched upon, but will be studied in much more detail in Part III.

Before undertaking such an analysis we extend in Part II the KMG approach towards a small open economy with a more detailed sectoral structure, including a housing sector. Such a structure is suggested by the empirical model presented in detail in Powell and Murphy (1997) and there applied to the Australian economy. We use their approach to derive a theoretical continuous-time model comparable in extent to their applied approach in order to study again the interaction of feedback channels we have introduced in this chapter and the additional ones suggested by the Powell and Murphy (1997) modelling approach. The higher dimensional models in Part III are in fact then based on the theoretical framework we will establish in Part II, concerning the further analysis of debt deflation in the sector of firms as well as in the housing sector.

Part II

Theoretical foundations for structural macroeconometric model building

5 Keynesian macroeconometric model building: a point of departure

5.1 Introduction

In this part of the book we lay the theoretical foundations for the construction of larger macroeconometric models where large means the approximate size of, for example, the Murphy model of the Australian economy (approximately a hundred equations). In practice this implies that about twenty laws of motion have to be considered in order to describe the evolution of such an economy. Yet, in contrast to many models that are actually applied we insist here that such models must be completely specified in terms of budget equations (identities or restrictions) and the stock-flow interactions that they imply. Moreover the models should not only be formulated on the extensive form level, but must also allow for a representation in intensive terms as well (trendless variables as far as the theoretical representation of the model is concerned). This intensive form representation should then also allow the determination of at least one steady state solution, the stability of which is to be discussed from the perspective of the partial feedback structures which are included in the general formulation of the model.

In this chapter we extend the hierarchically structured continuous-time models of Keynesian monetary growth, that have been introduced and generalised in some respects in Chiarella and Flaschel (2000, Chs. 4–7), Chiarella *et al.* (2000, Chs. 4–6) and Asada *et al.* (2003) both for closed as well as open economies, along the lines of the macroeconometric Murphy model of the Australian economy. The resulting modelling framework leads towards an empirically motivated model of a small open economy with a Keynesian short and medium run and with classical or monetarist features in the medium- as well as the long-run behaviour of the economy. The Murphy model (see Powell and Murphy (1997) for its detailed description) and our theoretical reformulation of it in this chapter, therefore blend demand and supply side approaches into an integrated and coherent whole with a (from a theoretical point of view) very detailed description of the structure of a small open economy, like Australia (in the case of the Murphy model). The present chapter, however, approaches this task from the perspective of macrotheory developed in Chiarella and Flaschel (2000) and Chiarella *et al.* (2000, Chs. 4–6) and thus mirrors the approach chosen in Powell and Murphy (1997) only to a certain degree. We will go on to sketch what may be the consequences of the present approach for macroeconometric model building. In subsequent chapters we shall provide more details on the dynamic structure and analysis of the present model (its intensive form, steady state analysis, more or less complex attractors, transients, etc.). We shall also attempt to move closer to the structure of the Murphy model, by revising the equations of the model of this chapter towards the inclusion of smooth factor substitution and other flexibilities, as well as a more standard view of the money market and money supply (as contained in the Murphy model). We will continue to use a continuous-time approach (without any discrete lags) so as to allow for a compact representation and analysis of the dynamics implied by the model.

In this chapter we add to the structural form of the Murphy model a complete set of fully specified budget equations for all sectors and thereby take account of all feedback structures implied by such budget restrictions. Furthermore all equations are specified in a consistent way from the perspective of dimensional analysis and are at first chosen in as linear a fashion as possible. This allows for a discussion of intrinsic (natural) non-linearities before attempts are made to design non-linearities that may keep the economy a viable one should it depart too much from the steady state in its naturally non-linear design. This in particular means that we shall start our theoretical reconsideration of the Murphy model on the basis of a fixed proportions technology which has the additional advantage that the rate of capacity utilisation of the capital stock is easy to define and to analyse with regard to the economic consequences implied by under- or over-utilised capital.

This choice of starting point for the analysis of the dynamic properties of structural macroeconometric models of open economies thus allows us, on the one hand, to study the implications of its intrinsic or 'natural' non-linearities first, as they derive from unavoidable growth rate formulations, products or quotients of state variables and the like. We shall see in this set-up that viability or boundedness of the dynamics (and in particular convergence to the steady state) will often depend on the assumption of sufficiently low adjustment speeds for quantities, prices and expectations, while local and even global stability will normally get lost if these adjustment parameters are chosen sufficiently high.

Our approach will allow us to introduce extrinsic non-linearities into the assumed technological or behavioural relationships in a systematic way at a later stage of the analysis, as a (theoretically reflected) response of the economy to the specific local instabilities observed in the working of the basic form of the model, often already known from partial dynamic macro-models. For example, a kink in the money wage Phillips curve (PC) (which reflects the fact that money wages may rise quickly in a boom but will only fall slowly – if at all – in a depression) is often of itself sufficient to avoid the inflationary instability that derives in such models from the existence of the so-called Mundell effects (an institutional non-linearity that has been very much neglected in the theoretical and applied debate on PCs inflation and stagflation).

We therefore will attempt here and in future work to proceed step by step to a detailed and systematic theoretical and numerical analysis of the dynamic features (steady states, attractors, transients, etc.) of complete and coherently formulated structural macroeconometric models, including those applied to actual economies, a theoretical discussion that so far has been basically lacking in the literature.[1] The reader should consult Asada *et al.* (2011) for a good overview of our modelling philosophy as well as some policy prescriptions.

Similarities of the Murphy model with the theoretical work on hierarchically structured Keynesian monetary growth models of Chiarella and Flaschel (1999a,b,c,d), became more and more apparent as work on this book progressed. Extending the working model of Chiarella and Flaschel (2000, Ch. 6) to the open economy, as in Asada *et al.* (2003), then provided the impetus for not only continuing with the hierarchical structure of Keynesian monetary growth models established in Chiarella and Flaschel (2000) towards more and more elaborate versions. This impetus also became the starting point for a further project of developing fully integrated and coherent Keynesian models from a so to speak reverse perspective, namely from the structural forms of small (or large) open economies as they are used in macroeconometric model building. Here the Murphy model was particularly useful, not only due to its many similarities with the theoretical work of Chiarella and Flaschel (2000), Chiarella *et al.* (2000, Chs. 4–6), and Asada *et al.* (2003), as already observed above, but also due to its very detailed and thorough presentation and discussion in Powell and Murphy (1997).

We use the structural model of Powell and Murphy (1997) in a simplified as well as in a more complex way. We suppress many of the lags included in the Murphy model as well as some secondary structural components. We write down for the model all sectoral identities or budget equations of agents and include all the feedbacks that they imply (in particular for asset accumulation). Finally, we modify in the present chapter (and in subsequent work) more or less the equations of the Murphy model in the light of the dynamic equations used in the main parts of Chiarella and Flaschel (2000), Chiarella *et al.* (2000), and Asada *et al.* (2003). In this way we arrive at theoretical presentations of such structural macroeconometric models which at one and the same time intend to be descriptive (to a certain extent) and theoretically consistent in the sense of dimensional analysis and of the budget equations that the various agents of the model are facing.

In the basic version of the model, we have endogenous natural rates of growth, of Harrod neutral technical change and of NAIRU employment, but exogenous output growth in the rest of the world. There is a detailed set of direct and indirect taxation schemes, including various types of wage taxation and payroll taxes. We have two types of households, pure asset holders and workers, with differentiated saving habits, where the latter group only saves in the form of savings deposits (or fixed-price bonds). Wage income (of three types of workers' households) is taxed at a different rate than interest income of asset holders (and of workers). Sluggish price dynamics, accompanied by Metzlerian quantity dynamics and varying degrees of capacity utilisation of the capital

[1] See however Barnett and He (1999) for an interesting approach to the analysis of applied macroeconometric models from the theoretical and the numerical perspective. We believe that further investigations of this type are urgently needed with respect to applied macroeconometric model building.

stock characterises the market for the non-traded domestic commodity, and we have of course also sluggish adjustment of money wages and varying employment rates on the labour market, augmented by insider and outsider considerations combined with a sluggish adjustment of the outside employment rate in view of the over- or under-employment of the employed workforce (the insiders). We have as a module of the model the market for housing services and consider investment in housing besides the investment of firms in fixed business capital, both depending on profitability and rates of capacity utilisation. There is a detailed description of the government sector with respect to tax receipts and expenditures and – based on that and the pure equity financing of firms that is still assumed in this chapter – also a full set of asset accumulation equations accompanied by asset price or interest rate dynamics (in the place of a full portfolio approach to asset markets). Pensions and unemployment benefits and their financing via payroll taxes are treated explicitly. There is no role for money in the model at present, but only an interest rate policy rule of the monetary authority which fixes the short-term rate of interest of domestically traded bonds in the light of certain measures of economic activity adopted by the central bank. There are finally exports of finished goods and imports of raw materials or semi-finished goods and there is (although still somewhat limited) international trade in financial assets, and a foreign exchange market that is always cleared by the actions of the private sector and the government despite the assumption of only a finite speed of adjustment of the rate of exchange.

The foregoing brief list of some structural components of the model of monetary growth of this chapter indicates that it will include various elements that are of importance in the current discussion of the macroeconomic problems that governments confront. It goes without saying, however, that there are still important components of a macroeconomy that are missing in the present theoretical reformulation of the Murphy model. The model of the present chapter therefore only represents a first step in the direction of formulating an integrated model of monetary growth for an open economy, which, on the one hand, is related to empirical work and which, on the other hand, allows for a complete computation of the steady state values of the model as well as numerical and sometimes also theoretical analyses of the behaviour of the dynamics around the steady state of such a high dimensional dynamical system.

In the next section we provide an overview on the structure of the real and the financial parts of the model, characterising the sectors, markets and activities that will be included in our model. Section 5.3 then presents this structure from the viewpoint of the system of national accounts and provides thereby a detailed introduction to the notation that is used in this chapter. In Section 5.4 we present the structural equations of the model (in their extensive form) by way of an appropriate subdivision into important modules that build up the model. Section 5.5 finally gives an outlook on what to do with this model type when it is reduced from extensive form to per unit of capital expressions or intensive form, to the laws of motion for the state variables of the model. We will find that there is a (basically) uniquely determined interior steady state for this dynamical system which appears to be locally attracting for low adjustment speeds, but which generally is surrounded by centrifugal forces leading to limit cycles or more complex attractors or to pure explosiveness for large displacements from the steady state or for adjustment speeds that are chosen sufficiently large. Further (extrinsic) non-linearities are therefore needed in general to get bounded dynamics for a larger set of parameter constellations.

5.2 The real and the financial part of the economy

The two tables below provide a survey of the structure of the economy to be modelled that is related, but not identical, to the description of the Australian economy given in Powell and Murphy (1997). Note in this respect that the aim of the present chapter is to establish an integrated continuous-time model, leading to an autonomous system of differential equations, where all sectors are fully specified with respect to their behaviour and their budget constraints from the viewpoint of complete theoretical models of monetary growth. A bridge will thereby be provided between the Keynes–Metzler type monetary growth models of Chiarella and Flaschel (2000), Chiarella *et al.* (2005) and the Powell and Murphy (1997) approach. This perspective of the economy will allow us to highlight where we deviate from the framework given in Powell and Murphy (1997). In Section 5.4 we will briefly comment on the differences between their discrete time macroeconometric model and our continuous-time one.[2]

5.2.1 The structure of the real part

Let us start with a presentation of the variables that comprise the real part of the economy. Table 5.1 provides data on the temporary equilibrium position of the economy, based on given prices and expectations, and also shows real stocks and their rates of growth.

Table 5.1 describes the real sector of the economy. We have a labour market, three commodity markets and the housing market. Domestic production Y concerns one good that is only domestically used (for all private consumption $C_w + C_c$, all investment $I, I_h, \mathcal{I}$, also in housing, and all government consumption G and which uses up all the imports J^d as intermediate goods) and one that is only used for exports X. There is thus only a single commodity used in domestic absorption, apart from the housing services C_h^d demanded by workers.

Our model exhibits three domestic sectors: households, firms and the government, but with heterogeneous agents in the household sector, workers and (pure) asset holders, the former supplying their labour L at the wage level w^b (which includes payroll taxes) and the latter the housing services C_h^s for the workers as far as real flows are concerned.[3] Firms produce a non-traded domestic and an exported commodity and employ labour L_f^w (with varying rates of utilisation L_f^d) and imports J^d besides their capital stock K

[2] The real-financial market interaction is also studied in Chiarella *et al.* (2009a) from a quite different perspective. The reader may also consult this reference for applied work in this context.

[3] Powell and Murphy (1997) do not have an explicit description of heterogeneous agents in their household sector, but basically use a uniform life-cycle hypothesis for the modelling of the consumption demand of this sector; see however their p. 117 for a brief remark on income distribution.

Table 5.1. *The real part of the economy (foreign country data: γ, p_x^*, p_m^*, $\tau_c^* = \tau_c$)*

	Labour	Non-traded Goods	Exports	Imports	Dwellings
Workers	$L = \alpha_l L_1$	C_w	–	–	C_h^d
Asset holders	–	C_c	–	–	C_h^s, I_h
Firms	L_f^d, L_f^w	$Y^p, Y, I, \mathcal{I}$	X	J^d	–
Government	L_g^d	G	–	–	–
Prices	$w^b, w[w^r, w^u]$	$p_v = (1 + \tau_v)p_y$	$p_x = sp_x^*$	$p_m = (1+\tau_m) sp_m^*$	p_h, p_y
Expectations	$\pi^e = \hat{p}_v^e$	$\pi^e = \hat{p}_v^e$	–	–	$\pi^e = \hat{p}_v^e$
Stocks	L_1	K, N	–	–	K_h
Growth	$\hat{L}_1 = n$	$\hat{K} = I/K - \delta_k$ $\dot{N} = Y - Y^d$	–	–	$\hat{K}_h = \frac{I_h}{K_h} - \delta_h$

for these purposes, and invest in fixed business capital I and inventories $\mathcal{I}$. Government finally provides public consumption goods G, pays rents w^r and unemployment benefits w^u and also employs part of the workforce L_g^d. There are a number of variables needed to describe the laws of motion of the quantities, prices p_v (including value-added taxes), and expectations about their rates of change, which will be explained in detail when we turn to the description of the various equations of the model in Section 5.4. There is endogenous growth n of the potential labour force L_1, of the capital stock K, and of the stock of housing K_h (supplied at price p_h for rental services) and also actual change of inventories N that is different from their desired rate of change $\mathcal{I}$.

5.2.2 The structure of the financial part

Let us next consider the financial part of the economy. Table 5.2 provides data on the changes in financial stocks, corresponding prices, and the growth of stocks in the financial part of the economy.

The first column in Table 5.2 shows that we do not consider money holdings. Cash management and transactions money are introduced in Chiarella *et al.* (1999a,b), in the usual form of an aggregate Cagan money demand function and also in a more disaggregated form than in the Murphy type model. We exclude money holdings in our basic modelling framework, by assuming that money is a costless medium of exchange for firms, household and the government that returns at the 'end' of each point in time t to the 'local branches' of the central bank by the balancing of the budget restrictions of these sectors.[4] At present there are only (four) interest-bearing financial assets in our model that can be held by the (pure) asset owners and by the workers of our economy (as shown in Table 5.2). As in the Keynes–Metzler model of monetary growth of Chiarella and Flaschel (2000) we here assume, in order to start with a simple representation of

[4] There are no commercial banks in the model of this chapter.

Table 5.2. *The financial part of the economy (foreign country data: i^*)*

	Money	Short-term Bonds	Long-term Bonds	Equities	Foreign Bonds
Workers	–	$\dot{B}_w$	–	–	–
Asset holders	–	$\dot{B}_c$	$\dot{B}_1^l$	$\dot{E}$	$\dot{B}_2^l$
Firms	–	–	–	$\dot{E}$	–
Government	–	$\dot{B}$	$\dot{B}^l$	–	–
Prices	1	1 [i]	$p_b = 1/i_l$	p_e	$sp_b^* = s \cdot 1/i_l^*$
Expectations	–	–	$\pi_b = \hat{p}_b^e$	$\pi_e = \hat{p}_e^e$	$\epsilon_s = \hat{s}^e$
Stocks	–	$B = B_w + B_c$	$B^l = B_1^l + B_1^{l*}$	E	B_2^l
Growth	–	$\hat{B}, \hat{B}_w, \hat{B}_c$	$\hat{B}^l, \hat{B}_1^l$	$\hat{E}$	$\hat{B}_2^l$

financial flows, that bonds are only issued by the government, that firms use only equity financing and pay out expected earnings as dividends, and that there exist also long-term bonds issued by the 'foreign government'. Financial flows between the sectors of our economy are therefore very narrowly defined (in order to simplify the flow budget restrictions to a sufficient degree). The laws of motion of the real part of our economy do not yet depend too severely on this financial structure of the economy since, as in Powell and Murphy (1997), we do not use a full portfolio approach towards the description of the stock equilibria of the economy. Rather we determine asset prices and asset returns through certain simple laws of motion, while the inflow of financial assets is basically determined from the supply side.[5] This is done in a way that implies equilibrium on the market for foreign exchange with respect to the flows appearing in the current as well as in the capital account so that there is no change in reserves held by the central bank and thus no need to consider this item explicitly in the balance of payments to be discussed in the next section.

For initial work on the situation where loans to firms, inside debt of the household sector, supply side rationing, market imperfections and other realistic features may be introduced into the Keynes–Metzler framework of Chiarella and Flaschel (2000) we refer the reader to Chiarella *et al.* (2000).[6]

Note that we allow for savings out of wages (in a Kaldorian way) and that workers save only in the form of short-term debt (interest-bearing saving deposits[7] held at the local branches of the central bank). All other assets (plus the remainder of short-term debt) are exclusively held by the (pure) asset holders of our model. We stress that this approach serves the purpose of simplifying the budget constraints of the agents, but needs refinement in future reformulations of the model. Note that the government sector

[5] Powell and Murphy (1997) use perfect substitute assumptions, as for example the interest rate parity condition, and rational expectations to describe the behaviour of the asset markets, while we use certain delayed adjustment processes towards such an outcome and thus avoid use of the jump variable technique for the description of the financial part of the economy.

[6] See also Franke and Semmler (1999) for a full portfolio approach to asset market behaviour.

[7] These can be thought of as fixed-price bonds, which are thus perfectly liquid.

includes the activities of the central bank (and its branches), which in the following model type boil down to setting the interest rate of (only domestically held) short-term government bonds according to some type of Taylor rule.[8]

5.3 The structure of the economy from the viewpoint of national accounting

We shall consider in this section the production accounts, income accounts, accumulation accounts and financial accounts of the four internal agents in our economy:[9] firms, workers, asset holders and the government (including the monetary authority). These accounts, plus the balance of payments, provide basic information on what is assumed for these four sectors as well as which of their activities are excluded from the present theoretical framework. These accounts furthermore serve the purpose of checking that all ex post results of the economy are consistent with each other and showing how the usual basic identities of national accounting (concerning output and income, savings and investment) can be derived from them.

5.3.1 The four sectors of the economy

We start with the accounts of the sector of firms (shown in Table 5.3) that organise production Y, employment L_f^d of their workforce L_f^w and gross business fixed investment I and that use (in the present formulation of the model) only equities E as financing instrument (no debt in the form of bank loans or bonds issued by firms). There are value-added taxes τ_v on consumption goods, import taxes τ_m and payroll taxes τ_p with respect to hours worked L_f^d, but no further taxation in the sector of firms and there are no subsidies.

All accounts are expressed in terms of the domestic currency. Firms build dwellings, which are of the same type as all other domestic production, and sell them to the asset holders (as investors) and thus have no own investment in the housing sector. They sell consumption goods to workers, asset holders and the government, export goods to the world economy, organise fixed gross investments with respect to their capital stock (as well as voluntary inventory changes $\mathcal{I}$ with respect to finished goods) and experience involuntary inventory changes $Y - Y^d$ due to the deviation of aggregate demand Y^d from output Y (which is based on expected sales Y^e and planned inventories $\mathcal{I}$).[10]

Firms use up all imports as intermediate goods which thereby become part of the unique homogeneous good that is produced for domestic purposes. They have replacement costs with respect to their capital stock, pay indirect taxes and wages including payroll taxes. Their accounting profit is therefore equal to expected profits (based on

[8] Such a mechanism is in the place of the indirect steering of this rate of interest through a monetary supply rule and money market equilibrium as in Powell and Murphy (1997).

[9] The fifth agent, the foreign economy, is represented by the balance of payments at the end of this section and later on will be confined to steady state behaviour. All demands of the foreign sector are indexed by $*$, while its supply of long-term bonds B_2 to domestic residents is indexed by 2.

[10] No other type of inventory holding is considered in the model of this chapter.

Table 5.3. *The production, income, accumulation and financial accounts of firms*

Uses	Sources
Production Account of Firms:	
Imports $sp_m^* J^d$	Consumption $p_v C_w$
Depreciation $p_y \delta_k K$	Consumption $p_v C_c$
Indirect Taxes $\tau_v p_y (C_w + C_c + G) + \tau_m s p_m^* J^d$	Consumption $p_v G$
Wages (including payroll taxes) $w^b L_f^d$	Exports $p_x X$
	Gross Investment $p_y I$
	Durables (Dwellings) $p_y I_h$
Profits $\Pi = r^e p_y K + p_y \mathcal{I} = r^a p_y K + p_y \dot{N}$	Inventory Investment $p_y \dot{N}$
Income Account of Firms:	
Dividends $r^e p_y K$	Profits Π
Savings $S_f^n = p_y \mathcal{I}$	
Accumulation Account of Firms:	
Gross Investment $p_y I$	Depreciation $p_y \delta_k K$
Inventory Investment $p_y \dot{N}$	Savings S_f^n
	Financial Deficit FD
Financial Account of Firms:	
Financial Deficit FD	Equity Financing $p_e \dot{E}$

sales expectations and paid out as dividends to equity owners) and retained profits (equal to planned inventories). As is obvious from the narrow income account of firms, firms thus only save an amount equal to their intended inventory changes. The accumulation account is self-explanatory as is the financial account which repeats our earlier statement that the financial deficit of firms is financed solely by the issuing of new equities.

Note that all investment is valued (and performed) net of value-added tax and thus at producer prices p_y in the place of the consumer prices $p_v = (1 + \tau_v)p_y$. Indirect taxes (value-added taxes)[11] only fall on consumption activities and not on gross investment, thus not on housing investments and the inventory investment of firms. There are furthermore no direct (capital) taxes in the sector of firms, neither on property nor on profits, since all expected profits are distributed to asset holders and since there are no taxes on windfall profits (unexpected retained earnings – or losses – of firms that help to finance investment). Note however that the wages w^b paid by firms include payroll taxes $\tau_p w$ (for unemployment insurance, health and other social insurance, and retirement pensions) and that wage income w of workers is taxed at the rate τ_w. Note finally that the accumulation account of firms is based on realised magnitudes and thus does not refer explicitly to their intended inventory changes.

[11] There is however a tax on the imports made by the firms.

Table 5.4. *The production, income, accumulation and financial accounts of asset holders*

Uses	Sources
Production Account of Households (Asset Holders/Housing Investment):	
Depreciation $p_y \delta_h K_h$	Rent $p_h C_h^d$
Earnings Π_h	
Income Account of Households (Asset Holders):	
Tax Payment $\tau_c i B_c$	Interest Payment $i B_c$
Tax Payment $\tau_c B_1^l$	Interest Payment B_1^l
Taxes $\tau_c(p_h C_h^d - p_y \delta_h K_h)$	Interest Payment $s(1 - \tau_c^*) B_2^l$
Tax Payment $\tau_c r^e p_y K$	Dividend Payment $r^e p_y K$
Consumption $p_v C_c$	Earnings Π_h
Savings S_c^n	
Accumulation Account of Households (Asset Holders):	
Gross Investment $p_y I_h$	Depreciation $p_y \delta_h K_h$
Financial Surplus FS	Savings S_c^n
Financial Account of Households (Asset Holders):	
Short-term Bonds $\dot{B}_c$	Financial Surplus FS
Long-term Bonds $p_b \dot{B}_1^l$	
Foreign Bonds $s p_b^* \dot{B}_2^l$	
Equities $p_e \dot{E}$	

Consider next the sector of asset holders (see Table 5.4). Investment in housing as well as the supply of housing services has been exclusively allocated to this sector. The production account thus shows the actual sale (not the potential sale) of housing services (= demand for housing services by assumption) which is divided into replacement costs and actual earnings or profits on the uses side of the production account.

The income of asset holders comes from various sources: interest payments on short- and long-term domestic bonds and on long-term foreign bonds (net of tax payments which must be paid abroad), dividend payments of firms (based on their expected profit) and profits from housing rents. All domestic profit income is subject to tax payments at the rate τ_c and after tax income by definition is divided into the consumption of domestic commodities (including houses, but not housing services) and the nominal savings of asset owners.

The accumulation account shows the sources for gross investment of asset holders in the housing sector, namely depreciation and savings, the excess of which (over housing investment) is then invested in financial assets as shown in the financial account. Note here that short-term bonds are fixed-price bonds $p_b = 1$ (which are perfectly liquid), while long-term bonds have the variable price[12] $p_b = 1/i_l$ (and fixed nominal interest

[12] These bonds are thus not perfectly liquid, since there is no 'money back' guarantee here for the sector of asset owners as a whole.

Table 5.5. *The production, income, accumulation and financial accounts of worker households*

Uses	Sources
Production Account of Households (Workers):	
–	–
Income Account of Households (Workers):	
Taxes $\tau_w[wL^d + w^u(L - L^w) + w^r\alpha_l L_2] + \tau_c i B_w$	Wages wL^d
Consumption $p_v C_w + p_h C_h^d$	Unemployment Benefits $w^u(L - L^w)$
–	Pensions $w^r\alpha_l L_2$
Savings S_w^n	iB_w Interest Payments
Accumulation Account of Households (Workers):	
Financial Surplus FS	Savings S_w^n
Financial Account of Households (Workers):	
Short-term Bond Accumulation $\dot{B}_w$	Financial Surplus FS

payments of one unit of money per period) which shows that they are akin to consols or perpetuities (the same holds true for imported foreign bonds, which are of long-term type solely).[13]

There is no taxation of financial wealth (held or transferred) in the household sector. Furthermore, although asset holders will consider expected gross rates of return on financial markets in their investment decision, there is no taxation of capital gains on these markets, which descriptively seems realistic.

The next set of accounts, the ones of worker households in Table 5.5, is fairly simple and easy to explain. First, there is no production account in this sector. Income of the members of the workforce, which may be employed, unemployed or retired, thus derives from wages, unemployment benefits or pension payments where $L = \alpha_l L_1$ denotes the total number of persons in the current workforce (L^w the part that is employed) and $\alpha_l L_2$ the number of retirees who have access to pension funds (α_l=const. the participation rate of the potential workforce L_1). To this we have to add the interest income on saving deposits (short-term bonds) which is taxed at the general rate used for financial asset income. All wage type incomes are subject to taxation at the rate τ_w and are again by definition divided into nominal consumption (consumption goods and housing services) and savings. Note here that the employment L^d of the employed L^w can differ from their normal employment which is measured by L^w, the number of persons who are employed. Note also that wages w are net of payroll taxes (used to finance unemployment benefits, social insurance and pensions in particular).

13 Due to the assumption of a given nominal rate of interest on foreign bonds, these bonds can be liquidated if this is desired by domestic residents, but they are of course subject to exchange rate risk. Foreign bond purchases by domestic residents will be treated as a residual in the wealth accumulation decisions of the asset holders.

Table 5.6. *The production, income, accumulation and financial accounts of the monetary and fiscal authorities*

Uses	Sources
Production Account of Fiscal and Monetary Authorities:	
Government Expenditure for Goods $p_v G$	Costless Provision
Government Expenditure for Services $w^b L_g^d$	of Public Goods
Income Account of Fiscal and Monetary Authorities:	
Interest Payment iB	Wage Income Taxation $\tau_w[wL^d + w^u(L - L^w) + w^r \alpha_l L_2]$
Interest Payment B^l	Profit and Interest Taxation $\tau_c[r^e p_y K + iB + B^l]$
Pensions $w^r \alpha_l L_2$	Rent Income Taxation $\tau_c(p_h C_h^d - p_y \delta_h K_h)$
Unemployment Benefits $w^u(L - L^w)$	Payroll Taxes $\tau_p w L^d$
Government Consumption $p_v G$	Value Added Tax $\tau_v p_y (C_w + C_c + G)$
Salaries $w^b L_g^d$	Import Taxes $\tau_m s p_m^* J^d$
Savings S_g^n	
Accumulation Account of the Fiscal Authority:	
	Savings S_g^n
	Financial Deficit FD
Financial Account of Fiscal and Monetary Authorities:	
Financial Deficit FD	Short-term Debt $\dot{B}$
	Long-term Debt $p_b \dot{B}^l$

We assume in the following that workers have a positive savings rate and that they hold their savings in the form of short-term bonds solely, which is mirrored here in the accumulation and financial account in a straightforward way.

There are finally the accounts of the fiscal and monetary authorities (see Table 5.6), which due to the many taxation schemes and transfer payments that are assumed are more voluminous than the preceding accounts – at least with respect to the income account. There is first however a fictitious production account where the supply of public goods is valued at production costs which consist of government expenditures for goods and labour.

The sources of government income consist of taxes on the various forms of workers' income (taxed at a uniform rate), of taxes on the various forms of profit, interest and rental income (again taxed at a uniform rate), payroll taxes, value-added taxes and import taxes. Uses of the tax income of the government are interest payments, transfers to the unemployed and retirees, and the costs of the aforementioned government 'production'. In general all these uses of the tax income of the government will exceed its income so that there will result a negative amount of nominal savings S_g^n which balances the income account of the government.

There is no accumulation of real assets in the government sector, which means that we only have to look into the financial account of the government to see how the excess of government outlays over government revenue is financed through short- or long-term debt. Note that there is some type of accounting money in the economy that however only fuels the economy during the transactions period, but does not appear as flow in the financial accounts of asset owners, and workers, and the government, but instead returns to the banking sector at the end of each transaction period t by the settlement of all budget restrictions in the economy. In striking contrast to a cash in advance constraint we thus assume in this chapter that agents can obtain all money they need for transaction purposes during the transaction period t (as intra-day credit in one form or another), but that they have to satisfy their budget constraint at the end of each such period t where money holdings are not needed and are thus not present. Instead all liquid asset holdings concern the short-term bonds of the government as some form of interest bearing saving deposit.

There is a variety of further types of taxes that could have been included into the structure of the model as we have discussed it so far. The most important types from a macroeconomic point of view are probably: corporate profit taxation; investment taxes (or subsidies) – fixed business investment and housing investment – including a treatment of depreciation allowances; financial wealth taxation and inheritance taxes; capital gains taxation; real property taxation; taxes on the rents imputed in the case of asset holders.

In the model of this chapter corporate income taxation would reduce to taxation of the windfall profits of firms, since all expected earnings of firms are distributed to workers and as dividend payments to asset holders. We leave (gross) investment as untaxed in order to stress that this type of activity is to be supported for the future development of the economy by the government. Financial wealth taxation will be considered in future work where a more advanced and much more interdependent structure for the small open economy to be introduced in Section 5.4 is considered. Similarly capital gains are not taxed in order to stimulate financial investment in risky assets (and since it is also difficult to treat in its exact amount and dating and, from an institutional perspective, with respect to capital losses). Real property taxation is probably a major item in many countries, but is here left aside for simplicity as are the imputed rents of the housing services consumed by the asset owners of our economy.

There are further taxes on the state level and on the local level of government administration (which are here completely ignored), taxes on private insurance and pensions (which do not exist in our model), product specific taxes, subsidies for employment and investment on the margin, and turnover taxes, which may be important from a partial microeconomic analysis of public economics, but which have to be left aside here in our broad picture of the macroeconomy. Furthermore, we do not impose internal constraints on the uses of the taxes that are actually received by the government of our macroeconomy and which might restrict the use of certain taxes to certain expenditures or transfers made by the government.

Table 5.7. *The external account*

Uses	Sources
External Account:	
sp^*X	sp^*J^d
$s(1-\tau_c^*)B_2^l$	$(1-\tau_c)B_1^{l*}$
$\dot{B}_1^{l*}/i_l$	$s\dot{B}_2^l/i_{l*}$

Let us finally describe the balance of payments of the economy under consideration. This will be done from the viewpoint of the foreign sector which can be viewed as a fifth agent of the economic structure considered in this chapter. The description of the behaviour of this agent will however be confined to steady state behaviour in the subsequent presentation of the structural equations of the model.

Table 5.7 is viewed from the perspective of the foreign economy and in terms of the domestic currency.

The external, or balance of payments, account (see Table 5.7) shows the trade account (exports X and imports J^d), the international component of interest payments (to foreigners and from abroad) that are all assumed to cross borders and the outflow and the inflow of new capital (long-term bonds). Note that this account does not show any reserve changes of the central bank due to foreign exchange market operations. This is possible in the approach chosen in this chapter, despite a temporarily given exchange rate s, since on the one hand the supply of bonds of the government domestically and abroad of the equities of firms are channelled into the savings decisions of households without readjustments. On the other hand the excess of domestic private savings is going into foreign bonds, which in turn implies that the balance of payments must be balanced without any intervention from the central bank. This will be checked in the next subsection from the viewpoint of the ex post equality of aggregate savings with aggregate investment plus the current account balance on the one hand and with aggregate investment plus the capital account balance on the other hand, where both equalities can be established without any interference from the central bank. The result obtained is basically due to the fact that all foreign exchange market operations can be settled without any help from the central bank, and without any rationing processes, since the residually determined item $s\dot{B}_2^l/i_{l*}$ just provides the balancing item for this account.

This concludes our description of the four accounts of the three typical sectors of a small open economy (with heterogeneous agents in the household sector) plus a foreign sector that is here represented solely via the balance of payments.

5.3.2 Gross domestic product, savings, investment and further aggregates

In this subsection we derive some basic concepts of national accounting in the specific form they receive in our model economy and also the relationships between nominal aggregate savings and nominal total investment. Considering nominal gross domestic product first, we see that this concept aggregates (with respect to uses) total private and government consumption, net exports, total investment (including housing and all inventory investment $\dot{N}$) and finally the services of housing actually demanded and supplied. The sources of these expenditures are the depreciation of the capital stock of firms and of the housing stock, indirect taxes, wage payments of firms and profits in production and in housing supply.

Gross Domestic Product (GDP):[14]

$$p_y\delta_k K + p_y\delta_h K_h + \tau_v p_y(C_w + C_c + G) + \tau_m s p_m^* J^d + w^b L_f^d + \Pi + \Pi_h$$
$$= p_v(C_w + C_c + G) + p_x X - s p_m^* J^d + p_y I + p_y I_h + p_y \dot{N} + p_h C_h^d.$$

Net domestic product is then obtained (also in nominal terms and at market prices) by moving the depreciation items from the left-hand side of the preceding equation to its right-hand side and thus by deducting them from the corresponding gross investment, giving rise to net investment descriptions for firms as well as for the housing sector of the economy.

Net Domestic Product at market prices (NDP):[15]

$$\tau_v p_y(C_w + C_c + G) + \tau_m s p_m^* J^d + w^b L_f^d + \Pi + \Pi_h$$
$$= p_v(C_w + C_c + G) + (p_x X - s p_m^* J^d) + p_y(I - \delta_k K)$$
$$+ p_y(I_h - \delta_h K_h) + p_y \dot{N} + p_h C_h^d.$$

Net domestic product at factor costs follows from net domestic product at market prices by deducting indirect taxes from both sides of the preceding equation which simply leads to a revaluation of consumption goods and imports, both measured now at prices without value-added taxes and without import taxes.

Net Domestic Product at factor costs (NDP-F):[16]

$$w^b L_f^d + \Pi + \Pi_h$$
$$= p_y(C_w + C_c + G) + (p_x X - p_m J^d) + p_y(I - \delta_k K) + p_y(I_h - \delta_h K_h)$$
$$+ p_y \dot{N} + p_h C_h^d$$

On the basis of the uses of nominal savings of the four sectors considered (see their accumulation and financial accounts), one furthermore obtains via their aggregation the result

$$S^n = S_w^n + S_c^n + S_f^n + S_g^n = I^{na} + [s\dot{B}_2^l / i_l^* - (\dot{B}^l - \dot{B}_1^l)/i_l]$$

[14] Gross National Product (GNP) = GDP + $s(1 - \tau_c^*)B_2^l - (1 - \tau_c)(B^l - B_1^l)$.
[15] Net National Product (NNP) = NDP + $s(1 - \tau_c^*)B_2^l - (1 - \tau_c)(B^l - B_1^l)$.
[16] National Income is defined on this basis by NDP-F $+s(1 - \tau_c^*)B_2^l - (1 - \tau_c)(B^l - B_1^l)$.

with

$$I^{na} = p_e\dot{E} + p_y\mathcal{I} + p_y(I_h - \delta_h K_h) = p_y(I - \delta_k K) + p_y\dot{N} + p_y(I_h - \delta_h K_h).$$

We here see that total nominal savings are ex post always equal to total nominal net investment plus net capital exports. Note that the home country's capital exports are equal (in value) to the import $\dot{B}_2^l$ of foreign bonds and that its capital imports are given by the value of the export of the home country's long-term bonds $\dot{B}^l - \dot{B}_1^l$. Note also that actual net investment consists of business fixed investment, of actual inventory changes and of net investment in the supply of dwellings. This important identity of national accounting is based on the four identities that relate the nominal savings of the various sectors to the uses made of these savings. Approaching aggregate nominal savings from the definitions of the various savings items, that is from the income side, by contrast gives rise to

$$\begin{aligned} S^n &= S_w^n + S_c^n + S_f^n + S_g^n \\ &= I^{na} + [p_x X - s p_m^* J^d] + [s(1-\tau_c^*)B_2^l - (1-\tau_c)(B^l - B_1^l)], \\ I^{na} &= p_y(I - \delta_k K) + p_y\dot{N} + p_y(I_h - \delta_h K_h), \end{aligned}$$

so that aggregate nominal savings equals aggregate nominal actual net investment plus nominal net exports plus international nominal net transfers. The identities just discussed thus in sum show that basic concepts of the system of national accounts can already be quite complicated in our model economy.

We digress to add a detailed calculation to what has just been asserted and in particular shows that there indeed is no intervention needed from the monetary authority on the market for foreign exchange, due to the assumed budget restrictions for households, firms and the government.

Starting from the definitions of the nominal savings of the four sectors the identity on nominal savings and investment just stated can also be shown as follows:

$$\begin{aligned} S^n = {} & Y_w^{Dn} - p_v C_w - p_h C_h^d \\ & + Y_c^{Dn} - p_v C_c + p_y\mathcal{I} \\ & + T^n - w^u(L - L^w) - w^r \alpha_l L_2 - (iB + \dot{B}^l) - (p_v G + w^b L_g^d), \end{aligned}$$

which gives rise to

$$\begin{aligned} S^n = {} & wL^d + w^u(L - L^w) + w^r\alpha_l L_2 + iB_w - p_v C_w - p_h C_h^d \\ & + r^e p_y K + iB_c + B_1^l + p_h C_h^d - p_y\delta_h K_h + s(1-\tau_c^*)B_2^l - p_v C_c + p_y\mathcal{I} \\ & + \tau_m s p_m^* J^d + \tau_c(B^l - B_1^l) + \tau_p w L^d \\ & + \tau_v p_y(Y^d - I - I_h) - w^u(L - L^w) - w^r\alpha_l L_2 - (iB + B^l) - (p_v G + w^b L_g^d). \end{aligned}$$

These expressions can be rearranged as

$$\begin{aligned}
w^b L^d &- p_v C_w + r^e p_y K + iB + B_1^l - p_y \delta_h K_h + s(1-\tau_c^*)B_2^l - p_v C_c \\
&+ p_y \mathcal{I} + \tau_m s p_m^* J^d + \tau_c(B^l - B_1^l) \\
&+ \tau_v p_y (C_w + C_c + G) - (iB + B^l) - (p_v G + w^b L_g^d) \\
&= w^b L_f^d - p_y C_w + r^e p_y K - (1-\tau_c)(B^l - B_1^l) - p_y \delta_h K_h + s(1-\tau_c^*)B_2^l - p_y C_c \\
&\quad + p_y \mathcal{I} + \tau_m s p_m^* J^d - p_y G \\
&= p_y(Y^e - \delta_k K) + p_x X - s p_m^* J^d - (p_y C_w + p_y C_c + p_y G) \\
&\quad - (1-\tau_c)(B^l - B_1^l) + s(1-\tau_c^*)B_2^l - p_y \delta_h K_h + p_y \mathcal{I} \\
&= p_y(Y - Y^d) + p_y Y^d - (p_y C_w + p_y C_c + p_y G) - p_y \delta_k K + p_x X - s p_m^* J^d \\
&\quad + s(1-\tau_c^*)B_2^l - (1-\tau_c)(B^l - B_1^l) - p_y \delta_h K_h \\
&= p_y \dot{N} + p_y(I - \delta_k K) + p_y(I_h - \delta_h K_h) \\
&\quad + p_x X - s p_m^* J^d + s(1-\tau_c^*)B_2^l - (1-\tau_c)(B^l - B_1^l) \\
&= I^{na} + s(1-\tau_c^*)B_2^l - (1-\tau_c)(B^l - B_1^l).
\end{aligned}$$

This proves the asserted identity from the viewpoint of the definitions of nominal savings. Note here that $B^l - B_1^l = B_1^{l*}$ holds by definition for the international allocation of domestic long-term bonds and that aggregate goods demand is defined by the expression $Y^d = C_w + C_c + I + I_h + G$.

Having presented the model from the ex post point of view by means of structured tables and the system of national accounts we now turn to the structural form of the model and present in the following section its technological foundations, its behavioural relationships, various definitions and the budget equations of the four agents of the domestic economy, and finally also its laws of motion for quantities, prices and expectations.

5.4 The model

In this section we develop the extensive form equations of our model based on the structure laid out in Section 5.3. We reformulate the Murphy model for the Australian economy, as presented in Powell and Murphy (1997), from a macrotheoretic perspective, by making it a continuous-time dynamic model of monetary growth, suppressing all discrete lag structures of their quarterly period model in particular. The present reformulation of the Murphy model is furthermore based on the experience gained in Chiarella and Flaschel (1999b,c) in the modelling of integrated Keynes–Metzler models of monetary growth for closed as well as open economies. Certain features of this dynamical system approach to growth and fluctuations are therefore retained in the formulation of our continuous-time version of the Murphy model, which of course means that its dynamical structure will differ from that of the Murphy model to a certain degree.[17]

Our aim in this section is not so much to fully mirror the dynamical structure and implications of the Murphy model. Rather our aim is to formulate and to investigate, to a first approximation of this 100 equations approach to macroeconometric model building, the set of the most prominent feedback structures of macrodynamic theory it basically contains and the role they play for stability analysis. As we have stated, we set up an integrated macrotheoretic monetary growth framework that in its generality is comparable to this type of macroeconometric model building. The current section therefore attempts to build a bridge between empirically motivated work on structural model building (where there generally is no analysis of the mechanisms that are hidden in the formulated structure) and theoretical investigations of reasonably large representation of concrete economies, where the interest is to see what the steady state of such economies will look like in all of its details and what stabilising (or destabilising) effects are present around it, or have to be added far off the steady state in order to ensure the boundedness of the considered dynamics.

5.4.1 Preliminaries

Let us start with some notation to be used in the structural equations we shall employ in our approach to Keynesian monetary growth. Module 1 of the model provides definitions of important rates of return r^e, r^a, r^n, r_h, of nominal wealth W^n[18] and of hourly wages including payroll taxes, w^b, prices p_v including value-added tax, of pension payments per retired worker (in the workforce) per time unit, w^r, and unemployment benefits per unemployed worker (of the workforce) per time unit, w^u, with w denoting the money wage exclusive of payroll taxes but still including wage income taxes. We here in particular define the currently expected rate of profit based on the sales expectations Y^e of firms (net of depreciation $\delta_k K$) and on actual exports $X = x_y Y$, imports $J^d = j_y Y$ and the actual employment $L^d = l_y Y$ of the workforce of the firms. In a similar fashion also the actual and the normal rate of return on business fixed investment, r^a, r^n, based on actual sales and normal rates of capacity utilisation of the capital stock. Our choice of notation of production coefficients already indicates that we are assuming a technology with fixed input/output coefficients where export supply is in fixed proportion to actual output Y, as is import demand and labour demand. Furthermore, potential output is defined on the basis of a given capital stock as $Y^p = y^p K, \ y^p = const$, and is used in the definition of normal profits in a specific way that has still to be explained. We use fixed coefficients technology for the same reasons as in Chiarella and Flaschel (2000), namely that it allows clearer insight into the dynamic feedback structure of the

[17] This remark in particular applies to our treatment of financial markets where we attempt to avoid the so-called jump variable technique of models with only rational expectations by allowing for heterogeneous expectations formation and somewhat delayed adjustments towards interest rate parity conditions.

[18] Wealth effects will however only be studied in future extensions of the model of this chapter, but should of course be kept in mind when interpreting the behaviour of the present model.

model without altering the qualitative features of the dynamics under smooth factor substitution technology.

1. Definitions (Rates of Return, Nominal Wealth, Wages and Prices):

$$r^e = \frac{p_y Y^e + p_x x_y Y - w^b l_y Y - p_m j_y Y - p_y \delta_k K}{p_y K}, \tag{5.1}$$

$$r^a = \frac{p_y Y^d + p_x x_y Y - w^b l_y Y - p_m j_y Y - p_y \delta_k K}{p_y K}, \tag{5.2}$$

$$Y^{dp} = \frac{\bar{u} Y^p}{1 + \gamma \beta_{n^d}}, \qquad Y^n = \bar{u} Y^p, \tag{5.3}$$

$$r^n = \frac{p_y Y^{dp} + p_x x_y Y^n - w^b l_y Y^n - p_m j_y Y^n - p_y \delta_k K}{p_y K}, \tag{5.4}$$

$$r_h = \frac{p_h C_h^d - p_y \delta_h K_h}{p_y K_h}, \tag{5.5}$$

$$i^r = (1 - \tau_c) i_l - \pi^c, \tag{5.6}$$

$$W^n = B + B_1^l / i_l + s B_2^l / i_l^* + p_e E + p_y K_h, \tag{5.7}$$

$$w^b = (1 + \tau_p) w, \tag{5.8}$$

$$w^r = \alpha^r w, \tag{5.9}$$

$$w^u = \alpha^u w, \tag{5.10}$$

$$p_v = (1 + \tau_v) p_y. \tag{5.11}$$

Note that the various rates of profits are defined on the basis of output prices p_y net of value-added tax, since they measure what can actually be distributed to equity owning households (with the rate r^e measuring actual dividend payments at each moment in time, while r^a measures the actual rate of profit of firms based on their actual sales).

Firms have a desired rate of capacity utilisation $\bar{u} < 1$ (which is not endogenised in the present model) and thus plan a normal output $Y^n = \bar{u} Y^p$ less than potential output in order to have capacity reserves in the case of unforeseen demand shocks. Furthermore they have to hold inventories $N^d = \beta_{n^d} Y^n$ which have to grow at the given world growth rate γ in the steady state which means that the demand Y^{dp} they consider as adequate in the light of their potential output (or as satisfying in the steady state) must be less than normal production since part of the latter is going into inventories). The normal rate of profit, r^n, is then defined on the basis of this concept of normal output as the other rates of profits just discussed. The rate of return r_h, finally, refers to the housing sector and its actual sale of (= demand for) housing services C_h^d at price p_h. It is diminished through the depreciation of dwellings at rate δ_h and set in relation to the net value of the capital stock K_h in the housing sector. All capital goods are (or have been) purchased at price p_y in the market for non-traded (domestic) goods, since value-added taxes only concern consumption expenditures in the present model.

We often compare profitability as measured by the above rates of return with required profitability given by the expected long-term real rate of interest $(1-\tau_c)i_l - \pi^c$ which is related to the price of long-term bonds (consols or perpetuities) in the following well known way $p_b = 1/i_l$, π^c a weighted (long-term) expected rate of inflation to be defined in module 5b of the model. Note that we calculate this required rate of return net of interest taxation, while all other rates in this block are gross rates of return.

Aggregate nominal wealth of asset holders and workers (the latter only hold short-term debt of the government as saving deposits) is composed of short-term fixed-price (= perfectly liquid) bonds of the domestic government, B, held only domestically, long-term bonds issued by the domestic and the foreign government in the amounts held by domestic residents, B_1^l, B_2^l, equities E and the value of the housing capital stock K_h, again measured at producers' prices. We assume that there is no resale market for houses (and goods in general) and thus do not have a secondary market in this segment of the economy in order to keep things simple in our one domestic good economy (once these commodities are sold they do not reappear on the market). Financial assets by contrast are traded in secondary markets and give rise to certain price adjustment equations that are implicitly based on stock reallocations in the financial markets considered. Asset markets are therefore still treated in a preliminary way, since portfolio decisions are not yet modelled explicitly (see module 6 of the model).

Note that government bonds are treated as net wealth.[19] However, since wealth effects are still excluded from the behavioural equations to be introduced later on, this concept of wealth is here presented solely in order to point to the necessity of treating such wealth effects in future extensions of the model. Note furthermore that central bank money is not treated as a component of financial wealth in the present chapter. Such money is here assumed to be used for intra-day transaction purposes solely and is supplied by branches of the central bank without user costs (cash, ATM and credit cards) for the public during the day, but which however transfers this type of money back to these branches at the end of each 'trading period', by fulfilling their budget equations and due to the loss of interest rate payments that would otherwise arise. Households, firms and the government thus do not need to hold money balances for intra-day trading (due to flexibilities in the management of their intra-day income accounts) and are thus not forced to devote part of their asset holdings to pure cash holdings. Paper money fuels the economy within each period, but is simply stored in the banking sector at the end of it, while all savings decisions go into interest-bearing assets solely.[20] A

[19] A Ricardian equivalence argument might lead to the exclusion of workers' saving deposits B_w from aggregate wealth, since the wage taxation rate is endogenous and is varied by the government in order to establish a desired 'government debt/GDP ratio' in the economy.

[20] Since there is no need to hold non-interest-bearing cash balances in our type of economy.

Keynesian liquidity preference function, if it were explicitly present in our model, thus would concern the allocation of wealth (of wealth owners) between liquid short-term and illiquid long-term bonds and is thus not related to the specific treatment of cash or the means of exchange management chosen in the present chapter.

The remaining equations in this module define (on the basis of before tax money wages w) gross wages w^b that include payroll taxes (as the intended basis for government transfers to the unemployed, the retired, etc.), pensions w^r and unemployment benefits w^u, which are all in constant proportion to money wages w. Finally, p_v is the consumer price of the domestic good that is assumed to be in fixed proportion to the producer price p_y on the basis of a given value-added tax rate τ_v.

Module 1 finally provides the definitions of unemployment benefits, rents paid to retired worker households and consumer prices (producer prices plus value-added tax) which are not explicitly represented in the consolidated list of equations that Powell and Murphy (1997) supply, but which are not different from their use of these concepts. Crucial differences in the equations considered so far therefore basically concern the use by Powell and Murphy of model consistent inflations in the calculation of the required rate of return used by investors and their definition of private wealth that they use in the single optimal consumption function of their model.

Module 2 concerns the household sector where two types of households are distinguished, pure workers and pure asset holders or wealth owners. Of course, these two types of households are only polar opposite cases in the actual distribution of household types. Nevertheless we believe that it is useful to start from such polar opposite household types before intermediate cases are introduced and formalised. Powell and Murphy (1997) consider only one type of household explicitly (although they briefly refer to the effects of income distribution implicitly contained in their formulation of a consumption function) the consumption behaviour of which is based on the life-cycle hypothesis with respect to wage income and wealth. We shall use differentiated saving habits for the two types of households instead (as they can be derived from Cobb–Douglas utility functions[21]) and we will ignore wealth as a direct argument in our consumption functions (leaving this issue for later reformulations of the model).

5.4.2 Households

We consider the behavioural equations of worker households first:

2*a*. Households (Workforce):

$$\begin{aligned} Y_w^{Dn} &= (1-\tau_w)[wL^d + w^u(L - L^w) + w^r\alpha_l L_2] + (1-\tau_c)iB_w \\ &= Y_{w1}^{Dn} + (1-\tau_c)iB_w \qquad (5.12) \\ L^w &= L_f^w + L_g^w \qquad (5.13) \end{aligned}$$

[21] Note in this respect also that the relative price p_v/p_h does not yet play a role in the consumption decisions of workers.

$$L^d = L^d_f + L^d_g = L^d_f + L^w_g \tag{5.14}$$

$$C^{on}_w = c_y(1-\tau_w)[wL^d + w^u(L - L^w) + w^r\alpha_l L_2], \quad C^o_w = C^{on}_w / p_v \tag{5.15}$$

$$\hat{C}_w = \alpha^w_1(C^o_w / C_w - 1) + \alpha^w_2(e - \bar{e}) + \gamma \tag{5.16}$$

$$p_h C^{do}_h = c_h(1-\tau_w)[wL^d + w^u(L - L^w) + w^r\alpha_l L_2] \tag{5.17}$$

$$\hat{C}^d_h = \alpha^h_r(C^{do}_h / C^d_h - 1) + \alpha^h_i(e - \bar{e}) + \gamma \tag{5.18}$$

$$S^n_w = Y^{Dn}_w - p_v C_w - p_h C^d_h = \dot{B}_w \tag{5.19}$$

$$\hat{L}_1 = \hat{L}_2 = \hat{L}_0 = n \qquad (L_0(0), L_1(0), L_2(0) \quad \text{given}) \tag{5.20}$$

$$\dot{n} = \beta_{n_w}(\tilde{n} - n), \quad \tilde{n} = \tilde{n}(e, \hat{e}) \tag{5.21}$$

$$L = \alpha_l L_1 \tag{5.22}$$

The first equation in this module defines the aggregate disposable income of workforce households by the sum of the wage incomes of the employed, unemployment benefits for the unemployed, unemployment being measured by $\alpha_l L_1 - L^w$,[22] and the pensions of retirees, after taxes (with the tax rate τ_w uniformly applied to these three types of workers' incomes). Furthermore workers as a group also have interest income from their holding of saving deposits which is taxed as all other interest payments (which goes to pure asset owners) by means of the rate τ_c. Note that retirees L_2 receive pension payments in an amount that is scaled down by the given participation rate α_l (of the persons L_1 between 16 and 65) which is constant in the present model. Pensions are thus paid to both employed and unemployed workers in the workforce once they retire.[23]

Next we consider the number of employed workers L^w who are working in the sector of firms, L^w_f, or for the government, L^w_g, there providing public services. In contrast to L^w we denote by L^d the actual employment of the employed which can be larger or smaller than the normal hours of work L^w of the employed workforce due to over- or undertime work (such situations by assumption only occur in the firm sector, but not in the government sector, see equation 5.14).

Desired consumption (in nominal and in real terms) C^{on}_w, C^o_w of workers is proportional to their nominal and real wage income, respectively, with c_y denoting the uniform marginal propensity to consume of both employed and unemployed workers as well as for retirees. Note that we always use consumer prices p_v when going from nominal to real magnitudes (we thus ignore the influence of the price p_h of housing services here and later on). Note also that the interest income of worker households does not influence their consumption plans here, since we assume that all of their interest income is saved in order to simplify the feedback from asset accumulation into the

[22] α_l the participation rate of the workforce which is endogenously determined in the Murphy model for the Australian economy.

[23] The participation rate is also applied – for reasons of simplicity – to the growth rate in pension-receivers that is caused by the assumed migration of whole families.

real part of the model. Following Powell and Murphy (1997) we assume that actual consumption plans C_w of all types of workers adjust towards desired consumption with a time delay that depends on their deviation from desired consumption and on the state of the labour market which is measured by the rate of employment e (plus a trend term γ that ensures the existence of steady growth paths later on). The demand for desired housing services is treated in the same way as the demand of workers for consumption goods which means that we assume for this type of consumption: $p_h C_h^{do} = c_h(1 - \tau_w)[wL^d + w^u(L - L^w) + w^r \alpha_l L_2]$, with c_h as marginal propensity to consume these services. Note that we have to use the price for these services on the left-hand side of this consumption function. Note also that adjustment towards desired levels is of the same type as the one for the consumption of the domestic goods produced by firms.

It is of course questionable whether the considered marginal propensities to consume are really uniform with respect to the three types of situations adult workers may be in and whether they all use the actual rate of employment as an expression on the prospects of their future incomes. Introducing different behaviour in this place is easily possible, but should be left to investigations with a more pronounced empirical orientation.

The next equation defines nominal savings S_w^n of workers and states that these savings are held in the form of short-term bonds solely. As already explained in the preceding section money is assumed to fuel real transactions via its circulation, since there is no cash or income in advance constraint for obtaining such means of payments for intra-day trading.[24] It is thus considered to be stored in the banking sector (here only the branches of the central bank) after each round of transactions. Note that workers do not accumulate wealth in the form of real estate which is of course not true for example for the Australian economy. Including this into the present module and adding a resale market for houses is thus left here for future extensions of the model.[25]

When we say 'workers' we have, as already noted above, three groups of persons in mind: L_1, the potential workforce, L_0 the young people (below 16 years) and L_2, the retirees (above 65 years). All three components of the workforce households grow – via migration into the considered country (and possibly also by reasons internal to the economy) – at the same rate n, for reasons of simplicity and for the purpose of later steady state analysis. Note that these new members of the workforce are immediately treated as the residents of the country under consideration. This rate n follows with a delay the growth rate $\tilde{n}$ which represents the desire to migrate (with constant population shares) into the labour market of our economy and which is here endogenously determined through the state of the labour market e and its rate of change $\hat{e}$.

[24] Note again that the temporal budget equations of all agents in the economy must be fulfilled at each end of the trading period t.

[25] It is however possible to assume that the consumption of the domestic good through workforce households is partly going into the purchase of houses if it is assumed that goods purchased cannot be sold anymore at a later point in time to another sector of the economy.

Actual labour supply (in terms of persons), finally, is given by $\alpha_l L_1$ with α_l the participation rate, and is divided according to the state of the economy into employed and unemployed people, $L^w, L - L^w$. Note again that we have assumed that the participation rate is constant in time and thus do not make any use of the encouraged/discouraged worker effect as in Powell and Murphy (1997, Ch. 6.7).

Summing up the module 2a thus basically describes the two consumption decisions of workers' households based uniformly on their various sources of wage income. It is easy to derive such consumption functions by assuming Cobb–Douglas utility functions. Powell and Murphy (1997) make use of a life-cycle approach in the place of our description of the consumption behaviour of workers and thus immediately include wealth effects into the consumption decisions of their single type of household. We shall apply their approach to consumption behaviour in our two agents framework in another paper, see Chiarella *et al.* (1999a,b), and will then study the role of wealth effects in such an extended framework.

Next, we consider the other type of household of our model, the (pure) asset owners who desire to consume C_c (goods and houses as supplied by firms through domestic production Y) at an amount that is growing exogenously at the rate γ and which is thus in particular independent of their current nominal disposable income Y_c^{Dn}. The consumption decision is thus not an important decision for pure asset holders. Their nominal income diminished by the nominal value of their consumption $p_v C_c$ is then spent on the purchase of financial assets (three types of bonds and equities) as well as on investment in housing supply (for worker households). Note here that the one good view of the production of the domestic good entails consumption goods proper and houses (both at consumer prices p_v) so that asset holders buy houses for their consumption as well as investment purposes.

2*b*. Households (Asset Holders):

$$Y_c^{Dn} = (1 - \tau_c)[r^e p_y K + i B_c + B_1^l + p_h C_h^d - p_y \delta_h K_h] + s(1 - \tau_c^*) B_2^l \tag{5.23}$$

$$\hat{C}_c = \gamma \tag{5.24}$$

$$S_c^n = Y_c^{Dn} - p_v C_c \tag{5.25}$$

$$= \dot{B}_c + \dot{B}_1^l / i_l + s \dot{B}_2^l / i_{l*} + p_e \dot{E} + p_y (I_h - \delta_h K_h), \quad \dot{B}_c = \dot{B} - \dot{B}_w$$

$$C_h^s = K_h \quad [\hat{C}_h^d = \alpha_r^h (C_h^{do} / C_h^d - 1) + \alpha_i^h (e - \bar{e}) + \gamma] \tag{5.26}$$

$$g_h^d = (I_h / K_h)^d$$

$$= \alpha_r^h ((1 - \tau_c) r_h^l - i^r) + \alpha_i^h (i_l - (i + \xi)) + \alpha_u^h \left(\frac{C_h^d}{C_h^s} - \bar{u}_h \right) + \gamma + \delta_h \tag{5.27}$$

$$\dot{r}_h^l = \beta_{r_h^l} (r_h - r_h^l) \tag{5.28}$$

$$\dot{g}_h = \beta_{g_h}(g_h^d - g_h), \; g_h = I_h/K_h \tag{5.29}$$

$$\hat{p}_h = \beta_{p_h}\left(\frac{C_h^d}{C_h^s} - \bar{u}_h\right) + \kappa_h \hat{p}_v + (1 - \kappa_h)\pi^c \tag{5.30}$$

$$\hat{K}_h = I_h/K_h - \delta_h \tag{5.31}$$

Equation (5.23) defines the disposable income of asset holders that consists of dividend payments of firms (which distribute their whole expected profit to equity holders), interest on government bonds, $iB_c + B_1^l$, insofar as they are held by domestic residents, rents for housing services net of depreciation, and interest payments on foreign bonds held by domestic households (after foreign taxation and expressed in domestic currency by means of the exchange rate s). Private savings of asset holders S_c^n concerns short-term and long-term bonds (domestic and foreign ones with respect to the latter), equities and net housing investment.

We assume in the following that the amount of savings of asset holders that goes into short-term bonds, $\dot{B}_c$ is given by $\dot{B} - \dot{B}_w$, which means that asset holders passively accept the inflow (or even the outflow) of short-term bonds that is implied for them by independent decision of the government on its short-term debt policy and by the savings decision of workers (that only concerns short-term bonds). This is clearly a very restrictive assumption which – together with the treatment of the other flows of financial asset accumulation – must be improved in further elaborations of the asset market dynamics of the model.

Note that there is no inside debt of the household sector (lending of asset owners to worker households). Note also that we have supplied – and not only here – a full treatment of budget equations including all feedbacks on asset accumulation that are implied by them, a degree of completeness which is missing in the Powell and Murphy (1997) model.

The supply of housing services C_h^s is assumed to be proportional to the existing stock of houses that is devoted to the supply of such services (there are no maintenance costs in the housing sector as in Powell and Murphy (1997)). We assume for simplicity that there is no resale market for dwellings. Note again that the production of dwellings is part of the production activities of firms and thus part of the homogeneous supply of the domestic (non-traded) output.

The demand for housing services has already been defined in module 2a. We assume that housing demand is always served and we can guarantee this in general – up to certain extreme fluctuations in the demand for housing services – by assuming that house owners voluntarily hold excess capacities as measured by the exogenously given desired rate of capacity utilisation $\bar{u}_h$ of the housing service supply. We have assumed in the workforce sector that their demand for housing services grows beside short-term influences with trend rate γ (underlying the steady state of the model). This implies that housing services per household grow with trend rate $\gamma - n$, where n is the natural rate of growth of the workforce. Therefore, over the growth horizon of the economy, we have that worker households consume more and more housing services (measured by square metres per housing unit for example).[26]

Equation (5.27) of module 2b describes the desired rate of gross investment of asset holders, which depends on the (expected!) long-run profit rate r_h^l in the housing sector compared with the required rate of return, measured in reference to government consols by $i^r = i_l - \pi^c$ (via Tobin's q as relative profitability measure), on the interest spread $i_l - (i + \xi)$ as a measure for the tightness of monetary policy (here based on an interest rate policy rule) and its perceived (or only believed) effects on the level of economic activity and employment,[27] on the actual rate of capacity utilisation[28] with respect to housing services (representing the demand pressure in this investment behaviour), $\frac{C_h^d}{C_h^s} - \bar{u}_h$, on the trend rate of growth γ and on the rate of depreciation δ_h in the housing sector. We assume that the actual rate of investment g_h in houses follows the desired one, g_h^d, with some delay.[29] Furthermore, the long-term rate of profit r_h^l in the housing sector follows the actual profit rate in this sector, r_h, with a delay, an approach towards long-run views in investment behaviour that will also be used in the description of the dynamics of the capital stock of firms.

The rate of inflation of the rental price in housing, $\hat{p}_h$, depends as investment on the rate of capacity utilisation in the housing sector (the demand pull component) and on a weighted average formed by the actual rate of inflation of consumer or producer prices in the production of the domestic good and on the level of this inflation that is expected as a long-term average, the rate π^c, whose law of motion will be provided later on (the cost-push components).[30] Finally actual gross investment plans are always realised and thus determine the rate of growth of the housing stock by deducting depreciation from them.

Summing up we can state that consumption decisions of asset owners are basically driven by exogenous habits that are independent of their income and wealth position and that their investment decision into the housing sector is preceding the other asset accumulation decisions as they derive from their choice of nominal savings. These latter decisions are in the present framework governed by supply side forces based on the new issuing of bonds by the domestic government and of equities by firms. Note here that asset holders accumulate or decumulate short-term bonds depending on the difference between their flow supply by the government and the flow demand of workers. Asset holders are thus simply adapting themselves to the decisions of these two other agents. Furthermore, their choice of accumulating or decumulating foreign long-term bonds is here determined as the residual to all these flows in or out of short-

26 Such a construction is needed for the discussion of steady states of the considered economy.

27 ξ a liquidity and risk premium with respect to long-term bond holdings.

28 Powell and Murphy (1997) use the rate of employment on the labour market in the place of this rate which is a more indirect way of expressing the demand conditions on the market for housing services.

29 Related to but also different from the approach chosen in Powell and Murphy (1997), which introduces some inertia into the housing investment decisions of asset owners.

30 This adjustment equation for rental prices in housing differs considerably from the one chosen in Powell and Murphy (1997).

and long-term domestic debt of the government and the flow of new equities issued by firms and is thus determined as a last step in the savings decision of asset holders. The essential decisions in this block of the model are therefore the housing investment decision and the pricing rule for housing services which is based on demand pressure as well as cost-push elements.

5.4.3 Firms

In the following module 3 of the model we describe the sector of firms, whose planned investment demand is also assumed to be always served, just as all other consumption and investment plans. We thus assume for the short run of the model that it is always of a Keynesian nature since aggregate demand is never rationed, due to the existence of excess capacities, inventories, overtime work and other buffers that exist in real market economies. There is thus only one regime possible, the Keynesian one, for the short run of the model, while supply side forces come to the surface only in the medium and the long run of the model. Up to certain extreme episodes in history this may be the appropriate modelling strategy for the macro-level of a market economy. This is shown in more detail in Chiarella *et al.* (2000, Ch. 5) for an integrated Keynes–Metzler model of monetary growth of a closed economy.

3. Firms (Technology, Production, Employment and Investment):

$$Y^p = y^p K, \quad y^p = const \tag{5.32}$$

$$J^d = j_y Y, \quad j_y = const \tag{5.33}$$

$$X = x_y Y, \quad x_y = const \tag{5.34}$$

$$L_f^d = l_y \exp(-n_l t) Y, \quad l_y = 1/z = const \tag{5.35}$$

$$\dot{n}_l = \beta_z(\widetilde{n}_l - z), \quad \widetilde{n}_l = \widetilde{n}_l(g_k) \tag{5.36}$$

$$u = Y/Y^p \tag{5.37}$$

$$\dot{L}_f^w = \beta_l(L_f^d - \bar{u}_f^w L_f^w) + (\gamma - n_l)L_f^w, \quad \bar{u}_f^w \in (0, 1) \tag{5.38}$$

$$\begin{aligned} g_k^d &= (I/K)^d \\ &= \alpha_1^k((1-\tau_c)r^e - i^r) + \alpha_2^k(i_l - (i + \xi)) + \alpha_3^k(u - \bar{u}) + \gamma + \delta_k \end{aligned} \tag{5.39}$$

$$\dot{r}^l = \beta_{r^l}(r^e - r^l) \tag{5.40}$$

$$\dot{g}_k = \beta_{g_k}(g_k^d - g_k), \; g_k = I/K \tag{5.41}$$

$$Y_f = Y - Y^e = \mathcal{I} \tag{5.42}$$

$$S_f^n = p_y Y_f \tag{5.43}$$

$$p_e \dot{E} = p_y(I - \delta_k K) + p_y(\dot{N} - \mathcal{I}) \tag{5.44}$$

$$I^a = I + \dot{N} \tag{5.45}$$

$$\hat{K} = I/K - \delta_k = g_k - \delta_k \tag{5.46}$$

As already stated we assume in the sector of firms a fixed proportions technology, with respect to the three inputs, labour L^d_f, imports (raw materials) J^d, and capital K, and its two outputs (internationally), non-traded and traded goods, Y, X (which are not constrained on the world markets for these two goods). Imports and exports are thus inelastically demanded and supplied by domestic firms. In addition we have endogenous Harrod neutral technological progress at the rate z with respect to labour productivity $z = Y/L^d$ – which follows the rate of innovations $\widetilde{n}_l(g_k)$ with some delay. We stress that the capital stock is used to measure potential output $Y^p = y^p K$ in the following, while all other magnitudes are provided by the Keynesian regime and its demand determined output rate Y. The rate of capacity utilisation u is defined on the basis of this concept of potential output and will receive importance when describing the investment behaviour and the pricing policy of firms. Firms employ a labour force of amount L^w_f which supplies labour effort of amount L^d_f as determined by the present state of sales expectations (plus voluntary inventory production). This labour force of firms is adjusted in a direction that reduces the excess or deficit in the utilisation of the employed labour force, $L^d_f - \bar{u}^w_f L^w_f$, which means that firms intend to return to the normal usage of their labour force thereby.[31] An additional growth term for the employed labour force takes account of the trend growth γ of domestic output, but is diminished by the effect of Harrod neutral technical change which when working in isolation would allow to reduce the workforce of the firms.

Next there is the formulation of the desired gross rate of capital stock accumulation of firms which depends on four factors. First, relative profitability, measured by the deviation of the long-term rate of profit r^l from the required rate of interest $i^r = i_l - \pi^c$ via the type of calculations underlying Tobin's q. Second, on the interest rate spread $i_l - (i + \xi)$, again representing the tightness of monetary policy and its believed effects on economic activity and employment. Third, on the rate of capacity utilisation u of the capital stock of firms in its deviation from the desired rate of capacity utilisation[32] $\bar{u}$, which is given exogenously. Fourth, on trend growth γ and the rate of depreciation δ_k of business fixed investment. As in the case of housing investment, we assume that the actual rate of accumulation g_k is following the desired one with some time delay. Furthermore, also the expected long-term rate of profit r_l is adjusted towards the currently expected rate of profit r^e with some time delay.

Firms produce output to cover expected demand for it and intended additions to inventories. Expected sales are also the basis of the dividend payments of firms and thus do not allow for retained earnings of firms, whose income Y_f is by definition equal

[31] Note that this normal usage includes a certain amount of absentism and is thus less than the full normal usage of this labour force ($\bar{u}^w_f < 1$).

[32] We could include here a dependence of the gross rate of investment on the rate of change of the rate of capacity utilisation which would add Harrod's accelerator to the present framework (which is in fact done in a similar fashion in Powell and Murphy (1997)).

to their output Y minus the expected sales Y^e, which in turn must be equal to desired inventory changes, to be defined below. Valued at producer prices p_y these inventory changes thus also represent the nominal savings of firms.

Due to these assumptions, on the dividend policy of the firm in particular, and due to our assumption that firms only use equities for financing their expenditures, we get as budget equation of firms

$$p_e \dot{E} = p_y(I - \delta_k K) + p_y(\dot{N} - \mathcal{I}),$$

implying that firms finance net investment and unintended inventory changes by issuing new equities (no bonds and no bank loans are allowed at present). Note here that unintended inventory disinvestment gives rise to windfall profits to firms which are retained, not subject to taxation and used to finance part of the fixed business investment as shown in the above equation. We stress once again that this particular financing rule is not crucial for the dynamic evolution implied by the model, but should of course give way to more realistic financing conditions in later reformulations of the model. The last two equations of module 3 then define the total actual investment of firms (for national accounting purposes) and the growth rate of the capital stock which is determined by the net rate of capital accumulation planned by firms.

Powell and Murphy (1997) allow for substitution in production by using a nested input technology of Constant Elasticity of Substitution (CES) type and CES transformation curves with respect to the two outputs that are produced by firms. With respect to such smooth transformation functions they then define medium-run marginal cost and revenue pricing procedures which act as attractors for the development of short-run prices in a particular way. We reconsider their approach to substitution and competitive pricing in Chiarella *et al.* (1999a,b). Furthermore, Powell and Murphy (1997) do not distinguish between actual working time and the normal working time of the employed, but use a single employment equation in their place which differs from our definitions of (efficient) employment L^d of the employed L^w and which is not backed up by budget equations. Finally there are some minor differences in the description of the investment behaviour of firms which, however, do not matter very much (it can be shown that the medium-run target prices of Powell and Murphy (1997) can be reformulated in terms of rates of capacity utilisation; see Chiarella *et al.* (1999a,b) in this regard).

Note finally that there is here no value-added tax on depreciation, investment and planned or unplanned inventories as in the housing sector considered beforehand and that there is no direct taxation of firms. Summing up the above module of the model basically provides descriptions of the output, the employment and the investment decisions undertaken in the sector of firms and this on the basis of various delays concerning employment, investment and underlying profitability measures (the delayed output adjustment decision is described under the heading 'quantity adjustment' in module 5a and the price adjustments undertaken by firms are considered in block 5b of the model).

Next, import and export prices are treated in the simplest way possible by assuming that they are fixed in terms of the foreign currency and thus need only to be multiplied with the exchange rate in order to arrive at domestic producer prices. There is no subsidy or tax on exports, but there is a tax rate on imported commodities of size τ_m. This module of the model basically impacts the profitability of firms as measured by the expected rate of profit r^e in the first block of our model.

3*a*. Export Prices and Import Prices in Domestic Currency

$$p_m = (1+\tau_m)sp_m^* \tag{5.47}$$

$$p_x = sp_x^* \tag{5.48}$$

In contrast to Powell and Murphy (1997) there are here no inventories held with respect to imports or exports. Since imports only serve as intermediate inputs of firms there is also no need to represent them in the consumer price index of the domestic country. Note furthermore that imports are demanded and exports supplied independently of their price changes, since they are in fixed proportions to the output Y of the domestic commodity. Note finally that the Purchasing Power Parity (PPP) theory cannot be valid here, since there is no common basket of goods that is produced and used internationally.

Powell and Murphy (1997) allow for certain price responses on the world market – due to varying imports and exports of the Australian economy – which we briefly consider in Chiarella *et al.* (1999a,b). Furthermore, they divide exports (in fixed proportions) into agricultural and non-agricultural exports which from a theoretical perspective does not contribute much to the generality of the model, but which may provide extra descriptive relevance.

5.4.4 The government

In module 4 we describe the public sector of the economy in a way that allows for government debt in the steady state and for a monetary policy that fixes the rate of interest on short-term debt in view of the level of the long-term world rate of interest, the domestic rate of inflation and the domestic level of activity of firms.

4. Government (Fiscal and Monetary Authority):

$$\begin{aligned} T^n &= \tau_w[wL^d + w^u(L-L^w) + w^r\alpha_l L_2] + \tau_p wL^d + \tau_v p_y(C_w + C_c + G) \\ &\quad + \tau_c[r^e p_y K + iB + B^l + p_h C_h^d - \delta_h K_h] + \tau_m s p_m^* J^d \end{aligned} \tag{5.49}$$

$$p_v G = g p_v Y^e, \quad g = \text{const.} \tag{5.50}$$

$$L_g^d = L_g^w = \alpha_g G/\exp(\hat{z}t) \tag{5.51}$$

$$\dot{i} = -\beta_{i_i}(i + \xi - i_{l*}) + \beta_{i_p}(\hat{p}_v - \bar{\pi}) + \beta_{i_u}(u - \bar{u}) \tag{5.52}$$

$$\hat{\tau}_w = \alpha_{\tau_{w1}}(d/\bar{d} - 1) + \alpha_{\tau_{w2}}\hat{d}, \qquad d = \frac{B + B^l/i_l}{p_v Y^e} \tag{5.53}$$

$$\hat{\tau}_m = \alpha_{\tau_m}\frac{p_x X - p_m J^d}{p_x X} \tag{5.54}$$

$$S_g^n = T^n - w^u(L - L^w) - w^r\alpha_l L_2 - (iB + B^l) - (p_v G + w^b L_g^d) \tag{5.55}$$

$$\dot{B} = \alpha_b^g(p_v G + iB + B^l - T^n + w^u(L - L^w) + w^r\alpha_l L_2 + w^b L_g^d) \tag{5.56}$$

$$\dot{B}^l/i_l = (1 - \alpha_b^g)(p_v G + iB + B^l - T^n + w^u(L - L^w) + w^r\alpha_l L_2 + w^b L_g^d) \tag{5.57}$$

$$\dot{B}_1^l = \alpha_{b1}^g \dot{B}^l \tag{5.58}$$

$$\dot{B}_1^{l*} = (1 - \alpha_{b1}^g)\dot{B}^l \tag{5.59}$$

The first equation in the government module describes the tax collection by the government which consists of taxes on wages, unemployment benefits and pensions, payroll taxes as the basis of state transfers to worker households, value-added taxes on consumption goods, capital taxes on profit, interest and rent (net of depreciation), and import taxes. Note that – symmetric to the treatment of interest payments received and taxed abroad – we have here that all interest payments of the government (to domestic residents or foreigners) are taxed domestically and thus contribute to a reduction in domestic government debt. Note also that there are no taxes on wealth, investment, depreciation and inventories and of course none on firm income which is equal to intended inventories plus windfall profits or losses, $Y^d - Y^e$, solely.

Government expenditures are assumed to be a fixed proportion of expected sales[33] (at consumer prices) and employment in the government sector is a fixed proportion of real government expenditure. In view of later steady state calculations we assume that this employment relationship is also subject to Harrod neutral technical change (of the same type as in the sector of firms), but that government employees have fixed normal working hours and thus are never over- or under-employed as is the case for the workers in the sector of firms. Note that this implies that there is no lag in the employment policy of the government in view of its employment function shown above.[34]

With respect to monetary policy we assume that monetary authorities determine by legislature (the change in) the nominal rate of interest on short-term bonds (which are not traded internationally) by means of a Taylor type policy rule.[35] There are no money holdings in the private sector of the economy and there is therefore no need to specify the new supply of money, used for open market operations as well as foreign exchange market operations. With respect to the first type of operation we observe

33 An easy extension of this rule for government expenditures would be to assume the ratio g depends negatively on short- and long-term interest rates i, i_l, which could also be extended to the consumption decision of workforce households and which thereby give extra power to the interest policy rule of the central bank to be considered below. Note also that we do not consider delays in the adjustment of government expenditure (and the employment decisions that accompany it).

34 Note here that the employment level in this part of the economy is much larger than any other employment level within each firm and may therefore allow for such a direct employment policy simply due to retirement effects and the like.

35 See Flaschel *et al.* (2001) with respect to this particular choice of an interest rate policy rule.

that there is no need for it in an economy where the short-term rate of interest is directly set by the monetary authority and where transactions are performed by costless temporary credit by the branches of the central bank that must be settled in accordance with the budget constraints at the end of each day. With respect to foreign market operations we have shown in the preceding section that they are not needed as long as the private sector just absorbs the inflows of domestic bonds and equities and invests the remaining savings into long-term foreign bonds. This considerably simplifies the feedback structure between the real and the financial sector of the economy, but of course should give way to more realistic descriptions of the financial markets in future extensions of the model.

With respect to the interest rate policy of the central bank we assume that it attempts to move the actual rate of interest, i, toward the steady state short-term rate of interest, i_o,[36] as it is determined by the world rate of interest on long-term bonds minus the liquidity premium that applies to them, but that it at the same time aims at moving the actual rate of inflation, $\hat{p}$, toward some target rate, $\bar{\pi}$, for example from above by raising the rate of interest in order to reduce economic activity (as measured by the rate of capacity utilisation u) and thus the demand pressure on the rate of inflation. Of course, high levels of economic activity u will make this decision for a tight monetary policy more pronounced than low levels of activity which explains the third term in our interest rate policy rule. In view of the fact that we will not consider inflationary processes in the world economy, but shall assume given world market prices for imports and exports in module 8 of the model, we set the target rate of inflation $\bar{\pi}$ of the central bank equal to zero throughout this chapter (in order to simplify the presentation of the interior steady state of the model).[37]

Note again that money is not held as a store of liquidity and wealth by the private sector of the economy, but is only used as means of transactions that flow from banks (here only branches of the central bank) to households, firms and the government and then back to the banking sector on each trading day, without any income-in-advance restrictions.

We use d to denote the ratio between government debt and expected sales (debt-GDP ratio) at consumer prices and assume as policy rule for the tax rate on wages that this rate is adjusted such that government moves debt into the direction of a desired debt-GDP ratio $\bar{d}$ augmented by a term that describes reactions to the rate of change of the debt-GDP ratio d as in a derivative control feedback loop. The burden of too high debt thus falls entirely on wage income which supports our view that government bonds are net wealth. In addition, the import tax rate τ_m is adjusted in order to reduce any possible surplus or deficit in the trade balance in terms of the domestic prices for exports and imports (which include import taxation).

36 Or at least attempts to not let it go too far away from it.

37 We shall show in future work however that this rate should be chosen positive in order to avoid certain problems caused by the actual behaviour of money wages (and that central banks actually generally have a target that is greater than zero).

The next two equations, on the debt financing of the government, are based on their left-hand sides on the actual government deficit or surplus. Government revenue is based on nominal taxes T^n and is used to finance nominal government expenditures $p_v G$, interest payments on short- and long-term debt ($iB+B^l$), unemployment benefits, pensions and the wage sum of state employees. The deficit that generally will come about in this way is then financed by issuing new short-term or long-term debt. We here assume that the portion α_b^g of the new government debt is financed short term, while the remainder is financed long term.

For accounting purposes we have added the definition of nominal government savings S_g^n which – if negative – is financed in the just stated way through short- and long-term debt. Finally we have to state how the new long-term government debt is distributed in the world. As before we here too assume that this is done in constant proportions with respect to the domestic and the foreign market for domestic long-term debt.

New assets are therefore distributed to asset owners in fairly rigid proportions (on primary asset markets) supplemented by a procedure whereby we will only introduce laws of motion for the various asset prices in the following, but will not develop a full portfolio approach to the determination of asset prices (or their rates of change) and the implied portfolio adjustments on secondary as well as on primary asset markets. Hence, asset markets are represented here solely by way of certain interest rate adjustment processes (and their impact on the investment decisions of firms and in dwellings). Asset markets are in this chapter thus surely modelled less complicated than in a full portfolio approach (and the liquidity preference schedule this approach would imply for the holding of short-term debt). More or less assets therefore just flow into the private sector of the economy in proportions that are determined by the government and the firms, which represents a very tranquil way of asset absorption. It is therefore quite obvious that asset markets are the substructure of the model that need improvement most urgently; see also the module on asset price dynamics.[38]

For the moment we justify this approach to asset accumulation and their price dynamics by the fact that we at least provide by it a complete – although not yet really convincing – description of the dynamics of asset markets, which must be improved later on by a static or dynamic portfolio approach to the behaviour of these markets that gives more role to the demand side. At present however supplies of new assets just flow into the economy – up to the foreign investment of asset holders – and lead through some type of not explicitly formulated process to interest rate differentials and the dynamics of asset prices and expectations about them as they are described in Section 5.4.

Note that this description of the government sector excludes open market operations as well as foreign exchange operations of the central bank. The first type of policy is not

[38] Köper and Flaschel (2000) integrate a portfolio approach into the real dynamics of the 6D Keynes–Metzler model of Chiarella and Flaschel (2000) and find that the implications of this portfolio approach to the real-financial interaction share many similarities with model types where the present approach to asset market dynamics is used instead.

needed in an economy where the interest rate on short-term bonds is set by the central bank and where accounting money only serves the purpose of intra-day trading until all budget equations are settled again. The second type of policy is not needed since the supply side description of asset markets and the accommodating behaviour of asset holders with respect to foreign bonds always clears the market for foreign exchange as we have seen in the preceding section.

In sum we have a target rate of inflation $\bar{\pi}$ of the central bank which is here zero by assumption, a debt target per unit of expected nominal GDP which is given by $\bar{d}$, government's expenditures which are a given share in expected GDP, and the attempts of the government to establish external trade equilibrium via import taxation. In a sense the behaviour of the government is therefore still fairly neutral, although we allow for steady state debt and deficit according to certain rules. There are certain similarities between our description of the government sector and the one of Powell and Murphy (1997), in particular with respect to the wage tax rate adjustment rule. It is not difficult to add further policy rules to this module of the model, as e.g. an anticyclical government expenditure and employment policy rule, an anticyclical behaviour of payroll taxes or other formulations of the Taylor interest policy rule. Later extensions and modifications of the model should concern the introduction of a banking industry (which transforms short-term debt into long-term debt, issues loans to firms and the like) and a less rigid diversification and distribution scheme for the allocation of government debt to the various other agents of the model (where we in principle have followed Powell and Murphy (1997) for the time being).

5.4.5 Quantity and price adjustment processes

We now come to the description of the dynamics of quantities (module 5a) and prices (module 5b). Module 5a of the model basically describes a Metzlerian inventory adjustment process for the non-traded good produced by firms.[39] Module 5b describes the nominal adjustments in the goods and in the labour market, as well as the adjustment of long-term inflationary expectations π^c.

5a. Quantity Adjustments in the Production of the Domestic (Non-traded) Good:

$$Y^e \neq Y^d = C_w + C_c + I + I_h + G \tag{5.60}$$

$$S^n = S_p^n + S_f^n + S_g^n = I^{na} + NCX^n = I^{na} + NX^n + NFX^n \tag{5.61}$$

$$I^{na} = p_y(I - \delta_k K) + p_y(I_h - \delta_h K) + p_y\dot{N} \tag{5.62}$$

$$N^d = \beta_{n^d} Y^e \tag{5.63}$$

$$\mathcal{I} = \beta_n(N^d - N) + \gamma N^d \tag{5.64}$$

$$Y = Y^e + \mathcal{I} \tag{5.65}$$

39 There are no sales and delivery constraints for traded goods and there is thus no direct need to consider inventory adjustment processes in their case.

$$\dot{Y}^e = \beta_{y^e}(Y^d - Y^e) + \gamma Y^e \quad (5.66)$$

$$\dot{N} = Y - Y^d \quad (5.67)$$

The first equation in 5a contrasts expected sales Y^e with aggregate demand and actual sales Y^d of the non-traded good for our Keynesian description of the short run of the model. Actual sales = aggregate demand consists of five different items here (two types of consumers' demand, two types of investors' demand and the government's demand for domestic goods). Next we consider once again (for consistency reasons) the accounting identity for actual total savings, actual total investments and the balance in the current or the capital account, where nominal actual total investment I^{na} is defined by net fixed business investment and net investment in houses and by total inventory changes – everything valued at producers' prices. This equation provides an important consistency check for our analysis of goods market disequilibrium in the context of a small open economy. It also implies, see Section 5.3.2, that the flows of new assets supply are equal to the absorption of these supplies by the household sector (workers and asset holders).

The remaining five equations describe the inventory adjustment process. Desired inventories N^d are a constant fraction of expected sales Y^e. Intended inventory changes $\mathcal{I}$ are proportional to the gap between desired inventories and actual ones, N, plus a term that accounts for the fact that inventory formation takes place in a growing economy with trend growth γ. Output decisions Y are based on the sum of expected sales and intended inventory changes, while sales expectations Y^e are changed in an adaptive way through the observation of the discrepancy between actual sales Y^d and the expected ones Y^e, again augmented by a term γY^e that accounts for the trend growth underlying the evolution of this economy. Finally, actual inventory changes $\dot{N}$ are just given by the difference between actual output and actual sales, which once again gives expression to our general assumption that the short run of our economy is always of a Keynesian nature and not perfectly foreseen by the agents of our economy. This inventory adjustment process is the same as the one in Powell and Murphy (1997) with the exception that sales expectations are always correct in the Murphy model.

Next we consider the wage-price dynamics of the model. This type of dynamics is receiving more and more attention in recent studies of primarily empirical orientation[40] and thus represents an important module of the present stage of modelling the details of a small open economy with an integrated treatment of its short-, medium- and long-run behaviour. We stress however that we do not yet treat consumer price indices and the role of import prices in the formation of the money wage and the price level PCs respectively; see Chiarella *et al.* (1999a,b) in this regard.

5*b*. Wage-Price Adjustment Equations, Expectations:

$$\hat{w}^b = \beta_{w_e}(e - \bar{e}) + \beta_{w_u}(u_f^w - \bar{u}_f^w) + \kappa_w(\hat{p}_v + \widetilde{n}_l) + (1 - \kappa_w)(\pi^c + \widetilde{n}_l) \quad (5.68)$$

[40] See Fair (1997, 2000), and Stock and Watson (1999).

$$\hat{p}_v = \hat{p}_y = \beta_p(u - \bar{u}) + \kappa_p(\hat{w}^b - \widetilde{n}_l) + (1 - \kappa_p)\pi^c \tag{5.69}$$

$$\dot{\pi}^c = \beta_{\pi^c}(\alpha_{\pi^c}(\hat{p}_v - \pi^c) + (1 - \alpha_{\pi^c})(\bar{\pi} - \pi^c)) \tag{5.70}$$

$$L^w = L^w_f + L^w_g = L^w_f + L^d_g \tag{5.71}$$

$$e = L^w/L = e_f + e_g = L^w_f/L + L^w_g/L \tag{5.72}$$

$$u^w_f = L^d_f/L^w_f, \qquad [u^w_g = L^d_g/L^w_g = 1] \tag{5.73}$$

$$\dot{\bar{e}} = \beta_{\bar{e}}(e - \bar{e}) \tag{5.74}$$

Wage inflation $\hat{w}^b = \hat{w}$ is nearly of the same type as in Powell and Murphy (1997). Wage inflation responds in the traditional PC manner; to the state of the demand pressure in the labour market as measured by the deviations of the rate of employment e from its NAIRU level $\bar{e}$; to the deviation of the employment rate u^w_f of the employees of firms from their norm (including absentism) which is measured by $\bar{u}^w_f$ (and which corresponds to the derivative term for the rate of employment, $\dot{e}$, that Powell and Murphy (1997) employ in this place); and to the usual accelerator term of price inflation which is here measured as a weighted average of actual price inflation based on short-term perfect foresight (plus the actual rate of productivity growth) and expected long-term price inflation (plus the long-run rate of productivity growth) in the place of the simple adaptive scheme used by Powell and Murphy (1997). Wage inflation is therefore governed by demand pull terms augmented by a weighted average of cost-push expressions.

The law of motion for consumer prices p_v of the non-traded commodity is formulated in a similar way, as a second type of PC. In the place of the concept of medium-run prices used by Powell and Murphy (1997) we use the demand pressure measure $u - \bar{u}$, the deviation of actual capacity utilisation from its norm, as one cause of price inflation. In Chiarella *et al.* (1999a,b) we show that this measure is closely related to the medium-run price concept of Powell and Murphy (1997) in the case of smooth factor and output substitution. The cost-push term in the price inflation equation is given as a weighted average of current wage inflation and the one expected for the long run (both made less severe in their influence on price inflation by the existence of a positive growth rate of labour productivity, now and in the longer run).

Expected long-term inflation π^c in turn is based on a weighted average of two expectations mechanisms, an adaptive one with weight α_π and a forward-looking one with weight $1-\alpha_\pi$. Forward-looking expectations are here simply based on the inflation target of the central bank $\bar{\pi}$, in the usual way of a regressive scheme of expectations revision. Inflationary expectations are thus following a weighted average of actual inflation and the target rate of the monetary authority.

This description of the wage-price spiral is based on formulations used extensively in Chiarella and Flaschel (2000) and is therefore not explained in more detail here.

Equations (5.71) to (5.73) describe some definitions concerning total employment (through firms and the government) and the outside rate of employment e as well as the inside rate of employment u^w of the employed. The last equation, finally, assumes that the NAIRU rate of employment follows the actual rate of employment with some delay. We here deviate again from Powell and Murphy (1997) who consider this rate of employment as being determined exogenously. Note that firms follow the rate u^w when deciding on the change in the workforce they employ.

We can see from the above description that only the inflation rate of non-traded domestic goods matters in the wage-price module of our economy. Housing, meaning the rental price of dwellings (and its rate of change $\hat{p}_h$), is thus completely ignored in this description of the wage-price interaction. This simplifies the feedback structure of the model, but should give way to a domestic price index of the form $p_c = p_y^a p_h^{1-a}$ and its rate of change in the wage equation in future reformulations of the model.

5.4.6 The dynamics of asset market prices and expectations

The sixth module lists the dynamic adjustment equations we assume to hold for the asset prices of our model: long-term domestic bonds, p_b, equities, p_e, and for the exchange rate (in view of the given US $ rate of return on foreign bonds). We stress that reallocations of the stock of wealth are not considered explicitly in the present version of the model (which also does not yet allow for wealth effects in the behavioural assumptions that are employed).

As already discussed in the preceding descriptions of the modules of the model, asset flows and asset accumulation are determined by supply side conditions in the main in the present form of the model and are thus just absorbed by asset holders, at least as far as short-term bonds (leaving aside those already purchased by worker households), long-term domestic bonds and equities are concerned. In contrast to this, asset holders are supplied with an investment demand function as far as their housing investment is concerned (which is never rationed) and they balance their savings account thereafter by purchasing or selling foreign bonds on the world market. This is surely only a preliminary approach to the accumulation of financial wealth and its distribution to the two household sectors we consider. We return to this question in Chiarella *et al.* (1999a,b) where money holdings are added to the model and are adjusted in time via changes in the short-term rate of interest.

The adopted approach to asset accumulation is acceptable in a continuous-time framework, if there is subsequent stock reallocation according to a specified money demand function and if all other assets can be considered as perfect substitutes for each other, since asset holders are in such a case indifferent with respect to their holding of interest bearing bonds, see Sargent (1987) for example. In the present approach there is however no stock demand for transaction balances and thus no explicit reallocation of stock positions that have been changed by flows of new assets into the asset markets. Furthermore, due to somewhat delayed responses of asset prices to expected interest rate differentials we depart in the following from the perfect substitutability assumption. Thus we have to acknowledge that asset market dynamics are not yet well-founded as far as conceivable behaviour of individual holders of financial assets is concerned.

Franke and Semmler (1999) provide a portfolio approach with imperfect substitutabilities to the determination of the temporary structure of interest rates of the economy which will be adapted to the present framework in either stock or flow form in future extensions of the model.

6. Asset Prices, Expectations and Interest Rate Adjustments:

$$\hat{p}_b = \beta_{p_b}[(1-\tau_c)i_l + \pi_b - ((1-\tau_c)i + \xi)], \quad \hat{p}_b = -\hat{i}_l \tag{5.75}$$

$$\hat{p}_e = \beta_{p_e}[(\frac{(1-\tau_c)r^e p_y K}{p_e E} + \pi_e) - ((1-\tau_c)i_l + \pi_b)] \tag{5.76}$$

$$\hat{s} = \beta_s[(1-\tau_c^*)i_{l*} + \epsilon_s - ((1-\tau_c)i_l + \pi_b)] \tag{5.77}$$

$$\dot{\pi}_{bs} = \beta_{\pi_{bs}}(\hat{p}_b - \pi_{bs}), \qquad p_b = 1/i_l \tag{5.78}$$

$$\pi_{bc} = \hat{p}_b \tag{5.79}$$

$$\pi_b = \alpha_s \pi_{bs} + (1-\alpha_s)\pi_{bc} \tag{5.80}$$

$$\dot{\pi}_{es} = \beta_{\pi_{es}}(\hat{p}_e - \pi_{es}) \tag{5.81}$$

$$\pi_{ec} = \hat{p}_e \tag{5.82}$$

$$\pi_e = \alpha_s \pi_{es} + (1-\alpha_s)\pi_{ec} \tag{5.83}$$

$$\dot{\epsilon}_s = \beta_{\epsilon_s}(\hat{s} - \epsilon_s) \tag{5.84}$$

$$\epsilon_c = \hat{s} \tag{5.85}$$

$$\epsilon = \alpha_s \epsilon_s + (1-\alpha_s)\epsilon_c \tag{5.86}$$

Note first of all with respect to the three laws of motion for the bond price, the share price and the nominal rate of exchange, that they have to be based on interest rate differentials after taxes, but that there is no taxation of actual capital gains in the model, and thus no tax term applied to expected capital gains in the formulae shown above.

Instead of a full portfolio approach to asset market equilibria it is assumed in the above adjustment equations for asset prices p_b, p_e and the exchange rate s that stocks in asset markets give rise to forces that imply certain laws of motion for their prices. The law of motion for the price of long-term domestic bonds, $p_b = 1/i_l$, for example, states that the rate of change of p_b is determined by the differential between the net rate of return $(1-\tau_c)i_l + \pi_b$ on long-term bonds (including expected capital gains π_b) and the short-term rate of interest $(1-\tau_c)i$ (of fixed-price bonds and after taxes) augmented by a liquidity and risk premium ξ that is exogenously given. In the limit, $\beta_{p_b} = \infty$, we interpret this dynamic law as an equilibrium relationship: $(1-\tau_c)i_l+\pi_b = ((1-\tau_c)i+\xi)$ which could then be used as in Blanchard (1981) to study the conventional type of saddlepoint adjustment processes based on the jump variable technique. Yet it is not at all clear under which circumstances fast, but finite adjustments of consols prices will lead to dynamics that mirror such saddlepoint dynamics obtained in the limit. On the contrary, considerations of small size models as in Flaschel *et al.* (1997) have shown that nothing of this type can be expected in general. Therefore, we stick to the assumption that the rate of interest $i_l = 1/p_b$ of long-term bonds follows the movement of the short-term rate of interest i (in the above assumed way) with some delay which may be very short, but which is larger than zero.

The next equation describes the evolution of equity prices, p_e, in a similar way. Their rate of change, p_e, is driven by the discrepancy between the rate of return on equities (dividend payments of firms after taxes and expected capital gains π_e per equity value) and the rate of return on long-term bonds after taxes (including expected capital gains). Note here that $\frac{(1-\tau_c)r^e p_y K}{p_e E}$ describes the actual dividend payments per unit of equity value and represents a nominal rate of return which – leaving capital gains aside – has to be compared with the nominal rate of interest on bonds $(1 - \tau_c)i_l$ in order to make the correct rate of return comparison. Assuming $\beta_{p_e} = \infty$ would again imply the often used assumption that long-term bonds and equities are considered as perfect substitutes and would thus lead to asset market representations of a more conventional type.

Finally, we assume that the dynamic of the exchange rate, $\hat{s}$, is also based on an expected interest rate differential, namely between domestic and foreign long-term bonds (both after taxes), the latter augmented by the expected capital gains from possible devaluations, ϵ_s, of the domestic currency and the former by expected capital gains on domestic bonds. Note here that the foreign rate of interest is exogenously given so that there is no comparable capital gain on long-term foreign bonds. An increase in the above differential makes foreign bonds more attractive which leads to a capital outflow and thus an increase of the demand for the foreign currency which is the (here implicit) cause for the increase of the exchange rate s implied by equation (5.77). Assuming $\beta_s = \infty$ would lead us to the limit assumption of uncovered interest rate parity (UIP) – often employed in the literature – which in this chapter is however subject to some time delay.

With respect to expected capital gains on long-term bonds and equities we assume heterogeneous expectation formation. On the one hand, there is technical or time series analysis (for a certain group of asset owners), which here boils down to an exponentially weighted formula based on past observations or simply an adaptive formation of expectations with speeds of adjustment $\beta_{\pi_{bs}}, \beta_{\pi_{es}}$ (less ambitious 'retired' or less well-informed asset owning agents which we here identify with the fraction of elderly people among the asset holders). On the other hand, there exists a portion of asset owners with correct expectations $\hat{p}_b$, $\hat{p}_e$ (ambitious 'younger' or well-informed agents who achieve myopic perfect foresight by sacrificing leisure time).

We thus assume that the establishment of myopic perfect foresight is very time consuming (reducing the leisure time of the ambitious wealth owners significantly). There is thus only a certain fraction, the 'younger' ones of the population of all pure asset owners, who devote themselves and their leisure time to this formidable task (represented by $1 - \alpha_s$), while the other (the less ambitious ones among the wealth owners) rely on less time consuming time series analysis in order to make their predictions of temporary asset price changes. The market opinion is then simply reflected on the macroeconomic level by the average of these two expectations generating mechanisms formed by means of the weight α_s, $1 - \alpha_s$ in each case (long-term bonds and equities).

In line with the dominant view of currently prevailing economic theory we consider the less ambitious agents as the stupid ones and the ambitious agents as the clever ones.

Due to their myopic perfect foresight clever agents of course perform better than the stupid ones and thus will have a higher overall rate of return than this latter group. Yet, since they will change their behaviour in later parts of their lives (due to changing habits and obligations of people that get older) they will only temporarily outperform the market and accumulate wealth at a higher pace. The overall effect of the existence of these two groups of people among the pure asset holders is that markets would adjust their prices according to the interest rate differentials perceived by the stupid agents, but that the existence of clever agents and their perfect short-run expectations works such that the former interest rate differentials are transformed and corrected to some extent into the directions the clever agents see them to be. This is due to the redirection of portfolio demands as they come from this second group of agents which are not made explicit here. Adaptive expectations that are too high with respect to actual changes in asset prices are thereby made less severe in their impact on asset demands and resulting asset price changes.

In order to justify this approach to expectations formation further we now insert this average expectation on asset price or exchange rate changes into the corresponding price formation rule which in the case of long-term bonds, for example, implies the following final form for the adjustment of bond prices:

$$\hat{p}_b = \frac{\beta_{p_b}}{1 - \beta_{p_b}(1 - \alpha_s)}[(1 - \tau_c)i_l + \alpha_s \pi_{bs} - ((1 - \tau_c)i + \xi)]$$

together with equation (5.78) for π_{bs}. Increases in the population and the weight $1 - \alpha_s$ of the clever ones among the asset owners (with their time-consuming establishment of myopic perfect foresight), starting from $\alpha_s = 1$ therefore increases the volatility of bond prices and the difficulties to predict them perfectly, since it increases the adjustment speed with which the interest rate differentials as viewed by stupid agents (weighted by their fraction in the total population of asset owners) is transferred into bond price changes.

There is an absolute upper limit with respect to this increase in volatility which is represented by the critical proportion α_s^* of 'less ambitious' asset owners given by:

$$\alpha_s^* = (\beta_{p_b} - 1)/\beta_{p_b} < 1.$$

At α_s^* the speed of adjustment of bond prices has become infinite while it is still finite (and working into the right direction) for all admissible α_s that are larger than α_s^*. Decreasing the number of less ambitious asset owners therefore is bounded by this critical value α_s^* where the young workaholics must finally lose sight of the true behaviour of asset prices and the exchange rate. We do not however investigate in this chapter the adjustments that may take place in the share α_s of time series based expectations according to some switching mechanism between the two groups of asset owners here considered, but assume instead that this proportion is constant in time at a 'balancing age' where asset owners switch from ambitiousness to laziness. Endogenous changes in this dividing line and also other reasons for such a switch should be incorporated at a later stage.[41]

Whatever the outcome of such a discussion may be, we thus here simply assume that there is a mechanism at work that creates heterogeneous asset owner behaviour and heterogeneous expectation formation of a type and extent that prevents the model converging to situations of overall myopic perfect foresight in the financial markets. Rather a situation is reached where asset price reactions to interest rate differentials are still normal with respect to direction and are finite.

Of course, these considerations of long-term bond price dynamics apply to the dynamics of equities in the same way and as the above module of asset prices shows also to the dynamics of the exchange rate and the expectations mechanisms there assumed. In all three cases we assume therefore a lower limit for the proportion or market share of 'less ambitious' or 'stupid' asset owning households given by

$$\alpha_x^* = (\beta_x - 1)/\beta_x$$

where x stands for the asset market under consideration. Note that we must assume that α_s is larger than all three critical ratios that are generated on the three considered asset markets in order to have normal reactions of asset prices and exchange rates on all three markets.

We stress that all interest rate comparisons are made with respect to gross levels of these rates (not net of taxes at the rate τ_c), so that the tax rate τ_c does not show up in these laws of motion for interest rates, asset prices and the rate of exchange. Taking net rate in the place of gross ones would only complicate the above formulae without any change in substance.

This closes the description of the behaviour we assume for the asset markets of the economy. Powell and Murphy (1997) assume only 'clever' agents or 'workaholics' to exist in their formulation of asset market behaviour and assume in addition that adjustment speeds of asset revaluations are always infinite, leading them to the usual interest rate parity conditions as for example for the comparison of domestic and foreign long-term bonds: $(1-\tau_c)i_{l*} + \hat{s} = (1-\tau_c)i_l$. Their model thus is based on the limiting case of myopic perfect foresight in the asset markets which leads them to the then usual jump variable technique as assumed representation of the forward-looking behaviour of agents and restricts the dynamics of the model to its stable manifold (thereby removing *all* local instability from sight). We do not follow this procedure in our formulation of the dynamics of the model, which only partly incorporates forward-looking behaviour on the asset markets, whose dynamical implications are – as will be seen – radically different from those with complete myopic foresight on the asset markets and perfect adjustments of asset price (no interest rate differentials).

[41] See Brock and Hommes (1997), Chiarella and Khomin (1999) and Sethi (1996) for examples of analysis of the implication of such switching mechanisms.

The consequence is of course that we will have differentiated rates of return at each moment in time, without formulating a full portfolio approach to take account of the non-uniformity of these rates. In sum, we must state that the description of the asset market adjustment processes represents the module of our model where future improvements are needed the most. At present 'causality' runs from the interest rate policy of the central bank (with respect to short-term debt which is not traded internationally) to adjustments in the rate of interest of long-term debt to adjustments of the exchange rate (in view of internationally traded long-term bonds) to changes in the rate of profit expected by firms. There are also adjustments in equity prices based on the rate of return for long-term bonds but these adjustments do not feed back into the model due to the lack of wealth effects and more advanced financing rules for firms (and due to the hierarchy chosen for the adjustment of asset prices). With the exception of the latter type of dynamics we have effects of the above changes in asset markets on business fixed investment and housing investment, but this is basically all that relates the real and the financial part of our economy. Note here also that the monetary authority is steering the short-term rate of interest basically from an anti-inflationary perspective and that it can do so to some extent since short-term debt is not traded internationally. Of course, it has to accept then the consequences that result from the adjustments of the long-term rate of interest and nominal exchange rates.

5.4.7 External accounts and foreign country data

The next module, 7, describes the various items that appear in the balance of payments Z, nominal net exports NX^n, nominal net (international) interest payments NFX^n and nominal net capital exports NCX^n. Concerning nominal net interest payments, which are normally interpreted as net 'factor' exports NFX^n and which need not cross borders and thus need not appear as an item in the current account, we have in fact assumed that they do cross borders. They are fully present in the calculation of the disposable income of wealth owners and also in the current account of the balance of payments Z. We stress again that the balance of payments must be balanced in our model due to assumed behaviour of asset holders with respect to the domestic supply of debt and equities and the international adjustments that residually follow from them.

7. Balance of Payments:

$$NX^n = EX^n - IN^n = sp_x^* X - sp_m^* J^d \tag{5.87}$$

$$NFX^n = s(1-\tau_c^*)B_2^l - (1-\tau_c)B_1^{l*} \tag{5.88}$$

$$NCX^n = s\dot{B}_2^l / i_{l*} - \dot{B}_1^{l*} / i_l \tag{5.89}$$

$$Z = NX^n + NFX^n - NCX^n = 0 \tag{5.90}$$

Module 8 finally provides the data needed from the 'foreign' economy in the simplest form possible. It is assumed that the modelling of the foreign economy is based on the same qualitative principles we used for the description of the domestic economy and that it is inflation free, exhibits a constant rate of growth and a constant rate of interest on long-term bonds.

8. Foreign Country Data:

$$i_{l*} = const. \quad \text{(world interest rate)} \tag{5.91}$$

$$\tau_c^* = const. \quad \text{(foreign tax rate} = \tau_c \quad \text{by assumption)} \tag{5.92}$$

$$\gamma = const. \quad \text{(world growth rate)} \tag{5.93}$$

$$p_x^* = const. \quad \text{(world price level of the export good)} \tag{5.94}$$

$$p_m^* = const. \quad \text{(world price level of the import good)} \tag{5.95}$$

This closes the description of the extensive or structural form of the model of a small open economy and its detailed comparison with the structure of the Murphy model for the Australian economy.

We stress once again that the short run of the model is Keynesian throughout which means that supply bottlenecks can either be avoided through appropriate buffers or have to be added still for larger deviations of the economy from its steady state behaviour as described in Chiarella *et al.* (1999a,b).[42]

Summarising our comparison with the Murphy model as presented in Powell and Murphy (1997) we can state that their model basically differs in the range of assets they allow in the financial part of the economy where we use a disequilibrium approach to asset market dynamics and expectations while the Murphy model rests on interest rate parity conditions coupled with perfect foresight of investors, both with respect to financial as well as real investment which is a limit case of the approach we have adopted. It may be that this limit case is the only convincing case of the situations we allow for asset market dynamics as far as a pure flow treatment of these markets is concerned. In our view this would imply that the asset market module of our model must be replaced by a full portfolio approach in later reformulations of the model as it is presented in Franke and Semmler (1999).

The largest difference is the difference in the treatment of production as far as formal difficulties are concerned. Powell and Murphy (1997) have to solve an eight dimensional non-linear equation system in their treatment of the objectives of firms on the background of their nested CES technology while we have only explicit linear expressions for the same procedures in the case of a fixed proportions technology of the same type. We show in Chiarella *et al.* (1999a,b), however, how the approach chosen for the Murphy model, its so-called neoclassical heart, can be integrated into the model of the present chapter and that the qualitative dynamic behaviour of the model remains the same.

Further differences concern household behaviour where we show in Chiarella *et al.* (1999a,b) how the representative life-cycle approach of the Murphy model can be

42 See Chiarella *et al.* (2000) for the details of such an extension which explicitly includes the possibility of and the reaction to supply bottlenecks.

integrated into our heterogeneous household framework. There we also allow again for the conventional type of money holding and a Cagan type money demand function for the two types of households we consider. There are also many further, but generally minor, differences to the Murphy model which will not be investigated here. In view of this we would nevertheless claim, even at the present stage of the investigation, that the model of this chapter and the Murphy model are very similar in spirit, although of course different in purpose still, with respect to the weights these two model types give to theoretical or applied considerations.

5.5 The next steps

We have introduced and discussed in this chapter in great detail an integrated macrotheoretical model of monetary growth for a small open economy in extensive or level form which has many features in common with the macroeconometric model for the Australian economy as presented in Powell and Murphy (1997). Our aim in this chapter was to provide a starting model which can provide macrofoundations to applied models of the Murphy type, in the twofold sense that all budget equations of all agents that are considered be spelt out in their details and in their consequences (the assumed behaviour of economic agents of course being consistent with these budget restrictions) and second that there be a fully specified steady state solution to be used as a consistency check and as a reference path for the dynamics implied by the model.

For the moment we have used fairly conventional macro descriptions for the behaviour of households, firms and the government without demonstrating how they can and have been microfounded in the literature. Specific microfoundations may be provided later on and may change some of the modules we have presented here to a certain degree, but we expect that they will not change the general outlook and type of investigation of the presented description of labour, goods, and asset market dynamical (disequilibrium) adjustment processes. In our view, macrofoundations (or macroperspectives) come first (before microfoundations), since they provide the overview across the modules of the structure to be studied in their dynamic interdependence, while microfoundations are needed later on to obtain hopefully a firmer basis and more convincing formulation of the modules used in the initial macrostructure.

Our next steps in pursuing the project of macrofoundations and macro analysis in this way will aim at obtaining first of all a thorough presentation of the intensive or state variable form of the model (explaining its characteristics in detail also on this level). We then calculate (with respect to real magnitudes) on this basis a uniquely determined interior steady state solution of the model and study the comparative dynamic implications to which it gives rise. This will lead us to a 34 dimensional non-linear dynamical model and its steady state solution which in this general form is difficult to understand with respect to the many economic features it contains and which generally can only be investigated from the numerical point of view.

In order to approach the understanding of such large disequilibrium growth models in a systematic way we shall simplify them in various ways in the subsequent chapters.

We shall make use of a core 18D model that is obtained from the general version by suppressing certain secondary feedback structures of the full 34D dynamics. This 18D model can be further reduced to a basic 6D Keynes–Metzler–Goodwin type real dynamical model of a closed economy as it was introduced in Chiarella and Flaschel (2000, Ch. 6). Starting from this model type various routes for extending it back to the 18D structure will then be investigated and compared in their numerical behaviour, see Chiarella *et al.* (2003b) for details.

Next, from the theoretical point of view, we shall isolate all the partial feedback mechanisms that are contained in the 18D core case in order to discuss their stabilising or destabilising potential from a theoretical point of view. This will add extra insights to the numerical investigations already carried out and will often allow us to predict how the full 18D model behaves when some of these feedback mechanisms become more pronounced; see Chiarella and Flaschel (1999b) for details. In this way we will arrive at a method of understanding large theoretical (but small applied) macrodynamical models that is quite new, since these models have rarely been studied in the literature from the theoretical perspective, although Barnett and He (1999) is one important exception. It is our opinion that there is an urgent need for similar investigations of the dynamical features of applied or applicable integrated macrodynamical models and that tools are now indeed available for the achievement of progress at this frontier. We expect that one outcome of this analysis will be that applied structural disequilibrium models of monetary growth will exhibit a rich menu of attractors (points, limit cycles, quasi periodic orbits and also more complex ones) and also interesting transient behaviour towards such attractors that will severely question the narrow, but still prevalent, view of only steady state attractors as far as the deterministic part of published macroeconometric models is concerned. In our view this understanding will drastically change the way such models are conceived and utilised in theory as well as in applications in the future.

6 Intensive form and steady state calculations

6.1 Introduction

In this chapter we derive and investigate the 34D intensive (state variable) form of the applied structural model of disequilibrium growth we have introduced and discussed in its originally extensive form level in great detail in Chiarella and Flaschel (1999b) and in the preceding chapter. We will represent the resulting 34 dimensional dynamical system from various perspectives, providing compact intensive form representations of the real and the financial sector of this economy in tabular form and also in the form of a system of national accounts. We will then discuss to some extent the economic content of the resulting laws of motion from their intensive form perspective, thereby showing that the model can be understood from the outset on the intensive form level.

Presenting the system from these various perspectives serves the purpose of making the reader acquainted with the notation and the relationships that apply on the intensive form level of the model. We hope that this approach will increase the readability of the laws of motion for quantities (including rates of growth), for prices (including wages, asset prices and also expectations), financial asset accumulation and feedback fiscal and monetary policy rules to be presented and discussed in Section 6.3. Section 6.4 then calculates the (up to the determination of nominal variables) uniquely determined steady state solution of this dynamical system and briefly considers its comparative dynamic properties which are generally very simple in nature. We then go on and show that the dimension of the dynamics can be significantly decreased by only a few simplifying assumptions (leading us from 34D to 18D dynamics) whereby we obtain what we will call the 18D core dynamics of our approach to disequilibrium growth.

We shall briefly compare these dynamics in Section 6.6 with the fourteen equations second order system of Bergstrom *et al.* (1994), a prominent example from the literature on continuous-time macroeconometric model building and testing.[1] We then use an approach similar to the one by Barnett and He (1999), who reconsider the fourteen-equation model just mentioned from the numerical perspective, in order to study the numerical properties of our 18D core dynamics in particular with respect to the role

[1] See also Bergstrom and Nowman (2007) for a survey on this literature.

played by speeds of price and quantity adjustment. In the present chapter, however, we shall for the time being use only eigenvalue calculations based on one-parameter changes in order to see which adjustment speeds (and their corresponding feedback chains) are stabilising in the full 18D dynamics, and which are destabilising when they are increased. In future work we will also calculate, as in Barnett and He (1999), bifurcation boundaries in various two-parameter spaces (which bound the regions of local asymptotic stability of the system) and will then show that the bifurcations that occur are essentially of the Hopf type (which at present is only a conjecture based on earlier work on such disequilibrium growth dynamics).

6.2 The real and the financial structure on the intensive form level

Tables 6.1 and 6.2 provide a survey of the structure of the economy to be investigated in the following and they do so on the basis of what has been presented and discussed in Chiarella and Flaschel (1999b) with respect to the extensive structural form of a general disequilibrium monetary growth model by transferring this discussion to the intensive form level and related steady state calculations.[2] This chapter therefore continues the analysis begun in Chiarella and Flaschel (1999b) by showing that this model type has a well-defined intensive form state variable representation and also a basically (up to the level of nominal variables) uniquely determined interior steady state or balanced growth path solution.

6.2.1 The real part of the economy

Let us start with a presentation of the variables that comprise the real part of the economy to be considered which, as already stated, are all recalculated here in per unit of capital form as far as the side of quantities is concerned, plus in efficiency units in the case of labour, and also in efficiency units in the case of wage rates, since these variables also would exhibit a positive trend otherwise (since they rise with labour productivity on average). Price levels, however, are at present without trend in the considered model, since it is assumed that the central bank follows an interest rate policy rule with a zero target rate of inflation, which restricts the steady state solution of the dynamics to zero.

Table 6.1 describes the real sector of the considered economy. We have a labour market, three commodity markets and the housing market. Domestic production $y = Y/K$, per unit of capital, concerns one good that is only domestically used (for all private consumption $c_w + c_c$, all investment $g_k^d, g_h^d, \mathcal{I}/K$, also into housing, and all government consumption $g = G/K$ and which uses up all the imports j^d as intermediate goods) and one good that is only used for exports x. There is thus only a single commodity used in domestic absorption – up to the housing services c_h^d demanded by workers. We denote the demand for this domestically produced and absorbed commodity by $y^d (= Y^d/K)$.

[2] In order to clarify the notation used and the contents it represents the reader should therefore utilise this original presentation of the model.

Table 6.1. *The real part of the economy*

	Labour	Non-traded Goods	Exports	Imports	Dwellings
Workers	$l^e = \alpha_l l_1^e$	c_g^o	–	–	c_h^o
Asset holders	–	g_h^d	–	–	c_h^s, g_h^d
Firms	l_f^{de}, l_f^{we}	$y^p, y, g_k^d, \mathcal{I}/K$	x	j^d	–
Government	$l_g^{de} = l_g^{dw}$	g	–	–	–
Prices	$w^e, w^{re}, w^{be}, w^{ue}$	$p_v = (1+\tau_v)p_y$	$p_x = sp_x^*$	$p_m = (1+\tau_m)sp_m^*$	p_h, p_y
Expectations	$\pi^e = \hat{p}_v^e$	$\pi^e = \hat{p}_v^e$	–	–	$\pi^e = \hat{p}_v^e$
Stocks	l_1^e	ν=N/K	–	–	k_h
Growth	n	$\hat{K} == g_k^d - \delta_k$ $\hat{N} = (y - y^d)/\nu$	–	–	$\hat{K}_h = g_h^d - \delta_h$

Our model exhibits three domestic sectors: households, firms and the government, but with heterogeneous agents in the household sector, workers and (pure) asset holders, the former supplying their labour l^e (measured here in efficiency units) at the gross wage level w^{be} (which includes payroll taxes) and the latter the housing services c_h^s for the workers. Firms produce a non-traded domestic and an exported commodity and employ labour l_f^{we} (with varying rates of utilisation l_f^{de}) and imports j^d (besides their capital stock K) for these purposes, and invest into fixed business capital g_k^d (per unit of capital) and inventories $\mathcal{I}/K$. Government finally provides public consumption goods g, pays rents w^{re} and unemployment benefits w^{ue} and also employs part of the workforce l_g^{de}. There is endogenous growth n of the potential labour force L_1, of the capital stock K, by $g_k^d - \delta_k$ and of the stock of housing K_h, by $g_h^d - \delta_h$ (supplied at price p_h for rental services) and also actual change of inventories $\nu = N/K$ that is different from their desired rate of change $\mathcal{I}/K$.

6.2.2 *The financial part of the economy*

Let us next consider the financial part of the economy. Note that all stock variables $B, B_w, B_c, B^l, B_1^l, B_2^l, E$ (and their rates of change) appearing here are measured relative to the gross value of the capital stock $p_v K$ based on prices p_v that include value-added tax. They are then denoted by lower case Latin letters (and by ε in the case of equities E).

The first column in Table 6.2 shows that we do not consider money holdings in the model of this chapter; see Chiarella and Flaschel (1999b) for details. At present there are only (four) interest-bearing financial assets in our model that can be held by the (pure) asset owners and by the workers of our economy (as shown in Table 6.2). As in the Keynes–Metzler model of monetary growth of closed and open economies – see Chiarella and Flaschel (1999a,b,c,d, 2000) – we here assume, in order to start with a

Table 6.2. *The financial part of the economy*

	Short-term Bonds	Long-term Bonds	Equities	Foreign Bonds	
Workers	$\dot{B}_w/(p_v K) = \hat{B}_w b_w$	–	–	–	
Asset holders	$\dot{B}_c/(p_v K) = \hat{B}_c b_c$	$\dot{B}_1^l/(p_v K)$	$\dot{E}/(p_v K)$	$\dot{B}_2^l/(p_v K)$	
Firms	–	–	–	$\dot{E}/(p_v K)$	–
Government	$\dot{B}/(p_v K) = \hat{B} b$	$\dot{B}^l/(p_v K)$	–	–	
Prices	1 [i]	$p_b = 1/i_l$	p_e	$s p_b^* = s \cdot 1/i_l^*$	
Expectations	–	$\pi_b = \hat{p}_b^e$	$\pi_e = \hat{p}_e^e$	$\epsilon_s = \hat{s}^e$	
Stocks	$b = B/(p_v K)$	$b^l = B^l/(p_v K)$, $b_1^l = B_1^l/(p_v K)$	$\varepsilon = E/(p_v K)$	$b_2^l = B_2^l/(p_v K)$	
Growth	$\hat{B}$	$\hat{B}^l$, $\hat{B}_1^l$	$\hat{E}$	$\hat{B}_2^l$	

simple representation of financial flows, that bonds are only issued by the government, that firms use only equity financing and pay out expected earnings as dividends, and that there exist also long-term bonds issued by the 'foreign government'. Financial flows between the sectors of our economy are therefore very narrowly defined. Note that we allow for savings out of wages in the present model (in a Kaldorian way) and that workers save only in the form of short-term debt (interest-bearing saving deposits[3] held at the local branches of the central bank).[4] All other assets (plus the remainder of short-term debt) are exclusively held by the (pure) asset holders of our model. We stress that this formulation has served the purpose of simplifying the budget constraints of the agents in Chiarella and Flaschel (1999b), but should be extended in future developments of the model.

This is the basic structure we assume for our economy which will be further explained in the next section from the viewpoint of national accounting before we present and discuss the intensive form of the model of Chiarella and Flaschel (1999b).

6.3 The implied 34D dynamics

In order to study the dynamics of our stylised disequilibrium growth model analytically and numerically it is necessary to reduce the equations of the model presented in Chiarella and Flaschel (1999b) to intensive or per (value) unit of capital form. This has already been indicated and discussed in the preceding section from the viewpoint of the system of national accounts by dividing all (nominal) level magnitudes through (the value of) the capital stock K of firms (measured at consumer prices p_v) and by taking note of the fact that the model exhibits Harrod neutral technological change

[3] Or fixed-price bonds, which are perfectly liquid, while the other type of bonds, long-term bonds (here consols or perpetuities, held by asset holders), cannot be redeemed at a given price from the viewpoint of the sector of asset holders as a whole.

[4] For the purpose of financing government expenditures with no explicit reserve requirements.

which means that all variables involving labour must be measured in efficiency units, so they are to be multiplied by the term $\exp(n_l t)$ in order to remove the trend in labour productivity from them. Note that this procedure must also be applied to the nominal wage w which is to be replaced by the term $w^e = w/\exp(n_l t)$ since nominal wages w will rise with labour productivity in the steady state and must therefore be detrended and replaced by the wage rate per efficiency unit of labour in order to get a variable that in principle allows for stationarity ($\hat{w}^e = \hat{w} - n_l$).

Note here again that the model has been formulated in a way that implies zero price inflation in the steady state if it is assumed that the target inflation rate of the central bank, $\bar{\pi}$, equals zero – an assumption that will be made for the remainder of the chapter. The variables such as w^e, p_y, p_h therefore need not be detrended any further, but represent state variables of the dynamical system to be formulated below. The first two laws of motion of these state variables are easily obtained from module 5b of Chiarella and Flaschel (1999b) by inserting there the definitions for $u_f^w = l_f^{de}/l_f^{we}$, $u = y/y^p$ in particular and by replacing level variables by their intensive form measures. In the same way we obtain the dynamical laws for long-run inflationary expectations π^c by making use of $\hat{Y}^p = \hat{K}$, and also the law of motion for the price of dwelling services p_h, see module 2b of Chiarella and Flaschel (1999b).

Note finally that the magnitude $c_c = C_c/K$, the consumption of asset holders of the domestic good per unit of capital, is a given magnitude in the steady state of the model (but not off the steady state), due to the assumption $\hat{C}_c = \gamma$ made in Chiarella and Flaschel (1999b).

6.3.1 *The laws of motion*

Let us start our presentation of the model in intensive form by first considering the quantity dynamics it implies,[5] which are given by

1. The Quantity Dynamics (seven laws of motion):

$$\dot{y}^e = \beta_{y^e}(y^d - y^e) + (\gamma - (g_k - \delta_k))y^e, \tag{6.1}$$

$$\dot{\nu} = y - y^d - (g_k - \delta_k)\nu, \tag{6.2}$$

$$\hat{c}_w = \alpha_1^w(c_w^o/c_w - 1) + \alpha_2^w(e - \bar{e}) + \gamma - (g_k - \delta_k), \tag{6.3}$$

$$\hat{c}_h^d = \alpha_r^h(c_h^{do}/c_h^d - 1) + \alpha_i^h(e - \bar{e}) + \gamma - (g_k - \delta_k), \tag{6.4}$$

$$\hat{c}_c = \gamma - (g_k - \delta_k), \tag{6.5}$$

$$\hat{l}_f^{we} = \beta_l(u_f^w - \bar{u}_f^w) + \gamma - (g_k - \delta_k), \tag{6.6}$$

$$\dot{\bar{e}} = \beta_{\bar{e}}(e - \bar{e}). \tag{6.7}$$

These formulae are obtained from the extensive form presented in Chiarella and Flaschel (1999b) by the usual growth rate formula for intensive expressions, for example

[5] These dynamics, as well as the growth dynamics, will be considerably more complicated if substitution is allowed for in the production possibilities of firms: see Chiarella *et al.* (1999a,b) on this matter.

$\widehat{Y^e/K} = \hat{Y}^e - \hat{K}$ with $\hat{K} = g_k - \delta_k$ by reformulating such expression in terms of time derivatives whenever necessary. The dynamical laws for quantities describe sales expectations dynamics, actual inventory dynamics, three types of consumption demand dynamics for workers (domestic goods and housing services) and asset holders (domestic goods including houses), the dynamic employment policy of firms and finally the dynamics of the NAIRU rate of employment.

Next we describe the price dynamics as far as real markets are concerned:

2. Wage/Price Dynamics (four laws of motion):

$$\hat{w}^e = \beta_{w_e}(e - \bar{e}) + \beta_{w_u}(u_f^w - \bar{u}_f^w), \tag{6.8}$$

$$+ \kappa_w(\hat{p}_y + n_l) + (1 - \kappa_w)(\pi^c + \widetilde{n}_l) - n_l,$$

$$\hat{p}_y = \beta_p(y/y^p - \bar{u}) + \kappa_p \hat{w}^e + (1 - \kappa_p)\pi^c, \tag{6.9}$$

$$\dot{\pi}^e = \beta_{\pi^c}(\alpha_{\pi^c}(\hat{p}_y - \pi^c) + (1 - \alpha_{\pi^c})(0 - \pi^c)), \tag{6.10}$$

$$\hat{p}_h = \beta_h\left(\frac{c_h^d}{k_h} - \bar{u}_h\right) + \kappa_h \hat{p}_y + (1 - \kappa_h)\pi^c. \tag{6.11}$$

These equations for wage and price dynamics (including medium-run inflationary expectations) and rental price dynamics are straightforward consequences of the laws of motion as they were formulated in Chiarella and Flaschel (1999b).

We have next the dynamics of asset prices, expectations about the dynamics and the dynamics of certain long-run concepts of interest and profits. Note that we here make use of Tobin's $q = \frac{p_e E}{p_y K}$ as an aggregate expression for the joint dynamics of equity prices p_e and the number of equities E. Given the formulation of the model in Chiarella and Flaschel (1999b) it suffices to describe the dynamics of q in the intensive form which moreover, due to the lack of wealth effects and the like, does not feed back into the rest of the dynamics. Note however that the expression for $\hat{p}_e$ from Chiarella and Flaschel (1999b),

$$\hat{p}_e = \frac{\beta_{p_e}}{1 - \beta_{p_e}(1 - \alpha_s)}[(1 - \tau_c)r^e/q + \alpha_s \pi_{es} - ((1 - \tau_c)i_l + \pi_b)], \tag{6.12}$$

with aggregate expectations π_b being determined by $\alpha_s \pi_{bs} + (1 - \alpha_s)\hat{p}_b$, has to be inserted into the law of motion for Tobin's q in order to get a description of these dynamics that is complete. Due to the isolated nature of these dynamics it is however not necessary here to go into more detail.

3. Asset Prices and Expectations (eight laws of motion):

$$\hat{p}_b = \frac{\beta_{p_b}}{1 - \beta_{p_b}(1 - \alpha_s)}[(1 - \tau_c)i_l + \alpha_s \pi_{bs} - ((1 - \tau_c)i + \xi)], \quad (p_b = 1/i_l), \tag{6.13}$$

$$\dot{\pi}_{bs} = \beta_{\pi_{bs}}(\hat{p}_b - \pi_{bs}), \tag{6.14}$$

$$\hat{q} = \hat{p}_e - \hat{p}_y + \frac{g_k - \delta_k + y - y^d - (\beta_n(\beta_{n^d} y^e - \nu) + \gamma\beta_{n^d} y^e)}{q} - (g_k - \delta_k), \tag{6.15}$$

$$\dot{\pi}_{es} = \beta_{\pi_{es}}(\hat{p}_e - \pi_{es}), \tag{6.16}$$

$$\hat{s} = \frac{\beta_s}{1 - \beta_s(1 - \alpha_s)}[(1 - \tau_c^*)i_l^* + \alpha_s\epsilon_s - ((1 - \tau_c)i_l + \pi_b)], \tag{6.17}$$

$$\dot{\epsilon}_s = \beta_{\epsilon_s}(\hat{s} - \epsilon_s), \tag{6.18}$$

$$\dot{r}^l = \beta_{r_l}(r^e - r^l), \tag{6.19}$$

$$\dot{r}_h^l = \beta_{r_h^l}(r_h - r_h^l). \tag{6.20}$$

We have first the law of motion for the price of long-term bonds, $p_b = 1/i_l$, which is here expressed in terms of the interest rate that these bond prices (consols) represent. This interest rate adjusts in the direction of the risk free interest rate on short-term bonds after taxes $(1 - \tau_c)i$, augmented by a risk and liquidity premium ξ for long-term bonds. Note that we have removed the perfect foresight expectations from the left side of this adjustment equation which, as shown in Chiarella and Flaschel (1999b), gives rise to the fraction in front of the shown formula. Note furthermore that only the law of motion of 'less ambitious' expectations is then needed in order to make this substructure determinate, but that aggregate expectations on these bond price changes π_b are needed in the subsequent laws of motion of asset prices.

Making use of the formula for the rate of change of equity prices π_e expected on average we can transform the law of motion for equity prices just as the law of motion for long-term bond prices and also remove the explicit representation of 'ambitious' agents, as shown in the representation of the p_e dynamics. This law is again to be supplemented by the law of motion for the expectations of 'less ambitious' agents.

The next law of motion concerns Tobin's q which, as already shown, is measured by the ratio between the value of equity stock and the producer price of the existing capital stock, that is $q = \frac{p_e E}{p_y K}$. We have $\hat{q} = \hat{p}_e - \hat{p}_y + \hat{E} - \hat{K}$ where the first two inflation rates have already been determined in equations (6.12) and (6.9). For the remaining expression $\widehat{E/K} = \hat{E} - \hat{K}$ we have

$$\begin{aligned}\widehat{E/K} = \hat{E} - \hat{K} &= \frac{p_e \dot{E}}{p_y K} \cdot \frac{p_y K}{p_e E} - \hat{K} \\ &= [g_k - \delta_k + y - y^d - (\beta_n(\beta_{n^d} y^e - \nu) + \gamma\beta_{n^d} y^e)]/q - (g_k - \delta_k),\end{aligned}$$

which yields the law of motion for Tobin's q shown in module 3. Note again that the expression for $\hat{p}^e$ can be inserted into the q dynamics and thus gives rise to one law of motion in Tobin's q solely.

The method used to describe the dynamics of p_e also applies to the law of motion for the exchange rate s by removing again the correct expectations of the 'ambitious' agents from its right-hand side after having inserted the expression for average expectations $\epsilon = \alpha_s \epsilon_s + (1-\alpha_s)\hat{s}$ into this formula. Again this is to be supplemented by the law that describes the evolution of the expectations of 'less ambitious' agents in the postulated adaptive way.

There follow the two laws of motion for expected long-run profitability, r^l, which is used in the investment equation for the capital stock, and r_h^l, which is used in the investment equation for the capital stock in housing. Both of these measures follow their short-run equivalents with some time delay.

Next we consider the laws of growth that apply to the economy under consideration:

4. Growth Dynamics (six laws of motion):

$$\dot{n} = \beta_{n_w}(\tilde{n} - n), \quad (\tilde{n} = \tilde{n}(e, \hat{e})), \tag{6.21}$$

$$\hat{l}^e = n + n_l - (g_k - \delta_k), \tag{6.22}$$

$$\dot{g}_k = \beta_{g_k}(g_k^d - g_k), \tag{6.23}$$

$$\hat{k}_h = g_h - \delta_h - (g_k - \delta_k), \tag{6.24}$$

$$\dot{g}_h = \beta_{g_h}(g_h^d - g_h), \tag{6.25}$$

$$\dot{n}_l = \beta_{n_l}(\tilde{n}_l - n_l), \quad \tilde{n}_l = (\tilde{n}_l(g_k)). \tag{6.26}$$

The growth equations represent the time rate of change of the so-called natural rate of growth, the law of motion for the full employment labour intensity (in efficiency units), the time rate of change of gross investment per unit of capital (also for the housing sector), the growth rate of the relative magnitude of the stock of houses to the capital stock employed by firms and finally the time rate of change of the rate of Harrod neutral technological change. There is no further comment needed with respect to the above presentations of the growth laws of the economy which again use the formula $\hat{K} = g_k - \delta_k$ in the formulation of intensive expressions.

Next the dynamic feedback rules for government behaviour are collected. These concern the steering of the short-term nominal rate of interest by the central bank, the dynamic wage taxation rule based in reaction to the evolution of government debt d and the motion of the tax rate on imports, which is here used to establish a balanced trade account in the steady state.

5. Monetary and Fiscal Policy Rules (three laws of motion):

$$\dot{i} = -\beta_{i_i}(i + \xi - i_l^*) + \beta_{i_p}(\hat{p}_y - \bar{\pi}) + \beta_{i_u}(y/y^p - \bar{u}), \quad (\bar{\pi} = 0), \tag{6.27}$$

$$\hat{\tau}_w = \alpha_{\tau_{w1}}(d/\bar{d} - 1) + \alpha_{\tau_{w2}}\hat{d}, \qquad \left(d = \frac{b + b^l/i_l}{y^e}\right), \tag{6.28}$$

$$\hat{\tau}_m = \alpha_{\tau_m}\frac{p_x x - p_m j^d}{p_x x}. \tag{6.29}$$

Note with respect to module 5 that the aggregate accumulation of government bonds cannot be divorced from the real sector (even though wealth effects are not yet included in the model) due to the assumed wage income taxation rule whereby the government attempts to steer a certain ratio for government debt to a desired ratio $\bar{d}$.

There remain the dynamics of aggregate and individual asset holdings which represent the most involved block in our dynamical system. We have already stressed that the individual allocation of government bonds (between workers and asset holders and also throughout the world) does not feed back into the remaining dynamics, since only total government bonds matter in the present context due to the absence of wealth effects in consumption and due to the independence of consumption of workers and asset holders from their interest income. In the current version of the dynamics only the laws of motion for b and b^l feed back into the real part of the dynamics via the wage tax collection rule of the government.

6. Assets Dynamics (six laws of motion):

$$\dot{b} = \alpha_b^g[gy^e + ib + b^l - t^n + (w^{ue}/p_v)(l^e - l^{we}) + (w^{re}/p_v)\alpha_l l_2^e + (w^{be}/p_v)l_g^{de}] - (\hat{p}_y + g_k - \delta_k)b, \tag{6.30}$$

$$\dot{b}^l = i_l(1-\alpha_b^g)[gy^e + ib + b^l - t^n + (w^{ue}/p_v)(l^e - l^{we}) + (w^{re}/p_v)\alpha_l l_2^e + (w^{be}/p_v)l_g^{de}] - (\hat{p}_y + g_k - \delta_k)b^l, \tag{6.31}$$

$$\dot{b}_w = y_w^D - c_w - \frac{p_h}{p_v}c_h^d - (\hat{p}_y + g_k - \delta_k)b_w, \qquad (\dot{b}_c = \dot{b} - \dot{b}_w), \tag{6.32}$$

$$\dot{b}_1^l = i_l\alpha_{b1}^g(1-\alpha_b^g)[gy^e + ib + b^l - t^n + (w^{ue}/p_v)(l^e - l^{we}) + (w^{re}/p_v)\alpha_l l_2^e + (w^{be}/p_v)l_g^{de}] - (\hat{p}_y + g_k - \delta_k)b_1^l, \tag{6.33}$$

$$\dot{b}_1^{l*} = i_l(1-\alpha_{b1}^g)(1-\alpha_b^g)[gy^e + ib + b^l - t^n + (w^{ue}/p_v)(l^e - l^{we}) + (w^{re}/p_v)\alpha_l l_2^e + (w^{be}/p_v)l_g^{de}] - (\hat{p}_y + g_k - \delta_k)b_1^{l*}, \tag{6.34}$$

$$\dot{b}_2^l = \dot{B}_2^l/(p_vK) - (\hat{p}_y + g_k - \delta_k)b_2^l, \tag{6.35}$$

where we have

$$\frac{\dot{B}_2^l}{p_vK} = \frac{i_l^*}{s}[y_c^D - c_c - \frac{\dot{B}_c}{p_vK} - \frac{\dot{B}_1^l/i_l}{p_vK} - \frac{p_e\dot{E}}{p_vK} - \frac{p_y}{p_v}(g_h - \delta_h)k_h]$$
$$= \frac{i_l^*}{s}\{y_c^D - c_c - (\alpha_b^g + (1-\alpha_b^g)\alpha_{b1}^g)[gy^e + ib + b^l - t^n$$

$$+ (w^{ue}/p_v)(l^e - l^{we}) + (w^{re}/p_v)\alpha_l l_2^e + (w^{be}/p_v)l_g^{de}]$$
$$- (p_y/p_v)[g_k - \delta_k + y - y^d - (\beta_n(\beta_{n^d} y^e - \nu) + \gamma\beta_{n^d} y^e)]$$
$$- (p_y/p_v)(g_h - \delta_h)k_h)\}$$

according to the flow budget constraint of asset holders.

This part of the dynamics is to some extent missing in the Murphy model; see Powell and Murphy (1997), with which we compared our model in detail in Chiarella and Flaschel (1999b), due to the lack of a complete treatment of the budget equations of the three sectors that form the basis of this model. As indicated above the laws of motion of the individual assets that are held by the household sector in our model however do not feed back into the rest of the dynamics, since they do not show up in the real part of the economy. Therefore, only the two laws of motion for short- and long-term government debt are really needed at present in the discussion of the growth pattern and the fluctuations that may occur around them which are implied by the disequilibrium growth model under consideration.

Note with respect to the right-hand sides of these stock accumulation equations that they are based on a fixed ratio α_b^g describing the allocation between the short- and long-term financing of government debt done by the government (as in the Murphy model) and that the term in square brackets, the government budget equation

$$gy^e + ib + b^l - t^n + (w^{ue}/p_v)(l^e - l^{we}) + (w^{re}/p_v)\alpha_l l_2^e + (w^{be}/p_v)l_g^{de},$$

in both cases represents the sum of government expenditure for goods, labour, interest and transfer payments to the unemployed and retirees minus t^n, the sum of all taxes that are raised by the government (per value unit of capital).[6]

The total amount of debt financing is thus represented through the expression shown above, leading to $\dot{b} + \dot{b}_l/i_l$, and it is split via the weights α_b^g, $1 - \alpha_b^g$, applied to the Government Budget Restraint (GBR) in the above intensive form, into short-term financing $\dot{b}$ (equation (6.30)) and long-term financing $\dot{b}_l/i_l$ (equation (6.31)). Note that $(\hat{p}_y + g_k - \delta_k)b$ and $(\hat{p}_y + g_k - \delta_k)b^l$ have to be deducted from the resulting expression, due to the fact that these bond variables are in intensive form and are thus divided by $p_v K$.

The dynamic equation (6.32) for real savings of workers per unit of capital, $b_w = B_w/(p_v K)$, follows from the definition of this expression and from the definition of the disposable income of worker households and their saving plans, while the law of motion for short-term debt of asset holders per capital, $b_c = B_c/(p_v K)$, is a simple consequence of the two laws of motion assumed for the expressions b and b_w.

The next two dynamic laws (6.33) and (6.34) for the distribution of new domestic long-term debt throughout the world basically follow again from the budget restriction of the government shown above (expressed in intensive form), since there is also a

[6] Note that all wage concepts in the above intensive form of the GBR are in efficiency units (to allow for stationarity) and are deflated by consumer prices p_v.

fixed proportion α^g_{b1} assumed to apply with respect to the distribution of long-term debt between domestic and foreign asset holders. The expressions for the proportions of long-term financing that go to domestic and foreign residents, $\dot{b}^l_1, b^l_1 = B^l_1/(p_v K)$ and $\dot{b}^{l*}_1, b^{l*}_1 = B^{l*}_1/(p_v K)$, are thus obtained by applying the weights $\alpha^g_{b1}, 1 - \alpha^g_{b1}$ to $\dot{b}^l$ and again noting the fact that now $(\hat{p}_y + g_k - \delta_k)b^l_1$ and $(\hat{p}_y + g_k - \delta_k)b^{l*}_1$ have to be deducted from the resulting expressions (due to the intensive form formulation) in the place of the former expression $(\hat{p}_y + g_k - \delta_k)b^l$.

There remains the law of motion of foreign assets held by domestic residents which, due to the definition of the intensive variable $b^l_2 = B^l_2/(p_v K)$, basically demands the determination of the variable $\dot{B}^l_2/(p_v K)$ in terms of intensive expressions. This task is solved residually by referring to the fact that $\dot{B}^l_2$ is given by the disposable income of asset holders minus their consumption minus all other asset accumulation that these households undertake. This provides the last law of motion shown in the above block of asset accumulation equations, which is thus purely residual in nature.

6.3.2 *Static relationships*

There is a variety of definitions and static relationships used in the above collection of the laws of motion of our disequilibrium model of monetary growth. These abbreviations are collected in the next six blocks of the intensive presentation of the model and are generally immediate consequences of the corresponding equations in extensive form presented in Chiarella and Flaschel (1999b).

7. Output and Demand on the Market for Goods (including Housing Services):

$$y^d = c_w + c_c + g_k + g_h k_h + g y^e, \tag{6.36}$$

$$y = y^e + \beta_n(\beta_{n^d} y^e - \nu) + \gamma \beta_{n^d} y^e, \tag{6.37}$$

$$x = x_y y, \tag{6.38}$$

$$j^d = j_y y, \tag{6.39}$$

$$c^o_w = c_y(1 - \tau_w)[w^e l^{de} + w^{ue}(l^e - l^{we}) + w^{re}\alpha_l l^e_2]/p_v, \tag{6.40}$$

$$c^{do}_h = c_h(1 - \tau_w)[w^e l^{de} + w^{ue}(l^e - l^{we}) + w^{re}\alpha_l l^e_2]/p_h. \tag{6.41}$$

Note with respect to block 7 of the static equations that all variables are obtained here by dividing the extensive expressions by K, giving rise for example to $k_h = K_h/K$. The same procedure applies to block 8 of the algebraic equations underlying our dynamic model:

8. Employment, Labour Supply and Retirees:

$$l^{de}_f = l_y y, \quad \text{(see block 1 for the law of motion for } l^{we}_f\text{)}, \tag{6.42}$$

$$l^{de}_g = l^{we}_g = \alpha_g g y^e, \tag{6.43}$$

$$l^{de} = l^{de}_f + l^{de}_g, \quad (u^w_f = l^{de}_f / l^e), \tag{6.44}$$

$$l^{we} = l_f^{we} + l_g^{we}, \quad (e = l^{we}/l^e), \tag{6.45}$$

$$l_2^e = (L_2(0)/L_1(0))l^e/\alpha_l. \tag{6.46}$$

Note again that all magnitudes concerning labour inputs and supply are expressed in efficiency units – due to the technological condition $L_f^d = l_y \exp(-n_l t)Y$ that represents Harrod neutral technical change. When multiplied with wages measured in efficiency units the term $\exp(-n_l t)$ just cancels from the resulting expression and gives the corresponding wage payments in both efficiency units and original levels. Note, finally, that we need initial conditions in order to relate the sizes of the intensive expression for potential labour supply and retirees.

9. Desired Growth Rates of the Capital Stocks (Firms/Dwellings):

$$g_k^d = \alpha_1^k((1-\tau_c)r^e - i^r) + \alpha_2^k(i_l - (i+\xi)) + \alpha_3^k(y/y^p - \bar{u}) + \gamma + \delta_k, \tag{6.47}$$

$$g_h^d = \alpha_r^h((1-\tau_c)r_h^l - i^r) + \alpha_i^h(i_l - (i+\xi)) + \alpha_u^h(\frac{c_h^d}{k_h} - \bar{u}_h) + \gamma + \delta_h. \tag{6.48}$$

The growth rates of the capital stocks for fixed investment of firms and housing investment of asset holders (here shown as gross rates) are an immediate consequence of their original formulation in Chiarella and Flaschel (1999b), and simply state that these ratios are assumed to be influenced by long-run profitability measures, by the interest rate spread and by the rate of capacity utilisation. The same immediate correspondence to what has been introduced in Chiarella and Flaschel (1999b) holds true for the following definitions of rates of return needed for the dynamical laws or just for the discussion of the steady state of the model.

10. Rates of Return on Real and Financial Assets:

$$r^e = y^e - \delta_k + (p_x/p_y)x - (w^{be}/p_y)l_f^{de} - (p_m/p_y)j^d, \tag{6.49}$$

$$y^{dp} = \frac{\bar{u}y^p}{1+\gamma\beta_{n^d}}, \quad (y^n = \bar{u}y^p),$$

$$r^n = y^{dp} - \delta_k + (p_x/p_y)x_y y^n - w^{be}l_y y^n - (p_m/p_y)j_y y^n, \tag{6.50}$$

$$i^r = (1-\tau_c)i_l - \pi^c, \tag{6.51}$$

$$r_h = (p_h/p_y)c_h^d/k_h - \delta_h. \tag{6.52}$$

The following definitions of the various prices we use in our model in addition to the prices that appear as state variables in the dynamics are also an immediate consequence of their definitions in the extensive form of the model in Chiarella and Flaschel (1999b) when account is again taken of the fact that wages have to be expressed in efficiency units in order to ensure their stationarity in the steady state: $w^e = w/\exp(n_l t)$.

11. Consumer Prices, Gross Wages and Transfers:

$$p_x = sp_x^*, \tag{6.53}$$

$$p_m = (1+\tau_m)sp_m^*, \tag{6.54}$$

$$w^{be} = (1+\tau_p)w^e, \tag{6.55}$$

$$w^{ue} = \alpha^u w^e, \tag{6.56}$$

$$w^{re} = \alpha^r w^e, \tag{6.57}$$

$$p_v = (1+\tau_v)p_y. \tag{6.58}$$

Finally the short-cut expressions for the intensive forms of disposable incomes and taxes are easily obtained from their extensive form analogues and are of the form shown below. Note that the expressions for disposable income of workers and asset holders are only needed in their bond accumulation equations and, as the model is currently formulated, are not yet involved in the consumption decisions of the two types of households considered.

12. Disposable Incomes and Government Taxes per Value Unit of Capital:

$$y_w^D = (1-\tau_w)[w^e l^{de} + w^{ue}(l^e - l^{we}) + w^{re}\alpha_l l_2^e]/p_v + (1-\tau_c)ib_w, \tag{6.59}$$

$$y_{w1}^D = (1-\tau_w)[w^e l^{de} + w^{ue}(l^e - l^{we}) + w^{re}\alpha_l l_2^e]/p_v, \tag{6.60}$$

$$\begin{aligned} y_c^D &= (1-\tau_c)[r^e(p_y/p_v) + ib_c + b_1^l + (p_h/p_v)c_h^d - (p_y/p_v)\delta_h k_h] \\ &\quad + s(1-\tau_c)b_2^l, \end{aligned} \tag{6.61}$$

$$\begin{aligned} t^n &= \tau_w[w^e l^{de} + w^{ue}(l^e - l^{we}) + w^{re}\alpha_l l_2^e]/p_v + \tau_p(w^e/p_v)l^{de} \\ &\quad + \tau_v(y^d - g_k - g_h k_h)(p_y/p_v) \\ &\quad + \tau_c[r^e(p_y/p_v) + ib + b^l + (p_h/p_v)r_h k_h] + \tau_m s(p_m^*/p_v)j^d. \end{aligned} \tag{6.62}$$

In closing the discussion of the intensive form of our disequilibrium model of monetary growth we stress again that the law of motion for equity prices p_e is not needed, since it can be substituted into the law of motion for Tobin's q. It can thus be removed from explicit representation, since there is here no feedback from Tobin's q on the real part of the economy, due to the lack of wealth effects in the current version of the model.

6.4 Steady state analysis

In this section we show that there is, up to the level of nominal variables, a uniquely determined economically meaningful balanced growth path or steady state solution of our model. This steady state provides us with a useful reference path for the dynamical evolution implied by the model, which may or may not converge to this steady state solution, not even if long-run moving averages are used in the place of the temporary positions that the economy will pass through.

The calculation of this interior, economically meaningful, steady state[7] of the full model (which up to the level of nominal magnitudes for wages and goods prices is uniquely determined) is in many respects simple due to the given growth rate of the world economy and the given interest rate (on consols) abroad. Note that we only consider expressions for the total supply of domestic bonds in the following, and not their distribution at home and abroad which can be easily obtained from the savings decisions of workers and pure asset owners.

To simplify subsequent presentations of the dynamics of the model, and also its steady state solution, we assume in the remainder of this chapter for the consumption of asset owners that $C_c = 0$ and for the liquidity premium applied to long-term debt that $\xi = 0$. These two assumptions do not restrict the dynamical behaviour of the system in any significant way.

The first set of steady state conditions presented below concerns the growth rates of our small open economy, and are given by

$$\gamma = g_k - \delta_k = g_k^d - \delta_k \quad \Rightarrow g_k = g_k^d = \gamma + \delta_k, \tag{6.63}$$

$$\gamma = g_h - \delta_h = g_h^d - \delta_h \quad \Rightarrow g_h = g_h^d = \gamma + \delta_h, \tag{6.64}$$

$$\gamma = \widetilde{n}(\bar{e}) + \widetilde{n}_l(g_k) = \widetilde{n}(\bar{e}) + \widetilde{n}_l(\gamma + \delta_k) \quad \Rightarrow \bar{e}, \quad (n = \widetilde{n}, n_l = \widetilde{n}_l). \tag{6.65}$$

These equations state that capital (and thus also output) will grow with the external rate γ, to which also the natural rate of growth adjusts. This means that the steady state value of NAIRU rate of employment $\bar{e}(= e)$ has to adjust such that $\gamma = \widetilde{n}(\bar{e}) + \widetilde{n}_l(g_k)$ holds. This determines a unique NAIRE $\bar{e} = e$ for the long run of the model under suitable (but simple) assumptions on the function $\widetilde{n}$.

The next set of steady state conditions concerns inflation and expected inflation (for all prices that exist in our model, except wage rates) and also the various rates of interest and profit of our model:

$$\hat{p}_v = \hat{p}_y = \hat{p}_h = \pi^c = \pi_{bs} = \pi_b = \pi_{es} = \pi_e = \epsilon_s = \epsilon = 0, \tag{6.66}$$

$$i_l^* = i_l = i^r = i = 1/p_b, \tag{6.67}$$

$$i_l^* = r^e = i_l = r^n = r_h = r_h^l. \tag{6.68}$$

These conditions state that there is no steady state inflation and thus no non-zero expectations of it, which is due to the interest rate policy rule of the central bank. Furthermore, all (expected) rates of return are equalised in the steady state and determined by the world rate of interest on long-term bonds i_l^*.

The next block concerns the steady state determination of various quantities, of the steady state ratio of government debt to aggregate demand and of the tax rate on

[7] We thus neglect as alternative steady state positions all zeros which can be obtained mathematically from the growth law formulations that our model employs. Note also the steady state depends parametrically on the initial conditions for $\frac{L_2(0)}{L_1(0)}$, p_v, $\frac{C_c(0)}{L_1(0)}$ that characterise the initial composition of the labour force, the initial output price level (including value-added taxes) and a relative expression for the consumption of asset owners.

imports:

$$y = y^p \bar{u}, \quad c_h^d = k_h \bar{u}_h, \tag{6.69}$$

$$l_f^{de} = l_f^{we} = l_y y, \tag{6.70}$$

$$l_g^{de} = l_g^{we} = \alpha_g g y^e, \tag{6.71}$$

$$l^{we} = l^{de} = l_f^{we} + l_g^{we}, \tag{6.72}$$

$$l^e = l^{de}/\bar{e} \quad [e = \bar{e}], \; l_1^e = l^e/\alpha_l, \; l_2^e = (L_2(0), L_1(0)) l_1^e, \tag{6.73}$$

$$x = x_y y, \quad j^d = j_y y, \tag{6.74}$$

$$d = (b + b^l / i_l^*)/y^e = \bar{d}, \tag{6.75}$$

$$\tau_m = \frac{p_x^* x - p_m^* j^d}{p_m^* j^d}. \tag{6.76}$$

These equations still depend on the steady state value of y^e, which will be given below, and they reveal certain supply side influences on the steady behaviour of our economy.

Further steady state relationships on the side of quantities are

$$y^e = \frac{y}{1 + \gamma \beta_{n^d}}, \tag{6.77}$$

$$y^d = y^e, \quad \nu = \beta_{n^d} y^e, \tag{6.78}$$

$$c_w^o = c_y y_{w1}^D, \quad c_h^{do} = c_h p_v y_{w1}^D / p_h, \tag{6.79}$$

$$y_{w1}^D = (1 - \tau_w)[w^e l^{de} + w^{ue}(l^e - l^{we}) + w^{re} \alpha_l l_2^e]/p_v. \tag{6.80}$$

By using the distribution laws for government bonds we furthermore find that

$$b = \alpha_b^g \bar{d} y^e, \tag{6.81}$$

$$b^l = i_l^* (1 - \alpha_b^g) \bar{d} y^e, \tag{6.82}$$

from which the individual distribution of bonds can be derived if desired.

Next, one can determine the nominal steady state expressions on the basis of an (arbitrarily) given price level p_v. This indeterminacy of the general price level of domestically produced goods is due to the fact that the central bank has adopted an interest rate policy rule and allows for intra-day deviations from the budget constraints of the two types of households, the firms and the government and that therefore, in our present model, money is not held as cash balances by the agents of our economy.

$$p_v = \text{undetermined and thus a parameter,} \tag{6.83}$$

$$p_y = p_v/(1+\tau_v), \tag{6.84}$$

$$w^{be} \quad via \quad i_l^* = y^e - \delta_k - \frac{w^{be}}{p_y} l_f^{de} : \quad w^{be} = \frac{y^e - \delta_k - i_l^*}{l_y y} p_y, \tag{6.85}$$

$$w^e = w^{be}/(1+\tau_p), \; w^{ue} = \alpha^u w^e, \; w^{re} = \alpha^r w^e. \tag{6.86}$$

The equation for the determination of gross wages in efficiency units holds since we have balanced trade in the steady state (see the above), and thus no influence of the international trade in goods on the rate of profit in the steady state. Note here that net real wages ω^e (excluding payroll taxes, but before wage taxation), measured in terms of consumer prices p_v and efficiency units, are given by

$$\omega^e = \frac{w^e}{p_v} = \frac{1}{(1+\tau_v)(1+\tau_p)} \frac{y^e - \delta_k - i_l^*}{l_y y}$$

and thus do not depend on the arbitrarily determined nominal price level p_v. This observation also applies to all other real magnitudes implying that there are no real effects of shocks which lead to a different consumer price level p_v in the long run.

The equations $c_h^d = \bar{u}_h k_h$ and $i_l^* = p_h c_h^d/(p_y k_h) - \delta_h$, on the one hand, and $c_h y_{w1}^D = p_h c_h^d / p_v$, $y^e = c_y y_{w1}^D + \gamma + \delta_k + (\gamma + \delta_h) k_h + g y^e$, on the other hand,[8] allow us to determine the price ratio p_h/p_y and k_h, y_{w1}^D, τ_w according to

$$p_h/p_y = (i_l^* + \delta_h)/\bar{u}_h, \tag{6.87}$$

$$k_h = \frac{y^e(1-g) - \gamma - \delta_k}{c_y(i_l^* + \delta_h)/(c_h(1+\tau_v)) + \gamma + \delta_h}, \tag{6.88}$$

$$y_{w1}^D = p_h \bar{u}_h k_h / (c_h p_v), \tag{6.89}$$

$$\tau_w = 1 - \frac{y_{w1}^D}{[w^e l^{de} + w^{ue}(l^e - l^{we}) + w^{re} \alpha_l l_2^e]/p_v}. \tag{6.90}$$

Note also that this determination of y_{w1}^D and k_h must be used above for the determination of consumption plans per unit of capital.

There remains the determination of the steady state value of the exchange rate s,[9] since the price of long-term bonds, $p_b = 1/i_l^*$, has already been determined and since

[8] Note that the last equation represents goods market equilibrium in the steady state.
[9] This in turn determines the prices p_x, p_m.

the price of equities does not matter in the core 34D dynamics of the model.[10] The calculation of the steady state exchange rate is economically complex, but mathematically quite simple. Mathematically it is provided by the implicit equations for the variables t^r, s on the basis of the expression for t^c, namely

$$0 = gy^e + ib + b^l - t^w - t^c + [w^{ue}(l^e - l^{we}) + w^{re}\alpha_l l_2^e + w^{be} l_g^{de}]/p_v - \gamma b/\alpha_b^g,$$

$$\begin{aligned} 0 &= \tau_w y_{w1}^D/(1-\tau_w) + \tau_p(w^e/p_v)l^{de} \\ &\quad + \tau_v(p_y/p_v)(y^d - g_k^d - g_h^d k_h) + \tau_m s p_m^* j^d/p_v - t^r, \end{aligned}$$

where

$$\begin{aligned} t^c &= \tau_c[r^e(p_y/p_v) + i_l^* b + b^l + (p_h/p_v)c_h^d - (p_y/p_v)\delta_h k_h] \\ &= \tau_c[(r^e + i_l^* k_h)/(1+\tau_v) + i_l^* b + b^l]. \end{aligned}$$

These equations lead to

$$t^r = gy^e + ib + b^l - t^c + [w^{ue}(l^e - l^{we}) + w^{re}\alpha_l l_2^e + w^{be} l_g^{de}]/p_v - \gamma b/\alpha_b^g, \tag{6.91}$$

$$s = \frac{t^r - [\tau_w y_{w1}^D/(1-\tau_w) + \tau_p(w^e/p_v)l^{de} + \tau_v(p_y/p_v)(y^d - g_k^d - g_h^d k_h)]}{\tau_m p_m^* j^d/p_v}. \tag{6.92}$$

We see that the long-run rate of exchange is neither determined in the market for goods, nor through the trade balance, nor by international capital flows, but rather is a complicated expression of many parameters and steady state values of the model and is in particular heavily dependent on the form of the GBR and its components.

Note finally that the dynamics of equity prices imply that $q = 1$ must hold true in the steady state, so that $p_e E = p_y K$ and that the steady state distribution of long-term bonds can be derived from block 6 of Chiarella and Flaschel (1999b), while the steady state value of b_w (and b_c) follows by setting (6.32) equal to zero. This gives rise to[11]

$$b_w = \frac{(1 - c_y - (p_h/p_v)c_h)y_{w1}^D}{\gamma - (1-\tau_c^*)i_l^*},$$

due to the difference that exists between the definitions of y_{w1}^D and y_w^D.

Summarising, we see that the steady state of the considered economy depends heavily on the data assumed to apply to the rest of the world (generally in a fairly straightforward and simple way) and that the steady values of the wage taxation rate and in particular the exchange rate are complicated functions of the parameters and various other steady

[10] The same holds true for the disposable income of asset holders y_c^D.

[11] This solution implies by economic reasoning that $\gamma > (1-\tau_c^*)i_l^*$ should hold true in the world economy (because of the particular interest income policy of workers).

state solutions of the dynamics. Furthermore, since the steady rate of profit r^e and thus also the real wage rate $\omega^e = w^e/p_v$ (see the above expressions) are determined through the foreign rate of interest, we obtain for the real wage ω^{ne} (after taxes, at consumer prices and in efficiency units) the expression

$$\omega^{ne} = (1-\tau_w)\omega^e = \frac{1-\tau_w}{(1+\tau_v)(1+\tau_p)} \frac{y^e - \delta_k - i_l^*}{l_y y},$$

which implies that all increases in the three tax rates shown (value-added tax, payroll taxes and – endogenously determined – wage income taxes) fall on real wages of workers (measured in this chapter solely by the consumer price of domestic goods). There is however also an influence of the value-added tax on overall interest rate income per value unit of capital, besides of course a dependence of this income on the capital taxation rate τ_c.

Output levels (per unit of capital) and also steady employment (per unit of capital and measured in efficiency units) are basically determined through supply side considerations (technology and desired steady rates of capacity utilisation), but the former also depend on government expenditures g per unit of capital and thus will change with this ratio.

We stress again that the external growth rate γ determines the NAIRU rate of employment via

$$\gamma = \widetilde{n}(\bar{e}) + \widetilde{n}_l(\gamma + \delta_k),$$

which implies that an increase in γ will increase the NAIRU rate of employment $\bar{e}$ if $\widetilde{n}' > 0, \widetilde{n}_l \in (0,1)$ holds.

The above has also shown that no inflation occurs in the steady state of the 34D dynamics as far as goods and asset prices are concerned. It is of course important to also consider economies which allow for (moderate) price inflation in the steady state, in the place of stationary price levels that here prevail in the steady state. Just as rates of growth, the steady levels of interest and profit rates are here all fixed and given through the external rate of interest i_l^* so that there is no possibility that the considered country may exhibit an extraordinary level of profitability in the steady state.

6.5 The 18D core dynamics of the model

In order to get (as a starting point for our dynamical investigations of the model in subsequent chapters) a dynamical system that is, on the one hand, as close as possible in spirit to the one of the general model of this chapter and, on the other hand, also as low dimensional as possible, we consider in this section a simplified structure for our Keynesian disequilibrium dynamics of monetary growth which reduces its 34D representation to the following 18D core dynamics. This reformulation makes use of the assumptions $C_c = 0$ and $\xi = 0$ that have already been used in the preceding section (there to simplify slightly the calculation of the interior steady state of the model), and it removes furthermore certain delayed adjustment processes from the considered dynamics, which gives the dynamic model an outlook that is not too far from the theoretical models introduced and analysed in Chiarella and Flaschel (2000, Chs. 6, 7). Furthermore, the natural rate of growth, of Harrod neutral technological change, and of employment are assumed as constant in the following analysis. Finally, the parameter $\alpha_{\tau_{w1}}$ is set equal to zero, implying that there is only a proportional influence of government debt on the wage taxation rate (and no longer an additional derivative one).

6.5.1 The laws of motion

1. The Quantity Dynamics (three laws of motion):

$$\dot{y}^e = \beta_{y^e}(y^d - y^e) + (\gamma - (g_k^d - \delta_k))y^e, \tag{6.93}$$

$$\dot{\nu} = y - y^d - (g_k^d - \delta_k)\nu, \tag{6.94}$$

$$\dot{l}_f^{we} = \beta_l(l_f^{de} - \bar{u}_f^w l_f^{we}) + [\gamma - (g_k^d - \delta_k)]l_f^{we}. \tag{6.95}$$

In the quantity dynamics we have removed the adjustment equations (6.3), (6.4), (6.5) for the actual consumption of workers (for goods and housing services) and replaced these consumption plans by the desired consumption targets which are now immediately realised (without any lag). Furthermore, the NAIRU rate of employment, $\bar{e}$, is no longer considered as endogenously determined by (6.7), but is now a given parameter of the model. There remain the equations for the adjustment of sales expectations, for inventories and for the workforce employed by firms.

2. The Wage/Price Dynamics (four laws of motion):

$$\hat{w}^e = \beta_{w_e}(l^{we}/l^e - \bar{e}) + \beta_{w_u}(l_f^{de}/l_f^{we} - \bar{u}_w^f) + \kappa_w\hat{p}_y + (1 - \kappa_w)\pi^c, \tag{6.96}$$

$$\hat{p}_y = \beta_p(y/y^p - \bar{u}) + \kappa_p\hat{w}^e + (1 - \kappa_p)\pi^c, \tag{6.97}$$

$$\dot{\pi}^c = \beta_{\pi^c}(\alpha_{\pi^c}(\hat{p}_y - \pi^c) + (1 - \alpha_{\pi^c})(0 - \pi^c)), \tag{6.98}$$

$$\hat{p}_h = \beta_h\left(\frac{c_h^{do}}{k_h} - \bar{u}_h\right) + \kappa_h\hat{p}_y + (1 - \kappa_h)\pi^c. \tag{6.99}$$

There is no direct change to the dynamics of the various types of price adjustment rules of the model, on the market for labour, goods and housing services (including the expectations formation mechanism for medium-run inflation rate of the domestically produced good), but an indirect one due to the assumptions $\gamma = n + n_l = \widetilde{n} + \widetilde{n}_l\bar{e}$, on natural growth and employment (which are now considered as given and together with all constant).

3. The Growth Dynamics (two laws of motion):

$$\hat{l}^e = \gamma - (g_k^d - \delta_k), \tag{6.100}$$

$$\hat{k}_h = g_h^d - \delta_h - (g_k^d - \delta_k). \tag{6.101}$$

In block 3 we assume that the natural rates of growth and of technical change, n, n_l, are given exogenously and equal in sum to γ. Furthermore actual accumulation rates are assumed to adjust with infinite speed to their desired targets and thus are no longer represented as lagged adjustment rules. Moreover we have removed here the adjustment equations for the rates of return r^l, r^l_h by assuming that these rates adjust with infinite speed to their short-run equivalents, which are now used in the corresponding behavioural equations in their place.

Next, we present the set of equations that represent the dynamics of asset accumulation and asset prices that are needed for the analysis of the real part of the dynamics of the model:

4. Asset Market Dynamics (six laws of motion):

$$\dot{b} = \alpha_b^g[(gy^e + ib + b^l - t^w - t^c + (w^{ue}/p_v)(l^e - l^{we}) + (w^{re}/p_v)\alpha_l l_2^e + (w^{be}/p_v)l_g^{de}] - (\hat{p}_y + g_k^d - \delta_k)b, \tag{6.102}$$

$$\dot{b}^l = i_l(1-\alpha_b^g)[gy^e + ib + b^l - t^w - t^c + (w^{ue}/p_v)(l^e - l^{we}) + (w^{re}/p_v)\alpha_l l_2^e + (w^{be}/p_v)l_g^{de}] - (\hat{p}_y + g_k^d - \delta_k)b^l, \tag{6.103}$$

$$\hat{p}_b = \frac{\beta_{p_b}}{1-\beta_{p_b}(1-\alpha_s)}[(1-\tau_c)i_l + \alpha_s\pi_{bs} - ((1-\tau_c)i)], \quad \left(i_l = \frac{1}{p_b}\right), \tag{6.104}$$

$$\dot{\pi}_{bs} = \beta_{\pi_{bs}}(\hat{p}_b - \pi_{bs}), \qquad (\pi_b = \alpha_s\pi_{bs} + (1-\alpha_s)\hat{p}_b),$$

$$\hat{s} = \frac{\beta_s}{1-\beta_s(1-\alpha_s)}[(1-\tau_c)i_l^* + \alpha_s\epsilon_s - ((1-\tau_c)i_l + \pi_b)], \tag{6.105}$$

$$\dot{\epsilon}_s = \beta_{\epsilon_s}(\hat{s} - \epsilon_s). \tag{6.106}$$

The price adjustment rules in block 4 concern the nominal value of long-term bonds p_b and the nominal exchange rate s and they are based (as explained in Chiarella and Flaschel [1999b] and also in this chapter) on heterogeneous expectations of the pure wealth owners of the model. Note that, as in the larger model, the dynamics of equity prices and of Tobin's q are not needed in the investigation of the core dynamics of the model.

Next, the dynamic policy rules are presented which are basically the same as in the larger model. Note however that we have removed the derivative term from the right-hand side of the wage tax rate dynamics (6.28) to obtain (6.108).

5. The Feedback Policy Rules (three laws of motion):

$$\dot{i} = -\beta_{i_i}(i - i_l^*) + \beta_{i_p}(\hat{p}_y - 0) + \beta_{i_u}(y/y^p - \bar{u}), \tag{6.107}$$

$$\hat{\tau}_w = \alpha_{\tau_{w1}}(d/\bar{d} - 1), \quad \left(d = \frac{b + b^l/i_l}{y^e}\right), \tag{6.108}$$

$$\hat{\tau}_m = \alpha_{\tau_m} \frac{p_x x - p_m j^d}{p_x x}. \tag{6.109}$$

Summing up we have thus arrived at an 18D dynamical system by setting certain adjustment speeds equal to infinity or equal to zero, by cutting certain feedback effects of the individual distribution of bonds on aggregate demand (based on the facts that $C_c = 0$ holds and that workers save all their interest income), and by assuming constant 'natural' rates of growth as well as of employment. Note that the housing services sector feeds back into this core dynamics of the model through the investment demand for dwellings (on the market for domestic goods) and through its rate of return which is in particular determined by the law of motion for the rent price of housing services.

6.5.2 *Static relationships*

As abbreviations and static relationships we now have the following reduced and modified list of equations underlying this 18D dynamical system.

1. Output and Demand:

$$y^d = c_w^o + g_k^d + g_h^d k_h + g y^e, \tag{6.110}$$

$$c_w^o = c_y y_{w1}^D, \tag{6.111}$$

$$c_h^{do} = p_v c_h y_{w1}^D / p_h, \tag{6.112}$$

$$y = y^e + \beta_n(\beta_{n^d} y^e - \nu) + \gamma \beta_{n^d} y^e, \tag{6.113}$$

$$x = x_y y, \tag{6.114}$$

$$j^d = j_y y. \tag{6.115}$$

2. Employment and Labour Supply:

$$l_f^{de} = l_y y, \tag{6.116}$$

$$l_g^{de} = l_g^{we} = \alpha_g g y^e, \tag{6.117}$$

$$l^{de} = l_f^{de} + l_g^{de}, \tag{6.118}$$

$$l^{we} = l_f^{we} + l_g^{we}, \tag{6.119}$$

$$l_2^e = (L_2(0)/L_1(0)) l_1^e = (L_2(0)/L_1(0)) l^e / \alpha_l. \tag{6.120}$$

3. Growth Rates of the Capital Stocks of Firms and Asset Owners:

$$g_k^d = \alpha_1^k((1-\tau_c)r^e - i^r) + \alpha_2^k(i_l - i) + \alpha_3^k(y/y^p - \bar{u}) + \gamma + \delta_k, \tag{6.121}$$

$$g_h^d = \alpha_r^h((1-\tau_c)r_h - i^r) + \alpha_i^h(i_l - i) + \alpha_u^h\left(\frac{c_h^d}{k_h} - \bar{u}_h\right) + \gamma + \delta_h. \tag{6.122}$$

4. Rates of Return:

$$r^e = y^e - \delta_k + (p_x/p_y)x - (w^{be}/p_y) l_f^{de} - (p_m/p_y) j^d, \tag{6.123}$$

$$i^r = (1-\tau_c)i_l - \pi^c, \tag{6.124}$$

$$r_h = (p_h/p_y)c_h^{do}/k_h - \delta_h. \tag{6.125}$$

5. Prices, Wages and Transfers:

$$p_x = sp_x^*, \tag{6.126}$$

$$p_m = (1+\tau_m)sp_m^*, \tag{6.127}$$

$$w^{be} = (1+\tau_p)w^e, \tag{6.128}$$

$$w^{ue} = \alpha^u w^e, \tag{6.129}$$

$$w^{re} = \alpha^r w^e, \tag{6.130}$$

$$p_v = (1+\tau_v)p_y. \tag{6.131}$$

6. Disposable Income of Workers and Taxes Per Value Unit of Capital:

$$y_{w1}^D = (1-\tau_w)[w^e l^{de} + w^{ue}(l^e - l^{we}) + w^{re}\alpha_l l_2^e]/p_v, \tag{6.132}$$

$$y_w^D = y_{w1}^D + (1-\tau_c)ib_w, \tag{6.133}$$

$$t^w = \tau_w[w^e l^{de} + w^{ue}(l^e - l^{we}) + w^{re}\alpha_l l_2^e]/p_v + \tau_p(w^e/p_v)l^{de} + \tau_v(p_y/p_v)(y^d - g_k^d - g_h^d k_h) + \tau_m sp_m^* j^d/p_v, \tag{6.134}$$

$$t^c = \tau_c[r^e(p_y/p_v) + ib + b^l + (p_h/p_v)c_h^d - (p_y/p_v)\delta_h k_h]. \tag{6.135}$$

The steady state of the model is the same as in the preceding section. The dimension of this dynamical system can be further reduced, to dimension 16, if the housing sector is removed from the model.

6.6 Outlook: feedback structures and stability issues

We have presented a structural model of disequilibrium growth which is fairly complete with respect to markets, sectors and agents. We believe it is sufficiently detailed to capture the essential dynamic features of modern macroeconomies, while at the same time abstracting from the welter of detail that inevitably must characterise large-scale macroeconometric models such as the Fair model for the US economy or the Murphy model for the Australian economy.

We considered the model from the point of view of national accounts, and then discussed the development of its extensive form and finally expressed its dynamic structure in terms of intensive form state variables. We saw in particular that in intensive form we are dealing with a 34D dynamical system. We further found that with a small number of further assumptions (concerning consumption of asset holders and certain secondary delayed adjustment processes) the dynamics reduce to an 18D dynamical system which we call the core model.

There turn out to be eight main partial feedback mechanisms contained in the 18D core model. First, the labour and goods market interaction, the tendency of which to become destabilising is determined by an interplay between wage and price flexibility. Second, the expected sales and inventory accumulation interaction. The tendency to instability of this mechanism is determined by the relative values of speeds of adjustment of expected sales and inventory changes. Third, the dynamics of the housing sector are determined largely by the strength of investment into this sector and the speed of adjustment of the prices for housing services. This partial feedback mechanism is always stabilising. Fourth, the dynamic interaction between the level of economic activity and the nominal interest rate (the so-called Keynes effect). The stabilising/destabilising tendency of this mechanism is very dependent on the sensitivity of the nominal interest rate to the price level. We note that when considered in conjunction with the Taylor-style interest rate rule used in our model this mechanism is by and large stabilising. Fifth, the inflation/expected inflation mechanism. This is essentially a destabilising effect (associated with the names of Mundell and Cagan) determined by the interplay of speeds of adjustment of prices and inflationary expectations. Sixth, the bond and stock market dynamics (originally considered by Blanchard (1981)), first in isolation and then in their interaction, are driven by rates of return and expectations feedback. The mainly destabilising tendency of this mechanism is driven by the speeds of adjustment of bond prices and expectations of bond price inflation. Seventh, the dynamics of the GBR. This mechanism, when considered in isolation, is stabilising provided the rate of growth of government debt is restricted in certain ways. Eighth, the exchange rate/expected exchange rate (Dornbusch) mechanism where stabilising/destabilising tendencies essentially depend upon the relationship between the speed of adjustment of exchange rates and exchange rate expectations.

The 18D core model of this chapter has been studied in a series of papers; see Chiarella and Flaschel (1999b,c,d), Chiarella *et al.* (1999a,b, 2003b). These papers discuss the feedback structure of the 18D core dynamics in great detail with respect to the partial stabilising or destabilising feedback chains that are present. They also present further numerical investigations of the model both from the local and the global point of view (adding also extrinsic non-linearities in order to achieve global boundedness) and extending the theoretical basis of the disequilibrium growth model employed so far (by allowing for smooth input and output substitution and other flexibilities).

Prototype subdynamics of the 18D system which are often discussed in the literature in isolation, and which we have briefly discussed above, will be derived and analysed in subsequent chapters. The current chapter provides more insights into the stability properties of the 18D dynamics by investigating the partial feedback chains it contains (often well known from comparative static analysis) with respect to the partial dynamics to which they give rise. The interaction of these partial dynamics has been studied in Chiarella *et al.* (2003b), there basically from the numerical point of view as in Barnett and He (1999) who as we have seen in Section 6.1, use a 14D second order dynamical representation of the UK economy to study the bifurcation loci to which such a model type can give rise.

We close this chapter by giving a graphical representation of the disequilibrium growth approach that will be considered in the subsequent discussion on the intensive form level. Figure 6.1 shows the various points we wish to stress in this book in different fonts. The figure presents as a starting point the basic market hierarchy of Keynes' (1936) General Theory as we interpret it. This view asserts that asset markets dominate (in a casino-like fashion) the outcome in the real markets basically by way of the investment decision of firms that here still simply depend on financial markets and the structure of nominal interest rates that they generate, but does not exercise a feedback influence on them. Effective demand (with a Metzlerian feedback mechanism included) that derives from the investment decision determines the outcome on the market for goods which is therefore purely demand determined. Finally, at the lowest level of the hierarchy, there are the labour markets which just have to accept the amount of employment that is generated by (expected) goods demand and the technology with which firms produce their demand determined supply of goods (including intended inventory changes).

This 'prejudice' on the fundamental macroeconomic forces that may (or may not) shape the temporary equilibrium position of the economy represents in our view a way of thinking that allows one to approach the full situation in a systematic hierarchically ordered way, and which does not just state that everything depends on everything else as far as financial decisions, and quantity and price determination, are concerned. Of course, one has to address the question of which feedback mechanisms have to be added to this picture (and those which may be left aside due to their minor importance) and in what way they would alter the temporary equilibrium position (or its evolution) as determined by the fundamental 'causal nexus' from the asset market to the labour market shown by the grey boxes in Figure 6.1. Therefore, the proposed feedback mechanisms (or repercussions) have to be discussed as to their importance for full employment positions or (if they work with a delay) as to their role as a stabilising or destabilising mechanism in the evolution of the temporary equilibrium positions of the economy. Of course, there may be feedback mechanisms of great importance that are still missing in Figure 6.1. An example for this is given by the Fisher debt effect relating firms with households or banks which is still missing in our model due to the limited (supply side oriented) treatment of asset markets and the financial decisions made by firms.[12] By contrast, it may be questioned whether for example the Keynes short-term interest rate effect on investment or the Pigou effect on consumption demand are really of importance in the picture of the real and financial interaction shown by the black portions in Figure 6.1. There are also feedback mechanisms that are internal to the asset markets and that may create cumulative processes in them that are bounded by certain switches in expectational regimes.

An important controversial aspect of Figure 6.1 is given by its presentation of supply side influences. In our view this is basically the question of the wage-price interaction (including expectations) which should be approached from the viewpoint of a separate

[12] Note however that we have a Fisher debt effect in the present model as far as the sector of households is concerned where we can have the situation that workers with a high marginal propensity to consume become debtors to asset holders (with a low or zero marginal propensity to consume) which in this way implies that consumption will be depressed in deflationary periods and will accelerate in periods of inflation.

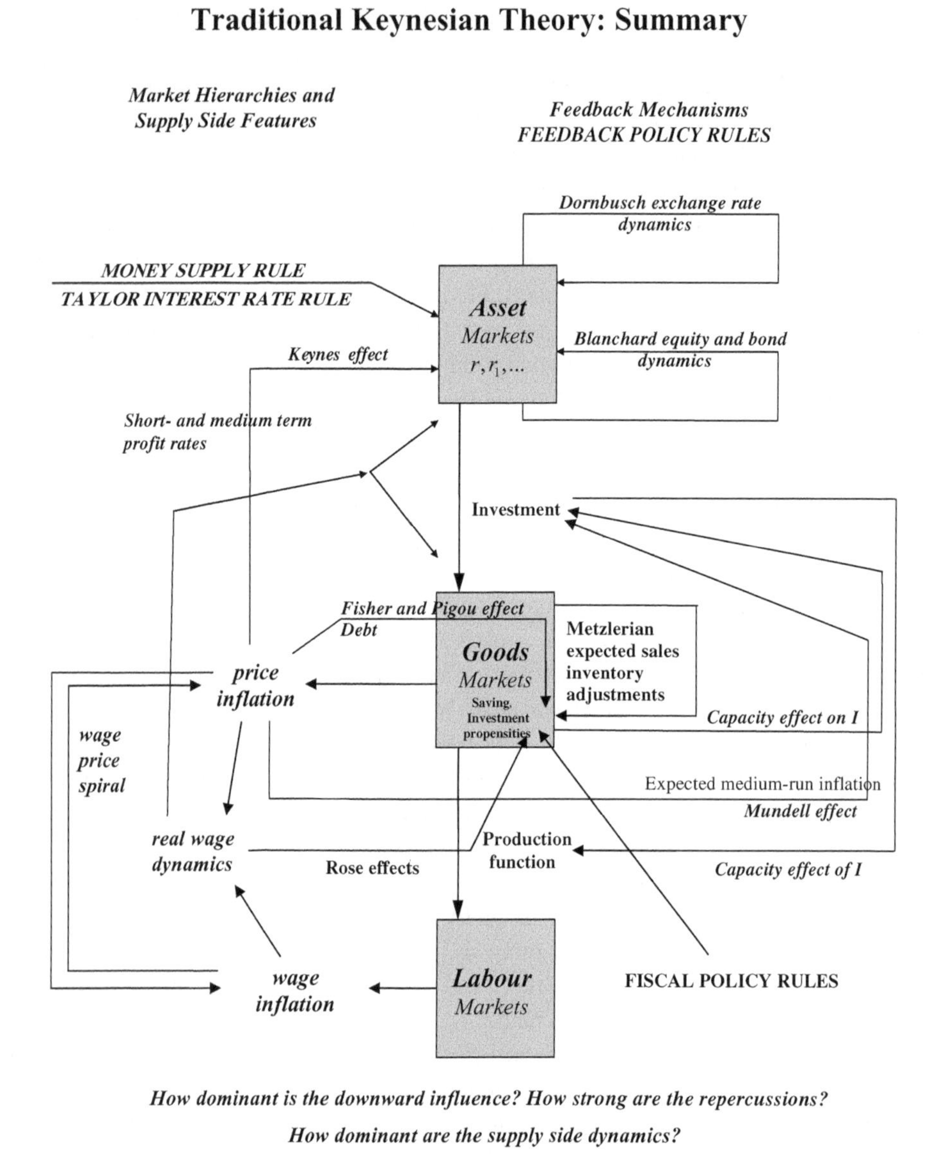

Figure 6.1 Advanced traditional disequilibrium growth dynamics: graphical summary. Different fonts and shading represent the market hierarchies, supply side features, feedback mechanisms and feedback policy rules

treatment of Phillips curves (PCs), one for the nominal wage and one for the price level. Such an approach allows the analysis to escape from the narrow perspective of a unique monetarist type of expectations augmented price inflation labour market PC which does not really allow for the discussion of wage-price spirals, which is needed in a full approach to disequilibrium growth where both labour and capital can be over- or under-utilised. Such a view on the working of the wage-price mechanism, which allows for a sluggish adjustment of both of these nominal magnitudes, will include Rose (1967) effects in the interaction of the goods and the labour markets, which generally imply that either wage or price flexibility will lead to instability in the process that is usually considered as the medium run of macrodynamic model building.

Finally we assume that certain policy feedback rules interact with the dynamics of the private sector. Such rules are present in the approach investigated in the present chapter, but are not yet at the centre of interest in the present stage of the investigation.

Figure 6.1 therefore summarises and contrasts the main substructures we have introduced in greater detail in Chiarella *et al.* (1999a,b) and which we describe on the intensive form level in this chapter and also investigate further in subsequent chapters. At the bottom of Figure 6.1 we also see a summary of the main questions that should find some answers in the course of the investigations of this general approach to disequilibrium growth. First, we have the question to what extent the asset markets dominate the outcome of the real/financial interaction (which, as we shall see, is here still of a very particular type and thus demands further extensions of the model if the dynamics of asset prices are to be linked more closely to the stocks supplied and demanded on these markets). Second, there is the question as to what the various feedback mechanisms shown add to the real/financial interaction and to what extent they will contribute to or undermine, when working together, the local stability of the balanced growth solution(s) of the model. Third, the dynamics of income distribution, as they find expression in the wage-price spiral, have to be investigated, in particular in their role of shaping the long-run outcome of this model which has a strictly Keynesian short-run outcome. Finally, the perspective of our approach is of course to contribute to the analysis of policy issues which due to the fact that we want to treat medium- and long-run dynamics as well is more oriented to the treatment of monetary policy rules than to a treatment of the consequences of isolated fiscal or monetary shocks that occur only once in time. In the present chapter we have only set the stage for such investigations, while subsequent work is needed, starting from special cases of the model as in Chiarella *et al.* (2003b), in order to understand in a systematic way the implications that are contained in our approach to disequilibrium growth.

7 Partial feedback structures and stability issues

7.1 Introduction

In this chapter we continue the analysis of our applied structural model of disequilibrium growth initiated in Chiarella and Flaschel (1999b,c,d). In those earlier papers we developed a model of disequilibrium growth which is fairly complete with respect to markets, agents and sectors and consistent with respect to the various budget constraints between them. We showed in Chiarella and Flaschel (1999b,c,d) that the model could be expressed as a dynamical system of 34D intensive state variables together with a number of static relationships. We further showed how a small number of not unreasonable simplifying assumptions reduced this dynamical system to one of eighteen laws of motion solely, which we have dubbed the core model of this approach with fixed proportions in production. Our aim in this, and in the next two chapters, is to analyse in quite some detail the properties of this 18D core model. In this chapter in particular we focus on the basic partial feedback structures of the core model and their stability characteristics.

We can distinguish qualitatively at least seven important feedback chains (plus stabilising or destabilising policy reaction functions), which we will describe below in isolation from each other. These will of course interact with each other in the full 18D dynamics of the core model, so that one or another may become dominant when the parameters of the model are chosen appropriately.[1]

The structure of the chapter is as follows: Section 7.2 describes the accounts of the various agents of our modelling framework. In Section 7.3 we summarise the special 18D case of the preceding chapter from the perspective of the various accounts of the sectors of our structural macroeconometric model of Chapter 5. In Section 7.4 we then briefly recapitulate the obtained 18D core dynamics subject to the 'scissor and paste' methodology we use in the present chapter to study the feedback chains it contains. In Section 7.4 and Section 7.5 we then start the investigation of the partial feedback mechanisms contained in the core dynamics of our model by isolating the dynamic

[1] To simplify the presentations in this chapter we assume in the following without loss of generality $\tau_c = 0$, $\xi = 0$, $c_c = 0$; see the following compact representation of the 18D core dynamics.

interaction of income distribution with various measures of economic activity on the market for labour and for goods which will push income distribution in favour of labour or of asset holders depending on marginal propensities to demand goods for consumption and investment purposes and on the speeds of adjustment of nominal wages and prices in the market for labour and goods, respectively. This multi-faceted feedback mechanism is related to early (and later) work of Rose; see Rose (1966, 1990) in particular, and also to Goodwin's (1967) growth cycle model, but there in a less multi-faceted way due to the simpler real wage mechanism of this model type. Goodwin's (1967) growth cycle model nevertheless constitutes the core dynamics that, married with goods market adjustment processes, will provide the basic 5D situation from which our numerical analysis of the model of Chiarella *et al.* (2003b) will start.

In Section 7.6 we consider the Metzlerian inventory mechanism describing the dynamic interaction of expected sales and inventory accumulation. We also discuss in this section a certain non-linearity (in the adjustment speed of inventories) which can 'tame' the instabilities that this mechanism is capable of generating. Section 7.7 discusses the dynamics of the housing sector, while Section 7.8 analyses the well-known Keynes effect which describes the interaction between economic activity and the nominal interest rate. Section 7.9 describes the Mundell–Tobin mechanism of the interaction between inflation and expected inflation, and discusses how an interest rate policy rule may help to overcome this largely destabilising adjustment process.

Section 7.10 outlines the infrequently discussed Blanchard mechanism for the dynamic adjustments on, and the dynamic interaction between, bond and stock markets. This section also discusses some non-linear mechanisms which can tame the rapid tendency to instability in the price dynamics of long-term bonds (or equities). Section 7.11 describes the dynamics of the government budget constraint, which, unlike in other studies and due to the assumptions made, we find to be locally stabilising at least when considered in isolation. Section 7.12 considers briefly the dynamics of import taxation. Section 7.13 discusses in some detail the Dornbusch mechanism for the dynamic interaction between the exchange rate and expectations of its appreciation (or depreciation), identifying the factors leading to stability and instability of this mechanism. Section 7.14 draws some conclusions and points to future directions in the research agenda initiated by this chapter.

7.2 National accounting (in intensive form)

The structure of the considered economy from the viewpoint of national accounting is shown in Table 7.1 (everything being measured in nominal domestic currency units per gross value of the capital stock).

7.2.1 Firms

The firms produce two kinds of output, the pure export good which is tradable only on the world market and the domestic good which can only be sold in the domestic

Table 7.1. *The accounts of firms*

Uses	Resources
Production Account of Firms:	
Imports $sp_m^* j^d / p_v$	Consumption c_g^o
Depreciation $\delta_k p_y / p_v$	–
Value-added Taxes $\tau_v(c_g^o + g)p_y/p_v$	Consumption g
Taxes on Imports $\tau_m sp_m^* j^d / p_v$	Exports $sp_x^* x / p_v$
Wages (excluding payroll taxes) $w^e/p_v l_f^{de}$	Gross Investment $g_k^d p_y/p_v$
Payroll Taxes $\tau_p w^e / p_v l_f^{de}$	Durables (Dwellings) $g_h^d p_y / p_v$
Profits $(r^e + \mathcal{I}/K)p_y/p_v$	Inventory Investment $p_y \dot{N}/(p_v K) = p_y(y - y^d)/p_v$
Income Account of Firms:	
Dividends $r^e p_y / p_v$	Profits $(r^e + \mathcal{I}/K)p_y/p_v$
Savings $\mathcal{I}/K p_y/p_v$	
Accumulation Account of Firms:	
Gross Investment $g_k^d p_y / p_v$	Depreciation $\delta_k p_y / p_v$
Inventory Investment $\dot{N}/K p_y / p_v$	Savings $S_f^n/(p_v K)$
	Financial Deficit $FD/(p_v K)$
Financial Account of Firms:	
Financial Deficit $FD/(p_v K)$	Equity Financing $p_e \dot{E}/(p_v K)$

economy. The domestic good serves as the consumption good for the workforce and the government (in our simplified 18D dynamical version of the model). It can also be used for investment in inventories, in business fixed capital and in housing. Firms use three kinds of inputs for their production: imports, capital and labour. The capital stock in the sector of firms depreciates by a given rate δ_k. Value-added taxes (on consumption goods solely) appear on the left side of the production account and have to be paid to the government. The balance of this account is the profit of the sector of firms. Note that all expressions are in intensive form (they have all been measured in domestic currency units in Chiarella and Flaschel (1999b,c,d)) and are here divided uniformly by $p_v K$, the value of the capital stock (including value-added taxation by assumption).[2] We stress that the profits are not subject to any direct tax. By assumption profits are only used to be paid as dividends to asset holders (and then taxed) or to be used for planned inventory investments. One can clearly see this in the income account. The accumulation account displays again that investments in business fixed capital and in inventories are the only stocks which can be accumulated by firms. There is no

[2] Note that all investment and thus also the value of the capital stock and the measure of the rate of profit based on it are in prices p_y net of value-added tax, since these taxes are only applied to consumption purchases and not to investment purchases in the present model. Note also that the following uniform intensive form representation of the model does not immediately apply to the structural form of the model in intensive form, since we do not need accounting homogeneity in this structural form as is necessary in the present subsection.

possibility of accumulating financial stocks, that is no holding of bonds by firms in the present context. The financial deficit of firms must be financed in our present model by selling new equities. This assumption is of course not very realistic, and thus should be modified in future reconsideration of the model to allow in particular for bond financing and loans of firms.

7.2.2 Asset holders

While firms produce and sell two types of goods, the sector of the private asset holders sells dwelling services. Hence there is a production account for this sector. The income of this sector consists of interest payments (long- and short-term bonds, the former also from abroad), dividend payments from the sector of firms and the profits from selling dwelling services. This income is reduced through profit income taxation. The remaining amount is the saving of this sector (since asset holders do not consume in the 18D core dynamics of our general model to be considered in this chapter). Savings plus depreciation is split into gross investment in housing and the financial surplus in the following account. The financial surplus is distributed by asset owners to all kinds of financial assets that exist in our model. See Table 7.2 for the accounts of asset holders.[3]

7.2.3 Workers

This sector does not take part in private ownership production, but only provides the labour input for firms. Therefore the production account remains empty. The income account includes wages, unemployment benefits and pensions. Workers' income is allocated to income taxes and consumption and savings. All savings is allocated to short-term bonds. See Table 7.3 for the accounts of workers.

7.2.4 Fiscal and monetary authorities

The government sector's production account takes up the costless provision of public goods which is defined to be identical to consumption of the government. In order to provide the economy with public goods the government has to buy goods and pay wages to the workers it employs.

The only sources of income for the government are the various taxes, which are used for interest payments, pensions, unemployment benefits and salaries. The balance of this account are the savings of the government. Generally these savings are negative, hence there is a financial deficit in the accumulation account, rather than a financial surplus in general.

In financial accounting of the government one can see the sources from which the deficit is financed, namely by issuing short- and long-term bonds. See Table 7.4.

[3] Expressions such as $\hat{B}b(=\dot{B}/(p_v K))$ are used to indicate the way the law of motion, of here $b=B/(p_v K)$, has to be derived.

Table 7.2. *Accounts of households (asset owners)*

Uses	Resources
Production Account of Households (Asset Owners/Housing Investment):	
Depreciation $\delta_h k_h p_y / p_v$	Rent $p_h c_h^o / p_v$
Earnings $\Pi_h / (p_v K)$	
Income Account of Households (Asset Owners):	
Tax Payment $\tau_c i b$	Interest Payment ib
Tax Payment $\tau_c b_1^l$	Interest Payment b_1^l
Taxes $\tau_c (p_h c_h^o / p_v - \delta_h k_h p_y / p_v)$	Interest Payment $s(1 - \tau_c^*) b_2^l$
Tax Payment $\tau_c r^e p_y / p_v$	Dividend Payment $r^e p_y / p_v$
Savings $S_c^n / (p_v K)$	Earnings $\Pi_h / (p_v K)$
Accumulation Account of Households (Asset Owners):	
Gross Investment $g_h^d p_y / p_v$	Depreciation $\delta_h k_h p_y / p_v$
Financial Surplus $FS / (p_v K)$	Savings $S_c^n / (p_v K)$
Financial Account of Households (Asset Owners):	
Short-term Bonds $\hat{B} b$	Financial Surplus $FS / (p_v K)$
Long-term Bonds $p_b \hat{B}_1^l b_1^l$	
Foreign Bonds $s \hat{B}_2^l b_2^l / i_l^*$	
Equities $p_e \hat{E} \varepsilon$	

Table 7.3. *Accounts of households (workers)*

Uses	Resources
Production Account of Households (Workers):	
–	–
Income Account of Households (Workers):	
Taxes $\tau_w [w^e l^{de} + w^{ue}(l^e - l^{we}) + w^{re} l_2^e] / p_v$	Wages $w^e l^{de} / p_v = (w^e l_f^{de} + w^e l_g^{de}) / p_v$
Consumption $c_g^o + p_h c_h^o / p_v$	Unemployment Benefits $w^{ue}(l^e - l^{we}) / p_v$
Savings $S_w^n / (p_v K)$	Pensions $w^{re} l_2^e / p_v$
Accumulation Account of Households (Workers):	
Financial Surplus $FS / (p_v K)$	Savings $S_w^n / (p_v K)$
Financial Account of Households (Workers):	
Short-term Bond Accumulation $\hat{B}_w b_w$	Financial Surplus $FS / (p_v K)$

7.2.5 International relationships

The external account contains all transactions with the foreign countries. It exhibits the amounts of goods, capital and interest payments that cross the borders. See Table 7.5. This closes this section on the national accounts of the model that will be investigated numerically in the following sections.

Table 7.4. *Accounts of the fiscal and monetary authorities*

Uses	Resources
Production Account of Fiscal and Monetary Authorities:	
Government Expenditure for Goods g	Costless Provision of
Salaries $w^{be}l_g^{de}/p_v = (w^e l_g^{de} + \tau_p w^e l_g^{de})/p_v$	Public Goods = Self Consumption
Income Account of Fiscal and Monetary Authorities:	
Interest Payment ib	Wage Income Taxation
	$\tau_w[w^e l^{de} + w^{ue}(l^e - l^{we}) + w^{re}l_2^e]/p_v$
Interest Payment $b_1^l + b_1^{l*}$	Profit and Interest Taxation
	$\tau_c r^e p_y/p_v + \tau_c ib + \tau_c b_1^l + \tau_c b_1^{l*}$
Pensions $w^{re}l_2^e/p_v$	Rent Income Taxation $\tau_c(p_h c_h^o/p_v - \delta_h k_h p_y/p_v)$
Unemployment benefits $w^{ue}(l^e - l^{we})/p_v$	Payroll Taxes $(\tau_p w^e l_f^{de} + \tau_p w^e l_g^{de})/p_v$
Self consumption g	Value-added Tax $\tau_v(c_g^o + g)p_y/p_v$
Savings $S_g^n/(p_v K)$	Import Taxes $\tau_m s p_m^* j^d/p_v$
Accumulation Account of the Fiscal Authority:	
	Savings $S_g^n/(p_v K)$
	Financial Deficit $FD/(p_v K)$
Financial Account of Fiscal and Monetary Authorities:	
Financial deficit $FD/(p_v K)$	Short-term Debt $\hat{B}b$
	Long-term Debt $\hat{B}^l b^l/i_l$

Table 7.5. *International relationships*

Uses	Resources
External Account:	
Exports $sp_x^* x/p_v$	Imports $sp_m^* j^d/p_v$
Factor Income from Abroad $s(1-\tau_c^*)b_2^l$	Factor Income to Abroad $(1-\tau_c)b_1^{l*}$
Capital Imports $\hat{B}_1^{l*}b_1^{l*}/i_l$	Capital Exports $s\hat{B}_2^l b_2^l/i_l^*$

7.3 The core 18D dynamical system: a recapitulation

We will base our subsequent numerical investigation of the 18D core model of Chiarella and Flaschel (1999b,c,d) in this chapter on the following condensed form of its eighteen laws of motion (which is the one used for the simulations reported below) and the unique interior steady state that this dynamical model exhibits (up to the level of nominal magnitudes). In order to simplify the notation to some degree we modify the model of the previous chapters by assuming in the following for the risk and liquidity premium $\xi = 0$ and thus will have $r^e = i = i_l = i_{l*}$ in the steady state. For the same reason we also assume for the normal employment rate $\bar{u}_f^w = 1$, and also $C_c = 0$, thus there is no consumption goods demand of asset holders who thus save all of their income. All these assumptions have only slight influences on the steady state position of the economy, and do not alter at all the dynamics around the steady state.

We consider the steady state values of the model first. All these values should have an index 'o' (denoting their steady state character). In order not to overload the notation, we do not add this index to the list of steady state values (7.1)–(7.18). Note again that all steady state values are expressed in per unit of capital form and if necessary in efficiency units:

$$y^e = \frac{y^p\bar{u}}{1+\gamma\beta_{n^d}}, \quad [y = y^p\bar{u}], \tag{7.1}$$

$$\nu = \beta_{n^d} y^e, \tag{7.2}$$

$$l_f^{we} = l_f^{de} = l_y y^p \bar{u} \quad [\text{total employment: } l^{we} = l_f^{we} + l_g^{we}, l_g^{we} = \alpha_g g y^e], \tag{7.3}$$

$$l^e = (l_f^{we} + \alpha_g g y^e)/\bar{e}, \tag{7.4}$$

$$p_y = \frac{p_v}{1+\tau_v}, \quad [p_v \quad \text{arbitrarily given}], \tag{7.5}$$

$$w^e = \frac{\omega^{be} p_y}{1+\tau_p}, \quad \left[\omega^{be} = \frac{w^e}{p_y} = \frac{y^e - \delta_k - i_l^*}{l_f^{we}}\right], \tag{7.6}$$

$$\pi^c = 0, \tag{7.7}$$

$$p_h = p_y(i_l^* + \delta_h)/\bar{u}_h, \tag{7.8}$$

$$k_h = \frac{c_h(y^e(1-g) - (\gamma + \delta_k))}{c_y(i_l^* + \delta_h)/(1+\tau_v) + (\gamma + \delta_h)c_h}, \tag{7.9}$$

$$b = \alpha_b^g \bar{d} y^e, \tag{7.10}$$

$$b^l = i_l^*(1 - \alpha_b^g)\bar{d} y^e, \tag{7.11}$$

$$p_b = 1/i_l^*, \tag{7.12}$$

$$\pi_{bs} = 0, \tag{7.13}$$

$$\epsilon_s = 0, \tag{7.14}$$

$$i = i_l^* \quad [= r^e], \tag{7.15}$$

$$\tau_m = \frac{p_x^* x_y - p_m^* j_y}{p_m^* j_y}, \tag{7.16}$$

$$\tau_w = 1 - \frac{p_h \bar{u}_h k_h}{c_h(1+\tau_v) p_y y_{w1}}, \tag{7.17}$$

$$s = \frac{s_o - [\tau_w y_{w1} + \frac{\tau_p}{1+\tau_v}\frac{w^e}{p_y} l^{we} + \frac{\tau_v}{1+\tau_v}(y^e - (\gamma + \delta_k) - (\gamma + \delta_h)k_h)]}{\tau_m p_m^* j_y y/((1+\tau_v)p_y)}. \tag{7.18}$$

With respect to the last two of the above equations, for the taxation rate τ_w and for the rate of exchange s of the model, we have to apply (besides the above definitions of y, l^{we} and ω^{be}, see the above) the further defining expressions

$$c_h^o = \bar{u}_h k_h,$$

$$t_o^c = \tau_c[i_l^*/(1+\tau_v) + ib + b^l + (p_h/p_y)c_h^o/(1+\tau_v) - \delta_h k_h/(1+\tau_v)],$$

$$s_o = gy^e + ib + b^l - t_o^c + \frac{w^e}{(1+\tau_v)p_y}[\alpha^u(l^e - l^{we}) + \alpha^r L_2(0)/L_1(0)l^e]$$

$$+ (1+\tau_p)\frac{w^e}{(1+\tau_v)p_y}\alpha_g g y^e - \frac{\gamma b}{\alpha_b^g},$$

$$y_{w1} = w^e[l^{we} + \alpha^u(l^e - l^{we}) + \alpha^r L_2(0)/L_1(0)l^e]/((1+\tau_v)p_y)$$

in order to have a determination of the steady state that is complete.

Note that the value of the exchange rate s will be indeterminate when we have $\tau_m = 0$ in the steady state, in which case the above formula for s cannot be applied. Note furthermore that the parameters of the model have to be chosen such that k_h, τ_w, s are all positive in the steady state.[4] Note finally that the parameter α_s must always be larger than $1 - 1/\beta_x$ for $x = p_b, s, p^e$ in order to satisfy the restrictions established in Chiarella and Flaschel (1999b,c,d).

Equation (7.1) gives expected sales per unit of capital K, while equation (7.2) provides the steady inventory-capital ratio N/K. Equation (7.3) provides the amount of workforce employed by the firms which in the steady state is equal to the hours worked by this workforce (assuming that the normal working day or week is represented by 1). It also shows total employment per K where account is taken of the employment in the government sector in addition. Equation (7.4) is the full employment labour intensity. Equation (7.5) provides the price level (net of value-added tax) and equation (7.6) gives the wage level (net of payroll taxes) based on the steady state value for the real wage ω^{be}. The steady state value of the inflation rate expected to hold over the medium run is zero, since the inflationary target of the central bank is zero.

Next we have the price level for housing rents (in equation (7.8)) and the stock of houses per unit of the capital stock K (in equation (7.9)). There follows the steady state value of $b = B/(p_v K)$ as well as the one for long-term domestic bonds. The price of these bonds is given by the given price $1/i_l^*$ of foreign long-term bonds in the steady state; see equation (7.12). The steady state value of the short-term rate of interest settles at its long-run equivalent as there is no risk or liquidity premium allowed for.

Import taxes τ_m just balance the trade balance in the steady state, see equation (7.16), while the wage tax rate τ_w must be calculated from gross steady wage income y_{w1} and the marginal propensity to spend for housing services, see equation (7.17). Equation

[4] There are further simple restrictions on the parameters of the model due to the economic meaning of the variables employed.

(7.18), finally, provides the steady state value of the rate of exchange which depends on nearly all parameters of the model, due to the definitional terms shown (to be inserted into the expression for s shown in equation (7.18)).

Next we present the eighteen laws of motion of our dynamical system which have been derived in Chiarella and Flaschel (1999b,c,d) and which of course also make use of the state variables we have just discussed.

Making use of the formula

$$\Delta\hat{p}_y = \hat{p}_y - \pi^c = \kappa[\kappa_p(\beta_{w_e}(e-\bar{e}) + \beta_{w_u}(l_f^{de}/l_f^{we} - 1)) + \beta_p(y/y^p - \bar{u})]$$

for the deviation of the actual inflation rate from the expected one, the laws of motion around the above steady state solutions of the dynamics read as

$$\dot{y}^e = \beta_{y^e}(y^d - y^e) + (\gamma - (g_k^d - \delta_k))y^e, \tag{7.19}$$

$$\dot{\nu} = y - y^d - (g_k^d - \delta_k)\nu, \tag{7.20}$$

$$\dot{l}_f^{we} = \beta_l(l_f^{de} - l_f^{we}) + [\gamma - (g_k^d - \delta_k)]l_f^{we}, \tag{7.21}$$

$$\hat{l}^e = \gamma - (g_k^d - \delta_k), \tag{7.22}$$

$$\hat{w}^e = \pi^c + \kappa[\beta_{w_e}(l^{we}/l^e - \bar{e}) + \beta_{w_u}(l_f^{de}/l_f^{we} - 1) + \kappa_w\beta_p(y/y^p - \bar{u})], \tag{7.23}$$

$$\hat{p}_y = \pi^c + \kappa[\kappa_p(\beta_{w_e}(l^{we}/l^e - \bar{e}) + \beta_{w_u}(l_f^{de}/l_f^{we} - 1)) + \beta_p(y/y^p - \bar{u})], \tag{7.24}$$

$$\dot{\pi}^c = \beta_{\pi^c}(\alpha_{\pi^c}\Delta\hat{p}_y + (1-\alpha_{\pi^c})(0 - \pi^c)), \tag{7.25}$$

$$\hat{p}_h = \beta_h\left(\frac{c_h^o}{k_h} - \bar{u}_h\right) + \kappa_h\Delta\hat{p}_y + \pi^c, \tag{7.26}$$

$$\hat{k}_h = g_h^d - \delta_h - (g_k^d - \delta_k), \tag{7.27}$$

$$\dot{b} = \alpha_b^g[gy^e + ib + b^l - t^a - t^c + g^a] - (\Delta\hat{p}_y + \pi^c + g_k^d - \delta_k)b, \tag{7.28}$$

$$\begin{aligned}\dot{b}^l &= (1-\alpha_b^g)/p_b[gy^e + ib + b^l - t^a - t^c + g^a]\\ &\quad - (\Delta\hat{p}_y + \pi^c + g_k^d - \delta_k)b^l,\end{aligned} \tag{7.29}$$

$$\hat{p}_b = \frac{\beta_{p_b}}{1-\beta_{p_b}(1-\alpha_s)}[(1-\tau_c)i_l + \alpha_s\pi_{bs} - (1-\tau_c)i], \quad i_l = 1/p_b, \tag{7.30}$$

$$\dot{\pi}_{bs} = \beta_{\pi_{bs}}(\hat{p}_b - \pi_{bs}), \tag{7.31}$$

$$\dot{i} = -\beta_{i_i}(i - i_l^*) + \beta_{i_p}(\Delta\hat{p}_y + \pi^c) + \beta_{i_u}(y/y^p - \bar{u}), \tag{7.32}$$

$$\hat{\tau}_m = \alpha_{\tau_m}\frac{p_x^*x - (1+\tau_m)p_m^*j^d}{p_x^*x}, \quad (x = x_y y,\ j^d = j_y y), \tag{7.33}$$

$$\hat{\tau}_w = \alpha_{\tau_{w1}}\left(\frac{d}{\bar{\bar{d}}} - 1\right), \quad d = \frac{b + p_b b^l}{y^e}, \tag{7.34}$$

$$\hat{s} = \frac{\beta_s}{1-\beta_s(1-\alpha_s)}[(1-\tau_c)i_l^* + \alpha_s\epsilon_s - ((1-\tau_c)i_l + \pi_b)], \quad (i_l = 1/p_b), \tag{7.35}$$

$$\dot{\epsilon}_s = \beta_{\epsilon_s}(\hat{s} - \epsilon_s). \tag{7.36}$$

These laws of motion make use of the supplementary definitions and abbreviations

$$y = y^e + \beta_n(\beta_{n^d} y^e - \nu) + \gamma\beta_{n^d} y^e,$$

$$l_f^{de} = l_y y,$$

$$l_g^{de} = l_g^{we} = \alpha_g g y^e,$$

$$l^{de} = l_f^{de} + l_g^{de},$$

$$l^{we} = l_f^{we} + l_g^{we},$$

$$y_{w1} = w^e[l^{de} + \alpha^u(l^e - l^{we}) + \alpha^r \frac{L_2(0)}{L_1(0)} l^e]/[(1+\tau_v)p_y],$$

$$c_g^o = c_y(1-\tau_w)y_{w1},$$

$$c_h^o = (1+\tau_v)p_y c_h(1-\tau_w)y_{w1}/p_h,$$

$$r^e = y^e - \delta_k + (sp_x^*/p_y)x_y y - ((1+\tau_p)w^e/p_y)l_f^{de} - ((1+\tau_m)sp_m^*/p_y)j_y y,$$

$$g_k^d = \alpha_1^k((1-\tau_c)r^e - ((1-\tau_c)i_l - \pi^c)) + \alpha_2^k(i_l - i),$$
$$+\alpha_3^k(y/y^p - \bar{u}) + \gamma + \delta_k, \quad i_l = 1/p_b,$$

$$g_h^d = \alpha_r^h((1-\tau_c)((p_h/p_y)c_h^o/k_h - \delta_h) - ((1-\tau_c)i_l - \pi^c)) + \alpha_i^h(i_l - i)$$
$$+\alpha_u^h\left(\frac{c_h^o}{k_h} - \bar{u}_h\right) + \gamma + \delta_h, \quad i_l = 1/p_b,$$

$$y^d = c_g^o + g_k^d + g_h^d k_h + g y^e,$$

$$\pi_b = \alpha_s\pi_{bs} + (1-\alpha_s)\hat{p}_b,$$

$$g^a = w^e\left[\alpha^u(l^e - l^{we}) + \alpha^r\frac{L_2(0)}{L_1(0)}l^e + (1+\tau_p)l_g^{de}\right]/(1+\tau_v)p_y,$$

$$t^a = \tau_w w^e\left[l^{de} + \alpha^u(l^e - l^{we}) + \alpha^r\frac{L_2(0)}{L_1(0)}l^e\right]/((1+\tau_v)p_y) + \tau_p w^e l^{de}/((1+\tau_v)p_y)$$
$$+\frac{\tau_v}{1+\tau_v}(y^d - g_k^d - g_h^d k_h) + \tau_m sp_m^* j_y y/((1+\tau_v)p_y),$$

$$t^c = \tau_c[r^e/(1+\tau_v) + ib + b^l + (p_h/p_y)c_h^o/(1+\tau_v) - \delta_h k_h/(1+\tau_v)].$$

Inserting these equations into the above eighteen laws of motion gives an explicit system of eighteen autonomous non-linear differential equations in the eighteen state variables (7.19)–(7.36) shown above. Note that we have to supply as initial conditions the relative magnitude $\frac{L_2(0)}{L_1(0)}$ in order to get a complete characterisation of the dynamics and that the evolution of price levels is subject to hysteresis, since it depends on historical conditions due to our assumptions on costless cash balances for the behaviour of the four agents of the model.

Our strategy for analysing the 18D core model is to discuss, in the subsequent sections of this chapter, the various partial feedback mechanisms it contains. In Chiarella *et al.* (2003b) we have considered the interaction of these partial mechanisms, and via a series of partial analyses built up to an analysis of the full 18D dynamics. We refer the reader to Chiarella *et al.* (2009b) for a more complete description of the business fluctuations and long-phased cycles that the 18D core model is capable of generating.

7.4 A Goodwin wage income/insider-outsider labour market dynamics

In order to isolate this extended feedback mechanism between functional income distribution and capital accumulation we assume for the parameter κ_w that it equals 1. Furthermore we abstract from the government sector and its employment decisions and from exports and imports and also assume that fixed business investment is simply given by $g_k^d = \alpha_1^k(r^e - \bar{i}^r) + \gamma + \delta_k$ based on the assumptions $\alpha_2^k = 0$, $y = y^p$, implying that there is no impact of interest rates on fixed business investment and firms also face no demand constraint, but produce at full capacity $Y^p = y^p K$ throughout.[5]

It is easy to show then that the law of motion of real wages ω^e is in this case given by

$$\hat{\omega}^e = \beta_{w_e}(e - \bar{e}) + \beta_{w_u}(l_f^{de}/l_f^{we} - \bar{u}_f^w),$$

so that the demand pressure on outside and inside labour markets are here the sole determinants of the dynamics of real wages (since the short-run inflation rate is fully reflected in the adjustment of money wages).[6] The obtained law of motion for real wages is easily rewritten as

$$\hat{\omega}^e = \beta_{w_e}(l^{we}/l^e - \bar{e}) + \beta_{w_u}(u_f^w - \bar{u}_f^w), \tag{7.37}$$

with $u_f^w = l_f^{de}/l_f^{we}$ ($l_f^{de} = l_y y^p$) and $e = l^{we}/l^e$. The laws of motion of these latter two variables can then be obtained from the complete model of the preceding section, in fact specifically from the equations

$$\hat{l}^e = \gamma + \delta_k - \alpha_1^k(r^e - \bar{i}^r),$$

$$\hat{l}_f^{we} = \beta_l(l_y y^p / l_f^{we} - \bar{u}_f^w) + \gamma + \delta_k - \alpha_1^k(r^e - \bar{i}^r),$$

5 Aggregate demand may and will here differ from aggregate supply, but is assumed to have effects on the rate of price inflation solely with no feedback on the growth dynamics considered below.

6 See the next section for a more complicated real wage mechanism which also takes account of the imbalance that exists in the market for goods.

with r^e given by $y^e - \delta_k - (1+\tau_p)\omega^e l_f^{de}$. After some manipulations the differential equations for u_f^w and e can be written as

$$\hat{u}_f^w = \alpha_1^k(r^e - (\gamma + \delta_k) - \bar{i}^r) - \beta_l(u_f^w - \bar{u}_f^w), \tag{7.38}$$

$$\hat{e} = \beta_l(u_f^w - \bar{u}_f^w). \tag{7.39}$$

These laws of motion basically represent the assumed investment behaviour and the employment policy of firms which indeed influence both of these dynamics. On the basis of the above assumptions we thus obtain a 3D dynamical system in the state variables ω^e, u_f^w, e, of the real wage in efficiency units, of the rate of employment of the employed and of the outside rate of employment.

Proposition 7.1 *1. The dynamical system (7.37), (7.38), (7.39) for ω^e, u_f^w and e has a unique interior steady state given by*

$$\omega_o^e = \frac{y^p - \delta_k - \bar{i}^r}{(1+\tau_p)l_y y^p}, \quad u_{f0}^w = \bar{u}_f^w, \quad e_o = \bar{e}.$$

2. The steady state is locally asymptotically stable if $\beta_{w_u}\bar{u}_f^w > \beta_{w_e}\bar{e}$ holds.
3. At the value $\beta_{w_u}^H = \beta_{w_e}\bar{e}/\bar{u}_f^w$ of the parameter β_{w_u} there occurs a Hopf bifurcation, a cyclical loss of stability, of either subcritical, supercritical or degenerate type.

Proof:
1. Obvious.
2. The Jacobian of the dynamics at the steady state is given by

$$J = \begin{pmatrix} 0 & \beta_{w_u}\omega_o & \beta_{w_e}\omega_o \\ -\alpha_1^k(1+\tau_p)l_y y^p u_o^w & -\beta_l u_o^w & 0 \\ 0 & \beta_l u_o & 0 \end{pmatrix}$$

Therefore, $-a_1 = \text{trace } J = -\beta_l u_o^w < 0$ and $-a_3 = \det J = -\beta_{w_e}\omega_o\alpha_1^k(1+\tau_p)l_y y^p u_o^w \beta_l e_o < 0$. For a_2 (the sum of the principal minors) we get $a_2 = \beta_{w_u}\omega_o\alpha_1^k(1+\tau_p)l_y y^p u_o^w > 0$. According to the Routh–Hurwitz conditions – see Gantmacher (1959) – we have to consider in addition the positivity of

$$a_1 a_2 - a_3 = \beta_l u_o^w \omega_o \alpha_1^k(1+\tau_p)l_y y^p(\beta_{w_u}\bar{u}_f^w - \beta_{w_e}\bar{u}_o).$$

Hence $a_1a_2 - a_3 > 0$ if $\beta_{w_u}\bar{u}_f^w > \beta_{w_e}\bar{u}_o$. The assertion of a Hopf bifurcation at $\beta_{w_u} = \beta_{w_e}\bar{e}_o/\bar{u}_f^w$ is then proved by means of the above expression for $a_1a_2 - a_3$ as in Benhabib and Miyao (1981).
3. As in Benhabib and Miyao (1981), due to the above expression for $a_1a_2 - a_3$. □

We thus in particular have that fast inside wage adjustments speeds, β_{w_u}, are enhancing local asymptotic stability, while the opposite holds true for the adjustment speed of outside wage claims, β_{w_u}. All other parameters of these dynamics (up to the levels of the employed rates of Non-Accelerating Inflation Rate of Unemployment (NAIRU) type) do not matter for the stability of this partial dynamics between real wages and the inside and outside rate of employment. This holds in particular for the speed of adjustment β_l of the hiring and firing policy of the firms. If the steady state is locally explosive, because of a high adjustment speed with respect to outside labour demand pressure, it is easy to establish global stability or boundedness of the dynamics through simple further (extrinsic) non-linearities as in Flaschel (2000), the main results of which read as follows:

Proposition 7.2 *1. The interior steady state of the dynamical system (7.37)–(7.39), with smooth factor substitution*[7] $z = f(k)$ *in the place of fixed coefficients in production, is of the same type as before, but now with the endogenous determination of the steady state ratios* $x_o = f(k_o)$, $y_o = f(k_o)/k_o$ *and* $k_o = k(\omega_o)$, *where* ω_o *is given by the solution of the equation* $\gamma/\alpha_r^k = f'(k(\omega_o))$.

2. This steady state is locally asymptotically stable if $\beta_{w_u} - \beta_{w_e}\bar{e} - c > 0$ *holds for some suitably chosen* $c > 0$. *The size of* c *can be chosen the larger the term* $\epsilon_s(\omega) = k'(\omega)\omega/k(\omega)$, β_l, β_{w_u} *becomes.*

Proof: See Flaschel (2000). □

Proposition 7.3 *1. The dynamical system (7.37)–(7.39) with smooth factor substitution and supply constraints exhibits the sub domain* $(0, \infty) \times (0, 2) \times (0, 1)$ *of its phase space as invariant subset which it therefore cannot leave. The dynamics can therefore be bounded to an economically meaningful domain and may, depending on parameters and functional shapes, give rise in this domain to a variety of simple or complex motions.*

2. The so-called classical regime of non-Walrasian disequilibrium analysis – see Flaschel (2000) for its definition – is the only regime that is possible in this domain.

Proof: See Flaschel (2000). □

Figure 7.1 provides an example for this type of bounded dynamics where the attracting set that is shown is still of a simple limit cycle type. The figure top left shows the stable limit cycle of the dynamics with the additional non-linearity in the growth rate of the labour supply assumed in Flaschel (2000), while the two cycles that border this figure show its projection into the adjacent planes, now with the variable v, the share of wages, in the place of ω, the real wage in order to show that profits remain positive along the cycle (and on the way to it). The figure bottom right finally shows the time series for the outside and inside rate of employment (with the full employment ceiling for

[7] Denoting by k the actually prevailing capital intensity K/L we know from the Solow model of neoclassical growth that this gives rise to equations of the type

$$z = f(k) \quad [y =: f(k)/k], \ \omega = f(k) - f'(k)k = g(k).$$

For the function g there then holds

$$g'(k) = f'(k) - f'(k) - f''(k)k = -f''(k)k > 0$$

so that the function g is strictly increasing (due to decreasing marginal products of labour). We denote by $k = k(\omega)$ the inverse of g and by $\epsilon_s(\omega) = k'(\omega)\omega/k(\omega) > 0$ the elasticity of this function k.

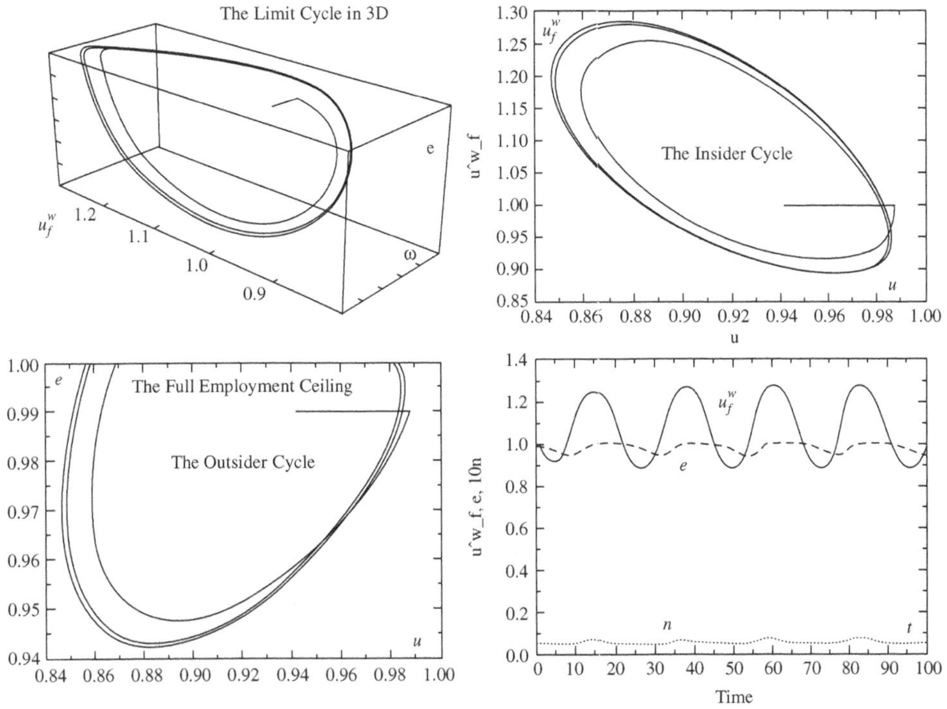

Figure 7.1 A limit cycle of the dynamics (7.37), (7.38), (7.39) showing the full employment ceiling

the first rate sometimes in operation and with a rate of employment of inside workers that stays below 130 per cent). When inside employment approaches this level it is furthermore clearly visible that the rate of growth of labour supply responds to this as assumed in Flaschel (2000) but as in the case of the inside rate of employment only in a moderate way in order to create the volume of labour supply and its rate of growth that is demanded by firms.

The result established by this section therefore is that labour demand pressure within the firms, when operating on wage adjustment in a sufficiently strong way, can destabilise the interior steady state of the model, but only locally if smooth factor substitution and certain labour supply adjustment processes are added to the model. This global aspect of the considered dynamics is investigated in detail in Flaschel (2000) and is therefore not considered here again, where local feedback mechanisms are at the centre of interest.

7.5 Adding the Rose real wage feedback chain

In order to sketch the details of this further economic feedback chain which now integrates goods market dynamics into the growth cycle dynamics of the preceding section we have to derive anew the law of motion for real wages from the wage-price dynamics first. Starting from the corresponding equations of the general 18D dynamics we have

$$\hat{w}^e - \pi^c = \beta_{w_e}(e - \bar{e}) + \beta_{w_u}(l_f^{de}/l_f^{we} - \bar{u}_f^w) + \kappa_w(\hat{p}_y - \pi^c), \tag{7.40}$$

$$\hat{p}_y - \pi^c = \beta_p(y/y^p - \bar{u}) + \kappa_p(\hat{w}^e - \pi^c). \tag{7.41}$$

We can see that these equations form a linear equation system in the two unknowns: $\hat{w}^e - \pi^c$, $\hat{p}_y - \pi^c$. This system can be uniquely solved if $\kappa = 1 - \kappa_w\kappa_p \neq 0$ holds true for $\kappa_w, \kappa_p \in [0, 1]$, which is so if both of these parameter values are not equal to 1, meaning that the cost-push terms in both the wage and the price dynamics are not solely based on currently observed price and wage inflation rates. The explicit solution of this equation system is

$$\hat{w}^e - \pi^c = \kappa[\beta_{w_e}(e - \bar{e}) + \beta_{w_u}(l_f^{de}/l_f^{we} - \bar{u}_f^w) + \kappa_w\beta_p(y/y^p - \bar{u})],$$

$$\hat{p}_y - \pi^c = \kappa[\kappa_p(\beta_{w_e}(e - \bar{e}) + \beta_{w_u}(l_f^{de}/l_f^{we} - \bar{u}_f^w)) + \beta_p(y/y^p - \bar{u})],$$

which in turn implies for the real wage, $\omega^e = w^e/p_y$, measured in efficiency units and relative to producer prices, the expression

$$\hat{\omega}^e = \kappa[(1 - \kappa_p)(\beta_{w_e}(e - \bar{e}) + \beta_{w_u}(l_f^{de}/l_f^{we} - \bar{u}_f^w)) - (1 - \kappa_w)\beta_p(y/y^p - \bar{u})].$$

The dynamics of the real wage therefore depend positively on the demand pressure in the market for labour and negatively on the demand pressure in the market for goods, while the cost-push terms of the nominal dynamics have neutralised themselves in this relative expression for the wage dynamics. The economic reason for and the meaning of this result is easy to understand, since real wages should generally also depend on what happens in the market for goods. It is therefore astonishing to see that studies of Phillips curves (PCs), that integrate labour market phenomena with price inflation, are often built on only one of these demand pressures (the one in the labour market) in the theoretical as well as in the empirically oriented literature.

On the basis of the foregoing discussion we can now describe the feedback chain of real wage increases onto their rate of change implied by the core 18D model of this chapter. Increases in real wages will either increase or decrease aggregate demand y^d for the domestic good (per unit of capital) depending among others on the consumption propensity c_y of workers in comparison with the marginal propensity to invest i_1 that mirrors the influence of the expected profit rate

$$r^e = y^e - \delta_k + (p_x/p_y)x - (1 + \tau_p)\omega^e l_f^{de} - (p_m/p_y)j^d$$

in the investment demand function of firms.

Let us consider first the situation where economic activity y or $u = y/y^p$ is reduced through this channel by real wage increases. We know from the model that this decreases the employment of the employed and with some time delay also the rate of outside employment e. According to the above dynamical law for real wages we thus get that real wage increases are slowed down if wage flexibility is high and price flexibility is low, since the money wage will then react more strongly than the price level to this reduction in economic activity and will thus dominate the response of real wages to reduced economic activity. In this situation, the interaction between economic activity and real wages is therefore stabilising, since real wage increases are then checked by decreases in economic activity through their impact on real wages. However, in the opposite case of high price flexibility and low wage flexibility real wages will increase in the case of a reduction of economic activity and will thus amplify the initial increase in real wages, which creates a destabilising feedback chain between real wages and economic activity.

Consider next the case where economic activity increases with real wage increases, since consumption demand responds more strongly than investment demand of firms to changes in the real wage. Of course, we then get the opposite conclusions to the case just considered. Price flexibility will now be enhancing economic stability while wage flexibility will be detracting from it. We thus find that the real wage/economic activity interaction depends crucially on the parameters that characterise the market for goods and the labour market.

Either price or wage flexibility must however always be destabilising. The destabilising Rose effect (of whatever type) will be weak if both wage and price adjustment speeds $\beta_{w_e}, \beta_{w_u}, \beta_p$ are low, at least as far as situations of a depressed economy are concerned. The working of the Rose mechanism in integrated models of monetary growth is explored in detail in Flaschel *et al.* (1997) and Chiarella and Flaschel (2000), where also the original approach of Rose (1967) is reconsidered and discussed.

We now go on to consider the situation in which we add growth dynamics to the above considerations as in the considered extended Goodwin (1967) case, but will now neglect inside employment adjustments ($\beta_{w_u} = 0$) so that increases in the output of firms are immediately transferred to new employment with respect to the external labour market. We thus assume $l_f^{de} = l_f^{we}$ and again neglect any employment in the government sector. This gives rise to the following growth dynamics

$$\hat{\omega}^e = \kappa[(1-\kappa_p)(\beta_{w_e}(l_f^{de}/l^e - \bar{e}) - (1-\kappa_w)\beta_p(y/y^p - \bar{u})],$$

$$\hat{l}^e = \gamma + \delta_k - \alpha_1^k(r^e - \bar{i}^r) - \alpha_3^k(y/y^p - \bar{u}),$$

where $l^{de} = l_y y$ and $r^e = y - \delta_k - (1+\tau_p)\omega^e l_f^{de}$ and where the second law of motion is derived as usual from the growth law for the capital stock. Note here that we have included now the third term $\alpha_2^k(>0)$ of the fixed business investment function again, since the rate of capacity utilisation is variable in the Rose type labour and goods market interaction. Note also that we do not distinguish here between output and the (expected) demand for goods and thus ignore the quantity adjustment process of firms and the details of the formation of aggregate demand. Instead we shall now simply assume that output per capital y is a function of real wages ω^e measured in efficiency units and that this function is increasing if we assume that the impact of real wage changes on y is positive (if consumption demand is more sensitive than investment demand to real wage changes) while it is decreasing in the opposite case.

We thereby arrive at the autonomous non-linear system of differential equations of dimension 2,

$$\hat{\omega}^e = \kappa[(1-\kappa_p)\beta_{w_e}(l_y y(\omega^e)/l^e - \bar{e}) - (1-\kappa_w)\beta_p(y(\omega^e)/y^p - \bar{u})], \tag{7.42}$$

$$\hat{l}^e = \gamma + \delta_k - \alpha_1^k(y(\omega^e) - \delta_k - (1+\tau_p)\omega^e l_y y(\omega^e) - \bar{i}^r) - \alpha_3^k(y(\omega^e)/y^p - \bar{u}), \tag{7.43}$$

in the two state variables ω^e, l^e. We consider here only the case where the rate of profit $r^e = y(\omega^e) - \delta_k - (1+\tau_p)\omega^e l_y y(\omega^e)$ depends negatively on the real wage ω^e, namely where the mass purchasing effect of real wage increases is not so large that it outweighs the wage cost effect on the rate of profit.[8] In this case we get for the Jacobian J of the above 2D dynamics at the steady state the following sign structure (that is typical for the Rose (1967) employment cycle mechanism)

$$J = \begin{pmatrix} \kappa[(1-\kappa_p)\beta_{w_e} l_y y(\omega^e)/ & -\kappa(1-\kappa_p)\beta_{w_e} l_y y(\omega^e)/(l^e)^2 \\ \quad l^e - (1-\kappa_w)\beta_p y'(\omega^e)/y^p] & \\ -\alpha_1^k (r^e)'(\omega^e) - \alpha_3^k y'(\omega^e)/y^p & 0 \end{pmatrix}$$

$$= \begin{pmatrix} \pm & - \\ + & 0 \end{pmatrix}.$$

The sign of J_{11} in the trace is therefore the decisive element that determines the local stability or instability of the Rose real wage mechanism in isolation as well as its interaction with economic growth.

A wage mechanism of the extrinsically non-linear type shown in Figure 7.2, as it was used in Rose (1967),[9] will therefore generally only be successful in bringing boundedness to the dynamics of the economy for a given speed of adjustment β_p of the price inflation rate when the sign in J_{11} is negative. If the opposite holds true, then one would need an extrinsic non-linearity with respect to price adjustment, not wage adjustment, which would need to be assumed to be limited in its speed, in order to get boundedness for the dynamics in this case. Depending on propensities to consume and to invest we therefore have to assume more flexible adjustments in the labour market or in the market for goods in order to get boundedness of the dynamics. Not knowing which situation in fact prevails it may therefore be best to assume that both speeds of adjustment are fairly low in which case the entry J_{11} in the trace of J will be small, but positive or negative. It can then be hoped that this germ of instability – which in the general 18D dynamics need not and will not appear in the trace of their Jacobian – is overcome by the other stabilising mechanisms in the dynamics.

[8] In addition the parameter α_3^k needs to be chosen sufficiently small.
[9] The function displayed, $\beta_{w_e}(e)$, replaces the linear term $\beta_{w_e}(e - \bar{e})$ in equation (7.40).

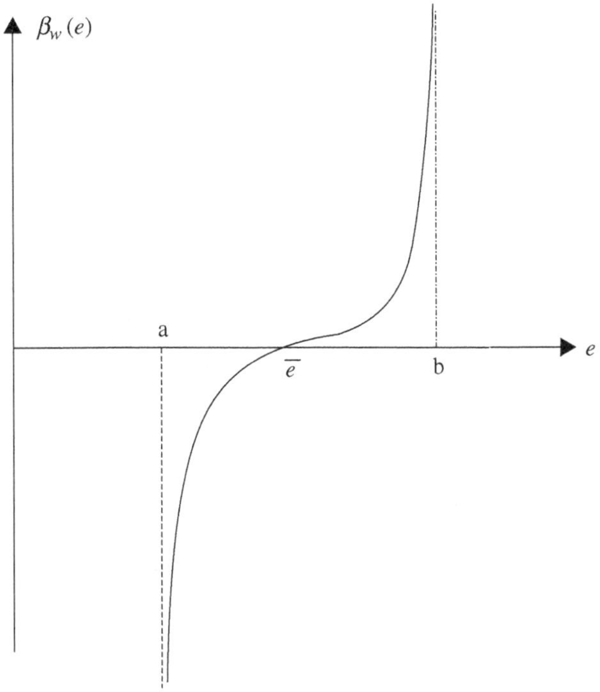

Figure 7.2 A non-linear law of demand in the labour market

If we however are sure that y and therefore also r^e depend negatively on the real wage ω^e, the above dynamical system (7.42), (7.43) will imply the phase portrait representation shown in Figure 7.3.[10]

This diagram indicates that the growth dynamics of this section are globally asymptotically stable if price flexibility is sufficiently low such that the steady state of these dynamics is locally asymptotically stable. Then – as we shall assert without proof – the growth dynamics are also globally asymptotically stable with respect to the triangular domain shown in Figure 7.3 and only globally stable. The dynamics will give rise to stable limit cycles around the steady state if the steady state is locally a repeller (which could occur for a given value of price flexibility that is chosen sufficiently high).[11]

[10] We neglect technical change and therefore efficiency units in Figure 7.3.

[11] The isoclines $\dot{\omega}^e = 0, \dot{l}^e = 0$ of (7.42), (7.43) are given by

$$l^e = l_y y(\omega^e)\left(\beta_w^{-1}\left[\frac{1-\kappa_w}{1-\kappa_p}\beta_p\right] + \bar{e}\right)^{-1},$$

$$\omega^e = \omega_o^e$$

where ω_o^e is given by that level of real wages that implies the required rate of profit $\bar{i}^r$. Due to the assumed shape of the β_{w_e} function we know that the first expression is always well defined and must always lie between $y(\omega^e)/b$ and $y(\omega^e)/a$; see Figure 7.2. The above two isoclines then divide the phase space as shown in Figure 7.3.

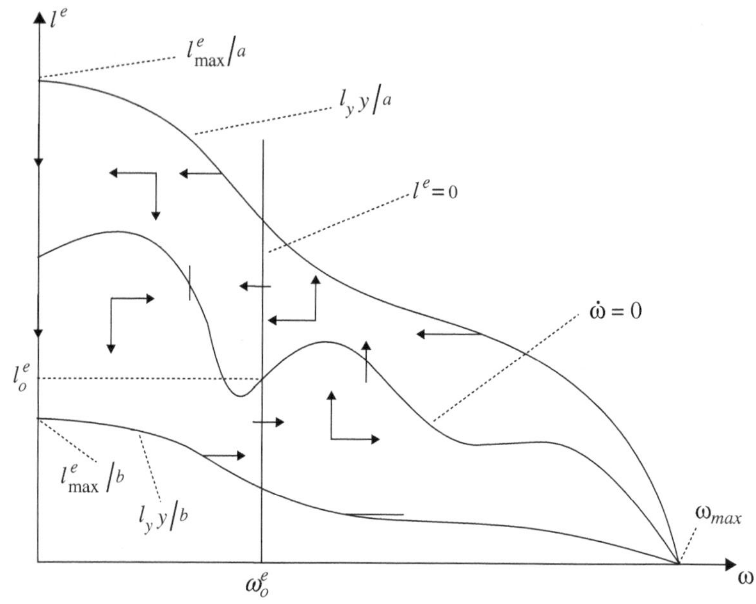

Figure 7.3 The viability domain of the Rose dynamics for $y'(\omega^e) < 0$

The details underlying the construction of the viability domain shown in Figure 7.3 are given in also Chiarella and Flaschel (2000, Ch. 5). We conclude from the above that large values of β_{w_u} and either β_{w_e} or β_p provide problems for the local asymptotic stability of the interior steady state of the dynamics, but that extrinsic non-linearities in fact can be tailored so that they tame local explosiveness and bound the considered growth dynamics to an economically meaningful domain.

7.6 The Metzlerian expected sales/inventory dynamics

In order to isolate this mechanism we assume that fixed business investment is given by its trend component solely: $g_k^d = \gamma + \delta_k$. In this case we get for the interaction of expected sales y^e and actual inventories ν from the 18D core dynamics of the general model, the equation system

$$\begin{aligned}
\dot{y}^e &= \beta_{y^e}(y^d - y^e),\\
\dot{\nu} &= y - y^d - \gamma\nu\\
y^d &= c_w^o + \gamma + \delta_k + \gamma k_h + \delta_h + g y^e,\\
c_w^o &= c_y y_{w1}^D,\\
y_{w1}^D &= (1-\tau_w)[w^e l_y y + w^{ue}(l^e - l^{we}) + w^{re}\alpha_l l_2^e]/p_v,\\
y &= y^e + \beta_n(\beta_{n^d} y^e - \nu) + \gamma\beta_{n^d} y^e.
\end{aligned}$$

These equations provide us with two linear differential equations in the state variables expected sales and actual inventories (per unit of capital). To simplify our argument we have ignored here the delay in the firms' employment policies and of course do not take wage-price reactions to the change in economic activity into account in the investigation of this partial feedback structure. It is then easy to see that a sufficiently large adjustment parameter value β_n (which can approach infinity in continuous-time if this is needed) implies that the dependence of y^d on y and thus on y^e obtains a slope that is larger than one, in which case the law of motion for y^e then depends positively on the size of y^e, or in other words, the entry J_{11} of the Jacobian J of the above dynamics at the steady state becomes positive under these circumstances. We conclude that the trace of J must then become positive if the parameter β_{y^e} is chosen sufficiently large in addition, since this parameter is not involved in the second component that defines the trace of J.

The above equations for the 2D inventory dynamics thus show that output y depends positively on expected sales y^e and this more and more strongly the higher the speed of adjustment β_n of planned inventories becomes. The time rate of change of expected sales therefore depends positively on the level of expected sales when the parameter β_n is chosen sufficiently large. Flexible adjustment of inventories coupled with a high speed of adjustment of sales expectations are thus bad for obtaining economic stability. There will, however, exist other situations (with a low inventory accelerator) where an increase in the latter speed of adjustment may increase the stability of the dynamics. The question of local explosiveness and global boundedness of this inventory cycle dynamics has been discussed in detail in Franke and Lux (1993), Franke (1996) and Chiarella and Flaschel (2000, Ch. 6).

In view of these contributions we add the following further simplified modelling and analysis to the observations just made. We now assume, as a simple expression for aggregate demand in the place of the static equations employed above, that there holds

$$y^d = d_1 y + d_0, \quad \text{with} \quad d_0 > 0, d_1 \in (0,1)$$

and also set the exogenous growth rate γ of the general 18D model equal to zero. On this basis, the isolated inventory dynamics of the model read

$$\dot{y}^e = \beta_{y^e}(y^d - y^e) = \beta_{y^e}(d_1 y + d_0 - y^e), \tag{7.44}$$

$$\dot{\nu} = y - y^d = (1 - d_1)y - d_0, \tag{7.45}$$

where the output y produced by firms is again given by

$$y = y^e + \beta_n(\beta_{n^d} y^e - \nu), \tag{7.46}$$

that is as the sum of expected sales and intended inventory changes. The steady state of the model (7.44)–(7.46) of sales and inventory dynamics is given by

$$y_o^d = y_o^e = y_o = \frac{1}{1 - d_1} d_0, \qquad \nu_o = \beta_{n^d} y_o.$$

Inserting (7.46) into (7.44), (7.45) one obtains a linear system of two differential equations with the matrix of partial derivatives

$$J = \begin{pmatrix} (d_1 - 1 + d_1 \beta_n \beta_{n^d}) \beta_{y^e} & -d_1 \beta_n \beta_{y^e} \\ (1 - d_1)(1 + \beta_n \beta_{n^d}) & -(1 - d_1) \beta_n \end{pmatrix}.$$

For the determinant of this matrix we find

$$|J| = \beta_{y^e}(1 - d_1)\beta_n > 0.$$

and for the trace

$$\text{trace } J = -\beta_{y^e}(1 - d_1 - \beta_n \beta_{n^d} d_1) - \beta_n(1 - d_1).$$

From these expressions we see that the dynamics (7.44), (7.45) can only be unstable if $1 - d_1 - \beta_n \beta_{n^d} d_1 < 0$ holds and then if and only if

$$\beta_{y^e} > \beta_{y^e}^H = -\frac{\beta_n(1 - d_1)}{1 - d_1 - \beta_n \beta_{n^d} d_1}$$

applies. Since we want to show in this section the existence of inventory oscillations and in the limit also of relaxation oscillations for inventory dynamics of sales expectations, we assume in the following that the adjustments speed β_n for inventory changes satisfies

$$\beta_n > \frac{1 - d_1}{d_1 \beta_{n^d}} > 0$$

at the steady state, which means that the above necessary condition for instability is fulfilled at the steady state. In this case, the dynamics (7.44), (7.45) would be totally unstable when sales expectations are adjusted with a sufficiently high speed. In view of such a situation, Franke and Lux (1993) assume that the inventory adjustment speed that firms choose is slowed down the further the economy departs from the steady state (since firms become more cautious then). We add to this assumption the motivation that firms slow down their inventory adjustment far off the steady state, since they expect a turn in economic activity which would by itself give rise to the desired direction of inventory changes. In making this assumption the action of firms will then in fact lead to such a turn in economic activity which thus confirms the cautious policy adopted by firms. In their paper, Franke and Lux (1993) present a set of related assumptions which in sum allow them to show that despite local instability, such an inventory dynamics will be globally stable or viable and give rise to persistent oscillations (or relaxation oscillations when expectations tend to myopic perfect foresight).

In the following, we will not reproduce the details of such an analysis, but only sketch in an intuitive way[12] how such global boundedness of the dynamics and the implied limit cycle (or limit limit cycle in the limit case of relaxation oscillations) can be obtained in principle.

[12] We also appeal to the special example of the non-linearity introduced by Franke and Lux in the adjustment speed of inventories.

To this end, we choose for the adjustment speed β_n of inventories the functional form of their dependence on sales expectations (per unit of capital) given by

$$\beta_n = (\beta_n^* - \beta_n^0)\exp(-\beta_n^1(y^e - y_o^e)^2) + \beta_n^0, \tag{7.47}$$

where $\beta_n^* - \beta_n^0 > \frac{1-d_1}{d_1\beta_{n^d}}$ and $0 < \beta_n^0 < \frac{1-d_1}{d_1\beta_{n^d}}$ holds.

On the basis of this modification of the model, the dynamics (7.44), (7.45) become non-linear, with a steady state that is identical to the one of the linear system and which must be unstable for a high adjustment speed of sales expectation since the Jacobian J is the same for the linear and the non-linear system at the steady state. It is not difficult to show that this non-linear version of the inventory dynamics implies again the existence of persistent fluctuations or even relaxation oscillations, as in Kaldor (1940) and by means of diagrams as in Chiarella and Flaschel (2000) and Asada *et al.* (2003). This analysis is here simply exemplified for the limit case of relaxation oscillations by means of the numerical simulation shown in Figure 7.4.

The bottom left panel of Figure 7.4 shows the relaxation oscillations in sales expectations y^e. Inventories ν, on the other hand, exhibit no jump in their levels (as is reasonable), but of course their growth rate is subject to such jumps whenever a regime switch occurs in the perfect foresight regime from optimistic (nearly perfect) sales expectations to pessimistic ones and vice versa. The bottom right panel of Figure 7.4 however reveals that such sales expectations are not always perfect, since sales expectations may overshoot aggregate demand during a regime switch – at least for the discretisation we have chosen here to simulate this model.

Figure 7.4, at the top right, shows the development of output as compared with sales expectations (and aggregate demand). Of course, the path of output must depart in a systematic way from that of expected sales, since firms pursue an active inventory policy. Finally, the top-left panel of Figure 7.4 shows again the relaxation cycle in the phase space, revealing part of the ye isocline as well as of the nearly horizontal adjustments that occur in sales expectations when phases of boom give way to phases of recession or depression by way of a regime switch in sales expectations.

The panels of Figure 7.4 also show that the cycle period is approximately three years. We note that the phase length of this cycle can be decreased if the parameter β_{n^d} is reduced in size. Of course, the amplitude of the cycle is completely determined by the shape of the non-linearity that has been assumed for its generation; see equation (7.47) for the parameter β_n.

The discussion of this section may be summarised in the following proposition:

Proposition 7.4 *The dynamics of the Metzlerian inventory feedback mechanism are dominated by a trade-off between β_{y^e} (speed of adjustment of sales expectations) and β_n (speed of adjustment of planned inventories). At low values of both of these parameters, this mechanism is locally stable. For β_n larger than a certain value, β_{y^e} acts as a bifurcation parameter, giving rise to local instability and limit cycles via a Hopf bifurcation beyond a certain critical value.*

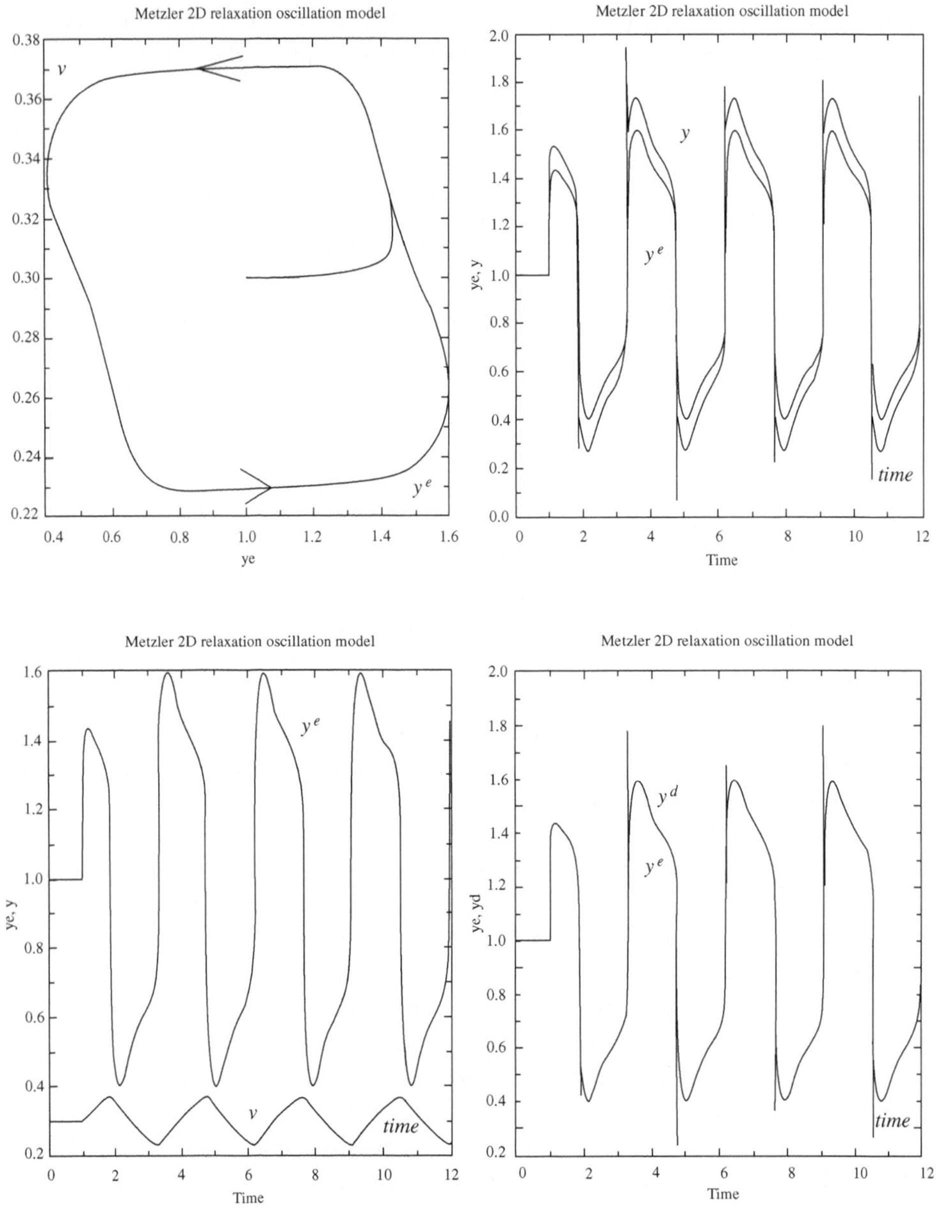

Figure 7.4 A numerical representation of the limiting relaxation oscillations in the Metzlerian 2D dynamics

7.7 The dynamics of housing supply

In order to study the dynamics of housing investment and housing rents in isolation we assume that the capital stock of firms grows with constant rate $\gamma = g_k^d - \delta_k$, that the rate of investment in dwellings does not depend on bond interest rates and that the price level of domestic goods (and thus of the supply of dwellings) p_y is a given magnitude. Furthermore, total wage income of workers (per unit of capital) is held constant at $\bar{y}^D_{w1}$. The laws of motions in the housing sector are in this case given by[13]

$$\hat{k}_h = g^d_h - \delta_h - \gamma = \alpha^h_r(r_h - \bar{i}^r) + \alpha^h_u\left(\frac{c^{do}_h}{k_h} - \bar{u}_h\right), \tag{7.48}$$

$$\hat{p}_h = \beta_h\left(\frac{c^{do}_h}{k_h} - \bar{u}_h\right), \tag{7.49}$$

with

$$r_h = c_h\bar{y}^D_{w1}/k_h - \delta_h,$$
$$c^{do}_h = \bar{p}_v c_h \bar{y}^D_{w1}/p_h.$$

This system of equations can be reduced to two autonomous differential equations in the state variables k_h, p_h with a uniquely determined point of rest in the positive domain of the real plane, given by

$$k_{h0} = c_h\bar{y}^D_{w1}/(\bar{i}^r + \delta_h), \quad p_{h0} = \bar{p}_v c_h\bar{y}^D_{w1}/(k_{h0}\bar{u}_h),$$

due to
$$r_h = \bar{i}^r = c_h\bar{y}^D_{w1}/k_h - \delta_h.$$

Proposition 7.5 *The interior steady state of the dynamics of the housing sector, given by (7.48) and (7.49), is always locally asymptotically stable with monotonic convergence back to the steady state for small displacements out of the steady state, so that it is a stable node.*[14]

Proof: Let us first consider the above dynamics in the case $\alpha_3 = 0$. In this case we get for the Jacobian of the dynamics at the steady state the sign structure

$$J = \begin{pmatrix} J_{11} & J_{12} \\ J_{21} & J_{22} \end{pmatrix} = \begin{pmatrix} - & 0 \\ - & - \end{pmatrix}.$$

This implies the assertion of Proposition 7.5 in this special case, since such a dynamical system has only real eigenvalues with negative sign due to

$$(\text{trace } J)^2/4 - \det J = (J_{11} - J_{22})^2/4 \geq 0.$$

In the case $\alpha_3 > 0$ it is however easy to see that the trace will become more negative than compared with the situation when $\alpha_3 = 0$ while the determinant remains unchanged, which implies local asymptotic stability also in this case, and of course

$$(\text{trace } J)^2/4 - \det J = (J_{11} - J_{22})^2/4 > 0.$$

□

[13] All tax rates are set equal to zero in the present subsystem of the general 18D dynamics.

[14] We here only assert that these dynamics are also globally stable and that this can be proved by means of Olech's theorem in a similar way to what is presented in Flaschel (1984).

The adjustments that take place in the stock of dwellings and the price of dwelling services thus do not give rise to the results we derived for business fixed capital investment (as in Goodwin (1967)) and for the Tobin (1975) nominal dynamics considered below, since there is no labour market involved in this subdynamics and also no inflationary expectations mechanism with respect to p_h. The latter may be considered a shortcoming of the present model type which should find better treatment in later reformulations of this macroeconomic dynamics.

Adjustment processes in this segment of the economy therefore do not cause problems for economic stability, at least as the model is presently formulated.

7.8 The Keynes effect

In order to discuss this effect in the conventional way one has to reformulate the model by means of a money supply rule and IS–LM equilibrium (in the place of the Taylor interest rate policy rule that we have used in the general 18D dynamics of Section 7.2). According to conventional LM equilibrium the nominal rate of interest i depends positively on the price level p, with all other variables kept fixed. Aggregate demand and thus output and the rates of capacity utilisation therefore depend negatively on the price level implying a negative dependence of the inflation rate on the level of prices through this channel. A high sensitivity of the nominal rate of interest with respect to the price level, the opposite of the liquidity trap, should thus exercise a strong stabilising influence on the dynamics of the price level and on the economy as a whole, which is further strengthened if price and wage flexibility increase. We expect that this effect is also present (in modified form) in the case of the interest rate policy rule, as we shall show succinctly below.

Monetary policy rules that attempt to control money supply in order to achieve inflationary and real stability may for example be formulated as

$$\hat{M} = \mu = \mu_o + \beta_m(\bar{\pi} - \hat{p}), \tag{7.50}$$

$$\hat{M} = \mu = \mu_o + \beta_m(\mu_o - n - \hat{p}), \tag{7.51}$$

$$\hat{M} = \mu = \mu_o + \beta_m(\bar{\pi} - \hat{p}^*). \tag{7.52}$$

The first rule (equation (7.50)) states that the growth rate of money supply is adjusted in view of the discrepancy that exists between the target rate of inflation of the central bank and the actual rate of inflation, implying for example that the growth rate of the money supply is reduced below its desired level μ_o if the actual rate of inflation exceeds the target rate (based on the assumption that this will dampen economic activity and the inflationary pressure that derives from it). The second rule (equation (7.51)) can be considered a special case of the first one, since it uses the steady state rate of inflation as the target rate. The third rule (equation (7.52)) assumes the so-called p^* theory of the rate of inflation, which assumes that the actual rate of inflation will tend to the p^* rate $\hat{p}^*$ as its centre of gravity where p^* is given by the application of the quantity theory of money to the case where the economy operates at its potential output level (or a certain fixed percentage below it). This would therefore give

$$p^* = vM/Y^p, \quad \text{so that,} \quad \hat{p}^* = \mu - \hat{K},$$

where v denotes the constant velocity of money[15] and Y^p the potential output of firms which is a fixed multiple of the capital stock K in our model. Of course, we could have also used the rate π^c, expected to hold for the medium run, in the place of the actual rate of inflation or the p^* rate (where π^c is in turn partly based on the knowledge of $\hat{p}^*$). Equations (7.50), (7.51) and (7.52) show that there is a variety of possibilities by which a money supply rule that pays attention to economic activity and inflationary pressure can be formulated.

Yet, in our general model, presented in Section 7.2 and in Chiarella and Flaschel (1999b,c,d), we have adopted a different approach to monetary policy that is based on a direct setting of the short-run rate of interest (or its time rate of change) in the place of the more indirect approach that attempts to influence this rate of interest via changes in the supply of money as described above. We believe that this latter approach is, on the one hand, less ambiguous as far as the definition of the instrument that is being used is concerned and, on the other hand, more successful in the attempt to stabilise the economy and to remove inflationary pressure from it. Furthermore in Chiarella and Flaschel (1999b,c,d) we have treated money in a way that makes it redundant in the presentation of the structural equations of the model.

In order to show this last point in as simple a way as possible consider again our formulation of the Taylor interest rate policy rule, given by

$$\dot{i} = -\beta_{i_i}(i - i_l^*) + \beta_{i_p}(\hat{p}_y - 0) + \beta_{i_u}(y/y^p - \bar{u})$$

in the light of the definition of aggregate demand, which we recall in

$$\begin{aligned}
y^d &= c_w^o + g_k^d + g_h^d k_h + g y^e, \\
g_k^d &= \alpha_1^k(r^e - i^r) + \alpha_2^k(i_l - i) + \alpha_3^k(y/y^p - \bar{u}) + \gamma + \delta_k, \\
g_h^d &= \alpha_r^h(r_h - i^r) + \alpha_i^h(i_l - i) + \alpha_u^h\left(\frac{c_h^{do}}{k_h} - \bar{u}_h\right), \\
i^r &= i_l - \pi^c.
\end{aligned}$$

Keeping all variables fixed at their steady state values, with the exception of the short-run rate of interest rate i, immediately implies the conventional situation that aggregate demand depends negatively on this nominal rate of interest – due to investment behaviour of firms and in dwellings. This implies again that expected sales and actual output of firms will also respond (*ceteris paribus*) negatively to increases in the

[15] Here assumed to be constant for simplicity of exposition.

nominal interest rate i, although in a somewhat delayed fashion, depending on adjustment speeds of the sales expectations of firms. Furthermore, domestic price inflation $\hat{p}_y$ depends positively on the degree of capacity utilisation of firms.

Taken together, this implies that there are only negative feedback mechanisms involved in the above formulation of the Taylor rule, so that inflation or capacity utilisation rates above the norm will be diminished through this interest rate policy of the central bank (the opposite is of course true in the case of price deflation and less than normal activity of firms). The Taylor rule therefore has the same stabilising features as is known for the Keynes effect, and it has the additional advantage that it incorporates these features in the form of a more direct steering of the economy than a rule that attempts to control the money supply in a counter-cyclical fashion. Note again that this stabilising adjustment process will not simply appear as a negative trace component in the local stability analysis of the full 18D dynamical system.

7.9 The Mundell–Tobin effect

The assumption that $\kappa_p = 0, \alpha_{\pi^c} = 1$ in the 18D model of Section 7.3 implies that equation (7.25) for the evolution of adaptively formed inflationary expectations π^c becomes

$$\dot{\pi}^c = \beta_{\pi^c}\beta_p(y/y^p - \bar{u}).$$

In order to derive from this formula the basic way in which $\dot{\pi}^c$ is influenced by the level of π^c, we make the further assumption that there holds the simplified equations

$$\begin{aligned} y^d &= const. + g_k^d + g_h^d k_h, \\ g_k^d &= \alpha_1^k(\bar{r}^e - (\bar{i}_l - \pi^c)) + \gamma + \delta_k, \\ g_h^d &= \alpha_r^h(\bar{r}_h - (\bar{i}_l - \pi^c)) + \gamma + \delta_h. \end{aligned}$$

In these expressions we consider only investment expenditures as variable and only in their dependence on the expected rate of inflation π^c, that is we allow only for profitability effects in investment behaviour by freezing the rate of profit r^e and the long-term rate of interest i_l at their steady state values (k_h is also considered a given magnitude). On the basis of these simplifications we see that aggregate demand (per unit of capital) depends positively on the expected rate of inflation, since an increase in this rate improves the profitability differential and thus increases the rate of investment, both for fixed business investment and housing. Since the sales expectations mechanism implies that sales expectations y^e (and thus also output y) follow aggregate demand y^d with a time delay, we get from that a (delayed) positive response of output to increases in inflationary expectations and hence (according to the above law of motion for these expectations) a positive feedback of inflationary expectations on their time rate of change. Due to the delays just discussed this dependence is an indirect one, so that it does not show up in the trace of the Jacobian of the dynamics at the steady state, but is distributed in a specific way in the Jacobian's off-diagonal elements.

Nevertheless, we have that increases in inflationary expectations have a (somewhat delayed) positive effect on economic activity and, due to the additional inflationary pressure this creates, a positive impact effect on their time rate of change. This effect has come to be known as the Mundell effect in the literature. Its working in a Keynesian dynamic multiplier/money market equilibrium framework with a Friedmanian type of PC has been investigated in a 3D approach to such Keynesian/Monetarist dynamics in a prominent paper by Tobin (1975). In that paper a critical level of the adjustment speed of inflationary expectations is determined at which the system loses its local stability by way of a Hopf bifurcation, similar to Proposition 7.1 that we have established in Section 7.4 for the adjustment speeds in the wage formation process. We claim – but do not prove here – that the destabilising Mundell effect becomes dominant also in our 18D core dynamics of Section 7.3 if the parameter β_{π^c} is chosen sufficiently large (for $\alpha_{\pi^c} > 0$.)

The destabilising Mundell effect can be checked if an interest rate policy rule is chosen that attempts to steer the expected real rate of interest as in Flaschel and Groh (1997). Such a feedback policy rule counteracts the source of the inflationary process which lies in the expansionary forces that are created by inflation and which in turn further stimulate the inflationary climate already in existence. We shall demonstrate this briefly here for the type of interest rate policy rule we have introduced in the preceding section.

For this purpose we assume that there is no delayed quantity adjustment process of Metzlerian type, but that there is goods market equilibrium $y = y^e = y^d$ throughout, based on the aggregate demand function y^d of this section, which is now however augmented by the terms that describe the sensitivity of investment with respect to short-term interest and the monetary policy rule applied by the central bank. In sum this gives rise to the dynamical system

$$\begin{aligned}
\dot{\pi}^c &= \beta_{\pi^c}\beta_p(y^d/y^p - \bar{u}),\\
y^d &= const. + g_k^d + g_h^d k_h,\\
g_k^d &= \alpha_1^k(\bar{r}^e - (\bar{i}_l - \pi^c)) + \alpha_2^k(\bar{i}_l - i) + \gamma + \delta_k,\\
g_h^d &= \alpha_r^h(\bar{r}_h - (\bar{i}_l - \pi^c)) + \alpha_i^h(\bar{i}_l - i) + \gamma + \delta_h,\\
\hat{p}_y &= \beta_p(y^d/y^p - \bar{u}) + \pi^c,\\
\dot{i} &= -\beta_{i_i}(i - i_o) + \beta_{i_p}(\hat{p}_y - 0) + \beta_{i_u}(y^d/y^p - \bar{u}).
\end{aligned}$$

This system can be reduced to a two-dimensional system in the two state variables π^c, i as

$$\dot{\pi}^c = \beta_{\pi^c}\beta_p(y^d(\pi^c, i)/y^p - \bar{u}) \tag{7.53}$$

$$\dot{i} = -\beta_{i_i}(i - i_o) + (\beta_{i_p}\beta_p + \beta_{i_u})(y^d/y^p - \bar{u}) + \beta_{i_p}\pi^c \tag{7.54}$$

where $y^d(\pi^c, i)$ is given by the linear function

$$y^d(\pi^c, i) = const. + \alpha_1^k \pi^c - \alpha_2^k i + \alpha_r^h \bar{k}_h \pi^c - \alpha_i^h \bar{k}_h i.$$

The system (7.53), (7.54) is thus a linear system of differential equations with a system matrix J that obviously has a positive determinant if β_{i_i} is zero (or chosen sufficiently small).[16] For the trace of this matrix J in the case of $\beta_{i_i} = 0$ one finds

$$-(\beta_{i_p}\beta_p + \beta_{i_u})(\alpha_2^k + \alpha_i^h)/y^p + \beta_{\pi^c}\beta_p(\alpha_1^k + \alpha_r^h)/y^p,$$

which implies that any instability that is caused by the positive term J_{22} of the matrix J can in principle (but maybe not in practice) be overcome and neutralised by choosing the policy parameters β_{i_p}, β_{i_u} sufficiently large – if and only if investment is influenced by short-term interest rate changes. We thus see how the destabilising Mundell effect of inflationary expectations may be overcome by a policy that makes the usual Keynes effect of models of IS–LM type sufficiently large by way of an appropriately tailored monetary policy rule.

7.10 The Blanchard bond and stock market dynamics

Blanchard (1981) has investigated the dynamic adjustment processes in the market for long-term bonds and for equities on the basis of myopic perfect foresight and perfect asset substitutability by means of the saddlepath dynamics that is then present and the jump variable technique that is then typically applied in order to have asymptotically stable adjustment processes after the occurrence of unanticipated shocks or changes in the expectations of future events.

We have assumed in the presentation of the structural form of our model that rate of return differentials are not instantaneously removed, but give rise to somewhat delayed adjustments in asset prices. We have also argued that there are always heterogeneous expectations present, here of asset holders who fall into two groups – ambitious agents who devote significant parts and their time (and resources) to the effort of forming perfect anticipations, and less ambitious (or perhaps less well-informed) asset holders who behave in an adaptive fashion. We have argued furthermore that the market share of the latter agents, despite their less accurate predictions of asset price dynamics, does not tend to zero due to the fact that all asset owners have a life-cycle profile that lets them act in an ambitious fashion when they are young and in a less ambitious fashion when they become old (due to changes in their preference relations). Although ambitious agents have more profitable investments (a fact that is only implicitly present in our model) their influence is bounded since they become less ambitious later on.

16 It is however interesting to see that a parameter β_{i_i} that is chosen too large may lead to saddlepath instability of the steady state solution.

For the laws of motion for the price of long-term bonds and expectations about its rate of change we have assumed

$$\hat{p}_b = \frac{\beta_{p_b}}{1-\beta_{p_b}(1-\alpha_s)}\left[\frac{1}{p_b} + \alpha_s\pi_{bs} - \bar{i}\right], \tag{7.55}$$

$$\dot{\pi}_{bs} = \beta_{\pi_{bs}}(\hat{p}_b - \pi_{bs}). \tag{7.56}$$

Note that the short-term rate of interest i is considered as given in this partial analysis of the market for consols. Insertion of (7.55) into (7.56) yields

$$\dot{\pi}_{bs} = \beta_{\pi_{bs}}\left[\left(\frac{\alpha_s\beta_{p_b}}{1-\beta_{p_b}(1-\alpha_s)} - 1\right)\pi_{bs} + \frac{\beta_{p_b}}{1-\beta_{p_b}(1-\alpha_s)}\frac{1}{p_b} + const.\right]. \tag{7.57}$$

We see that the trace of the Jacobian J of the 2D dynamical system (7.55), (7.57) at the steady state can be made as positive as desired. This is so, since the parameter β_{p_b} can always be chosen to make J_{22} positive, then $\beta_{\pi_{bs}}$ can be chosen so as to scale up J_{22} in the trace to an arbitrarily large value without changing the other coefficient J_{11} of the trace. It is easy to show that the determinant of the Jacobian J of the full 2D dynamics shown above is always positive and that the system switches from stable nodes to stable foci to unstable foci to unstable nodes when the adjustment speed of expectations of less ambitious agents is increased from zero towards infinity. Therefore all local stability scenarios – apart from saddlepoint dynamics – are possible, depending on the adjustment speed of adaptively formed expectations.

In sum, the foregoing analysis implies that there is a tendency for the price dynamics of long-term bonds to become at least locally explosive when the adjustment speed of bond prices becomes sufficiently large and when the expectations adjustment speed of less ambitious asset owners approach the limit case of myopic perfect foresight $\beta_{\pi_{bs}} \to \infty$. We stress that the bond rate dynamics influence investment behaviour of firms and of asset holders and thus will transfer its instability to the rest of the full 18D dynamical system.

Let us next investigate the isolated bond market dynamics shown above in more detail, again on the basis of a given short-term interest-rate $i = i_o$. To simplify the notation we rewrite the system as

$$\dot{p}_b = \beta_1\left(1 + (\alpha_s\pi_{bs} - i_o)p_b\right),$$

$$\dot{\pi}_{bs} = \beta_2(\hat{p}_b - \pi_{bs}) = \beta_2\left(\beta_1\left(\frac{1}{p_b} + \alpha_s\pi_{bs} - i_0\right) - \pi_{bs}\right),$$

where for convenience we set $\beta_1 = \beta_{p_b}(1-\beta_{p_b}(1-\alpha_s))$ and $\beta_2 = \beta_{\pi_{bs}}$. For local stability analysis we have to calculate the determinant and the trace of the Jacobian J of this system at the steady state $p_b = 1/i_{lo}, \pi_{bs} = 0$. The Jacobian J is given by

$$J = \begin{pmatrix} -i_o\beta_1 & \beta_1\alpha_s/i_o \\ -\beta_2\beta_1/i_o^2 & \beta_2\beta_1\alpha_s - \beta_2 \end{pmatrix}.$$

Therefore, $\det J = i_o\beta_1\beta_2 > 0$ and $\text{trace } J = -i_o\beta_1 + \beta_2\beta_1\alpha_s - \beta_2 = \beta_2[\beta_1\alpha_s - 1] - i_o\beta_1$. The critical condition for stability thus is $\beta_2^H = i_o\beta_1/(\beta_1\alpha_s - 1) =$

$i_o/(\alpha_s - 1/\beta_1)$.[17] Below this value for β_2, J has a negative trace and thus the dynamics display a stable node or focus, and above it J has a positive trace and the dynamics display either an unstable focus or a node. In the latter case of an explosive motion of asset prices on the bond market we have to ask ourselves of course what can limit these dynamics and thus prevent economic collapse.

We propose the following stylised solution to this problem. Assume that there are subjective thresholds for the adaptive expectations mechanism, based on deviations of the long-term rate of interest i_l from the given international rate i_l^*, beyond which (for large deviations) the adjustment parameter β_2 is significantly reduced, since the agents who form their expectations in this way believe that the market will not deviate much further from the norm i_l^*. Should the market, however, continue to do so, they slow down their response to this fact by following this development with a much lower error correction speed β_2, becoming more cautious and thus responding in a more reserved way to such a development (by lowering β_2). We shall see that this in turn will indeed stop the explosive motion and thus confirm the reasons on which this response is based.

To provide a simple example for this (which can, however, be modified in many ways) assume now that β_2 is a function of the rate of interest i_l in its deviation from the rate i_l^* of the simple form displayed in Figure 7.5, where β_2^H is the critical parameter

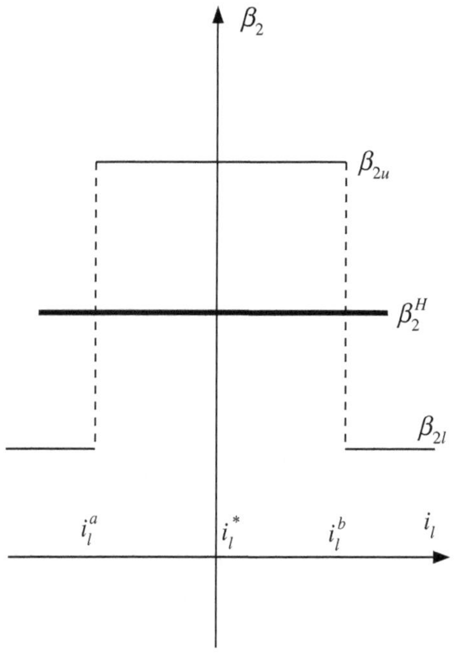

Figure 7.5 Variable speed of adjustment of expected bond price inflation

[17] We assume that $\beta_1 \alpha_s > 1$ holds true.

value at which the dynamics investigated above turn from local asymptotic stability to instability.

Outside the interval $[i_l^a, i_l^b]$ adaptive expectations are thus made in a cautious way, as further deviations are considered as suspect and thus followed with lower speed, whereas inside this interval there is a rapid adjustment towards observed changes in i_l.

Calculating the isoclines of the bond price dynamics with the above threshold behaviour gives rise to the formulae

$$\dot{p}_b = 0 : p_b = \frac{1}{i_o - \alpha_s \pi_{bs}}$$

$$\dot{\pi}_{bs} = 0 : p_b = \frac{1}{i_o - (\alpha_s - 1/\beta_1)\pi_{bs}} = \frac{1}{i_o - \alpha_s \pi_{bs} + \frac{1}{\beta_1}\pi_{bs}}$$

and the phase diagram displayed in Figure 7.6.

The assumed threshold behaviour of Figure 7.5 makes the dynamics shown in the phase portrait of Figure 7.6 stable for large deviations of i_l from i_l^* and explosive in the vicinity of i_l^*. We conjecture that this creates a limit cycle when these aspects are combined with each other and will look for numerical confirmations of this conjecture in further extensions of this chapter, also in combination with the impact this has on the real part of the economy.

The claim just made can be more easily shown if an alternative non-linearity is added to the dynamics of long-term interest rates. To show this we now assume (for a given speed of adjustment β_2 of bond price expectations) that the parameter β_p (we assume further that $\alpha_s = 1, \beta_2 > i_o$, for simplicity) depends on the deviation of long-term interest i_l from the steady state rate i_l^* in the way displayed in Figure 7.7.

The functional form shown in Figure 7.7 may be justified by stating that the bond price dynamics slow down far off the steady rate of interest due to a slowdown in

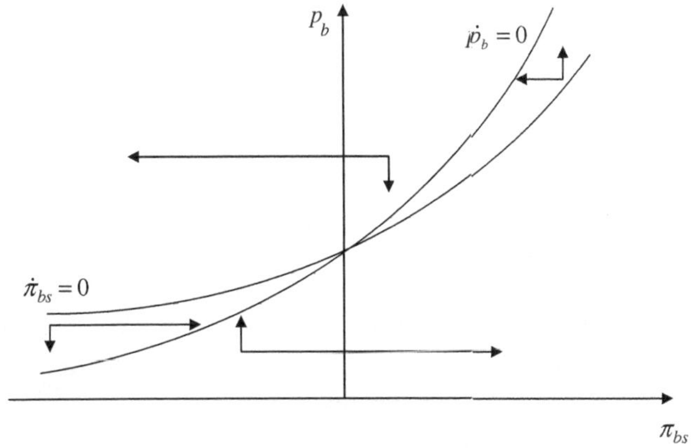

Figure 7.6 The phase diagram of the bond price dynamics with the assumed threshold behaviour in Figure 7.5

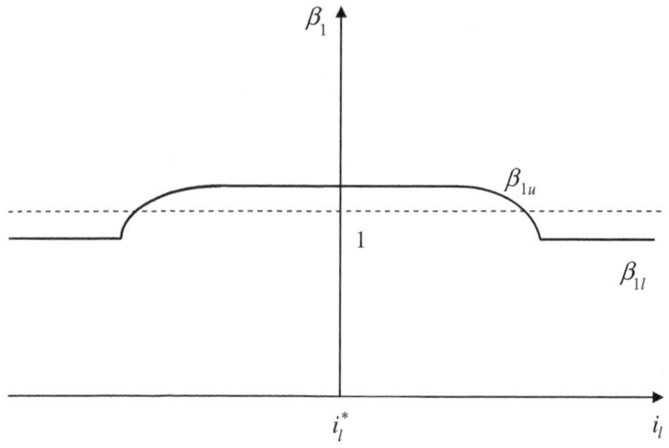

Figure 7.7 A variable speed of bond price adjustment

capital movements. We admit however that this type of occurrence is more difficult to rationalise in the heterogeneous agent framework we have postulated for our general model. We assume that β_2 is chosen such that the speed β_{1u} (β_{1l}) leads to local instability (stability) when combined with this adjustment speed of inflationary expectations. We know furthermore from the above local stability analysis that we have asymptotic stability for all parameter values β_2 if $\beta_1 < 1/\alpha_s$. We therefore again have the situation that the 2D bond price dynamics are locally unstable, but subject to stabilising forces when they departs too much from the steady state i_l^* of the foreign rate of interest.

If such a threshold behaviour exists, it would give rise to the type of phase diagram shown in Figure 7.8. In this phase diagram we have in fact already assumed that the adaptive revision of expectations is very fast so that there is a nearly horizontal movement in situations of the perfect foresight line $\dot{\pi}_{bs} = 0$. In this situation it can be judged from the phase portrait shown that there is a single attracting limit cycle for this type of dynamics (in fact a limit limit cycle or a so-called relaxation oscillation in the case $\beta_2 = \infty$). We assert that there will also exist a unique attracting limit cycle in situations where expectations are fast but not infinitely so.

Markets that slow down in their adjustment behaviour far off the steady state (in the expectation of turning points of the considered dynamics or simply in their speed of adjustment) may therefore stabilise what is in fact a cumulative process close to the steady state and thus induce in fact the turning points that are expected by less ambitious (adaptively behaving) asset owners or the market as a whole. We have therefore at least two possibilities at our disposal by which we can generate bounded asset market dynamics and on this basis also bounded dynamics in the real part of the economy, as long as these latter dynamics are bounded by themselves.

It is not difficult to show that the results on long-term bond price dynamics hold also for the dynamics of stock market prices p_e; see Asada *et al.* (2003), which (when

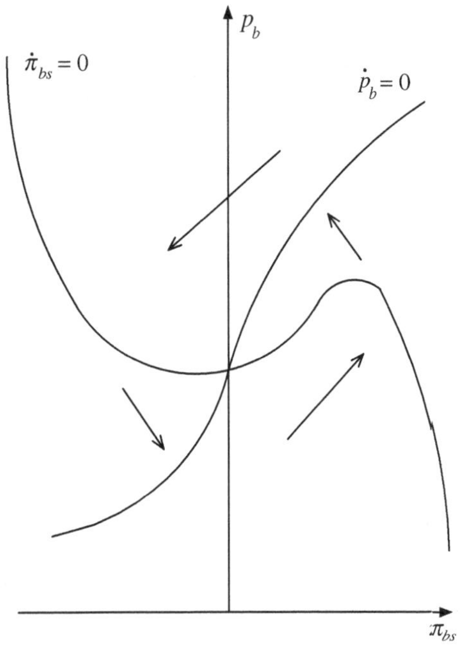

Figure 7.8 The phase diagram for variable speed of bond price adjustment

formulated in isolation) can be described as

$$\hat{p}_e = \frac{\beta_{p_e}}{1 - \beta_{p_e}(1 - \alpha_s)}[r^e/q + \alpha_s \pi_{es} - (i_l + \pi_b)] \qquad \left(q = \frac{p_e E}{p_y K} \text{ Tobin's } q\right),$$

$$\hat{q} = \hat{p}_e - \hat{p}_y + (g_k - \delta_k + y - y^d - (\beta_n(\beta_{n^d} y^e - \nu) + \gamma \beta_{n^d} y^e))/q - (g_k - \delta_k),$$

$$\dot{\pi}_{es} = \beta_{\pi_{es}}(\hat{p}_e - \pi_{es}),$$

and which is here thus to be investigated on the basis of frozen (steady state) values for the bond market and for the expected rate of profit of firms, due to the partial perspective adopted in this chapter. From these equations we get for the isolated adjustment of equity price change expectations the differential equation

$$\dot{\pi}_{es} = \beta_{\pi_{es}}\left[\left(\frac{\beta_{p_e}\alpha_s}{1 - \beta_{p_e}(1 - \alpha_s)} - 1\right)\pi_{es} + \frac{\beta_{p_e}}{1 - \beta_{p_e}(1 - \alpha_s)} r_o^e/q + const.\right]$$

which allows us to draw the same conclusions on the trace of the q, π_{es} dynamics as we have obtained for the dynamics of the price of long-term bonds. High adjustment speeds of expectations in the stock market therefore give rise to unstable spirals or unstable nodes as in the case of bonds, if the adjustment speed of equity prices to rates of return differentials is chosen sufficiently high. Again, the dynamics can be made viable or bounded by assuming changes in adjustment speeds as in the case of long-term bonds. We however do not go into details here as the dynamics of equity prices do not feed back into the 18D dynamics whose theoretical and numerical analysis is the theme of this chapter.

7.11 The dynamics of the government budget constraint

In order to isolate the dynamics of government debt from the rest of the dynamics we assume that all of its state variables are frozen at the steady state with the exception of the variables b, b^l, τ_w which describe the evolution of short- and long-term government debt together with the adjustments in the wage taxation rate that have been assumed to take place in view of the deviation of government debt from a certain target ratio (per unit of expected sales). The remaining dynamics then can be expressed as

$$\dot{b} = \alpha_b^g \left[i_o b + b^l - \tau_w c^1 + c^2 \right] - \gamma b, \tag{7.58}$$

$$\dot{b^l} = i_{lo}(1 - \alpha_b^g) \left[i_o b + b^l - \tau_w c^1 + c^2 \right] - \gamma b^l, \tag{7.59}$$

$$\hat{\tau}_w = \alpha_{\tau_{w1}} \left(\frac{b + b^l / i_{lo}}{y^e \bar{d}} - 1 \right), \tag{7.60}$$

where $c^1 > 0$, c^2 denote certain constants and where $i_o^l = i_o$.

Proposition 7.6 *The interior steady state of the government debt dynamics (7.58), (7.59), (7.60) is locally asymptotically stable if*

$$\alpha_b^g i_o - \gamma \ \ \textit{and} \ \ i_{lo}(1 - \alpha_b^g) - \gamma$$

are both smaller than zero.

Proof: The Jacobian of the dynamical system (7.58), (7.59), (7.60) at the steady state reads

$$J = \begin{pmatrix} \alpha_b^g i_o - \gamma & \alpha_b^g & -c^1 \alpha_b^g \\ i_{lo}(1 - \alpha_b^g) i_o & i_{lo}(1 - \alpha_b^g) - \gamma & -c^1 i_{lo}(1 - \alpha_b^g) \\ \alpha_{\tau_{w1}} / (y^e \bar{d}) & \alpha_{\tau_{w1}} / (i_{lo} y^e \bar{d}) & 0 \end{pmatrix}.$$

Due to the assumptions made we immediately have the result that the trace of the matrix J is negative and thus $a_1 > 0$.[18] Multiplying the second row of this matrix J by

$$-\frac{\alpha_b^g}{i_{lo}(1 - \alpha_b^g)}$$

and adding the resulting vector to the first row does not alter the determinant of J, which is therefore based on the sign structure

$$J = \begin{pmatrix} - & 0 & 0 \\ + & - & - \\ + & + & 0 \end{pmatrix}.$$

The determinant of J is therefore negative. We thus also have $a_3 > 0$.

[18] We recall that a_1, a_2, a_3 refers to the Routh–Hurwitz coefficients and thus we require $a_1 > 0, a_2 > 0, a_3 > 0$, $a_1 a_2 - a_3 > 0$ for local asymptotic stability.

Next we show that the principal minors of J are all positive so that also $a_2 > 0$ holds true. This is easily obtained from the full sign structure of the matrix J which is given by

$$J = \begin{pmatrix} - & + & - \\ + & - & - \\ + & + & 0 \end{pmatrix}.$$

First, $J_{11}J_{33} - J_{13}J_{31}$ and $J_{22}J_{33} - J_{23}J_{32}$ are obviously positive, since only the off-diagonal elements are of importance in these cases. Furthermore, also $J_{11}J_{22} - J_{12}J_{21}$ must be positive as can be seen by means of the same row operation we have used above for the calculation of the sign of the determinant of the matrix J, again based on the factor $-\frac{\alpha_b^g}{i_{lo}(1-\alpha_b^g)}$. The sum a_2 of these three expressions is therefore unambiguously positive.

Finally, also the expression $a_1a_2 - a_3$ must be positive since the $-a_3$ expression, the determinant of J (due to the above calculation) is neutralised by one of the products in the expression a_1a_2 which are all positive. □

The assumptions of Proposition 7.6 compare steady rates of return with the steady rate of growth and thereby restrict the rate with which government debt grows due to the debt service that has to be made. The two conditions of the proposition weaken the assumption that is normally made if only one debt financing instrument is considered. However, we state without proof that there is also one aggregate stability condition that is sufficient for the stability result of the proposition, namely $i_o - \gamma < 0$. Note in this respect also that one can of course assume that the government relies only on debt instruments, in which case the dynamical system (7.58), (7.59), (7.60) becomes two-dimensional. Finally, if Proposition 7.6 does not apply and if furthermore the dynamics are even monotonically explosive we get, due to the assumed tax rate policy rule, that the tax rate τ_w tends monotonically to either zero or one. This suggests that the dynamics are only valid over a restricted domain in such a case and that further adjustments will come into operation if certain thresholds in wage taxation are crossed. One possibility that may help to avoid the occurrence of such a situation is given by adding a derivative term for debt evolution based on a parameter $\alpha_{\tau_{w2}} > 0$ to the tax rate adjustment rule of the general model of Section 7.2. We assert that the addition of such a term, a derivative control in fact, will improve the stability properties in the fiscal policy part of the model. Nevertheless it may be necessary to add further or other adjustment mechanisms, in this module of the model, in order to really get dynamics that stay at least bounded if they are not locally asymptotically stable.

Proposition 7.6 shows that the evolution of government debt (due to the interest payments that have to be made, to the steady state size of government expenditures and revenues and also due to the taxation rule that has been assumed for wage taxation) contributes to the local asymptotic stability of the 18D dynamical system. The dynamic instability found in other studies of the evolution of the GBR is thus not a problem in the present formulation of government debt and its evolution, at least when considered in isolation. The extent to which this result holds is dependent on the suppression of other feedback mechanisms that are involved in the GBR, which may come into operation when the general 18D core dynamics of Section 7.3 are investigated. We refer the reader to the much further reaching generalisations of this model type considered in Chiarella *et al.* (1999a,b) and also Chiarella *et al.* (2000).

The monetary and fiscal policy rules we have considered so far have been of a fairly orthodox type: an anti-inflationary interest rate policy rule, a target debt fiscal policy rule and an import taxation rule that attempts to reduce the impact of nominal exchange rate changes on the business sector of the economy. There exist however a variety of other policy rules that might be helpful in reducing the disequilibria that can occur in our model economy. At present we only wish to point to four further extensions of a rule determined behaviour of the government, without attempting to integrate these features into the general 18D core dynamics model of this chapter or even to discuss the role of these rules for economic stability and the like. These extensions are:

1. A counter-cyclical adjustment rule for payroll taxes τ_p.
2. A labour market policy rule that attempts to raise the NAIRE level $\bar{e}$.
3. A counter-cyclical policy rule for government expenditures g per unit of social product (appropriately measured).
4. A counter-cyclical employment policy in the government sector which endogenises the parameter α_g.

This brief list must here suffice to indicate that there is a lot of room in our 18D core model for designing, testing and evaluating various fiscal (and monetary) policy rules.

7.12 Import taxation

The evolution of import taxation, when treated in isolation, is particularly easy, since its law of motion

$$\hat{\tau}_m = \alpha_{\tau_m} \frac{p_x x - p_m j^d}{p_x x}$$

can be reduced to

$$\hat{\tau}_m = \alpha_{\tau_m} \frac{p_x^* x - (1 + \tau_m) p_m^* j^d}{p_x^* x}$$

where p_m^*, p_x^*, x, j^d are given magnitudes of the model.

We thus have only to consider one law of motion here, which is based on a negative feedback of the rate of import taxation on to itself and therefore is globally asymptotically stable and establishes balanced trade in the limit. This simply serves the important purpose of making the solution of the private sector of the economy independent of trade flows and the revenues and costs these trade flows generate for the sector of firms (off the steady state). We expect that this subsector of the model needs further improvements in future reformulations. At present international trade of goods has only limited but well defined effects on the behaviour of firms, but not on the domestic goods market or Keynesian aggregate demand in general.

7.13 The Dornbusch exchange rate dynamics mechanism

The evolution of the exchange rate and expectations about its behaviour can be reduced to an independent 2D subsystem of the general 18D dynamics of Section 7.3 if the data concerning bond price dynamics are considered as given for the time being. In that case the dynamics of s and ϵ_s read (see equations (7.35), (7.36)).

$$\hat{s} = \frac{\beta_s}{1 - \beta_s(1 - \alpha_s)}[i_l^* + \alpha_s \epsilon_s - (i_l + \pi_b)],$$

$$\dot{\epsilon}_s = \beta_{\epsilon_s}(\hat{s} - \epsilon_s).$$

To study the resulting dynamics in isolation we again assume that the other asset market situations are frozen at their steady state values which fixes the expression $(i_l + \pi_b)$ involved in the above equations to i_{lo}. From this we thus derive as law of motion for the change in exchange rate expectations of the less ambitious agents

$$\dot{\epsilon}_s = \beta_{\epsilon_s}\left(\frac{\beta_s \alpha_s}{1 - \beta_s(1 - \alpha_s)} - 1\right)\epsilon_s,$$

which clearly provides (trivial) monotonically explosive dynamics if the parameters in the fraction are chosen such that it becomes larger than one. Increasing the parameter β_{ϵ_s} beyond any bound then makes this process as explosive as desired and thus will significantly contribute to local instability of the full 18D dynamics. Compared with the isolated dynamics for long-term bonds and equities considered in Section 7.10 we therefore here find a particularly simple representation of the centrifugal forces that surround asset market dynamics in our approach to their behaviour.

Increasing the parameters β_s for exchange rate flexibility will increase the positive influence of the expected exchange rate changes ϵ_s on the actual rate of change of the exchange range without bound. For positive α_s we get in this way a positive feedback of exchange rate expectations on their time rate of change which becomes the more destabilising the faster these expectations are adjusted. This effect is similar to the Mundell effect we considered previously.

The influence of the dynamics of the nominal exchange rate on the rest of the dynamics is limited in the model of monetary growth investigated in this chapter, since it only works through the rate of profit of firms which depends on the rate s via exports and imports and the tax revenue that is generated from import taxation.

The above extremely one-sided situation in the adjustments of the exchange rate is partly due to our hierarchical treatment of the asset market dynamics, where we have assumed that the short-run rate of interest is set by the monetary authority, where the long-term rate of interest adjusts into the direction of this short-term interest rate and where the exchange rate is driven by the differential that expectations about its rate of change create between the expected rate of return on foreign as compared with the expected rate of return on domestic long-term bonds. The positive feedback mechanisms that exist in the dynamics of asset prices and the exchange rate are therefore built on a sequential reasoning in our model and lead to an extreme type of instability when the foreign exchange market is considered in isolation – without its feedback through the real part of the economy.

A similar observation is not so obvious, if we allow the exchange rate s to influence the evolution of the real part of the dynamics, by removing the assumption that the rate of import taxation is always set such that the trade account of firms is balanced (when measured in domestic prices). In this latter case, the expected rate of profit of firms does not depend on their export and import levels and thus on exchange rate changes. As long as there are no wealth effects in the model and as long as the individual allocation of bonds on the various sectors does not matter, there is indeed only this one channel through which the nominal exchange rate can influence the real economy (besides of course through the GBR which includes the tax income of the government) that derives from import taxation, but which does not play a role for the real part of the model unless wage taxation is responsive to the evolution of government debt (as we have seen in the preceding section). To have this influence of the exchange rate we thus have to extend the 9D real dynamics by the three laws of motion[19]

$$\hat{\tau}_m = \alpha_{\tau_m} \frac{p_x^* x - (1+\tau_m) p_m^* j^d}{p_x^* x}, \tag{7.61}$$

$$\hat{s} = \frac{\beta_s}{1-\beta_s(1-\alpha_s)} \left[i_l^* + \alpha_s \epsilon_s - \left(\frac{1}{p_b} + \pi_b \right) \right], \tag{7.62}$$

$$\dot{\epsilon}_s = \beta_{\epsilon_s} (\hat{s} - \epsilon_s). \tag{7.63}$$

The exchange rate dynamics are now more difficult to analyse, since their two laws of motion require the influence of the bond dynamics in order to be meaningful. Otherwise the two laws of motion (7.62), (7.63) would imply monotonic implosion or explosion of exchange rate expectations and the actual exchange rate depending on whether the adjustment speed of the exchange rate is smaller or larger than one (for $\alpha_s = 1$), as we have seen earlier. The financial dynamics are therefore in this respect immediately of dimension 5 and one also needs input from the real dynamics in order to get the effects from the exchange rate s on bond prices p_b and thus an interdependent dynamics and not one of the appended monotonic form just discussed. Yet, the effect of changes in s via the rate of profit r^e of firms and the investment decisions that are based on it needs to reach a long way in order to influence the market for long-term bonds. Changes in investment lead to changes in aggregate goods demand and thus to changes in sales expectations and actual output. This leads to changes in capacity utilisation of firms and domestic price inflation which (if and only if monetary policy responds to them) are transferred to changes in the short-term rate of interest and thus to changes in the long-term rate of interest. In this way there is a feedback of a change in the exchange rate on its rate of change, which has to be analysed if the full dynamics are to be investigated.

For the moment we consider that this feedback chain is too long and complicated for a first discussion of the dynamics of asset markets that integrate exchange rate dynamics.

[19] Note that the first law is independent of the changes in the exchange rate.

We thus consider the following simplification of this feedback mechanism, which here serves to demonstrate that there is some similarity between the isolated bond price dynamics and the dynamics of the exchange rate. In models of the Dornbusch (1976) type of overshooting exchange rates there is generally a very determinate mechanism that leads to a positive impact effect of an increase in the exchange rate s on the nominal rate of interest i, via increasing exports and decreasing imports, the resulting increases in economic activity and in the price level and thus to i increases via an LM theory of the money market. This mechanism is here used as a basis for the design of a monetary policy rule that copies this feedback chain according to

$$i = i_o + \beta_i(s - s_o), \quad i_o = i_l^*,$$

where i_o, s_o denote the steady state values of i, s. In a first application of this rule we in addition assume that it applies immediately to the long-term rate of interest $i_l = 1/p_b$.

The dynamical equations for the exchange are thereby transformed to[20]

$$\hat{s} = \beta_s[i_l^* + \epsilon_s - (i_o + \beta_i(s - s_o) + \pi_{bs})],$$
$$\dot{\epsilon}_s = \beta_{\epsilon_s}(\hat{s} - \epsilon_s).$$

In order to consider these dynamics in the simplest possible way we finally assume $\pi_{bs} \equiv 0$. Rearranging terms we then obtain

$$\hat{s} = \beta_s[-\beta_i s + \epsilon_s + \beta_i s_o],$$
$$\dot{\epsilon}_s = \beta_{\epsilon_s}(\hat{s} - \epsilon_s).$$

In this form the system is of the same type as the one for the long-term bond dynamics shown above. It therefore will give rise to the same conclusions as the bond dynamics that we have considered in Section 7.10.

Yet this similarity is based on a number of artificial assumptions as far as our original 18D dynamics are concerned. Therefore using (as is necessary) as policy rule the short-term interest rate policy of the 18D dynamics would imply for example the extended dynamics (again assume for $\alpha_s = 1$ for simplicity)

$$\hat{p}_b = \beta_{p_b}\left[\frac{1}{p_b} + \pi_{bs} - i\right],$$
$$\dot{\pi}_{bs} = \beta_{\pi_{bs}}(\hat{p}_b - \pi_{bs}),$$
$$\hat{s} = \beta_s\left[i_l^* + \epsilon_s - \left(\frac{1}{p_b} + \pi_{bs}\right)\right],$$
$$\dot{\epsilon}_s = \beta_{\epsilon_s}(\hat{s} - \epsilon_s),$$
$$i = i_o + \beta_i(s - s_o)$$

[20] We again assume $\alpha_s = 1$ for simplicity. Note that import taxation was of no importance in the presently considered dynamics.

which is already a 4D dynamical system (as can be seen by inserting the last equation into the first one) representing in isolation those financial markets that will have impact on the real part of the economy. The question then arises as to what extent the 2D analysis of the market for long-term bonds also applies to this two asset approach and its four laws of motion from the local as well as from the global perspective (giving rise again to limit cycles or limit limit cycles or possibly also more complex types of attractors).

Rearranging the above system slightly reduces it to

$$\hat{p}_b = \beta_{p_b}\left[\frac{1}{p_b} + \pi_{bs} - \left(i_l^* + \beta_i(s - s_o)\right)\right], \tag{7.64}$$

$$\dot{\pi}_{bs} = \beta_{\pi_{bs}}(\hat{p}_b - \pi_{bs}), \tag{7.65}$$

$$\dot{\epsilon}_s = \beta_{\epsilon_s}(\hat{s} - \epsilon_s), \tag{7.66}$$

$$\hat{s} = \beta_s\left[i_l^* + \epsilon_s - \left(\frac{1}{p_b} + \pi_{bs}\right)\right]. \tag{7.67}$$

The interior steady state of these dynamics is given by $p_b = 1/i_l^* = 1/i_o^*, \pi_{bs} = 0, s = s_o, \epsilon_s = 0$. The Jacobian of the dynamics at the steady state in the case $\beta_{\pi_{bs}}, \beta_{\epsilon_s} < 1$, has the sign distribution

$$J = \begin{pmatrix} - & + & 0 & - \\ - & - & 0 & - \\ + & - & - & 0 \\ + & - & + & 0 \end{pmatrix}.$$

It is easy to see from this form that the dynamics must be locally asymptotically stable if the parameter β_s is chosen sufficiently small. Setting this parameter equal to zero and considering only the remaining 3D dynamical system one obtains for the Jacobian the sign structure

$$J = \begin{pmatrix} - & + & 0 \\ - & - & 0 \\ + & - & - \end{pmatrix}.$$

It is fairly obvious that this matrix must fulfil the Routh–Hurwitz conditions for local asymptotic stability, since this is obviously true for the upper principal minor

$$\begin{pmatrix} J_{11} & J_{12} \\ J_{21} & J_{22} \end{pmatrix}.$$

Thus the system is obviously composed of two stable subdynamics with all three eigenvalues having negative real part and determined only by their respective subsystem.

Furthermore as far as the determinant of the full Jacobian is concerned we can easily remove linear dependencies from this Jacobian in order to get for its determinant

$$\det J = \det \begin{pmatrix} - & + & 0 & - \\ 0 & - & 0 & 0 \\ 0 & 0 & - & 0 \\ + & - & + & 0 \end{pmatrix},$$

which is easily calculated to be positive. Due to the continuity of eigenvalues with respect to the entries of the matrix J we see that a negative eigenvalue must be born adding to the three of the 3D dynamics when the parameter β_s is changed from zero to small positive values. We conjecture that this remains valid as long as the parameter β_s remains less than one. We thus have the result:

Proposition 7.7 *1. The dynamical system (7.64), (7.65), (7.66), (7.67) for bond price/exchange rate dynamics has a unique interior steady state which is locally asymptotically stable for adjustment speeds of prices and expectations sufficiently low.*

2. The steady state will generally lose its stability in a cyclical fashion by way of a Hopf bifurcation if in particular the adjustment speeds of the adaptively formed expectations are chosen sufficiently high.

The second part of Proposition 7.7 holds true since we have shown that the determinant of the full Jacobian J is always positive, so that eigenvalues cannot become zero (in particular when the imaginary axis in the complex phase plain is crossed. We conjecture but cannot show this here that all eigenvalues will become real and will thus give rise to saddlepath dynamics with monotonic features if the adjustment speeds in the above model are all chosen sufficiently high.

If all adjustment speeds are set equal to infinity the dynamical system (7.64)–(7.67) reduces to the 2D form

$$\hat{s} = \beta_i(s - s_o),$$

$$\hat{p}_b = i_l^* - \frac{1}{p_b} + \beta_i(s - s_o).$$

In this representation the order of dependence of the two asset markets is reversed and the saddlepath dynamics that are then implied are clearly visible. In the case of unanticipated shocks that concern these dynamics, the traditional mode of analysis would then be to apply the jump variable technique which would here imply that the system immediately jumps to its new steady state values $(s_o, 1/i_l^*)$ when these values have been moved to a new location through the assumed type of shock.

We thus see that the rational expectations solution in our deterministic model is a limit case of our approach that demands a new solution technique if one wants to suppress the explosiveness of the asset market subdynamics under perfect foresight and infinitely fast price adjustments as far as the obtained 2D dynamics are concerned. We believe however that the considered limit case is too ideally chosen and that one should apply the relaxation oscillation methodology of Section 7.6 in the derivation of the limiting properties instead of simply setting all adjustment speeds equal to infinity and of only discussing the consequences of replacing certain laws of motion by simple algebraic conditions when deriving this ideal situation of perfect flexibility and perfect anticipation of asset market prices. We admit however that the relaxation oscillation methodology is difficult to apply to the 4D dynamics considered above due to the assumed hierarchical structure in the interaction of long-term bond prices with the rate of exchange. The task would be much easier if the expected rate of return on foreign bonds could be compared with the short-term rate of interest in the law of motion for the exchange rate, which however would demand a reformulation of the asset market structure of our general model.

7.14 Conclusions

Summing up the isolated stability or instability results we have obtained in this chapter we can state the following conclusions.

We have found that either wage or price level flexibility is bad for local economic stability. Whenever wage flexibility is good its flexibility on the outside labour market will nevertheless be bad for local stability if it becomes too large compared with the demand pressure that originates from the inside labour market. Next, a very flexible adjustment speed of planned inventory holdings has been shown to lead to local instability when coupled with a rapid adjustment of sales expectations. We have in addition described situations where some of these local instabilities can be overcome by certain bounds on the behaviour of these subdynamics.

On the nominal side there was still more room for the occurrence of centrifugal forces around the steady state of the model, since the price level of goods and long-term bonds as well as equity prices and the nominal exchange rate all gave rise to local explosiveness if adjustment speeds in these markets are sufficiently high and coupled with a rapid adjustment of the expectations of workers (in the market for goods) and less ambitious asset holders (in the remaining markets).

Stability only came about, first, through the Keynes effect and the nominal interest rate policy of the central bank that derives from it; second, through assumptions on the size of steady rates of returns as compared with the size of steady economic growth coupled with a stabilising feedback rule between government debt and wage taxation; and third, through a simple adjustment rule for import taxes. Stabilising forces therefore mainly originate in the behaviour of the government and the central bank, unless the relaxation oscillations mechanism considered in Section 7.6 and Section 7.10 can be successfully applied to the expected rate of inflation, sales expectations, long-term bond price expectations and expectations on exchange rate changes as far as the adaptive component of these expectations is concerned.

This brief discussion of the basic partial feedback mechanisms of our full 18D dynamics on balance suggests that increases in the speeds of adjustments of the dynamics will generally be bad for economic stability or viability. Exceptions to this rule are given by either wage or price flexibility and by the sales expectations mechanism, in the case where inventories are adjusted in a sufficiently slow fashion. Mathematically speaking it should be noted finally that the destabilising effects we have discussed in this chapter will generally not appear as obviously destabilising mechanisms in the guise of positive entries in the trace of the Jacobian of the system at the steady state. Rather such destabilising effects will be hidden somewhat in the many principal minors that underlie the calculation of the Routh–Hurwitz conditions for local asymptotic stability in high dimensional dynamical models.

Due to our simple formulation of the investment and pricing behaviour with respect to dwellings and housing services we have also found local asymptotic stability in this part of the private sector. The overall impression nevertheless surely is that the steady state of the private sector is more likely to be subject to centrifugal forces than to centripetal ones, which moreover generally will not remain bounded to an economically meaningful domain around this steady state if the 18D dynamics are considered from a more global perspective. This is in particular shown by the numerical simulations in Chiarella *et al.* (2003b). Extrinsic non-linearities, such as the assumptions underlying relaxation oscillations, therefore have to be added, at least far off the steady state, in order to obtain economic boundedness for the considered dynamics. Further important and still very fundamental candidates in this respect are downward inflexibilities of nominal wages and/or prices, supply bottlenecks as in non-Walrasian macroeconomic theory, further non-linearities in the inventory mechanism and in investment behaviour, and the like. Such extrinsic non-linearities have to be added later on to the intrinsic ones that are 'naturally' present in the dynamics we have considered so far[21] in order to obtain a dynamic model that can generate viability for the orbits it implies. These are studied in a systematic way in Chiarella *et al.* (2003b).

[21] Due to growth rate expressions, products or quotients of state variable as they derive from multiplicative value magnitudes ($w^e l_f^{de}$ for example) or certain quantity ratios (l_f^{de}/l_f^{we} for example), and the like.

Part III

Debt crises: firms, banks and the housing markets

8 Debt deflation: from low to high order macrosystems

8.1 Introduction

At the beginning of the current century, in the public debate on problems of the world economy, 'deflation' or more specifically 'debt deflation' has once again become an important topic. The possible role of debt deflation in triggering the Great Depression of the 1930s has long been the subject of academic studies. It has been observed that there are similarities between recent global trends and the 1930s, namely the joint occurrence of high levels of debt and falling prices: the dangerous downside to cheaper credit when debt is high. Debt deflation thus concerns the interaction of high nominal debt of firms, households and nations and shrinking economic activity due to falling output prices and therefore increasing real debt.

There is often another mechanism accompanying the first one. That other mechanism deals with how large debt may exert its impact on macroeconomic activity, and works through the asset market. Asset price inflation during economic expansions normally gives rise to generous credit extension and lending booms. Assets with inflated prices serve as collateral for borrowing by firms, households or nations. On the other hand when asset prices fall the borrowing capacity of economic agents shrinks, financial failures may set in, macroeconomic activity decreases and consequently large output losses may occur.

Countries that have gone through such booms and busts are Asian countries, in particular Japan, as well as Russia and Brazil in the years 1998 and 1999. In all of those countries as well as during the financial crisis in Mexico in 1994 asset price inflation and lending booms entailed subsequent debt crises and asset price deflation. Thus, usually the mechanism of debt deflation due to falling output prices has been accompanied by the asset price deflation mechanism.[1]

Concerning the public debate on problems of the world economy, 'debt deflation' is surely one of the key expressions that has significantly shaped this discussion, although it is now much less debated than the current subprime crisis. The behaviour of firms

[1] For a detailed study employing asymmetric information theory, see Mishkin (1998).

relying on rounds of downsizing and cost-cutting from the perspective of short-run profitability solely (short-term maximisers), thereby demolishing their productivity over the medium run, was noted as a dangerous strategy caused by their dependence on financial markets. Criticism however has also been raised with respect to the single-minded preoccupation of certain central banks with inflation and it has been suggested that some inflation could be of help in preventing a global economic crisis. The viewpoint of the FED, and of the government in the USA, of course received particular attention in this respect and the former chairman of the FED, Alan Greenspan, was quoted with passages such as:[2]

> Deflationary forces that emerged a year ago were expanding 'and there's no evidence of which I am aware which suggests that the process ... has stabilized'.

Moreover, global growth strategies, and the elements they should contain, continue to be discussed in academic and policy circles. The need for a fundamental restructuring of the IMF and World Bank and a new financial architecture is continuously stressed based on the judgement that the world has, since the years 1998 and 1999 and particularly in the last two years, faced its biggest financial challenge since the 1930s. Debt deflation and its destabilising potential therefore appears to be an important problem that the world economy is still facing.

Deflation, at least in certain sectors of the economy, combined with high indebtedness of firms, although currently not the focus of interest, therefore appears to be an important problem for the world economy, and – as is sometimes stressed – one that it will continue to face for a considerable period into the future; see in particular Shilling's (1999) detailed study of the long-run forces driving deflation. The destabilising potential of debt deflation without and with its interaction with other economic feedback mechanisms that concern the danger of deflationary processes (to be discussed in this chapter) should therefore be modelled and investigated thoroughly. One should also take into consideration the possibilities for monetary and fiscal policies that allow a cessation of the processes of rising debt and falling output prices that can lead to depression or in the extreme even economic breakdown as in the Great Depression.

Modern macroeconomic theory, as it has evolved since the Second World War, has paid scant attention to the above described mechanism of debt deflation. No doubt this is due to the fact that during that time the major economies in the world experienced a long period of growth followed by a long period of inflation from which we have recently emerged. The classic study of debt deflation remains Fisher (1933), though Minsky (1975, 1982) in his writings on the financial instability hypothesis continued to warn of the dangers of another great depression. There is therefore an urgent need for economists to model the process of debt deflation in its interaction with monetary and fiscal policies that may stop the process of rising debt, falling output and asset prices and a subsequent collapse into depression. We here note that the current subprime crisis at present primarily concerns the financial sector of the economies involved, but may

[2] *The Sydney Morning Herald*, 21 September 1998.

easily give rise to subsequent processes of debt deflation if it spreads into the real part of these and other economies.

In this chapter we embed the process of debt accumulation and debt deflation into a fully integrated and consistent – with respect to budget constraints – macroeconomic model as it has already been formulated in Chiarella *et al.* (2001a,b); see Part II for a detailed formulation of the underlying structure. At the core of the model will be firms that finance fixed investment not from retained earnings, but by loans from the credit market. In the current chapter we therefore neglect the equity financing of the earlier approach of Part II. Our model will thus focus mainly on the first mechanism of the debt deflation process, the destabilising role of flexible wages and prices in economies with high nominal debt, while the destabilising role of asset prices will be neglected here.[3]

Our macroeconomic model contains a sufficient number of agents and markets to capture the essential dynamic features of modern macroeconomies, and stresses the dynamic interaction between the main feedback loops of capital accumulation, debt accumulation, price and wage inflation (and deflation), income distribution, inventory accumulation and government monetary and fiscal policies. Our modelling framework relies on previous work by the authors and contributions by other co-authors underlying Part II. The essential difference is that we here focus on debt-financed investment of firms in place of pure equity financing. We will thus add a further important feedback loop that was missing in our earlier approach to macro modelling, namely, from a partial point of view, the destabilising Fisher debt effect of deflationary (or inflationary) phases of capital accumulation arising from the creditor–debtor relationship between banks and firms.

The Fisher debt deflation mechanism is easily described, for example by means of the diagram shown in Figure 8.1. This diagram shows that price (and wage) deflation, caused by depressed markets for goods (and for labour), increase the real debt of firms (and indebted households), thereby leading to reduced investment (and consumption), which gives further impetus to the depression already under way and its subsequent consequences for further price (and wage) deflation. This partial reasoning thus suggests that debt deflation may end up in a deflationary spiral and economic breakdown, if this downward movement in prices (and wages) cannot be stopped.

Further issues in this context concern subjects that can aggravate the development of debt deflation (stock price collapses, credit rationing, large scale bankruptcy, banking and foreign exchange crisis and domestic or foreign policy intervention). These issues will be approached to a certain degree in the chapters of Part III, but remain to be integrated and investigated into the model of the present chapter in future work in order so as to allow a full treatment of the dangers of the joint occurrence of debt and deflation in certain regions of the world economy or even on a worldwide scale.

[3] For work on the credit market, economic activity and the destabilising role of asset price inflation and deflation, see Minsky (1975).

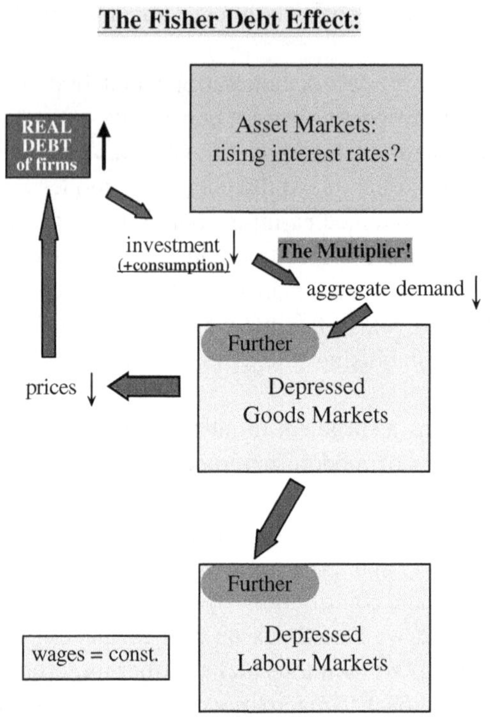

Figure 8.1 The Fisher debt deflation effect

However, such deflationary spirals do not work in isolation and may be counteracted by well-known Keynes or Pigou effects. This chapter will, however, primarily pay attention to another aspect of falling wages and prices, namely the so-called normal or adverse Rose (1967) or real wage effects. The working of such effects is explained by means of the following two diagrams. Considering normal Rose effects first, there are two possibilities for their occurrence:

1. The case where aggregate demand depends positively on the real wage and a price flexibility which is sufficiently higher than wage flexibility, in which case real wages fall in a boom and rise in a depression, which is stabilising.
2. The case where aggregate demand depends negatively on the real wage and a wage flexibility which is sufficiently higher than price flexibility in which case real wages also fall in a boom and rise in a depression, which is again stabilising.

Such stabilising real wage adjustments are exemplified in Figure 8.2 and they would – just as do Keynes or Pigou effects – work against the depressing forces of the Fisher debt deflation mechanism. The question however is whether such stabilising forces can really overcome the depressing effects of rising real debt. This question will be investigated in Section 8.3.

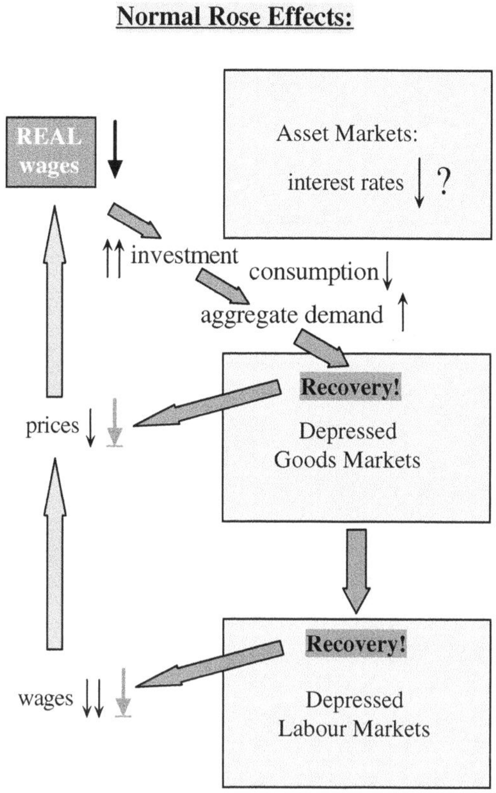

Figure 8.2 Normal Rose effects

However, Rose effects can also be adverse or destabilising, namely when in the first of the above considered two situations wage flexibility is sufficiently high or in the second case when price flexibility is sufficiently high. These adverse Rose effects are exemplified in Figure 8.3. Price and wage flexibility may, therefore, be destabilising through two channels, the Fisher debt effect and the adverse Rose real wage effects. These two mechanisms are at the core of the high dimensional analysis of AS–AD disequilibrium growth type which this chapter provides, while further traditional mechanisms such as the Keynes effect or the dynamic multiplier process are also addressed, but are of secondary importance here.

In this chapter we therefore start a series of investigations that attempt to apply the general approach to disequilibrium growth theory of Part II of this book to contemporary topics of applied economic analysis and to policy issues that are debated in the economics literature and amongst the public. These issues were not included in or not sufficiently stressed in our approach in Part II to disequilibrium growth. The main purpose of the present and of subsequent applications and extensions of our integrated disequilibrium approach to economic growth is therefore to bring the models used by this approach closer to the applied macroeconomic literature, by considering the (often)

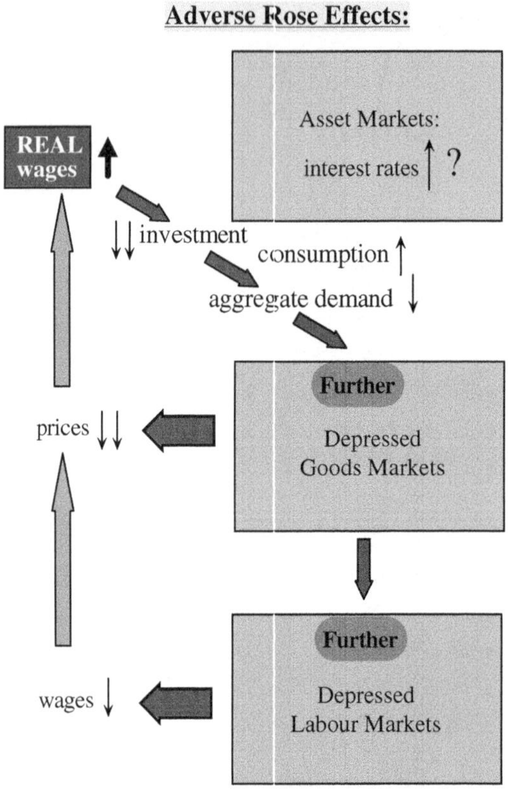

Figure 8.3 Adverse Rose effects

partial models of this literature and their theoretical or empirical results from the general perspective and model formulation reached in Part II.

Topics that will in this way be integrated or be the focus of our investigations are (among others): situations of high indebtedness of firms (bank loans) and households (mortgages) and the danger of deflationary processes in such an environment; other aspects of financial markets and their implications for fixed business investment, in particular for the housing sector (see Chapter 11) as well as the commercial office market in view of the fluctuations that are there observed. Such topics will be integrated one after another into our general approach to disequilibrium growth and then investigated with respect to the changes their inclusion may imply for the dynamics of the whole economy and, in turn, what the general approach to fluctuating growth chosen in Part II may imply for the outlook of the new partial mechanism that is imbedded into it and investigated from this perspective. In this way we believe we can demonstrate to the reader the power of our approach to treat those real world applications or topics that have received a great deal of attention from the viewpoint of applied macroeconomics.

Keen (2000) has investigated the Fisher debt effect (between firms and financial intermediaries) in the context of an augmented Goodwin growth cycle model and has found that such an effect may imply local asymptotic stability for the overshooting mechanism of the Goodwin growth cycle, but can lead to instability (for high debt) outside a corridor around the steady state of the model. His paper in addition provides an interesting discussion of Fisher's vision of the interaction of over-indebtedness and deflation and also of Minsky's financial instability hypothesis. It then extends the proposed model of the interaction of indebted firms and income distribution to an inclusion of the role of government behaviour in such an environment and of nominal adjustment processes in place of the real ones of the Goodwin model. Details of his approach to debt deflation will be mentioned in the following sections of the chapter.

To introduce such a debt effect into our model of integrated disequilibrium growth demands, of course, that firms finance their fixed business investment expenditures not only by issuing new equities, as was the case in the approach chosen in Part II, but also by loans which they obtain (via certain intermediaries, not explicitly considered in this chapter; see however the subsequent ones) from pure asset owners, so that they finance these expenditures by a combination of equity (or retained earnings) and debt. Such a situation however calls for some rule by which firms split their financial needs into new equity supply and loan demand. There is a variety of possibilities for formulating such a rule which however makes the discussion of debt deflation more involved than is really necessary in a first treatment of its occurrence in a fully specified macrodynamic model. We therefore assume in this chapter for reasons of simplicity that firms finance their investment decisions (fixed business investment as well as involuntary inventory investment) exclusively via loans – apart from pure profits, as will be made clear below. The accumulation of debt is thus a simple consequence of the budget constraint of firms which only needs to be transferred to per unit of capital terms in order to provide one of the two new laws of motion of this chapter compared with the 18D case developed in Part II (the other new law of motion concerns the dynamics of the rate of interest on loans).

Introducing debt financing and removing equity financing from the general approach of Part II has the further implication that there are now fluctuations in the income of firms that go beyond the windfall losses or profits caused by disappointed or over-satisfied sales expectations. There are now also pure profits (or losses) to be considered as they will result from systematic deviations of actual (or expected) sales from the factor costs of firms now including interest payments besides wage and import costs. The budget equations and financing behaviour of firms, and their impact on their investment behaviour, therefore have to be reformulated in an appropriate way in order to take account of this deviation between total factor costs and the total proceeds of firms and the retained earnings based upon them.

Such a revision is however not needed if it were assumed that there are further investment expenditures (over and above those based on debt financing) that are financed by issuing new equities, as in Chiarella *et al.* (1999a,b),[4] and that all expected (pure) profits, based on total factor costs (including interest payments) and on the sales expectations

[4] In this regard see also Chiarella *et al.* (2000).

of firms, are paid out as dividends to asset owners (who besides providing the loans, also hold the total stock of equities that was issued in the past). This is a second way of investigating the role of debt of firms in inflationary or deflationary environments (not yet pursued in this chapter). As already stated it requires, in contrast to the case of a pure loan financing, some rule describing how firms choose between debt and equity financing in view of their intended fixed business investment.

In Section 8.2 we briefly present the changes to the model of Part II that are needed for a discussion of debt deflation from the perspective of national accounting. Section 8.3 then provides the new equations of the debt deflation model on the extensive form level and discusses these changes in comparison with the extensive form model of Part II and also their relationships to the work of Keen (2000). Section 8.4 gives a short description of the interior steady state of the model, its twenty laws of motion (now including loans and interest on loans) for its intensive form state variables, including various algebraic equations that supplement the dynamical laws.

Section 8.5 then approaches the issue of debt deflation by first starting from the basic 3D model of Keen (2000) which only allows for debt accumulation, but not yet for deflationary processes, by presenting some propositions relevant to this starting situation. We then extend the model to dimension 4 by including nominal price dynamics and again derive certain propositions on this extended situation with nominal price level adjustments. Section 8.6 then considers the 3D, the 4D and the general 20D dynamics from the numerical perspective and thereby illustrates what has been shown analytically. Section 8.7 concludes and gives a perspective on future developments.

8.2 Reformulating the structure of the economy

Tables 8.1 to 8.9 (and subsequent accounting presentations) provide a brief survey of the changes we shall make in this chapter with respect to the structure of the 18D core dynamics of the small open economies considered and investigated in Part II. These changes basically concern the financing conditions and the investment behaviour of firms assumed in Part II. We thus do not repeat here many of the structural details of this 18D model of disequilibrium growth, in particular of the real part of the economy, but refer the reader back to Part II for the full details of this model type (with fixed proportions in production).[5] When presenting the new intensive form of the now 20D dynamics we will however attempt to motivate its equations to some extent. These equations concern

- quantity adjustment processes and growth (sales expectations, inventories and the stock of labour besides the capital stock growth and growth of the housing stock of the economy);
- price adjustment processes (wages, prices, inflationary expectations and the price of housing services);

[5] The case of neoclassical smooth input and output substitution is considered in detail in Chiarella *et al.* (1999a,b), see also Chiarella *et al.* (2000).

- asset market dynamics (bond price and exchange rate dynamics, both including capital gain expectation formation);
- policy rules and government debt (the accumulation of short- and long-term bonds, wage and import taxation and a Taylor interest rate policy rule);
- as new laws of motion the dynamics of the debt to capital ratio and the dynamics of interest on loans.

Note that we will ignore value-added taxes on consumption goods in the following and thus set the parameter τ_v of the original 18D dynamics equal to zero for notational simplicity.

8.2.1 Changes in the financial sector of the economy

Let us first reformulate the financial part of the economy where all additions made with respect to the general framework presented in Part II are marked by bold letters. Note that we here switch from pure equity financing to pure loan financing as far as the external fund-raising of firms is concerned and that therefore the expected returns of firms are no longer distributed to households (but retained) in this revision of the 18D core model of Part II in order to allow concentration on the effects of debt financing for firms' performance (and also for worker households later on).

Table 8.1 shows that firms now use loans in the place of equities as instrument to finance (part of) their investment expenditures. These loans are supplied by pure asset holders in the gross amount $\dot{\Lambda}_f^b$ following the loan demand of firms. Loans are just an amount of money lent to firms (with a price of unity) and they exhibit a variable rate of interest i_λ which is applied to all loans (old and new ones, Λ_f, $\dot{\Lambda}_f^b$) in a uniform manner so that there is no term structure of interest rates as far as loans are concerned. Furthermore, in order to keep things simple, we assume that a certain fraction δ_λ of the stock of loans Λ_f existing at each moment in time is repaid in this moment of time, and that only net amounts of new debt $\dot{\Lambda}_f = \dot{\Lambda}_f^b - \delta_\lambda \Lambda_f$ need to be considered as far as budget equations and asset accumulation are concerned, in order to ease the presentation of the model in later sections of the chapter. Note that money is not treated as an asset in this chapter, due to specific assumptions made in Part II (where 'money' has been treated as a pure medium of account).

8.2.2 Changes from the viewpoint of national accounting

We shall consider in this subsection briefly the production and income accounts, and the accumulation and financial accounts of two of the four agents of our economy, firms and asset holders, whose relationship to each other is changed by the introduction of loans from asset holders to firms (in place of the equities and the dividend payments assumed in the version of the model presented in Part II). These accounts provide basic information on what has been changed compared with the general disequilibrium growth model of Part II.

Table 8.1. *The financial part of the economy (Foreign country data: i_l^*)*

	Short-term Bonds of the Government	Long-term Bonds of the Government	Loans to Firms	Foreign Bonds of the Foreign Government
Workers	$\dot{B}_w$	–	–	–
Asset holders	$\dot{B}_c$	$\dot{B}_1^l$	$\dot{\Lambda}_f = \dot{\Lambda}_f^b - \delta_\lambda \Lambda_f$	$\dot{B}_2^l$
Firms	–	–	$\dot{\Lambda}_f = \dot{\Lambda}_f^b - \delta_\lambda \Lambda_f$	–
Government	$\dot{B}$	$\dot{B}^l$	–	–
Prices	$1\ [i]$	$p_b = 1/i_l$	$1\ [i_\lambda]$	$sp_b^* = s \cdot 1/i_l^*$
Expectations	–	$\pi_b = \hat{p}_b^e$	–	$\epsilon_s = \hat{s}^e$
Stocks	$B = B_w + B_c$	$B^l = B_1^l + B_1^{l*}$	Λ_f	B_2^l
Growth	$\hat{B}, \hat{B}_w, \hat{B}_c$	$\hat{B}^l, \hat{B}_1^l$	$\hat{\Lambda}_f = \dot{\Lambda}_f^b/\Lambda_f - \delta_\lambda$	$\hat{B}_2^l$

Table 8.2. *Production account of firms*

Uses	Resources
Depreciation $p_y \delta_k K$	Consumption $p_y C_w + p_y C_c + p_y G$
Imports (including import taxes) $p_m J^d$	Durables (Housing) $p_y I_h$
Wages (including payroll taxes) $w^b L_f^d$	Exports $p_x X$
Interest on Loans $i_\lambda \Lambda_f$	Gross Fixed Business Investment $p_y I$
Actual Profits + Inventories $\Pi = r^a p_y K + p_y \dot{N}$	Actual Inventory Investment $p_y \dot{N}$
= Intended Profits + Inventories: $r^e p_y K + p_y \mathcal{I}$	Intended Inventory Investment $p_y \mathcal{I}$

We start with the accounts of the sector of firms – shown in Table 8.2 – which organise production Y, employment L_f^d of their workforce L_f^w and gross business fixed investment I and which use (in the present formulation of the model) loans Λ_f and expected retained earnings (plus windfall profits) as financing instruments for their desired net investment. There are import taxes τ_m on imported commodities and payroll taxes τ_p (with respect to hours worked L_f^d in the sector of firms). There are no subsidies and no longer value-added taxes τ_v on the consumption goods produced by firms, for reasons of simplicity. Note that all accounts are expressed in terms of the domestic currency. Note also that our one-good economy assumes that this good can be used for consumption and investment purposes (also for new housing supply).

Firms use up all imports J^d as intermediate goods which thereby become part of the unique homogeneous good Y that is produced for domestic purposes. They have replacement costs with respect to their capital stock, pay import taxes and wages including payroll taxes, and, as a new item, have to pay interest $i_\lambda \Lambda_f$ on their stock of loans Λ_f. Their accounting profit is therefore equal to actual pure profits $r^a p_y K$ (based on actual sales) and notional income gone into actual inventory changes (besides the depreciation fund for capital stock replacement).

Table 8.3. *Income account of firms*

Uses	Resources
Savings S_f^n	Profits Π

Table 8.4. *Accumulation account of firms*

Uses	Resources
Gross Fixed Investment $p_y I$	Depreciation $p_y \delta_k K$
Inventory Investment $p_y \dot{N}$	Savings S_f^n
–	Financial Deficit FD

Note that firms have sales expectations that follow actual sales in an adaptive fashion. They therefore experience (unexpected) windfall profits (or losses) for the financing of their fixed investment when their actual inventory changes are smaller than (larger than) their desired ones. Firms save all the income they receive and spend it on net fixed investment and on inventories of finished goods. The accumulation account is therefore self-explanatory as is the financial account which only repeats our statements made above that the financial deficit of firms is financed by new loans from pure asset holders.

Note also that the amount $\delta_\lambda \Lambda_f$ of existing loans must be repaid to asset holders (and replaced by new loans by assumption on credit market contracts) in each moment of time which means that the sum of all new loans $\dot{\Lambda}_f^b$ must be diminished by this magnitude in order to arrive at the rate of change of the stock of loans $\dot{\Lambda}_f$ to be considered later on. Note also that all goods are now valued at producer prices p_y which do not differ from consumer prices $p_v = (1 + \tau_v)p_y$ in the presently considered model ($\tau_v = 0$). There are also no direct (capital) taxes in the sector of firms, neither on property nor on profits. Note finally that the accumulation account of firms is based on realised magnitudes and thus refers to their intended inventories plans only implicitly. In the production account of the firms shown in Table 8.2, the important (single) change is depicted in bold-face letters.

The income account of firms is formally seen the same as in Part II and shown in Table 8.3.

The change in the accumulation account is also only an implicit one (based on the change in profits) and shown in Table 8.4.

There is finally the financial account of firms (see Table 8.5) where the debt financing of investment is the (single) new element (bold-face letters).

Turning next to the sector of asset holders we know from Part II that investment in housing as well as the supply of housing services has been exclusively allocated to

Table 8.5. *Financial account of firms*

Uses	Resources
Financial Deficit FD	**Loans** $\dot{\Lambda}_f = \dot{\Lambda}^b_f - \delta_\lambda \Lambda_f$

Table 8.6. *Production account of households (asset holders)*

Uses	Resources
Depreciation $p_y \delta_h K_h$	Rent $p_h C^w_h$
Rent Earnings Π_h	

Table 8.7. *Income account of households (asset holders)*

Uses	Resources
Tax Payment $\tau_c r B_c + \tau_c B^l_1$	Interest Payment $r B_c + B^l_1$
Taxes $\tau_c(p_h C^w_h - p_y \delta_h K_h)$	Interest Payment $s(1 - \tau^*_c) B^l_2$
Tax Payment $\tau_c i_\lambda \Lambda_f$	**Interest on Loans** $i_\lambda \Lambda_f$
Consumption $p_y C_c$	Rent Earnings Π_h
Savings S^n_c	

this sector. The production account of asset holders (see Table 8.6) therefore shows the actual sale (not the potential sale) of housing services (set equal to the demand for housing services by assumption) which is divided into replacement costs and actual earnings or profits on the uses side of the production account.

The income account of asset holders (see Table 8.7) comes from various sources: interest payments on short- and long-term domestic bonds and on long-term foreign bonds (net of tax payments which must be paid abroad), interest income on loans to firms and profits from housing rents. All domestic profit income is subject to tax payments at the rate τ_c and after tax income is by definition divided into the consumption of domestic commodities (including houses, but not housing services) and the nominal savings of asset owners.

The accumulation account (see Table 8.8) shows the sources for gross investment of asset holders in the housing sector, namely depreciation and savings, the excess of which (over housing investment) is then invested into financial assets as shown in the financial account. Note here that short-term bonds are fixed-price bonds $p_b = 1$ (which are perfectly liquid), while loans as well as long-term bonds are not perfectly liquid, the latter since they have the variable price $p_b = 1/i_l$ which shows that they are of the

Table 8.8. *Accumulation account of households (asset holders)*

Uses	Resources
Gross Investment $p_y I_h$	Depreciation $p_y \delta_h K_h$
Financial Surplus FS	Savings S_c^n

Table 8.9. *Financial account of households (asset holders)*

Uses	Resources
Short-term Bonds $\dot{B}_c$	Financial Surplus FS
Long-term Bonds $p_b \dot{B}_1^l$	
Foreign Bonds $s p_b^* \dot{B}_2^l$	
Loans $\dot{\boldsymbol{\Lambda}}_f = \dot{\boldsymbol{\Lambda}}_f^b - \delta_\lambda \boldsymbol{\Lambda}_f$	

type of consols or perpetuities (the same holds true for imported foreign bonds, which are of long-term type solely).[6]

The central new topic in the income account of asset holders is of course the interest on the loans supplied to the worker households. The accumulation account is formally seen the same as in Part II. The loans of pure asset holders to worker households is again the single new topic as compared with Part II of the book.

The financial account of asset holders is shown in Table 8.9. There is no taxation of financial wealth (held or transferred) in the household sector and there is also no real property tax. Furthermore, although asset holders will consider expected net rates of return on financial markets in their investment decision, there is no taxation of capital gains on these markets as the model is presently formulated, which descriptively seems realistic.

We do not present the accounts of the worker households here as there is no change in their treatment as compared with Part II). Later on we shall however reinterpret the quantity B_w, their stock of short-term assets, as liabilities to the sector of asset holders, in other words as a negative quantity, and thus will get also debtor–creditor relationships between our two types of households, workers and pure asset holders, in addition to the one between firms and asset holders. We also do not present the foreign

[6] Due to the assumption of a given nominal rate of interest on foreign bonds, these bonds can always be sold at a given international price if this is desired by domestic residents, but they are then of course subject to exchange rate risks. Note that foreign bond purchases by domestic residents are treated as residual in the wealth accumulation decisions of the asset holders of the model of this chapter.

account, the balance of payments, here, as there is also no change in this single account, representing trade in goods, in capital and interest payments.

There are finally the accounts of the fiscal and the monetary authority which are slightly altered through the above additions to the accounts of firms and asset holders. We simply state in this regard that the term $\tau_c i_\lambda \Lambda_f$ has now to be added to the resources side of the income account of the government as the sole change in the activity accounts of the government.

Having presented the model from the ex post point of view as far as its new elements as compared with Part II are concerned we now turn to the structural form of the model and present in the following section its technological and behavioural relationships, various definitions and the budget equations of the agents of the domestic economy, and finally also the laws of motion for quantities, prices and expectations to the extent they are experiencing change by the modifications of the model described above.

8.3 The augmented 18+2D system: investment, debt and price level dynamics

We now start with the presentation of the structural equations of the advanced model of disequilibrium growth, here only with respect to the changes needed for a treatment of the problem of debt deflation. We will compare these changes with the building blocks of the Keen (2000) model step by step.

Module 1 of the model provides definitions of important rates of return r^e, r^a, an expected one based on sales expectations Y^e of firms and the actual one based on the actual sales Y^d of firms. Note that actual production Y exceeds expected sales by planned inventory changes $\mathcal{I}$ and that it differs from actual sales by actual inventory changes. Note also that the currently expected and the actual pure rate of profit (net of depreciation $p_y \delta_k K$ and of interest payments $i_\lambda \Lambda_f$) are both based on actual exports $X = x_y Y$, actual imports $J^d = j_y Y$ and the actual employment $L^d = l_y Y$ of the workforce of the firms. Our choice of notation of production coefficients indicates that we are assuming a technology with fixed input/output coefficients ($Y^p = y^p K$ the potential output of firms) where export supply is in fixed proportion to actual output Y, as is import demand and labour demand (the latter coefficients are however subject to Harrod neutral technological change: $\hat{l}_y = -n_l$). For the details of all the notation as well as further explanations of the equations used in this model the reader is referred to Part II. Note again that the changes made to the model are represented by bold letters in the following.[7]

1. Definitions (Rates of Return and Real Growth):

$$r^e = \frac{p_y Y^e + p_x x_y Y - \boldsymbol{i_\lambda \Lambda_f} - w^b l_y Y - p_m j_y Y - p_y \delta_k K}{p_y K}, \tag{8.1}$$

[7] Note also that there holds as a relationship between actual and expected profits: $r^a p_y K = r^e p_y K + p_y(\mathcal{I} - \dot{N}) = r^e p_y K + p_y(Y^d - Y^e)$.

$$r^a = \frac{p_y Y^d + p_x x_y Y - i_\lambda \Lambda_f - w^b l_y Y - p_m j_y Y - p_y \delta_k K}{p_y K}, \tag{8.2}$$

$$\gamma = n + n_l \quad \text{all given magnitudes.} \tag{8.3}$$

The two rates of profits used in Part II are now defined by subtracting the interest payments of firms to asset holders based on the amount of loans Λ_f they have accumulated over the past. Furthermore trend growth in the world economy is given by the rate γ which is identified with the natural rate of growth n of the domestic working population plus the given rate of Harrod neutral technological progress n_l for reasons of simplicity.

Keen (2000, p. 83) considers a prototype 3D model of classical growth where besides the direct investment of capitalists (who own the firms and who reinvest all of their profit income, based on the pure profits of firms) there is also only pure loan financing of the remaining investment expenditure of the firms. These loans are supplied by financial asset holders (called banks in his paper) which are to be treated explicitly if his approach is to be compared with the one we present in the following. There are no demand constraints on the market for goods in Keen's (2000) paper which implies that his (uniquely determined) measure of the profitability $r = r^e = r^a$ of the firms' activities is based on actual = potential output $Y^p = y^p K$ throughout (with no reference to export or import activities of firms due to the assumption of a closed economy in his case). This gives as pure actual (= expected) rate of profit, used to describe the investment behaviour of firms in his paper, a rate of the type:

$$r = \frac{p_y Y^p - i_\lambda \Lambda_f - w l_y Y - p_y \delta_k K}{p_y K}.$$

These profits accrue directly to the real capital owning households who do not consume, but only invest (and are therefore named firms in Keen (2000) and in the following for simplicity).

Module 2 provides the equations that concern the household sector where two types of households are distinguished, workers and pure asset or wealth owners. Of course, these two types of household are only polar cases in the actual distribution of household types. Nevertheless we believe that it is useful to start from such polar household types before intermediate cases are introduced and modelled. There is no change in the behavioural equations of worker households, as compared with Part II, which are therefore not repeated in the present chapter. In Keen (2000) workers spend what they get: $p_y C_w = wL^d$ (as in the original Goodwin (1967) growth cycle model) and wage income wL^d is not taxed since there is no government sector in the basic form of his model.[8]

The other type of household of our model, the asset owners, desire to consume C_c (goods and houses as supplied by firms through their domestic production Y) at an

[8] We denote by e the rate of employment L^d/L and assume for labour supply natural growth at a given rate $n = \hat{L}$.

amount that is growing exogenously at the rate γ which is therefore independent of their current nominal disposable income Y_c^{Dn}. The consumption decision is thus not treated here as an important decision of these pure asset holders. Their nominal interest and rent income (after taxes) diminished by the nominal value of their consumption $p_y C_c$ is then spent on the purchase of financial assets as well as on investment in housing services supply (for worker households). Note here that our one good representation of the production of domestic commodities entails consumption goods proper and houses so that asset holders buy houses for their consumption as well as for investment purposes.

2. Households (Asset Holders):

$$Y_c^{Dn} = (1-\tau_c)[\boldsymbol{i_\lambda \Lambda_f} + iB_c + B_1^l + p_h C_h^w - p_y \delta_h K_h] + s(1-\tau_c^*)B_2^l, \tag{8.4}$$

$$\hat{C}_c = \gamma, \tag{8.5}$$

$$S_c^n = Y_c^{Dn} - p_v C_c = \dot{B}_c + \frac{\dot{B}_1^l}{i_l} + \frac{s\dot{B}_2^l}{i^{l*}} + \boldsymbol{\dot{\Lambda}_f} + p_y(I_h - \delta_h K_h), \quad \dot{B}_c = \dot{B} - \dot{B}_w. \tag{8.6}$$

Changes in this sector of the economy are again quite small, since we only have to add interest income (from loans) to the income of asset holders (and of course to remove dividend payments as there are no equities in the changed model) and to describe later on how much of their savings goes into new loans $\dot{\Lambda}_f$ to firms, both shown above in bold-face letters. Note that the term $s\dot{B}_2^l/i^{l*}$ adjusts residually to the other changes in the wealth composition of asset holders in this chapter.

Keen (2000) does not consider explicitly the agents that supply credit to firms in the forms of loans (called 'banks' in his chapter). Yet there must be a budget equation for these agents, since their interest income will generally differ from their supply of new loans. This means that something like

$$i_\lambda \Lambda_f = \dot{\Lambda}_f + p_y C_c,$$

must be assumed in his approach since there is no demand constraint for the supply of output in his model, which can only be true if the budget constraints for the three types of agents imply that the demand for goods is always equal to their supply: $Y^p = C_w + C_c + I$. The budget equation just shown together with the one that has been assumed above for workers (workers spend what they get) and below for firms – as in Keen (2000) – indeed just guarantee this type of outcome. Note that the consumption of these 'credit institutions' may become negative in the Keen (2000) model, if they lend more than they get as interest rate income, in which case they must be considered as supplying commodities to the goods market (from their stock of goods).[9] Note finally

[9] Such an occurrence of negative consumption for 'banks' may be considered as problematic and must at least be based on the assumption that their accumulated stock of (durable) goods stays non-negative in time which means this type of agent is considered to build up stocks of finished commodities in certain times from which it sells (in order to provide additional loans) in other times (when this is demanded by firms). Note that nothing of this sort is needed in our general model (as long as firms have positive inventories) where moreover the output of firms is always demand determined.

that debt accumulation in Keen (2000) as well as in the present model does not consider debt repayments explicitly (but does consider only the net effect in this respect).

In the next module 3 of the model we describe the sector of firms, whose planned gross investment demand I is assumed to be always served, just as all consumption. We thus assume for the short run of the model – see Part II for the details – that it is always of a Keynesian nature, so that aggregate goods demand is never rationed, due to the existence of excess capacities, inventories, overtime work and other buffers that exist in this model type as well as in real market economies. There is thus only one regime possible, the Keynesian one, for the short run of the model, while supply side forces – concerning price dynamics – come to surface only in the medium and the long run (Keen's (2000) model by contrast is completely supply side based in its evolution of quantities). Note that we only display the investment relationships of the model, since there is no change in the description of technology, the employment policy of the firms and the like; see Part II for the details.

3. Firms (Investment Behaviour):

$$g_k = \alpha_r^k(r^e - i_\lambda) + \alpha_i^k(i_l - i) + \alpha_u^k(u - \bar{u}) + \gamma + \delta_k, \tag{8.7}$$

$$\dot{\Lambda}_f = p_y(I - \delta_k K) + p_y(\dot{N} - \mathcal{I}) - r^e p_y K = p_y(I - \delta_k K) - r^a p_y K, \tag{8.8}$$

$$\hat{K} = I/K - \delta_k = g_k - \delta_k. \tag{8.9}$$

We assume in the sector of firms, without showing this explicitly here, a fixed proportions technology.[10] The capital stock of firms is used to measure potential output $Y^p = y^p K$ in the following, while all other magnitudes are provided by the Keynesian regime and its demand determined output rate $Y = Y^e + \mathcal{I}$, $\mathcal{I}$ the inventory changes desired by firms. The rate of capacity utilisation $u = Y/Y^p$ is defined on the basis of the above concept of potential output and will receive importance when describing the investment behaviour and the pricing policy of firms. Firms employ a labour force of amount L_f^w which supplies labour effort of amount L_f^d as determined by the present state of sales expectations Y^e (plus voluntary inventory production). This labour force of firms is adjusted in a direction that reduces the excess or deficit in the utilisation of the employed labour force, $L_f^d - L_f^w$, which means that firms intend to return to the normal usage of their labour force thereby. An additional growth term for the employed labour force takes account of the trend growth γ of domestic output, but is diminished by the effect of Harrod neutral technical change, n_l, which when working in isolation would allow to reduce the workforce of the firms.

Explicitly presented above is the formulation of the desired gross rate of capital stock accumulation of firms, $g_k = I/K$, which depends on relative profitability, measured by the deviation of the expected rate of profit, r^e, from the interest rate, i_λ, firms have

[10] Smooth input and output substitution is considered, as in Powell and Murphy (1997), in Chiarella *et al.* (1999a,b), see also Chiarella *et al.* (2000), with respect to the three inputs, labour L_f^d, imports (raw materials) J^d, and capital K, and its two outputs (internationally) non-traded and traded goods, Y, X.

to pay on their debt, on the interest rate spread $i_l - i$, between long- and short-term government debt, representing the tightness of monetary policy and its believed effects on economic activity, on the rate of capacity utilisation u of the capital stock of firms in its deviation from the desired rate of capacity utilisation, $\bar{u}$, which is given exogenously, and on trend growth γ and the rate of depreciation δ_k of business fixed investment. When comparing the rates r^e, i_λ in their investment decision firms decide to increase their investment projects via additional debt if $r^e - i_\lambda > 0$ holds (and vice versa). They do not pay attention here to (expected) inflation and the implied real rate of interest on their loans when making this decision. This would make the considered dynamics much more involved, in particular through the medium-run rates of return then to be used as in Chiarella *et al.* (2000, Part III) in conjunction with the expected medium-run rate of inflation used in the wage-price module of this chapter. We expect that such an extension would add further momentum to the debt effects to be investigated in later sections of this chapter.

The budget equation (8.8) of firms says that firms have to finance net investment and all inventory changes $\dot{N}$ (unintended inventory changes $\mathcal{I}$) by the profits that are based on actual output Y (expected sales Y^e, respectively) or by making new loans. Note here that unintended inventory disinvestment gives rise to windfall profits to firms which are retained and thus used to finance part of the fixed business investment as shown by the above budget equation if $\dot{N} - \mathcal{I} < 0$ holds true. The last equation of the above module of the model finally defines the growth rate of the capital stock which is determined by the net rate of capital accumulation planned by firms (due to the Keynesian nature of the short run of the model).

Keen (2000) assumes as budget equation of firms (owned by capitalists) the following equation

$$\dot{\Lambda}_f = p_y(I - \delta_k K) - rp_yK,$$

where r is the actual pure rate of profit. Firms therefore finance net investment $I - \delta_k K$ by means of pure profits rp_yK (which are always reinvested) and new debt, the latter being determined residually. There are no (unintended) inventory changes, but there is full capacity growth with goods demand always equal to goods supply. Furthermore, he assumes that gross investment is driven by the pure rate of profit (net of interest) $r = r^e$ solely which gives

$$I/K = \alpha^k(r - r_{min}) + \delta_k \quad \text{in place of his equation} \quad I/Y = \alpha^k(r),$$

if we use the notation of our modelling approach and neglect the non-linearity in the investment behaviour considered in Keen (2000). These two equations constitute two of the three laws of motions of his basic model of debt accumulation and wage inflation or deflation.

The next equation describes the change in the public sector of the economy, as compared with Part II, which only concerns tax collection, where taxes on the interest paid for loans are to be added (and taxes on dividends to be ignored) in the equation describing the tax income of the government.

4. Government (Fiscal Authority):

$$T^n = \tau_w[wL^d + w^u(L - L^w) + w^r\alpha_l L_2] + \tau_p wL^d,$$
$$+ \tau_c[i_\lambda \Lambda_f + iB + B^l + p_h C_h^w - \delta_h K_h] + \tau_m s p_m^* J^d. \tag{8.10}$$

Keen (2000) considers the government sector in a later section of his paper, there based on dynamic government expenditure and taxation rules that differ from the ones underlying the present approach. This module of the model may be used as in Keen (2000) to consider the topic of automatic stabilisers and the like.

There is no change in the description of the dynamics of quantities and prices. We however here present briefly the two Phillips curves (PCs) that describe money wage and price level dynamics since these equations are of course of importance when the problem of debt accumulation is to be approached in a deflationary (and of course also in an inflationary) environment.

5. Wage-Price Adjustment Equations, Expectations:

$$\hat{w}^b = \beta_{w_e}(e - \bar{e}) + \beta_{w_u}(u_f^w - \bar{u}_f^w) + \kappa_w(\hat{p}_y + n_l) + (1 - \kappa_w)(\pi^c + n_l), \tag{8.11}$$

$$\hat{p}_y = \beta_p(u - \bar{u}) + \kappa_p(\hat{w}^b - n_l) + (1 - \kappa_p)\pi^c. \tag{8.12}$$

The two equations just shown describe the dynamics of nominal (gross) wages as dependent on demand pressure terms, here specifically the outside and the inside employment of workers, $e - \bar{e}$, $u_f^w - \bar{u}_f^w$, measured as deviation from Non-Accelerating Inflation Rate of Unemployment (NAIRU) levels, and on cost pressure terms, here the short-term actual and the medium-term expected rate of price inflation, $\hat{p}_y, \pi^c$, augmented by the rate of productivity growth, n_l. We shall set $\bar{u}_f^w$ equal to 1 in the following which means that each employed worker provides one unit of labour if there is no over- or under-employment within firms. Similarly, price inflation depends on demand pressure in the market for goods, here solely measured by the rate of capacity utilisation, $u - \bar{u}$, in its deviation from the NAIRU rate of capacity utilisation,[11] and on wage cost pressure, diminished by productivity growth. These equations have been explained in their details in Part II and here serve the purpose of indicating how inflationary or deflationary processes (based on demand pressure as well as cost-push terms) are to be integrated into an environment where firms use debt to finance at least part of their investment expenditures.

Keen (2000) considers a money wage PC, $\hat{w} = \beta_w(e)$, based on demand pressure on the (outside) labour market solely, and assumes with respect to the price level p_y that it is a given magnitude ($\equiv 1$ implying of course $\pi^c = 0$). His third law of motion of

[11] The term NAIRU is used in an extended way in this chapter and should be read as Non-Accelerating Inflation Rate of Utilisation. Note here also that a second term in the price PC could be given by the deviation of desired inventory holdings from actual inventory holdings.

the considered growing economy can thus be obtained from the first of the above two PCs by assuming $\beta_{w_u} = 0, \kappa_w = 1$. This gives for the dynamics of the share of wages v in national income of the Keen model:

$$\hat{v} = \beta_{w_e}(e - \bar{e}) - n_l,$$

where we again use a linear form for the time being. In a final section, he briefly considers prices for consumption and capital goods separately, but does not yet represent their dynamics by way of formalised laws of motion.

The module of asset price dynamics of Part II is to be augmented in the present context by just one equation describing the dynamics of the interest rate on loans (while all other adjustment processes in these markets remain as before):

6. Asset Prices, Expectations and Interest Rate Adjustments:

$$\dot{i}_\lambda = \beta_{i_\lambda}(i_l - i_\lambda). \tag{8.13}$$

We here simply assume that the rate of interest on loans follows the rate of interest on long-term government bonds with some time delay, measured by the speed of adjustment β_{i_λ}, similar to the other delayed interest rate parity conditions used in our model. In Keen (2000) the rate of interest i_λ on loans is a given magnitude, so that there is no need there to formulate a law of motion for this interest rate variable. Note that it may take considerable time until the steering of the short-term rate of interest i by the central bank (via a Taylor interest rate policy rule) can actually exercise a significant effect on the interest rate on loans governing the firms' investment decision in the present model.

Summing up the dynamics of the core model in Keen (2000) builds on a money wage dynamics of type $\hat{w} = \beta_w(e - \bar{e}), e = L^d/L$ with only labour market demand pressure influences (since the price level is still kept constant), on an investment-demand driven growth path $\alpha^k(r - r_{min})$ that is partly financed by loans (at a given rate of interest) and on the budget equation of firms $\dot{\Lambda}_f = p_y(I - \delta_k K) - rp_y K$ where r is given by $\frac{p_y Y^p - i_\lambda \Lambda_f - wl_y Y^p - p_y \delta_k K}{p_y K}$. These three dynamic laws operate in a fixed proportions technological environment (exhibiting Harrod neutral technical change) with natural labour force growth, no savings out of wages and no effective demand constraint on the market for goods. We shall reconsider this fundamental approach to debt-financed economic growth in intensive form, and also its implications, in the next sections of the chapter.

We have added to this model type in particular an endogenous determination of the price level and of the rate of interest paid on loans, and also a Keynesian demand constraint. Furthermore, as shown in Chiarella *et al.* (2000), there are detailed descriptions of the behaviour of the fiscal and the monetary authority in our extension of this model, more advanced types of structural relationships for consumption, investment and financial wealth accumulation (still without feedback effect on the real side of the economy due to the lack of wealth effects in consumption) and also a detailed treatment of asset markets and their dynamics with heterogeneous expectations formation on these markets as well as with respect to wage and price formation.

8.4 Intensive form representation of the 20D dynamics

In this section we present our modification of the 18D core model of Part II in intensive form in order to allow for the consideration of debt financing of the investment undertaken by firms and the problem of debt deflation in this model type. To simplify the model slightly we assume in the following that $C_c(0)$ holds initially (and thus for all times) and thus neglect the consumption of asset holders altogether (which does not contribute to the present investigation very much under the assumptions made). We stress that the resulting dynamics on the state variable level are then of dimension twenty, due to the additional laws of motion formulated in the preceding section for the accumulation of debt by firms and for the interest rate paid by them on their loans.

We start with a compact presentation (including brief comments on their contents) of these twenty laws of motion (now including the state variables $\lambda_f = \Lambda_f/(p_y K)$ and i_λ), and will present thereafter the unique interior steady state solution of these dynamics. These laws of motion around the steady state of the dynamics, appropriately grouped together and all in per (value) unit of capital form, and in efficiency units if necessary, are the following ones.

As first group we consider the quantity adjustment mechanisms with respect to the market for goods, concerning sales expectations y^e and actual inventories ν, and for labour, concerning the employment policy of firms, l_f^{we}, and also concerning the evolution of full employment labour intensity l^e (both in efficiency units) and of the stock of housing (everything per unit of the capital stock of firms):

$$\dot{y}^e = \beta_{y^e}(y^d - y^e) + (\gamma - (g_k - \delta_k))y^e, \tag{8.14}$$

$$\dot{\nu} = y - y^d - (g_k - \delta_k)\nu, \tag{8.15}$$

$$\dot{l}_f^{we} = \beta_l(l_f^{de} - l_f^{we}) + [\gamma - (g_k - \delta_k)]l_f^{we}, \tag{8.16}$$

$$\hat{l}^e = \gamma - (g_k - \delta_k), \tag{8.17}$$

$$\hat{k}_h = g_h - \delta_h - (g_k - \delta_k). \tag{8.18}$$

The first of these five laws for quantity movements describes the adjustment of sales expectations y^e in view of the observed expectational error $y^d - y^e$ based on currently realised sales y^d, augmented by a term that takes account of the fact that this adjustment is occurring in a growing economy. Next, inventories ν change according to the gap between actual output y and actual sales y^d, again reformulated such that growth of the capital stock, the measurement base for the considered intensive form variables, is taken account of. Employment of firms, l_f^{we}, is changed in order to reduce the discrepancy that currently exists between the actual employment l^{de} of the employed and their normal employment, here measured both by l_f^{we} (everything measured in efficiency units). The growth rate of the factor endowment ratio l^e (in efficiency units) is simply given by the difference between the natural rate of growth (including Harrod neutral technical change) and the growth rate of the capital stock $g_k - \delta_k$. Similarly, the growth rate of the housing stock (per unit of the capital stock of firms) is simply given by the difference of the accumulation rates of the stock of houses and the capital stock.

Next we consider the nominal dynamics in the real sector of the economy which are described by four dynamical laws. Note here that the laws of motion for wages, w^e, net of payroll taxes and in efficiency units, and prices, p_y, are here formulated independently from each other and show that reduced form or across markets PCs (exhibiting only one rate of inflation as remaining cost-push term) are generally not as simple as is often assumed in the literature:[12]

$$\hat{w}^e = \pi^c + \kappa[\beta_{w_e}(l^{we}/l^e - \bar{e}) + \beta_{w_u}(l_f^{de}/l_f^{we} - 1) + \kappa_w\beta_p(y/y^p - \bar{u})], \quad (8.19)$$

$$\hat{p}_y = \pi^c + \kappa[\kappa_p(\beta_{w_e}(l^{we}/l^e - \bar{e}) + \beta_{w_u}(l_f^{de}/l_f^{we} - 1)) + \beta_p(y/y^p - \bar{u})], \quad (8.20)$$

$$\dot{\pi}^c = \beta_{\pi^c}(\alpha_{\pi^c}(\hat{p}_y - \pi^c) + (1 - \alpha_{\pi^c})(0 - \pi^c)), \quad (8.21)$$

$$\hat{p}_h = \beta_h(\frac{c_h^w}{k_h} - \bar{u}_h) + \kappa_h\hat{p}_y + (1 - \kappa_h)\pi^c. \quad (8.22)$$

As already noted we now use reduced form PCs for wage inflation $\hat{w}^e$ and price inflation $\hat{p}_y$ which both depend on the demand pressures in the markets for labour (external and internal ones: $l^{we}/l^e - \bar{e}, l_f^{de}/l_f^{we} - 1$) as well as for goods, $y/y^p - \bar{u}$. The change of the rate of inflation expected over the medium run, π^c, is determined as a weighted average of adaptively formed expectations and regressive ones (which implies that the steady state rate of inflation is zero in the present model). Finally, the inflation rate for housing services depends on the demand pressure term $\frac{c_h^w}{k_h} - \bar{u}_h$ in the market for these services,[13] and on actual and perceived cost-push expressions, here simply based on a weighted average concerning the inflation rate of domestic output.

There follow below the dynamical laws for long-term bond price dynamics and exchange rate dynamics (including expectations) which basically formulate a somewhat delayed adjustment towards interest rate parity conditions and are supplemented by heterogeneous expectations formation (of partially adaptive and partially perfect type). Note that perfect foresight, concerning the proportion $1-\alpha_s$ of market participants, can be removed from explicit representation as it coincides with the left-hand side of the

[12] Such disentangled laws of motion for nominal prices and wages are obtained from their originally interdependent presentation – see the preceding section – by solving the two linear equations of this section with respect to the variables $\hat{w}^e - \pi_l$, $\hat{p}_y - \pi_l$. This implies the expressions shown in equations (8.19) and (8.21), which both depend, via demand-pull and cost-push inflation pass through considerations, on our measures of demand pressure on the market for labour *as well as* on the market for goods; and on the expected medium-run inflation π^c in addition, the only cost-push term that is still explicitly shown in the equations (8.19) and (8.21). It is intuitively obvious that the removal of wage or price inflation cost-push pressure, $\hat{w}^e$, $\hat{p}_y$, from price or wage dynamics must imply that both the goods and the labour market demand pressure will be present in the resulting disentangled PCs which thus are in a significant way more general than the ones usually considered in the theoretical or applied literature on price PCs unless one assumes – as some kind of Okun's law – that the two demand pressure variables used are positive multiples of each other. But even then the composed parameters of our reduced form equations (8.19) and (8.21) clearly show the complex way the labour and the goods market are interrelated in these two equations.

[13] Where $\frac{c_h^w}{k_h}$ represents the rate of capacity utilisation demanded on this market and $\bar{u}_h$ its NAIRU level.

corresponding price adjustment equation, giving rise to the fractions in front of these adjustment equations (see Chiarella *et al.* (2000) and here Part II for the details):[14]

$$\hat{p}_b = \frac{\beta_{p_b}}{1-\beta_{p_b}(1-\alpha_s)}[(1-\tau_c)i_l + \alpha_s\pi_{bs} - (1-\tau_c)i], \quad i_l = 1/p_b, \tag{8.23}$$

$$\dot{\pi}_{bs} = \beta_{\pi_{bs}}(\hat{p}_b - \pi_{bs}), \tag{8.24}$$

$$\hat{s} = \frac{\beta_s}{1-\beta_s(1-\alpha_s)}[(1-\tau_c)i_l^* + \alpha_s\epsilon_s - ((1-\tau_c)i_l + \pi_b)], \quad i_l = 1/p_b, \tag{8.25}$$

$$\dot{\epsilon}_s = \beta_{\epsilon_s}(\hat{s} - \epsilon_s). \tag{8.26}$$

Note that the literature generally only considers the border case where $\alpha_s = 0$ is used in conjunction with infinite adjustment speeds on the two considered markets. This gives rise to two interest parity conditions coupled with myopic perfect foresight on bond price and exchange rate movements, a situation of knife-edge instability, which is stabilised by means of the so-called jump variable technique.[15]

The next set of dynamical laws concerns the evolution of short- and long-term debt of the government (the relative issuing of which is here subject to fixed proportions $\alpha_b^g, 1-\alpha_b^g$), its wage and import taxation policy and the interest rate policy of the central bank.

$$\dot{b} = \alpha_b^g[gy^e + rb + b^l - t^w - t^c + w^a] - (\hat{p}_y + g_k - \delta_k)b, \tag{8.27}$$

$$\dot{b}^l = (1-\alpha_b^g)/p_b[gy^e + rb + b^l - t^w - t^c + w^a] - (\hat{p}_y + g_k - \delta_k)b^l, \tag{8.28}$$

$$\hat{\tau}_w = \alpha_{\tau_{w1}}\left(\frac{\lambda_g}{\bar{\lambda}_g} - 1\right), \quad \lambda_g = \frac{b + p_b b^l}{y^e}, \tag{8.29}$$

$$\hat{\tau}_m = \alpha_{\tau_m}\frac{p_x^* x - (1+\tau_m)p_m^* j^d}{p_x^* x}, \quad x = x_y y, \; j^d = j_y y, \tag{8.30}$$

$$\dot{i} = -\beta_{i_i}(i - i_l^*) + \beta_{i_p}\hat{p}_y + \beta_{i_u}(y/y^p - \bar{u}). \tag{8.31}$$

Since these laws of motion, with the exception of the interest rate policy rule, are not of central interest in the following analysis we here only briefly state that the first two are immediate consequences of the government budget constraint (based in particular on various sources of tax income), that wage taxation is here adjusted in the direction of a target ratio of government debt, $\bar{\lambda}_g$, and that import taxes are adjusted in a way that ensures a balanced trade account in the steady state (which greatly simplifies the calculation of the steady state of the model). The interest rate policy rule (8.31) is of interest since it could be of help to counteract accelerating debt deflation, by lowering, if still possible, nominal interest rates in situations of depressed output and price deflation.

14 These laws of motion are made of secondary importance in this chapter as we shall assume in this part of model low adjustment speeds for the time being (which is not realistic). More appropriate treatments are thus left here for future research.

15 See Blanchard (1981) for an early and typical example of this type of macro-modelling.

This rule states that the central bank attempts to steer the domestic short-term interest rate i towards its international level, i_l^*, but deviates from this general target in view of current price inflation $\hat{p}_y$ and the current state of the business cycle as measured by demand pressure on the market for goods $u - \bar{u}$. Note here that the inflationary target of the central bank and thus steady state inflation is assumed as zero in the present chapter in order to ease the presentation of the state variables of the model.

There remain the two dynamical laws that are new to the model:

$$\dot{\lambda}_f = g_k - \delta_k + y - y^d - \beta_n(\beta_{n^d} y^e - \nu) - \gamma\beta_{n^d} y^e - r^e - (\hat{p}_y + g_k - \delta_k)\lambda_f, \tag{8.32}$$

$$\dot{i}_\lambda = \beta_{i_\lambda}(i_l - i_\lambda). \tag{8.33}$$

Although the dynamical law for absolute debt accumulation considered in the preceding section is by and large a simple one, its representation on the intensive form level is somewhat complicated due to the fact that unintended inventory changes are involved (and expressed in intensive form) besides the rate of capital accumulation $g_k - \delta_k$, and due to the fact that debt is now calculated in per value unit of capital (divided by $p_y K$) which transformed to growth rates gives rise the addition of $-(\hat{p}_y + g_k - \delta_k)\lambda_f$. By contrast, there is no change needed in the law of motion for interest on loans since it only involved state variables of the model right from the start. We shall consider in the next section the evolution of the ratio λ_f in situations of increasing generality, at first only coupled with laws of motion for nominal wage adjustment (and thus given prices) and the evolution of labour intensity in a supply side growth model. Thereafter we include a static simplification of the quantity adjustment processes on the goods market considered above (leading to a demand driven growth model) and add the price level dynamics (8.20) to not only allow for debt accumulation, but also for goods price deflation in situations of depressed rates of capacity utilisation. Finally we will also study the more general case where quantity and price adjustment processes interact (still without much stress on fiscal policies, asset markets, all kinds of expectations, the housing sector and the openness of the economy).

The above twenty laws of motion for the state variables of the model make use in addition of the following supplementary intensive form definitions and abbreviations (which are not explained here in detail, since we only provide the essential features of the modelling approach of Part II of the book):

$$y = y^e + \beta_n(\beta_{n^d} y^e - \nu) + \gamma\beta_{n^d} y^e,$$

$$l_f^{de} = l_y^e y, \quad (l_y^e \text{ the labour coefficient in efficiency units}),$$

$$l_g^{de} = l_g^{we} = \alpha_g g y^e,$$

$$l^{de} = l_f^{de} + l_g^{de},$$

$$l^{we} = l_f^{we} + l_g^{we},$$

$$y_{w1} = w^e \left[l^{de} + \alpha^u (l^e - l^{we}) + \alpha^r \frac{L_2(0)}{L_1(0)} l^e \right] / p_y,$$

$$c_g^w = c_y (1 - \tau_w) y_{w1},$$

$$c_h^w = p_y c_h (1 - \tau_w) y_{w1} / p_h,$$

$$r^e = y^e - \delta_k + (s p_x^* / p_y) x_y y - i_\lambda \lambda_f - ((1 + \tau_p) w^e / p_y) l_f^{de} - ((1 + \tau_m) s p_m^* / p_y) j_y y,$$

$$g_k = \alpha_r^k (r^e - i_\lambda) + \alpha_i^k (i_l - i) + \alpha_u^k (y / y^p - \bar{u}) + \gamma + \delta_k, \quad (i_l = 1/p_b),$$

$$g_h = \alpha_r^h ((1 - \tau_c)((p_h / p_y) c_h^w / k_h - \delta_h) - ((1 - \tau_c) i_l - \pi^c)) + \alpha_i^h (i_l - i)$$
$$+ \alpha_u^h \left(\frac{c_h^w}{k_h} - \bar{u}_h \right) + \gamma + \delta_h, \quad (i_l = 1/p_b),$$

$$y^d = c_g^w + g_k + g_h k_h + g y^e,$$

$$\pi_b = \alpha_s \pi_{bs} + (1 - \alpha_s) \hat{p}_b,$$

$$t^w = \tau_w w^e \left[l^{de} + \alpha^u (l^e - l^{we}) + \alpha^r \frac{L_2(0)}{L_1(0)} l^e \right] / p_y + \tau_p w^e l^{de} / p_y + \tau_m s p_m^* j_y y / p_y,$$

$$t^c = \tau_c \left[i_\lambda \lambda_f + i b + b^l + (p_h / p_y) c_h^w - \delta_h k_h \right],$$

$$w^a = w^e \left[\alpha^u (l^e - l^{we}) + \alpha^r \frac{L_2(0)}{L_1(0)} l^e + (1 + \tau_p) l_g^{de} \right] / p_y.$$

These equations state how output y depends on expected demand and inventories, how employment is determined in the private and the public sector, how disposable wage income y_{w1}^{Λ} of workers is formed and used for goods and housing services consumption, how the expected rate of pure profits and the rates of accumulation for capital and houses are defined on the intensive form level, how aggregate demand per unit of capital y^d is composed from consumption, investment and government demand and how average bond price expectations are composed from adaptive and perfect expectations. There are finally three expressions for wage and import taxation, property income taxation and transfer payments to and from the government.

Inserting these equations into the above twenty laws of motion gives rise to an explicit system of twenty autonomous non-linear differential equations in the twenty state variables of the model, given by equations (8.14)–(8.33). Note that we have to supply as initial conditions the relative magnitude $\frac{L_2(0)}{L_1(0)}$ in order to get a complete characterisation of the dynamics and that the evolution of price levels is subject to zero-root hysteresis, since it depends on historical conditions due to our assumptions on the interest rate policy rule of the central bank and the accompanying assumption of costless cash transactions (during each trading period) for the four agents of the model; see Part II for details.

We present next the twenty steady state values of the model. All these values should normally have an index 'o' to denote their steady state character. As we have done earlier, to not overload the notation we do not add this index to the following list of steady state values. Note that the steady state values of level magnitudes are all expressed in per unit of capital form and if necessary in efficiency units; see Part II for the details in the case of the 18D core model.

Note also that we have now debt of firms and of the government in the model and that we therefore denote their actual and steady debt to capital ratios by choosing appropriate indexes in both cases: λ_f, λ_g. Note finally that the steady state is parametrically dependent on a given output price level p_y which is not determined by the model (due to the Taylor type interest rate policy pursued by the central bank) and thus can be supplied from the outside in an arbitrary fashion:

$$y^e = \frac{y^p \bar{u}}{1+\gamma\beta_{n^d}} \quad [y = y^p \bar{u}], \tag{8.34}$$

$$\nu = \beta_{n^d} y^e, \tag{8.35}$$

$$l_f^{we} = l_f^{de} = l_y^e y^p \bar{u} \quad [\text{total employment: } l^{we} = l_f^{we} + l_g^{we}, l_g^{we} = \alpha_g g y^e], \tag{8.36}$$

$$l^e = (l_f^{we} + \alpha_g g y^e)/\bar{e}, \tag{8.37}$$

$$k_h = \frac{d_h(y^e(1-g) - (\gamma+\delta_k))}{d_y(i_l^* + \delta_h) + (\gamma+\delta_h)d_h}, \tag{8.38}$$

$$w^e = \frac{\omega^{be} p_y}{1+\tau_p} \quad \left[\omega^{be} = \frac{y^e - \delta_k - i_l^*\lambda_f - i_l^*}{l_f^{we}}\right], \tag{8.39}$$

$$p_y = \text{arbitrary}, \tag{8.40}$$

$$\pi^c = 0, \tag{8.41}$$

$$p_h = p_y(i_l^* + \delta_h)/\bar{u}_h, \tag{8.42}$$

$$p_b = 1/i_l^*, \tag{8.43}$$

$$\pi_{bs} = 0, \tag{8.44}$$

$$s = \frac{s_o - [\tau_w y_{w1} + \tau_p \frac{w^e}{p_y} l^{we}]}{\tau_m p_m^* j_y y/p_y}, \tag{8.45}$$

$$\epsilon_s = 0, \tag{8.46}$$

$$b = \alpha_b^g \bar{\lambda}_g y^e, \tag{8.47}$$

$$b_l = i_l^*(1-\alpha_b^g)\bar{\lambda}_g y^e, \tag{8.48}$$

$$\tau_w = 1 - \frac{p_h \bar{u}_h k_h}{c_h p_y y_{w1}}, \tag{8.49}$$

$$\tau_m = \frac{p_x^* x_y - p_m^* j_y}{p_m^* j_y}, \tag{8.50}$$

$$i = i_l^*, \tag{8.51}$$

$$\lambda_f = \frac{\gamma - i_l^*}{\gamma}, \tag{8.52}$$

$$i_\lambda = i_l^* = [r^e]. \tag{8.53}$$

With respect to the two equations for the wage tax rate τ_w and for the rate of exchange s of the model we have to apply (besides the steady values calculated for of y, l^{we}, and ω^{be}, see the above) the further defining expressions

$$c_h^w = \bar{u}_h k_h,$$

$$t_o^c = \tau_c[i_l^*\lambda_f + i_l^* b + b^l + (p_h/p_y)c_h^w - \delta_h k_h],$$

$$s_o = gy^e + i_l^* b + b^l - t_o^c + \frac{w^e}{p_y}\left[\alpha^u(l^e - l^{we}) + \alpha^r \frac{L_2(0)}{L_1(0)} l^e\right]$$

$$+ (1 + \tau_p)\frac{w^e}{p_y}\alpha_g g y^e - \frac{\gamma b}{\alpha_b^g},$$

$$y_{w1} = w^e \left[l^{we} + \alpha^u(l^e - l^{we}) + \alpha^r \frac{L_2(0)}{L_1(0)} l^e\right] / p_y,$$

in order to have a determination of the interior steady state solution that is complete.

Note that the value of the exchange rate s will be indeterminate when we have $\tau_m = 0$ in the steady state and that the above formula for s cannot be applied then. Note furthermore that the parameters of the model have to be chosen such that k_h, τ_w, s are all positive in the steady state.[16] Note finally that the parameter α_s, the proportion of adaptive forecasters, must always be larger than $1 - 1/\beta_x$ for $x = p_b, s, p_e$ in order to satisfy the restrictions established in Chiarella *et al.* (2000) and here in Part II.

Equation (8.34) gives the steady state solution of expected sales y^e per unit of capital K (and also output y per K) and equation (8.35) provides on this basis the steady inventory-capital ratio N/K. Equation (8.36) represents the amount of workforce (per K) employed by firms which in the steady state is equal to the hours worked by this workforce. It also shows total employment (per K) where account is taken of the employment in the government sector in addition. Equation (8.37) represents full employment labour intensity (in the steady state), while the last expression for the quantity side of the model, in equation (8.38), provides the steady value of the housing capital stocks per unit of the capital stock of firms.

Equation (8.39) concerns the nominal wage level (net of payroll taxes and in efficiency units) to be derived from the steady state value for gross real wages ω^{be}, which include payroll taxes, which depends on the amount of interest to be paid on the loans of firms. The steady state value of the price inflation rate expected to hold over the medium run is zero – see equation (8.41) – since the inflationary target of the central bank is zero in the present formulation of the model. This also implies that all nominal magnitudes

[16] There are further simple restrictions on the parameters of the model due to the economic meaning of the variables employed.

(up to nominal wages) have no long-run trend in them and that all expected rates of change – see equations (8.41), (8.44), (8.46) – must be zero in the steady state. Again, in equation (8.40), p_y can be any value due to the assumptions made on monetary policy and money balances. Note that all nominal magnitudes, up to the price for long-term bonds p_b – see equation (8.43) – depend on p_y and thus change proportionally when this price level magnitude is changed. As remaining nominal magnitudes we have the price level p_h for housing rents (in equation (8.42)), to be calculated from the uniform rate of interest i_l^* of the economy in the steady state (provided by the world economy), and the nominal exchange rate, s, in equation (8.45), which is given by a complicated expression to be obtained from the government budget constraint, due to the import taxation rule followed by the government. Note here that the equations for the steady state of the economy are presented in the same order as its laws of motion. They have to be reordered from the mathematical point of view when solved in a recursive fashion.

There follows the steady state value of short-term government debt per unit of capital $b = B/(p_v K)$ as well as the one for long-term domestic bonds, in equations (8.47) and (8.48), which are both simple consequences of the debt adjustment rule of the government and the rigid proportions by which government splits its debt in short- and long-term components. The steady state value of the wage tax rate – see equation (8.50) – is obtained from wage income-spending relationships of worker households, here performed on the basis of the housing services demanded and supplied in the steady state,[17] while the steady value of the import tax rate, in equation (8.50), just balances the trade account (when import taxes are included into it). With respect to the public sector, there is finally the interest rate policy rule of the central bank, which due to its formulation implies that the interest rate on short-term government debt must settle down at the given foreign rate, i_l^*, in the steady state.[18]

Again, the new equations are equations (8.52) and (8.53), where the steady debt to capital ratio of firms is easily obtained from the budget constraint of firms and is positive if and only if the world rate of interest is smaller than the natural rate of growth (including the rate of technical progress) of the domestic economy. Finally, the steady value of the rate of interest on loans, i_λ, is provided which quite obviously must settle down at $i = i_l^*$. This closes the presentation of the interior steady state solution of our 20D dynamical model.

We have used in the preceding section as point of reference for the general 20D model the extended supply side growth cycle dynamics formulated and investigated in Keen (2000) which includes loans to firms and thus debt financing of (part of) their investment expenditures in a very fundamental way. We have thus now at our disposal two polar cases for the discussion of debt accumulation and debt deflation, a very basic classical one where the stress should lie on analytical results and a proper inclusion

17 Making use of gross steady wage income y_{w1} and the marginal propensity to spend this income on housing services.

18 The steady value of the short-term rate of interest equals its long-run equivalent as there is no risk or liquidity premium in the 18D version of Part II as well as in the present 20D extension of it.

of deflationary processes – see the next section – and a very detailed Keynesian one where the question should be how it compares numerically with the insights obtained for the smaller models.

Taken together, and based on the linear behavioural assumptions used in our approach to debt and deflation, the equations of the theoretical starting point of the investigation can be represented as 3D dynamical systems in the state variables $v = wL^d/p_yY^p$, the wage share, $e = L^d/L$, the rate of employment, and $\lambda_f = \Lambda_f/p_yK$, the debt to capital ratio of the firms, as follows:[19]

$$\hat{v} = \beta_w(e - \bar{e}) - n_l, \tag{8.54}$$

$$\hat{e} = \alpha^k(r - r_{min}) - (n + n_l), \tag{8.55}$$

$$\dot{\lambda}_f = \alpha^k(r - r_{min})(1 - \lambda_f) - r, \tag{8.56}$$

where $r = y^p(1 - v) - \delta_k - i_\lambda\lambda_f$ is the actual rate of profit in this supply driven approach to economic growth.[20] As stated, we use a linear PC mechanism and a linear investment function in this representation of the Keen (2000) model and leave the discussion of behavioural non-linearities for future investigations. Note that we have made use of the notation of our general model presented above in order to express the laws of motion of the Keen (2000) core dynamics.

There is not yet a foreign and a government sector in this form of the Goodwin growth cycle model (up to the indication of credit supplying institutions: see our discussion in the preceding section), but only the interaction of firms (capitalists) and worker households. The first two equations of this model would in fact be identical to the original Goodwin (1967) growth cycle approach if debt would not be there in the formulation of the pure profit rate of the model and if $\alpha^k = 1, r_{min} = 0$ would hold, in which case capitalists would just invest all income not going into wages and thus would determine the rate of growth of the employment rate as the difference between capital stock growth $\hat{K} = r$ and effective labour supply growth $n + n_l$. But α^k will here be assumed as larger than 1 – see the next section – which in particular means that investment must be financed to some extent via loans which, of course, then implies the redefinition of the rate of profit of firms as shown above.

The third equation of this model is easily derived from the budget equation of firms[21]

$$\dot{\Lambda}_f = \alpha^k(r - r_{min})K - rK,$$

by making use of the definitional relationship $\dot{\lambda}_f = \dot{\Lambda}_f/K - \hat{K}\lambda_f,\ \lambda_f = \Lambda_f/K$. We stress that the dynamics automatically guarantee that v, e stay positive when they start positive, but that $r = y^p(1-v) - \delta_k - i_\lambda\lambda_f \geq 0,\ e \leq 1$ need not be fulfilled at all times. Furthermore, we should have $\alpha^k(r - r_{min}) + \delta_k \geq 0$ at all times, since disinvestment

[19] Note again that the price level p_y is kept fixed in the core version of the Keen model (and set equal to one) and that the rate of interest i_λ is also a given magnitude in this model.

[20] Due to the assumption $Y^d \equiv Y \equiv Y^p$ in the Keen (2000) paper.

[21] Note again that this model assumes $p_y = 1$.

can by assumption at most occur at rate δ_k. Note that this last inequality can be used to argue that $r \geq 0$ is not really needed for the viability of the model under the assumed investment behaviour. Referring in addition to overtime work when the labour market is exhausted may finally be used to argue that the constraint $r \geq r_{min} - \delta_k/\alpha^k$ is really the only one that is crucial for a meaningful working of the model.

We shall explore in the next section these growth dynamics (with debt accumulation) with respect to the state variables v, e, λ_f analytically in order to see what we can learn from their properties for the general 20D dynamics. Conversely, these 20D dynamics provides us with the perspective of how to augment the 3D core case by price level dynamics in order to obtain a basic case where debt accumulation and deflation can be investigated in their interaction analytically, then in a 4D situation of supply driven growth.

This basic proper model of debt deflation is augmented in the 20D situation by Rose effects in the wage-price interaction (which say that either wage or price flexibility must be destabilising with respect to the implied real wage adjustments), by Keynes effects (which here are more direct than is usually the case due to the monetary policy rule assumed), by Mundell effects (which state that the interaction between price inflation and expected price deflation must be destabilising if the adaptive component of these expectations is operating with sufficient speed), by Metzler effects (which imply accelerator-type instability of the inventory adjustment mechanism when it operates with sufficient speed) and by cumulative (destabilising) effects in financial markets (if adjustments are fast) due to positive feedback loops between expected changes and resulting actual changes of financial variables in our delayed adjustment processes towards overall interest rate parity (uniform rates of return). All these effects are of course partial in nature and must be studied in their interaction in a full analysis of the 20D model. However, we will only consider in the next section effects that concern the real part of the economy in its interactions with the debt accumulation of firms and thus leave the other markets in the financial sector of the economy for later investigations (by assuming low adjustment speeds in the market for long-term domestic and foreign bonds). These two financial markets are thus very 'tranquil' in the present chapter which concentrates on the effects of credit relationships between households and firms (not households and the government) and the possibilities of the central bank to neutralise the destabilising nature debt deflation by way of its interest rate policy rule.

8.5 Debt effects and debt deflation

In subsection 1 of this section we shall consider the Keen (2000) 3D growth cycle dynamics from the analytical point of view. We then extend these dynamics in subsection 2 by a law of motion for the price level that is a special case of the one used in the 20D case and analyse the features of these 4D dynamics (now including deflation or inflation besides debt accumulation of firms). In Section 8.6 we then approach these 3D and 4D and also the general 20D dynamics from the numerical perspective, with particular stress on the occurrence of debt deflation. We then provide a brief discussion of another possibility where the combination of high debt and deflation may lead the economy into recessions or depressions, namely the situation of a debtor–creditor relationships within the household sector coupled with marginal propensities to consume that are higher for debtors than for creditors.

8.5.1 *3D debt accumulation*

Let us first consider the steady state of the dynamics (8.54)–(8.56) presented in the preceding section as the simplest case that allows for debt-financed (cyclical) growth. This steady state is uniquely determined, since no situation on the boundary of the positive orthant (or economic state space) can be steady in these growth dynamics. This unique steady state is given by:

$$e_o = \bar{e} + n_l/\beta_w, \tag{8.57}$$

$$v_o = \frac{y^p - \delta_k - r_o - i_\lambda \lambda_f^o}{y^p} \quad (r_o = r_{min} + (n + n_l)/\alpha^k), \tag{8.58}$$

$$\lambda_f^o = 1 - \frac{r_o}{n + n_l} = \frac{\alpha^k - 1}{\alpha^k} - \frac{r_{min}}{n + n_l}. \tag{8.59}$$

This set of steady state values shows that steady employment increases with the rate of technical progress and decreases with the speed of adjustment of nominal wages. Profitability depends positively on the minimum rate of profit (which separates positive from negative net investment) and on the natural rate of growth, and negatively on the speed of adjustment of investment with respect to changes in the pure rate of profit earned by firms, while just the opposite holds true for the debt to capital ratio in the place of the pure rate of profit.

Note that the rate of pure profits need not coincide with the rate of interest on loans in the steady state as there is no mechanism in the model that would promote their equalisation. We will assume in this subsection that $i_\lambda < n + n_l$ and $\alpha^k > 1$ holds (a necessary condition for a positive debt to capital ratio in the steady state which needs to be coupled with an assumption on the relative size of r_{min} in order to get a positive steady state value for λ_f).[22] Furthermore, the size of output per capital y^p should be such that the steady share of wages v_o is positive (and less than one which is always the case under the assumption just made).

To show that this steady state solution is the only one it suffices to exclude that $e_o = 0$ or $v_o = 0$ can be steady state values of the model. With respect to $e_o = 0$ this is obvious, since the state variable v cannot be steady in this case. With respect to $v_o = 0$ we first note that there is a unique solution of equations (8.58), (8.59) – set equal to zero – with respect to the values of r, λ_f as they are shown above (since $e_o > 0$ holds).

22 Note that the steady debt ratio must always be smaller than one.

Assume now with respect to the parameter y^p of the Keen (2000) model that it satisfies

$$y^p > \delta_k + r_o + i_\lambda \lambda_f^o,$$

which means that there is a meaningful steady state solution $v_o > 0$ to the model.

Since r_o, λ_f^o are uniquely determined there cannot therefore be an additional steady state with $v_o = 0$. We thus know that there is not only a uniquely determined interior steady state solution of the dynamics (8.54)–(8.56), but have shown in addition that there cannot be another steady state solution on the boundary on the positive orthant of the considered three dimensional state space (in contrast to many other systems that involve rates of growth formulation).

Referring again to overtime work (here assumed to come about when the labour market is exhausted),[23] we do not exclude the case $e_o > 1$ from consideration in the following, and do also allow for steady rates of profit r that are larger than $n + n_l$. Note that the Goodwin (1967) growth cycle is obtained if $\alpha^k = 1, r_{min} = 0$ is assumed which gives $\dot{\lambda}_f = r(1 - \lambda_f) - r$ which remains zero when we start from a situation of no debt: $\lambda_f(0) = 0$.

Proposition 8.1 *Assume $\alpha^k > 1, 0 < i_\lambda < n + n_l$.[24] Then: the steady state (8.57)–(8.59) of the dynamics (8.54)–(8.56) is locally asymptotically stable for all admissible parameter values.*

Proof: Concerning the calculation of the determinant of the Jacobian of the dynamics (8.54)–(8.56) at the steady state we can first of all state that its third row can be reduced to $(0, 0, -(n + n_l))$ by the addition of an appropriate multiple of its second row without changing its size. This immediately implies that this determinant is equal to $-\beta_w v_o \alpha^k y^p e_o(n + n_l)$ and thus negative which provides one of the Routh–Hurwitz conditions for local asymptotic stability. With respect to the sum a_2 of the principal minors of order 2 one furthermore immediately gets the expression $\beta_w v_o \alpha^k y^p e_o < 0$ since two of these minors are equal to zero. Furthermore one has for the entry J_{33} of the Jacobian J (which gives the trace of J) in the considered situation the expression:

$$\begin{aligned} J_{33} &= -(n + n_l) + i_\lambda(1 - \alpha^k) + \alpha^k i_\lambda \lambda_f^o \\ &= -(n + n_l) + i_\lambda - \alpha^k i_\lambda(1 - \lambda_f^o) = -(n + n_l) - i_\lambda \alpha^k r_{min}/(n + n_l). \end{aligned}$$

The trace of J is therefore negative since $i_\lambda < n + n_l$ by assumption and since $\lambda_f^o < 1$ holds. The coefficients $a_1 = -\text{trace } J, a_2, a_3 = -\det J$ of the Routh–Hurwitz polynomial are therefore all positive and thus all support the local asymptotic stability claimed by the above proposition. Finally, we also have $a_1 a_2 - a_3 > 0$, since the expression for det J is part of the all positive expressions contained in $a_1 a_2$ and thus cannot make the expression $a_1 a_2 - a_3$ less or equal to zero (the latter if $i_\lambda > 0$ holds). □

[23] See the 20D model for a more plausible treatment of overtime work.

[24] In the case $i_\lambda = 0$ we have the Goodwin growth cycle dynamics coupled with an isolated adjustment process in the debt to capital ratio.

We thus have the strong result that a partial debt financing of investment demand turns the centre type dynamics of the original Goodwin (1967) growth cycle (all orbits are closed) into ones that imply convergence to the steady state, at least in a certain neighbourhood of this steady state.

Proposition 8.2 *We consider again the situation* $\alpha^k > 1, 0 < i_\lambda < n + n_l$. *Assume furthermore as a special case that* $\beta_w = 0, n_l = 0$ *holds, so that there is no adjustment in the wage share occurring when the other two state variables of (8.54)–(8.56) are changing. Then: for each level of the wage share* v *satisfying* $y^p(1-v) - \delta_k - r_{min} > 0$ *there exists a threshold value* $\bar{\lambda}_f \geq 0$ *of the debt to capital ratio* λ_f *above which this ratio will increase beyond any bound according to the dynamics (8.54)–(8.56).*

Proof: If the state variable v is stationary by assumption we get that the third law of motion of the dynamics is independent of the remaining two state variables. It is then given by:

$$\dot{\lambda}_f = \alpha^k i_\lambda \lambda_f^2 + [(1-\alpha^k)i_\lambda - \alpha^k \tilde{r}]\lambda_f + (\alpha^k - 1)\tilde{r} - r_{min},$$

with $\tilde{r}$ being given by $y^p(1-v) - \delta_k - r_{min} > 0$. The right-hand side of this equation represents a polynomial of degree 2 $p(\lambda_f) = c_o\lambda_f^2 + d_y\lambda_f + d_h$ with $c_o > 0, d_y < 0$. The minimum of this function is at $\lambda_f = -d_y/(2c_o) > 0$ and it exhibits of course only positive values after the larger of its two roots has been passed (if it is real, otherwise all values of $p(\lambda_f)$ are positive even for all $\lambda_f > 0$). Initial values of the debt to capital ratio λ_f which lie to the right of this root therefore imply a purely explosive behaviour of this ratio as long as there is no sufficiently strong counteracting change in the wage share v. □

We have pointed out at the end of the preceding section that, in the minimum, the side condition $r \geq r_{min} - \delta_k/\alpha^k$ should always be fulfilled in order to allow for economically meaningful trajectories (along which gross investment should always stay non-negative). The threshold for an explosive evolution of the debt to capital ratio found to exist in Proposition 8.2 may however still be so large that explosiveness can only occur in a domain where the system is not economically viable. In this case the proposition simply states that the dynamics will not always be globally stable from the purely mathematical point of view, but does not yet prove that critical developments in the debt to capital ratio may also come about at initial situations to which there corresponds an economically meaningful environment. To show that such situations will indeed exist is the aim of the following Proposition 8.3.

Proposition 8.3 *We assume as before* $\alpha^k > 1, 0 < i_\lambda < n + n_l$ *and as a special case again that* $\beta_w = 0, n_l = 0$ *holds. Then: for the steady state value of the wage share,* v_o,[25] *the threshold value* $\bar{\lambda}_f \geq 0$ *of the debt to capital ratio* λ_f *of Proposition 8.2 implies a rate of profit* $\bar{r} \in (0, r_{min})$. *The considered dynamics (8.54)–(8.56) therefore*

[25] Note here that the steady state value of e, the rate of employment, is no longer uniquely determined in the considered case.

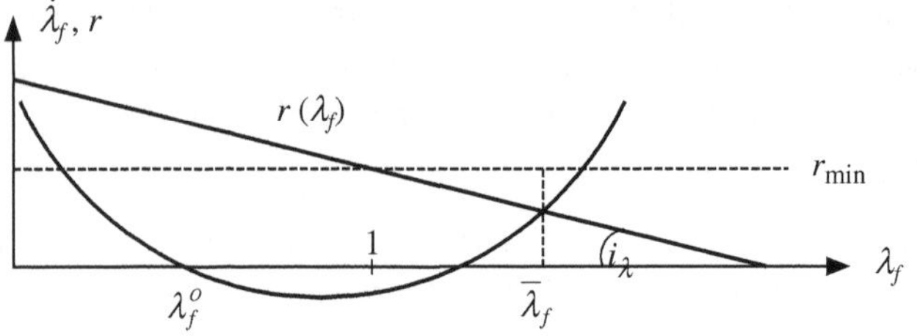

Figure 8.4 Debt and profit curves around the steady state share of wages

become divergent for values of λ_f that lie in an economically meaningful part of the state space.

Proof: We shall show below that the situation depicted in Figure 8.4 holds true under the assumed assumptions.

First, we show that the threshold value $\bar{\lambda}_f$ must be larger than one in the considered situation. To see this it suffices to show that the polynomial considered in Proposition 8.2 is still negative at $\lambda_f = 1$. At $\lambda_f = 1$ we have $\dot{\lambda}_f = -r = y^p(1 - v_o) - \delta_k - i_\lambda$. This gives $\dot{\lambda}_f = -[r_o + (i_\lambda \lambda_f^o - i_\lambda)]$. Inserting the steady state values (8.58), (8.59) into this expression then implies

$$\dot{\lambda}_f = -[r_{min} + \frac{n}{\alpha^k} + i_\lambda(\frac{\alpha^k - 1}{\alpha^k} - \frac{r_{min}}{n} - 1)].$$

Rearranging the shown items then gives

$$\dot{\lambda}_f = -[r_{min}(1 - \frac{i_\lambda}{n}) + \frac{1}{\alpha^k}(n - i_\lambda)] < 0$$

due to the assumption $n > i_\lambda$. From this result there follows immediately that the second root of the considered polynomial $\bar{\lambda}_f$ must be larger than one (while the first coincides with the steady state due to our assumption $v = v_o$).[26]

Let us now calculate the rate of profit at this threshold value $\bar{\lambda}_f$. Since we have $\dot{\lambda}_f = 0$ at this value (yet not a steady rate of employment, but instead a falling one), we get for $\bar{r} = y^p(1 - v_o) - \delta_k - i_\lambda \bar{\lambda}_f$ the expression

$$0 = \alpha^k(\bar{r} - r_{min})(1 - \bar{\lambda}_f) - \bar{r},$$

which in turn gives

$$\bar{r} = \frac{\alpha^k r_{min}(1 - \bar{\lambda}_f)}{\alpha^k(1 - \bar{\lambda}_f) - 1} = \frac{r_{min}}{1 - 1/(\alpha^k(1 - \bar{\lambda}_f))}.$$

Due to the above considerations we know however that the denominator of this expression is larger than one which implies that $\bar{r}$ must lie in the open interval $(0, r_{min})$. □

[26] Note that the smaller root can be negative, meaning that firms are creditors not debtors in the steady state, if $r_{min} > 0$ and if the parameter α^k is sufficiently close to one.

Should a shock throw the economy out of the steady state to a value of λ_f slightly above the threshold value $\bar{\lambda}_f$ it will be caught in a situation where λ_f is monotonically increasing accompanied by a falling rate of employment e until the domain of economically meaningful values for these two state variables is left. We stress that this result is obtained on the basis of a wage share that remains fixed at its steady state value and which therefore neither improves nor worsens the considered situation through its movements in time. This result will also hold true for all adjustments in the wage share that are sufficiently slow. At present it is however not clear whether a strongly falling wage share (based on a high value of the parameter β_w), which significantly improves the profitability of indebted firms, can lead us back to the steady state. This may depend on the size of the implied change in gross investment and its consequences for the change of the debt of firms.

For sufficiently small parameter values β_w we however know that the dynamics will produce explosiveness of the debt to capital ratio λ_f and implosiveness for the rate of employment e beyond threshold values $\bar{\lambda}_f, \bar{r}$. For sufficiently high debt, measured relative to the level of the capital stock, we thus get that debt accumulation feeds itself and will lead to larger and larger debt to capital ratios at least if there is no sufficient support for the pure rate of profit from downward changes in the wage share. Yet, as there is no price deflation, there cannot be a 'perverse' adjustment (a rise) of the wage share in such a situation of depressed profitability and high debt accumulation. Such a problematic situation comes about when there is sluggish or no downward adjustment in the level of nominal wages, but – due to insufficient goods demand, which is not yet a possibility in the considered model of Keen (2000) – downward adjustment in the price level causing increases in the real wage and the wage share. This scenario will be investigated by a suitable 4D simplification of the general 20D model in the next subsection.

8.5.2 4D debt deflation

Let us thus now extend the model (8.54)–(8.56) to include into it in a minimal way the possibility for price level deflation and thus the possibility for the occurrence of debt deflation (high levels of debt combined with declining profitability due to falling output prices). In order to achieve this, we set all parameters of the general 20D model that characterise the fiscal and monetary authority, the foreign sector, the housing sector and the asset markets equal to zero and thus get in particular given rates of interest (no Keynes effect, no cumulative asset market behaviour), with all interest rates equal to the then given rate of interest on loans. We will furthermore ignore the delayed Metzlerian quantity adjustment on the market for goods and assume that firms adjust their labour force with infinite speed which identifies employment l^{de} with the employed workforce l^{we} as now unique expression for the utilisation of the labour force. We assume finally that inflationary expectations remain fixed at their steady state level (no Mundell effect) by setting adjustment coefficients equal to zero there too. This gives rise to the following type of nominal dynamics for wages w^e, prices p_y and debt λ_f

coupled with an investment driven growth path, here represented by the dynamics of full employment labour intensity l^e (measured in efficiency units):[27]

$$\hat{w}^e = \kappa[\beta_{w_e}(l^{de}/l^e - \bar{e}) + \kappa_w \beta_p(y/y^p - \bar{u})], \tag{8.60}$$

$$\hat{p}_y = \kappa[\kappa_p \beta_{w_e}(l^{de}/l^e - \bar{e}) + \beta_p(y/y^p - \bar{u})], \tag{8.61}$$

$$\hat{l}^e = -[\alpha_r^k(r - i_\lambda) + \alpha_u^k(y/y^p - \bar{u})], \tag{8.62}$$

$$\dot{\lambda}_f = [\alpha_r^k(r - i_\lambda) + \alpha_u^k(y/y^p - \bar{u}) + \gamma](1 - \lambda_f) - r - \hat{p}_y \lambda_f. \tag{8.63}$$

Where the Metzlerian feedback mechanism from actually observed aggregate demand to expected demand to planned output and income and back to aggregate demand,

$$y^d = d_y \frac{w^e}{p_y} l^{de} + \alpha_r^k(r - i_\lambda) + \alpha_u^k(y/y^p - \bar{u}) + \gamma + \delta_k \to y^e \to y \to y^d$$

will be simplified and specialised to the following static (and again linearised) relationship:

$$\begin{aligned} y^d &= y^e = y = y\left(\frac{w^e}{p_y}, \lambda_f\right) \\ &= \bar{u} y^p + d_w\left(\frac{w^e}{p_y} - (\frac{w^e}{p_y})_o\right) + d_\lambda(\lambda_f - \lambda_f^o) \qquad (d_w, d_\lambda \leq 0), \end{aligned}$$

which will be used in the following as a shortcut for the delayed feedback chain of the general case (and its richer concept of aggregate demand) in order to integrate the effects of price inflation and deflation into the Keen (2000) model as presented and analysed in the preceding subsection.[28] Otherwise the 4D dynamics are just a subdynamics of the general 20D dynamics considered in this chapter. Note that the budget equations of the credit-giving institution (here the pure asset holders) are no longer subject to the problem we observed for the banks of the 3D Keen model. Note furthermore that Goodwin type dynamics are obtained when $i_\lambda, \lambda_f(0), d_w, d_\lambda$ are all zero,[29] while the more general Rose (1967) type of real wage dynamics demands $i_\lambda, d_\lambda = 0$ (with wage flexibility as a stabilising factor and price flexibility destabilising if (as is assumed) $d_w < 0$ holds). Finally, the Fisher debt mechanism is obtained (due to $d_\lambda < 0$) by setting $\beta_{we}, \kappa_w, d_w = 0$. The above goods market representation therefore allows for Rose effects of traditional type (where price flexibility is destabilising) and for Fisher debt effects (where price flexibility should also be destabilising), but it excludes Mundell effects for example (that would also demand the inclusion of inflationary expectations into the above model).

27 $\bar{e}, \bar{u}$ the NAIRU utilisation rates of the labour force and the capital stock.

28 Note that this shortcut of the originally delayed quantity adjustment process of Metzlerian type demands that the steady state value of this function y must be equal to $y^p \bar{u}$ in order to get a steady state solution for this 4D simplification of the 20D dynamics.

29 Also in the further special case where $\alpha_r^k = 1, \alpha_u^k = 0, \gamma = i_\lambda$ holds.

We assume that the propensity to invest dominates the propensity to consume with respect to the impact of real wages $\frac{w^e}{p_y}$ on consumption and investment (the orthodox point of view) and take also from the above feedback chain and its shown shortcut the assumption that output depends negatively on the debt to capital ratio λ_f. The partial derivatives of the function $y(\frac{w^e}{p_y}, \lambda_f)$ are therefore both assumed as negative in the following ($d_w, d_\lambda < 0$). Since l^{de} is strictly proportional to output y, due to the fixed proportions technology assumed, we have that this employment magnitude exhibits the same type of dependence on the real wage and the debt to capital ratio as output y. Finally we of course again have $r = y - \delta_k - \frac{w^e}{p_y} l^{de} - i_\lambda \lambda_f$ for the rate of pure profits r.

The above represents the simplest way to integrate from the perspective of the 20D model the dynamics of the price level into our representation of the Keen (2000) model by abstracting from Metzlerian delayed output adjustment, from the distinction between the inside and the outside employment rate, from inflationary expectations, the housing sector, a fiscal and monetary authority, a foreign sector and from endogenous interest rate determinations.

Let us first calculate the interior steady state of the dynamics (8.60)–(8.63). This steady state is uniquely determined up to the steady level of prices p_y and is characterised by[30]

$$\lambda_f^o = 1 - i_\lambda / \gamma, \tag{8.64}$$

$$y_o = y^p \bar{u}, \tag{8.65}$$

$$l_o^{de} = y_o l_y^e, \tag{8.66}$$

$$l_o^e = l_o^{de} / \bar{e}, \tag{8.67}$$

$$r_o = i_\lambda, \tag{8.68}$$

$$\left(\frac{w^e}{p_y}\right)_o = \frac{y_o - r_o - \delta_k - i_\lambda \lambda_f^o}{l_o^{de}}, \tag{8.69}$$

$$p_y^o = \text{determined by initial conditions}, \tag{8.70}$$

$$w_o^e = p_y^o \left(\frac{w^e}{p_y}\right)_o. \tag{8.71}$$

Due to the new form of the investment function[31]

$$I/K = \alpha_r^k (r - i_\lambda) + \alpha_u^k (y/y^p - \bar{u}) + \gamma + \delta_k$$

we now have a different steady debt to capital ratio which is solely determined by trend growth γ in its deviation from the given rate of interest i_λ on loans. We again assume that $\gamma - i_\lambda > 0$ holds in order to get a positive steady state ratio λ_f. The two NAIRUs

[30] We use l_y^e to express employment per unit of output measured in efficiency units (a given magnitude).
[31] Which must be non-negative along the relevant trajectories of the dynamics.

on the labour and the goods market, $\bar{e}, \bar{u}$, and our consistency assumption that y is equal to $y^p\bar{u}$ in the steady state imply (on the basis of the given technology) the steady state ratios for actual and full employment labour intensity (in efficiency units), l^{de}, l^e in the usual way. Having determined the rate of profit through the rate of interest on loans implies on this basis a well-defined level of real wages measured in efficiency units, $(\frac{w^e}{p_y})_o$, which is positive if y^p is chosen sufficiently high relative to $\gamma, \delta_k, i_\lambda$ and $\bar{u}$. This real wage level then determines the nominal wage level on the basis of a given price level which is determined through historical (initial) conditions.

Proposition 8.4 *Assume* $0 < i_\lambda < \gamma, d_\lambda = 0$ *and* $\beta_p, \kappa_p = 0$,[32] *implying that the price level is a given magnitude in this special case. Assume furthermore that the investment parameter* α_r^k *is chosen such that* $\alpha_r^k i_\lambda - \gamma > 0$ *holds true. Then: the steady state (8.64)–(8.71) of the dynamics (8.60)–(8.63) is locally asymptotically stable for all other admissible parameter values.*

Proof: Note first of all that the dynamics are now of dimension three by assumption. Concerning the calculation of the determinant of the Jacobian of these reduced dynamics (8.60), (8.62), (8.63), at the steady state, we can first of all state that its third row can be reduced to $(0, 0, -\gamma)$ by the addition of an appropriate linear combination of the first two rows of this determinant without changing its sign. This immediately implies that this determinant can be characterised by the following remaining sign structure:

$$\det J = \begin{vmatrix} - & - & 0 \\ + & 0 & - \\ 0 & 0 & -\gamma \end{vmatrix}$$

and must thus be negative which provides one of the Routh–Hurwitz conditions for local asymptotic stability. With respect to the sum a_2 of the principal minors of order 2 one furthermore gets from the full sign structure of the Jacobian matrix J in the case $d_\lambda = 0$:

$$J = \begin{pmatrix} - & - & 0 \\ + & 0 & - \\ - & 0 & - \end{pmatrix},$$

thus the Jacobian is the sum of two positive and one zero determinant and thus unambiguously positive. Note furthermore that the entry

$$J_{33} = -\gamma + i_\lambda - \alpha_r^k i_\lambda (1 - \lambda_f) = -\gamma - i_\lambda \gamma (\alpha_r^k i_\lambda - \gamma)$$

in the preceding matrix is negative and larger in amount than γ due to the assumption made with respect to the parameter α_r^k. The trace of J is therefore negative, too, since $i_\lambda < \gamma$ by assumption and since $\lambda_f^o < 1$ holds again. The coefficients $a_1 = -\text{trace } J, a_2, a_3 = -\det J$ of the Routh–Hurwitz polynomial are therefore all positive and thus all support the local asymptotic stability claimed by the above proposition. Finally, we also have $a_1 a_2 - a_3 > 0$, since the expression for $\det J$ is part of

[32] This implies $\kappa = 1$.

the all positive expressions contained in a_1a_2 and thus cannot make the expression $a_1a_2 - a_3$ less or equal to zero. □

We thus have that the steady state of the reduced dynamics (8.60), (8.62), (8.63) (where there is no adjustment of prices due to the demand pressure on the market for goods) is locally asymptotically if the influence of the debt to capital ratio λ_f on the level of output and employment, both in intensive form, is sufficiently weak. Furthermore, since the determinant of the full 4D dynamics is always zero these dynamics will be convergent with respect to the three state variables w^e, l^e, λ_f also for all speeds of adjustments β_p (and parameters κ_p) chosen sufficiently small, since the eigenvalues of the full dynamics are continuous functions of the parameters of the model.

Proposition 8.5 *Assume now (as was originally the case) that $d_\lambda < 0$ holds. Then: the steady state (8.64)–(8.71) of the dynamics (8.60)–(8.63) is not locally asymptotically stable for all price adjustment speeds β_p chosen sufficiently large.*

Proof: The interdependent part of the dynamics (8.60)–(8.63) can be reduced to the dynamics of the state variables $\omega^e = \frac{w^e}{p_y}$, the real wage, and again l^e, λ_f, as follows:

$$\hat{\omega}^e = \kappa[(1-\kappa_p)\beta_{w_e}(l^{de}/l^e - \bar{e}) - (1-\kappa_w)\beta_p(y/y^p - \bar{u})], \tag{8.72}$$

$$\hat{l}^e = -[\alpha_r^k(r - i_\lambda) + \alpha_u^k(y/y^p - \bar{u})], \tag{8.73}$$

$$\begin{aligned}\dot{\lambda}_f &= [\alpha_r^k(r - i_\lambda) + \alpha_u^k(y/y^p - \bar{u}) + \gamma](1-\lambda_f) - r \\ &\quad - \kappa[\kappa_p\beta_{w_e}(l^{de}/l^e - \bar{e}) + \beta_p(y/y^p - \bar{u})]\lambda_f.\end{aligned} \tag{8.74}$$

Regarding the terms in the trace of the Jacobian of these dynamics at the steady state that depend on the parameter β_p one obtains

$$\omega_o^e\kappa(1-\kappa_w)\beta_p(-d_w)/y^p + \kappa\beta_p(-d_\lambda)/y^p,$$

which is based on positive expressions throughout (up to the possibility that either κ_w or κ_p can be equal to one).[33] Therefore the trace of J can always be made positive by choosing the parameter β_p sufficiently large. □

The local stability result for the 3D Keen model is therefore overthrown in the case where relative goods demand is negatively dependent on the debt to capital ratio and where the price level adjusts with respect to demand pressure on the market for goods with sufficient speed. In such a case, we conjecture and will test this assertion numerically, that a process of deflation will continue without end accompanied by higher and higher debt ratios of firms which eventually will lead to zero profitability and bankruptcy.

Proposition 8.6 *Assume again that $d_\lambda < 0, \beta_p > 0$ holds. Assume now that nominal wages are completely fixed ($\beta_w = \kappa_w = 0$). Then: the dynamics (8.60)–(8.63) are*

[33] The first expression shows the strength of the destabilising Rose or price level flexibility effect and the second is the Fisher debt effect.

monotonically explosive, implying higher and higher real wages and debt to capital ratios, for initial debt to capital ratios chosen sufficiently high (in particular larger than one) and all real wage levels above their steady state value.

Proof: The real economic dynamics considered in the proof of the preceding proposition can then be reduced to

$$\hat{\omega}^e = -\beta_p(y/y^p - \bar{u}), \tag{8.75}$$

$$\dot{\lambda}_f = [\alpha_r^k(r - i_\lambda) + \alpha_u^k(y/y^p - \bar{u}) + \gamma](1 - \lambda_f) - r - \beta_p(y/y^p - \bar{u})\lambda_f, \tag{8.76}$$

since l^e does no longer feed back on the state variables of these dynamics. Since both ω^e and λ_f are larger than their steady state values, we get from the first law of motion that ω^e must be rising further (due to falling price levels caused by $y < y^p\bar{u}$). Furthermore, since also $r - i_\lambda$, $1 - \lambda_f < 0$ holds we get that $\dot{\lambda}_f$ must be larger than

$$\gamma(1 - \lambda_f) - i_\lambda - \beta_p(y/y^p - \bar{u})\lambda_f > -\gamma\lambda_f - \beta_p(y/y^p - \bar{u})\lambda_f.$$

If therefore $-\beta_p(y/y^p - \bar{u}) > \gamma$ has come about by choosing λ_f sufficiently high we have that $\dot{\lambda}_f > 0$ must be true so that both ω^e and λ_f will be rising which further strengthens the conditions for their monotonic increase. □

We thus get as in Proposition 8.3, but much easier and much more severe (through the occurrence of price deflation), that there will indeed occur situations of now debt *deflation* where profitability falls monotonically and where the debt of firms is increasing beyond any limit, therefore leading to economic collapse sooner or later.

Proposition 8.7 *Assume as always $0 < i_\lambda < \gamma$ and $\alpha_r^k > 1$. Assume furthermore that $\beta_p = 0$, $\kappa_p = 1$, so that the price level is determined by cost-push considerations solely and hence by a conventional markup equation of the type*

$$p_y = (1 + m)\frac{wL^d}{Y} = (1 + m)wl_y = (1 + m)w^e l_y^e.$$

Assume that the given markup m is such that the implied real wage ω^e (in efficiency units) is equal to its steady state level. Next, assume a given level of nominal wages (measured in efficiency units), which means that $\beta_{we} = 0$, $\kappa_w = 0$.[34] *Assume finally that the investment parameter α_u^k is chosen such that $\alpha_u^k > y^p(1 - \omega^e l_y^e)\frac{\gamma - i_\lambda}{i_\lambda}$ holds true.*[35] *Then: the steady state (8.64)–(8.71) of the dynamics (8.60)–(8.63), which can then be reduced to adjustments of the debt to capital ratio basically, is locally asymptotically stable for all values of the parameter $d_\lambda < 0$.*

[34] The nominal wage is therefore growing in line with labour productivity.
[35] This inequality is equivalent to the inequality

$$\alpha_u^k > [(\gamma - i_\lambda)^2 + 2(\gamma - i_\lambda) + \delta_k(\gamma/i_\lambda - 1)]/\bar{u}.$$

Proof: In the assumed situation we have $\hat{p}_y = 0$ due to the given level of nominal wages and thus get a single independent law of motion for the debt to capital ratio λ_f:

$$\dot{\lambda}_f = [\alpha_r^k(r(\lambda_f) - i_\lambda) + \alpha_u^k(y(\lambda_f)/y^p - \bar{u}) + \gamma](1 - \lambda_f) - r(\lambda_f).$$

We have to show that the derivative of the right-hand side of this equation is negative at λ_f^o. Note first that $r'(\lambda_f) = y'(\lambda_f)(1 - \omega^e l_y^e) - i_\lambda = d_\lambda(1 - \omega^e l_y^e) - i_\lambda$ holds with a real wage ω^e that stays at this steady state level. Next, the derivative of the $\dot{\lambda}_f$ equation with respect to λ_f evaluated at the steady state is calculated and reads:

$$-\gamma + [\alpha_r^k r'(\lambda_f) + \alpha_u^k y'(\lambda_f)/y^p](1 - \lambda_f) - r'(\lambda_f).$$

This expression can be rearranged as follows:

$$-\gamma + (\alpha_r^k - 1)r'(\lambda_f)(1 - \lambda_f) + \alpha_u^k d_\lambda/y^p(1 - \lambda_f) - r'(\lambda_f)\lambda_f.$$

From this expression we get through further rearrangement

$$-(\gamma - i_\lambda\lambda_f) + (\alpha_r^k - 1)r'(\lambda_f)(1 - \lambda_f) - d_\lambda(-\alpha_u^k/y^p(1 - \lambda_f) + (1 - \omega^e l_y^e)\lambda_f)$$

with $\lambda_f = 1 - i_\lambda/\gamma$, $1 - \lambda_f = i_\lambda/\gamma$. This expression must be negative since $i_\lambda < \gamma$, $\lambda_f < 1$, $\alpha_r^k > 1$, $r' < 0$ and due to

$$\alpha_u^k > y^p(1 - \omega^e l_y^e)\lambda_f/(1 - \lambda_f) = y^p(1 - \omega^e l_y^e)\frac{\gamma - i_\lambda}{i_\lambda}.$$

In a similar way it can also be shown that the above derivative is negative for all $\lambda_f \in (0, \lambda_f^o)$, hence there is convergence to the steady state for all positive debt to capital ratios below the steady state ratio. It is however not possible to provide an easy expression for the upper limit of the basin of attraction of the steady state (which may be less than one). □

We have formulated Proposition 8.7 in view of an intended policy application which however can only be sketched here. Consider the case where the debt to capital ratio λ_f is so large that there are cumulative forces at work (as in Proposition 8.6) which would lead to higher and higher debt and lower and lower profitability in the considered economy. In the case considered in Proposition 8.7 there are three possible ways to break this catastrophic tendency in the evolution of the economy:

- An increase in nominal wages w^e which under the assumptions of Proposition 8.7 causes an immediate increase in the price level p_y and thus an immediate decrease in the ratio λ_f, which (if strong enough) may lead the economy back to the basin of attraction of its steady state.
- A decrease in the rate of interest i_λ on loans which moves the steady state of the economy to a higher sustainable debt to capital ratio.
- A decrease in the sensitivity of output y (through appropriate fiscal policies) with respect to λ_f, meaning a value of the parameter d_λ that is smaller in amount (which may enlarge the basin of attraction of the steady state).

There is therefore scope for economic policy to move the economy out of regions of developing debt deflation into regions where it converges back to the steady state. The details of such possibilities must however be left for future research.

8.6 Numerical simulations: from low to high order dynamics

In this section we provide numerical examples for the propositions on the 3D and 4D dynamics presented in the preceding sections and will also present some simulation runs of the general 20D dynamical system. Part II has discussed the various feedback mechanisms it contains and given some indication of the shape and size of the basins of attraction in the 18D case.[36]

8.6.1 The 3D dynamics

We start the numerical analysis of the 3D dynamics (8.54)–(8.56) by stressing again that they are of the Goodwin (1967) growth cycle type (where all orbits are closed curves around the steady state) when one assumes the parameter values: $i_\lambda = 0, r_{min} = 0$, $\alpha^k = 1$. There are also further cases where the closed orbit structure is obtained as we shall see in the following.

As a first example we now consider the case where there holds: $\alpha^k = 1.5$; $\beta_w = 0.5$; $n = 0.03$; $n_l = 0.03$; $r_{min} = 0$; $\bar{e} = 0.9$; $i_\lambda = 0.05$; $y^p = 0.45$; $\delta_k = 0.1$; and where we exercise a very large shock on the debt to capital ratio, giving it three times the size of its steady state value (from which the dynamics starts). The first thing to notice is that the debt to capital ratio converges back to its steady state value in a time span of approximately fifty years and does so monotonically while the real cycle keeps its basic shape. The result is that the size of this cycle is shock dependent since the disappearance of motion in the debt ratio makes the wage-share employment-rate dynamics again self-contained and thus of the Goodwin (1967) closed orbit type (the size of which depends as in the Goodwin growth cycle model on the history of the economy). If there is strong convergence of λ_f back to its steady state value (and this appears to be the case in many situations even when shocks are large) the involved Goodwin cycle mechanism comes to a rest once the debt ratio comes sufficiently close to its steady state value again. Figure 8.5 provides an example of such dynamics.

In the next 3D example in Figure 8.6 we make use of less sensitive investment behaviour now based on a minimum rate of profit that is larger than zero. In this case we get sluggishly convergent Goodwin-type growth cycle behaviour which we exhibit in the lower graphs of Figure 8.6 for the time interval (200, 260). As in many other convergent cases we have here only a weak reduction in amplitude over time, in particular since debt is relatively small for many reasonable choices of the parameters α^k and r_{min}. We now also observe a basically positive correlation of the employment rate and the debt to capital ratio.

[36] The simulation studies in this and the preceding chapters were performed in Fortran, Gauss or SND. See Chiarella *et al.* (2002) with respect to the latter simulation package.

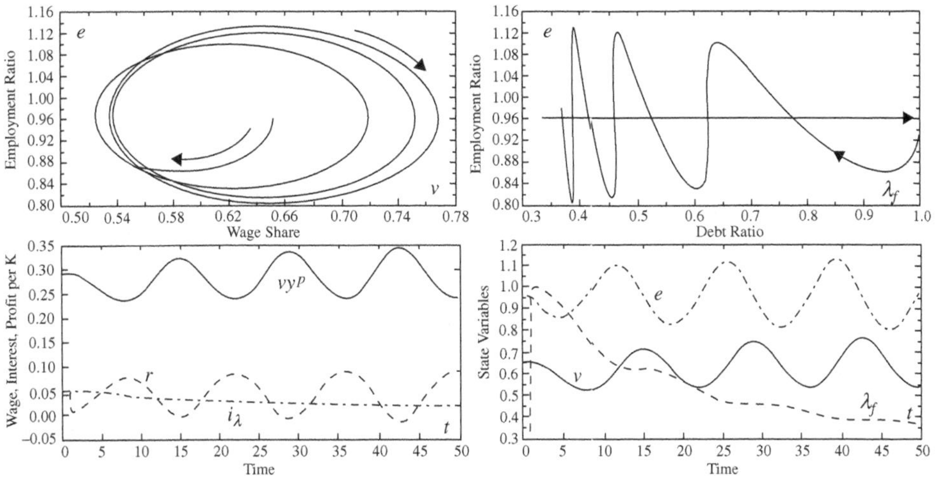

Figure 8.5 Debt convergence and shock-dependent persistent cyclical growth

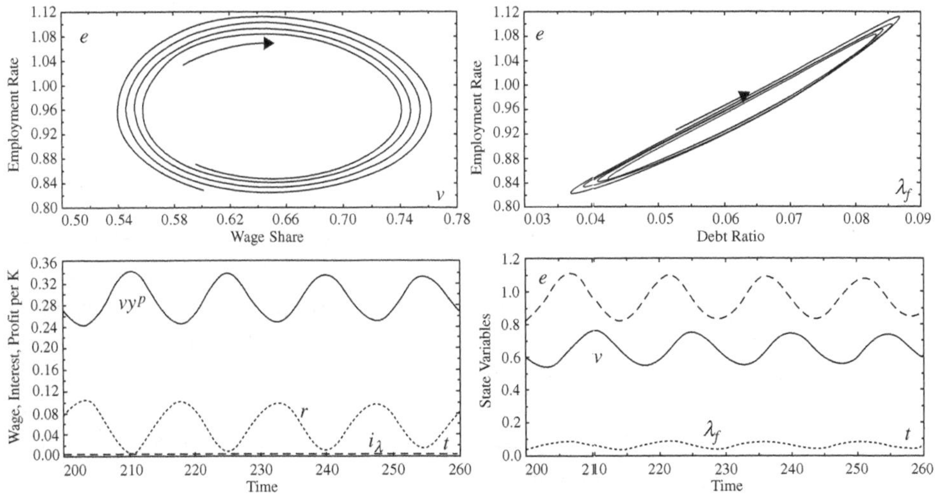

Figure 8.6 Slow convergence through debt-financed investment

The parameters underlying Figure 8.6 are given in Table 8.10 where we see that the change only concerns the assumed investment behaviour in comparison with the situation of Figure 8.5.

We conclude from these and various other simulations that the Goodwin real growth cycle often plays a dominant role in the shaping of the dynamics, while the debt dynamics either die out, lead to Goodwin cycles with slowly declining amplitude, or lead to strongly explosive behaviour (not shown) if the shocks in the debt ratio are made very large. It is therefore time to add the nominal price dynamics to the real growth model which is characterised by firms that finance part of their investment through new debt.

Table 8.10. *Parameter values underlying the simulations of Figure 8.8*

$\alpha^k = 1.3$; $\beta_w = 0.5$; $n = 0.03$; $n_l = 0.03$; $r_{min} = 0.01$; $\bar{e} = 0.9$; $i_\lambda = 0.05$; $y^p = 0.45$; $\delta_k = 0.1$

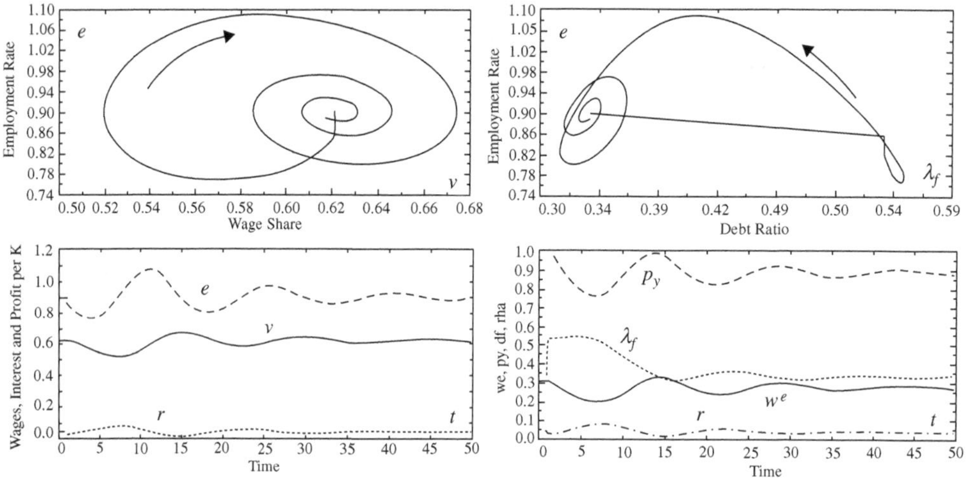

Figure 8.7 Faster convergence through a stabilising Rose effect

8.6.2 The 4D dynamics

We consider now the 4D dynamics (8.60)–(8.63) with both wage and price level adjustment.[37] We thus assume now that price adjustments are based on demand pressure as well as a wage cost-push term, and that wage adjustments (expressed in efficiency units) fully incorporate price inflation ($\kappa_w = 1$), a situation in which the real wage dynamics depend only on demand pressure in the market for labour and not on that in the market for goods. There is thus only a stabilising Rose (1967) effect present with respect to real wage adjustment (since $d_w < 0$ holds and since goods market equilibrium is in this situation irrelevant for real wage dynamics). This effect is of course the stronger the larger the parameter β_{we} becomes. Furthermore the debt effect on output is comparably weak here since $d_\lambda = -0.1$, and the steady debt ratio as well as the dynamic one (and thus also interest payments) are small in the present situation, which in sum gives rise here to a fast cyclical adjustment of the employment rate, of the wage share and of the debt to capital ratio to their steady state positions.

Note however that the initial phase of the dynamics (see Figure 8.7) exhibits high (and even rising) debt and falling price levels which however in the current situation create no long-lasting problem for the economy. We expect that this situation will change when the wage adjustment speed is decreased or the price adjustment speed increased and the parameter d_λ made more negative, because of the normal Rose effect

[37] We assume as a starting point the following parameter set: $\alpha_r^k = 1.3$; $\alpha_u^k = 1.3$; $\beta_{we} = 0.3$; $\beta_p = 0.5$; $\kappa_w = 1$; $\kappa_p = 0.5$; $\gamma = 0.06$; $\bar{e} = 0.9$; $\bar{u} = 0.9$; $i_\lambda = 0.04$; $y^p = 0.45$; $\delta_k = 0.1$; $l_y^e = 2$; $d_w = -0.5$; $d_\lambda = -0.1$.

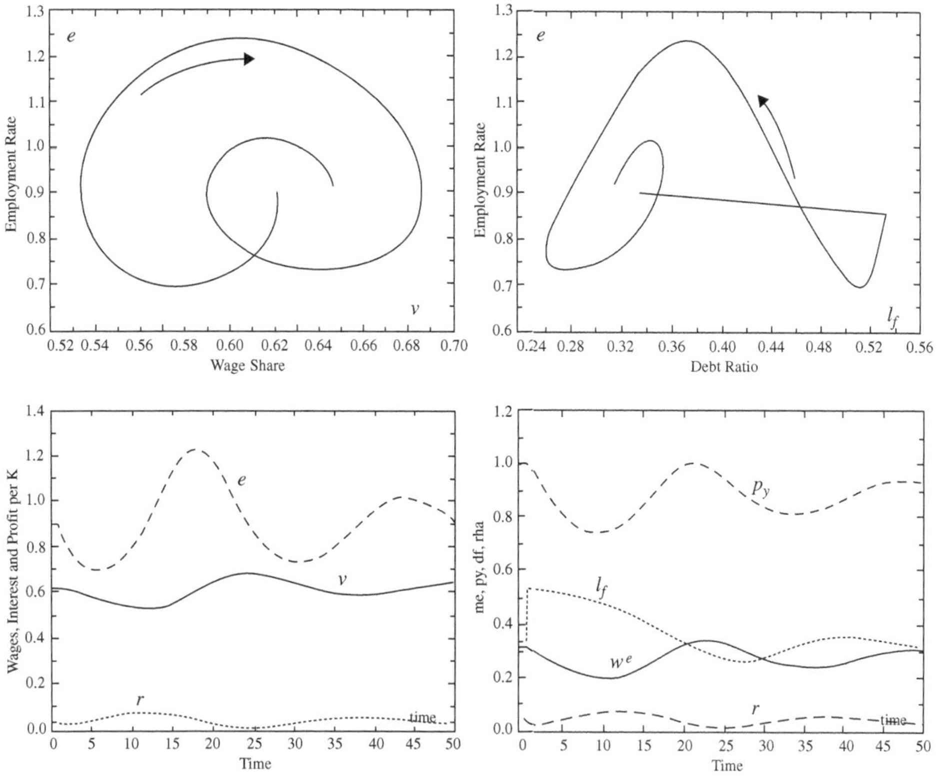

Figure 8.8 Slower convergence through more sluggish wages

with respect to real wage adjustments and a destabilising Fisher debt effect. A partial example for this is shown in Figure 8.8. Yet, even in this figure we have still a rising rate of profit despite high debt and falling prices and thus still a situation where the conflict about income distribution helps to prevent debt deflation from becoming a real threat to the rate of pure profits of firms.

Such a situation is assumed away in Figure 8.9 where we have $\beta_{we} = 0$ coupled with $\kappa_w = 1$, which implies that wages are following prices passively such that the wage share stays constant (furthermore we now also assume $d_\lambda = -0.2$ and $\beta_p = 0.552$).

As Figure 8.9 shows, we have a marked dip in the rate of profit when the sudden increase in the debt ratio occurs (at $t = 1$), which nevertheless slowly reverses thereafter since the debt ratio declines back to its steady value and since deflation no longer causes the dynamics to collapse. Note however that, although the rate of capacity utilisation converges back to its normal rate, the rate of employment does not show a similar tendency as there is no demand pressure effect from the rate of employment on the share of wages.[38] Increasing further the size of the shock in the debt to capital ratio will, however, eventually lead to monotonic divergence and thus to economic breakdown.

[38] See Fair (2000) for an empirical study of wage and price PCs where only demand pressure in the goods market is important.

Table 8.11. *The parameter set for Figure 8.10*

$\alpha_r^k = 1.3$; $\alpha_u^k = 1.3$; $\beta_{we} = 0.1$; $\beta_p = 0.1$; $\kappa_w = 1$; $\kappa_p = 0.5$; $\gamma = 0.06$; $\bar{e} = 0.9$;
$\bar{u} = 0.9$; $i_\lambda = 0.025$; $y^p = 0.45$; $\delta_k = 0.1$; $l_y^e = 2$; $d_w = 0$; $d_\lambda = -0.03$

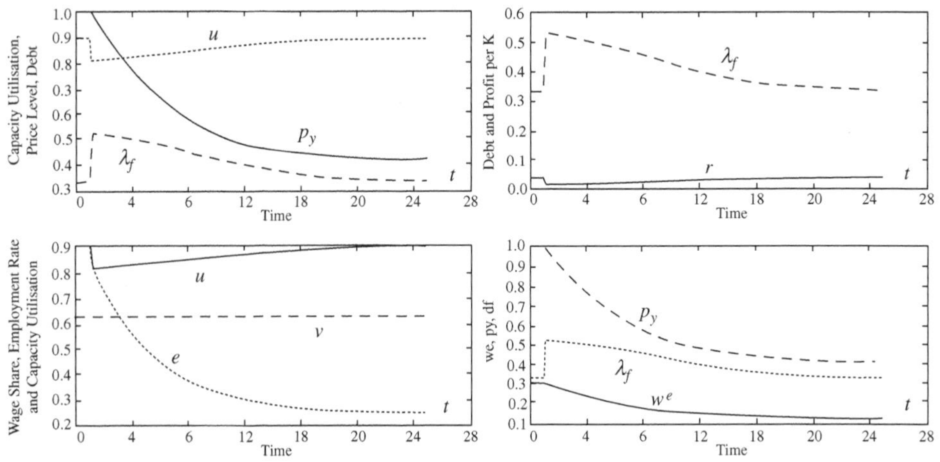

Figure 8.9 Deflation and converging debt

Figure 8.10 is based on the parameter set shown in Table 8.11 so that we have sluggishly reacting price and wage levels, now coupled with a low rate of interest on loans and thus a higher steady state ratio for λ_f. There is little movement in the wage share at first and no real wage effect on output (no Rose effect), but only a small negative effect of increasing debt on y. As we can see the dynamics are explosive in the present case, with at first rapidly rising profitability, due to the decline in debt and in the wage share occurring after the initial increase of debt at $t = 1$. Later on, however, the wage share starts rising, lowering the rate of profit significantly which then leads to increasing debt to capital ratios, falling capacity utilisation and falling prices, and to economic breakdown soon thereafter (although the wage share seems to start declining again).

Clearly, there is debt deflation in the final phase of the time series shown, and the question may therefore be posed whether positive price shocks, placed appropriately in such periods of deflation, can prevent economic collapse, extending its life beyond the 70 years that it here runs before (numerical) breakdown occurs. To obtain some insight into this issue, in Figure 8.11 we have added such positive price shocks (at $t = 58.70$) to the dynamics shown in Figure 8.10 and do indeed observe that these shocks counteract debt deflation for some time, by stopping the occurrence of falling price levels, restoring profitability and lowering the debt to capital ratio, which also leads to higher capacity utilisation due to its negative dependence on debt to capital

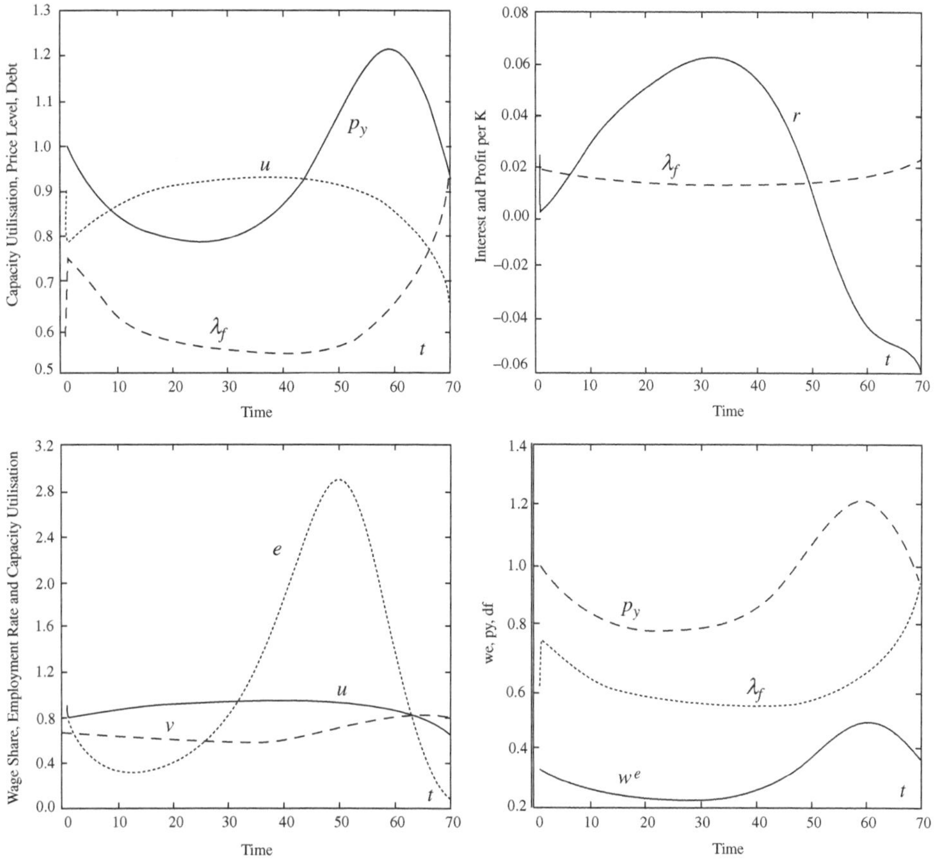

Figure 8.10 Debt deflation in the case of a sluggishly adjusting wage share

ratio λ_f. Note however that employment reacts in an extreme fashion and with long swings (basically due to the sluggish adjustment of nominal wages in the face of a large disequilibrium in the market for labour).

This closes our investigation of basic growth cycle models with debt financing, the possible occurrence of deflation and the role of the wage share in such a situation. Further numerical investigation is provided in Chiarella *et al.* (2001a,b) concerning the Fisher debt effect and the Rose real wage feedback mechanism. We have seen that (with and without profitability increasing adjustments in the wage share) debt will often converge back to its steady state value after debt shocks of considerable size. Undamped fluctuations are however possible and may lead to periods of strong debt deflation where positive price shocks may help to avoid economic collapse. Further increases in price flexibility will, however, lead to strong explosiveness (not shown), in the present model due to the joint working of the Rose real wage and the Fisher debt effects if both of the parameters d_w and d_λ are chosen significantly below zero.

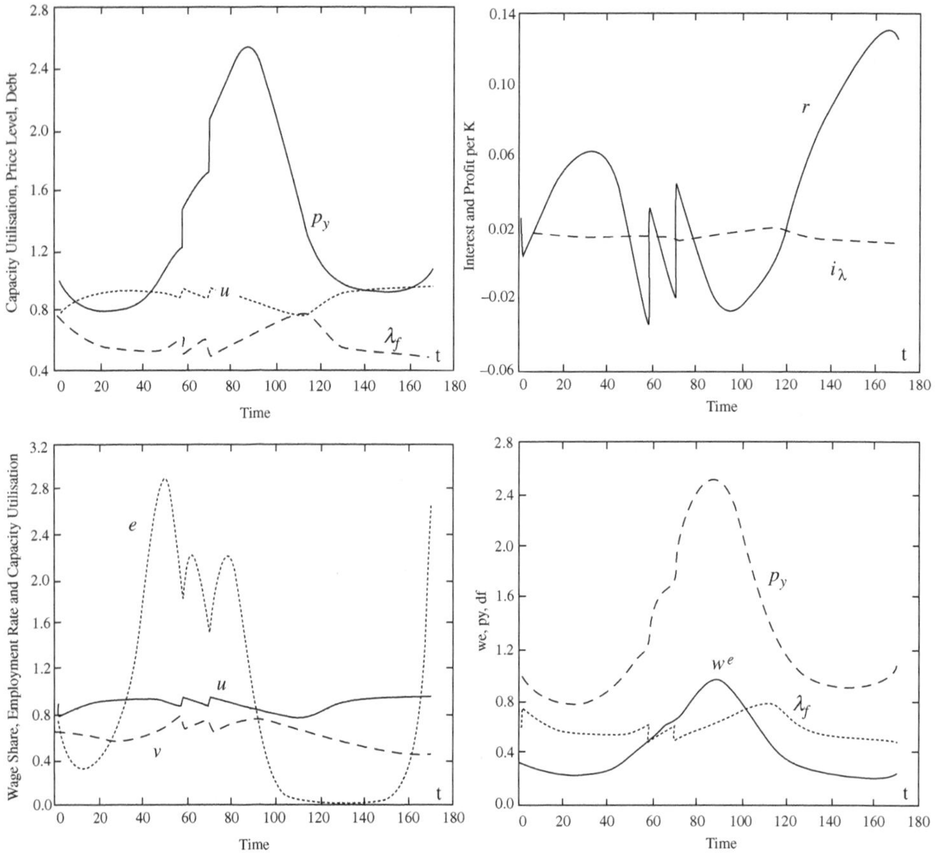

Figure 8.11 Positive price shocks (temporarily) stop debt deflation

8.6.3 The 20D dynamics

Now we consider simulations of the intensive form of the 20D dynamics laid out in Section 8.5. Let us first of all stress that debt financing is the least involved in the 20D dynamics in the case where the parameter values $\alpha_r^k = 1$, $\alpha_i^k = \alpha_u^k = 0$, $\beta_{i_\lambda} = 0$ and $i_\lambda(0) = \gamma$ hold. We then have $g_k = r^e + \delta_k$, which implies that only unexpected inventory changes have to be financed by loans (which should not matter very much for the dynamics of the model and thus should not allow debt deflation to play a significant role in this case). Furthermore, the qualitative properties of the original 18D dynamics considered in Part II should not change radically as far as the role of adjustment speeds is concerned if all expected profits are retained and not paid out as dividends, as was assumed in the 18D model (where fixed business investment was financed – in the background via the issuing of new equities). In our numerical simulations we have used the above simplified situation to find cases where the steady state is asymptotically stable (not shown) and from where we could then start, through

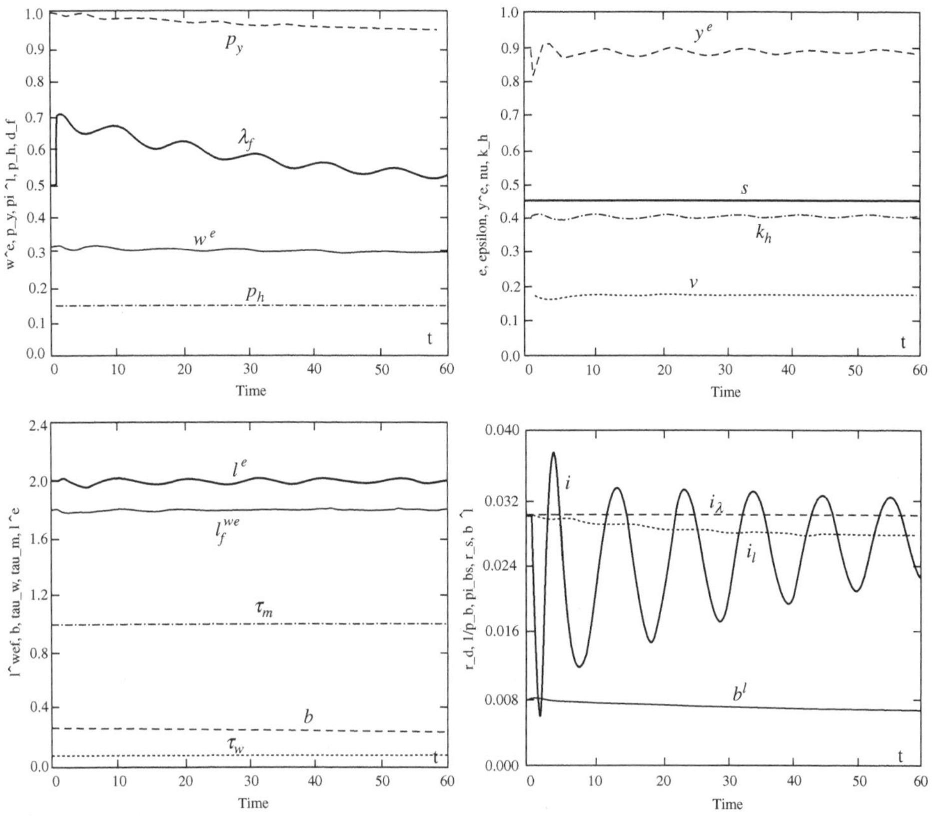

Figure 8.12 Asymptotic stability in the 20D case

parameter modifications, the investigation of destabilising debt deflation in the 20D case.

We first show in Figure 8.12 a case of asymptotic stability of the steady state of the 20D dynamics. The parameter values underlying Figure 8.12 are those specified in Table 8.12, with the exception that $\beta_{i_p} = 0.5$, $\kappa_w = 0$ and $\beta_p = 0.2$. We stress that the steady state is indeed asymptotically stable since also the price level will converge to a given level (and thus not fall forever) in the considered situation. Note that this case already departs from the above reference situation to a considerable degree and that we have assumed that monetary policy works with sufficient strength in order to overcome the instabilities here already present in the private sector of the economy. These destabilising forces again basically derive from the Rose and the Fisher debt effect which in this extended framework can be schematically presented as

$$p_y \downarrow \rightarrow \omega^e \uparrow \rightarrow y^d \downarrow \rightarrow y^e \downarrow \rightarrow y \downarrow \rightarrow \hat{p}_y \downarrow \quad \text{(the Rose effect),}$$

$$p_y \downarrow \rightarrow \lambda_f \uparrow \rightarrow r^e \downarrow \rightarrow y^d \downarrow \rightarrow y^e \downarrow \rightarrow y \downarrow \rightarrow \hat{p}_y \downarrow \quad \text{(the Fisher effect).}$$

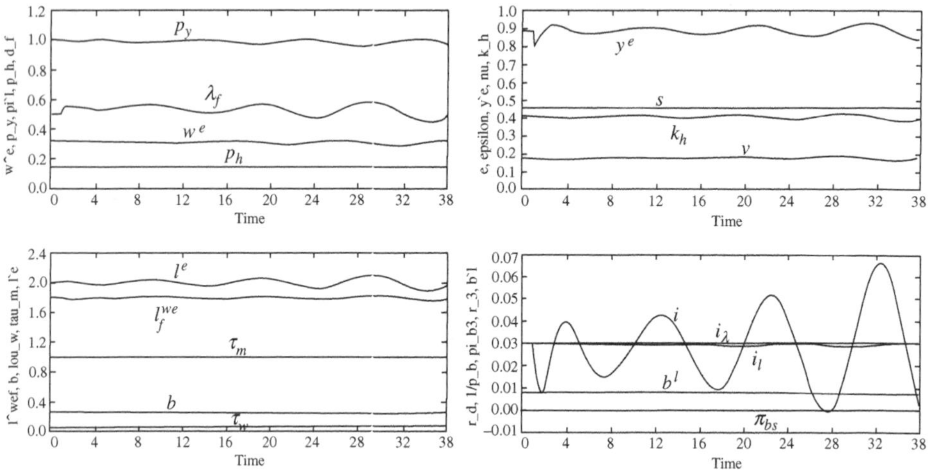

Figure 8.13 Destabilising price flexibility

Note that the partial Rose effect only works in this way if investment reacts more sensitively to real wage changes than consumption, in which case the cost effect of increasing real wages dominates the purchasing power effect they have in this model (as is the case in the following numerical simulations of the 20D dynamics). Note furthermore that asset markets react very sluggishly in the situations considered in this subsection and that the inventory adjustment mechanism exhibits slow inventory adjustments coupled with fast sales expectations which give it (from a partial perspective) the features of a stable dynamic multiplier process. Finally, the Mundell effect of inflationary expectations is also absent, due to the parameter choices made in the following. We consequently concentrate in this subsection on the two effects shown in the above boxes and on the role of the interest rate policy rule as a stabilising instrument in such an environment (because of its close relationship to the Keynes effect in the alternative case of a money-supply policy rule). Note finally that rates of return are equalised in the 20D case, in contrast to the 3D and 4D situations considered in the preceding subsections.

Next, we increase the parameter reflecting price flexibility to $\beta_p = 0.35$ and indeed in Figure 8.13, get a situation where the steady state is no longer attracting. We stress that monetary policy (the stabilising Keynes effect) is needed in order to obtain this only slightly explosive situation. However, the type of monetary policy that is assumed seems to be too weak here to again enforce convergence to the steady state.

Next, in Figure 8.14 we consider a case where there is some sort of isolated debt deflation, over the horizon shown, coupled with declining government debt and corresponding rates of interest. There are however no real effects visible over the horizon shown, which only occur later on when the situation becomes more and more extreme. The parameters specific to this situation are obtained from Table 8.12 but with $\beta_p = 1$, $\beta_{i_p} = 1$, $\kappa_w = 1$.

Table 8.12. *The simulation of the 20D dynamics – parameter values for Figures 8.12–8.15 with the exceptions noted in the text*

$\beta_{w_e} = 1; \beta_{w_u} = 0; \beta_p = 1; \beta_{\pi_l} = 0; \beta_{p_b} = 0.4; \beta_{\pi_{bs}} = 0;$
$\beta_e = 0; \beta_\epsilon = 0; \beta_n = 0.1; \beta_{n_d} = 0.2; \beta_{y_e} = 10; \beta_{lh} = 0;$
$\beta_l = 0.5; \beta_{i_i} = 0.5; \beta_{i_p} = 1; \beta_{i_u} = 0.5; \beta_{r_d} = 0;$
$\alpha_g = 0; \alpha_l = 0.5; \alpha_b^g = 0.5; \alpha_{\pi^c} = 0; \alpha_r^h = 0; \alpha_u = 0; \alpha_i^h = 0; \alpha_r = 0;$
$\alpha_u^h = 0; \alpha_{\tau_w} = 0; \alpha_r^k = 1; \alpha_{\tau_m} = 0.5; \alpha_i^k = 0.5; \alpha_s = 1; \alpha_u^k = 0;$
$L_1(0) = 20,000; L_2(0) = 5,000; \kappa_p = 0; \kappa_w = 1; \kappa_h = 0;$
$\bar{u} = 0.9; \bar{u}_h = 0.9; n = 0.03; \bar{e} = 0.9; n_l = 0.03; \bar{d} = 0.6; p_m^\star = 1;$
$g = 0.33; p_x^\star = 1; c_l = 0.7; r_l^\star = 0.03; \delta = 0.1; \tau_c = 0.5;$
$\delta_h = 0.1; \tau_p = 0.3; \gamma = 0.06; c_h = 0.1; x_{x_y} = 0.2; j_y = 0.1;$
$l_y^e = 2; y^p = 1; p_y(o) = 1; i_o = r_l^\star;$

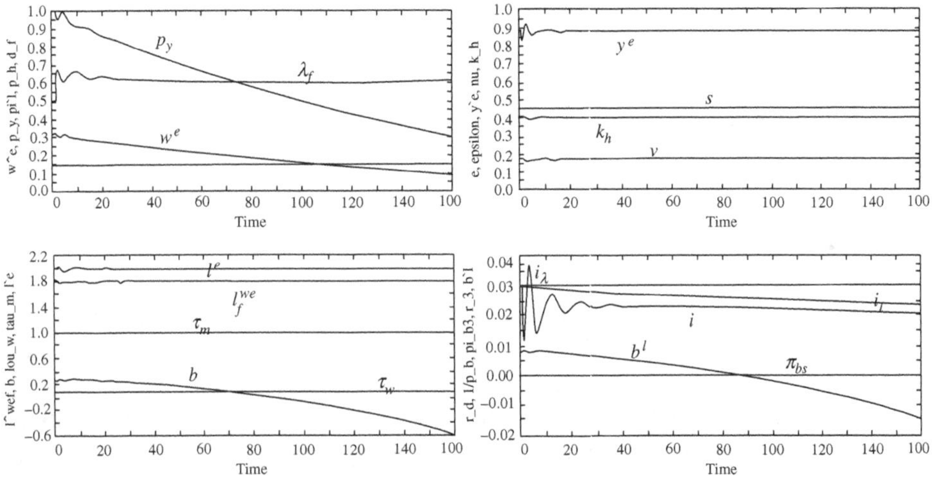

Figure 8.14 Pure debt deflation

The final situation presented in this subsection is given by Figure 8.15 where the deflationary process just considered is interrupted from time to time by positive price shocks which stop the monotonic development shown in Figure 8.14, decrease the real debt of firms and add fluctuations to the real magnitudes also shown in Figure 8.14.

These few numerical examples of the working of the 20D dynamics (still with a simplified choice of parameter values) show that much remains to be done for a proper demonstration of the consequences of debt deflation in a fully specified Keynesian model of monetary growth. Such investigations, which call for more refined numerical tools and more carefully considered parameter choices (in particular with respect to empirically observed parameter sizes), must however be left for future research. In addition, changes need to be made in the specification of the investment behaviour of firms and the way interest on loans is determined in order to extend the here still very

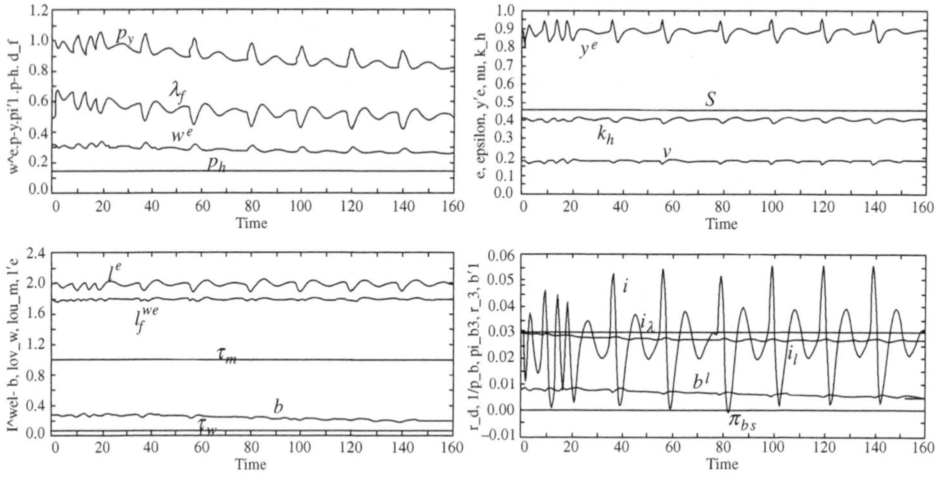

Figure 8.15 Positive price shocks in order to stop debt deflation

basic treatment of debt and deflation to more virulent cases of debt deflation than could be considered here.

8.7 Summary and outlook

In this chapter we have applied the integrated Keynesian 18D dynamics of Part II, with their price and quantity adjustment processes, their growth laws, asset market descriptions and fiscal and monetary policy rules, to the problem of describing and investigating situations where high debt of firms becomes combined with deflationary processes on the goods market, leading to falling profitability when there is no accompanying sufficiently large fall in real wages.[39]

To achieve this we have assumed as modification of Part II that firms use debt (in addition to retained pure profits) in place of equities to finance their investment expenditures (fixed business investment and inventories) and have derived the growth law of the debt to capital ratio from the budget equation of firms. In contrast to the very stylised situation of pure equity financing considered in Part II, where firms basically had no retained earnings, we now have pure profits of firms (over and above their debt service and factor costs) that in their relation to the interest rate on loans determine their investment plans. Although wealth effects on consumption and asset holdings are lacking in both of the considered dynamics we have seen in the present chapter that the level of debt and corresponding interest rate payments influence economic activity via investment behaviour and thus may significantly influence the fluctuating growth patterns to which this model type generally gives rise. Using loans in place of equities

[39] Real wages may even rise in such situations if prices fall faster than nominal wages.

implies that the rate of interest on loans has to be added to the endogenous variables of the model and this has been done in this chapter in the simplest way possible, by assuming that it adjusts to the long-term rate of interest on government bonds with a given time delay. The original 18D dynamical system thereby became a 20D dynamical system that served as point of reference for various types of simpler dynamics that we have considered in this chapter.

The most basic type of debt accumulation in a growing economy was obtained by making use of Keen's (2000) extension of the Goodwin (1967) growth cycle model. In addition to the reinvestment of the pure profits of firms this model also allows for debt financed investment in this supply driven growth context, thereby extending the dynamic interaction of the share of wages with real capital accumulation by the law of motion for the debt to capital ratio which feeds back into the real part of the dynamics via the pure rate of profit that it defines. The wage squeeze of the Goodwin model has thereby been augmented by a certain type of interest rate squeeze mechanism. This basic situation was investigated both analytically and numerically and gave rise to local stability assertions as well as global instabilities, depending on the size of the shock applied to the debt to capital ratio in particular. Integrating debt financing into the Goodwin growth cycle therefore gives rise to a new phenomenon, the occurrence of corridor stability, in this classical model of fluctuating growth. The interest rate squeeze mechanism therefore introduces a different type of behaviour as compared with the classical profit squeeze mechanism of real wage adjustments in view of demand pressure on the labour market. This may be explained by the lack of a PC mechanism as far as the credit market of the model is concerned.

Yet, in this basic approach, debt accumulation occurs without the possibility that firms have to face falling output prices simultaneously, a possibility that is not easily incorporated into a model where there is full capacity growth. In view of the established general 20D model, as a next step we have therefore integrated into the 3D dynamics a demand constraint for firms on the market for goods, reflecting two basic goods market characteristics of the general case. These two characteristics are represented by a negative impact effect of both real wages and real debt per unit of capital on this demand constraint. Using this shortcut to a full description of goods market adjustment processes of the 20D case, we then made use of the price PC of the 20D case in order to add as a fourth law of motion to the 3D dynamics a theory of price inflation based on demand pressure terms and cost-push elements. In this extended 4D model, we could again show asymptotic stability of the steady state for sluggishly adjusting price levels and, by as appropriate choice of parameters for debt deflation, instability for price flexibility chosen sufficiently large. Furthermore, if wages do not fall by a sufficient degree, the possibility of debt deflation could be demonstrated and policies that possibly could stop such an outcome were sketched (again analytically as well as numerically).

The decisive step away from supply side driven capital accumulation to demand side determined growth patterns was however to a certain extent preliminary, as the static shortcut of the dynamic feedback chain leading from expected demand to actual output to aggregate demand and back to expected demand is not an exact representation of the features of this delay driven feedback chain. The full feedback chain must therefore be used eventually if Keynesian growth is formulated, as it should be, with sluggish price as well as quantity adjustment processes. In this respect this chapter has offered however only a range of preliminary numerical illustrations that also downplayed important, but for the current question not central, aspects of the general model, namely activities of the state (the exception being the use of a Taylor type monetary policy rule), asset market behaviour, international aspects and the housing sector. As in the 4D dynamics we therefore concentrated in these examples on Rose type real wage dynamics and Fisher type debt deflation,[40] which both stress the destabilising potential of price flexibility in depressed situations due to its adverse effects on real wages and real debt. With the fully integrated 20D dynamics as a perspective we thus have been able to show how the question of debt deflation may be approached with respect to integrated models of monetary growth of an applicable nature. However we must also admit that much remains to be done in order to develop a deeper understanding of processes of debt deflation, which, as has been argued, are currently an important theme in public discussions on the state of the world economy.

The present chapter, with its general 20D model, has in fact not fully exploited the possibilities for a strong debt deflation mechanism that its 4D simplification may contain. This is due to the fact that debt operates on investment behaviour solely via the budget constraint of firms and not as in the 4D case through a direct adverse effect on effective demand. In addition interest rates were following long-term bond market interest rates with a time delay and thus did not have any direct relationship to the level of loans per unit of capital. The role played by debt accumulation in the 20D model thus resembles more the role the government budget constraint has for economic stability or instability than in fact the situation where debt and falling prices significantly depress investment behaviour and thus economic activity. By reducing pure profits, debt and deflation can however put the evolution of the debt of firms on an explosive path that cannot be counteracted in the way the government can counteract the explosive evolution of its own debt.

We shall return to the above issues and additional ones in future investigations of the general 20D model where more advanced mathematical tools will be used to determine regions of stability with respect to speed of adjustment parameters and boundaries where stability gets lost and basins of attraction; a preliminary investigation of these issues has been carried out by Chiarella *et al.* (2003b). In this way we hope to contribute to the understanding of the adjustment features of structural macroeconometric dynamic models for the USA, Germany, Australia and other countries to the point that the insights developed can actually be applied.

40 We also had stabilising Keynes as well as destabilising Mundell effects.

9 Bankruptcy of firms, debt default and the performance of banks

The preceding chapters have shown that debt accumulation when combined with price dynamics may give rise to instability. A stylised fact of periods of financial fragility is that over-indebtedness leads to the insolvency of borrowers. Firms go bankrupt and default on loans. The impact of the failure of firms and non-performing loans plays a central role in the theories of financial fragility developed by Minsky and Fisher.[1] Non-performing loans may have a boomerang effect on the financial sector, by undermining the profitability of commercial banks. In this chapter, the preceding models are extended to take into account three aspects of debt over-indebtedness over the business cycle:

1. Bankruptcy of firms
2. Debt default
3. Non-performing loans and banking crises.

Bankruptcies may have ambiguous effects on the business cycle. On the one hand, the market sanctions bad performance by bankruptcy. It eliminates the weakest and most fragile firms and establishes favourable conditions for economic recovery. Similarly, in a Schumpeterian approach, the creative destruction argument points in the same direction. Recessions are productive as they are periods during which new technologies and new organisations are implemented. Likewise, bankruptcy also improves the average output to capital ratio, which paves the way for economic recovery. This is in fact a key element of the so-called reproductive cycle (see Gordon *et al.* (1983)). On the other hand, using a Keynesian line of argument bankruptcies may have a destabilising effect on consumption through unemployment and nominal wages. In addition, in situations of widespread over-indebtedness such as during a currency crisis, a strict enforcement of bankruptcy procedures would eliminate firms that would be profitable in a normal environment. Perverse effects may outweigh positive effects and impede recovery. In such a situation, public intervention might be required to steer the economy out of recession.

Bankruptcies can also generate debt default. Debt default may be seen as a way to solve the debt crisis, as it may reduce the Fisher effect – to the extent that investment

[1] See for instance Fisher (1933) or Minsky (1986).

depends negatively on the debt level.[2] Just as over-indebtedness may reduce firms' access to credit in the downturn and worsen the depression, debt default may ease credit constraints and may enable a faster economic rebound. It may well be seen as a reverse Fisher effect. Neo-institutionalism[3] highlights however the misallocation of resources that may result. Sgard (2002), for instance, notes that debt default requires a redefinition of the microeconomic relationships between borrowers and lenders. If debt default is not sanctioned by bankruptcy, moral hazard may spread and worsen bad credit allocation. Andrieu-Lacu (2006) argues that debt default without the sanction of bankruptcy explains the length and protracted nature of the Japanese crisis.

In turn, debt default generates non-performing loans and may affect the credit supply of the banks. As debt defaults constitute a loss for banks, financial fragility may lead to a banking crisis and may trigger additional unstable mechanisms. The extent to which banks can absorb these losses is likely to explain the depth and protracted nature of financial crises. As a matter of fact, the resilience of the banking sector determines the length of time it takes to resolve a crisis. The cost of banking crises in terms of GDP can actually be quite large – the IMF has estimated around 11 per cent for the twin crises in 1998; see IMF (1998).

In order to take into account the impact of bad debt on banks, commercial banks must be modelled more precisely. In the previously discussed models, households financed firms directly in the absence of a commercial bank. We here model a commercial bank, which collects deposits and supplies loans to firms as well as invests in public bonds. This detailed banking sector is necessary to take into account the role of banks' performance on the business cycle. There are different approaches to modelling commercial banks. Most of the literature on commercial banks focuses on the role of reserve requirements in the transmission of monetary policy. The so-called 'lending channel' disregards the role of bank profits and capital. More recently the so-called 'banks' capital channel' has received more attention and evidence has been found that bank performance affects credit supply (see Van den Heuvel (2002)). Banks' balance sheets and profitability are pro-cyclical and add a further channel to the financial accelerator. During periods of expansion, bank health improves and banks tend to take more risks and to extend credit beyond normal limits. Borio *et al.* (1999) show that bank profitability is strongly pro-cyclical and that risks, interest rate spreads and provisions for bad loans are counter-cyclical. Risks are often underestimated in periods of booms and overestimated in periods of recessions and contribute to a rapid growth of credit in

[2] As shown by the vast literature on the financial accelerator in closed and open economies. See for instance Bernanke *et al.* (1996).

[3] Institutional economics is a field of economics which studies the institution at the basis of capitalist economies. Five groups of institutions are usually considered: the monetary regime, the degree of competition, the labour nexus, the organisation of firms and the state/private sector interactions. A central question is what set of institutions produces an economic path which is stable and viable over time. Another central theme is to understand how institutions evolve over time and what are the key factors driving these changes. Institutional economics has been flourishing in France with the Regulation school Aglietta (1976), Boyer (1986) as well as in the US with the work of Epstein and Gintis (1995). Neo-institutionalism usually refers to a neoclassical interpretation of the aforementioned questions; see North (1990).

the upturn and a fast contraction of credit in the downturn. Gambacorta and Mistrulli (2004) show for a panel of Italian banks over the 1990s that excess capital of banks, as well as maturity mismatch, explain credit supply. Specifying the budget constraint of banks enables one to take into account the impact of bank performance on credit supplied. From this perspective, debt defaults weaken the financial situation of the banks and may lead to a credit crunch and banking crises. The financial accelerator in fact produces a boomerang effect on financial institutions.

Public authorities have two main policy options for supporting banks. Monetary authorities can rely on decentralised policies, which consist of organising the support of failing banks by the banking sector. This procedure belongs to a buy-in principle, which requires little public funding. On the other hand, fiscal and monetary authorities may step in directly. The bailout principle implies large public spending, and may differ slightly depending on the type of public intervention: for example, recapitalisation, fund injections, transfers of non-performing loans to a public entity, and partial or total nationalisation. The bailout principle implies a transfer of losses from the banking sector to the public sector, or inversely a transfer of funds from taxpayers to financial institutions. This model also extends public intervention beyond monetary and fiscal policy to account for bailout procedures.

We first present the main modifications undertaken with respect to the preceding chapter. We then present our artificial economy through the stocks and flows tables as in Godley (1999) and Dos Santos and Zezza (2004), before discussing the main equations of our model with a special focus on the strategy for modelling debt default, bankruptcy and commercial banks. The discrepancies between debt default with and without bankruptcy are discussed in a small three dimensional model. We then perform simulations to identify the impact of bankruptcy and debt default as well as bank performance on the business cycle. We briefly discuss loss socialisation and its impact on credit supply. Note that we also show that the main properties of the models presented in the previous chapters are still at work, especially with respect to the wage-price dynamics, debt deflation as well as with respect to monetary and fiscal policies.

9.1 Debt targeting, debt default and bankruptcy

In this section we provide a description of how the general model of the preceding chapter may be further extended and modified in order to allow for further stabilising or destabilising feedbacks caused by the simultaneous occurrence of high debt and deflation, concerning in particular debt default, the bankruptcy rate of firms and the resilience of the banking system.

The main changes undertaken in this chapter are threefold. First, the equations for capital and debt accumulation are modified to take into account the rate of bankruptcy and debt default. Second, the model considers the case of a commercial bank, which plays the role of a financial intermediary between lenders and borrowers. In this chapter, banks supply credit as in the endogenous theory of money. Modelling a commercial bank requires us to make a choice between the exogenous and the endogenous theories of money, as the causality between deposits and credits differs across these two theories. Third, the investment function of firms is slightly modified to address the question of credit rationing, which constitutes the main transmission channel between bank performance and the real economy. Credit supply depends positively on both the net wealth of borrowers as well as the profitability of banks.

To this end we first reformulate the equation for debt and capital accumulation of Section 8.3 as follows:

1. Firms: Actual Debt and Actual Capital Stock Growth

$$\dot{\Lambda}_f = p_y(I - \delta_k K) - r^a p_y K - \varphi_d(r)\Lambda_f, \quad (\varphi_d'(r) < 0), \tag{9.1}$$

$$\hat{K} = g_k - \delta_k - \varphi_b(r), \quad (\varphi_b'(r) < 0). \tag{9.2}$$

The equations (8.8) and (8.9) for the dynamics of firm debt and capital accumulation are modified to reflect the impact of bankruptcy. Thus in equations (9.1) and (9.2) the default rate φ_d as well as the bankruptcy rate φ_b enter negatively the equations for firm debt and capital accumulation respectively. It is here assumed that they both depend negatively on firm profitability r. The chapter will discuss explicitly the case in which the rates of debt default and bankruptcy differ. Assuming identical rates of bankruptcy and debt default in Equations (9.1) and (9.2) leaves the debt to capital ratio of firms unaffected, implying no feedback effects from the debt dynamic to the real economy. Both rates differ because of a composition effect, which arises as firms that go bankrupt have zero net wealth. The rate of debt default is then greater than the rate of bankruptcy, which improves the net wealth of firms at the macroeconomic level.

Defaults here reduce the debt level of firms in their dependence on the sector of commercial banks (since these firms stop paying interest) and therefore happen as if there were a debt-reducing gift from these banks to firms. The chapter also discusses the case in which debt default does not result from bankruptcy. Past episodes of financial crisis show that bankruptcy procedures are not necessarily enforced strictly. In Japan for instance (see the following chapter), debt default was massive while bankruptcy was relatively rather limited.

The second set of changes concerns commercial banks. In the preceding chapter, households financed firms directly in the absence of financial intermediation. The financial system now consists of a commercial bank that makes profits and has a non-zero net wealth. Debt default affects bank balance sheets and income statements in two ways. First, default reduces the interest payments received every period from borrowers by reducing the value of outstanding loans. Second, debt default is a loss that must be reported by banks and that enters banks' net wealth negatively.

Lastly in equation (9.3) we reformulate the investment function of firms given by (8.7) to address the case of credit rationing. The investment function is augmented by two elements: firms' debt to capital ratio λ_f and banks' profitability r_{nb}. The former captures the idea that credit supply is made on the basis of borrower net wealth as in the financial accelerator literature. Any improvement of the debt to capital ratio of firms loosens credit rationing and fosters investment. On the one hand, this implies a negative feedback of debt on its rate of change. On the other hand, increasing real debt – caused by a falling price level – will reduce investment behaviour and lead via goods demand to further (destabilising) downward pressure on the output price level of firms. The latter captures the idea that credit supply is made on the basis of bank profitability. Credit supply increases with bank performance and pushes investment upward. This transmission channel is potentially destabilising as new loans mechanically improve bank profits up to the point where over-indebtedness produces debt default. The investment function can be seen here as a reduced form equation reflecting firms' heterogeneity with respect to credit rationing as in Duménil and Lévy (1999).

2. Firms: Investment Behaviour

$$g_k = \alpha_r^k(\cdot) + \alpha_i^k(\cdot) + \alpha_u^k(\cdot) - \alpha_\lambda^k(\lambda_f - \lambda_{f0}) + \alpha_{irb}(r_{nb} - r_{nb0}) + \gamma + \delta_k. \quad (9.3)$$

In this chapter we will consider in more detail situations where the direct debt relationship between firms and pure asset holders is replaced by commercial bank intermediation. We will then use lower dimensional dynamical models to shed more light on the role of firm bankruptcy and indebtedness for the stability of the macroeconomy.

9.2 Tabular representations of stocks and flows

Tables 9.1 and 9.2 give a broad view of the economic system considered in this chapter. Table 9.1 displays the balance sheets of the different agents and Table 9.2 displays their income and expenditure.

Our economy is composed of six kinds of agents: workers, asset holders or rentiers, firms, commercial banks, a central bank and a government. With the exception of workers, other agents have assets and/or liabilities. The assets of firms consist of the stock of capital (machines, buildings) resulting from past investments and the stock of inventories. Firms hold no financial assets but have financial liabilities in the form of credit Λ.[4] Banks make use of deposits from households D_c to meet reserves requirements R, to supply credit Λ and to hold short-term public bonds B_b^s, the residual. The latter quantity plays the role of a buffer and is such that banks satisfy their budget constraints. Reserves are held at the central bank, which also creates money, B_{cb}^s through open market operations. Money is seen here as high-powered money. It only includes cash held by households H_c and reserves.[5] The central bank accommodates all demand for money in line with the usual post-Keynesian tradition of endogenous money. Open market operations consist in buying or selling short-term government bonds B^s issued by the government to finance its deficit. Another source of financing is available to the government in the form of long-term bonds $p_b B^l$. Eventually, rentiers are the ultimate lenders to all other agents. They have only financial assets and no liabilities. They hold cash H_c, deposits D_c, as well as short- and long-term bonds B_c^s and $p_b B^l$.

[4] Equities are ignored at this stage since they make the portfolio much more complicated.

[5] Deposits and short-term bonds are not included in this restrictive definition of money but would fit a broader definition as they are very liquid at near zero cost.

Table 9.1. *Balance sheets*

	Rentiers	Firms	Banks	CB	Government	Total
Capital		$+pK$				$+pK$
Inventories		$+p$N				$+p$N
Cash	$+H_c$			$-H_c$		0
Deposits	$+D_c$		$-D_c$			0
Reserves			$+R$	$-R$		0
Loans		$-\Lambda$	$+\Lambda$			0
ST bonds	$+B_c^s$		$+B_b^s$	$+B_{cb}^s$	$-B^s$	0
LT bonds	$+p_b B^l$				$-p_b B^l$	0
Total	W_c	W_f	W_b	0	W_g	$+p(K+\text{N})$

Table 9.2. *Flows of funds*

	Workers	Rentiers	Firms	Banks	CB	Gvt	Total
Consumption	$-pC$		$+pC$				0
Investment			$+pI$				$+pI$
Gvt spending			$+pG$			$-pG$	0
Wages	$+wL^d$		$-wL^d$				0
Taxes	$-pT_w$	$-pT_c$	$-pT_f$			$+pT$	0
Inventory accumulation			$+p\dot{N}$				$+p\dot{N}$
Loan interest			$-i\Lambda$	$+i\Lambda$			0
ST bond interest		$+iB_c^s$		$+iB_b^s$	$+iB_{cb}^s$	$-iB^s$	0
LT bond interest		$+B^l$				$-B^l$	0
Bank transfers		$+\alpha_{rb}r_b$		$-\alpha_{rb}r_b$			0
CB transfers					$-iB_{cb}^s$	$+iB_{cb}^s$	0
Total	0	S_c	S_f	S_b	0	S_g	S_T

Concerning income flows, firms pay wages wL^d to workers and interest rate $i\Lambda$ to banks. They sell goods that are consumed by workers pC and the government pG. The demand for investment goods pI is made by firms to themselves as there is no distinction between firms in charge of producing investment and consumption goods. They also finance inventories by use of profits rather than debt. They are eventually taxed at a rate τ_f. Workers receive wages and consume their entire income net of taxes pT_w. Banks receive interest payments on credit and short-term bonds $i\Lambda + iB_b^s$ while deposits are not remunerated. Banks distribute part of their profits to asset holders. It is assumed that rentiers own commercial banks but that they are not traded on the stock market. The share of non-distributed profits increases banks' own funds. To ensure that the central bank's net wealth is zero, its profits are transferred to fiscal authorities.[6] Government

[6] Introducing the central banks' own funds is left for future research.

income is also composed of taxes raised on households and firms. Spending is made up of demand for goods pG to firms and of interest on public debt $iB^s + B^l$. Eventually, asset holders also receive interest payments on public bonds $iB^s_c + B^l$, and banks' income $i\Lambda + iB^s_b$.

9.3 Commercial banks and pro-cyclical credit supply

This section presents the equations of the model for each type of agent.

9.3.1 Firms

The first block of equations for firms is similar to the equations of the model of Section 5.4.3. Firms still have a fixed proportion production function as in Chapter 5. Potential output Y^p is a certain proportion y^p of the stock of capital K as a constant production function is assumed. Labour demand L^d grows together with the level of production. The rate of employment e is the ratio of people employed over the active labour population, and u (the rate of capacity utilisation) is simply the ratio of actual production over potential production.

3. Firms

$$Y^p = y^p K, \tag{9.4}$$

$$L^d = Y/x, \tag{9.5}$$

$$e = L^d/L, \tag{9.6}$$

$$u = Y/Y^p, \tag{9.7}$$

$$\dot{Y}^e = \beta_{ye}(C + I + G - Y^e) + nY^e, \tag{9.8}$$

$$\mathcal{I} = \beta_n(N^d - N) + nN^d, \tag{9.9}$$

$$Y = Y^e + \mathcal{I}, \tag{9.10}$$

$$N^d = \beta_{nd} Y^e, \tag{9.11}$$

$$\dot{N} = Y - Y^d, \tag{9.12}$$

$$r = (pY - wL^d - \delta_k pK - i\Lambda)/(pK), \tag{9.13}$$

$$Y^d = pC + pI + pG. \tag{9.14}$$

The stock-flow principle of our model also requires the specification of inventories explicitly. There are implicit inventories as the discrepancy between production and demand is met either by increasing or decreasing inventories. Disequilibrium on the goods market requires that we distinguish output from aggregate demand and expected production. Firms produce Y, which is the sum of expected production Y^e and expected inventories $\mathcal{I}$. On the basis of aggregate demand Y^d, firms form expectations regarding the level of production. Similarly, firms have a desired stock of inventories N^d which is proportional to expected output. Expected inventories $\mathcal{I}$ adjust to the discrepancy between desired and actual inventories. The actual change in inventories $\dot{N}$ is simply the difference between output and aggregate demand. The profit rate r is the difference between the revenue from selling goods produced and the different costs that firms face (mainly wages, depreciation and interest payments). Aggregate demand consists of consumption, investment and public expenditure.

There are three new elements in the block of equations of firms: bankruptcy of firms, debt default of firms and credit rationing.

$$\varphi_b = \beta_{\varphi_b}(\bar{r} - r) + \delta_{\varphi}, \tag{9.15}$$

$$\hat{K} = I/K - \delta_k - \varphi_b, \tag{9.16}$$

$$\dot{\Lambda} = p(I - \delta_k K) - (1 - \tau_f) r_{\ell} p K + (Y - Y^d) - \varphi_d \Lambda, \tag{9.17}$$

$$\varphi_d = \varphi_b / \lambda, \tag{9.18}$$

$$\lambda = \Lambda / pK, \tag{9.19}$$

$$I/K = \alpha_{iu}(u - \bar{u}) + \alpha_{i\lambda}(\lambda_0 - \lambda) + \alpha_{ir}(r - r_0) + \alpha_{irb}(r_{nb} - r_{nb0}) + n + \delta. \tag{9.20}$$

There are two ways to model firm bankruptcy, and these are not equivalent in terms of the model properties and in terms of wealth transfers. On the one hand, firms might be homogeneous and the rate of bankruptcy is the same as the rate of default. On the other hand, firms might be heterogeneous. Bankrupt firms are firms that have zero net wealth. In this case, the rate of default is greater than the rate of bankruptcy.

Assuming that firms are homogeneous and that they have a debt to capital ratio of 50 per cent, which also entails a net wealth to capital ratio of 50 per cent. A 40 per cent rate of bankruptcy entails a 40 per cent rate of default and a 40 per cent rate of wealth loss. In such a case, the debt and net wealth to capital ratio is constant and equal to $\frac{1}{2}$. Bankruptcy leaves the debt to capital ratio unaffected and therefore does not affect the Fisher effect. What may change the properties of the model is the fact that the output to capital ratio and the labour to capital ratio both rise. The former increases the rate of utilisation of the productive capacity u. It might have a positive effect on investment and real wages. It may also have a negative effect on employment, which may reduce real wages and aggregate demand.

The assumption that the firms are heterogeneous leads to slightly different results. It may in fact be more realistic to assume that firms that go bankrupt are firms that have a net zero wealth $K_2 = \Lambda_2$ (see Figure 9.1). The rate of bankruptcy and default are now different and bankruptcy modifies the debt to capital ratio. The rate of bankruptcy is $\varphi_b = K_2/(K_1 + K_2)$. The rate of default is $\varphi_d = \Lambda_2/\Lambda = K_2/\Lambda > \varphi_b$. Put differently, $\varphi_d = \frac{K_2}{K}\frac{K}{\Lambda} = \frac{\varphi_b}{\lambda}$.[7] In terms of wealth transfers, bankruptcy reduces the stock of capital while debt default reduces the stock of borrower liabilities. The net effect is an increase of the net wealth to capital ratio. Bankruptcy is here associated with an

[7] Note that $K = K_1 + K_2$, $\Lambda = \Lambda_1 + \Lambda_2$ and $\lambda = \Lambda/K$.

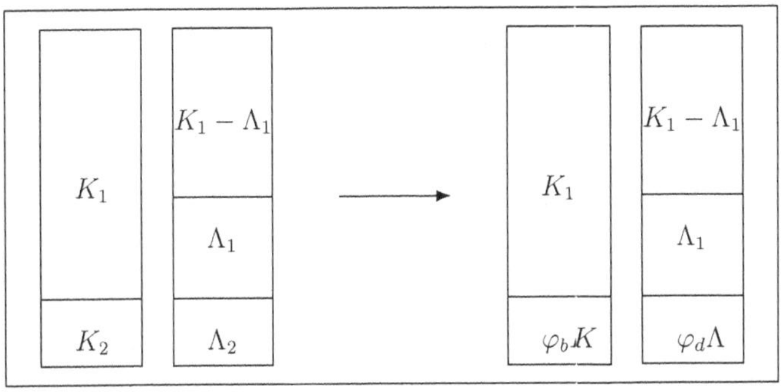

Figure 9.1 Bankruptcy – heterogenous firms

increase in borrowers' aggregated wealth, and with a transfer of losses to lenders. This specification integrates a form of balance sheet composition effect.

Formalising bankruptcies modifies the block of equations of firms. The main difference concerns the equation for the capital stock and debt change. Bankruptcy is expressed as a negative function of the difference between the steady state and current profit rate $(\bar{r} - r)$. In a downturn, firms go bankrupt only when profits are very low. It is here assumed that closing physical assets are not bought out by existing firms. There is therefore no secondary market for the stock of capital. Physical assets are destroyed at no cost. The bankruptcy function could include a much greater variety of elements, such as the output capacity or the level of indebtedness. We choose to keep the model as simple as possible in order to ease the analysis of the feedback channels. At the equilibrium, the rate of bankruptcy is constant at a rate δ_φ. Given that investment is already a function of profits, these enter twice into the equation of the capital stock and with the same sign. It might therefore be more meaningful to replace the investment and the bankruptcy function by only one equation that would deal with a form of net investment function. Nevertheless, investment and bankruptcy might not be exactly of the same nature, and bankruptcy might not be equivalent to a negative investment. If negative investment or bankruptcy reduces the stock of capital, bankruptcy does not appear directly in the aggregate demand, while investment does. In other words, reducing investment or increasing bankruptcy do not have the same effect on aggregate demand Y^d. The stock of fixed capital grows with investment I and decreases with depreciation δ and bankruptcy φ_b. Bankruptcy affects the economy by reducing the stock of capital. The creative destruction mechanism is captured by the increasing output to capital ratio, while the Keynesian effect is captured by the higher labour to capital ratio.

The rate of debt default φ_d reduces the stock of existing debt Λ. It is equal to the rate of bankruptcy divided by the debt to capital ratio. Given that the rate of debt default is larger than the rate of bankruptcy, firms' net wealth increases with bankruptcy. Debt default is likely to be stabilising through two main mechanisms represented in Figure 9.2. By reducing the stock of debt, firms restore their profitability as debt service decreases.

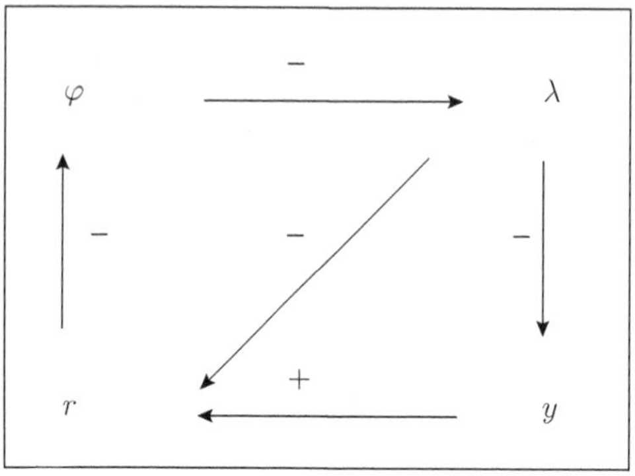

Figure 9.2 Stabilising debt default – intensive form

Lower debt is also likely to reduce the Fisher effect and to restore investment. Default has an opposite effect to debt deflation – it alleviates the debt burden while the Fisher effect magnifies the debt burden. The level of debt depends on retained profits on the one hand and on investment on the other hand. It also decreases with bankruptcy as it generates debt default. As explained previously, to the extent that bankrupt firms have zero net wealth, the rate of default is larger than the rate of bankruptcy. The debt to capital ratio therefore decreases with bankruptcy. In addition, inventories affect the quantity of external funds. As they are financed by profits, change in inventories reduces internal funds by the quantity $Y - Y^d$.

It is necessary to introduce some type of credit rationing into the model if the impact of bank performance on firms' investment is taken into account. Thus we write

$$I^d/K = I^d(u, r),$$
$$I^r/K = I^r(r, \dot{\lambda}^s).$$

Credit rationing is here introduced in a very simple way. The investment function I displayed in this chapter is seen as a reduced form equation for desired investment I^d and restricted investment I^r. Firms might not be able to invest this quantity as they might be rationed by financial institutions. In the case of rationing, investment I^r is equal to internal plus external funds: the quantity of debt supplied by banks and firms' retained earnings $I^r = \dot{\Lambda}^s + (1 - \tau_f)rpK$. Realised investment is therefore the minimum between firms' desired investment and restricted investment $I = min(I^d, I^r)$. When such a *min* function is specified it is no longer possible to derive the stability conditions. We therefore make use of a reduced form equation for investment I, similar to Duménil and Lévy (1999). This equation can be interpreted as reflecting the heterogeneity of firms. The economy is made up of firms which are not rationed and firms which are rationed. It gathers the various elements of desired and restricted investment. Investment

I is still a basic function that includes a Harrodian accelerator u and the profit rate rpK. Credit rationing is also a function of the basic financial accelerator λ, but is also augmented by variable for banks. Note that λ is similar to the net wealth to capital ratio:

$$\left[\frac{pK-\Lambda}{pK} - \left(\frac{pK-\Lambda}{pK}\right)_0\right] = \left[\left(\frac{\Lambda}{pK}\right)_0 - \frac{\Lambda}{pK}\right].$$

Restricted investment is also a positive function of bank profitability net of default losses with a sensitivity α_{irb}. The latter parameter therefore captures the sensitivity of credit supply to bank performance. At the steady state, investment grows at a constant rate equal to the growth rate of the population n and the rate of depreciation of the capital stock δ.

9.3.2 Commercial banks: credit rationing and money creation

This subsection presents a detailed banking sector that tries to overcome some of the usual shortcomings related to the formalisation of financial institutions. Although post-Keynesian theories usually give a central role to financial intermediaries, banks' assets and liabilities are usually not modelled. Here we shall focus in particular on the link between bank performance and credit supply.

The balance sheet of banks is displayed in Table 9.3[8] and is composed as follows. Banks use deposits D_c to grant loans Λ. Part of the deposits, R, must be held as reserves at the central bank for prudential requirements. They are a fixed proportion θ of deposits. Eventually, banks adjust their budget constraint by selling or buying government bonds $B_b^s = D_c + OF - \Lambda - R$. In case deposits are not large enough to finance reserves and loans, banks sell public bonds. There are therefore no idle resources. Financial institutions make the best use of existing resources and invest excess reserves in financial assets. Holding of public bonds acts as a buffer that adjusts to changes in deposits, loans and reserves. In the absence of central bank advances, banks adapt their asset structure to finance investment. As banks' assets are greater than liabilities and as profits are positive, banks have a positive net wealth, called own funds (OF). Own funds increase with banks' profits and decrease with debt default. Debt default must appear twice in the balance sheet. It reduces the value of the existing stock of debt. It also appears as a loss in bank own funds. The stock of debt cannot be greater than the stock of deposits plus own funds minus compulsory reserves as banks have no advances from the central bank $\Lambda \leq D_c + OF - R$. Eventually, profits are made out of interest on loans and public bonds. Both interest rates are the same and deposits are not remunerated for simplicity. This type of banking system behaviour is close to the behaviour of North American banks, and it may be expressed as the set of equations

[8] This table is from Lavoie and Godley (2004).

Table 9.3. *The balance sheet of banks: assets adjustments*

Assets		Liabilities
Λ		D_c
R		OF
B_b		
	Assets - Liabilities = 0	

Table 9.4. *Banks' balance sheets: CB advances*

Assets		Liabilities
Λ		D_c
R		A
		OF
	Assets - Liabilities = 0	

4. Commercial Banks

$$\dot{R} = \theta \dot{D}_c, \tag{9.21}$$

$$\dot{B}_b^s = \dot{D}_c + \dot{OF} - \dot{\Lambda} - \dot{R}, \tag{9.22}$$

$$r_b p K = i\Lambda + iB_b^s, \tag{9.23}$$

$$\dot{OF} = (1 - \alpha_{rb}) r_b p K - \varphi_d \Lambda. \tag{9.24}$$

An alternative, which takes into account the European banking system would specify central bank advances. Instead of adjusting their assets structure to finance investment, banks would rely on central bank advances, which are defined as $A = \Lambda + R - D_c - OF$ (see Table 9.4).[9] To better understand this specification, it is useful to make an analogy with firms. In the case of the central bank's advances, it is straightforward. The change in bank assets results from bank investment. Investment has an active component in the form of credit supply, and a passive component in the form of compulsory reserves. Banks then raise external funds to meet the need for external finance.

The presentation of financial intermediaries given here is in line with what the reader will find in Lavoie and Godley (2004).

The supply of credit is a function of borrowers' characteristics as specified in the base line model. The quantity of loan supplied depends on firms' net wealth. A cumulative loop takes place, as easing credit supply increases capital accumulation, which improves firms' net wealth in return, as illustrated in Figure 9.3. In addition, we express credit rationing with respect to bank performance as shown in equations (9.25) and (9.26) below.

[9] This table is also from Lavoie and Godley (2004).

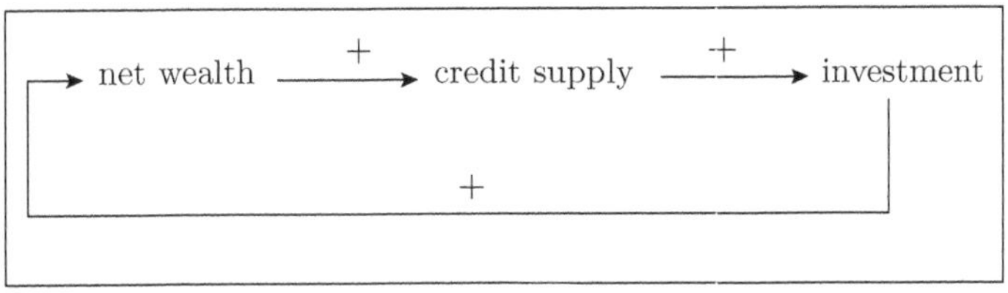

Figure 9.3 Credit rationing

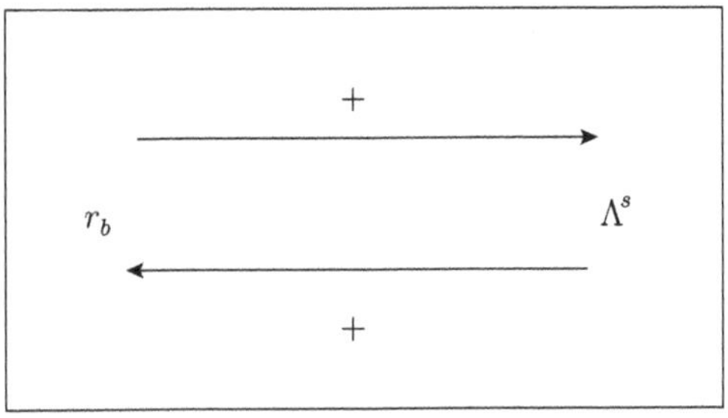

Figure 9.4 Banks' profitability and credit supply

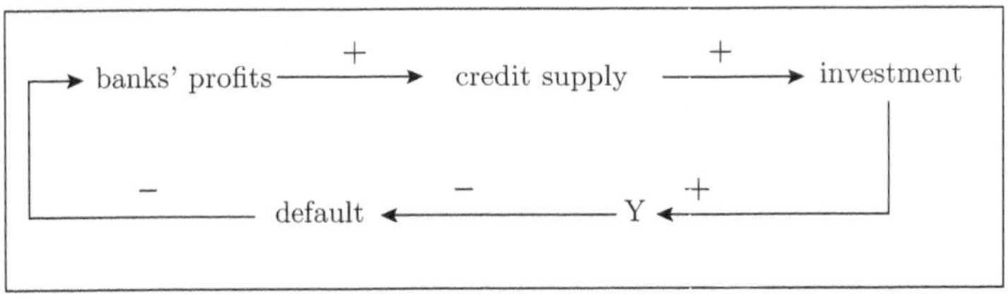

Figure 9.5 Debt default and banks' profits

$$\dot{\Lambda}^s = \Lambda^s(W_f, r_{nb}) \tag{9.25}$$

$$r_{nb} = i_\lambda \Lambda + i B_b - \varphi_d \Lambda \tag{9.26}$$

We argue that banks increase credit when their profitability r_b increases. When bank profits increase, banks are more willing to expand their assets further. In addition, banks may be less selective with respect to borrowers' ability to serve debt commitments (Figure 9.4). Banks' income is in fact strongly pro-cyclical and amplifies the financial accelerator, as shown by Borio *et al.* (1999). Another pro-cyclical mechanism goes through the dynamics of debt default. Debt defaults are losses for banks. Debt defaults reduce the value of banks' assets and their profits. As debt defaults decline in the upturn, firms' profitability increases further and stimulates credit supply. On the contrary, large scale debt defaults in the downturn depress credit supply further, Figure 9.5 illustrates this process.

9.3.3 *Asset holders: Blanchard asset market dynamics*

We improve the behavioural equations of asset holders by specifying a Tobin type portfolio function to allocate asset holders' savings between the different assets. They allocate their savings to three kinds of financial assets: short-term bonds B_c^s, long-term bonds $p_b B^l$ and money M_c, which includes deposits D_c and cash H_c. Their income Y^c is made up of interest on public short-term bonds, iB_c^s, and on long-term bonds, B^l, as well as a share of banks' income $\alpha_{rb}(i\Lambda + iB_b^s)$ to ensure stock-flow consistency. Asset holders are taxed at a rate τ_c and do not consume their income.

The choice between short- and long-term bonds B_c^s, B^l follows a Tobin like portfolio decision while money is a function of asset holder wealth.[10] Bonds are held in a certain proportion of the agent's wealth[11] and this proportion varies with respect to the differential rate of return between the different assets.[12] The return on short-term bonds is the interest rate i set by the central bank, whereas the rate of return on long-term bonds is the inverse of their price $1/p_l$. The long-term bonds considered here yield a fixed income of one money unit (e.g. euro, dollar) per bond. The interest rate or the return on long-term bonds is given by the sum paid as interest B^l over the nominal value of bonds $p_b B^l$. The equations for asset holders are:

5. Asset Holders

$$S_c^n = \dot{B}_c^s + p_b \dot{B}^l + \dot{H}_c + \dot{D}_c, \tag{9.27}$$

$$Y_c^n = (1 - \tau_c)(r_b pK + iB_c^s + B^l), \tag{9.28}$$

$$S_c^n = Y_c^n, \tag{9.29}$$

$$B^l = f_l(i, r_b^e) W_c^n / p_b, \tag{9.30}$$

$$B_c^s = f_b(i, r_b^e) W_c^n, \tag{9.31}$$

$$W_c^n = W_c - M_c = B_c^s + p_b B^l, \tag{9.32}$$

$$r_b^e = 1/p_b, \tag{9.33}$$

$$M_c^d = \alpha_m (p_b B^l + B_c^s), \tag{9.34}$$

$$\dot{M}_c = \beta_{mc}(M_c^d - M_c) + (n + \bar{\pi}) M_c, \tag{9.35}$$

$$\dot{H}_c = c\dot{M}_c, \tag{9.36}$$

$$\dot{D}_c = (1 - c)\dot{M}_c. \tag{9.37}$$

The bond demand functions satisfy $f_l + f_b = 1$. Assets demands follow the gross substitution principle, which implies that $\partial f_b/\partial i > 0$, $\partial f_b/\partial r_b^e < 0$, $\partial f_l/\partial i < 0$ and $\partial f_l/\partial r_b^e > 0$. The bond price is the clearing variable that ensures the equilibrium of financial markets. If the interest rate is set by the central bank and does not

[10] Net of money.
[11] Net of money.
[12] Taxes are assumed to be lump sum such that they do not affect rentiers' portfolio allocation.

clear the short-term bond market, it is shown that flows consistency holds and ensures equilibrium in the short-term bond market.

In addition to equities and public bonds, rentiers' wealth is composed by money M_c. Money demand is excluded from the portfolio decision for simplicity as the assumption of endogenous money does not allow the interest rate to clear the market for short-term bonds. Asset holders have a desired quantity of money holdings M_c^d that is expressed as a proportion of their wealth net of money. The effective change in money demand $\dot{M}_c$ adjusts towards this ratio. The expression for money demand is similar to the Metzler inventory formulation (see Chiarella *et al.* (2005) for instance). Money is held in two forms. In order to have cash and deposits in the model, it is assumed that a proportion c of M_c is held as cash H_c and a proportion $(1 - c)$ is held as deposits in banks in line with the basic IS–LM model without a portfolio (Sargent, 1987). Even if the portfolio formulation does not include all assets, the key point is that there is a portfolio allocation between one risky and one safe asset.

9.3.4 Public sector

The public sector gathers both fiscal authorities and a central bank.

<u>6. Fiscal Authorities</u>

$$pT_w = \tau_w w L^d, \tag{9.38}$$

$$pT_c = \tau_c Y_c^n, \tag{9.39}$$

$$pT_f = \tau_f r p K, \tag{9.40}$$

$$pG = \psi p K, \tag{9.41}$$

$$\begin{aligned}\dot{\psi} &= \psi\big(- \beta_{gd}(B^s + p_b B^l - (B_0^s + p_{b0} B_0^l)) \\ &\quad - \beta_{ge}(e - \bar{e}) - \beta_{gg}(\psi - \psi_0)\big),\end{aligned} \tag{9.42}$$

$$\begin{aligned}\dot{B}_{cb}^s + \dot{B}^s &= \alpha_b\big(pG + iB^s + B^l - pT_c - pT_w - pT_f\big), \\ &\quad \text{with } \dot{B}^s = \dot{B}_c^s + \dot{B}_b^s,\end{aligned} \tag{9.43}$$

$$p_b \dot{B}^l = (1 - \alpha_b)\big(pG + iB^s + B^l - pT_c - pT_w - pT_f\big). \tag{9.44}$$

The government taxes profits, financial and labour incomes and consumes goods in a proportion ψ of the capital stock. This proportion changes with respect to two elements: the level of public debt in line with some kind of Maastricht criteria and the level of employment in a very Keynesian fashion. The budget deficit is financed by either short- or long-term bonds in the proportions α_b and $(1 - \alpha_b)$ respectively. The quantity B^s is now the quantity of short-term bonds available to the public (household and banks). It is the fraction of the deficit financed by short-term bonds minus bonds bought by the central bank through open market operations $\dot{B}^s = \alpha_b(pG + iB^s + B^l - pT_c - pT_w - pT_f) - \dot{B}_{cb}^s$. It is now possible to define bonds held by asset holders as the difference between bonds available to the public minus bonds held by banks $B_c^s = B^s - B_b^s$.

7. Monetary Authorities: Endogenous Money and the Taylor Rule

$$\dot{i} = \alpha_i(i^* - i), \tag{9.45}$$

$$i^* = (i_0 - \bar{\pi}) + \hat{p} + \gamma_{ip}(\hat{p} - \bar{\pi}) + \gamma_{iu}(u - \bar{u}), \tag{9.46}$$

$$\dot{B}_{cb}^s = \dot{H}_c + \dot{R} = \mu \dot{M}_c \text{ with } \mu = \theta(1 - c) + c. \tag{9.47}$$

The assumption of endogenous money is a key pillar of the post-Keynesian research agenda and is seen as one of the arguments against orthodox approaches (Godley, 1999).[13] Surprisingly, post-Keynesian models that explicitly formulate endogenous money rarely specify the role of the central bank or how monetary policy is conducted (Godley, 1999; Tadeu Lima and Meirelles, 2003, for instance), even if the use of a Taylor rule is an implicit recognition of endogenous money. In fact, the supply of money must adjust to the demand of money as the interest rate is fixed. In our case, monetary authorities steer the interest rate towards a target $\alpha_i(i^* - i)$ that depends on the long-term interest rate and on two measures of the business cycle: deviations from the output gap $\gamma_{iu}(u - \bar{u})$ and from the long-term inflation rate $\gamma_{ip}(\hat{p} - \bar{\pi})$ (Taylor, 1993). In this framework, the interest rate policy is strongly counter-cyclical as interest rates are raised when output and inflation are higher than their long-term value, as shown schematically in Figure 9.6.

In an endogenous money framework (Deleplace and Nell, 1996), money creation results from the supply of loans by commercial banks. Meanwhile in the presence of a central bank, their interaction and the path of money creation is more difficult to trace. It must be shown that the demand for high-powered money by economic agents is accommodated by the central bank and equals money injected through open market operations. On the one hand, loan supply generates investments by firms and the distribution of bank profits to asset holders. It generates a demand for high-powered money, as part of asset holders' income is held as cash ($\dot{H}_c$) and part of asset holders' deposits are held as reserves ($\theta(1 - c)\dot{M}_c$) by banks at the central bank. On the other hand, the demand for short-term bonds by private agents changes as asset holders allocate their new revenue through the portfolio and as banks' holdings of bonds are adjusted to finance new credit. In order to fix the interest rate through the Taylor rule, given a change in bond demand, the central bank must implement open market operations.[14] The quantity of bonds bought by the central bank is equal to the total

[13] According to Godley, p.394 "It is no exaggeration to say that the endogenous money view is potentially lethal not merely to monetarism, which has now been discredited, but to the neoclassical paradigm itself."

[14] In the case where banks rely on central banks' advances to finance credit operations, the role of the central bank in the process of money creation is more easily identified. Banks demand advances to finance the share of loans that is not covered by new deposits. The central bank acts as the bank of commercial banks and prints money for that purpose. It leads us to one of the points of disagreement about endogenous money. Some who argue in favour of a weak hypothesis of endogenous money consider that the central bank can still influence

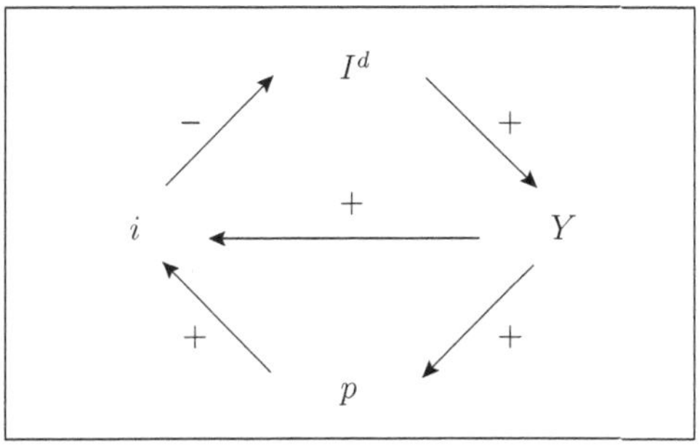

Figure 9.6 Taylor rule

demand of cash $\dot{H}_c + \dot{R}$ as given in equation (9.47). It follows that the amount of high-powered money in the economy is smaller than the amount of money in the broad sense $c\dot{M}_c + \theta(1-c)\dot{M}_c < \dot{M}$, which gives us the definition of the money multiplier $\mu = \theta(1-c) + c$.

9.3.5 Workers

Workers' households receive labour income wL^d that is a function of nominal wage and labour demand from which taxes must be subtracted. Workers consume all their income to underline that savings out of wages are small and relatively lower than savings out of profits.[15] The Kaldor neo Pasinetti theorem provides a theoretical rationale for this assumption (Kaldor, 1966) that has strong empirical support (Marglin, 1984). The active labour population grows at a constant rate n. These assumptions lead to the following equations:

8. Wage-price Interaction: the Rose Effect

$$pC = (1-\tau_w)wL^d, \tag{9.48}$$

$$S_w^n = 0, \tag{9.49}$$

$$\hat{L} = n. \tag{9.50}$$

The so-called Rose effect comes from the wage-price interaction formulated by Rose (1967) and used by Chiarella *et al.* (2003a) to model a Goodwinian conflict over income distribution. In this formulation, wages and prices are adjusting to some measures of labour and goods market disequilibrium. Two Phillips curves (PCs) are specified instead of the usual single one by expressing price changes as a function of the goods market disequilibrium. In this framework, inflation not only results from wage inflation but also from the ability of firms to increase or decrease prices. In other words, the

money creation to some degree by restricting the quantity of money advances. Contrarily, those advocating a strong assumption of endogenous money consider that in such a case, commercial banks can still adjust the structure of their financial assets or rely on financial innovations (Palley, 2002).

15 Asset holders' saving rate equals 1.

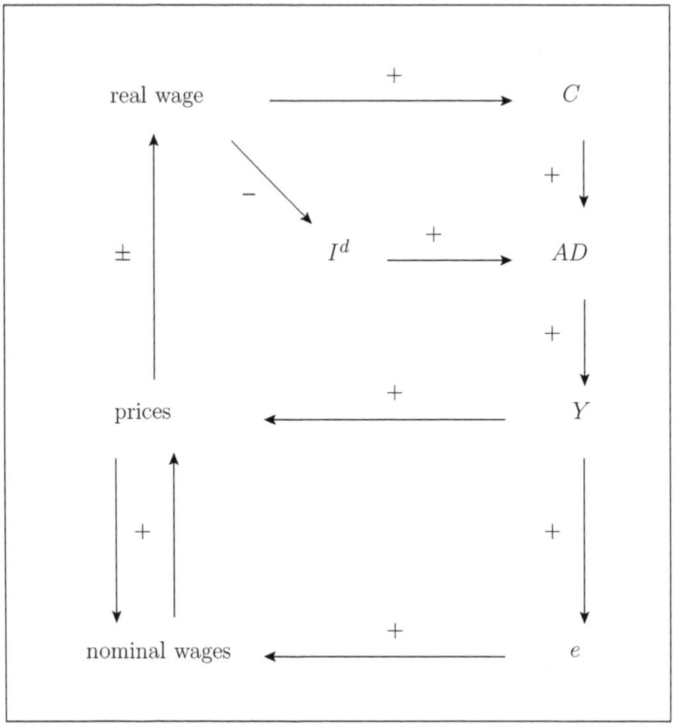

Figure 9.7 Rose effect

markup on wage cost is not fixed. In this respect, it shares some similarities with the conflict approach to inflation by Rowthorn (1977). Thus prices and nominal wages adjust according to

$$\hat{p} = \beta_p(u - \bar{u}) + \kappa_p\hat{w} + (1 - \kappa_p)\bar{\pi}, \tag{9.51}$$

$$\hat{w} = \beta_w(e - \bar{e}) + \kappa_w\hat{p} + (1 - \kappa_w)\bar{\pi}. \tag{9.52}$$

Nominal wages adjust to some measure of the disequilibrium on labour market $\beta_w(e-\bar{e})$ to which is added a cost-push element linked to changes in inflation $\kappa_w\hat{p}$. Prices react to deviation of the rate of capacity utilisation of the capital stock from its steady state value $\beta_p(u - \bar{u})$. And a cost-push element linked to variations of the nominal wage is also added $\kappa_p\hat{w}$. We adopt here a very simple formulation of the wage-price spiral by considering constant expectations $\bar{\pi}$ about price inflation instead of the usual backward and/or forward expectations that we considered in Chapter 6.

Four possible scenarios may arise and these are displayed in Figure 9.7. The relative speeds of adjustment of nominal wages and prices determine the sign of real wage change. Taking for instance the case of a positive shock on output, a faster speed of adjustment of prices entails a reduction of real wage. The overall effect of the real wage adjustment depends on the sensitivity of aggregate demand on the real wage

(Bhaduri and Marglin, 1990).[16] In a wage-led economy, aggregate demand lowers and the disequilibrium on the output market is counterbalanced. Inversely, in a profit-led economy, aggregate demand increases and excess demand worsens. The other two cases take place when nominal wages are more flexible than prices. The positive shock on output raises the real wage. These speeds of adjustment are destabilising in a wage-led economy and stabilising in a profit-led economy.

9.4 Reduced form equations and steady state

The reduced form equations give rise to an eleven-dimensional system of differential equations with respect to real wage, labour population, expected output, inventories, interest rate, expected capital gains, short- and long-term bonds, public spending, money and debt. Thus we write[17]

$$\begin{aligned}
\dot{\omega} &= \omega\kappa\big((1-\kappa_p)\beta_w(e-\bar{e}) + (\kappa_w - 1)\beta_p(u-\bar{u})\big),\\
\dot{l} &= l\big(n - \delta_\varphi - (g_k - \delta_k - \varphi_b)\big),\\
\dot{y}_e &= \beta_{ye}(y^d - y_e) + (n - \delta_\varphi + \delta_k - g_k + \varphi_b)y_e,\\
\dot{i} &= \beta_{ii}(i_0 - i) + \beta_{ip}(\hat{p} - \bar{\pi}) + \beta_{iu}(u - \bar{u}),\\
\dot{b}^s &= \alpha_g(\psi + ib^s + b^l - t_c - t_w - t_f) - \mu\dot{m}_c - (\hat{p} + g_k - \delta_k - \varphi_b)b^s,\\
\dot{b}^l &= (1-\alpha_g)(\psi + ib^s + b^l - t_c - t_w - t_f)/p_b - (\hat{p} + g_k - \delta_k - \varphi_b)b^l,\\
\dot{\psi} &= \psi(-\beta_{gd}(b^s + p_b b^l - b^s_0 + p_{b0}b^l_0) - \beta_{ge}(e-\bar{e}) - \beta_{gg}(\psi - \psi_0)),\\
\dot{m}_c &= \beta_{mc}(\alpha_m(b^s_c + p_b b^l) - m_c) + (n + \bar{\pi} - \delta_\varphi - \hat{p} - g_k + \delta_k + \varphi_b)m_c,\\
\dot{\lambda} &= g_k - \delta - (1-\tau_f)r - \varphi_b + (y - y^d) - (\hat{p} + g_k - \delta - \varphi_b)\lambda,\\
\dot{of} &= (1-\alpha_{rb})r_b - \varphi_b - (\hat{p} + g_k - \delta_k - \varphi_b)\ of.
\end{aligned}$$

Finally some algebraic relationships must be added for investment g_k, the rate of profit r, bankruptcy φ_b, labour demand l^d, taxes t, asset holders' bonds b_c, the money multiplier μ, the employment e and output rate u, the long-term interest rate i_l, bank holding of bonds b^s_b as well as the growth rate of price $\hat{p}$. These are summarised by

$$\begin{aligned}
g_k &= \alpha_{iu}(u-\bar{u}) + \alpha_{i\lambda}(\lambda_0 - \lambda) + \alpha_{ir}(r - \bar{r}) + \alpha_{irb}(r_{nb} - r_{nb0}) + n + \delta_k,\\
r_f &= y - \omega y/x - \delta_k - i\lambda,\\
\kappa &= 1/(1-\kappa_w\kappa_p),\\
\varphi_b &= \beta_{\varphi_b}(\bar{r} - r) + \delta_\varphi,\\
l^d &= y/x,
\end{aligned}$$

[16] Bhaduri and Marglin formulate the dichotomy between a wage-led and a profit-led economy.
[17] With regard to the last of these equations, for of, note that OF is defined by equation (9.24) and $of = OF/K$.

$$
\begin{aligned}
t &= t_w + t_c = \tau_w \omega l^d + \tau_c (i b^s + i\lambda + b^l) + \tau_f r,\\
y^d &= (1-\tau_w)\omega l^d + g_k + \psi,\\
b_c^s &= b^s - b_b^s,\\
\mu &= \theta(1-c) + c,\\
e &= l^d/l,\\
u &= y/y^p,\\
i_l &= 1/p_b,\\
r_b &= 1/p_b,\\
r_b &= i_\lambda \Lambda + i B_b,\\
r_{nb} &= 1 - \alpha_{rb} r_b - \varphi_b,\\
b_b^s &= (1-\theta)(1-c)m_c + of' - \lambda,\\
\hat{p} &= \kappa\big(k_p \beta_w (e-\bar{e}) + \beta_p (u-\bar{u})\big) + \bar{\pi}.
\end{aligned}
$$

Note that p_b clears the long-term bond market and ensures that $b^{ls} = b^{ld}$. The market clearing values of p_b are the solutions of a polynomial expression of second order.[18]

Setting $\hat{w} = 0$ and $\hat{p} = 0$ give the steady state value for e_0 and u_0, which yield y_0 and l_0. At the steady state, output y_0 equals normal production $y^p\bar{u}$ such that there is no disequilibrium on the goods market. The steady state for labour demand l_0^d is given by the steady state level of production $y^p\bar{u}$ and the proportion between production and employment given by x. Choosing the steady state value of the profit rate $r_0 = \bar{r}$ and setting $\dot{d} = 0$ give the steady state debt. It depends on the steady state of the population growth rate, retained earnings and price growth rate. From the government budget constraint you get the steady state for public bonds b_0^s and b_0^l. The steady state value of the expected capital gain on bonds dynamic is calculated from $\dot{\pi}_{b0} = 0$. Given b_{c0}^s and substituting into $\dot{m}_c = 0$ gives m_{c0}. From the definition of the rate of profit we get i_0 and assuming that the rate of return on bonds is equalised ($i_0 = r_{b0}^e$) gives us p_{b0}.

[18] One may calculate that

$$p_{bi} = \frac{-b \pm \sqrt{b^2 - 4ac}}{2a} \qquad (i = 1, 2),$$

where

$$
\begin{aligned}
a &= b^l(\alpha_{b0} - \alpha_{b1}(i - i_0) + \alpha_{b2}(\pi_b - r_{b0}^e) - 1),\\
b &= b_c^s(\alpha_{b0} - \alpha_{b1}(i - i_0) + \alpha_{b2}(\pi_b - r_{b0}^e)) + \alpha_{b2} b^l,\\
c &= b_c^s \alpha_{b1}.
\end{aligned}
$$

There are two solutions and it is assumed that $p_b = \max\{p_{b1}, p_{b2}\}$.

The steady state calculations may be summarised as:

$$
\begin{aligned}
r_0 &= \bar{r},\\
y_0 &= y^p\bar{u},\\
y_{e0} &= y_0/(1+\beta_{nd}(n-\delta_\varphi)),\\
l_0^d &= y_0/x = y^p\bar{u}/x,\\
l_0 &= l_0^d/\bar{e} = y^p\bar{u}/\bar{e}/x,\\
v_0 &= \beta_{nd}y_{e0},\\
u_0 &= (y_{e0}-n-delta-g)x_0/(y_0(1-\tau_w)),\\
\lambda_0 &= (-\delta-g-y_0u_0(1-\tau_w)/x_0+y_0-(1-\tau_f)r_0-\delta_\varphi)/(n+\bar{\pi}-\delta_\varphi),\\
i_0 &= (y-u_0y/x-\delta_k-r_0)/\lambda_0,\\
p_{b0} &= 1/i_{l0},\\
A &= 1+(1-\theta)(1-c)\alpha_m,\\
b_0^s &= \alpha_b\big(g-\tau_w\omega_0y_0/x_0-\tau_ci_0\lambda_0-\alpha_rr_{f0}\big)/(n+\bar{\pi}-\delta\varphi),\\
B_0^l &= (1-\alpha_b)\big(g-\tau_w\omega_0y_0/x_0-\tau_ci_0\lambda_0-\alpha_rr_{f0}\big)/(n+\bar{\pi}-\delta\varphi)p_b,\\
of_0 &= \big((1-\alpha_{rb})i_{\lambda 0}\lambda_0-\delta_\varphi+\delta_{\varphi_s}+(1-\alpha_{rb})i_0((1-\theta)(1-c)\alpha_m(b_0+p_{b0}b_0^l)\\
&\quad -\lambda_0)/A\big)/(\bar{\pi}+n-\delta_\varphi-(1-\alpha_{rb})i_0/A),\\
b_{c0} &= b_0-b_{b0},\\
m_{c0} &= \alpha_m(b_{c0}+p_{b0}b_0^l),\\
\hat{p}_0 &= \bar{\pi},\\
r_{nb0} &= i_0\lambda_0+i_0b_{b0}-\delta_\varphi.
\end{aligned}
\tag{9.53}
$$

9.5 Debt default without and with bankruptcy

In this subsection, we raise the issue of debt default with and without bankruptcy. In a capitalist economy in which property rights are strictly enforced debt default results from firm bankruptcy, as in the model just presented. There are nevertheless numerous contemporary examples of debt default without bankruptcy as illustrated by the Japanese and Argentinian cases. Debt default and bankruptcy both reduce indebtedness. Debt default and bankruptcy differ with respect to loss sharing. In the case of bankruptcy, borrowers suffer some losses. In the case of debt default without bankruptcy, all losses are borne by creditors.

Bankruptcy and debt default therefore raise an important institutional issue: the role of property right enforcement in resolving over-indebtedness situations. Neoclassical institutionalism has pointed to the key aspect of the legal framework in various fields of economic theory. With regards to financial fragility, it puts forward that a necessary element to solve periods of financial fragility quickly is a strict enforcement of property rights, through bankruptcy procedures. There are two main issues. First, a virtuous microeconomic framework ensures in the neoclassical line of argument that the proper incentives are given to economic agents. The resulting efficient responses are transmitted to the macroeconomic level. Meanwhile, by focusing too much on the incentives given by the legal framework, mainstream economics minimises the direct and potentially powerful effects of debt default in alleviating the financial burden of firms. The moral hazard argument is over-emphasised. In addition, it may lead to extreme conclusions. Following this line of reasoning, it is better that firms go bankrupt today rather than adopting biased behaviours tomorrow. Put differently, a crisis today is better than a crisis tomorrow. Second, from a Schumpeterian perspective, bankruptcy is the instrument through which the market selects viable firms from the failing ones. In a Darwinist line of argument, bankruptcy eliminates the weakest. It is said that crises are creative. Our macro approach enables us to discuss whether debt default without and with bankruptcy can solve financial fragility. We also discuss the impact of demand regimes and labour and good markets' institutions.

The following sections discuss the respective properties of debt default without and with bankruptcy. For that purpose, the high order model of the previous section is reduced to three dynamic equations in order to better understand the mechanisms at work. In particular, we derive the stability conditions for two cases, debt default without bankruptcy and debt default with bankruptcy. For each situation, we discuss how the type of demand regime, wage-led or profit-led, affects the results. Lastly, in order to better understand the interaction of bankruptcy with the other equations of the model, we derive the stability conditions for the subsystem starting with two dimensions and ending at three dimensions.

9.5.1 Debt default without bankruptcy

The following 3D dynamical system consists of three equations for wages, output adjustment and debt:

$$\dot{\omega} = \omega\kappa\big((1-\kappa_p)\beta_w(e-\bar{e}) + (\kappa_w - 1)\beta_p(u-\bar{u})\big),$$

$$\dot{y} = \beta_y(y^d - y) + (n + \delta_k - g_k)y,$$

$$\dot{\lambda} = g_k - \delta_k - (1-\tau_f)r - \varphi_d\lambda - (\hat{p} + g_k - \delta_k)\lambda.$$

Debt default, $\varphi_d\lambda$, enters debt accumulation negatively. The rate of debt default φ_d, is a negative function of profitability. Debt default has a clear counter-cyclical effect on the business cycle as it contributes to the reduction of debt in the downturn and to an increase of debt in the upturn.

The following algebraic quantities, including the rate of default, are required on the right-hand side of the above 3D dynamical system for ω, y and λ:

$$g_k = \alpha_{iu}(u-\bar{u}) + \alpha_{i\lambda}(\lambda_0 - \lambda) + \alpha_{ir}(r - r_0) + n + \delta_k,$$

$$\varphi_d = \beta_{\varphi_d}(\bar{r} - r) + \delta_\varphi,$$

$$
\begin{aligned}
r &= y - \omega y/x - \delta_k - i\lambda, \\
\kappa &= 1/(1 - \kappa_w \kappa_p), \\
l^d &= y/x, \\
\hat{p} &= \kappa\big(\kappa_p \beta_w (e - \bar{e}) + \beta_p (u - \bar{u})\big) + \bar{\pi}, \\
y^d &= (1 - \tau_w)\omega l^d + g_k + \psi.
\end{aligned}
$$

Steady states are similar to the steady states of the preceding section with the exception that the rate of bankruptcy no longer appears. The steady state is thus given by

$$
\begin{aligned}
r_0 &= \bar{r}, \\
y_0 &= y^p \bar{u}, \\
l_0^d &= y^p \bar{u}/x, \\
l_0 &= y^p \bar{u}/\bar{e}/x, \\
u_0 &= \bar{u}, \\
\lambda_0 &= (n - (1 - \tau_f) r_0)/(n + \bar{\pi} + \varphi_d), \\
i_0 &= (y - \omega y/x - \delta - r_0)/\lambda_0, \\
\hat{p}_0 &= \bar{\pi}, \\
\omega_0 &= (y_0 - \delta - g - g_{k0}) x / \big((1 - \tau_w) y_0\big), \\
e_0 &= \bar{e}, \\
g_{k0} &= n + \delta.
\end{aligned}
$$

The 2D model As illustrated by Figure 9.2, the introduction of debt default modifies the interaction between debt and output. The stability conditions of the two dimensional model may be summarised as follows:

- Debt accumulation is stabilising when wage and price dynamics are not taken into account.
- Debt default tends to increase the stability of the economy. It reduces the debt to capital ratio, which sustains the profit rate and limits credit rationing.

Proposition 9.1 *Assuming that* $\beta_y > y_0$ *and* β_{φ_d} *is large enough such that*

$$
\beta_{\varphi_d} > ((1 - \tau_f)(1 - \omega_0/x_0) - (1 - \lambda_0) g_{ky})/\lambda_0 (1 - \omega_0/x_0),
$$

assume furthermore that

$$
(1 - \tau_w)\omega_0/x_0 + \alpha_{iu}/y^p + \alpha_{ir}(1 - \omega_0/x_0) < 1
$$

holds. Assume finally that the adjustment speeds of β_w, β_p *are all zero.*

Then:
The Jacobian of the independent subdynamics:

$$\dot{y} = \beta_y(y^d - y) + (n + \delta_k - g_k)y,$$
$$\dot{\lambda} = g_k - \delta_k - (1 - \tau_f)r - \varphi_d\lambda - (\bar{\pi} + g_k - \delta_k)\lambda,$$

has a stable steady state.

Proof: The entries of the Jacobian matrix are:

$$J_{11} = \beta_y\Big((1 - \tau_w)\omega_0/x_0 + g_{ky} - 1\Big) - y_0 g_{ky} < 0,$$
$$J_{12} = (\beta_y - y_0)g_{k\lambda} < 0,$$
$$J_{21} = (1 - \lambda_0)g_{ky} - (1 - \tau_f)(1 - \omega_0/x_0) + \lambda_0\beta_{\varphi_d}(1 - \omega_0/x_0) > 0,$$
$$J_{22} = (1 - \lambda_0)g_{k\lambda} + (1 - \tau_f)i_0 - \beta_{\varphi_d}i_0\lambda_0 - (\bar{\pi} + \delta_\varphi + n) < 0,$$

with $g_{k\lambda} < 0$ and $g_{ky} > 0$. Thus it follows that trace J < 0 and det $J > 0$. □

Remark 9.1 As β_{φ_d} enters J_{21} positively and J_{22} negatively, $J_{21} > 0$ and $J_{22} < 0$. In other words, a β_{φ_d} large enough ensures that debt is not cumulative with the output and is not cumulative with itself. Default is unambiguously stabilising at this stage. Output has a positive effect on profitability. In the upturn, default decreases and increases the debt to capital ratio. It limits the increase of firms' net wealth in the boom. By contrast, debt depresses profits and increases debt default, which smoothes the feedback effect of debt on itself.

The 3D model The stability conditions of the three dimensional model may be summarised as follows:

- Debt accumulation is prone to instability if $\alpha_{i\lambda}$ is large and if prices are flexible.
- Debt default seems to have a strong stabilising effect. It smoothes the depression-inducing effects of credit rationing and sustains profitability; and reduces the debt to capital ratio.

We discuss the stability conditions for the case of wage-led aggregate demand and profit-led aggregate demand. Debt default is stabilising in both cases.

9.5.1.1 The case of a wage-led aggregate demand

Proposition 9.2 *Assume in addition to what has been assumed in Proposition 9.1 that* $(1 - \tau_w) > \alpha_{ir}$ *holds, that* β_{φ_d} *satisfies* $\beta_{\varphi_d} > (1 - \tau_f - \alpha_{ir}(1 - \lambda_0))/\lambda_0$*, that* β_p *and* κ_p *are larger than* β_w *and* κ_w *and that* β_p *and* κ_p *are not too large such that*

$$g_{ky}(1 - \lambda_0) - (1 - \tau_f)(1 - \omega_0/x_0) > \lambda_0\kappa(\kappa_p\beta_w/x_0 l_0 + \beta_p/y^p).$$

Then:
The Jacobian of the then independent subdynamics

$$\dot{y} = \beta_y(y^d - y) + (n + \delta_k - g_k)y,$$
$$\dot{\lambda} = g_k - \delta_k - (1 - \tau_f)r - \varphi_d\lambda - (\hat{p} + g_k - \delta_k)\lambda,$$
$$\dot{\omega} = \omega\kappa\big((1 - \kappa_p)\beta_w(e - \bar{e}) + (\kappa_w - 1)\beta_p(u - \bar{u})\big),$$

has the properties $\det J < 0$, $trJ < 0$, $J_1 + J_2 + J_3 > 0$, $(-trJ)(J_1 + J_2 + J_3) + \det J > 0$.
Thus the steady state of these reduced dynamics is locally asymptotically stable.

Proof: Some of the entries of the Jacobian are left unchanged. They are $J_{11} < 0$, $J_{12} < 0$ and $J_{22} < 0$. Due to the introduction of price dynamics, the other entries are

$$\begin{aligned}
J_{13} &= \beta_y(1 - \tau_w)y_0/x_0 + g_{kw}(\beta_y - y_0) > 0,\\
J_{21} &= g_{ky}(1 - \lambda_0) - (1 - \tau_f)(1 - \omega_0/x_0) + \lambda_0\beta_\varphi(1 - \omega_0/x_0)\\
&\quad - \lambda_0\kappa(\kappa_p\beta_w/x_0 l_0 + \beta_p/y^p) > 0,\\
J_{23} &= g_{kw}(1 - \lambda_0) + (1 - \tau_f)y_0/x_0 - \lambda_0\beta_{\varphi_d}y_0/x_0 < 0,\\
J_{31} &= \omega\kappa\big((1 - \kappa_p)\beta_w/x_0 l_0 + (\kappa_w - 1)\beta_p/y^p\big) < 0,\\
J_{32} &= 0,\\
J_{33} &= 0,
\end{aligned}$$

with $g_{kw} = -\alpha_{ir}y_0/x_0 < 0$.
The result then follows from standard calculations. □

Remark 9.2 Increasing the dimension of the model modifies some of the entries of the Jacobian matrix. With respect to the 2D model, the entry J_{21} is increased by $-\lambda_0\kappa(\kappa_p\beta_w/x_0 l_0 + \beta_p/y^p)$ which may change the sign of the entry if β_p and κ_p are sufficiently large. In other words, price flexibility may produce a counter-cyclical real debt to capital ratio. Firms' net wealth to capital ratio is pro-cyclical and the financial accelerator is unstable.

The only new effect of debt default appears through J_{23} which is augmented by $-\lambda_0\beta_{\varphi_d}y_0/x_0$. Changes in real wage affect profits and debt default, which feeds back on output through debt. This new element tends to intensify the negative effect of real wage on real debt. It therefore increases stability (see Figure 9.8).

The last condition (that $(\mathrm{tr}J)(J_1 + J_2 + J_3) + \det J > 0$) holds as β_y enters quadratically in $(-\mathrm{tr}J)(J_1 + J_2 + J_3)$ but not in $\det J$. This is so since β_y enters both the trace and J_2 as well as J_3. In addition, β_{φ_d} tends to increase the sign of the four conditions. The last condition is increasing with β_{φ_d}. The trace is decreasing with β_φ, $J_1 + J_2 + J_3$ is increasing with β_φ while $\det J$ is decreasing with β_φ. □

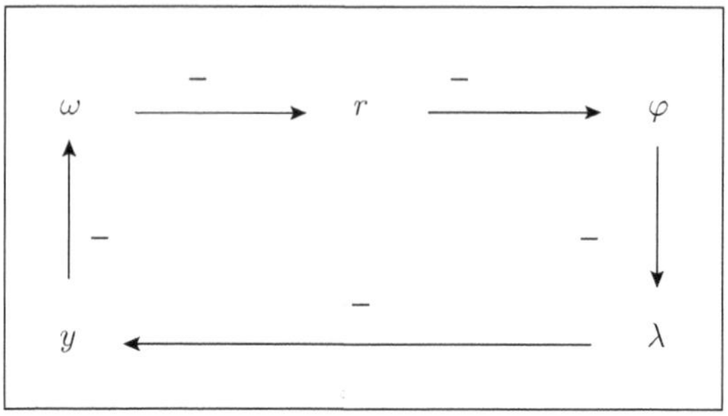

Figure 9.8 The intensive form dynamics – a stabilising channel of debt default via the effect of real wages on profits

9.5.1.2 The case of a profit-led aggregate demand

Proposition 9.3 *Assume in addition to what has been assumed in Proposition 9.1 that* $(1-\tau_w-\alpha_{ir})<0$ *holds, that* β_{φ_d} *satisfies* $\beta_{\varphi_d}>(1-\tau_f-\alpha_{ir}(1-\lambda_0))/\lambda_0$, *that* β_w *and* κ_w *are different from zero and sufficiently larger than* β_p *and* κ_p *and that* β_p *and* κ_p *are not too large such that*

$$g_{ky}(1-\lambda_0)-(1-\tau_f)(1-\omega_0/x_0)>\lambda_0\kappa(\kappa_p\beta_w/x_0l_0+\beta_p/y^p).$$

Assume furthermore that τ_w *is large enough and* τ_f *is small enough such that*

$$(1-\lambda_0)\beta_y(1-\tau_w)-(\beta_y-y_0)(1-\tau_f)<0.$$

Assume finally that $\alpha_{i\lambda}$ *is small enough and* α_{ir} *is large enough such that*

$$-\lambda_0\beta_{\varphi_d}(J_{12}y_0/x_0-i_0J_{13})<0.$$

Then:
The Jacobian of the independent subdynamics

$$\dot{y}=\beta_y(y^d-y)+(n+\delta_k-g_k)y,$$
$$\dot{\lambda}=g_k-\delta_k-(1-\tau_f)r-\varphi_d\lambda-(\hat{p}+g_k-\delta_k)\lambda,$$
$$\dot{\omega}=\omega\kappa\big((1-\kappa_p)\beta_w(e-\bar{e})+(\kappa_w-1)\beta_p(u-\bar{u})\big),$$

has the properties $\det J<0$, $trJ<0$, $J_1+J_2+J_3>0$, $(-trJ)(J_1+J_2+J_3)+\det J>0$. *Thus, the steady state of these reduced dynamics is locally asymptotically stable.*

Proof: The main results of the preceding section still hold. As aggregate demand is profit-led we have $J_{13}<0$, the real wage must be labour market-led so that $J_{31}>0$. We require investment to be sensitive to profitability (α_{ir} is large) and nominal wages to be more flexible than prices (β_w and κ_w are relatively larger than β_p and κ_p). As β_p and κ_p are relatively small, they do not make debt counter-cyclical, and so $J_{21}>0$. In addition, i_0 is sufficiently small such that $J_{22}<0$ holds. The propensity to consume is lower than 1 so that $J_{11}<0$; and β_y is still larger than y_0 to achieve $J_{12}<0$.

Eventually, $J_{32} = J_{33} = 0$, and $J_{23} < 0$. Note that similarly to the wage-led aggregate demand case, β_φ tends to reinforce the sign of the entries J_{2i}.

Although the trace is negative and the sub-determinants are positive, the sign of the determinant is not clear at first glance. Here again, the model is stable if $J_{12}J_{23} - J_{13}J_{22} < 0$. Taxes on profits must be small while taxes on wages must be sufficiently large such that $(1-\lambda_0)\beta_y(1-\tau_w)-(\beta_y-y_0)(1-\tau_f) < 0$ is true. In addition, the interest rate must be sufficiently small such that $(1-\tau_f)i_0 - n - \bar{\pi} < 0$ holds. It must also be the case that if $\alpha_{i\lambda}$ is small enough and α_{ir} is large enough then $-\lambda_0\beta_\varphi(J_{12}y_0/x_0 - i_0 J_{13}) < 0$ is true. Note that this latter condition may be hard to fulfil as i_0 is assumed to be small. Nevertheless, in such a case the determinant is decreasing with β_{φ_d}. Default stabilises the economy. In other words, if the destabilising Fisher effect $\alpha_{i\lambda}$ is smaller than the stabilising Rose effect α_{ir}, then default increases stability. □

9.5.2 Debt default with bankruptcy

The following 3D dynamic takes into account the case of debt default with bankruptcy:

$$\dot{\omega} = \omega\kappa\big((1-\kappa_p)\beta_w(e-\bar{e}) + (\kappa_w - 1)\beta_p(u-\bar{u})\big),$$

$$\dot{y} = \beta_y(y^d - y) + (n - \delta\varphi + \delta_k + \varphi_b - g_k)y,$$

$$\dot{\lambda} = g_k - \delta_k - (1-\tau_f)r - \varphi_b - (\hat{p} + g_k - \delta_k - \varphi_b)\lambda.$$

The equations are similar to the high order model of Section 9.4 except that inventories do not enter the debt dynamics and the distinction between expected and actual output. The rate of bankruptcy φ_b is a negative function of firms' profitability and reduces the stock of capital. Debt default is a consequence of bankruptcy and can be expressed as a function of the rate of bankruptcy.

The following variables must be introduced into the above equations.

$$g_k = \alpha_{iu}(u-\bar{u}) + \alpha_{i\lambda}(\lambda_0 - \lambda) + \alpha_{ir}(r - r_0) + n + \delta_k,$$

$$\varphi_b = \beta_\varphi(\bar{r} - r) + \delta_\varphi,$$

$$r = y - \omega y/x - \delta_k - i\lambda,$$

$$\kappa = 1/(1-\kappa_w\kappa_p),$$

$$l^d = y/x,$$

$$\hat{p} = \kappa\big(\kappa_p\beta_w(e-\bar{e}) + \beta_p(u-\bar{u})\big) + \bar{\pi},$$

$$y^d = (1-\tau_w)\omega l^d + g_k + \psi.$$

Steady states are left unchanged with the exception that inventories no longer appear. Thus

$$e_0 = \bar{e}, \qquad u_0 = \bar{u}, \qquad y_0 = y^p\bar{u},$$

$$r_0 = \bar{r}, \qquad g_{k0} = n + \delta_k, \qquad \hat{p}_0 = \bar{\pi},$$

$$l_0^d = y^p\bar{u}/x, \qquad l_0 = y^p\bar{u}/\bar{e}/x,$$

$$\lambda_0 = (n - (1-\tau_f)r_0 - \delta\varphi)/(n + \bar{\pi} - \delta\varphi),$$
$$\omega_0 = (y_0 - \delta - g - g_{k0})x/\big((1-\tau_w)y_0\big),$$
$$i_0 = (y - \omega y/x - \delta_k - r_0)/\lambda_0.$$

The 2D model The stability conditions for the two dimensional model may be summarised as follows:

- As seen previously, debt is stabilising in a two dimensional model. Debt accumulation has a strong disciplinary effect.
- Default with bankruptcy increases stability. It combines the stabilising effect of default and bankruptcy. In periods of depression and inversely in periods of expansion, the stock of capital is reduced, which increases the output to capital ratio. The remaining firms are on average more efficient which enables the economy to rebound.

Proposition 9.4 *Assume that $\beta_y > y_0$ and β_φ is large enough such that*

$$\beta_\varphi > ((1-\tau_f)(1-\omega_0/x_0) - (1-\lambda_0)g_{ky})/(1-\lambda_0)(1-\omega_0/x_0).$$

Assume furthermore that

$$(1-\tau_w)\omega_0/x_0 + \alpha_{iu}/y^p + \alpha_{ir}(1-\omega_0/x_0) < 1.$$

Assume finally that the adjustment speeds of β_w, β_p are all zero.
Then:

The Jacobian of the independent subdynamics:

$$\dot{y} = \beta_y(y^d - y) + (n - \delta\varphi + \delta_k + \varphi_b - g_k)y,$$
$$\dot{\lambda} = g_k - \delta_k - (1-\tau_f)r - \varphi_b - (\bar{\pi} + g_k - \delta_k - \varphi_b)\lambda.$$

has a stable steady state.

Proof: The entries of the Jacobian matrix are:

$$J_{11} = \beta_y\Big((1-\tau_w)\omega_0/x_0 + g_{ky} - 1\Big) - y_0 g_{ky} - y_0\beta_\varphi/y^p - \beta_\varphi(1-\omega_0/x_0) < 0,$$
$$J_{12} = (\beta_y - y_0)g_{k\lambda} + \beta_\varphi y_0 i_0 < 0,$$
$$J_{21} = (1-\lambda_0)g_{ky} - (1-\tau_f)(1-\omega_0/x_0) + \beta_\varphi(1-\lambda_0)(1-\omega_0/x_0) > 0,$$
$$J_{22} = (1-\lambda_0)g_{k\lambda} + (1-\tau_f)i_0 - \beta_\varphi i_0(1-\lambda_0) - (\bar{\pi} + n - \delta\varphi) < 0,$$

with $g_{k\lambda} < 0$ and $g_{ky} > 0$. The result readily follows as trace J < 0 and det J > 0. □

Remark 9.3 With respect to default without bankruptcy, default appears in the entries J_{21} and J_{22} with the same sign but with a weight $1-\lambda_0$ that reflects the balance sheet composition at the sectoral level.

Bankruptcy enters negatively in J_{11} and positively in J_{12}. The effect of bankruptcy on output is stabilising as J_{11} is decreasing with β_φ. Conversely, change in output with respect to debt tends to increase with β_φ. The entries J_{12} change sign only for very large and unrealistic values of β_φ.

Default increases the pro-cyclical tendency of debt with respect to output. It also increases the negative feedback effect of debt on itself. We do not need to assume that τ_f is large enough to ensure $J_{21} > 0$ and $J_{22} < 0$ as these conditions are fulfilled if β_φ is larger than $(1-\tau_f)/(1-\lambda_0)$ and smaller than $-g_{k\lambda}(\beta_y - y_0)/y_0 i_0$.

The 3D model The stability conditions for the full model may be summarised as follows:

- Debt accumulation is prone to instability when the wage-price dynamic is incorporated.
- When default results from bankruptcy, a wage-led real sector is stabilised by a higher output to capital ratio and lower debt level.
- With respect to a profit-led real sector, default resulting from bankruptcy may trigger an unstable feedback channel between wage flexibility, output and debt. Wage flexibility which is stabilising in a profit-led demand regime has some perverse effects when combined with debt. In periods of depression, real wage decreases, which reduces bankruptcies. In turn, the output to capital ratio decreases further. In other words, the real wage dynamics weaken the destructive creation effect. In addition, lower bankruptcies increase debt, which depresses output further. Nominal wage flexibility also weakens the positive effect of debt default.

9.5.2.1 The case of a wage-led aggregate demand

Proposition 9.5 *Assume in addition to what has been assumed in Proposition 9.1 that $(1-\tau_w) > \alpha_{ir} - y_0\beta_\varphi/\beta_y$ holds, that β_φ is sufficiently large that $\beta_\varphi > (1-\tau_f - \alpha_{ir}(1-\lambda_0))/(1-\lambda_0)$ holds, that β_p and κ_p are larger than β_w and κ_w and that β_p and κ_p are not so large such that*

$$g_{ky}(1-\lambda_0)-(1-\tau_f)(1-\omega_0/x_0)+(1-\lambda_0)\beta_\varphi(1-\omega_0 x_0) > \lambda_0\kappa(\kappa_p\beta_w/x_0 l_0+\beta_p/y^p).$$

Then:

The Jacobian of the independent subdynamics:

$$\begin{aligned}
\dot{y} &= \beta_y(y^d - y) + (n - \delta\varphi + \delta_k + \varphi_b - g_k)y,\\
\dot{\lambda} &= g_k - \delta_k - (1-\tau_f)r - \varphi_b - (\hat{p} + g_k - \delta_k - \varphi_b)\lambda,\\
\dot{\omega} &= \omega\kappa\big((1-\kappa_p)\beta_w(e-\bar{e}) + (\kappa_w - 1)\beta_p(u-\bar{u})\big),
\end{aligned}$$

has a stable steady state.

Proof: The entries J_{11}, J_{12} and J_{22} are left unchanged. The other new or modified entries are

$$
\begin{aligned}
J_{13} &= \beta_y(1-\tau_w)y_0/x_0 + (\beta_y - y_0)g_{kw} + y_0\beta_\varphi y_0/x_0 > 0,\\
J_{21} &= (1-\lambda_0)g_{ky} - (1-\tau_f)(1-\omega_0/x_0) + \beta_\varphi(1-\lambda)(1-\omega_0/x_0),\\
&\quad - \lambda_0\kappa(\kappa_p\beta_w/x_0l_0 + \beta_p/y^p) > 0,\\
J_{23} &= g_{kw}(1-\lambda_0) + (1-\tau_f)y_0/x_0 - \beta_\varphi(1-\lambda_0)y_0/x_0 < 0,\\
J_{31} &= \omega\kappa\big((1-\kappa_p)\beta_w/x_0l_0 + (\kappa_w - 1)\beta_p/y^p\big) < 0,\\
J_{32} &= 0,\\
J_{33} &= 0.
\end{aligned}
$$

It is straightforward to calculate that trace J < 0, det J $=< 0$, $J_1 + J_2 + J_3 > 0$, and $-\mathrm{tr}J(J_1 + J_2 + J_3) + \det J > 0$. The result then follows from application of the Routh–Hurwitz conditions. □

Remark 9.4 J_{11} and J_{12} are left unchanged with respect to the 2D case. In a wage-led real sector, default with bankruptcy increases J_{13} by $y_0\beta_\varphi y_0/x_0$. An increase of the real wage reduces profit and increases bankruptcies, which in turn further raises output. This effect is stabilising.

J_{21} is increased by $-\lambda_0\kappa(\kappa_p\beta_w/x_0l_0 + \beta_p/y^p)$ as prices affect real debt. As underlined in the baseline model, large price flexibility may lead debt to be counter-cyclical with $J_{21} < 0$. J_{22} is left unchanged. It is decreasing with bankruptcy. Debt is unlikely to feed back on itself when default is allowed. Eventually, J_{23} decreases with bankruptcies. Higher real wage increases bankruptcies and default, which in turn reduces the debt to capital ratio. These feedback channels are displayed in Figure 9.9.

In line with the preceding model, a wage-led aggregate demand is stabilised by a goods market-led real wage. Prices are more flexible than nominal wages if β_p and κ_p are greater than β_w and κ_w.

In the case of debt accumulation with a wage-led real sector, default with bankruptcy increases the stability of the economy. The positive feedback channel between real wage, bankruptcy, debt and output is represented in Figure 9.9.

9.5.2.2 *The case of a profit-led aggregate demand*

Lemma 9.1 *Assume in addition to what has been assumed in Proposition 9.1 that* $\alpha_{ir} > (1-\tau_w) + y_0\beta_\varphi/\beta_y$ *holds, that* β_φ *is sufficiently large that* $\beta_\varphi > (1-\tau_f - \alpha_{ir}(1-\lambda_0))/(1-\lambda_0)$ *holds, that* β_w *and* κ_w *are different from zero and sufficiently larger than* β_p *and* κ_p *are not too large such that these hold*

$$g_{ky}(1-\lambda_0)-(1-\tau_f)(1-\omega_0/x_0)+(1-\lambda_0)\beta_\varphi(1-\omega_0/x_0) > \lambda_0\kappa(\kappa_p\beta_w/x_0l_0+\beta_p/y^p).$$

In addition assume that τ_w *is large enough and* τ_f *is small enough such that*

$$(1-\lambda_0)\beta_y(1-\tau_w) - (\beta_y - y_0)(1-\tau_f) < 0.$$

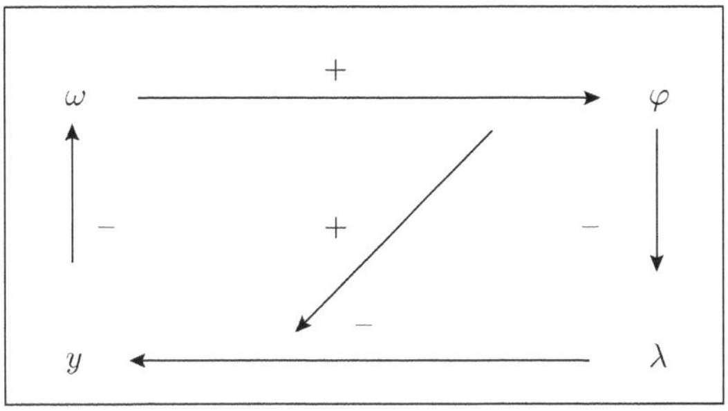

Figure 9.9 The intensive form dynamics – a stabilising channel of debt default via the effect of goods market-led real wage

Finally assume that $\alpha_{i\lambda}$ is small enough, α_{ir} is large enough and β_φ is not so large such that

$$-\lambda_0\beta_\varphi(J_{12}y_0/x_0 - i_0J_{13}) < 0.$$

Then:

The Jacobian of the independent subdynamics:

$$\dot{y} = \beta_y(y^d - y) + (n - \delta\varphi + \delta_k + \varphi_b - g_k)y,$$
$$\dot{\lambda} = g_k - \delta_k - (1 - \tau_f)r - \varphi_b - (\hat{p} + g_k - \delta_k - \varphi_b)\lambda,$$
$$\dot{\omega} = \omega\kappa\big((1 - \kappa_p)\beta_w(e - \bar{e}) + (\kappa_w - 1)\beta_p(u - \bar{u})\big)$$

has a stable steady state.

Proof: The following conditions hold: trace J < 0, det J $=< 0$, $J_1 + J_2 + J_3 > 0$ and $-\text{tr}J(J_1 + J_2 + J_3) + \det J > 0$. The result then follows from application of the Routh–Hurwitz conditions. □

Remark 9.5 With respect to a wage-led real sector, the entry J_{13} is negative in a profit-led real sector. The real wage tends to increase the output to capital ratio through bankruptcy, so reducing the degree to which the real sector is profit-led. J_{13} is negative if $\alpha_{ir} > (1 - \tau_w) + y_0\beta_\varphi/\beta_y$. A significant sensitivity of bankruptcy to the profit rate may turn a profit-led aggregate demand into a wage-led one. The entries J_{21}, J_{22} and J_{23} are similar to the wage-led case.

As seen previously, a profit-led aggregate demand is stabilised by a labour market-led real wage. The entry J_{31} is positive if β_w and κ_w are larger than β_p and κ_p. Although the stability conditions trace J < 0, $J_1 + J_2 + J_3 > 0$ and $-\text{tr}J(J_1 + J_2 + J_3) + \det J > 0$ are straightforward, the sign of the determinant is less clear. In the preceding sections, a destabilising feedback channel between real wage, debt and output was identified. We argued that nominal wage flexibility may lead to a debt-deflation spiral, and that its positive effect on profit may not be large enough to restore stability (det J < 0 if $J_{12}J_{23} - J_{13}J_{22} < 0$). We argue that bankruptcy generates an additional destabilising feedback channel with nominal wage flexibility. In other words, nominal wage flexibility tends

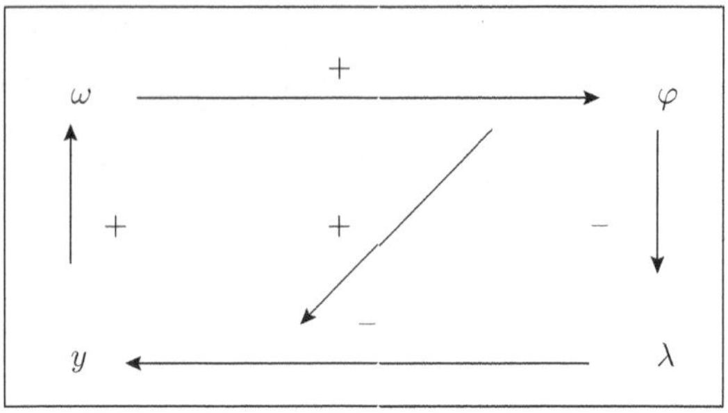

Figure 9.10 Destabilising channels of bankruptcy with a profit-led AD

to reduce the positive effects of bankruptcy and default. The quantity J_{13} is increased by $y_0\beta_\varphi y_0/x_0$. An increase of the real wage reduces profit, increases bankruptcies and output, which in turns raises the real wage further. Nominal wage flexibility reduces the stabilising interaction between output and the real wage through bankruptcy. In addition, J_{23} decreases with bankruptcies. Higher real wage increases bankruptcies and debt default, which reduces the debt to capital ratio. In turn, output increases and the real wage is pushed upward. In the case of debt accumulation with a profit-led real sector, default with bankruptcy decreases the stability of the economy. The unstable feedback channels between real wage, bankruptcy, debt and output are displayed in Figure 9.10.

9.6 Simulations: baseline scenarios

In this section, we seek to gauge by use of simulations the impact of debt default, bankruptcy and bank performance on the business cycle. We also consider the effect of the resulting supply of credit on the economy as a whole.

9.6.1 Debt default and bankruptcy

In Figure 9.11(a) and 9.11(b), debt default takes place without bankruptcy and is stabilising. Credit rationing is moderate $\alpha_{i\lambda} = 0.35$, aggregate demand is profit-led $\alpha_{ir} = 1.9$ and the real wage is labour market-led $\beta_w = 0.5$, $\beta_p = 0.05$, $\kappa_w = 0.75$ and $\kappa_p = 0.5$. In such a case, default is highly stabilising. Increasing the parameter of debt default from 0.1 to 0.5 accelerates the convergence of the economy. To the extent that the baseline finance-led model with a profit-led aggregate demand is very unstable, default smoothes out some of the destabilising feedbacks. An important channel is the profit rate channel. Eigenvalues diagrams clearly show that default is stabilising, as the maximum real part of the eigenvalues is decreasing in β_φ and β_{φ_d}.

Bankruptcy has ambiguous effects when aggregate demand is profit-led as can be seen in Figures 9.11(c) and 9.11(d). The sensitivity of aggregate demand to profit is large, $\alpha_{ir} = 1.9$, $\tau_w = 0.325$ and the real wage is labour market-led with $\beta_w = 1$ and

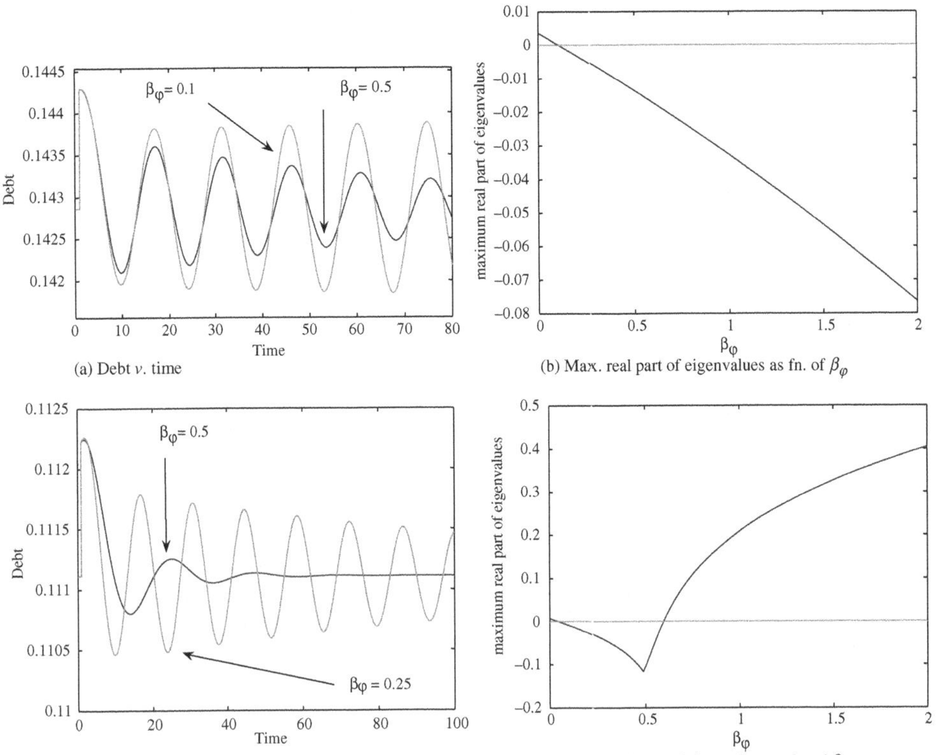

(a) Debt v. time

(b) Max. real part of eigenvalues as fn. of β_φ

(c) Debt v. time - Profit-led AD

(d) Max. real part of eigenvalues as fn. of β_φ

Figure 9.11 Debt default and bankruptcy – the 3D model

$\beta_p = 0.1$. With a moderate sensitivity of bankruptcy to profitability, bankruptcy is stabilising. Increasing β_φ from 0.25 to 0.5 stabilises the business cycle. As the weakest firms are eliminated and as debt default reduces the Fisher effect, the economy converges faster. By contrast, the maximum real part of the eigenvalues graph (Figure 9.11(d)) shows that after a certain point, a large β_φ destabilises the economy.

9.6.2 Banks' budget constraint

Figures 9.12 and 9.13 display banks' balance sheet. The main parameters involve a wage-led aggregate demand ($\alpha_{ir} = 0.1, \tau_w = 0.1$) and goods market-led real wage dynamics ($\beta_w = 0.05, \beta_w = 0.4$, $\kappa_p = \kappa_w = 0.4$). The monetary policy is active and weights inflation and the output gap similarly with $\alpha_{iu} = \alpha_{ip} = 0.4$. The fiscal policy is counter-cyclical ($\beta_{ge} = 0.2$) and there is no credit rationing with respect to the borrower or lender characteristics ($\alpha_{i\lambda} = \alpha_{irb} = 0$). A 1 per cent positive shock to output generates damped business cycle oscillations of approximately fifteen years. There are two main results. First, the banks' balance sheet sums to zero at every point in time. Second, when credit decreases, banks will hold excess reserves. Instead of having unused cash, they buy public bonds. And given the change in deposits, net wealth

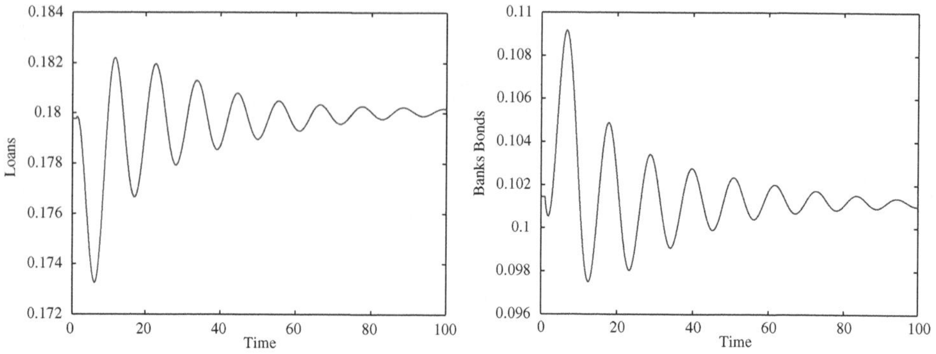

(a) Loans *v*. time (b) Bank bonds *v*. time

Figure 9.12 The balance sheet of banks - loans and bank bonds

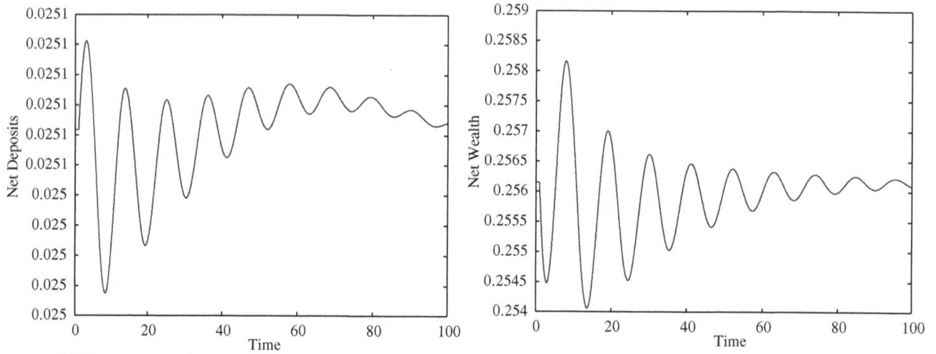

(a) Net deposits *v*. time (b) Net wealth *v*. time

Figure 9.13 The balance sheet of banks – net deposits and net wealth

decreases. The evolution of banks' net wealth is roughly in line with the dynamics of credit supply.

9.6.3 Pro-cyclical profits and credit supply

Figure 9.14 illustrates the case of credit rationing with respect to bank profits. In particular, we check whether the profitability of firms and therefore own funds are pro-cyclical. We then enquire whether the resulting credit supply is pro-cyclical as well. With respect to the parameters of the preceding simulations, we increase the sensitivity of credit supply with respect to bank profits from 0 to 0.1. In the boom, firms' desired investment increases and their need for external funds also increases. Credit expands and bank assets and profitability improve. As bank credit supply is now a function of bank income, they ease credit rationing. A cumulative loop is unleashed in which higher credit supply leads to better profitability of banks and larger credit supply. Note that this simulation confirms that bank profitability is pro-cyclical, which implies an expansion of the balance sheet of banks; see Figure 9.14(a). This bank based version of the financial accelerator brings instability. Increasing α_{irb} from 0.1 to 0.7 generates wider

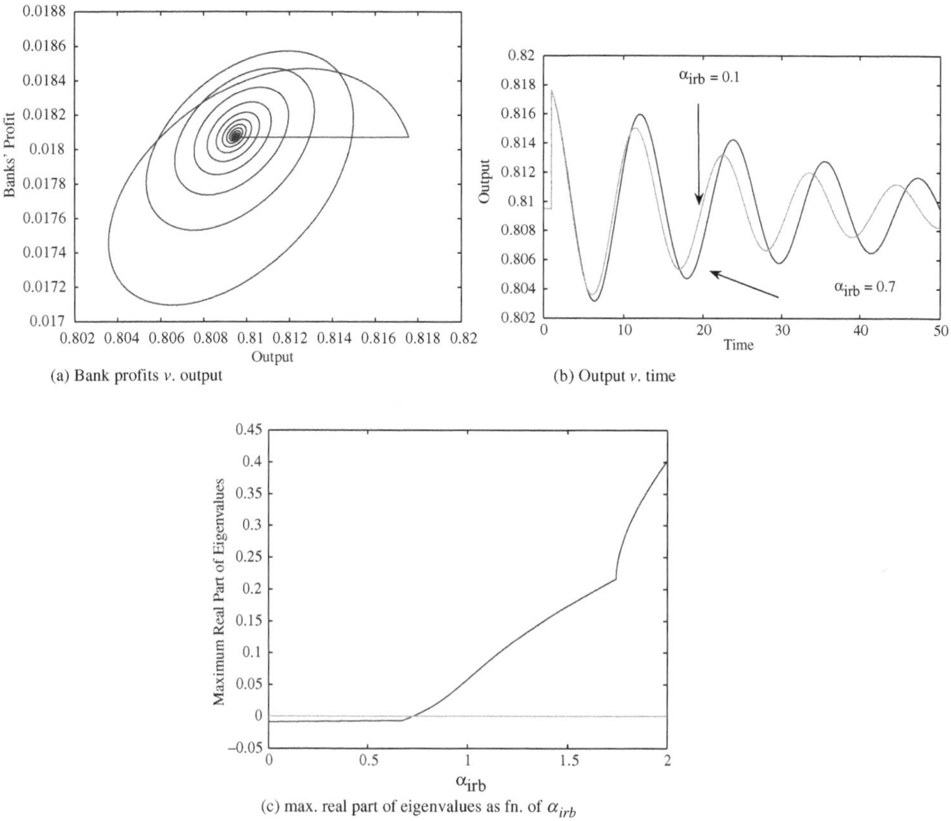

Figure 9.14 Banks' pro-cyclical profitability and credit supply

oscillations of the output as shown in Figure 9.14(b). Figure 9.14(c) displays the effect of a high sensitivity of credit supply to bank profitability on economic stability. The maximum real part of the eigenvalues are increasing with α_{irb}, so clearly pro-cyclical credit supply is destabilising.

9.6.4 Debt default and credit crunch

Figure 9.15 shows the impact of debt default on the credit supply of banks. In Figure 9.15(a) debt default takes place but credit rationing is independent of bank profitability and it is assumed here that the parameter for credit rationing (α_{irb}) is 0. The maximum real part of the eigenvalues decreases slightly with β_φ. As shown in the second model, bankruptcy may have some positive effects through debt default. In addition, active monetary and fiscal policies are likely to smoothe the negative effect of bankruptcy on unemployment. Now, increasing the sensitivity of credit supply to bank profitability reverses the effect of default. In the upturn, banks' profits and credit supply both increase. This effect is amplified by the reduction of debt default. As output increases, firms' general profitability improves. Meanwhile, in the downturn, debt default contributes to reducing credit supply further by reducing bank assets and

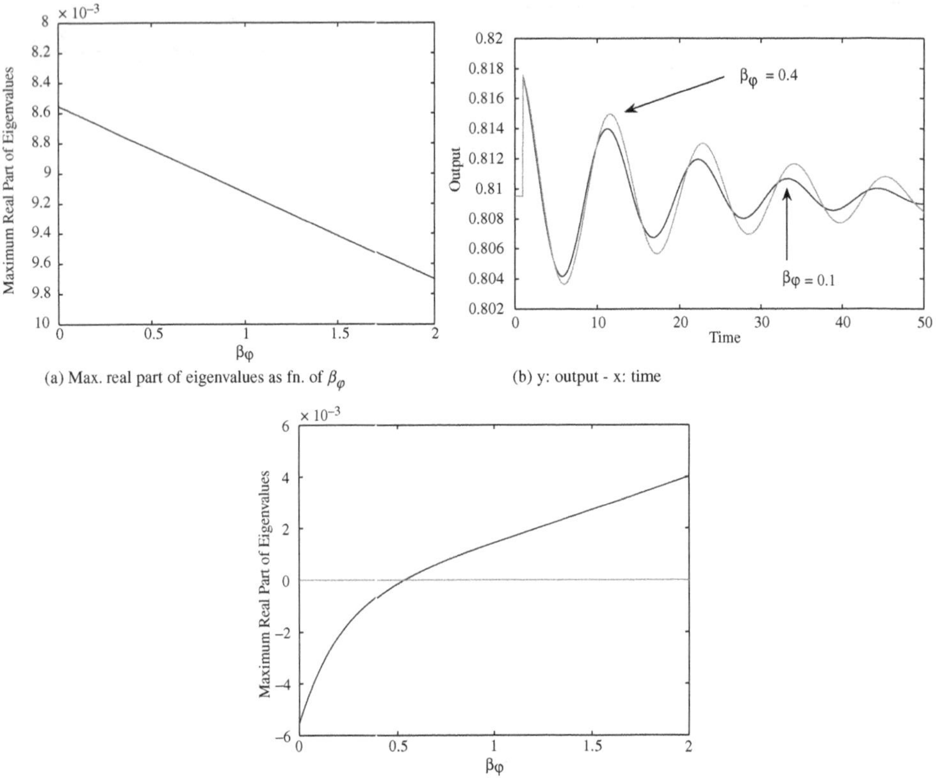

(a) Max. real part of eigenvalues as fn. of β_φ

(b) y: output - x: time

(c) Max. real part of eigenvalues as fn. of β_φ

Figure 9.15 Debt default and credit crunch

income (in addition to the deterioration brought by the depressed economic environment). Increasing the speeds of adjustment of bankruptcy to profitability from 0.1 to 0.4 increases output fluctuations. In the same line of argument, the maximum real part of the eigenvalues is increasing with β_φ as shown in Figure 9.15(c) where now the parameter for credit rationing (α_{irb}) is 0.7. Put differently, financial instability is enhanced when the banking sector's financial health is affected by debt default. In such a case, a banking crises may unfold and require public intervention.

9.6.5 Bank bailouts and loss socialisation

Large defaults deteriorate the own funds of banks and generate a credit crunch. To avoid a systemic crisis and to relax credit rationing, the government can bail out banks. There are different ways to support banks. In this framework, banks transfer part of the non-performing loans to the government, so a proportion $\varphi_s \Lambda$ is socialised in this way. This transfer allows banks to sustain net equity and increases government debt, with $\varphi_s < \varphi_d$. Such a transfer mechanism requires an adjustment to the budget constraints of banks and government. The change in own funds of banks still decreases with debt default, but it is sustained by loss socialisation $\varphi_s \Lambda$. The share of default socialised in this way appears positively in the government budget constraint. It slightly modifies the steady state for government debt, as well as for own funds of banks. The latter increase with loss socialisation, while at the same time government net wealth decreases.[19]

In extensive form the dynamics of the banks become:[20]

$$\dot{OF} = (1-\alpha_{rb})r_b pK - \varphi_d\Lambda + \varphi_s\Lambda, \tag{9.54}$$

$$\varphi_s = \beta_{\varphi s}(\varphi_b - \delta_\varphi) + \delta_{\varphi s}, \tag{9.55}$$

$$\dot{B}^s_{cb} + \dot{B}^s = \alpha_b\big(pG + iB^s + B^l + \varphi_s\Lambda - pT_c - pT_w - pT_f\big), \tag{9.56}$$

$$p_b\dot{B}^l = (1-\alpha_b)\big(pG + iB^s + B^l + \varphi_s\Lambda - pT_c - pT_w - pT_f\big). \tag{9.57}$$

The resulting effect is ambivalent. On the one hand, own funds of banks are sustained and the economy is stabilised. Increasing $\beta_{\varphi s}$ from 0.1 to 0.5 increases loss socialisation. For a given default, the own funds of banks decrease less. Credit rationing is smoothed and the recession is limited. The business cycle fluctuations are narrower as we see in Figure 9.16(b). Meanwhile, the government finances this spending by issuing additional public bonds. If public debt increases too much, public debt starts accumulating and brings instability. Loss socialisation contributes to the solution of the private debt problem, but is likely to lead to a public debt crisis. This effect appears through the maximum part of eigenvalues that turns positive for a large socialisation of bad debt, as shown in Figure 9.16(c). It is actually well known that public intervention has a direct positive effect but may have indirect and unexpected perverse effects.

9.7 Simulations: extended studies

In this section we reproduce some of the findings of the previous small size models (in particular of Chapter 8), using wage-led and profit-led aggregate demand. It turns out that the finance-led regime is still destabilising through credit rationing and may lead to debt-deflation spirals, whereas fiscal and monetary policies stabilise the business cycle.

9.7.1 Wage-led aggregate demand

The wage share plays an important role in the simulation of Figure 9.17 as the first difference of output with respect to real wages ($\dot{y}/\dot{w}$) is equal to 0.1236. Taxes on

[19] Steady state for banks' own funds and public debt is modified as follows:

$$\begin{aligned} of_0 &= \big((1-\alpha_{rb})i_{\lambda 0}\lambda_0 - \delta_\varphi + \delta_{\varphi_s} + (1-\alpha_{rb})i_0((1-\theta)(1-c)\alpha_m(b_0 + p_{b0}b^l_0) - \lambda_0)/A\big) \\ &\quad /(\bar{\pi} + n - \delta_\varphi - (1-\alpha_{rb})i_0/A), \\ A &= 1 + (1-\theta)(1-c)\alpha_m, \\ b^s_0 &= \alpha_b\big(g + \delta_{\varphi s} - \tau_w\omega_0 y_0/x_0 - \tau_c i_0\lambda_0 - \alpha_r r_{f0}\big)/(n + \bar{\pi} - \delta\varphi), \\ B^l_0 &= (1-\alpha_b)\big(g + \delta_{\varphi s} - \tau_w\omega_0 y_0/x_0 - \tau_c i_0\lambda_0 - \alpha_r r_{f0}\big)/(n + \bar{\pi} - \delta\varphi)p_b. \end{aligned}$$

[20] Note that Equation (9.54) is a modification of Equation (9.24), Equation (9.55) is new, and Equations (9.56) and (9.57) are modifications of Equations (9.43) and (9.44) respectively.

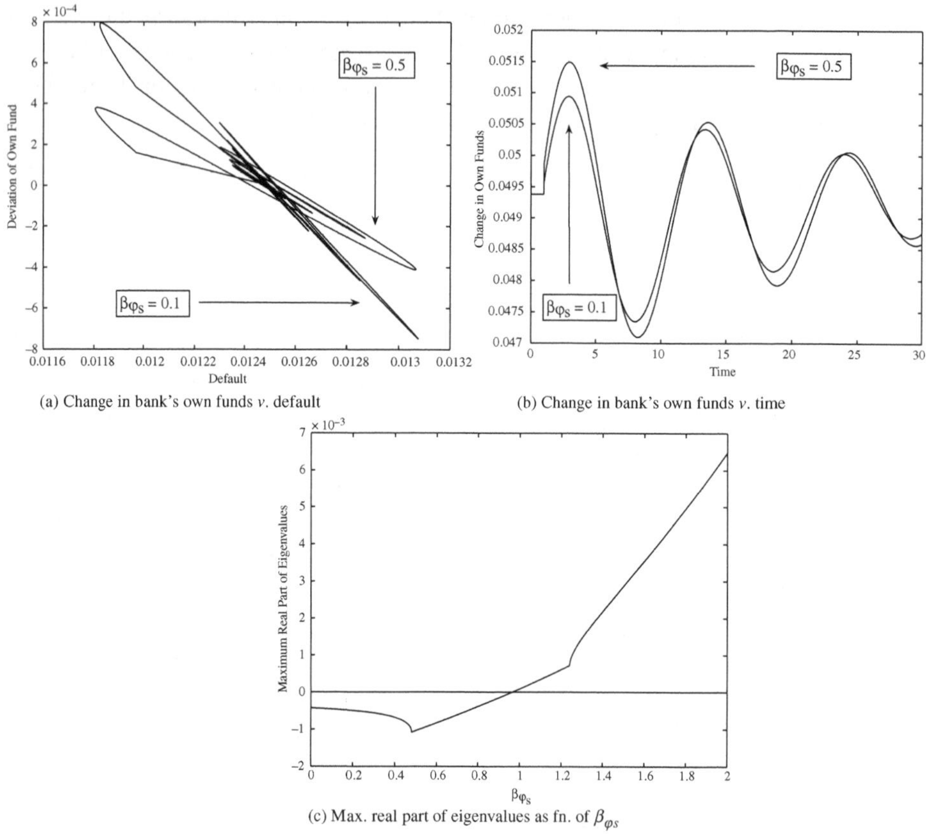

Figure 9.16 Bank bailout

wages amount (τ_w) 'only' to 50 per cent of real income, while investment strongly depends on the Harrodian multiplier with $\alpha_{iu} = 0.8$ and less on profitability since $\tau_f = 0.4$. Note also that the Fisher effect is kept relatively small at $\alpha_\lambda = 0.1$. The Rose effect is stabilising. Nominal wages are quite flexible ($\beta_w = 0.4$ and $\kappa_w = 0.4$) but prices are even more flexible ($\beta_p = 0.6$ and $\kappa_p = 0.75$). The Taylor rule is weak as the interest rate does not react much to the output gap or to inflation given that $\beta_{iu} = \beta_{ip} = 0.1$. Monetary authorities are more concerned with keeping the interest rate at its equilibrium value $\beta_{ii} = 0.4$. Public spending tends to be counter-cyclical as the debt target is almost zero ($\beta_{g1} = 0.001$) and the employment level is important ($\beta_{g2} = 0.4$). In this set-up, public intervention might be more effective through fiscal rather than monetary policy. The destabilising effects of long-term bond dynamics we kept small by making two assumptions: public spending is mainly financed through short-term debt ($\alpha_b = 0.85$), and there is a weak feedback effect between bond price and capital gain expectations ($\beta_{\pi_b^e} = 0.1$).

The outcome of a 5 per cent shock on output is a business cycle of approximately twelve years that converges towards the steady state at a somewhat slow speed. The

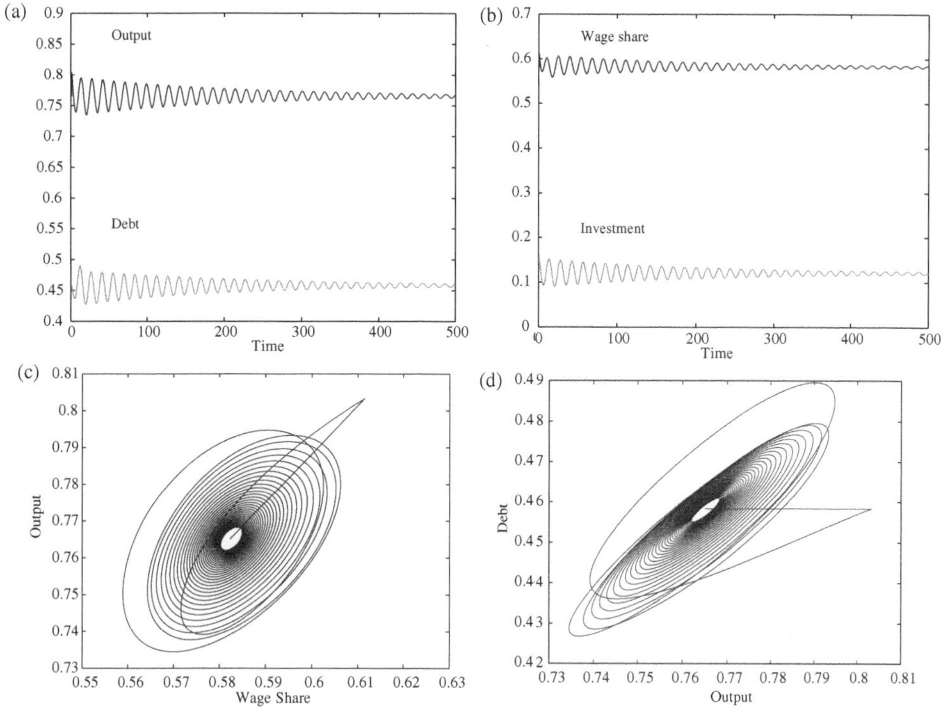

Figure 9.17 Business cycle – wage-led – stability

wage share is pro-cyclical, as is investment, due to its dependence on the output gap even if with a lag. As a result of high investment and high wage share in the upturn, indebtedness is also pro-cyclical. It entails that the Fisher effect is rather small when prices are slightly negative over the first cycles. The main stabilising element of the model is the wage-price dynamics that generate a counter-cyclical real wage. As prices react faster than nominal wages to the disequilibrium on the labour and goods markets, the real wage slows down in the upturn so smoothing aggregate demand and stabilising the economy. In line with theoretical intuition an increase in the price flexibility parameter β_p increases the stabilising influence of the Rose effect. Figure 9.18 displays all of the effects just discussed; note that β_p has been increased from 0.6 to 0.9. The economy converges much faster to its steady state compared with Figure 9.17.

Figure 9.19 shows the maximum real part of eigenvalue diagrams for the wage-price dynamics and confirms the properties of the wage-price dynamics with a wage-led aggregate demand. Fast adjustment of prices is stabilising as the maximum real part of the eigenvalues are negative for large value of β_p and κ_p. On the contrary, the maximum real part of the eigenvalues turns positive for a large coefficient of nominal wage β_w

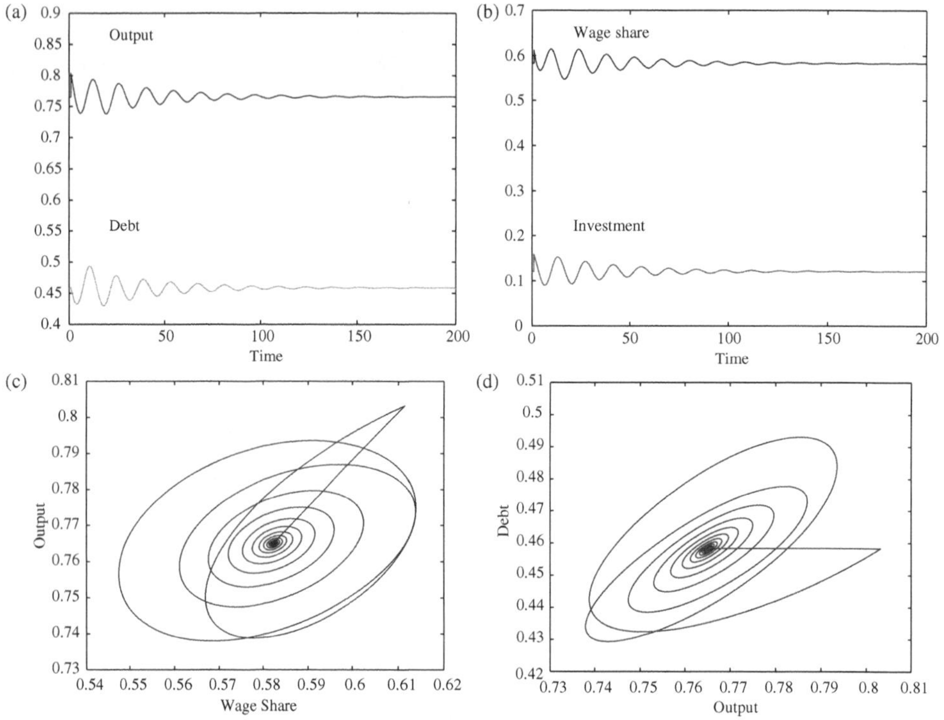

Figure 9.18 Business cycle – wage-led – stabilising higher price flexibility

and κ_w. More precisely, in a wage-led aggregate demand, the Rose effect is stabilising if the derivation of the change in real wage with respect to output is negative.

9.7.2 *Profit-led aggregate demand*

The mirror case of wage-led aggregate demand is profit-led aggregate demand where higher wages have a depressing effect on output. Increasing the coefficient for the sensitivity of investment to profit from 0.4 to 0.6 shifts the slope of $\frac{\dot{y}}{\omega}$ to -0.1234. Other parameters that do not affect the IS curve were also changed. The output gap sensitivity of investment α_{iu} is reduced from 0.8 to 0.4. In addition, given that aggregate demand is profit-led, nominal wages are made more flexible than prices ($\beta_p = 0.3$, $\beta_w = 0.6$, $\kappa_p = 0.7$ and $\kappa_w = 0.6$). In such a way, the real wage adjusts to dampen economic cycles.

The wage share has now an inverse relationship with the output while profit rate is positively related to output as shown in Figures 9.20(a) and (b). Decreasing β_p from 0.3 to 0.1 makes the Rose effect even more stabilising. As illustrated in Figures 9.20(c) and (d) the economy reaches the point of rest much faster. The sign of $\frac{\partial \dot{\omega}}{\partial y}$

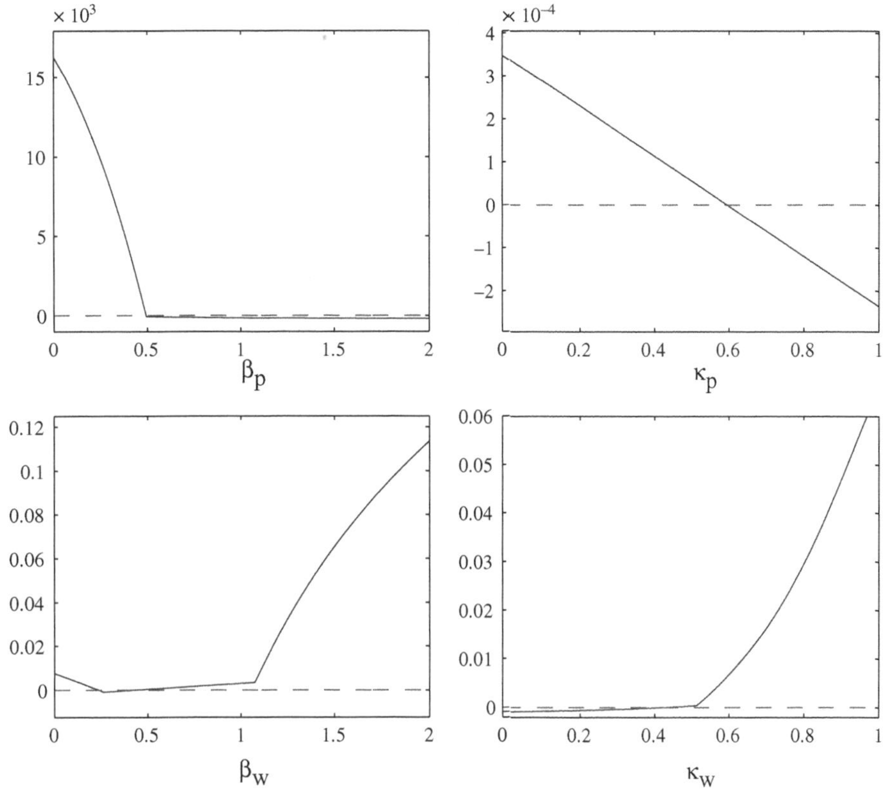

Figure 9.19 Maximum real parts of eigenvalues – wage-led – Rose effect

increases from 0.0346 to 0.0739, confirming that the Rose effect is stabilising in this case.

9.7.3 Debt deflation

In this subsection, we try to reproduce a debt-deflation spiral that is finance-led both in the cases of a wage-led and a profit-led aggregate demand set-up. It appears that debt deflation is more likely to occur in a profit-led demand regime as in this framework price flexibility has unambiguously destabilising effects contrary to wage-led aggregate demand. In the former case, price flexibility is destabilising in two ways, through the Rose and through the Fisher effect. In the latter case, price flexibility is stabilising through the Rose effect and destabilising through the Fisher effect.

Figure 9.21 illustrates the case of debt deflation. It is based on the parameters of Figure 9.17 except that the parameter $\alpha_{i\lambda}$ for the Fisher effect in the investment function is increased from 0.1 to 0.2 while the parameter α_{iu} for the Harrodian component of investment is decreased from 0.8 to 0.4. Due to the strong effect of $\alpha_{i\lambda}$ the speed of adjustment of price is slightly reduced from 0.6 to 0.5. If faster price adjustment

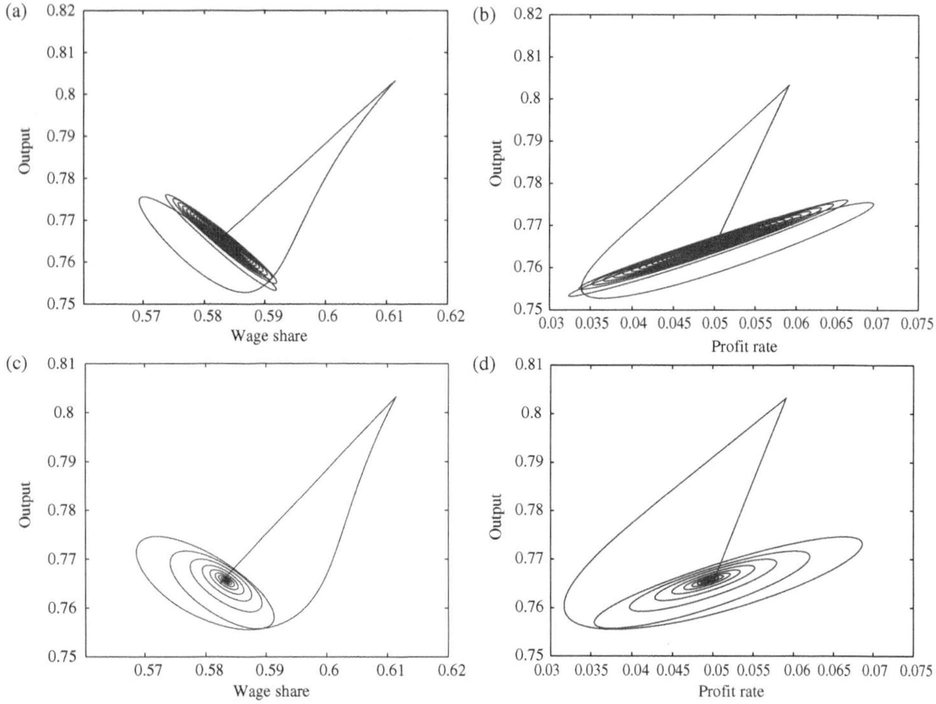

Figure 9.20 Business cycle – profit-led – stability

is stabilising through the Rose effect, then it is destabilising through the Fisher effect. Eventually, the interest rate is made more sensitive to the output gap by setting $\beta_{iu} = 0.2$ to counteract price deflation. As a result of the stronger Fisher effect, debt increases when price growth rate is negative. The cycle is exploding as illustrated in Figure 9.21(b). Figure 9.21(d) shows that the Fisher effect may be quite strong. For values of $\alpha_{i\lambda}$ greater than 0.2 the system loses stability. Contrary to Figures 9.19(a) and (d), Figures 9.21(b) and (c) show the maximum real part of the eigenvalues positive for large values of β_p and κ_p. Even if strong the Fisher effect may not necessarily lead to explosiveness. Price deflation may be contained within reasonable bounds as illustrated in Figures 9.21(e) and (f). A more stable Rose effect (which occurs when β_w and κ_w are reduced from 0.4 to 0.3 and 0.325 respectively) together with a 20 per cent shock to debt generates damped fluctuations where price deflation does not exceed 2 per cent.

Figure 9.22 illustrates the case of debt deflation in a situation of profit-led aggregate demand. The parameters are identical to Figure 9.20 except that the sensitivity of investment to indebtedness ($\alpha_{i\lambda}$) is increased from 0.1 to 0.115. This slight change generates debt deflation of a moderate magnitude. Price deflation does not exceed 1.5 per cent and fluctuations are converging slowly to the equilibrium. In Figures 9.22(c) and (d) the maximum real parts of eigenvalues with respect to β_p and

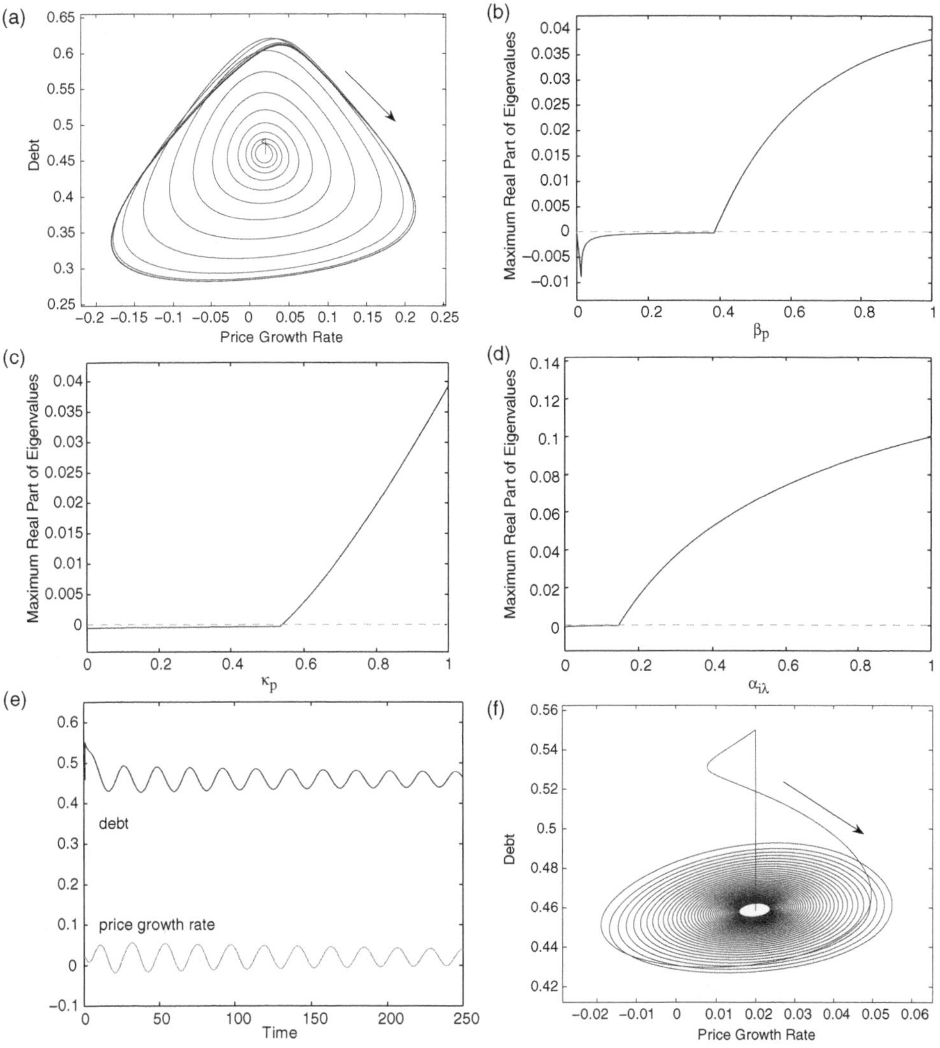

Figure 9.21 Debt deflation – wage-led AD

κ_p are always positive, underlining that price flexibility may very quickly become destabilising.

9.7.4 Interest rate policy rules

The conclusion of the first part of the model (Sections 9.7.1, 9.7.2 and 9.7.3) is that the private sector is prone to instability when the economy is finance-led and when nominal wages and prices are free to adjust to disequilibrium on the goods and labour markets. Public interventions might therefore play this stabilising role through monetary and

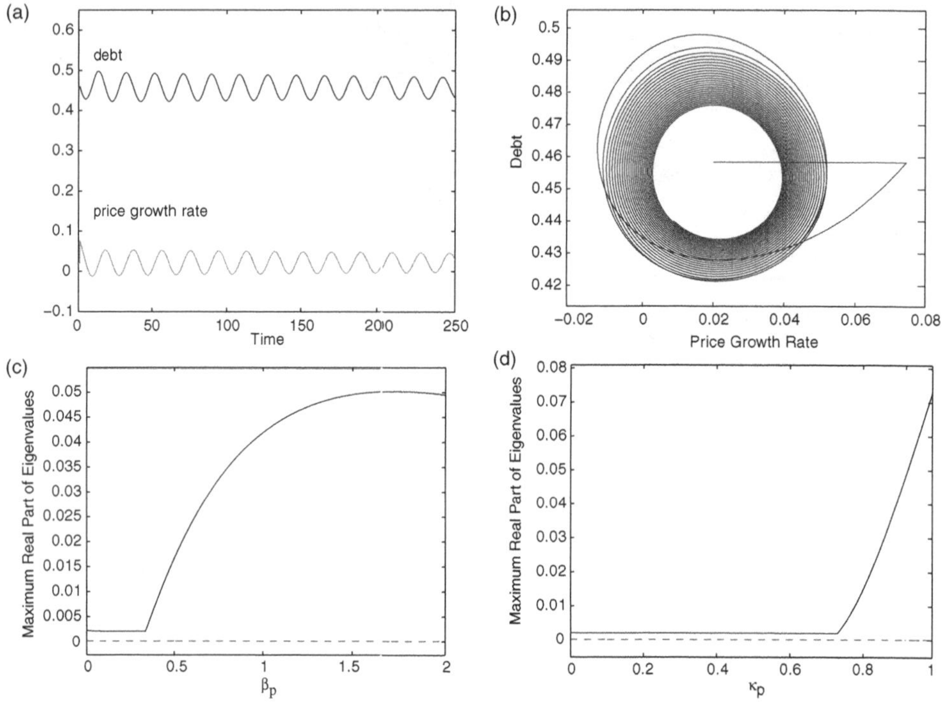

Figure 9.22 Debt deflation – profit-led AD

fiscal policy. Figure 9.23 assesses the effect of monetary policy on the stability of the model based on the parameters of the coefficients of Figure 9.17. Increasing the speed of adjustment of the interest rate with respect to the output gap, β_{iu}, from 0.1 to 0.4 has a positive effect. The economy converges much faster. Eigenvalue diagrams give additional evidence that monetary policy may be beneficial. It tells in addition that the speed of convergence of the interest to its steady state level β_{ii} must not be too large, here greater than 0.8. The reaction to the output gap, β_{iu}, must be kept within a certain corridor. This corridor is quite large in the present case, and is stabilising for values between 0.05 and 1.6. Eventually, the sensitivity of the interest rate to inflation is stabilising if the speed of adjustment is greater than 0.05. This efficiency of the interest rate policy might be linked with the strong destabilising forces generated by the output, price and debt dynamics through the Fisher effect. Chiarella *et al.* (2003a) found slightly different results. In a model without debt they argue that the Taylor rule is stabilising for speed of adjustments that belongs to a small corridor. Faster and slower speed of adjustment brings instability, indicating that the monetary authorities should be neither be too quick nor too slow to react.

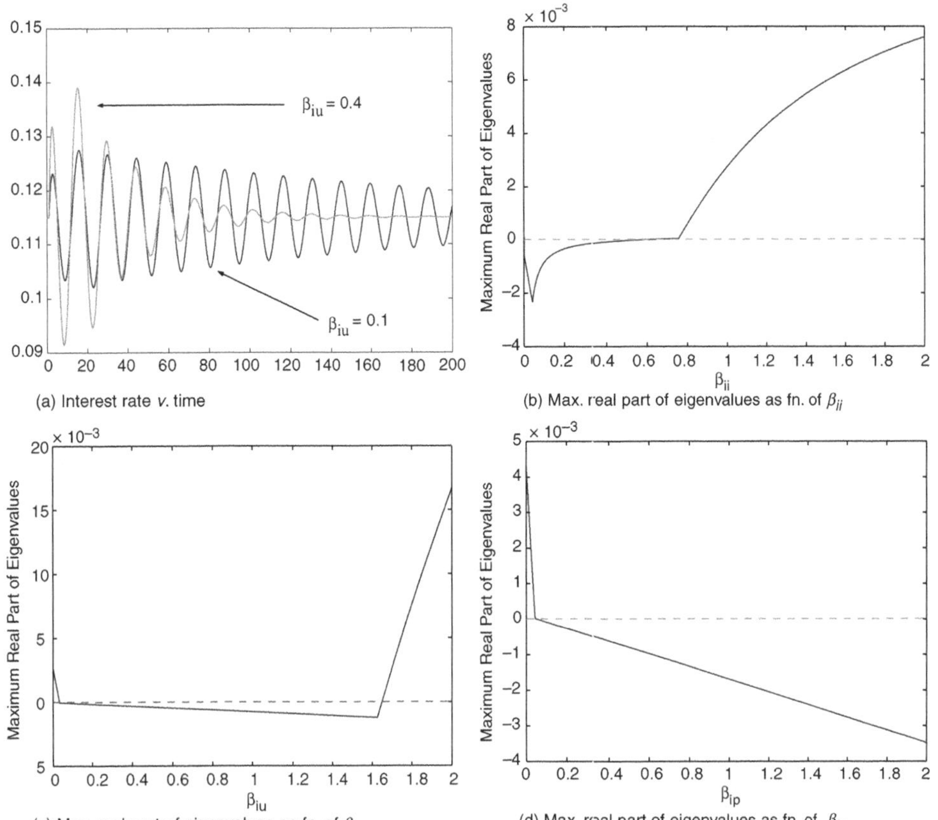

(a) Interest rate *v.* time

(b) Max. real part of eigenvalues as fn. of β_{ii}

(c) Max. real part of eigenvalues as fn. of β_{iu}

(d) Max. real part of eigenvalues as fn. of β_{ip}

Figure 9.23 Taylor rule

9.7.5 Fiscal policy

Figure 9.24 illustrates the effects of the fiscal policy on the stability of the model. Parameters are very similar to the coefficients of Figure 9.17. Few changes are applied: α_{iu} is decreased to 0.6, β_p is increased to 0.9 while the interest rate reacts slightly faster to inflation and to the output gap ($\beta_{ip} = \beta_{iu} = 0.2$). With the speed of adjustment of public spending to employment, β_{ge}, equal to 0.4, the economy fluctuates on a fifteen- to seventeen-year basis and converges towards the equilibrium. Increasing β_{ge} to 0.5 has a stabilising effect on the business cycle which converges faster. The maximum real parts of eigenvalues confirms the stabilising effects of a counter-cyclical fiscal policy. Eigenvalues are all negative between 0.2 and 1.4. Very slow or very fast speeds of adjustment are not stabilising; on the contrary, the economy loses stability when public spending reacts to the level of public debt. Eigenvalues are all positive for any speed of reaction. This illustration of some kind of Maastricht criteria underlines the destabilising effect of pro-cyclical policy when aggregate demand is fully taken into account.

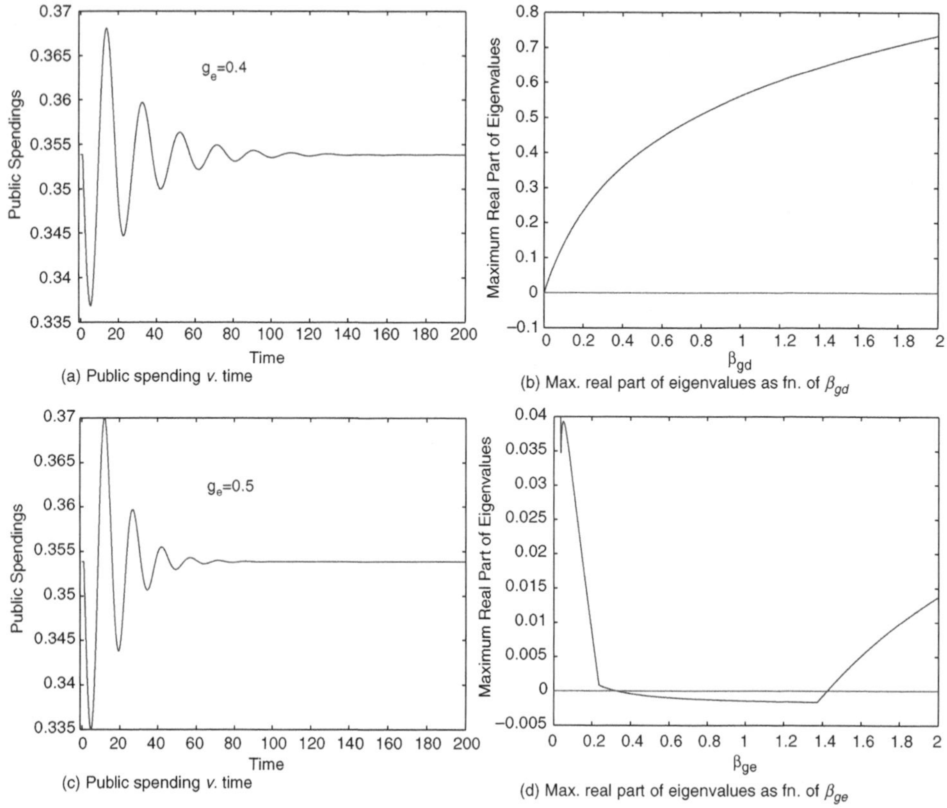

(a) Public spending *v.* time
(b) Max. real part of eigenvalues as fn. of β_{gd}
(c) Public spending *v.* time
(d) Max. real part of eigenvalues as fn. of β_{ge}

Figure 9.24 Fiscal policy

9.8 Conclusions

In the present period of financial instability, the fragility of banks has received increasing attention. The behaviour of banks is at the heart of the credit relationship. Bank performance alters the quantity of credit supplied and influences the accumulation of debt. In addition, there is a growing concern that debt defaults disrupt the credit relationship through their effect on the financial health of banks. Banking fragility from the asset side becomes very likely to the extent that over-indebtedness brings large scale debt defaults. In the case of a large credit loss, the government plays a central role in stabilising financial institutions. To avoid systemic risk, the socialisation of losses is necessary. The transfer of loss to public entities is a key instrument in the restoration of normal credit supply. A recession, in contrast, may be far worse.

In this section, we have tried to model some of the main mechanisms associated with the financial situation of banks and credit behaviour. There are three main aspects. First, it was shown that banks' profits are pro-cyclical and that their profits push up credit supply. In this sense, the behaviour of banks can cause economic oscillations to exhibit larger amplitude. This aspect also highlights an additional channel to the financial accelerator. Second, the over-indebtedness of borrowers reacts on the financial statements of banks and is an additional source of credit instability. By reducing banks' net equity in the downturn, credit disruption can worsen the recession. When financial institutions are brought into the picture, debt defaults become destabilising. This effect alters the conclusion of the preceding model. Debt defaults and bankruptcies are stabilising if they do not too much affect the financial system. These mechanisms are potentially strong and raise the question of the attitude of government to banks' financial distress. Third, bank bailouts by public authorities contribute to the restoration of the credit relationship. In line with the literature on banking crisis management, socialisation of losses is necessary when bank losses become very large. Meanwhile, the substitution of private debt by public debt carries the risk that a private debt crisis is transferred into a public sector one. It is in fact likely that loss socialisation triggers a self-accumulation of public debt.

10 Japan's institutional configuration and its financial crisis

In 1990, very few economists predicted that the stock market crash in Tokyo would trigger more than a decade of economic recession and stagnation. Unlike most developed economies, Japan had remained a dynamic economy over the 1970s and 1980s, experiencing neither stagflation nor rising unemployment even though economic growth had slowed. From 1973 to 1990, Japan grew at a rate of 3.9 per cent compared with the average of 2.5 per cent in Organization for Economic Co-operation and Development (OECD) countries and maintained close to full employment, with a 2 per cent unemployment rate.

The Japanese institutional setting[1] at the heart of this sustained period of growth was based on: i) a wages policy based on life employment and progressive income to ensure the support and the involvement of employees in the achievement of competitiveness; ii) an accommodating financial system that adjusted its profitability objectives to firms' performances and that formed tight links with borrowers; iii) governmental coordination of private sector strategies and expectations (Boyer, 2004).

Nevertheless, the 1980s were characterised by a growing disequilibrium linked to credit expansion and financial bubbles. The belief that Japanese organisations were able to dominate key industries led to a large expansion of credit. In reaction to these profit perspectives, financial assets, in particular real estate, attracted new investors and led to a large asset price inflation. The evolution of two factors modified the Japanese institutional setting. First, the increasing pressure on employees made their commitment to firm objectives ever more difficult. Second, the liberalisation of financial markets destabilised the main banking system and made the coordination of agents by public entities more hazardous. Increasing competition among banks led to a larger supply of credit and as a consequence to new sets of activities, including asset speculation, with far less monitoring.

With the burst of the real estate bubble, the large debt level pushed many borrowers into insolvency. The resulting non-performing loans degraded the health of financial institutions and prompted a deep and long lasting banking crisis (Hoshi and Kashyap, 1999; Calomiris and Mason, 2003). The length of the stagnation was subject to many

[1] See the definition of institutional economics in footnote 3 in Chapter 9.

interpretations (Wilson, 2000). Some stressed the weakening of aggregate demand resulting from lower investment and consumption. Others highlighted the macroeconomic mistakes of monetary and fiscal authorities (Kuttner and Posen, 2001). The liquidity trap, the asset bubble and price deflation, and the recession of 1998 have been interpreted as resulting from monetary mistakes (Bernanke, 2000; Nakaso, 2001), inadequate tax cuts and fiscal stimulus. Neo-institutionalists argued that the weak enforcement of bankruptcy laws led to the slow resolution of non-performing loans (Andrieu-Lacu, 2006), and that procedures put in place to resolve the banking crisis in fact delayed its management and prevented speedier reaction to it.

The main elements of the Japanese crisis consisted of debt and price dynamics, the effect of default on the banking sector, as well as the reaction of monetary and fiscal authorities. The theoretical models developed in Part III of this book provide a good framework to interpret the Japanese crisis as they combine these different elements and allow assessment of their respective effects.

In this chapter, we examine the three main elements that shape the behaviour of the private sector and the effect of their interaction in terms of stability. We first use estimation techniques to explore whether aggregate demand in Japan has been wage- or profit-led. While household consumption has been a key pillar of accumulation in Japan, firms' profitability has also been very important, and it is not clear which effect has dominated.

We then ask whether the real wage was labour market- or goods market-led. Again, the Japanese case is complex. Although mass lay-offs are not a key adjustment variable in Japan, the particularities of Japanese wage bargaining, and increasing job flexibility in the 1990s do not necessarily imply a relatively more rigid nominal wage.

Finally, we examine whether there has been a financial accelerator effect. While the main banking system involves close links between firms and banks, the progressive financial market liberalisation may have altered these relationships and favoured credit rationing.

Further, we discuss whether the private sector was shaped by unstable forces that may explain the crisis of the 1990s. The absence of institutional complementarity[2] may be an explanation for the Japanese crisis. We then assess what has been the overall effect of government intervention. As some have argued that the length of the crisis can be largely explained by policy mistakes, it is of interest to ask whether the speed of adjustment of the central bank interest rate falls within our theoretical stability corridors. In particular, it is challenging to ask why debt deflation was kept within a limited range and did not give rise to an increasing debt level. There are two possible answers. First, private sector instability was moderate which implied moderate debt deflation. Second, public intervention limited the extent of price deflation.

[2] A main result of institutional economics is actually to show that there is no single model of capitalist economies, but that different capitalist regimes are likely to coexist. To describe this variety of organisation, institutional economics uses the concept of institutional complementarity. Institutional complementarity can be defined following two principles. A first one is a Pareto-efficiency criterion -- institutions must be shaped such that all economic agents are better off. A second definition considers that a set of institutions is complementary, if it contains destabilising trajectories but maintains business cycles within viable magnitudes.

Given the lack of data for non-performing loans, we estimate the parameters of the following 5D model, which has equations for real wage, debt, output, the active population to capital ratio and a Taylor interest rate rule:

$$\dot{\omega} = \omega\kappa\big((1-k_p)\beta_w(e-\bar{e}) + (k_w-1)\beta_p(u-\bar{u})\big), \tag{10.1}$$

$$\dot{\lambda} = g_k - \delta - (1-\tau_f)r - (\hat{p} + g_k - \delta)\lambda, \tag{10.2}$$

$$\dot{y} = \beta_y(y^d - y) + (n + \delta_k - g_k)y, \tag{10.3}$$

$$\dot{l}^e = l^e\big(n - (g_k - \delta_k)\big), \tag{10.4}$$

$$\dot{i} = \beta_{ii}(i_0 - i) + \beta_{ip}(\hat{p} - \bar{\pi}) + \beta_{iu}(u - \bar{u}). \tag{10.5}$$

While small size models could be estimated from Japanese data, the lack of quarterly data concerning non-performing loans and the management of the banking crisis prevent such an exercise. We are nevertheless able to discuss two main aspects. First, as noted in the previous model, debt default is a possible way to resolve the debt problem. Nevertheless, its effect largely depends on whether it results from the bankruptcy of firms and how the real sector behaves. Second, debt default has potentially stabilising effects if it does not affect the banking sector on a large scale. The deep banking crisis in Japan suggests the opposite. Nevertheless, the various government interventions to tackle this issue potentially offset these deleterious effects.

10.1 A stable profit-led real sector

In this section, we estimate a version of the model restricted to the real side variables: namely, wages, prices, output and employment. One of the aims is to understand whether instability is purely related to real mechanisms. Price deflation might well result from real effect. In such a case, the Japanese financial disruptions may just be the result of a real crisis but not the triggering factor. An important source of instability in the real sector could be a lack of complementarity between income distribution and the determination of real wages. In fact, a profit-led economy with rigid nominal wages is prone to crisis.

The system of equations (10.1)–(10.5) is reformulated in discrete time in order to be estimated for the Japanese case. First, the active population to capital ratio is a definition and therefore cannot be estimated. Second, we decompose the real wage equation into two separate equations, for nominal wages and prices respectively. Third, the impact of firms' debt to capital ratio on capacity u is not considered here to abstract from financial variables. This leaves us with the following system of four equations:[3]

$$\hat{w}_t = \beta_{we}(e_{t-1} - e_0) + k_{wp}\hat{p}_t, \tag{10.6}$$

$$\hat{p}_t = \beta_{pu}(u_{t-1} - u_0) + k_{pw}\hat{w}_t, \tag{10.7}$$

[3] See Flaschel *et al.* (2009) for full details of how the system (10.6)–(10.9) is derived.

$$\hat{u}_t = \alpha_u(\hat{u}_{t-1} - \hat{u}_0) + \alpha_v(\hat{v}_{t-1} - \hat{v}_0), \tag{10.8}$$

$$\hat{e}_t = \alpha_{eu1}\hat{u}_{t-1} + \alpha_{eu2}\hat{u}_{t-2} + \alpha_{eu3}\hat{u}_{t-3}. \tag{10.9}$$

We rely on Generalized Method of Moments (GMM) type estimations for the coefficients. It is well known that GMM is suited for dealing with the issue of endogenous variables. As instruments, we use the past value of the explanatory variables up to three lags for production capacities. We make use of quarterly data over the period 1980–2004; a period that comprises the boom and bust aspect of the Japanese crisis. Data sources are described in the Appendix in Section 10.8. Of interest is the information published by the Ministry of Finance (MOF) related to firms' financial statements. This enables us to test directly for the effect of financial variables on economic activity.

In Section 10.2 production capacities are illustrated in Figure 10.1(a).[4,5] The 'boom and bust' aspect of the Japanese economy appears clearly. The 1980s are characterised by an increasing trend in economic activity and wider oscillations. Production capacities peak at 1.15 in 1991. The 1990s was a period of lower production capacity tending to follow a downward trend. From 1991 to 1993, it dropped to 0.95 and reached its lowest point in 2002 at 0.87. The recovery between 1993 and 1997 also appears clearly, as production capacities are restored to 1.07 in 1997 before the second depression of the 1990s starts in 1998. Production capacities drop to 0.87 in 2002 before the economy starts to recover and most financial disruptions end.[6]

The employment rate is closely linked with the business cycle (Figure 10.1(b)). The 1980s are characterised by near full employment. Employment deteriorates until 1987 to reach 97 per cent but it is only a 1 per cent drop over seven years. And the boom of the late 1980s raises employment back to its pre-1980s level. With the deterioration of economic activity, employment worsens. It decreases at first very slowly but it then decreases steadily. The fall starts in 1992 only and unemployment reaches 5.5 per cent in 2002. The economic rebound over the mid-1990s hardly appears in the data. The rapid deterioration of employment over the second half of the 1990s might be the result of the progressive deregulation of the labour market and the rise of unconventional employment.[7]

Wage change[8] follows the level of employment but has a clear negative trend (Figure 10.1(c)). Over the 1980s, periods of economic expansion generated accelerating wage inflation, e.g. between 1987 and 1991, but inflation is still cooling down over that period. The economic crisis increased (the rate of) wage disinflation. Wage inflation slowed three times over the 1990s. At the beginning of the crisis it drops from 0.04 to 0.02; during the years 1997–8 it drops from 0.02 to just below 0; and in 2000–1

4 They are normalised to 1 in 2,000, which explains why they are above 1 for the period of the 1980s.
5 The data sources used for the figures and tables of this chapter are listed in the Appendix in Section 10.8.
6 The problems of the banking system are almost all resolved at this date.
7 See Lechevalier (2003) for a detailed presentation of the debate about the changing nature of the Japanese labour market.
8 The graph represents the variation of the wage index in logarithm.

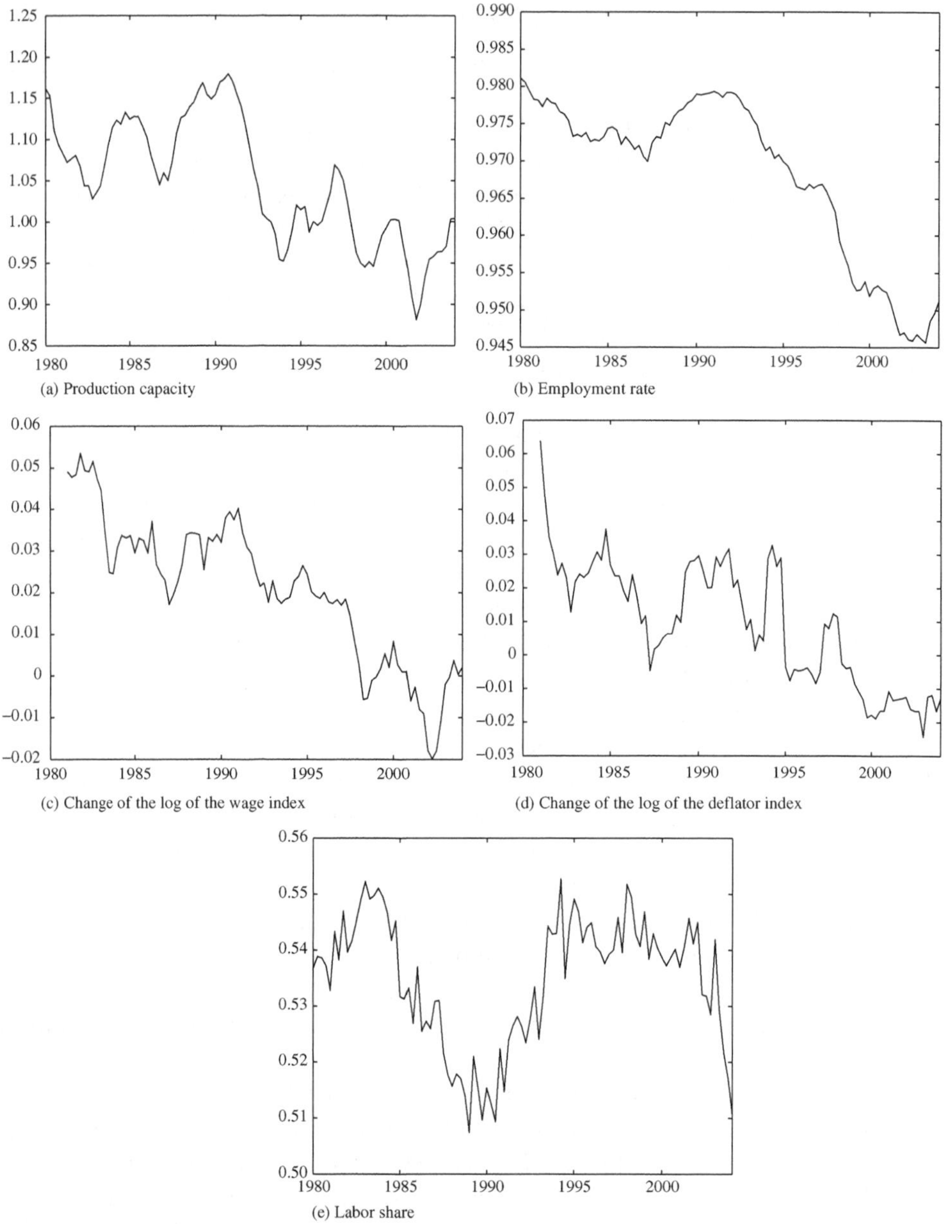

Figure 10.1 Japan – the main economic indicators

it drops from 0 to –0.02. In 1997 and 2001, wage inflation turns negative and wages decrease. It is surprising that nominal wages drop: this has been a rare occurrence in developed economies since the Second World War.

Similarly to wages, prices are also pro-cyclical. The change of the GDP deflator follows a downward trend, which underlines the strong disinflationary forces at work over that period. Inflation accelerates in the late 1980s up to 0.04 in 1991, before

Table 10.1. *Phillips–Perron unit test results for labour shave data*

Variable	Adj. Test Stat	Prob	Variable	Adj. Test Stat	Prob
u	–3.153	0.10	$d(u)$	–5.187	0.00
e	–1.330	0.87	$d(e)$	–7.663	0.00
$\ln(w)$	–0.123	0.99	$d\ln(w)$	–20.063	0.00
$\ln(p)$	0.371	0.99	$d\ln(p)$	– 9.696	0.00
v	–1.830	0.68	$d(v)$	–14.908	0.00

decreasing quickly in the 1990s. Price inflation is zero over the period 1994–6, before turning negative from 1998 onward (Figure 10.1(d)). Compared to the change in wages, disinflation seems to be much more gradual.[9] There is no abrupt decrease of inflation. On the contrary there are two peaks, in 1994 and in 1998.

The labour share appears in Figure 10.1(e). It fluctuates at around 53 per cent of GDP. It drops during the late 1980s and early 1990s from 55 per cent in 1984 to 51 per cent in 1990. The labour share then recovers in the first phase of the crisis, up to 55 per cent in 1994. From 1995, it follows a decreasing trend especially in the late 1990s. The labour share seems to be negatively linked with the business cycle. It actually decreases in the late 1980s during the boom years, while it increases in the early 1990s when the crisis starts. The same trend prevails after the early 1990s. The labour share decreases over the 1994–7 rebound, while it increases at the beginning of the deflation.

Given that we deal with times series, we must check for stationarity to avoid any problem related to spurious regressions. We carry out Phillips–Perron unit root tests for each series in order to account, not only for residual autocorrelation as is done by the standard Augmented Dickey-Fuller (ADF) tests, but also for possible residual heteroscedasticity when testing for stationarity. The Phillips – Perron test specifications and results are shown in Table 10.1. As often with linear economic series, variables are non-stationary. Nevertheless, taking the first difference is sufficient to provide stationarity.[10] An alternative possibility to make the series stationary is to divide each series by the stock of capital. Although the outcome is very much in line with our theoretical models, which express variables over the stock of capital in the reduced form equations, questions arise as a result of the implicit assumption that such a procedure entails – in particular dividing each series by the capital stock assumes that each series can be explained by the stock of capital with a unit root coefficient. In such a case, cointegration procedures are probably more suited than short-term estimation techniques such as GMM employed below. To correct for seasonality, we applied either the X12 procedure or we integrated quarterly dummies in the regressions.

The main results of this first estimation are given in Table 10.2 and indicate that wages are more flexible than prices in Japan.[11] Wages are more sensitive to the employment

[9] The graph represents the variation of the deflator index in logarithms.

[10] We write $d()$ to indicate first differences of the variable in the brackets.

[11] The number of stars gives the level of significance of the coefficient: *** is 1 percent, ** is 5 percent and * is 10 percent.

Table 10.2. *Estimations results: the real model*

$\hat{w}$	β_{we}	k_{wp}	$cst.$			R^2	DW
	0.363***	0.1	0.008***			0.79	1.77
$\hat{p}$	β_{pu}	k_{pw}	$cst.$			R^2	DW
	0.024**	0.459**	−0.001			0.32	2.17
$\hat{u}$	α_u	α_v	$cst.$			R^2	DW
	−0.067***	−0.276**	−0.002			0.94	0.84
$\hat{e}$	α_{eu1}	α_{eu2}	α_{eu3}	α_{eu4}	$cst.$	R^2	DW
	0.015***	−0.025**	0.029	−0.020	−0.003**	0.20	1.86

rate $\beta_{we} = 0.363$ than prices to capacity production $\beta_{pu} = 0.024$. Nevertheless, at this stage wages do not take into account inflation as κ_{wp} is non-significant while prices are very much sensitive to inflation costs $\kappa_{pw} = 0.459$. Put differently, nominal wages are largely determined by demand pressure while prices are largely determined by cost-push elements. Nonetheless, wages in Japan are more flexible than prices for the period 1980–2004. The Harrodian accelerator is negative and small, $\alpha_u = -0.067$, which implies stability of the output on itself. Finally, the labour share appears with a negative sign $\alpha_v = -0.267$ and is significant at 5 per cent. This suggests that the economy is profit-led and confirms the graphical analysis. Overall, the real sector is stable as aggregate demand is profit-led and the real wage is labour market-led. The real sector can be represented by a 2D model for output and wage dynamics (equations (10.1) and (10.3)) that we reproduce here:

$$\dot{\omega} = \omega\kappa\big((1 - k_p)\beta_w(e - \bar{e}) - (1 - k_w)\beta_p(u - \bar{u})\big),$$
$$\dot{y} = \beta_y(y^d - y) + (n - (g_k - \delta))y.$$

The estimation gives us the following signs of the Jacobian matrix, which imply stability:

$$J = \begin{vmatrix} - & - \\ + & 0 \end{vmatrix}$$

10.2 Pro-cyclical financial markets

A key aspect of our theoretical work is to integrate the effect of financial variables on the output dynamics. In particular, we make use of a measure of the net wealth of firms. Given that the theoretical model uniformly points to the destabilising effect of firms' net wealth on investment, any significant empirical evidence should identify a destabilising mechanism. Figure 10.2 displays a measure of firms' wealth. It is made up of assets minus liabilities divided by fixed assets. Data are taken from the MOF which publishes quarterly data on firms' financial statements. Firms' net wealth has a clear 'boom and bust' aspect over the 1980s and early 1990s. It increases continuously over the 1980s to reach 1.03 in 1990. It then drops to 0.88 in 1993 before rebounding to 0.97 in 1997.

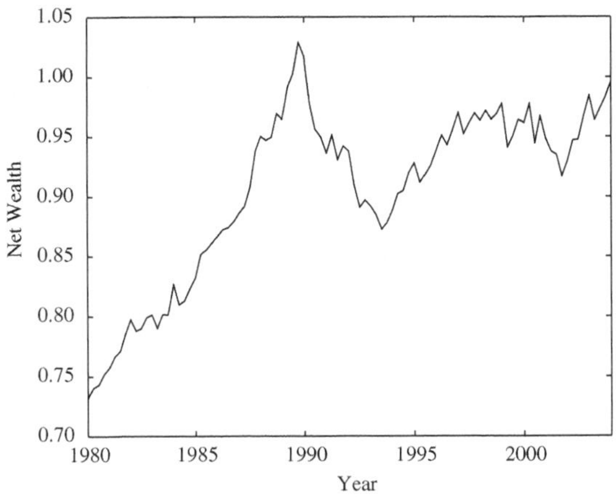

Figure 10.2 Japan - an indicator of firms' wealth (assets minus liabilities divided by fixed assets)

Nevertheless, the deflation of the late 1990s does not appear very clearly. Estimating the effect of banks' net wealth on investment requires inclusion of a measure of firms' assets and liabilities in the equation (10.8) for capacity u. Furthermore, firms' budget constraints are not directly estimated, as it is an accounting identity. The new IS curve to be estimated is now

$$\hat{u}_t = \alpha_u(u_{t-1} - u_0) + \alpha_v(v_{t-1} - v_0) + \alpha_{nw}(\lambda_{t-1} - \lambda_0). \tag{10.10}$$

Even if normalised by the stock of capital, firms' net wealth is non-stationary and would require differencing to become stationary (Table 10.3). Nevertheless, given that firms' net wealth enters capacity production as a function of the discrepancy between its value and its steady state value,[12] the resulting variable is very likely to be stationary. Concerning the real parameters, the estimated coefficients (see Table 10.4) are mostly the same as previously found. The real wage is still labour market-led, β_{we} increased slightly from 0.363 to 0.409 and κ_{wp} is still not significant. The sensitivity of prices to the output gap is slightly larger too, at 0.039 compared with 0.024 previously. The major change concerns the sensitivity of prices to wage costs which dropped from 0.459 to 0.15. The output gap is still negatively correlated to itself with $\alpha_u = -0.082$ and aggregate demand is still profit-led as the labour share is negatively correlated to output, $\alpha_v = -0.201$. The parameter for firms' net wealth is positive and significant, $\alpha_{nw} = 0.065$. There is evidence that firms' balance sheets matter for the output. Although the parameter may seem rather small, the theoretical models underline that the economy may lose stability for a very small value of α_{nw}. Given that the effect of firms' net wealth is unambiguously destabilising in the model, the firms' financial accelerator has contributed to instability.

12 The average of firms' steady state over the sample.

Table 10.3. *Phillips–Perron unit test results for interest rate data*

Variable	Adj. Test Stat	Prob	Variable	Adj. Test Stat	Prob
NW	-2.068	0.55	NW	-9.895	0.00

Table 10.4. *Estimations results: with credit rationing*

$\hat{w}$	β_{we}	k_{wp}	$cst.$			R^2	DW
	0.409***	0.20	0.009***			0.760	1.76
$\hat{p}$	β_{pu}	k_{pw}	$cst.$			R^2	DW
	0.039***	0.15*	0.001			0.31	2.12
$\hat{u}$	α_u	α_v	α_{nw}	$cst.$		R^2	DW
	−0.082***	−0.201*	0.065**	0.001		0.94	0.83
$\hat{e}$	α_{eu1}	α_{eu2}	α_{eu3}	α_{eu4}	cst.	R^2	DW
	0.022***	−0.023***	0.014***	−0.009**	−0.003***	0.237	1.94

10.3 Less than optimal fiscal and monetary policies

The Japanese government used a vast array of macroeconomic tools to try to lift Japan out of recession over the 1990s. The effectiveness of such tools has often been questioned. Public spending was considered inefficient, politically motivated and slowly implemented while monetary policy was considered inadequate, especially during the liquidity trap of the late 1990s. Our theoretical model underlines the fact that for fiscal and monetary policy, public intervention is efficient only to the extent that it is implemented at the right speed. A reaction that is either too slow or too rapid adds to the disequilibrium. We first estimate a Taylor rule and then discuss the various fiscal packages implemented by different governments in an attempt to stimulate the economy.

The question of monetary policy is a difficult question in the Japanese case. Although economists usually refer to the Taylor rule to assess whether monetary policy is too loose or too tight, the question arises whether this is still the required framework for the Japanese case. In the late 1990s, Japan's interest rate reached a zero bound and the central bank was not able to reduce the interest rate further to fight price deflation. Some have argued that evaluating monetary policy by use of a Taylor rule in such a case could give a negative interest rate. Others have focused on the alternative tools or channels that monetary policy should mobilise to fight deflation, such as the exchange rate (Eggertsson and Woodford, 2003, 2004, for instance).

For the estimation exercise, monetary policy is best illustrated by the call rate in Figure 10.3. The central bank interest rate decreased continuously until the late 1980s, and may have contributed to real estate speculation. Conversely, the interest rate increases in the late 1980s probably contributed to triggering the crisis. The interest rate more than doubled from 3.5 per cent to 8 per cent between 1987 and 1991.

Table 10.5. *Phillips–Perron unit root test results on the interest rate*

Variable	Adj. Test Stat	Prob
i	-3.611	0.007

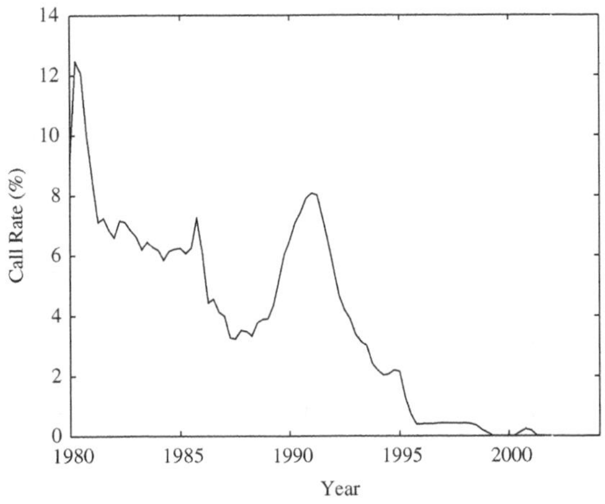

Figure 10.3 The call rate in Japan: 1980–2004

Once the crisis erupted, monetary authorities continuously decreased the interest rate to support the economy. Nonetheless, from 1999 monetary policy faced the zero bound interest rate and the so-called liquidity trap.

The unit roots test performed on the interest rate data shows that the series is stationary and does not need to be differenced (see Table 10.5). Introducing the interest rate estimation into the system does not modify the main results found previously. We have estimated the interest rate rule Equation (10.5) in the form

$$i_t = \beta_{ii} i_{t-1} + \beta_{ip} \hat{p}_t + \beta_{iu}(u_{t-1} - u_0). \tag{10.11}$$

The speeds of adjustment of nominal wages are still larger than prices, even though nominal wage sensitivity to employment is smaller at $\beta_{we} = 0.275$ (see Table 10.6).[13] The cost-push element in nominal wages is now positive and significant at $\kappa_{wp} = 0.207$ (again see Table 10.6), while it was not significant in the previous estimations. Price flexibility to the output gap is still relatively small $\beta_{pu} = 0.018$ while the cost-push element is large, being $\kappa_{pw} = 0.654$. Aggregate demand is still profit-led $\alpha_{uv} = -0.135$ which is consistent with the real wage. The sensitivity of output to itself and the effect

[13] Table 10.6 comes from the estimation of equations (10.6), (10.7), (10.9), (10.10) and (10.11).

Table 10.6. *Estimations results: with government policy*

$\hat{w}$	β_{we}	k_{wp}	$cst.$			R^2	DW
	0.275***	0.207***	0.008***			0.805	1.84
$\hat{p}$	β_{pu}	k_{pw}	$cst.$			R^2	DW
	0.018***	0.654***	−0.003***			0.311	1.99
$\hat{u}$	α_u	α_v	α_{nw}	$cst.$		R^2	DW
	−0.067***	−0.135*	0.100***	−0.003***		0.944	0.82
$\hat{e}$	α_{eu1}	α_{eu2}	α_{eu3}	α_{eu4}	cst.	R^2	DW
	0.053***	−0.081***	0.052***	−0.021***	−0.004***	0.376	2.57
i	β_{ii}	β_{ip}	β_{iu}			R^2	DW
	0.887***	0.074***	0.040***			0.981	1.13

of firms' balance sheets are left relatively unaffected. α_u and α_{λ_f} increased respectively from –0.082 to –0.067 and from 0.065 to 0.1. Up to this point, we still have a stable real sector with an unstable impact of financial variables. In this context, the Taylor rule appears to give mixed results. The interest rate is sensitive to both inflation and the output gap with a larger weight on the price rather than on the output component. Meanwhile, coefficients seem rather small, $\beta_{ip} = 0.074$ and $\beta_{iu} = 0.040$. Both coefficients are too small with respect to the existing empirical evidence of the Taylor rule. This might well be due to the liquidity trap as the interest rate was rigid downward to price and output dynamics. More generally, the numerous studies that test the Taylor rule in Japan do not give clear results. As underlined by Kuttner and Posen (2004), existing studies find opposite results, monetary policy being either too loose or too tight. In particular, they show that results depend largely on the measure of the output gap, on the trend estimate of the output gap by making use of real-time versus post-estimate data, and on the type of Taylor rule (backward or forward) estimated. All existing studies nevertheless show that the interest rate is more sensitive to prices than to the output gap in line with our own conclusion. With respect to the theoretical models, these coefficients lie on the boundary of the stability corridor. Faster reactions by the central bank would increase stability. A key point is that monetary policy did not provoke instability, although it lacked efficiency.

With respect to fiscal policy, we do not estimate the determinants of government policy (is it pro-cyclical or counter-cyclical?) as it is more difficult to estimate than a Taylor rule and as the size of the sample limits the number of equations that can be estimated. At the same time, it is well known that the government adopted numerous fiscal packages to sustain economic activity (OECD, 2002). The total amounted to 136 trillion yen, which is 27 per cent of GDP. This number is surprisingly much larger than the cost of the banking crisis. The vast majority was devoted to public works (25 per cent of total package), in an attempt to alleviate the loss of real estate and construction companies. Large real estate projects stimulated the construction sector and sustained land prices at the heart of the banking crisis. Another significant proportion of spending financed tax cuts (12 per cent of the total package). These various tax cuts aimed primarily at alleviating the fiscal burden of high income households. A temporary income cut was passed in 1994 for a three-year period. At the same time, the tax base was enlarged. It was balanced by a 2 per cent point increase (up to 5 per cent) of the value-added tax which falls more heavily on small incomes as they are mostly spent on consumption goods. The income tax was repealed in 1997 but was replaced by a permanent income tax for corporations and top incomes in 1998 (Kuttner and Posen (2001)). In Japan, taxes fall mostly on salaried urban workers rather than on small business owners and rural residents.

If the figures tend to show that spending increased in line with the various crises, the attitude of the government has been slightly more complex. In fact, fiscal authorities hesitated between sustaining aggregate demand and maintaining the deficit within reasonable limits. This explains why fiscal expansions followed fiscal contractions and why tax cuts followed tax increases. Announced projects were not always implemented as the central administration delegated the job to local government, but did not allocate the corresponding funds. The packages of August 1992 and April 1993 for instance amounted to 24 trillion yen, while originally targeting double this amount. Another example is the fiscal structural reform law in 1997 that aimed at restoring fiscal balance but which worsened the deflationary trends and was postponed (Kuttner and Posen (2001)).

10.4 Debt default without bankruptcy

A key feature of the Japanese crisis is that default was massive but bankruptcy was rare. Put differently, the transfer of losses from borrowers to lenders took place on a very large scale. We have seen in the theoretical sections of the previous chapter that debt default without bankruptcy has, to some extent, a stabilising effect when aggregate demand is profit-led. Contrary to some neo-institutionalist claims, the violations of property rights in Japan were probably not at the heart of the long-lasting recession.

Figure 10.4 shows the rate and the number of firm bankruptcies from 1975 onwards. The rate of bankruptcy decreases in the boom to reach its lowest point in 1990 at 0.05 per cent. It then increases during each recession, between 1991 and 1994, between 1997 and 1999, and between 2001 and 2002. Nevertheless, it is almost always contained at a low rate of between 0.1 per cent and 0.15 per cent. The number of bankrupt firms never exceeded 20,000 cases. Decomposition by types of industry tells us that all sectors incurred higher bankruptcies during the crisis, but that this was more concentrated within the construction sector as well as within the wholesale and retail trade sectors. The number of bankruptcies was thus relatively small with respect to the depth of the Japanese crisis.

Conversely, debt default was very large during the Japanese crisis, as can be seen from Figure 10.5. The Financial Supervisory Agency (FSA), which was set up to tackle the issue of bad debt in the early 1990s, has proposed two official measures of non-performing loans: the *risk management loans* and the *loans disclosed under the financial*

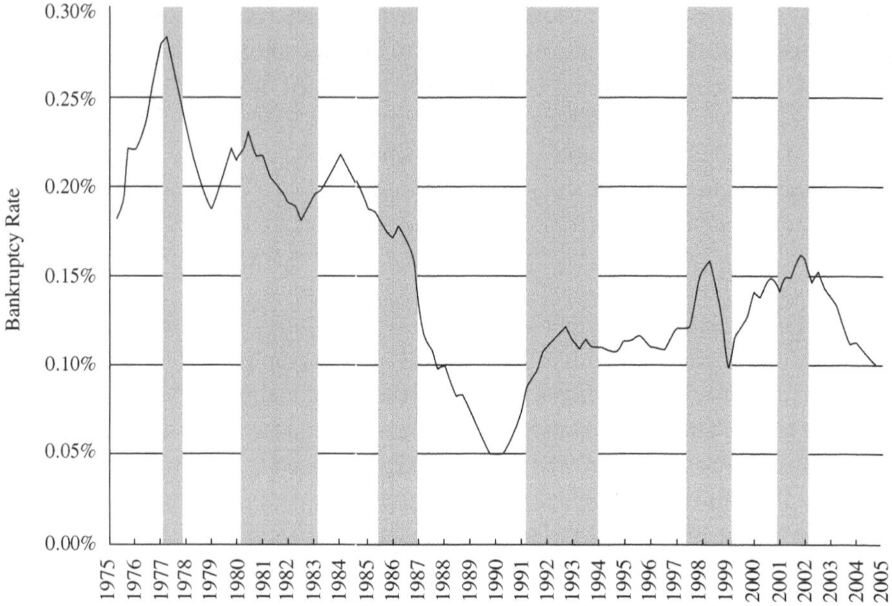

Figure 10.4 Firms' bankruptcy, reproduced from Kageyama and Harada (2007). The shaded zones indicate the recessionary periods.

reconstruction law. While their breakdowns differ slightly, their results are very similar: outstanding loans were 34.8 and 35.3 trillion yen respectively at the end of March 2003. Figure 10.5(a) gives an estimate of the stock of bad debt in Japanese financial institutions between 1993 and 2006 under the *risk management loans* measure.[14] Financial institutions hid the bad debt problem until 1995. From March 1995 to March 1996, the quantity of bad debt doubled, from 15,000 billion yen to 30,000 billion yen as financial institutions started to write them off. As a percentage of GDP, the stock of bad debt amounted to 6 per cent of GDP in March 1996. Bad debt levels then stayed constant over the mid-1990s and early 2000s despite the fact that they had been progressively written off. In fact, borrowers defaulted until 2002 and financial institutions encountered difficulties in absorbing non-performing loans. A peak was reached in March 2002, when the stock of bad debt amounted to 8.5 per cent of GDP. It then decreased quickly. In March 2006, it reached 2.5 per cent, the level prevailing in 1993. The cumulative loss for the disposal of non-performing loans reached 100,000 billion yen in 2006. This is equal to 20 per cent of GDP (Figure 10.5(b)). Banks also built provisions for non-performing loan losses. In terms of the stock of bad debt, the size increased from 30 per cent in 1993 to 60 per cent in March 1998. At the 1998 peak, provisions aggregated to 18,000 billion yen.

[14] Numbers are dated to March of each year.

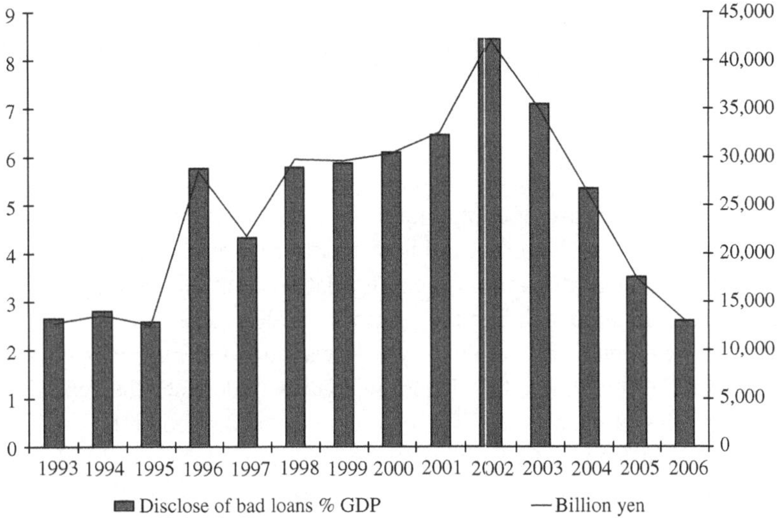

(a) Disclosed bad loans

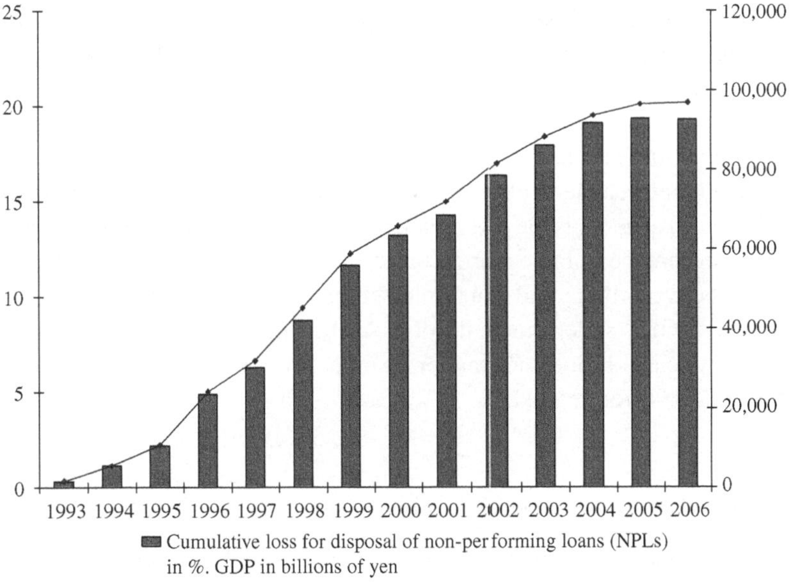

(b) Cumulative losses

Figure 10.5 Loss related to default. Source: FSA

10.5 Bad debt and banking crises

At the same time, although default alleviated borrowers' debt burden, the banking system was deeply affected by these large losses. The resulting destabilising effect on banks overturned the stabilising effects of default on non-financial firms. In line with the theoretical model, default becomes unambiguously destabilising if it deeply affects the banking sector and leads to credit rationing and a credit crunch.

Losses for NPLs[15] have affected banks' financial health negatively for more than a decade. Although lending margins and gross profits improved over the 1990s, loan losses generated negative profit before capital gains over almost the entire period of the Japanese stagnation. Banks' profitability reached its lowest points in 1995 (–7 trillion yen), 1997 (–7.9 trillion yen) and 1998 (–8.3 trillion yen) when loan losses were the largest (13.3, 13.5 and 13.5 trillion yen respectively). In 2002, profitability improved along the gradual decrease of debt default but was still negative (–1 trillion yen). As a result, many banks went bankrupt in Japan and the number of financial institutions fell dramatically. The large disruption to credit relations that the banking crisis generated is a key element to understanding the length of the Japanese recession.

The degree to which the banking system was affected by NPLs is controversial. According to Fukao (2002), the disclosed figures understate the real situation as a result of the rules of accounting. The bad loans of banks should be double in 2002 – 71 trillion yen, instead of 42 trillion yen. In addition, loan loss and therefore provisions, are underestimated as losses are assessed with respect to a one-year time frame, while automatic debt roll-over should imply a three-year time frame. The estimation of non-performing loans according to banks' self-assessment is actually far greater (see Figure 10.6). In the bank self-assessment procedure, the definition of credits that fall into the category *need special attention* is much wider. Included in this definition are loans that *need attention* while the *financial reconstruction law* considers only loans that *need special attention*. Figure 10.6 displays the difference between the *financial reconstruction law* and banks' self-assessment of NPLs. For each column of Figure 10.6(a), the first three elements equal the estimate by the *financial reconstruction law* while the fourth element is the discrepancy between FSA assessment and banks' assessment. The difference is large, for instance in September 2001 the banks' estimate of NPLs was between three and four times bigger than the official figures. NPLs reach 20 per cent of GDP under this definition. At the same time, the discrepancy concerns the less risky loans. It does not matter so much for the measure of banks' losses (see Inaba *et al.* (2004) for details).

10.6 Delayed and weak government response

The banking crisis has been actively combatted by the Japanese monetary authorities in order to limit credit disruption. As underlined in the theoretical model of Section 9.6.5, an appropriate answer by the government to the banking crisis may cancel most of the perverse effects linked to NPLs. Meanwhile, despite the effort of the monetary authorities, the length of the banking crisis can to some extent be attributed to a slow and inappropriate response.

In Japan, the management of the banking crisis can be divided into two main time periods. Until 1997, the resolution of failing institutions followed the usual procedure,

[15] NPL = non-performing loans.

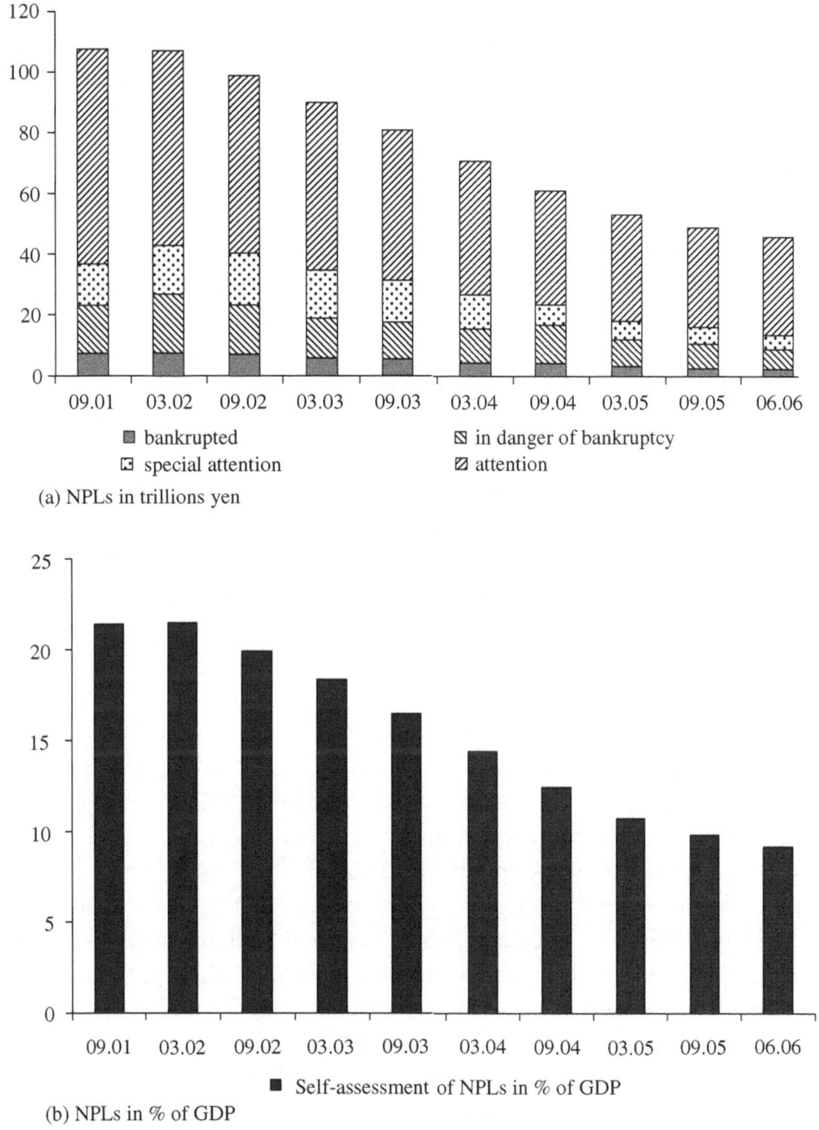

Figure 10.6 Banks' self-assessment of NPLs. Source: FSA

based on a buy-in principle. The first cases of distressed financial institutions were relatively small and specialised in the real estate market. Monetary authorities organised the distribution of loss between shareholders and creditors. The government assumed a small share of the losses in the Jusen case: 685 billion yen in the form of loss compensation. From 1997, although the government did not want to directly support financial institutions, the worsening of the banking crisis forced it to transfer public funds to financial institutions and to shift to buy-out procedures. A possible explanation of the length of the banking crisis lies in the reluctance of the Japanese government in the early 1990s to tackle the issue of bad debt on a large scale, as this would have required buying out banks.

10.6.1 The early response: buy-in of failing banks

In Japan, until 1997 banking failures were traditionally dealt with by the private sector. They took place under Merger and Acquisition assisted by public authorities or under Purchase and Assumption. The so-called 'cohort procedure' follows a buy-in principle and corresponds to a distribution of losses within financial institutions. This procedure is a direct consequence of the high degree of stability of the financial system since the Second World War. Financial institutions were very sound and there was no major bankruptcy until the 1990s. Furthermore, monetary authorities were concerned with avoiding any buy-out of the financial sector. They tried to avoid any incentives that would lead to moral hazard. In addition, the population strongly disapproved of such measures, as the banking sector had historically larger privileges than other sectors of the economy. Losses were distributed between shareholders, creditors and assuming institutions. Financial institutions purchased assets and assumed liabilities of the failed institutions or merged with them. The rescuing institutions agreed on the share of losses and public spending was not massively mobilised: at most limited to partial recapitalisation and by the transfer of assets to the Deposit Insurance Corporation (DIC). This type of procedure addressed the case of rather small bankruptcies and relied on the solidarity of the main financial actors.

A good illustration of the buy-in procedure is the famous Jusen case. Along with credit cooperatives, the Jusen companies were the first bankrupt financial institutions of the early 1990s. The Jusen companies were non-bank financial institutions founded by larger banks to grant housing loans to households. There were eight Jusen,[16] and the oldest was founded in 1971. The two banks (Long Term Credit Bank of Japan and Nippon Credit Bank)[17] that would be privatised in 1997 were in fact the mother banks of two Jusen companies: Daiichi Jutaku Kinyu and Nippon Housing Loan respectively. These institutions were created as larger banks had little interest in supplying small and complicated credits to households. Jusen could not accept deposits but received funds from mother banks. Nevertheless, the deregulation of the banking system in the early 1980s lowered profit margins of banks and the real estate bubble made real estate credit more worthwhile. Banks therefore started to compete with Jusen; which in turn were driven away from housing credit towards real estate and construction companies. Jusen loan portfolios were composed of 95.6 per cent housing loans in 1980, while

16 Nippon Jutaku Kinyu, Jutaku Loan Service, Juso, Sogojukin, Daiichi Jutaku Kinyu, Chigin Seiho Jutaku Loan, Nippon Housing Loan and Kyodou Jutaku Loan.

17 LTCB and NCB.

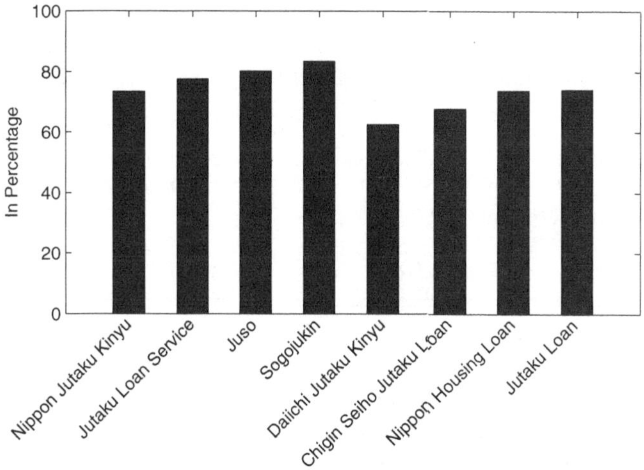

Figure 10.7 Bad assets of the Jusen companies in June 1995, reproduced from Kataoka (1997)

loans to companies amounted to 78.4 per cent by 1991. The major creditors of Jusen were agricultural cooperatives that benefited from special legislation.

In the late 1980s, the real estate market crash reduced Jusen assets and increased non-performing loans. The fall in real estate was aggravated by the credit crunch that followed as real estate assets were used as collateral for new loans. The real estate crash placed borrowers into insolvency. In addition, mother banks tended to transfer non-performing loans to their Jusen companies in the early 1990s. As a result, in 1995 the Jusen were plagued by non-performing assets up to 60–80 per cent of their total assets, as shown in Figure 10.7. The rapid increase of loan losses reduced their capital structure and pushed them into insolvency.

In December 1995, the MOF proposed a resolution plan that distributed losses between the different creditors of the Jusen according to Table 10.7. The main element was that assets that were likely to be recovered were sold to the Housing Recollection Company (HRCC), which tried to sell the collateral real estate assets at the best price. Losses linked to non-recoverable assets were divided between the different creditors. Out of the non-performing loans, bad assets of Category Four[18] were associated with a certain loss. These losses amounted to 6.3 trillion yen, and were borne by originating banks for 3.5 trillion yen, by other banks for 1.7 trillion yen and by agricultural cooperatives for 530 billion yen. Eventually, the government had to pay 680 billion yen. The small price paid by agricultural cooperatives gave rise to intense debate, as they were deeply involved in the Jusen. The cooperatives argued that banks were the effective

[18] Jusen assets are classified into four categories
1) asset tier 1; normal asset
2) asset tier 2; collectable, but not very soon
3) asset tier 3; difficult to collect
4) asset tier 4; a loss.

Table 10.7. *Jusen Resolution Corporation in December 1995 in billion yen. Source: MOF*

7 Jusen		First write-off		Sell HRCC		Capital subscription	
Normal assets	3,490	Mother banks	3,500	Normal assets	3,490	Mother banks	2,400
Bad asset 2	2,050	Other banks	1,700	Bad asset 2	2,050	Other banks	2,100
Bad asset 3	1,240	Agri-coops	530	Bad asset 3	1,240	Agri-coops	2,300
Bad asset 4	6,270	Government	680				
Deficit	140						
Total	13,190	Total	6,410	Total	6,780	Total	6,800

shareholders of the Jusen and that they should bear most of the losses. They considered themselves as simple creditors who should be served first. In 1994, their funding represented 42.5 per cent of total funds. NPLs of the other two categories were supposed to be at least partially recovered and transferred to the HRCC. The latter was financed by financial institutions at very low interest rates. Mother banks contributed 2.4 trillion yen, other banks 2.1 trillion yen and agricultural cooperatives 2.3 trillion yen. As the banking crisis deepened in the mid-1990s and came to involve a larger number of more significant institutions, the participation of public authorities became necessary, as existing banks were not financially strong enough to bear the costs associated with buy-in procedures.

10.6.2 The ineluctable buy-out of failing banks

Although monetary authorities were reluctant to buy out the financial sector, the depth of the crisis forced them to do so. It was not until 1997–8 that monetary authorities accepted such a response to the banking crisis. This delayed response is probably a major cause of the long-lasting banking crisis. Before that time, there were no adequate institutions to buy out financial institutions as the DIC could not raise large funds. In addition, the population was opposed to such use of public funds. In autumn 1997, the Bank of Japan (BOJ) refused to bring liquidity support to Sanyo Securities. The BOJ argued that its role was to help banking institutions, and not securities houses such as Sanyo. In addition, the amount of default was rather limited. Nevertheless, the shock triggered by the Sanyo default destabilised the interbank market and forced the BOJ to inject liquidity through the purchase of bonds. Three weeks later, the difficulties of Yamaichi Securities were this time answered by the BOJ with liquidity support. Meanwhile, the BOJ had no regulatory framework in which to act, as securities houses fell outside the scope of the DIC. It provided outstanding loans of 325 billion yen, that would eventually not be recovered. Consequently, a new law was passed in 1998 to enable the DIC to address the financial fragility of all financial institutions and raise larger funds.

These two examples highlight that 'lender of last resort' (LLR) activities evolved over the banking crisis to address new situations. The different types of LLR activities conducted by the BOJ, the MOF and the DIC may be classified into five categories (Nakaso, 2001).

1. **Emergency liquidity assistance to a failed deposit-taking institution.** This was the most frequent type of LLR. It provided funds to failed deposit-taking institutions to avoid disruptions of their activities. Assets and liabilities were transferred to the DIC, which covered its losses.
2. **Provision of liquidity to interbank markets.** The interbank liquidity crisis after the Sanyo default forced the government to inject liquidity through the purchase of eligible bills. It injected 22 trillion yen, which were fully paid back.
3. **Emergency liquidity assistance to a failed non-bank financial institution.** With the failure of Yamaichi, monetary authorities started to support non-banks in order to avoid systemic risks. The absence of an institutional framework raised the issue of who bears the losses.
4. **Provision of risk capital to a financial institution.** In the early stage of the crisis, systemic risk arose with the solvency of some banks. To ease the takeover by the assuming institutions, capital was injected into the failing institutions. Until 1998, there was no clear framework for capital injection, and so these turned out very costly.
5. **Emergency assistance to a temporarily illiquid institution.** This type of lending is very close to the theoretical definition of LLR activities. In Japan however no lending of this kind took place. A possible explanation is that this type of instrument is used as a crisis prevention measure rather than a crisis management measure.

The LLR types 2 and 5 are the typical situation and are usually neutral in terms of public funds, as loans are paid back quickly and on time. The other three types of LLR activities were implemented on a practical basis, in order to address the development of the banking crisis. The absence of pre-determined rules made the issues and cost of the crisis more unpredictable.

The DIC was the institution that was in charge of implementing LLR activities and transferring funds to financial institutions. It used three procedures, through which we are able to measure the cost of the banking crisis in terms of public funds: first, capital injections to weak banks to help them to meet their capital requirements; second, financial assistance in the form of monetary grant; and third, the purchase of non-performing assets.

Financial assistance was granted between 1992 and 1997. Over that period, the buy-in principle was dominant but the government injected funds to support either the failing or the assuming institution through two mechanisms: it purchased non-performing assets from failed institutions; and provided a monetary grant to assuming financial institutions. With the worsening of the crisis, financial assistance mobilised larger funds. In terms of resources, grants became much larger than asset purchases, amounting to 18.6 trillion yen between 1992 and 2002, mainly concentrated between

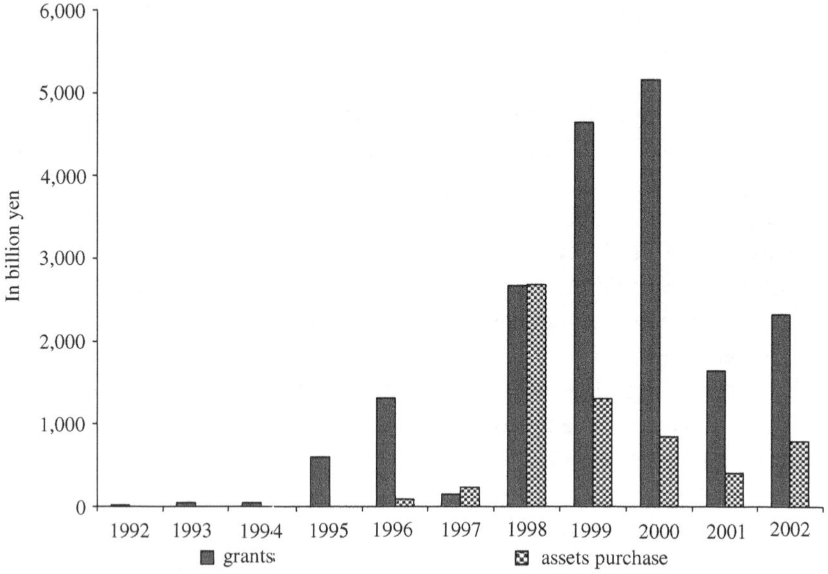

(a) Financial assistance

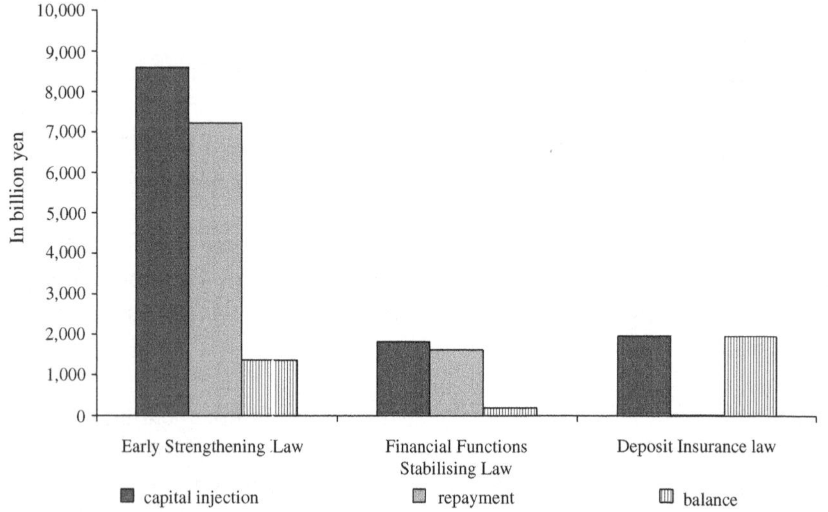

(b) Capital Injection

Figure 10.8 Financial assistance and capital injections. Source: FSA

1998 and 2000. Asset purchases were three times smaller, at around 6.3 trillion. Overall, financial assistance totalled almost 25 trillion yen for 180 cases, illustrated in Figure 10.8(a).

Another procedure was capital injections which are summarised in Figure 10.8(b). This took place from 1998 onwards, and was mainly related to buy-out procedures. As sound financial institutions were too weak to support failed institutions, the government adopted a more direct procedure called the open bank. This was mainly a massive injection of public funds to recapitalise banks. Capital injections took the form of purchase of preferred shares or subordinated bonds/loans. They were both very similar, as preferred shares can be viewed as the lowest-possible grade bond. They also paid a high return as they were very risky in the case of bankruptcy. Preferred shares were characterised by a fixed dividend paid on after-tax profit, while subordinated bonds/loans yielded a high interest rate. Subordinated debt was the last to be paid back among bond holders. Preferred shares are very risky too, as shareholders are paid back after creditors. In case of bankruptcy, they are very likely to entail a full loss. Finally, subordinated bonds/loans may be perpetual in the sense that there is no fixed date of repayment and it happens whenever the issuer so wishes. There were mainly subordinated bonds up to 1999, with preferred shares after this date. These injections were implemented through a series of new laws. They were made under the:

1. Financial Functions Stabilising Law in 1998;
2. Early Strengthening Law in 1999;
3. Deposit Insurance Law in 2003;
4. Financial Reorganisation Promotion Law in 2003;
5. Financial Function Strengthening Law in 2006.

The most important was the Early Strengthening Law that involved 8.6 trillion yen. Overall, capital injections aggregated to 12.4 trillion yen. Most of the injections were paid back after some time. The balances of each law are respectively 1,371, 190, 1,957, 6 and 40.5 billion yen. While they required large public funds, after a few years capital injections were mostly paid back.

The socialisation of losses also took the form of purchasing assets from financial institutions. This happened between 1999 and March 2005 through the Financial Revitalisation Law and was implemented by the Resolution and Collection Corporation (RCC).[19] Sound financial institutions transferred their risky loans to a public entity. The RCC resulted from the merger of two recollection agencies: the Housing Loan Administration Corporation (HLAC) in charge mainly of real estate assets, especially from the Jusen companies; and the Resolution and Collection Bank (RCB). Out of the total of asset transfers (from sound and failed financial institutions) the RCC had contrasting results depending on the nature of assets. HLAC and RCB both had similar amounts of claims, 4,653 and 5,071 billion yen respectively. At the same time, HLAC was only able to collect 66 per cent of claims while the RCB managed to get back more than 100 per cent. Collection by HLAC was made more complicated given the importance of real estate assets in its portfolio and the duration of depressed real estate prices, see Figure 10.9.

Nationalisation also took place over this period. Goods assets were transferred to a bridge bank affiliated to the DIC. Non-performing assets were transferred to the NCC, responsible for their recycling. Shareholders were sanctioned and it was the most costly

[19] The number of financial institutions is not counted for duplication of purchases.

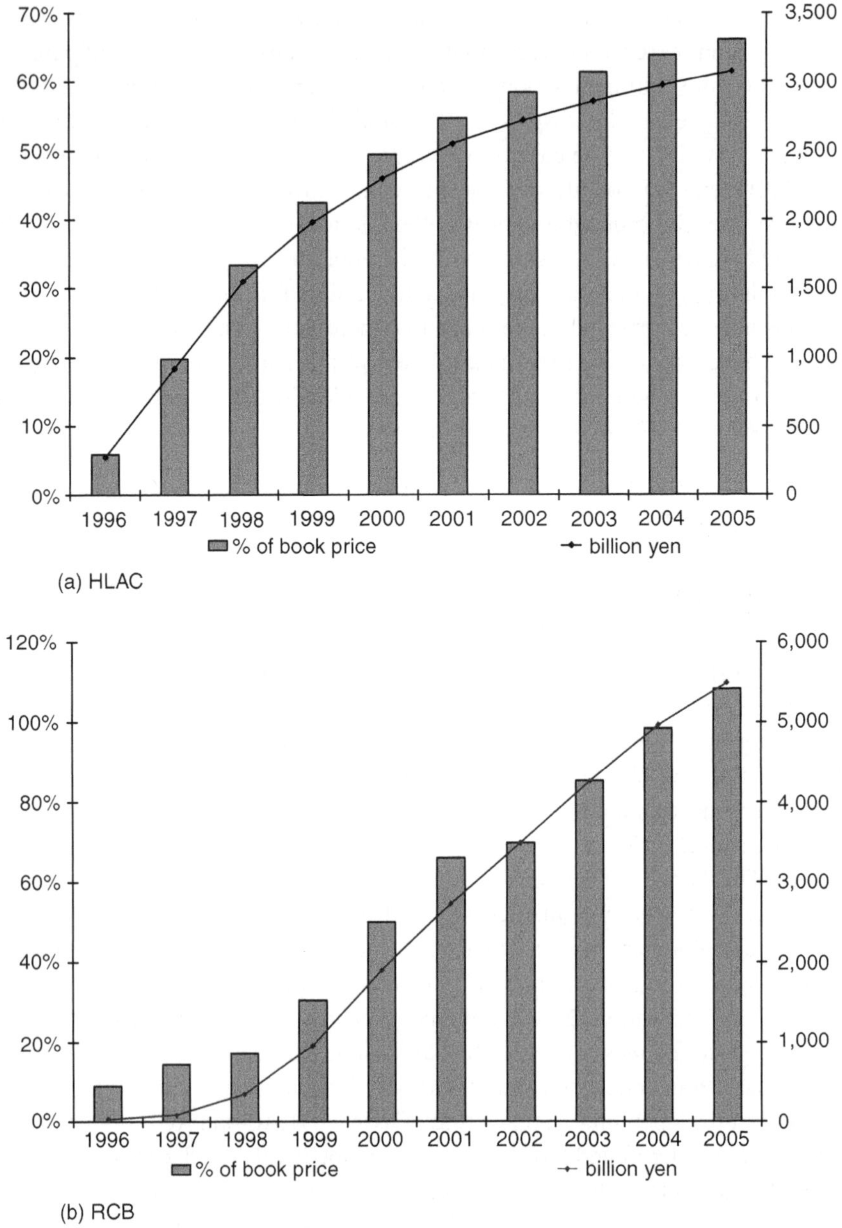

Figure 10.9 Asset purchases – Japan. Source: FSA

procedure in terms of public funds. There were two nationalisations: the Long Term Credit Bank (LTCB) in 1997 and the Nippon Credit Bank in 1998. They were privatised in 1999 and 2000 respectively.

Tax preferences were also mobilised to subsidise banks. From 1998, tax authorities enabled banks to integrate potential losses on assets in their fiscal deduction. In the

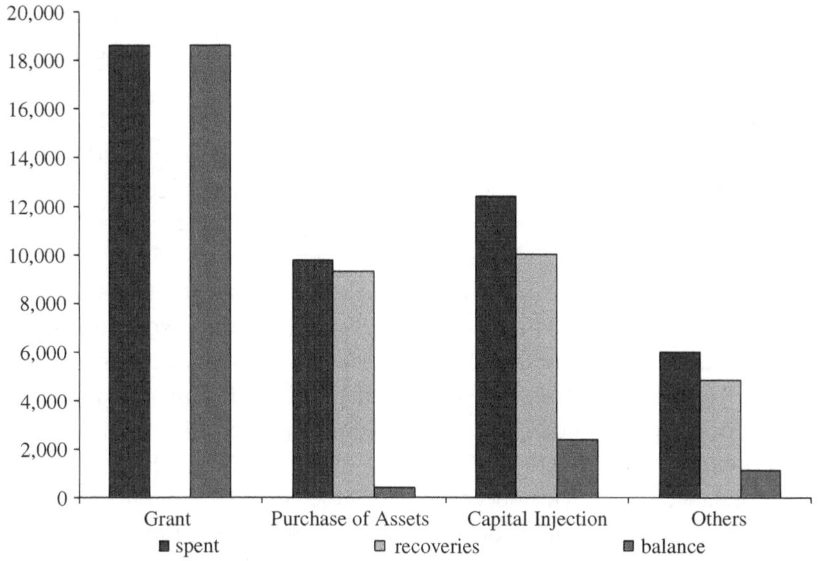

(a) In billions of yen

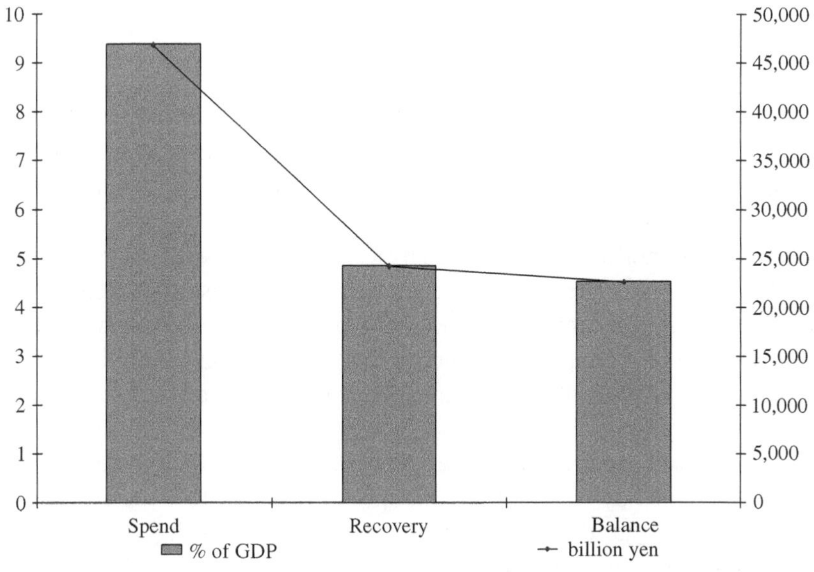

(b) In % of GDP

Figure 10.10 Transfers to the financial system – Japan. Source: FSA

case where bank income was so small that they were not submitted to taxation, this procedure enabled them to capitalise these tax reductions for the future. The time frame of this measure, about five years in 1998, was extended to seven years and became a disguised subsidy. Another fiscal procedure involved the use of related companies by banks to clean up their balance sheet. Before 1998, banks did not have to consolidate subsidiaries and affiliates with less than 50 per cent and 20 per cent stake respectively in their reports. They therefore transferred NPLs above market value to these structures (see Kanaya and David (2000)).

Overall, banking rescues by public authorities involved large transfers of funds towards failed financial institutions. Total transfers amounted to more than 9 per cent of GDP, which is roughly half of the cost of non-performing loans; Figure 10.10 displays the various transfers. Out of the 47 trillion yen, the government recovered 24 trillion and was left with a balance of 23 trillion which corresponds to 4.5 per cent of GDP (see figure 10.10b). Most of the cost was linked to monetary grants provided under financial assistance. Out of the 24 trillion yen recovered, 9 trillion yen were due to the sales of financial assets and were therefore not paid back by financial institutions (see figure 10.10b). The net transfers towards financial institutions amounted therefore to 32 trillion yen, or 6.4 per cent of GDP. To summarise, public action avoided systemic risk and contributed to the reduction of the stock of non-performing assets that destabilised banks' balance sheets. This success came at the cost of large transfers of wealth towards the financial sector. In addition, the difficulties of targeting solvent but illiquid, rather than insolvent, institutions combined with the systemic risk related to the failure of large institutions led authorities to rescue failed institutions.

10.7 Conclusions

In this chapter, we have explored how the Japanese institutional configuration can be characterised and whether it can be used to explain part of the financial crisis of the 1990s. We proceeded step by step: from a real model to a financial model with government intervention.

First, the real sector was characterised by a profit-led aggregate demand and a labour market-led real wage. The feedback channel between these two elements produces attracting forces and ensures that the crisis does not originate in the real sector. Second, there is evidence of a financial accelerator that has pro-cyclical effects and may be a source of instability. Nevertheless, its magnitude is not large enough to explain the deep economic crisis in Japan.

Third, legal institutions in Japan are such that borrowers were able to default without being sanctioned by bankruptcy. This special case has, to some extent, stabilising effects when aggregate demand is profit-led. It is therefore inaccurate to blame the Japanese bankruptcy procedure for the length of the Japanese crisis. Fourth, debt default affected negatively banks' financial health and gave rise to a long-lasting banking crisis. The resulting credit disruptions were largely responsible for the deterioration of economic activity. This underlines the fact that the key dimension to be taken into account to explain Japan's 'lost decade' is the effect of debt default on the banking system.

Further, the fifth result underscores the sluggish and inadequate government response to the crisis. Monetary policy was implemented slowly, and may have been more stabilising if more active. The banking crisis lasted for more than ten years, to a large extent because the government was reluctant to use public spending to solve the bad debt problem in the early 1990s. Monetary authorities preferred to rely on market-based solutions, which – although costless for the state – are not necessarily suited to solve widespread debt problems. Contrary to the moral hazard argument, it was actually the attempt by the government to avoid any moral hazard that resulted in the government response to the bad debt problem being so slow. Put differently, an economy based on banks' credit and intermediation should avoid financial deregulation that may disrupt the credit links between firms and borrowers. In addition, given the importance of the credit relationship, the management of the banking crisis should be fast and public funds should be mobilised if necessary.

From a distributive perspective, we have shown that the costs of over-indebtedness were mainly supported by creditors rather than borrowers. Creditors supported losses on credit equivalent to 20 per cent of GDP, while bankruptcy of the borrowers reached not even 0.25 per cent of the total number of firms at the worst point of the crisis. The overall transfers of public funds to the banking sector aggregated to 10 per cent of GDP, which is half of the financial sector losses. While part of the funds were paid back, the net transfers to financial institutions totalled 6.4 per cent of GDP. With respect to real transfers, the expansionary fiscal packages implemented by the government to sustain economic activities were far larger, at up to 27 per cent of GDP. This suggests that once the crisis became serious, large scale government intervention was unavoidable.

10.8 Appendix: data sources

Table 10.8. *Data sources for Japan*

Indicator	Source
GDP deflator	IMF
Monthly earnings	IMF
GDP	IMF
Index of capacity utilisation	METI
Compensation of employee	CAO
Number of employed	Labour force survey
Labour force	Labour force survey
Call rate	BOJ
Government spending	CAO
Net wealth, fixed assets, and liabilities	MOF

CAO (Central Application Office); IMF (International Monetary Fund); METI (Ministry of Economy, Trade and Industry)

11 Housing investment cycles, workers' debt and debt default

11.1 Introduction

A proper modelling of the housing sector in a structural macroeconomic and/or macroeconometric model needs to consider housing investment, the purchase of houses or housing services and the evolution of the prices charged for them. The main focus in the applied literature on this issue has often been the subsector of office space, but of course the sector of privately owned houses or private rental is also a very large and important sector of the macroeconomy.

What is particularly interesting from the macrodynamic point of view in this type of literature is that there are concepts and issues in the literature on the housing sector that are closely related to important topics of standard macrodynamic theorising. There is the concept of the natural vacancy rate, or of a Non-Accelerating Inflation Rate of Unemployment (NAIRU) in the housing sector, as discussed by Hendershott *et al.* (2002), the concept of overbuilt markets, see Hendershott (1996), and of persistent cycles in the housing sector that in our view bear close resemblance to what is happening in the unemployment-inflation dynamics in the interaction of the labour market with the market for goods and the wage-price spiral.

Due to the size of the housing sector it is therefore of great interest from the macrodynamic point of view to not only study this sector with its interaction of space demand and supply, rental and housing prices and the rates of return they imply and finally the investment behaviour in this sector, but to also consider its interaction with the rest of the macroeconomy where (at least) two real cycle generators may be at work leading to coupled oscillators and maybe to complex business cycle fluctuations. In the present chapter we want to lay foundations for such an investigation and to show that models of such type can even be handled from the theoretical perspective. Ultimately, though, numerical and empirical investigations will be needed, which however are beyond the scope of this chapter as far as empirical issues are concerned; see though the quoted literature for investigations of this issue.

In this chapter[1] we apply the general framework introduced in Part II[2] to the special issue of housing investment cycles, the supply and demand for housing services as part

[1] This chapter is based on Chiarella and Flaschel (2003).
[2] See also Chiarella *et al.* (2000, Part III) in this regard.

of the dynamics, and the price dynamics this implies in the housing sector. Rents in this sector then in turn determine rates of return for housing investment and interact with this investment in the generation of damped, persistent or even explosive cycles thus generated in the housing sector of the economy.

The necessary ingredients for this analysis have by and large already been provided in earlier chapters, but are here modified to a certain extent in order to allow a more specific analysis of the topics mentioned above. The following section will present in this regard the details we need for the analysis of the dynamics originating in the housing sector and that interact with the general business cycle of the model. However we will not repeat the general framework in all of its details, but simply refer the reader to Part II. The reader is therefore referred to earlier chapters for the full models on the extensive form level, the intensive form level and the many subdynamics to which this model type can give rise, as well as investigations of their interaction in the integrated 18D core dynamics of this approach. This overall framework has been motivated by an attempt to understand the basic dynamic feedback mechanisms of the macroeconomy, and their interaction, in large scale macroeconometric models such as that of Powell and Murphy (1997).

The new focus that the current chapter brings is on debt relationships in the household sector, composed of indebted worker households and pure asset holders as creditors. Worker households purchase houses as durable consumption goods (in addition to housing services by part of them) through credit from the asset holders and are thus now characterised by negative bond holdings in place of positive bond holdings in the chapters of Part II. They indeed have – in the aggregate – a marginal propensity to consume out of their disposable income that is larger than 1 (when consumption of non-durables and durables are taken together) and they finance the excess of consumption over their disposable income by new debt and thus credit from the asset holding part of the household sector. In the steady state we will have a constant debt to capital ratio and thus debt of workers growing at a constant rate over time.

Our interest however is to study endogenous fluctuations around this steady growth path and to investigate in addition the possibility that price and wage dynamics may be such that processes of debt deflation are generated, here not as in Chiarella *et al.* (2001a,b) and Chapter 7 with respect to firms and their indebtedness due to past investment behaviour, but rather within the household sector and its debtor-creditor relationship.[3]

In Section 11.2 we present the new components of the model on the extensive form level, in addition to the details from our earlier work that concern the housing sector. Section 11.3 then derives the laws of motion of the general 19D dynamics, which – with special focus on the housing sector – are simplified thereafter to give rise to the core 9D dynamics to be investigated in the remainder of the chapter. Section 11.4 considers 2D to 5D subcases of the integrated 6D real subdynamics of the 9D dynamics and

[3] We add here that the analysis in Chiarella *et al.* (2001a,b) may indeed be applicable to the sector of office space, while the present chapter focuses on private space.

formulates and proves a number of propositions on these subdynamics. The full 9D dynamics are investigated from the numerical perspective in Section 11.5. Section 11.6 concludes.

11.2 Debt relationships in the household sector

In this section we reformulate the general model of disequilibrium growth introduced and investigated in Part II with respect to assets supplied and demanded by the two types of households of our general model, workers and asset holders, who are assumed to make up the household sector.[4]

We will assume that worker households rent housing services and also buy new houses, and that they finance the resulting excess of their consumption over their disposable income via credit (bonds of the fixed-price/variable interest variety of the model of Part II). Such bonds are supplied by the other type of household of the model, the pure asset holders.

Firms produce for domestic purposes a unique good that can be used as a consumption good proper by the two types of households, as a business fixed investment good, as an investment good providing housing services to the workers by asset holders, for the purpose of government consumption and now also for representing the direct demand for houses by both asset holders and workers. These alterations of the original 18D core dynamics of Part II will increase the dimension of these dynamics by one, since debt accumulation of workers will now feed back into the rest of the dynamics due to their consumption habits. We will represent the resulting dynamical system in compact form in the following subsections.

11.2.1 Worker households

We consider the behavioural equations of worker households first, but only to the extent they are changed by the existence of a debtor-creditor relationship between our two types of agents in the household sector. In order to derive the new characteristics of this module of the model let us first present these equations in the form that they were used in the original approach of Part II of the book:

<u>Households (Workers – original formulation):</u>

$$Y_w^{Dn} = (1-\tau_w)[wL^d + w^u(L-L^w) + w^r\alpha_l L_2] + (1-\tau_c)iB_w$$
$$= Y_{w1}^{Dn} + (1-\tau_c)iB_w,$$
$$p_y C_g^w = c_y Y_{w1}^{Dn},$$

[4] If households are to be considered as heterogeneous in a macromodel then this should be the fundamental distinction in a model with labour supply and asset markets and with only two household types. Such polar types of households, which still appear in a very stylised way in the models of this book, are in our view much more relevant for macroeconomic model building than the distinction between workers and pensioners made in the Overlapping Generations (OLG) type of models.

$$p_h C_h^w = c_h Y_{w1}^{Dn},$$
$$S_w^n = Y_w^{Dn} - p_y C_g^w - p_h C_h^w = \dot{B}_w.$$

In these equations, the expression Y_w^{Dn} denotes total nominal disposable income of workers after taxes at the rate τ_w as far as their labour income $wL^d + w^u(L - L^w) + w^r \alpha_l L_2$ is concerned,[5] and after taxes at the rate τ_c with respect to their interest income iB_w, on the stock B_w of short-term bonds accumulated by workers.

We assumed in the original approach of Part II that workers save and thus hold and accumulate bonds in the amounts B_w and $\dot{B}_w$ respectively, but there they reinvested all of their interest income into bond accumulation, which thus did not feed back into the income term Y_{w1}^{Dn} that determined their nominal consumption of goods $p_y C_g^w$ and of housing services $p_h C_h^w$ (with marginal propensities to consume $c_y + c_h < 1$). These assumptions helped to simplify considerably the dynamics of that earlier study since the bond accumulation of workers did not influence aggregate demand and goods market behaviour in this case. Nominal savings S_w^n of workers was invested into short-term bonds solely, since money was not a financial asset in the model of Part II.

In the case of negative savings and thus debt accumulation (a negative B_w will be denoted by the positive expression Λ_w in the following), things are however not so easily disentangled. Since debt is in fact entered into in order to increase the consumption of workers (not only to rent houses as has so far been assumed, but also to buy houses as durable consumption goods), it follows that asset owners thereby become debtors to asset holders, just as the government. Interest payments[6] must then appear in the income expression to be used for determining the consumption demand of workers since these payments reduce the possibility of workers to spend more than they earn.[7] Assuming such a situation leads us to the following reformulation of the above representation of workers' behaviour, based on the augmented form of short-term loans, $\dot{B}_c = \dot{\Lambda}_g + \dot{\Lambda}_w$, supplied by the asset holders to the government as well as to worker households.

Households (Workers – new formulation):

$$Y_w^{Dn} = (1 - \tau_w)[wL^d + w^u(L - L^w) + w^r \alpha_l L_2] - (1 - \tau_c) i \Lambda_w$$
$$= Y_{w1}^{Dn} - (1 - \tau_c) i \Lambda_w, \quad (11.1)$$
$$p_y C_g^w = c_y Y_w^{Dn}, \quad (11.2)$$
$$p_h C_h^w = c_h Y_w^{Dn}, \quad (11.3)$$
$$\dot{\Lambda}_w = p_y C_g^w + p_h C_h^w - Y_w^{Dn}. \quad (11.4)$$

5 Labour income here consists of wage income, unemployment benefits and pension payments, which are all subject to tax payments here at the uniform wage tax rate τ_w. Note however that the model would not be changed very much if differential wage tax rates are allowed for, an observation which also applies to the consumption propensities shown, which at present are the same for employed, unemployed and retired workers.

6 For simplicity we assume that these are at the short-term rate i in place of i_λ.

7 Note here that interest payments are deducted before worker households decide on their consumption patterns. In the case where propensities to consume are applied to total wage income (after taxes) the dynamics of the capital to debt ratio to be considered later on do not feed back into the rest of the dynamics.

We assume in this chapter that $c_y + c_h > 1$ holds, so that worker households always consume more than they earn (after the deduction of interest payments).[8] Such an assumption for worker households amounts to assuming that there is no intertemporal budget constraint in the usual sense of the word for this type of household, just as for the government sector. In both cases we will have a given debt to capital ratio in the steady state meaning that part of expenditure is always financed by issuing new debt, which then grows (just as the stock of debt) with the given real growth rate of the world economy. Such an approach is admissible in a descriptively oriented disequilibrium growth model of monetary growth, in particular if it is understood that this model type (and its steady state solution) is to be applied to particular periods of the evolution of actual market economies. Assuming no debt of the government and of workers in the steady state by choosing the parameters of the model appropriately clearly is too limited an approach from the descriptive point of view.

We also note here that debt accumulation, and even more so debt deflation, is still of a fairly simple type. A study of the equations in the above module of the model clearly shows that workers' consumption demand depends negatively on their debt (due to their interest payments and their marginal propensities to consume being in sum larger than one) and thus on the debt to capital ratio $\lambda_w = \Lambda_w/(p_y K)$ to be considered later on. This means that aggregate demand depends negatively on the ratio λ_w and will thus shrink when this ratio is increasing, which happens in particular when there is goods price deflation (taken in isolation).

Such deflation therefore decreases aggregate demand, which via the Metzlerian goods market adjustment process leads to still lower economic activity and from there to further falling goods prices and so on. In this way a deflationary spiral may be established, which drives the economy into ever more depressed situations. The resulting downward spiral in prices and wages and in economic activity depends however on the precise way wages, goods prices and rental prices are falling and what happens to other components of aggregate demand. It should be noted that we have continued to ignore other feedback channels, in particular the ones that concern the effects of falling goods and rental prices.

One can interpret the above description of the behaviour of worker households also in the following way. Assume that workers accumulate debt basically due to their purchase of houses, which can be made explicit if it is assumed that c_y is split into c_y^g and c_y^h, where the first parameter describes the propensity to consume consumption goods proper and the second parameter denotes that portion of goods consumption that goes into purchase of houses. The equation that describes the evolution of the stock of houses K_h^w owned by workers is then given by

$$\dot{K}_h^w = c_y^h Y_w^{Dn}/p_y - \delta_h K_h^w \quad \text{or} \quad \hat{k}_h^w = c_y^h y_w^D / k_h^w - \delta_h - \hat{K},$$

[8] Note that we have assumed here for reasons of symmetry that interest paid on debt leads to tax reduction at the rate τ_c, which however is a detail of the model which is of secondary importance.

where δ_h, y_w^D and k_h^w denote the depreciation rate of houses, the real disposable income of workers (after interest deduction) per unit of capital K and K_h^w/K, respectively.

The steady state value of the stock of houses owned by workers per unit of capital is thus given by $k_h^w = c_y^h y_w^D/(\gamma + \delta_h)$, where γ denotes the steady state rate of growth of the economy. We shall show in Section 11.4 that the steady state value of the debt to capital ratio $\lambda_w = \Lambda_w/(p_y K)$ is given by $(c_y + c_h - 1)y_w^D/\gamma$. Assume now that Λ_w can be considered as the housing mortgage that can and will be bequeathed to the next generation if the side condition $\Lambda_w \leq p_y K_h^w$ is fulfilled (since the mortgage is then less than the reproduction value of the stock of houses owned by worker households). In the steady state this side condition amounts to

$$\lambda_w = \frac{c_y + c_h - 1}{\gamma} y_w^D \leq \frac{c_y^h}{\gamma + \delta_h} y_w^D,$$

which is fulfilled if

$$c_y + c_h - 1 \leq c_y^h \quad i.e., \quad c_y^g + c_h - 1 \leq 0.$$

The above thus gives a lower bound on the propensity to consume c_y^h such that the above side condition is fulfilled, at least along the steady state solution of the dynamics.

Note also that the dynamics of the model is based on a Keynesian determination of the short run throughout so that demand is always satisfied in this model type. Situations where this is not the case are analysed in detail in Chiarella *et al.* (2000) and do not lead to important changes in the behaviour of the models described there. Due to the two consumption functions just presented we have that Keynesian goods market features now depend on the stock of debt of workers (through the interest payments that they imply). The debt to capital ratio of workers will therefore now influence the dynamics of the real part of the model in contrast to the situation considered in Part II where workers accumulated a positive stock of short-term bonds.

11.2.2 Pure asset holder households

Next, we consider the other type of households of our model, the pure asset holders who are assumed to consume C_c (goods and houses as supplied by firms through their domestic production Y) at an amount that is growing exogenously at the rate γ, which is thus in particular independent of their current nominal disposable income Y_c^{Dn}. The consumption decision is thus not an important decision for pure asset holders. Their nominal income diminished by the nominal value of their consumption $p_v C_c$ is then spent on the purchase of financial assets, three types of bonds (short-term domestic, long-term domestic and foreign) and equities, as well as on investment in housing supply (for rent to part of the worker households). Note here that the one good view of the production of the domestic good entails consumption goods proper and houses so that asset holders buy houses for their consumption as well as for investment purposes.

Households (Asset Holders):

$$Y_c^{Dn} = (1 - \tau_c)[r^e p_y K + i B_c + B_1^l + p_h C_h^w - p_y \delta_h K_h] + s(1 - \tau_c^*) B_2^l, \quad (11.5)$$

$$\hat{C}_c = \gamma, \quad (11.6)$$

$$S_c^n = Y_c^{Dn} - p_y C_c \quad (11.7)$$

$$= \dot{B}_c + \dot{B}_1^l / i_l + s \dot{B}_2^l / i_l^* + p_e \dot{E} + p_y (I_h - \delta_h K_h) \quad (\dot{B}_c = \dot{\Lambda}_g + \dot{\Lambda}_w),$$

$$C_h^s = K_h, \quad (11.8)$$

$$r_h = (p_h C_h^w - \delta_h p_y K_h)/(p_y K_h), \quad (11.9)$$

$$g_h = I_h / K_h$$

$$= \alpha_r^h ((1 - \tau_c) r_h - i^r) + \alpha_i^h (i_l - i) + \alpha_u^h \left(\frac{C_h^w}{C_h^s} - \bar{u}_h \right) + \gamma + \delta_h, \quad (11.10)$$

$$\hat{p}_h = \beta_{p_h} \left(\frac{C_h^w}{C_h^s} - \bar{u}_h \right) + \kappa_h \hat{p}_y + (1 - \kappa_h) \pi^c, \quad (11.11)$$

$$\hat{K}_h = I_h / K_h - \delta_h. \quad (11.12)$$

This part of the model is basically the same as the one considered in Part II, with the interpretational exception that asset holders in addition now lend to worker households. Equation (11.5) defines the disposable income of asset holders which consists of the dividend payments of firms (who distribute their whole expected profit to equity holders), interest on government bonds (short-term bonds and consols), $i B_c + B_1^l$, to the extent they are held by domestic residents, rents for housing services net of depreciation, and interest payments on foreign bonds held by domestic households (after foreign taxation and expressed in domestic currency by means of the exchange rate s).

Private savings of asset holders S_c^n thus also concern short- and long-term bonds (domestic and foreign with respect to the latter), equities and net housing investment (equation (11.8)). The supply of housing services C_h^s (in equation (11.8)) is assumed to be proportional to that part of the existing stock of houses K_h devoted to the supply of such services (here the factor of proportionality is set to unity for simplicity). We assume for simplicity that there is no resale market for houses as there are for the financial assets of the model, which however is a feature of the model that should be removed in further extensions. Note again that the production of houses is part of the production activities of firms and thus part of the homogeneous supply of the domestic (non-traded) output.

The return on housing services is given by equation (11.9). The demand for housing services C_h^w has already been defined in the preceding module. We assume that housing demand is always satisfied and we can guarantee this in general (up to certain extreme fluctuations in the demand for housing services) by assuming that there is a given benchmark rate of capacity utilisation $\bar{u}_h$ of the housing service supply beyond which there is additional pressure on the price p_h of housing services and also increased effort to invest into housing supply (which may be of such extent that rationing on the market for housing services is prevented).[9] We have assumed in the workforce sector that the demand for housing services is growing (apart from short-term deviations) with the trend rate γ (underlying the steady state of the model). This implies that housing services per household grow with trend rate $\gamma - n$, where n is the natural rate of growth of the workforce. Therefore, over the growth horizon of the considered economy, we have that worker households consume more and more housing services (measured by square metres per housing unit for example).[10] Equation (11.10) describes the rate of gross investment in housing of asset holders, which depends on the profit rate r_h in the housing sector compared with the required rate of return, which is measured in reference to government consols by $i^r = i_l - \pi^c$ (via Tobin's q as the relative profitability measure). It depends furthermore on the interest spread $i_l - i$ as a measure for the tightness of monetary policy and its perceived (or only believed) effects on the level of economic activity and employment, on the actual rate of capacity utilisation of housing services in its deviation from the natural rate of occupancy (representing short-run demand pressure), $\frac{C_h^w}{C_h^s} - \bar{u}_h$, on the trend rate of growth γ and on the rate of depreciation δ_h in the housing sector.

In equation (11.11) the rate of inflation of the rental price of housing services, $\hat{p}_h$, depends (as does investment) on the rate of capacity utilisation in the housing sector (the demand pressure component) and on a weighted average formed by the actual rate of inflation of producer prices in the production of the domestic good and on the level of this inflation that is expected over the medium term as a medium-term average (the rate π^c), whose law of motion will be provided later on (this weighted average represents the cost-push component in this dynamical equation for the price of housing services). Finally in equation (11.12) actual gross investment plans are always realised and thus determine the rate of growth of the housing stock by deducting the rate of depreciation.

Summing up we can state that the consumption decisions of asset owners are basically driven by exogenous habits[11] (which are independent of their income and wealth position) and that their investment decision in housing service supply precedes the other (financial) asset accumulation decisions. These latter decisions are in the present framework governed by supply side forces based on the new issuing of bonds by the domestic government and of equities by firms. Furthermore, their choice of accumulation (or decumulation) of foreign long-term bonds is here determined as the residual to all these flows in or out of short- and long-term domestic debt and the flow of new equities issued by firms and is thus determined as the last step in the savings decision of asset holders. The essential decisions in this module of the model are therefore the housing investment decision and the pricing rule for housing services. Due to the

9 See for example Shilling *et al.* (1987) and Rosen and Smith (1983) for such NAIRU approaches to the market for housing services.

10 Such a construction is needed for the discussion of steady states of the economy and of course is only applicable over certain periods of time in the evolution of market economies.

11 Here in a way that allows for a fixed parameter representation in the intensive form of the model.

assumptions made on the consumption of asset holders we do not need to consider the asset accumulation of these agents explicitly in the dynamical investigations that follow.

11.2.3 Wage, price and interest rate adjustment processes

Finally, we present the wage, price and interest rate dynamics of the model that are important for the integrated core 5D dynamics of the real part of the model to be investigated subsequently in this chapter. This type of dynamics has started to receive growing attention in recent studies with an empirical orientation. We stress however that we do not yet pay attention to consumer price indices and the role of import prices in the formation of the money wage and the price level Phillips curves (PCs), respectively, see however Chiarella *et al.* (1999a,b) for such additions to the model. This module is the same as the one employed in Chiarella and Flaschel (1999a), which in sum means that the basic change in this chapter with respect to these earlier integrated models of monetary growth concerns solely the budget restriction and the consumption behaviour of worker households.

Wage-Price-Interest Adjustment Equations:

$$\hat{w} = \beta_w(e - \bar{e}) + \kappa_w(\hat{p}_y + n_l) + (1 - \kappa_w)(\pi^c + n_l), \tag{11.13}$$

$$\hat{p}_y = \beta_p(u - \bar{u}) + \kappa_p(\hat{w} - n_l) + (1 - \kappa_p)\pi^c, \tag{11.14}$$

$$\dot{\pi}^c = \beta_{\pi^c}(\alpha_{\pi^c}(\hat{p}_y - \pi^c) + (1 - \alpha_{\pi^c})(\bar{\pi} - \pi^c)), \tag{11.15}$$

$$\dot{i} = -\beta_{i_i}(i - i_l^*) + \beta_{i_p}(\hat{p}_y - \bar{\pi}) + \beta_{i_u}(u - \bar{u}). \tag{11.16}$$

In equation (11.13) wage inflation $\hat{w}$ responds in the traditional PC manner to the state of the demand pressure in the labour market as measured by the deviations of the rate of employment e from its NAIRU level $\bar{e}$ and there is also the usual accelerator term of price inflation, which is here measured as a weighted average of actual price inflation based on short-term perfect foresight (plus the actual rate n_l of productivity growth) and expected medium-term price inflation (also augmented by the given rate of productivity growth). The law of motion (11.14) for goods prices p_y of the domestic commodity is formulated in a similar way, as a second type of PC. We use the demand pressure measure $u - \bar{u}$, the deviation of actual capacity utilisation of firms from its norm, as the demand pressure cause of price inflation. The cost-push term in the price inflation equation is given as a weighted average of current wage inflation and the one expected for the medium run (both made less severe in their influence on price inflation by the existence of a positive growth rate of labour productivity).

In equation (11.15) expected medium-term inflation π^c in turn is based on a weighted average of two expectations mechanisms, an adaptive one with weight α_π and a forward-looking one with weight $1 - \alpha_\pi$. Forward-looking expectations are here simply based on the inflation target of the central bank $\bar{\pi}$, in the usual way of a regressive scheme of expectations revision. Inflationary expectations are thus following a weighted average of actual inflation and the target rate of the monetary authority. We assume $\bar{\pi} = 0$ in the following and thus will have no inflation in the steady state of the model. Furthermore we will also not consider the destabilising role of inflationary expectations (the so-called Mundell effect) and thus will set $\beta_{\pi^c} = 0$ for reasons of simplicity, in order to concentrate on destabilising real debt and real wage adjustments.

We can see from the above description that only the inflation rate of the domestic good matters in the wage-price module of our economy. Housing, through its rental price (and its rate of change $\hat{p}_h$), is thus ignored in this description of the wage-price interaction. All of this simplifies the feedback structure of the model, but should give way to a domestic price index of the form $p_c = p_y^a p_h^{1-a}$ and its rate of change in the wage equation in future reformulations of the model, see Chiarella *et al.* (1999a,b) in this regard.

The interest rate adjustment rule, equation (11.16), of the monetary authority adjusts the short-term interest rate i towards the given rate of interest in the world economy, but also pays attention to the deviation of the actual rate of price inflation from the targeted one, implying a rising i if the actual rate is above the target (and vice versa). Finally, interest rates are more easily increased if there is demand pressure on the market for goods than in the opposite situation.

We do not go here into the other modules of the model as formulated in Part II, since they by and large will not matter very much in our subsequent investigation of housing investment cycles, consumer debt and wage deflation. These modules concern the sector of firms with its fixed proportions technology (including exports and imports) and an investment behaviour that is similar to the one assumed for asset holders with respect to the housing stock, the government sector whose fiscal policies do not matter here (due to assumptions to be made in the next section), but which makes use of a Taylor type interest rate policy rule (as shown above), asset markets that adjust towards a general prevalence of interest rate parity conditions and Metzlerian adjustment of inventories and sales expectations of firms that generally do not correctly perceive aggregate demand on the market for domestic goods. These equations will be summarised in compact form on the level of intensive or state variables in the next section.

11.3 Intensive form derivation of a simplified 9D dynamics

In this section we present the modification of the 18D core model, which was investigated in Part II from various numerical perspectives, in order to focus now on a detailed consideration of the possibility of housing cycles and the debt financing of the investment undertaken by workers into housing purchases as already contained, but not yet considered in detail, in this original approach to disequilibrium growth dynamics (where interest payments in the sector of worker households did not yet have an impact on their consumption behaviour). To simplify the model slightly we assume throughout the following that $C_c(0) = 0$ holds initially (and thus for all times) and thus neglect the consumption of asset holders altogether (which does not contribute very much to the present investigation under the assumptions to be made). We stress that the resulting dynamics on the state variable level are no longer of dimension 18 as in Part II, but now of dimension 19, since the law of motion of workers' debt (formerly workers' bond accumulation) now feeds back into the market for goods due to the dependence of workers' goods demand on the interest payments for their loans. The present model thus not only reinterprets the worker households' bond accumulation as debt accumulation and adjusts their behavioural equations to this new interpretation, but it also adds a feedback chain to the dynamics that were formerly missing and on which the possibility of the occurrence of debt deflation is now based.[12]

We start with a compact presentation (including brief comments on their contents) of the nineteen laws of motion of the full model analysed in this chapter, and will present thereafter a 9D core case (with a unique interior steady state solution) of these dynamics to be used in the analysis that follows. These laws of motion around the steady state of the dynamics, appropriately grouped and all in per unit of capital terms, are given by the following set of differential equations. As first group we consider here the quantity adjustment mechanisms with respect to the market for goods, concerning sales expectations y^e and actual inventories ν, and for the market for labour, concerning the employment policy of firms, l^{we}, and also concerning the evolution of full employment labour intensity l^e (both in efficiency units) and of the stock of housing (everything per unit of the capital stock of firms):[13]

$$\dot{y}^e = \beta_{y^e}(y^d - y^e) + (\gamma - (g_k - \delta_k))y^e,$$

$$\dot{\nu} = y - y^d - (g_k - \delta_k)\nu,$$

$$\dot{l}^{we} = \beta_l(l^{de} - l^{we}) + [\gamma - (g_k - \delta_k)]l^{we},$$

$$\hat{l}^e = \gamma - (g_k - \delta_k),$$

$$\hat{k}_h = g_h - \delta_h - (g_k - \delta_k).$$

The first of these five laws for quantity dynamics describes the adjustment of sales expectations y^e in view of the observed expectational error $y^d - y^e$ based on currently realised sales y^d, augmented by a term that takes account of the fact that this adjustment is occurring in a growing economy and is expressed in intensive form. Next, inventories ν (per unit of capital) change according to the gap between actual output y and actual sales y^d, again reformulated such that growth of the capital stock, the measurement base for the considered intensive form variables, is taken into account. Employment of firms, l^{we}, changes so as to reduce the discrepancy that exists in each moment of time between the actual employment l^{de} of the employed and their normal employment, here measured by l^{we} (everything in efficiency units due to the assumed form of technical change). The growth rate of the factor endowment ratio $l^e = L^e/K$ (in efficiency units) is simply given by the difference between the natural rate of growth (including Harrod neutral technical change) and the growth rate of the capital stock $g_k - \delta_k$. Similarly,

12 See Chiarella *et al.* (2001a,b) for similar, but possibly much more severe situations of debt deflation, there with respect to credit relationships between asset holders and firms.

13 We denote by γ the given trend growth rate in the world economy, which is used as a trend term in the investment equations that apply to the domestic economy.

the growth rate of the housing stock (per unit of the capital stock of firms) is given by the difference of the corresponding net accumulation rates. We will assume in the analytical treatment of the model that employment of firms adjusts with infinite speed ($\beta_l = \infty$) to the actual employment of their labour force so that there is no over- or under employment of this labour force. There thus remain only four laws of motion of quantities of which the first two will in addition be replaced by a static relationship in the further evaluation of the model.

Next we consider the nominal dynamics in the real sector of the economy, which are described by four dynamical laws. Note here that the laws of motion for wages, w^e, in efficiency units, and prices, p_y, are now formulated independently from each other[14] and show that reduced form PCs (exhibiting only price inflation) are generally not as simple as is often assumed in the literature:[15]

$$\hat{w}^e = \pi^c + \kappa[\beta_w(l^{de}/l^e - \bar{e}) + \kappa_w\beta_p(y/y^p - \bar{u})],$$

$$\hat{p}_y = \pi^c + \kappa[\kappa_p\beta_w(l^{we}/l^e - \bar{e}) + \beta_p(y/y^p - \bar{u})],$$

$$\dot{\pi}^c = \beta_{\pi^c}(\alpha_{\pi^c}(\hat{p}_y - \pi^c) + (1 - \alpha_{\pi^c})(0 - \pi^c)),$$

$$\hat{p}_h = \beta_h\left(\frac{c_h^w}{k_h} - \bar{u}_h\right) + \kappa_h\hat{p}_y + (1 - \kappa_h)\pi^c.$$

As already noted we now use reduced form PCs for wage inflation $\hat{w}^e$ and price inflation $\hat{p}_y$, which both depend on the demand pressures in the markets for labour as well as for goods, $y/y^p - \bar{u}$. The change of the rate of inflation expected over the medium run, π^c, is determined as a weighted average of adaptively formed expectations and regressive ones (which realise that the steady state rate of inflation is zero in the present model). Finally, the inflation rate for housing services depends on the demand pressure term $\left(\frac{c_h^w}{k_h} - \bar{u}_h\right)$ in the market for these services,[16] and on actual and perceived cost-push expressions, here simply based on a weighted average concerning the inflation rate of domestic output. We shall assume in the following that $\beta_{\pi^c} = 0$ holds and thus we will not consider the role of inflationary expectations (which would add extra instability to the model if the price level is adjusting with high speed and if β_{π^c} is chosen sufficiently large, the so-called Mundell effect of Keynesian type models that include a wage-price sector).

[14] We do not consider in the present simplified form of the model payroll taxes, and value-added taxes, which helps to simplify the notation.

[15] Such disentangled laws of motion for nominal prices and wages are obtained from their originally interdependent presentation – see the preceding section – by solving the two linear equations of this section with respect to the variables $\hat{w}^e - \pi^c$ and $\hat{p}_y - \pi^c$ that implies the expressions shown below, which make use of both of our measures of demand pressure on the market both for labour and for the goods market (and on expected medium-run inflation). It is intuitively obvious that the removal of wage or price inflation cost-push pressure ($\hat{w}^e$ and $\hat{p}_y$) from the original form of the price or wage dynamics must imply that both the goods and the labour market expressions will be present in the resulting disentangled PCs which thus are in a significant way more general than the ones usually considered in the theoretical or applied literature on price PCs (unless one assumes – as some sort of Okun's law – that all demand pressure variables used are positive multiples of each other).

[16] Where $\frac{c_h^w}{k_h}$ represents the rate of capacity utilisation on this market and $\bar{u}_h$ the corresponding NAIRU level.

Next follow the dynamical laws for long-term bond price dynamics and exchange rate dynamics (including expectations) which basically formulate a somewhat delayed adjustment towards interest rate parity conditions and are supplemented by heterogeneous expectations formation (of partially adaptive and partially perfect type). Note that perfect foresight, concerning the proportion $1 - \alpha_s$ of market participants, can be removed from explicit representation as it coincides with the left-hand side of the corresponding price adjustment equation, giving rise to the fractions in front of these adjustment equations; see Part II for details):

$$\hat{p}_b = \frac{\beta_{p_b}}{1 - \beta_{p_b}(1 - \alpha_s)}[(1 - \tau_c)i_l + \alpha_s \pi_{bs} - (1 - \tau_c)i],$$

$$\dot{\pi}_{bs} = \beta_{\pi_{bs}}(\hat{p}_b - \pi_{bs}),$$

$$\hat{s} = \frac{\beta_s}{1 - \beta_s(1 - \alpha_s)}[(1 - \tau_c)i_l^* + \alpha_s \epsilon_s - ((1 - \tau_c)i_l + \pi_b)],$$

$$\dot{\epsilon}_s = \beta_{\epsilon_s}(\hat{s} - \epsilon_s).$$

These laws of motion are not made use of in the following since we assume in this chapter that the required rate of return i^r used in the description of investment of firms and asset holders is a given magnitude, measured by the world rate of interest i_l^* and since we will also assume that the measure for the tightness of monetary policy, $i_l - i$, is not involved in the formation of these investment plans (by setting the corresponding coefficients of the investment functions of the preceding section equal to zero). A further assumption needed to avoid any further discussion of these laws of motion will be provided when the next block of laws of motion, concerning the government sector, is considered.

Note with respect to the above equations that the literature generally only considers the border case where $\alpha_s = 0$ is used in conjunction with infinite adjustment speeds on the two considered markets. This gives rise to two interest parity conditions which, when coupled with myopic perfect foresight on bond price and exchange rate movements, give rise to a situation of knife edge instability – which is then stabilised by the adherents of the Rational Expectations School through the application of the jump variable technique to those variables they consider as non-predetermined.

The next set of dynamical laws concerns the evolution of short- and long-term debt of the government (the issuing of which is here governed by the fixed proportions $\alpha_b^g, 1 - \alpha_b^g$), its wage and import taxation policy and the interest rate policy of the central bank. Note here that we continue to use the letter b to denote government debt per unit of capital and that its short-term debt, b_g, must now be indexed by g since there is also the debt of worker households (which we here denote by λ_w in order to stress their importance for the present investigation):[17]

[17] The expressions t^a, t^c, w^a represent tax payments out of wages and profits and transfer payments of the government that will be of no importance in the core 9D dynamics that is the focus of this chapter.

$$\dot{b}_g = \alpha_b^g[gy^e + ib_g + b^l - t^a - t^c + w^a] - (\hat{p}_y + g_k - \delta_k)b_g,$$
$$\dot{b}^l = (1 - \alpha_b^g)[gy^e + ib_g + b^l - t^a - t^c + w^a]/p_b - (\hat{p}_y + g_k - \delta_k)b^l,$$
$$\hat{\tau}_w = \alpha_{\tau_{w1}}\left(\frac{\lambda_g}{\bar{\lambda}_g} - 1\right), \quad \lambda_g = \frac{b_g + p_b b^l}{y^e},$$
$$\hat{\tau}_m = \alpha_{\tau_m}\frac{p_x^* x - (1+\tau_m)p_m^* j^d}{p_x^* x}, \quad (x = x_y y,\, j^d = j_y y),$$
$$\dot{i} = -\beta_{i_i}(i - i_l^*) + \beta_{i_p}(\hat{p}_y - \bar{\pi}) + \beta_{i_u}(y/y^p - \bar{u}), \quad \bar{\pi} = 0.$$

Since these laws of motion, up to the interest rate policy rule, are also suppressed by appropriate assumptions in the analysis that follows we here only briefly state that the first two are immediate consequences of the government budget constraint (based in particular on various sources of tax income, now diminished by subsidies that concern the interest payments of worker households), that wage taxation is here adjusted in the direction of a target ratio of government debt, $\bar{\lambda}_g$, and that import taxes are adjusted in a way that ensures a balanced trade account in the steady state (which greatly simplifies the calculation of the steady state of the model). The interest rate policy rule $\dot{i}$ is of interest however since it could be used in counteracting accelerating debt (wage) deflation, by lowering nominal interest rates in situations of depressed activity levels and price deflation. This rule has already been explained in the preceding section. We assume in the following that the wage tax rate is not adjusted at all ($\alpha_{\tau_{w1}} = 0$) and set equal to the steady state value of the general 19D model and that the import taxes are adjusted with infinite speed ($\alpha_{\tau_m} = \infty$). These two assumptions imply in the reduced formulation of the model given below that the evolution of government debt does not feed back into the core dynamics of the model and that the exchange rate does not matter for them (also due to the assumption of given world market prices for both import and export commodities).

As the nineteenth law of motion, which is not new to the model but is now interacting with its core dynamics due to the feedback on the spending behaviour of workers' households, we finally have

$$\dot{\lambda}_w = (c_y + c_h - 1)y_w^D - (\hat{p}_y + g_k - \delta_k)\lambda_w,$$

which determines the evolution of the debt to capital ratio of worker indebtedness to the other type of households, namely the asset holders. This law of motion, together with the possibility of housing cycles due to the investment in housing and the rate of return that characterises the housing sector and the possibility of price deflation, will be the focus of interest of this chapter. Note here that the debt to capital ratio λ_w influences its rate of change negatively as far as the term based on the disposable income of workers is concerned, since this income depends negatively on this ratio and since the sum of workers' marginal propensities to spend has been assumed to be larger than one. However, due to this situation, we also have that aggregate demand, economic activity and thus goods price inflation depend negatively on λ_w, which introduces a positive dependence between the rate of change of this ratio and its level. This is indeed the partial debt deflation mechanism of the model we have already described in the preceding section. Note here that we do not yet have credit rationing in the model which would establish a further channel by which aggregate demand may be reduced in deflationary episodes.

Summarising we can thus state that we will basically consider the following sub-dynamics of the general 19D dynamics in the next section and will do this by making use of further simplifications of these dynamics that allow for the possibility of an analytical treatment:

$$\dot{y}^e = \beta_{y^e}(y^d - y^e) + (\gamma - (g_k - \delta_k))y^e, \tag{11.17}$$

$$\dot{\nu} = y - y^d - (g_k - \delta_k)\nu, \tag{11.18}$$

$$\hat{l}^e = \gamma - (g_k - \delta_k), \tag{11.19}$$

$$\hat{k}_h = g_h - \delta_h - (g_k - \delta_k), \tag{11.20}$$

$$\hat{\omega}^e = \kappa[(1-\kappa_p)\beta_w(l^{de}/l^e - \bar{e}) - (1-\kappa_w)\beta_p(y/y^p - \bar{u})], \tag{11.21}$$

$$\hat{p}_y = \kappa[\kappa_p\beta_w(l^{de}/l^e - \bar{e}) + \beta_p(y/y^p - \bar{u})], \tag{11.22}$$

$$\hat{p}_h = \beta_h\left(\frac{c_h^w}{k_h} - \bar{u}_h\right) + \kappa_h\hat{p}_y, \tag{11.23}$$

$$\dot{\lambda}_w = (c_y + c_h - 1)y_w^D - (\hat{p}_y + g_k - \delta_k)\lambda_w, \tag{11.24}$$

$$\dot{i} = -\beta_{i_i}(i - i_l^*) + \beta_{i_p}\hat{p}_y + \beta_{i_u}(y/y^p - \bar{u}). \tag{11.25}$$

Note in these laws of motion we use the real wage $\omega^e = w^e/p_y$ in the place of the nominal wage. These laws of motion make use of the following supplementary intensive form definitions and abbreviations (which are not explained here in detail since we only provide the new features of the modelling approach of Part II):[18]

$y = y^e + \beta_n(\beta_{n^d}y^e - \nu) + \gamma\beta_{n^d}y^e$ (output per unit of capital),

$l^{de} = l_y^e y,\quad l_y^e$ (the labour coefficient in efficiency units),

$y_w^D = (1-\tau_w)\omega^e l^{de} - (1-\tau_c)i\lambda_w$ (real disposable income of workers),

$c_g^w = c_y y_w^D$ (goods consumption of workers – including the purchase of houses),

$c_h^w = p_y c_h y_w^D / p_h$ (housing services consumption of workers),

$r^e = y^e - \delta_k - \omega^e l^{de}$ (the expected real rate of profits of firms),

$g_k = \alpha_r^k(1-\tau_c)(r^e - i_l^*) + \alpha_u^k(y/y^p - \bar{u}) + \gamma + \delta_k$ (gross investment of firms),

$r_h = (p_h/p_y)c_h^w/k_h - \delta_h$ (real rate of profit for housing investment),

[18] Note that output y differs from expected sales y^e due to voluntary inventory investments of firms.

$$g_h = \alpha_r^h(1-\tau_c)(r_h - i_l^*) + \alpha_u^h\left(\frac{c_h^w}{k_h} - \bar{u}_h\right) + \gamma + \delta_h \quad \text{(gross investment in housing)},$$

$$y^d = c_g^w + g_k + g_h k_h + g y^e \quad \text{(aggregate demand – including government demand } gy^e\text{)},$$

$$\tau_w = 1 - (y_{wo}^D + (1-\tau_c)i_l^*\lambda_{wo})/(\omega_o^e l_o^{de}) \quad \text{(the taxation rule)}.$$

Insertion of these equations into the above nine laws of motion gives an explicit system of nine autonomous non-linear differential equations in the nine state variables of the model shown in equations (11.17)–(11.25). Note that we have removed pension payments and unemployment benefits from the above presentation of the model. Note also that the evolution of price levels is subject to zero-root hysteresis, since these depend on historical conditions due to our assumption on the interest rate policy rule of the central bank and the accompanying assumption of costless cash balances (during each trading period) for the four agents of the model; see Chiarella and Flaschel (1999a) for details.

We present next the nine steady state values of the model (including further definitional equations that are needed for their full determination). All of these values should have an index 'o' (denoting their steady state character); in order not to overload the notation we do not add this index to the following list of steady state values. Note that the steady state values of level magnitudes are all expressed in per unit of capital form and if necessary in efficiency units; see Chiarella *et al.* (2003b) for the details in the case of the 18D core model. Note also that we have now debt of workers and of the government in the steady state of the model and that we therefore denote their actual and steady state debt to capital ratios by choosing appropriate indices λ_w, λ_g in both cases.[19] Note finally that the steady state is parametrically dependent on a given output price level p_y which is not determined by the model (due to the Taylor type interest rate policy pursued by the central bank) and thus can be supplied from the outside in an arbitrary fashion:[20]

$$y^e = \frac{y}{1+\gamma\beta_{n^d}} \quad (y = y^p\bar{u}), \tag{11.26}$$

$$\nu = \beta_{n^d} y^e, \tag{11.27}$$

$$l^e = l^{de}/\bar{e} \quad (l^{de} = l_y^e y), \tag{11.28}$$

$$k_h = \frac{(1-g)y^e - (\gamma + \delta_k)}{c_y(i_l^* + \delta_h)/c_h + \gamma + \delta_h} \quad (c_h^w = \bar{u}_h k_h), \tag{11.29}$$

$$p_h/p_y = (i_l^* + \delta_h)/\bar{u}_h, \tag{11.30}$$

[19] Here λ_g is the aggregate debt of the government sector.

[20] The inflation target of the central bank, $\bar{\pi}$, is a zero rate of inflation here (which is not true for actual central bank behaviour in general). This implies in the present model that steady state inflation will be zero, too, which in turn implies that the levels of nominal magnitudes are fixed in the steady state (in efficiency units solely as far as nominal wages are concerned).

$$y_w^D = (p_h/p_y)k_h\bar{u}_h/c_h, \tag{11.31}$$

$$y_{w1}^D = y_w^D + (1-\tau_c)i_l^*\lambda_w, \tag{11.32}$$

$$\tau_w = 1 - y_{w1}^D/(\omega^e l^{de}), \tag{11.33}$$

$$\omega^e = \frac{y^e - \delta_k - i_l^*}{l^{de}} \quad (w^e = \omega^e p_y), \tag{11.34}$$

$$p_y = \text{determined by initial conditions}, \tag{11.35}$$

$$p_h = p_y(i_l^* + \delta_h)/\bar{u}_h, \tag{11.36}$$

$$i = i_l^*, \tag{11.37}$$

$$\lambda_w = \frac{c_y + c_h - 1}{\gamma} y_w^D. \tag{11.38}$$

Note that λ_w is positive in the steady state due to our assumption that $c_y + c_h > 1$, so that workers' debt grows in line with the capital stock in the steady state (as do workers' interest payments). Note also again that the steady state is inflation-free due to our assumption about monetary policy and that nominal wages rise with labour productivity in the steady state.

Equation (11.26) gives the steady state solution of expected sales ye per unit of capital K (and also of output y per K) as determined by the desired utilisation rate of firms and the inventory policy they have to adopt due to demand growth in the steady state. Equation (11.27) provides the steady inventory-capital ratio N/K, which says that inventories (to be produced in addition to actual sales) must grow at the same speed as the capital stock. Equation (11.28) represents (in efficiency units) the amount of workforce (per K) employed by firms in the steady state as well as full employment labour intensity which is larger than actual labour intensity (in efficiency units) due to the assumed NAIRU rate of employment, $\bar{e} < 1$. The last expression for the quantity side of the model – in equation (11.29) – provides the steady value of the housing capital stock per unit of the capital stock of firms, which is obtained on the basis of the calculation of the income magnitudes shown and the debt to capital ratio of worker households to be determined below. Equation (11.34) concerns the wage level (in efficiency units), real and nominal, to be derived from the steady state value for the rate of profit which is given by the world rate of interest i_l^*. Note that all nominal magnitudes (up to nominal wages) exhibit no long-run trend and that the steady price level of output prices p_y is not determined by the model.

As remaining nominal magnitude we have the price level p_h for housing rents (in equation (11.36)), to be calculated from the uniform rate of interest i_l^* of the economy in the steady state (which also characterises the rate of return in the housing sector). There follows the steady value of the debt to capital ratio λ_w of workers, the only debt ratio to be considered in the following due to the assumption of a given wage tax rate. With respect to the public sector, there is finally the interest rate policy rule of the central bank, which due to its formulation implies that the interest rate on short-term government debt must also settle down at the given foreign rate, i_l^*, in the steady state. Again, the new equation is equation (11.37), where the steady state debt to capital ratio of workers is easily obtained from their budget constraint of workers and is positive if and only if $c_y + c_h > 1$ holds true. This closes the presentation of the interior steady state solution of our reduced 9D dynamical model. We note that the debt to capital ratio of workers rises with $c_y + c_h$, y_{w1}^D and τ_c and falls with γ and i_l^*.

11.4 2D, 3D and 5D subcases of integrated 6D real subdynamics

Using an approach similar to that of Chapter 6 of Part II of the book we simplify the 9D dynamics of the preceding section further, by assuming in place of the Metzlerian delayed feedback chain that is based on a goods market disequilibrium adjustment process of the type

$$y^d = c_y y_w^D + \alpha_r^k (r^e - i_l^*) + \alpha_u^k (y/y^p - \bar{u}) + \gamma + \delta_k \rightarrow y^e \rightarrow y \rightarrow y^d,$$

a simplified static and linearised[21] equilibrium relationship of the kind

$$y^d = y^e = y = y(\omega^e, \lambda_w) = \bar{u} y^p + d_w(\omega^e - \omega_o^e) + d_\lambda(\lambda_w - \lambda_w^o), \qquad d_w, d_\lambda \leq 0.$$

This relationship between output, real wages and real debt will be used in the following as a shortcut for the delayed feedback chain of the general case (and its richer concept of aggregate demand and its determinants) in order to study the effects of wage and price inflation and deflation on debt and real wages in a significantly simplified version of the 9D model. Note that this shortcut of the originally delayed quantity adjustment process of Metzlerian type requires that the steady state value of this function y must be equal to $y^p \bar{u}$ in order to get a steady state solution for this 7D simplification of the 9D dynamics. Note also that we concentrate in this presentation of goods market equilibrium on the effects of real wage increases and debt ratio increases which both are assumed to have a (non)-negative influence on goods market behaviour, that is in the case of real wages that the resulting decrease in investment demand outweighs the implied increase in consumption.

Let us furthermore assume that $\kappa_h = 1$ holds, so that the cost-push term in the dynamics of rental prices is given solely by the current rate of inflation on the market for goods. This assumption allows us to reduce the dynamics to a consideration of relative prices only, namely the real wage (as before) and the real rental price. On the basis of this assumption and the above short cut for goods market dynamics the dynamical system to be investigated in the following reads

$$\hat{l}^e = \gamma - (g_k - \delta_k), \tag{11.39}$$

$$\hat{k}_h = g_h - \delta_h - (g_k - \delta_k), \tag{11.40}$$

$$\hat{\omega}^e = \kappa[(1 - \kappa_p)\beta_w(l^{de}/l^e - \bar{e}) - (1 - \kappa_w)\beta_p(y/y^p - \bar{u})], \tag{11.41}$$

[21] Around the interior steady state of the model, given by ω_o^e, λ_w^o.

$$\hat{q}_h = \beta_h \left(\frac{c_h^w}{k_h} - \bar{u}_h \right) \quad (q_h = p_h/p_y), \tag{11.42}$$

$$\dot{\lambda}_w = (c_y + c_h - 1)y_w^D - (\kappa[\kappa_p\beta_w(l^{de}/l^e - \bar{e}) + \beta_p(y/y^p - \bar{u})] + g_k - \delta_k)\lambda_w, \tag{11.43}$$

$$\dot{i} = -\beta_{i_i}(i - i_l^*) + \beta_{i_p}\kappa[\kappa_p\beta_w(l^{de}/l^e - \bar{e}) + \beta_p(y/y^p - \bar{u})] + \beta_{i_u}(y/y^p - \bar{u}), \tag{11.44}$$

now with the static relationships

$$\begin{aligned}
y &= \bar{u}y^p + d_w(\omega^e - \omega_o^e) + d_\lambda(\lambda_w - \lambda_w^o) \quad (d_w, d_\lambda \le 0),\\
l_f^{de} &= l_y^e y,\\
y_w^D &= (1-\tau_w)\omega^e l^{de} - (1-\tau_c)i\lambda_w,\\
c_h^w &= c_h(1-\tau_w)y_w^D/q_h,\\
r &= y - \delta_k - \omega^e l^{de},\\
g_k &= \alpha_r^k(1-\tau_c)(r - i_l^*) + \alpha_u^k(y/y^p - \bar{u}) + \gamma + \delta_k,\\
r_h &= q_h c_h^w/k_h - \delta_h = c_h(1-\tau_w)y_w^D/k_h - \delta_h,\\
g_h &= \alpha_r^h(1-\tau_c)(r_h - i_l^*) + \alpha_u^h\left(\frac{c_h^w}{k_h} - \bar{u}_h\right) + \gamma + \delta_h,\\
\tau_w &= 1 - y_{w1}^D/(\omega^e l^{de}) \quad (y_{w1}^D = y_w^D + (1-\tau_c)i_l^*\lambda_w).
\end{aligned}$$

Neglecting the interest rate policy (11.44) of the monetary authority for the moment (by setting the corresponding adjustment parameters equal to ∞, 0 and 0, respectively which implies $i = i_l^*$) we have that interest payments of workers are based on a given rate of interest. The resulting 5D dynamics are then based on the growth laws for full employment labour intensity, housing capital per unit of capital, real wages and real rental prices and finally as the financial variable the debt to capital ratio of worker households.

The underlying interior steady state solution of these 5D dynamics (and also of the 6D dynamics) is characterised by

$$\begin{aligned}
y &= y^p\bar{u},\\
l^{de} &= l_y^e y,\\
l^e &= l^{de}/\bar{e},\\
r &= r_h = i_l^*,\\
\omega^e &= \frac{y - \delta_k - i_l^*}{l^{de}},\\
q_h &= (i_l^* + \delta_h)/\bar{u}_h,
\end{aligned}$$

$$\lambda_w = \frac{c_y + c_h - 1}{\gamma + (c_y + c_h - 1)(1 - \tau_c)i_l^*} y_{w1}^D, \quad y_{w1}^D = (1 - \tau_w)\omega^e l^{de},$$
$$c_h^w = c_h y_w^D / q_h, \quad y_w^D = y_{w1}^D - (1 - \tau_c)i_l^* \lambda_w,$$
$$k_h = c_h^w / \bar{u}_h,$$
$$\tau_w = 1 - y_{w1}^D / (\omega^e l^{de}).$$

The above 5D dynamical system can be subdivided further into a natural real growth cycle model of the Goodwin (1967), Rose (1967) type concerning the interaction of capital accumulation and income distribution and into a 3D dynamical system where we can study the interaction of the growth of the housing stock (for rental purposes) with real rental price adjustments and the debt to capital ratio of workers used in particular to finance their investment into their own stock of houses.

In order to obtain the first set of subdynamics we have to assume in addition to the assumptions already made that $d_\lambda = 0$ holds true, so that there is no debt effect with respect to the state of the goods market used in the following dynamical subsystem for describing real wage and investment dynamics. The resulting dynamics in the full employment labour intensity l^e and the real wage ω^e are basically of Goodwin (1967) growth cycle type augmented by Rose (1967) type effects of the real wage on its rate of change (as we shall see in detail below), namely

$$\hat{l}^e = -(\alpha_r^k (1 - \tau_c)(r - i_l^*) + \alpha_u^k (y/y^p - \bar{u})), \tag{11.45}$$
$$\hat{\omega}^e = \kappa[(1 - \kappa_p)\beta_w (l^{de}/l^e - \bar{e}) - (1 - \kappa_w)\beta_p (y/y^p - \bar{u})]. \tag{11.46}$$

We now have as remaining static relationships

$$y = \bar{u} y^p + d_w(\omega^e - \omega_o^e) \quad (d_w < 0),$$
$$(l^{de} = l_y^e y),$$
$$r = y - \delta_k - \omega^e l^{de}.$$

The assumption $d_w < 0$ represents what we call a negative Rose effect since it implies that wage flexibility is stabilising and price flexibility destabilising just as in the original contribution of Rose (1967).

The steady state of these 2D dynamics is characterised by

$$y = y^p \bar{u},$$
$$l^{de} = l_y^e,$$
$$l^e = l^{de} / \bar{e},$$
$$r = i_l^*,$$
$$\omega^e = \frac{y - \delta_k - i_l^*}{l^{de}}.$$

Assuming on the other hand no fluctuations in the capital stock of firms, $\hat{K} = g_k - \delta_k = \gamma$, and in the real wage of workers, $\omega^e = \omega_o^e$, by contrast gives rise to interacting dynamics between the stock of houses, $k_h = K - h/\mathrm{K}$, offered for rent on the market for housing services, the real rental price of housing services, $q_h = p_h/p_y$, and the real debt to capital ratio $\lambda_w = \Lambda_w/(p_y K)$:[22]

$$\hat{k}_h = \alpha_r^h(1-\tau_c)(r_h - i_l^*) + \alpha_u^h(c_h^w/k_h - \bar{u}_h), \tag{11.47}$$

$$\hat{q}_h = \beta_h\left(\frac{c_h^w}{k_h} - \bar{u}_h\right), \tag{11.48}$$

$$\dot{\lambda}_w = (c_y + c_h - 1)y_w^D - (\kappa[\kappa_p\beta_w(l^{de}/l_o^e - \bar{e}) + \beta_p(y/y^p - \bar{u})] + \gamma)\lambda_w, \tag{11.49}$$

here with the static relationships:

$$\begin{aligned}
y &= \bar{u}y^p + d_\lambda(\lambda_w - \lambda_w^o) \quad (d_\lambda < 0),\\
l^{de} &= l_y^e y,\\
y_w^D &= (1-\tau_w)\omega_o^e l^{de} - (1-\tau_c)i_l^*\lambda_w,\\
c_h^w &= c_h y_w^D/q_h,\\
r_h &= q_h c_h^w/k_h - \delta_h,
\end{aligned}$$

which reduces further to a 2D system where the evolution of debt does not matter if $c_h^w = const$ is assumed.

The interior steady state of these 3D dynamics is characterised by

$$\begin{aligned}
y &= y^p\bar{u},\\
l^{de} &= l_y^e y,\\
r_h &= i_l^*,\\
q_h &= (i_l^* + \delta_h)/\bar{u}_h,\\
\lambda_w &= \frac{c_y + c_h - 1}{\gamma + (c_y + c_h - 1)(1-\tau_c)i_l^*}y_{w1}^D, \quad y_{w1}^D = (1-\tau_w)\omega^e l^{de},\\
c_h^w &= c_h y_w^D/q_h, \quad y_w^D = y_{w1}^D - (1-\tau_c)i_l^*\lambda_w,\\
k_h &= c_h^w/\bar{u}_h.
\end{aligned}$$

Note that the steady state values can be obtained from the above dynamics in this order and that these calculations in particular imply that the excess demand situations underlying the β_w, β_p terms in the dynamics (11.47)–(11.49) are both zero in the steady state which in particular again implies that the price level is stationary in the steady

[22] Note here that $\hat{K} = \gamma$ implies $l^e = l_o^e$ if we start from the steady state and if shocks only occur in the state variables of the presently considered dynamics.

state. Note also that this implies that the steady state value of λ_w is uniquely determined, as is claimed above.

We stress that the study of these partial subdynamics is not to be considered as being completely specified from the economic point of view, but should be viewed as an approach, eventually leading back to the fully specified 9D dynamics, that generates propositions of the 'as if' variety, in the case of the above 3D dynamics, as if the debt effect on output can be considered as the one that dominates the outcome of the interaction of aggregate demand, sales expectations and output decisions of firms on the market for goods (as formulated for the full 9D dynamics).

With respect to these latter dynamics we now have as first propositions:

Proposition 11.1 *Assume that c_h^w is fixed at its steady state value ($\hat{C}_h^w = \gamma$). Then: the steady state of the dynamics (11.47), (11.48) is globally asymptotically stable for all positive starting values for k_h, q_h, so that all trajectories in the positive orthant of $\Re^2$ converge to the steady state values of k_h, q_h shown above.*

Proof: Concerning the Jacobian or linear part of the growth dynamics (11.47), (11.48), and paying no attention to the fact that we have growth rates in the place of time derivatives on the left-hand side, we get at all positive tuples (k_h, q_h) the qualitative expression

$$J = \begin{pmatrix} J_{11} & J_{12} \\ J_{21} & J_{22} \end{pmatrix} = \begin{pmatrix} - & + \\ - & 0 \end{pmatrix}.$$

We thus in particular have trace $J < 0$, det $J > 0$ and $J_{12}J_{21} \neq 0$. As shown in Flaschel (1984) these three conditions imply the assertion, due to a particular application of Olech's theorem on global asymptotic stability. □

We observe with respect to Proposition 11.1 and its proof that these dynamics would be of the Goodwin (1967) centre type were there not the negative (stabilising) influence of the state variable k_h on its own evolution.

The next proposition adds the influence of the debt to capital ratio to the dynamics just considered (via the effect this ratio has on the output of firms) and it of course adds also the budget law that determines the evolution of real debt per unit of capital. Contrary to what one might expect, we here find that these additional aspects do not endanger the stability result just obtained, if price adjustment is sufficiently sluggish, which due to the increased dimension of the dynamics can now however only be shown in an appropriately chosen neighborhood of the steady state. Yet, the included debt effects will be destabilising if the adjustments caused by goods and labour market disequilibrium in the wage-price module of the model become sufficiently pronounced.

Proposition 11.2 *The steady state of the dynamics (11.47)–(11.49) is locally asymptotically stable, if the parameters β_p and κ_p (or β_w) are chosen sufficiently small (such that $J_{33} < 0$ holds; see the proof). Conversely, this steady state will be unstable if the parameters β_p or β_w, the latter for $\kappa_p > 0$, are chosen sufficiently large (such that $J_{33} > 0$ holds).*

Proof: Due to the continuity of eigenvalues with respect to parameter changes we only need to consider the assertion of local asymptotic stability in the case where $\beta_p = \kappa_p = 0$ holds. The Routh–Hurwitz theorem then states that all eigenvalues of the considered Jacobian will have negative real parts if the Routh–Hurwitz coefficients fulfil $a_1 = -\text{trace } J > 0$, $a_2 = J_1 + J_2 + J_3 > 0$, $a_3 = -\det J > 0$ and finally $a_1 a_2 - a_3 > 0$, a situation which, as just stated, is not changed if small variations of the parameters β_p and κ_p away from zero are allowed for. Note here that the coefficient a_2 represents the sum of the principal minors of order 2 of the Jacobian J.

It is easy to show that the trace $J_{11}+J_{22}+J_{33}$ of the Jacobian J must be negative in the assumed situation, since all auto-feedbacks of the system (11.47)–(11.49) are negative, thus all three coefficients making up the trace are negative here. Concerning J_1, J_2 and J_3, whose indices refer to the row and column not considered in these subdeterminants, one also gets immediately (from what has just been shown for the trace) that both J_1 and J_2 must be positive, since J_{31} and J_{32} are both zero so that only multiplication with respect to elements from the diagonal of J is involved here. With respect to J_3 one gets furthermore that the dynamical law for k_h can be reduced to

$$\hat{k}_h = \alpha_r^h (1 - \tau_c) q_h,$$

without changing the sign of J_3, by making use of the linear dependencies that exist with respect to the second dynamical law (for q_h) that is involved in the calculation of J_3. From this we see qualitatively that

$$J_3 = \begin{pmatrix} J_{11} & J_{12} \\ J_{21} & J_{22} \end{pmatrix} = \begin{pmatrix} 0 & + \\ - & - \end{pmatrix} > 0,$$

as was claimed above.

Calculating $\det J$ one can use a similar linear dependency in addition in order to arrive at

$$\det J = \begin{vmatrix} J_{11} & J_{12} & J_{13} \\ J_{21} & J_{22} & J_{23} \\ J_{31} & J_{32} & J_{33} \end{vmatrix} = \begin{vmatrix} 0 & + & 0 \\ - & - & - \\ 0 & 0 & - \end{vmatrix}.$$

This not only shows that $\det J$ must be negative, but also that $-\det J$ must be equal to or smaller than $J_1(-J_{33})$ which finally gives that also $a_1 a_2 - a_3 > 0$ must hold true, since $a_1 a_3$ is based on positive expressions throughout.

Concerning the second assertion, on instability, one simply has to note that the third law of motion implies (with positive parameters β_p, κ_p and β_w) for the entry J_{33} of J at the steady state:

$$J_{33} = (c_y + c_h - 1)((1 - \tau_w)\omega_o^e l_y^e d_\lambda - (1 - \tau_c) i_l^*) - \gamma$$
$$+ \kappa[\kappa_p \beta_w l_y^e (-d_\lambda)/l_o^e + \beta_p(-d_\lambda)/y^p]\lambda_w.$$

This immediately shows that trace J can be made as positive as is desired by choosing either β_p or β_w (the latter for $\kappa_p > 0$) sufficiently large, since $-d_\lambda > 0$ and $\lambda_{w^o} > 0$ hold.

Note finally that in the present formulation of the dynamics (11.47)–(11.49) we always have that the third law of motion is independent of the other ones, so that J_{31} and J_{32} are always zero (which simplifies the above stability arguments further). The benchmark for asymptotic stability therefore is the situation where $J_{33} < 0$ holds true and instability in the present situation is therefore solely due to the law of motion for the debt to capital ratio λ_w. □

In view of this last observation on the (in)stability of the model we should however stress that we have approached this proposition and its proof from a slightly more general perspective than was really necessary, in order to indicate how it can be applied to more general situations than considered above. Assume for example that the marginal propensities to consume c_y and c_h both depend positively on the relative price for housing services q_h such that real expenditure on housing services c_h^w depends negatively on q_h (but, as assumed, not nominal expenditures on these services). Assume also that domestic output y depends positively on q_h. Proposition 11.2 basically also holds true in such an augmented situation, since trace J stays negative, since linear dependencies again imply that J_1, J_2 and J_3 are all positive and since det J can in this way be reduced to the form

$$\det J = \begin{vmatrix} J_{11} & J_{12} & J_{13} \\ J_{21} & J_{22} & J_{23} \\ J_{31} & J_{32} & J_{33} \end{vmatrix} = \begin{vmatrix} 0 & + & 0 \\ - & 0 & 0 \\ 0 & 0 & - \end{vmatrix},$$

which again shows that this determinant is negative and dominated by the positive expressions in a_1a_2. The situation of Proposition 2 therefore can be generalised to cases where the third law of motion is no longer independent of the other two differential equations.

Proposition 11.3 *The steady state of the dynamics (11.47)–(11.49), if locally asymptotically stable, is never globally asymptotically stable, but will be explosive in the debt to capital ratio if this ratio is chosen sufficiently large.*

Proof: We know in the assumed situation that $J_{33} < 0$ holds true at the steady state. Considering the right-hand side of equation (11.49) it is, however, obvious from the preceding proof that there must be a second root of this equation; where $\dot{\lambda}_w = 0$ holds and where $J_{33} > 0$ is true. This follows from the fact that the right-hand side of this equation is a polynomial of order 2 in the state variable λ_w with a positive coefficient in front of the λ_w^2 term. To the right of this root, the debt to capital ratio will increase beyond any bound, since $\dot{\lambda}_w > 0$ is then given for all points in time. □

Let us now consider the other subdynamics (11.45)–(11.46) of the 5D system (11.39)–(11.43) where it is assumed that the rate of interest on the debt of workers is a given magnitude ($= i_l^*$) and not subject to policy considerations by the central bank. Neglecting again the growth rate formulation of these dynamics, the Jacobian of the right-hand side of this system reads, for all points in the state space,

$$J = \begin{pmatrix} 0 & -\alpha_r^k(1-\tau_c)r_{\omega^e} - \alpha_u^k d_w/y^p \\ -\kappa(1-\kappa_p)\beta_w l^{de}(l^e)^{-2} & \kappa(1-\kappa_p)\beta_w l_y^e d_w/l^e + \kappa(1-\kappa_w)\beta_p(-d_w)/y^p \end{pmatrix},$$

with r_{ω^e} given by $d_w(1-\omega^e l_y^e) - l_y^e y < 0$.

Proposition 11.4 *Assume that $\beta_p = 0$ (or $\kappa_w = 1$) holds. The interior steady state of the dynamical system (11.45) and (11.46) is globally asymptotically stable for all positive starting values l^e and ω^e, so that all trajectories in the positive orthant of $\Re^2$ converge to this steady state in the current situation.*

Proof: Concerning the Jacobian J just calculated we get in this case for all points of $\Re^2$ the qualitative expression

$$J = \begin{pmatrix} 0 & + \\ - & - \end{pmatrix}.$$

We thus in particular have trace $J < 0$, det $J > 0$ and $J_{12}J_{21} \neq 0$ and so obtain the asserted global asymptotic stability as in Proposition 11.1 by an appropriate application of Olech's theorem on global asymptotic stability. □

This method of proof cannot be applied in the case $\beta_p > 0$ since we then have opposing signs in the element J_{22} of the trace of J with respect to the β_w and β_p expressions. Trace J may therefore change its sign (for large l^e for example) in the considered state space, although it may be negative at the steady state and thus imply local asymptotic stability, but not global asymptotic stability. In view of this we define a critical value for the parameter β_p (in the case $\kappa_w < 1$, for the steady state) by the expression

$$\beta_p^H = \frac{1-\kappa_p}{1-\kappa_w}\frac{\beta_w l_y^e/l^e}{y^p}.$$

With respect to this value we then get:

Proposition 11.5 *1. The interior steady state of the dynamical system (11.45), (11.46) is locally asymptotically stable for $\beta_p < \beta_p^H$.*

2. It is unstable for $\beta_p > \beta_p^H$.

3. At β_p^H there occurs a Hopf bifurcation, where the steady state loses its stability (in general) by way of the death of an unstable limit cycle or the birth of a stable limit cycle as this parameter value is crossed from below.

Proof: We have $J_{33} = 0$ at the bifurcation point and < 0 (> 0) to the left (to the right) of it, which proves the first two assertions since det $J > 0$. The third assertion is a standard one in the case where det $J > 0$ holds throughout at the steady state. □

We observe that assertion 3 also holds with respect to Proposition 11.2 in a similar and more trivial way (although the resulting dynamical system is formally seen to be of dimension three). In sum we therefore have the result that increasing price flexibility may be dangerous for asymptotic stability for two reasons, applying in two different subdynamics of the 5D dynamics of this section; due to its adverse effects on the debt to capital ratio (a Fisher debt effect) and due to its adverse effect on real wage adjustment (a Rose effect). We expect of course that these two destabilising mechanisms are jointly present in the integrated 5D dynamics and thus do not overthrow economic intuition when brought together in a higher dimensional environment.

This is easily shown for the dynamical system (11.39)–(11.43) since the Jacobian J of this growth rate system at the steady state reads with respect to the elements that depend on the parameter β_p:

$$J = \begin{pmatrix} -- & -- & -- & -- & -- \\ -- & -- & -- & -- & -- \\ -- & -- & \kappa(1-\kappa_w)\beta_p(-d_w)/y^p & -- & \kappa(1-\kappa_w)\beta_p(-d_\lambda)/y^p \\ -- & -- & -- & -- & -- \\ -- & -- & \kappa\beta_p(-d_w)\lambda_w/y^p & -- & \kappa\beta_p(-d_\lambda)\lambda_w/y^p \end{pmatrix} \tag{11.50}$$

Note that this expression only applies to the steady state of the dynamics and that we have used in this respect in particular that inflation is zero in the steady state. Obviously the trace expressions and the instability arguments based on them in the case of the disentangled 2D and 3D dynamics considered earlier apply again, showing that the trace of J can be made positive if the parameter β_p is chosen sufficiently large. Note however that the point where trace J becomes zero, and positive thereafter, is now not given by a simple expression.

Proposition 11.6 *1. The interior steady state of the 5D dynamical system (11.39)–(11.43) is locally asymptotically stable if it is assumed that y_w^D depends positively on the real wage ω_e, if the parameters β_p, β_w and β_h are sufficiently small, and if κ_p is sufficiently close to* 1.

2. Asymptotic stability gets lost by way of a Hopf bifurcation, at least in the case where $\kappa_p < 1$ holds (no stabilising real wage based Rose effect), if the parameter β_w is sufficiently large.[23]

3. Increasing the parameter β_p leads from a negative to a positive determinant of the Jacobian of the considered dynamics at the steady state, so the loss of stability need not occur via a Hopf bifurcation as the parameter β_p is increased, since real parts of eigenvalues may now become positive by a movement along the real line.

We observe that the assumption that y_w^D depends positively on the real wage is a plausible one since it means that labour demand, which depends negatively on the real wage, is not so sensitive in this respect that the wage sum is in fact decreased by an increase in the real wage. The mathematical condition underlying this assumption is that output elasticity with respect to real wages (in absolute terms) is less than 1 which is true at the steady state if the condition $(-d_w)\omega^e < \bar{u}y^p$ holds.

[23] Loss of stability is not obvious for the parameter β_h, but is of the same type if it occurs.

Proof: 1. Let us first consider the case where $\beta_p = 0$, $\beta_h = 0$ and $\kappa_p = 1$ hold and where therefore ω^e and q_h stay fixed at their steady state values. The remaining 3D system in the state variables l^e, k_h, λ_w (in this order) then gives rise to a Jacobian J at its interior steady state which is of the form

$$J = \begin{pmatrix} 0 & 0 & + \\ 0 & - & - \\ - & 0 & - \end{pmatrix},$$

if the parameter β_w is chosen sufficiently small that $J_{33} < 0$ holds. It is again easy to show that the Routh–Hurwitz conditions are fulfilled in such a case, in the same way as they were shown to hold in Proposition 2.

Let us next investigate the case where $\beta_p = 0$, $\beta_h > 0$ and $\kappa_p = 1$ holds so that the resulting dynamics therefore have become of dimension four (with q_h as the fourth state variable). It is then again easy to show that the determinant of the enlarged Jacobian can be reduced to the form (if the assumption on β_w is again made)

$$\det J = \begin{vmatrix} 0 & 0 & + & 0 \\ 0 & - & - & 0 \\ - & 0 & - & 0 \\ 0 & - & - & - \end{vmatrix}.$$

This determinant is therefore positive (since the upper 3×3 minor has been shown to be negative). Parameter values β_h sufficiently close to zero therefore imply that the real parts of the three eigenvalues which were negative (in the case $\beta_h = 0$) must stay negative also for small positive β_h which implies that the fourth eigenvalue will move from zero to a negative value in order to have a positive determinant of the Jacobian of the 4D system.

We now move in the same way from $\beta_p = 0$ and $\kappa_p = 1$ to values of these parameters sufficiently close to this situation. This then gives a 5D system whose fifth eigenvalue is no longer zero by necessity. We show again that the determinant of the Jacobian of this 5D system is negative and thus get in the same way as in the preceding step that the fifth eigenvalue must change from zero to a negative value in order to fulfil the condition on the determinant just stated. Therefore if the parameter changes are again that small that the negative real parts of the first four eigenvalues remain negative we get in sum that all real parts of the eigenvalues of the Jacobian of the full 5D dynamics must be negative. So the interior steady state is in fact locally asymptotically stable under the stated conditions (the proof has in fact shown that there are at least three real eigenvalues in such a situation).

It remains to show that the determinant of the 5D Jacobian is indeed negative under the stated conditions. To this end we first of all observe that the right-hand side equations of the dynamical system (11.39)–(11.43) can be reduced to the following expressions (in the case $\beta_p = 0$):

$$\begin{aligned} (\hat{k}_h)\ldots &\quad +q_h,\\ (\hat{q}_h)\ldots &\quad -k_h,\\ (\hat{l}^e)\ldots &\quad -g_k,\\ (\hat{\omega}^e)\ldots &\quad +y/l^e,\\ (\dot{\lambda}_w)\ldots &\quad +y_w^D, \end{aligned}$$

without change in the sign of the determinant. Hence we obtain the following sign structure

$$\det J = \begin{vmatrix} 0 & + & 0 & 0 & 0\\ - & 0 & 0 & 0 & 0\\ ? & ? & 0 & + & +\\ ? & ? & - & - & -\\ ? & ? & 0 & + & - \end{vmatrix} < 0,$$

which gives the desired result.

2. Assertion 2 is easy to show in the case $\kappa_p = 1$ since we then have that the parameter β_w is only present in the fifth law of motion and there with a positive effect on the trace of J via

$$J_{55} = \kappa\beta_w l_y^e(-d_\lambda)/l_o^e\lambda_w,$$

which means that the trace of J can be made positive if β_w is chosen sufficiently large. Note that things are more difficult in the case $\kappa_p < 1$ since we then have a stabilising Rose effect of wage flexibility, which counteracts the destabilising debt deflation effect of wage-price inflation (of the case $\kappa_p = 1$) just considered.

3. In order to prove this assertion we have to calculate that part of the considered determinant of the 5D system which depends on the parameter β_p. We again only show the items that are relevant for this calculation (where $\beta_p > 0$ now holds):

$$\det J(\beta_p) = \begin{vmatrix} 0 & + & 0 & 0 & 0\\ - & 0 & 0 & + & -\\ 0 & 0 & 0 & + & +\\ ? & ? & ? & +\beta_p & +\beta_p\\ ? & ? & + & ? & ? \end{vmatrix}.$$

Here, $\det J(\beta_p)$ denotes only that part of the determinant which in fact depends on the parameter β_p. Inspecting the original 5D dynamics one of course notes that the parameter β_p also appears in its fifth law of motion, but that it can be removed from the row of the corresponding Jacobian with respect to the calculation of their signs by means of an appropriate multiple of the fourth row without change in the qualitative structure of the remaining terms. Furthermore, it can be shown that β_p can be removed from the fourth column of the above determinant (by means of $(-d_w/d_\lambda)$ times the fifth column) without changing the positive sign in J_{34}.[24] This implies as remaining terms for the considered determinant in its dependence on the parameter β_p:

$$\det J(\beta_p) = \begin{vmatrix} 0 & + & 0 & 0 & 0 \\ - & 0 & 0 & + & - \\ 0 & 0 & 0 & + & + \\ ? & ? & ? & + & +\beta_p \\ ? & ? & + & ? & ? \end{vmatrix}.$$

We therefore get that the linear function $\det J(\beta_p)$ is upward sloping. Since we know already that $\det J(\beta_p)$ is negative for $\beta_p = 0$ we thus have the result that there is a unique value for β_p where $\det J$ must be zero (and that it is positive thereafter). □

Let us finally consider the full 6D dynamical system (11.39)–(11.44) of this section and investigate to what extent monetary policy (11.44) can contribute to the stability of the 5D dynamics of the private sector. Due to the peculiar role of debt in the considered dynamics we however obtain a negative result in this regard:

Proposition 11.7 *1. The interior steady state of the 6D dynamical system (11.39)–(11.44), which in the 5D case was locally asymptotically stable for $\partial y_w^D/\partial \omega^e > 0$, $\beta_p, \beta_w, \beta_h$ sufficiently small and κ_p sufficiently close to 1, becomes unstable (for all parameter choices) if the interest rate policy rule is switched on by choosing a positive value for either β_{i_p} or β_{i_u} (the other parameters in this feedback policy still being zero).*

2. Asymptotic stability is regained in the situation considered in assertion 1, if either β_{i_p} or β_{i_u} is negative and sufficiently small (the other remaining at zero).

3. In the situation considered in assertion 2, stability gets lost (in general) by way of a Hopf bifurcation, if the parameter β_p is made sufficiently large.

Proof: 1. The 6D dynamical system (11.39)–(11.44) can now be reduced to the following form if attention is only paid to the calculation of the sign of the determinant of the Jacobian at the steady state and if the case $\beta_{i_u} > 0$ is considered for example (the case $\beta_{i_p} > 0$ may be proved in the same way):

$$(\hat{l}^e) \ldots \quad - g_k,$$

$$(\hat{k}_h) \ldots \quad + g_h,$$

$$(\hat{\omega}^e) \ldots \quad + \beta_w l^{de}/l^e,$$

$$(\hat{q}_h) \ldots \quad + \beta_h\left(\frac{c_h^w}{k_h} - \bar{u}_h\right),$$

[24] See (11.50) and note in this regard that r_{ω^e} is given by $d_w(1 - \omega^e l_y^e) - l_y^e y$ which implies that J_{34} is larger than J_{35} as was claimed above.

$$
\begin{aligned}
(\dot{\lambda}_w)\ldots &\quad + (c_y + c_h - 1)y_w^D - (g_k - \delta_k)\lambda_w, \\
(\dot{i})\ldots &\quad + \beta_{i_u}(y/y^p - \bar{u}).
\end{aligned}
$$

With the same objective in mind this situation can be reduced further to:

$$
\begin{aligned}
(\hat{l}^e)\ldots &\quad + \omega^e, \\
(\hat{k}_h)\ldots &\quad + q_h, \\
(\hat{\omega}^e)\ldots &\quad + 1/l^e, \\
(\hat{q}_h)\ldots &\quad + \beta_h \left(\frac{1}{k_h}\right), \\
(\dot{\lambda}_w)\ldots &\quad - i, \\
(\dot{i})\ldots &\quad - \lambda_w.
\end{aligned}
$$

It follows that the sign of det J must be negative, which turns around one of the necessary and sufficient Routh–Hurwitz conditions for local asymptotic stability.

2. In the case assumed by assertion 2 we get, in the place of the just shown result, that

$$
\begin{aligned}
(\hat{l}^e)\ldots &\quad + \omega^e, \\
(\hat{k}_h)\ldots &\quad + q_h, \\
(\hat{\omega}^e)\ldots &\quad + 1/l^e, \\
(\hat{q}_h)\ldots &\quad + \beta_h \left(\frac{1}{k_h}\right), \\
(\dot{\lambda}_w)\ldots &\quad - i, \\
(\dot{i})\ldots &\quad + \lambda_w,
\end{aligned}
$$

and thus det $J > 0$ in this case. Continuity of eigenvalues with respect to parameter changes then again ensures that the stability result shown for the 5D case is preserved by such an addition to the interest rate policy rule.

3. Since det J is unambiguously positive in the situation considered by assertion 2 we immediately obtain the assertion from the fact that the trace of J is an upward sloping linear function of the parameter β_p, due to the destabilising Rose effect and the destabilising Fisher effect as far as price level flexibility is concerned and due to the fact that the β_p term in the interest rate policy rule does not concern the trace of the matrix J. Note that we do not prove the (not very restrictive) speed condition of the Hopf bifurcation theorem here (which in the present case is very difficult to obtain), but only assume that it will be fulfilled in nearly all conceivable situations. □

Note that the seemingly perverse result of assertion 2 is not really implausible if one notes the following characteristic of the dynamics under consideration. A policy of decreasing nominal interest rates in the situation of a depressed economy (or a deflationary one) in order to push economic activity back to normal activity does not work well in the present context, since this tends to increase disposable income of workers and thus their consumption and indebtedness, which by assumption leads to a further decline in the output of firms and thus does not necessarily have the consequences intended by this monetary policy (inducing further interest rate reductions). Monetary policy of this type therefore can only be expected to work if interest rate reductions speed up economic activity. Such a situation is however only present in the general 19D model of this chapter, where investment behaviour responds positively to a chain of interest rate reductions in general. This to some extent shows that the 6D dynamical system investigated in this section must be embedded in not only the general 9D situation where sluggish quantity adjustments of Metzlerian type make the feedback chains on the market for goods less fast and more involved and where nominal price adjustments matter, but must allow for the case where long-term interest rates respond to short-term ones and thus lead to responses of investment behaviour in view of the adjustments that occur in the financial markets. Such a task can however at present only be undertaken numerically, some examples of which are discussed in the next section.

11.5 Numerical investigation of housing cycles and debt deflation

In this section we briefly present some numerical illustrations of the investment cycles that are implied by the model of this chapter and the processes of debt accumulation and debt deflation to which it can give rise. These numerical illustrations provide a first impression of the dynamics that the model is capable of generating and only serve the purpose of illustration. Detailed numerical simulations should take a closer look on the various feedback channels that characterise the dynamical models of this chapter.[25] These illustrations must therefore be continued and considered in more depth in future studies of this model type, where also more refined debt deflation mechanisms than the still simple one of this chapter should be integrated.

In Figure 11.1 we show a case where damped oscillations are generated by the 9D dynamics in the case of a positive rental price shock, here still in the presence of a peg of the nominal rate of interest. We see that capacity utilisation rates in the goods and the labour market are basically fluctuating in line with each other, while the capacity utilisation rate of space is first leading and later on lagging behind these two measures of the business cycle (which then also become weaker in their positive correlation). These rates are all decreasing initially, since we had a positive rental price shock, which not only reduces the demand for housing services but also other consumption demand and thus economic activity.

We have a less than normal return in the housing sector soon after the positive price shock in this sector due to a significant decrease in the demand for housing services,

[25] The parameters underlying the numerical illustrations are (up to the changes discussed within the figures themselves): $\beta_w = 0$; $\beta_p = 0$; $\beta_n = 0.3$; $\beta n^d = 0.1$; $\beta_{y^e} = 1$; $\beta_h = 0.2$; $\beta_{i_i} = 0$; $\beta_{i_p} = 0$; $\beta_{i_u} = 0$; $\alpha_r^h = 0.25$; $\alpha_u^h = 0.25$; $\alpha_r^k = 0$; $\alpha_u^k = 0$; $\kappa_p = 0$; $\kappa_w = 0$; $\bar{u} = 0.92$; $l_y = 2$; $\bar{U}_h = 0.9$; $\bar{e} = 0.95$; $c_y = 0.7$; $i_l^* = 0.08$; $\delta_k = 0.1$; $\tau_c = 0.5$; $\delta_h = 0.1$; $g = 0.1$; $\gamma = 0.06$; $c_h = 0.4$; $y^P = 1$; $\kappa_h = 0$; $p_o = 5$.

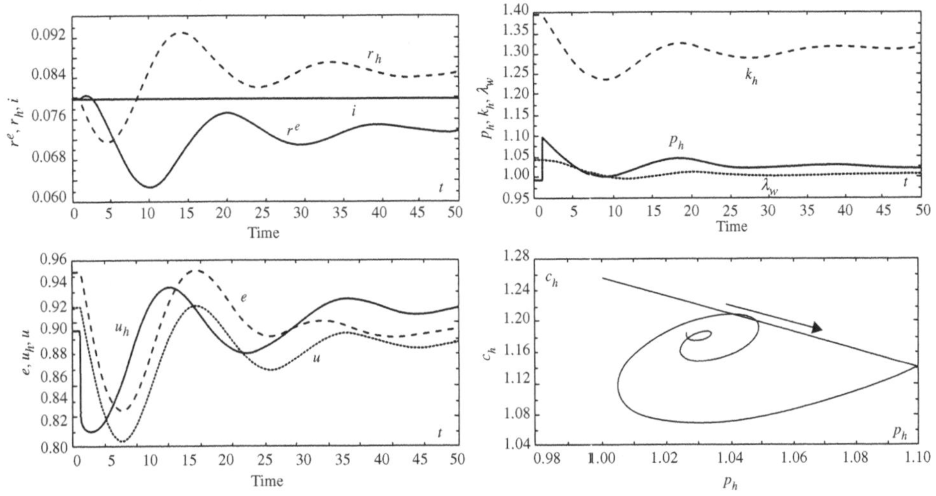

Figure 11.1 Damped fluctuations in the supply of housing services and rental prices

see the figure bottom right, which is accompanied by reduced capital formation in this sector relative to the goods-producing industry. This holds over a long-run horizon of fifty years, over which the demand for housing services does not return to its initial level again (although capacity utilisation in the housing sector does reach high levels in between). The opposite holds true, in particular with respect to the rate of return of the goods manufacturing sector. Bottom right we finally see a mild cyclical evolution with respect to occupied rental space and rental prices. We stress that the considered situation is still an extreme one, since neither wages nor goods prices respond to demand pressure on their respective markets so far, which allows for zero roots and thus path dependence and asymmetries in the time series that are shown. The considered situation is indeed a very sluggish one with respect to cycle lengths, since the economy does not yet respond to certain demand pressures to a sufficient degree.

In Figure 11.2 we have increased the adjustment speed of goods prices (away from its zero level to 0.2) which – due to an adverse real wage or Rose effect – destabilises the economy leading to higher volatility in all variables just discussed. This also removes the path-dependency from the shown time series, allows for basically symmetric fluctuations of utilisation rates around their steady state levels, with the rate of capacity utilisation of space now always leading the other two measures of the business cycle.

On average, profitability in the housing sector still remains depressed, while the opposite seems to hold in goods manufacturing, implying that the capital stock underlying the supply of housing services is still shrinking relative to the one in goods manufacturing. The variable that is subject to a positive shock is now the debt to capital ratio of worker households which leads to an immediate decline in their demand, in particular for housing services, a recession in all markets of the economy and the start of the business cycle from the resulting decrease in economic activity. There is now

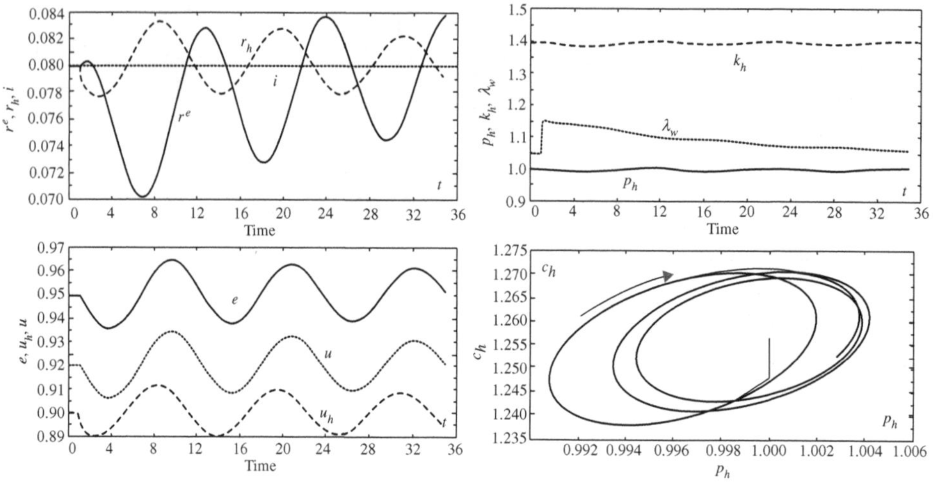

Figure 11.2 More volatile fluctuations through flexible goods-price level adjustments

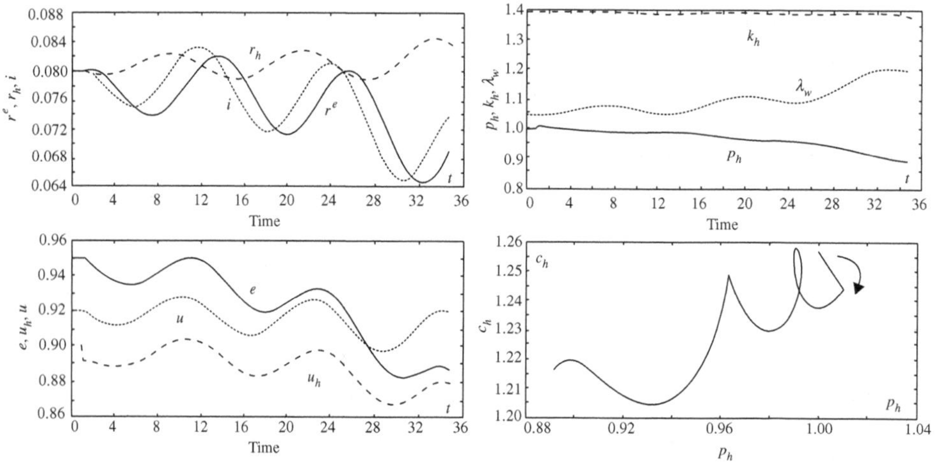

Figure 11.3 Implosive fluctuations and debt deflation

significant overshooting and a nearly persistent cycle in the interaction between rented space and rental prices and a pronounced negative correlation in the evolution of the rates of return in housing services and manufacturing.

Next, in Figure 11.3, we allow for much stronger price adjustments, and now also adjustment of wages with respect to demand pressure on the labour market, and return to the case of a positive shock in rental prices. We now indeed get price deflation with respect to all three price levels of the model. We also allow for an active interest rate policy of the central bank which here follows economic activity closely and is thus

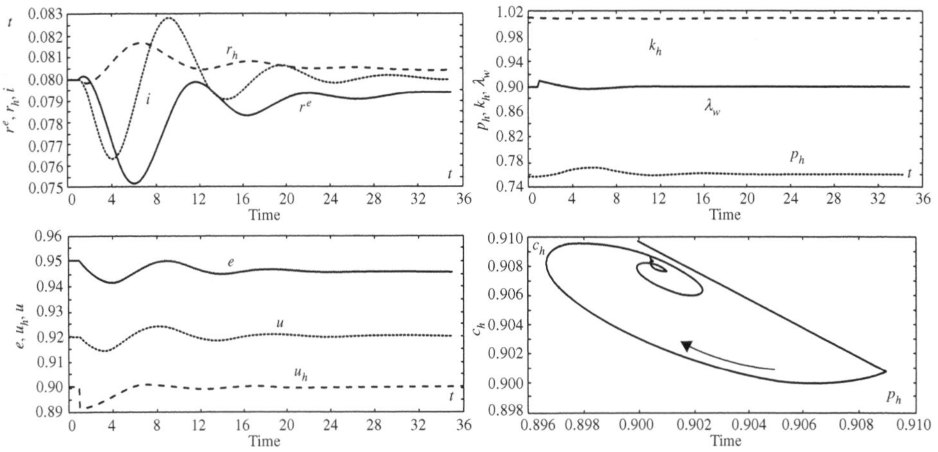

Figure 11.4 Damped fluctuations based on absolute downward wage rigidity

meant to be counter cyclical. The negative correlation between the rates of return in the provision of goods and space is still there and now there is a positive correlation between our three measures of economic activity, which in addition exhibit a significant downward trend. This is the novel thing in this cyclically fairly explosive situation accompanied by the significant upward trend in workers' debt to capital ratio and the shown downward trend in space rental prices as well as occupied space.

The explosive fluctuations of the preceding figure can however be removed and turned into damped oscillations when wages, although remaining flexible in the upward direction, are made downwardly rigid by an appropriate non-linearity in the money–wage PC.[26] This is shown in Figure 11.4 where the trends in the debt to capital ratio and the rental prices are removed by this downward rigidity in nominal wages (an important cost-pressure term in the evolution of space and goods prices). This asymmetric rigidity therefore helps to overcome the deflationary forces indicated in the preceding figure. Yet, due to the lack of a downward adjustment in the money wage we have no longer a uniquely determined NAIRU level on the labour market and need not have a situation in which the rate of employment recovers to its original steady state level (which is here still determined exogenously).

Figure 11.5 finally shows what indeed can happen in the economy if in particular this downward rigidity of money wages is removed to a larger degree. The shown situation of a strong process of debt deflation and increasing depression must however be considered in much more detail than is possible here. In this chapter we primarily attempted to supplement other work by the authors on the occurrence of debt deflation forces in the sector of firms by here considering debtor-creditor relationships in the

26 See Chiarella *et al.* (2000) for a detailed discussion of this type of downward rigidity in the money–wage PC.

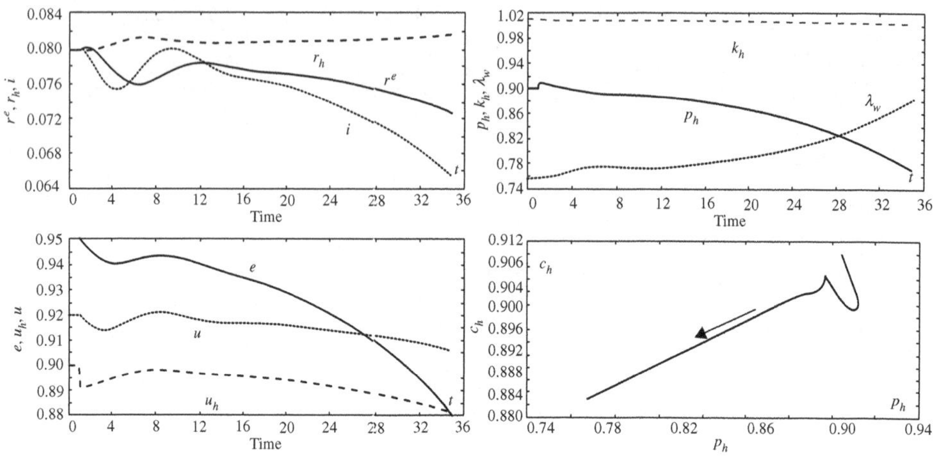

Figure 11.5 Monotonic debt deflation instead of cyclical recovery due to downward wage adjustment

household sector solely and the dynamics that this particular relationship may imply for the long-run evolution of the macroeconomy.

This closes the numerical investigation of the model, here still without worker households' debt default and bankruptcy as far as their past investment in houses (not the purchase of housing services) is concerned. In the next section we will add such debt default and bankruptcy to the housing market, comparable with what we considered for firms in Chapter 7 (to a certain degree). This is still done by adding certain leakages to the model, but not yet by considering housing booms and busts in the form of bubbles in the resale market for housing investment (which does not yet exist in this model type).

Note here also that we did not treat office space cycles explicitly in this chapter, but leave this for future investigation (see the introduction of this chapter for notes on the respective literature). Note also that the (p_h, c_h) cycle shown in Figure 11.4 bottom right is just another type of Goodwin (1967) cycle, in particular since c_h and the utilisation rate of housing space u_h are strictly positively correlated. Note finally that a similar, but not so strict correlation holds true with respect to the price levels p_h, p_y.

11.6 Debt default and bankruptcy in the private housing market

As an addition to the model of this chapter in this section we provide a description of how this general model may be extended and modified in order to allow for further stabilising or destabilising feedbacks caused by the simultaneous occurrence of high debt and deflation, here concerning in particular debt default and the bankruptcy rate of housing owned by worker households.

For this purpose we first reformulate the housing investment behaviour and the financing of this investment of the workers in the household sector:

Worker Households: Housing Investment Behaviour

$$\dot{K}_h^w = c_y^h Y_w^{Dn}/p_y - \delta_h K_h^w - \varphi_b(i) K_h^w, \quad \varphi_b'(i) > 0, \varphi_d \Lambda_w = \varphi_b p_y K_h^w,$$

see Section 11.2.1

$$\dot{\Lambda}_w = p_y C_g^w + p_h C_h^w - (1-\tau_w)[wL^d + w^u(L - L^w) + w^r \alpha_l L_2]$$
$$- (1-\tau_c) i \Lambda_w - \varphi_d(i)\Lambda_w.$$

We simply add in the first equation the situation of bankruptcy of some worker households as far as their holding of houses is concerned (as an additional leakage effect for the stock of houses K_h^w they are holding). Moreover, there will be in such situations debt default as far as these households are concerned (concerning Λ_w) which is here assumed to be of the extent: $\varphi_d \Lambda_w = \varphi_b p_y K_h^w$. We assume that the default rate φ_d as well as the bankruptcy rate φ_b depend (among other things) positively on the interest rate i, since φ_d is assumed to depend on this rate. We do not consider in this section a loan rate that differs from the short-term interest rate.

Defaults here just reduce the debt level of workers in their dependence on the sector of pure asset holders (since these workers stop paying interest) and are therefore happening as if there is a debt-reducing gift from these households to the worker households, in this extreme form doing no direct harm to the working of the economy as long as asset holder households do not react or are not forced to react to this situation (by credit rationing or – similar to commercial banks – by getting into liquidity difficulties). This is assumed to hold true in the income and savings statements of these households shown below, where part of the savings are no longer net savings, but mere replacement of the debt that has gone into default.

Pure Asset Holders: Debt Default, Income and Savings

$$Y_c^{Dn} = (1-\tau_c)[i_\lambda \Lambda_f + i B_c + B_1^l + p_h C_h^w - p_y \delta_h K_h] + s(1-\tau_c^*) B_2^l,$$

$$S_c^n = Y_c^{Dn} - p_v C_c = \dot{B}_c + \frac{\dot{B}_1^l}{i_l} + \frac{s\dot{B}_2^l}{i^{l*}} + p_y(I_h - \delta_h K_h) + \varphi_d(i)\Lambda_w + \dot{\Lambda}_w.$$

On the intensive form level we have now changes in two of the differential equations of the full model, yet one which does not feed back into its dynamics, changes that are simpler to add than the ones in the case of indebted firms. In fact we only show in the following two laws of motion the additions by which they are to be augmented.

The Extended Dynamics of the Workers' Housing Capital and their Indebtedness

$$\hat{k}_h^w = c_y^h y_w^D / k_h^w - \delta_h - (g_k - \delta_k) - \varphi_b(i), \quad \varphi_b = \varphi_d(i)\lambda_w / k_h^w \quad \text{or}$$

$$\dot{k}_h^w = c_y^h y_w^D - \delta_h k_h^w - (g_k - \delta_k) k_h^w - \varphi_d(i)\lambda_w \quad \text{and}$$

$$\hat{\lambda}_w = (c_y + c_h - 1) y_w^D / \lambda_w - \hat{p}_y + g_k - \delta_k - \varphi_d(i), \quad \varphi_d(i) = a_i(i - i_l^*).$$

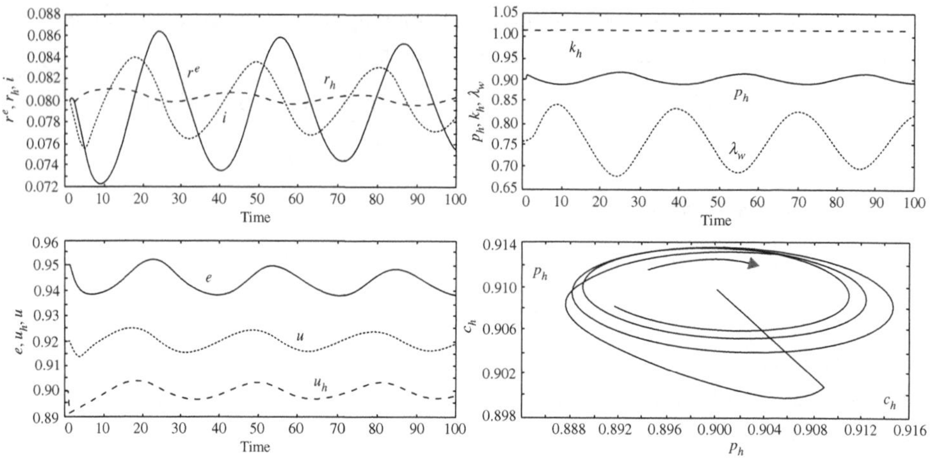

Figure 11.6 Increasing amplitude due to increasing interest rate effect on the default rate of worker households

Note that we do not yet allow that workers' consumption habits change when they go bankrupt with respect to housing capital. The first law of motion is therefore of no importance for the overall stability of the model, since it only describes the housing stock of workers, which may influence their well-being, but – by assumption – does not change their behaviour (since wealth effects are completely disregarded in this model type).

Default and bankruptcy do not have much impact in general and do indeed stabilise the dynamics for small values of the parameter a_i. This result is however not a general one, since larger choices of the parameter a_i may again increase the volatility of the implied trajectories. This is shown (in relation to Figure 11.4) in Figure 11.6 for the value $a_i = 4.5$.

The above high value for the parameter a_i (characterising the function φ_d) may appear as implausible, but may be chosen sufficiently smaller if further indirect effects of the default rate φ_d are taken into account, for example:

- a negative effect of the default rate φ_d, represented by a term $-\alpha_1(i - i_l^*)$, on the price inflation rate $\hat{p}_y$ which in our one good model represents the evolution of prices of all physical commodities (including house consumption and ordinary capital goods);
- a positive effect of the default rate φ_d, represented by a term $\alpha_2(i - i_l^*)$, on the investment rate g_h of pure asset holders into their housing capital stock and their provision of housing services;
- a negative effect of the rate φ_d on the propensity of workers to consume (purchase) houses; and
- the addition of a markup factor on the short-term rate of interest – as far as credit supplied to worker households that own houses is concerned – a markup that depends on the default rate φ_d.

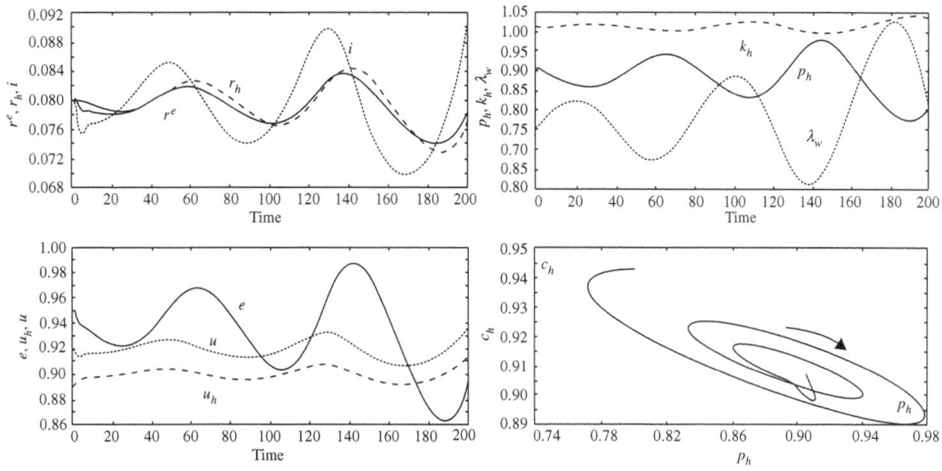

Figure 11.7 Increasing instability due to price level dependency on the default rate of worker households

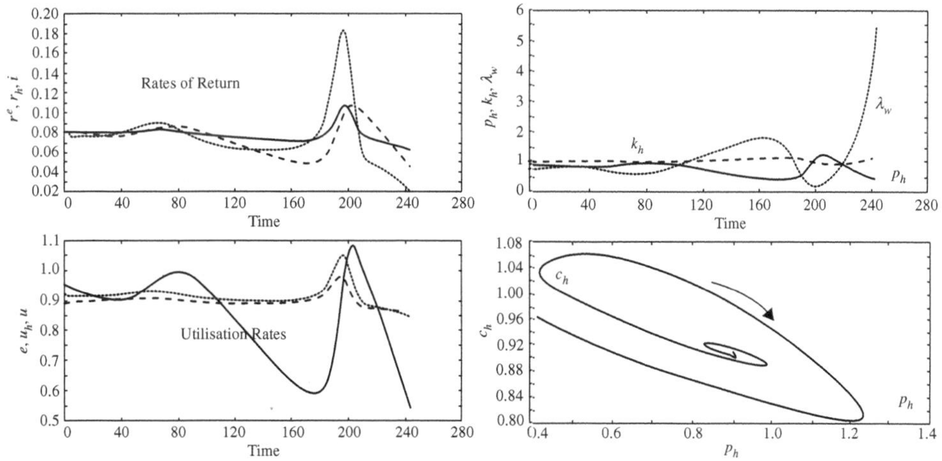

Figure 11.8 Economic breakdown through default dependent price deflation

In the first case, the combination of $a_i = 1$ and $\alpha_1 = 0.35$ is already sufficient to generate the explosive trajectories shown in Figure 11.7 – starting from the simulation shown in Figure 11.6. Introducing negative feedback of default on the price levels p_y, p_h therefore makes the economy subject to increased volatility in its activity levels.

A further slight increase of this parameter to $\alpha_1 = 0.37$ then ultimately produces a breakdown of the economy as shown in Figure 11.8 (if this outcome is not stopped by other means or policy actions).

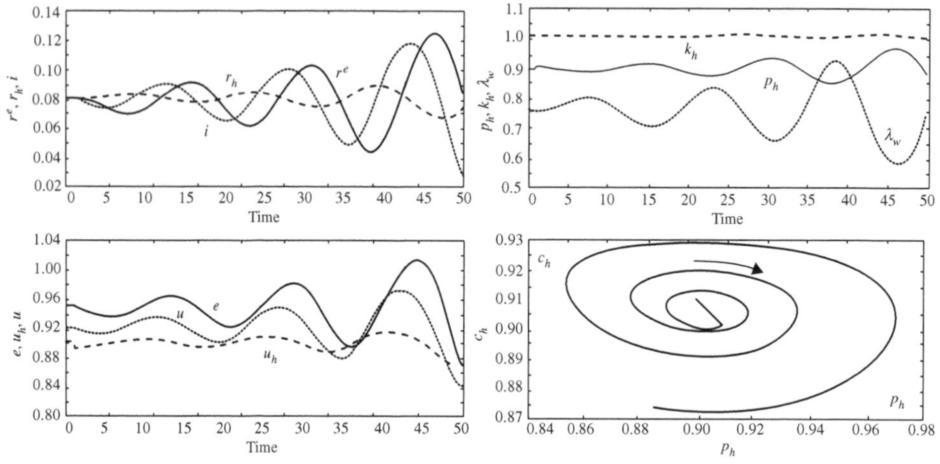

Figure 11.9 Increasing instability due to additional investment in the supply of housing services due to increases in the housing default rate of workers

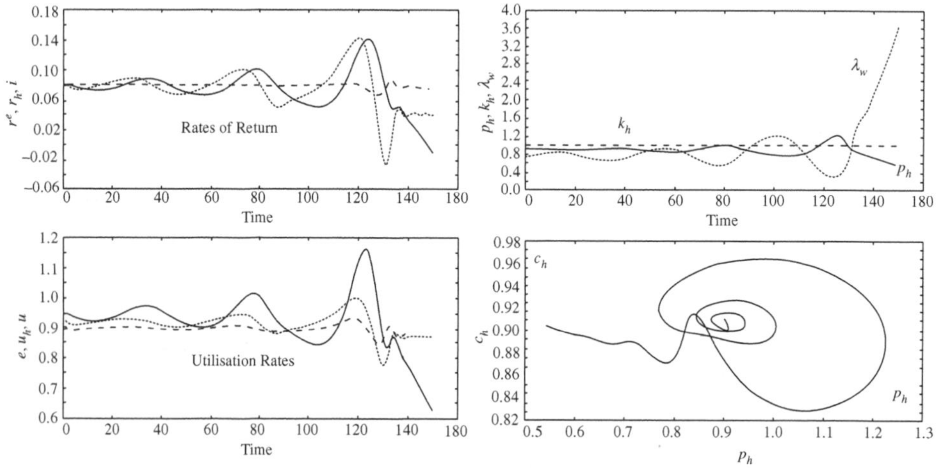

Figure 11.10 Economic breakdown through default dependent price deflation

In the second case the combination of $a_i = 1$ and $\alpha_2 = 0.35$ is sufficient to generate the explosive trajectories (again starting from the simulation shown in Figure 11.6) shown in Figure 11.9.

Finally, choosing both of the positive parameter values, $\alpha_1 = 0.25$, $\alpha_2 = 0.25$, again produces a breakdown of the economy as shown in Figure 11.10.

We refer the reader back to Part I of the book for a discussion of the current subprime crisis in the US and, spreading out from there, to parts of the world economy. This current debt and liquidity crisis is however much more multi-faceted than what could be included into the type of structural macroeconometric model which we extensively discussed in Part II of the book. In contrast to Chapters 8 and 9 we did not model commercial banks as intermediaries between pure asset holders and worker households (and thus also not the process of disintermediation). Furthermore, booms and busts in housing prices were here still coupled in a one-to-one fashion with what was happening on the other goods markets of the economy. Nevertheless inflationary and deflationary busts could be shown to be characteristic for the trajectories generated by the 9D subdynamics of this chapter, which however deserves much more investigation than could be done in this final chapter.

11.7 Conclusions

In this chapter we have reconsidered a general disequilibrium model, with an applied orientation and exhibiting a detailed modelling of the private housing sector, which we have developed in Part II, starting from the Murphy model for the Australian economy discussed in Powell and Murphy (1997). This modelling approach is complete with respect to budget equations and stock-flow interactions and can be reduced to a somewhat simplified 18D core model, the dynamics of which were intensively studied in Part II. In the present chapter we have modified this type of model towards the explicit consideration of debtor and creditor households, thus extending the dynamics of the core model by one dimension to 19D by the addition of the dynamics of the debt to capital ratio of the indebted worker households. The subdynamics of these 19D dynamics were investigated theoretically and illustrated numerically. The basic findings were that there is convergence to the balanced growth path of the model for sluggish disequilibrium adjustment processes, that persistent investment cycles in the housing sector can be generated for certain higher adjustment speeds by way of Hopf bifurcations in particular, and that processes of debt deflation may trigger monotonic depressions that become more and more severe when the real debt of debtor households is systematically increased by deflationary spirals in the manufacturing sector in particular.

References

Aghion, P., P. Bacchetta, and A. Banerjee (2004). A corporate balance-sheet approach to currency crises. *Journal of Economic Theory* 119, 6–30.

Aglietta, M. (1976). *Régulation et Crises du Capitalisme*. Paris: Odile Jacob.

Andrieu-Lacu, C. (2006). *Monnaie, Liquidité, Faillite: Une Histoire Analytique de la Crise Japonaise*. Doctoral Thesis, University Paris IX Dauphine, Place du Marechal de Lattre de Tassigny, 75775 Paris Cedex 16.

Asada, T., C. Chiarella, P. Flaschel, and R. Franke (2003). *Open Economy Macrodynamics. An Integrated Disequilibrium Approach*. Heidelberg: Springer.

— (2010). *Monetary Macrodynamics*. London: Routledge.

Asada, T., C. Chiarella, P. Flaschel, T. Mouakil, C. Proaño, and W. Semmler (2011). Stock-flow interactions, disequilibrium macroeconomics and the role of economic policy. *The Journal of Economic Surveys* 25, doi: 10.1111/j.1467-6419.2010.00661.x.

Ashcraft, A. and T. Schuermann (2007). Understanding the securitization of subprime mortgage credit. Working Paper, Federal Reserve Bank of New York.

Barnett, W. and Y. He (1999). Stability analysis of continuous-time macroeconomic systems. *Studies in Nonlinear Dynamics and Econometrics* 3(4), 169–88.

Beaudry, P. and A. Portier (2004). Stock prices, news, and economic fluctuations. NBER working paper no. 10548.

Benhabib, J. and T. Miyao (1981). Some new results on the dynamics of the generalized Tobin model. *International Economic Review* 22, 589–96.

Bergstrom, A. and K. Nowman (2007). *A Continuous Time Econometric Model of the United Kingdom with Stochastic Trends*. Cambridge University Press.

Bergstrom, A., K. Nowman, and C. Wymer (1994). Monetary and fiscal policy in a second-order continuous time macroeconometric model of the United Kingdom. *Journal of Economic Dynamics and Control* 18, 731–61.

Bernanke, B. (2000). Japanese monetary policy: a case of self-induced paralysis? In R. Mikitani and A. Posen (eds.), *Japan's Financial Crisis and its Parallels to US Experience*. Washington DC: Institute for International Economics.

Bernanke, B., M. Gertler, and S. Gilchrist (1996). The financial accelerator in a quantitative business cycle framework. *Review of Economics and Statistics* 78(1), 1–15.

Bernard, L. and W. Semmler (2009). Boom-bust cycles: leveraging, complex securities, and asset prices. CEM Working Paper, available at www.newschool.edu/nssr/cem/papers/wp/financial/SemmlerBernardNewversionSept2709_mrLucas_4.pdf.

Bhaduri, A. and S. Marglin (1990). Unemployment and the real wage: the economic basis for contesting political ideologies. *Cambridge Journal of Economics* 14(4), 375–93.

Blanchard, O. (1981). Output, the stock market and interest rates. *American Economic Review* 71, 132–43.
Blanchard, O. and S. Fischer (1989). *Lectures on Macroeconomics*. Cambridge, MA: The MIT Press.
Blanchard, O. and L. Katz (1999). Wage dynamics: Reconciling theory and evidence. *American Economic Review* 89(2), 69–74.
Borio, C., C. Furfine, and L. Phillip (1999). Procyclicality of the financial system and financial instability: issues and policy options. *Bank for International Settlements Papers* no. 1.
Boyer, R. (1986). *Théorie de la régulation. Une analyse critique*. Paris: La Découverte.
— (2004). Japon: de la décennie perdue à un improbable 'New Deal'. *Cepremap Working Paper* (2004-04).
Brock, W. A. and C. H. Hommes (1997). A rational route to randomness. *Econometrica* 65, 1059–95.
Burnside, C., M. Eichenbaum, and S. Rebelo (2001). Hedging and financial fragility in fixed exchange rate regimes. *European Economic Review* 45, 1151–93.
Calomiris, C. W. and J. R. Mason (2003). How to restructure failed banking systems: lessons from the US in the 1930's and Japan in the 1990's. NBER Working Paper 9624, 1–64.
Charpe, M., P. Flaschel, C. Proaño, and W. Semmler (2009). Overconsumption, credit rationing and bailout monetary policy from a Minskyan perspective. *Intervention* 6, 147–70.
Chiarella, C. and P. Flaschel (1996). Real and monetary cycles in models of Keynes-Wicksell type. *Journal of Economic Behavior and Organization* 30, 327–51.
— (1999a). Keynesian monetary growth in open economies. *Annals of Operations Research* 89(1), 35–59.
— (1999b). Towards applied disequilibrium growth theory: I. The starting model. School of Finance and Economics Working Paper no. 93, The University of Technology, Sydney.
— (1999c). Towards applied disequilibrium growth theory: II. Intensive form and steady state analysis of the model. School of Finance and Economics Working Paper no. 94, The University of Technology, Sydney.
— (1999d). Towards applied disequilibrium growth theory: III. Basic partial feedback structures and stability issues. School of Finance and Economics Working Paper no. 95, The University of Technology, Sydney.
— (2000). *The Dynamics of Keynesian Monetary Growth: Macro Foundations*. Cambridge University Press.
— (2003). Towards applied disequilibrium growth theory: V. Housing investment cycles, private debt accumulation and deflation. School of Finance and Economics Working Paper no. 97, The University of Technology, Sydney.
Chiarella, C. and A. Khomin (1999). Adaptively evolving expectations in models of monetary dynamics: The fundamentalists forward looking. *Annals of Operations Research* 89, 21–34.
Chiarella, C., P. Flaschel, G. Groh, C. Köper, and W. Semmler (1999a). Towards applied disequilibrium growth theory: VI. Substitution, money-holdings, wealth-effects and further extensions. School of Finance and Economics Working Paper no. 98, The University of Technology, Sydney.
— (1999b). Towards applied disequilibrium growth theory: VII. Intensive form analysis in the case of substitution. School of Finance and Economics Working Paper no. 99, The University of Technology, Sydney.
Chiarella, C., P. Flaschel, G. Groh, and W. Semmler (2000). *Disequilibrium, Growth and Labor Market Dynamics: Macro Perspectives*. Berlin and New York: Springer.

Chiarella, C., P. Flaschel, and W. Semmler (2001a). The macrodynamics of debt deflation. In R. Bellofiore and P. Ferri (eds.), *Financial Fragility and Financial Investment in the Capitalist Economy. The Economic Legacy of Hyman Minsky*, Volume II, pp. 133–84. Northampton, MA: Edward Elgar.

— (2001b). Price flexibility and debt dynamics in a high order AS-AD model. *Central European Journal of Operations Research* 9, 119–46.

Chiarella, C., P. Flaschel, A. Khomin, and P. Zhu (2002). *The SND Package: Applications to the Dynamics of Keynesian Monetary Growth*. Bern: Peter Lang.

Chiarella, C., P. Flaschel, G. Gong, and W. Semmler (2003a). Non-linear Phillips curves, complex dynamics and monetary policy in a Keynesian macro model. *Chaos, Solitons and Fractals* 18, 613–34.

Chiarella, C., P. Flaschel, and P. Zhu (2003b). Towards applied disequilibrium growth theory: IV. Numerical investigations of the core 18D model. School of Finance and Economics Working Paper no. 96, The University of Technology, Sydney.

Chiarella, C., P. Flaschel, and R. Franke (2005). *Foundations for a Disequilibrium Theory of the Business Cycle: Quantitative Analysis and Qualitative Assessment*. Cambridge University Press.

Chiarella, C., P. Flaschel, R. Franke, and W. Semmler (2009a). *Financial Markets and the Macroeconomy. A Keynesian Perspective*. London: Routledge.

Chiarella, C., H. Hung, P. Flaschel, and W. Semmler (2009b). *Business Fluctuations and Long-Phased Cycles in High Order Macrosystems*. NOVA Publishers: New York.

Christiano, L., R. Motto, and M. Rostagno (2006). Two reasons why money and credit may be useful in monetary policy. NBER working paper no. 13502.

— (2008). Monetary policy and stock market boom-bust cycles. ECB Working Paper no. 955.

Cohen, D. and E. Farhi (2001). The Phillips curves across the Atlantic: It is the price curves that differ. Discussion paper no. 3100, Centre for Economic Policy Research, London.

Corsetti, G., P. Presenti, and N. Roubini (1998). What caused the Asian currency and financial crisis. NBER working paper no. 2633.

Deleplace, G. and E. J. Nell (1996). *Money In Motion*. London: MacMillan Press.

Dell Ariccia, G., D. Igan, and A. L. Laeven (2008). Credit booms and lending standards: Evidence from the subprime mortgage market. CEPR Discussion Paper no. N6683.

Diamond, P. and P. Dybvig (1983). Bank runs, deposit insurance and liquidity. *Journal of Political Economy* 91(3), 401–19.

Dornbusch, R. (1976). Expectations and exchange rate dynamics. *Journal of Political Economy* 84, 1161–76.

Dos Santos, C. and G. Zezza (2004). A post-Keynesian stock-flow consistent macroeconomic growth model: Preliminary results. *The Levy Economic Institute Working Papers* (402).

Duménil, G. and D. Lévy (1999). Being Keynesian in the short term and Classical in the long term: The traverse to Classical long-term equilibrium. *The Manchester School* 67(6), 684–716.

Edwards, S. (1999). On crisis prevention: Lessons from Mexico and East Asia. NBER working paper no. 7233.

Eggertsson, G. and M. Woodford (2003). The zero bound on interest rates and optimal monetary policy. *Brookings Papers on Economic Activity* 2003(1), 139–211.

— (2004). Policy options in a liquidity trap. *American Economic Review* 94(2), 76–9.

Epstein, G. and H. Gintis (1995). *Macroeconomic Policy after the Conservative Era: studies in investment, saving and finance*. Oxford University Press.

Fair, R. (1997). Testing the NAIRU model for 27 countries. Yale University, available at http://fairmodel.econ.yale.edu/rayfair/pdf/1997C.PDF.

— (2000). Testing the NAIRU model for the United States. *The Review of Economics and Statistics* 82(1), 64–71.

Fisher, I. (1933). The debt-deflation theory of great depressions. *Econometrica* 1(4), 337–57.

Flaschel, P. (1984). Some stability properties of Goodwin's growth cycle. A critical elaboration. *Zeitschrift für Nationalökonomie* 44, 63–9.

— (2000). Disequilibrium growth theory with insider-outsider effects. *Structural Change and Economic Dynamics* 11(3), 337–54.

Flaschel, P. and G. Groh (1997). Textbook stagflation theory; narrow views and full implications; a note. Faculty of Economics, University of Bielefeld, Discussion Paper no. 359.

Flaschel, P. and H.-M. Krolzig (2006). Wage-price Phillips curves and macroeconomic stability: Basic structural form, estimation and analysis. In C. Chiarella, P. Flaschel, R. Franke, and W. Semmler (eds.), *Quantitative and Empirical Analysis of Nonlinear Dynamic Macromodels*, Volume 277 of *Contributions to Economic Analysis*, Chapter 2, pp. 4–48. Amsterdam: Elsevier.

Flaschel, P. and W. Semmler (2006). Currency crisis, financial crisis and large output loss. In C. Chiarella, P. Flaschel, R. Franke, and W. Semmler (eds.), *Quantitative and Empirical Analysis of Nonlinear Dynamic Macromodels*, Volume 277 of *Contributions to Economic Analysis*, Chapter 12, pp. 385–414. Amsterdam: Elsevier.

Flaschel, P., R. Franke, and W. Semmler (1997). *Dynamic Macroeconomics: Instability, Fluctuations and Growth in Monetary Economies*. Cambridge, MA: The MIT Press.

Flaschel, P., G. Gong, and W. Semmler (2001). A Keynesian macroeconometric framework for the analysis of monetary policy rules. *Journal of Economic Behavior and Organization* 25, 101–36.

Flaschel, P., R. Franke, and C. Proaño (2008). On equilibrium determinacy in new Keynesian models with staggered wage and price setting. *The B.E. Journal of Macroeconomics* 8(1), Article 31.

Flaschel, P., G. Gangolf, C. Proaño, and W. Semmler (2009). *Topics in Applied Macrodynamic Theory*. Heidelberg: Springer.

Franke, R. (1996). A Metzlerian model of inventory growth cycles. *Structural Change and Economic Dynamics* 7, 243–62.

Franke, R. and T. Lux (1993). Adaptive expectations and perfect foresight in a nonlinear Metzler model of the inventory cycle. *The Scandinavian Journal of Economics* 95, 355–63.

Franke, R. and W. Semmler (1999). Bond rate, loan rate and Tobin's q in a temporary equilibrium model of the financial sector. *Metroeconomica* 50(3), 351–85.

Fukao, M. (2002). Financial sector profitability and double gearing. *NBER Working Papers* (9638).

Gali, J. (2000). The return of the Phillips curve and other recent developments in business cycle theory. *Spanish Economic Review* 2, 1–10.

Gambacorta, L. and P. E. Mistrulli (2004). Does bank capital affect lending behavior? *Journal of Financial Intermediation* 13, 436–57.

Gantmacher, F. (1959). *Theory of Matrices*. New York: Interscience Publishers.

Godley, W. (1999). Money and credit in a Keynesian model of income determination. *Cambridge Journal of Economics* 23(4), 393–411.

Goodwin, R. (1967). A growth cycle. In C.H. Feinstein (ed.), *Socialism, Capitalism and Economic Growth*, pp. 54–8. Cambridge University Press.

Gordon, D., T. Weisskopt, and S. Bowles (1983). Long swings and the nonreproductive cycles. *American Economic Review, Paper and Proceedings* 73(2), 152–7.
Hendershott, P. H. (1996). Rental adjustment and valuation in overbuilt markets: Evidence from Sydney. *Journal of Urban Economics* 39, 51–67.
Hendershott, P. H., B. D. MacGregor, and R. Y. C. Tse (2002). Estimation of the rental adjustment process. *Real Estate Economics* 30(2), 165–83.
Hoshi, T. and A. Kashyap (1999). The Japanese banking crisis: where did it come from and how will it end? *NBER Working Paper 7250*, 1–86.
IMF (1998, May). Financial crises: Causes and indicators. *World Economic Outlook*.
Inaba, N., T. Kozu, T. Sekine, and T. Nagahata (2004). Non-performing loans and the real economy: Japan's experience. *BIS Working Paper* (22), 106–26.
Kageyama, N. and N. Harada (2007). Bankruptcy dynamics in Japan: A system estimation approach. In *Proceedings of the 51st Annual Meeting of the ISSS, Papers: 51st Annual Meeting*, Tokyo.
Kaldor, N. (1940). A model of the trade cycle. *Economic Journal* 50, 78–92.
— (1966). Marginal productivity and the macroeconomic theories of distribution. *Review of Economic Studies* 33, 309–19.
Kamin, S. (1999). The current international financial crisis: How much is new? *Journal of International Money and Finance* 18, 501–14.
Kanaya, A. and W. David (2000). The Japanese banking crisis of the 1990s: Sources and lessons. *IMF Working Paper* (WP/00/7).
Kataoka, T. (1997). Bank crisis, its causes and results. Working paper no. 9703, School of Business, Osaka City University.
Kato, M. and W. Semmler (2005). *Currency Crises and Monetary Policy Rules*. www.newschool.edu/gf/cem.
Keen, S. (2000). The nonlinear economics of debt deflation. In W. Barnett, C. Chiarella, S. Keen, R. Marks & H. Schnabl (eds.), *Commerce, Complexity and Evolution*, pp. 83–110. Cambridge University Press.
Keynes, J. (1936). *The General Theory of Employment, Interest and Money*. New York: Macmillan.
Kindleberger, C. (2000). *Manias, Panics, and Crashes: A History of Financial Crises*. New York: John Wiley.
King, R. (2000). The new IS–LM model: Language, logic, and limitations. *Federal Reserve Bank of Richmond Economic Quarterly* 86, 45–103.
Kiyotaki, N. and J. Moore (1995). Credit cycles. *Journal of Political Economy* 105, 211–248.
Köper, C. (2000). *Real–Financial Interaction in Contemporary Models of AS–AD Growth*. Berlin: Peter Lang.
Köper, C. and P. Flaschel (2000). Real–financial interaction: A Keynes–Metzler–Goodwin portfolio approach. Discussion Paper of the Faculty of Economics, University of Bielefeld, no. 442.
Krugman, P. (1999). Balance sheets, the transfer problem, and financial crises. *International Tax and Public Finance* 6, 459–72.
— (2000). Crises: The price of globalization. In *A Symposium: Global Economic Integration: Opportunities and Challenges*, Jackson Hole, Wyoming, pp. 75–106. Federal Reserve Bank of Kansas City.
Krugman, P. and M. Obstfeld (2003). *International Economics*. New York: Addison-Wesley.
Kuttner, K. and A. Posen (2001). The great recession: Lesson for macroeconomic policy from Japan. *Brookings Papers on Economic Activities* 2, 93–160.

— (2004). The difficulty of discerning what's too tight: Taylor rules and Japanese monetary policy. *North American Journal of Economics and Finance* 15, 53–74.
Lansing, K. J. (2008). Speculative growth and overreaction to technology shocks. Federal Reserve Bank of San Francisco, Working Paper Series no. 2008-08.
Lavoie, M. and W. Godley (2004). Features of a realistic banking system within a post-Keynesian stock-flow consistent model. CFAP Working Paper No. 12, Cambridge Judge Business School, University of Cambridge.
Lechevalier, S. (2003). *La Resegmentation du Marché du Travail Japonais depuis le Début des Années 1990: inégalités de sécurité de l'emploi, hétérogénéité des firmes et facteurs financiers*. Economics, Ecole des Hautes Etudes en Sciences Sociales, Blvd Raspail, 75005 Paris.
Marglin, S. (1984). *Growth Distribution and Prices*. Cambridge, MA: Harvard University Press.
Mehra, Y. (2000). Wage-price dynamics: Are they consistent with cost push? *Federal Reserve Bank of Richmond Quarterly Review* 86, 27–43.
Milesi-Ferretti, G. and A. Razin (1996). Current account sustainability: Selected East Asian and Latin American experiences. NBER working paper no. 5791, Cambridge.
— (1998). Sharp reduction in curent account deficits: An empirical analysis. NBER working paper no. 6310.
Miller, M. and J. Stiglitz (1999). Bankruptcy protection against macroeconomic shocks. CSGR Hot Topics: Research on Current Issues No.8.
Minsky, H. (1975). *John Maynard Keynes*. Columbia: New York University Press.
— (1982). *Can 'It' Happen Again? Essays on Instability and Finance*. Armonk: ME Sharpe.
— (1986). *Stabilizing an Unstable Economy*. New Haven: Yale University Press.
— (1992). The capital development of the economy and the structure of financial institutions. The Jerome Levy Economics Institute, Working Paper no. 72.
Mishkin, F. (1998). International capital movements, financial volatility and financial instability. National Bureau of Economic Research Working Paper no. 6390.
Nakaso, H. (2001). The financial crisis in Japan during the 1990s: How the Bank of Japan responded and the lessons learnt. BIS Working Papers no. 6.
North, D. (1990). *Institutions, Institutional Change and Economic Performance*. Cambridge University Press.
OECD (2002). Japan economic survey. Technical report, OECD.
Palley, T. (2002). Endogenous money: What it is and why it matters. *Metroeconomica* 53(2), 152–80.
Piazzesi, M. and M. Schneider (2009). Inflation and the price of real assets. Federal Reserve Bank of Minneapolis Staff Report no. 423.
Piazzesi, M., M. Schneider, and S. Tuzel (2005). Housing, consumption, and asset pricing. New York University, NBER Working Paper no. W12036.
Powell, A. and C. Murphy (1997). *Inside a Modern Macroeconometric Model. A Guide to the Murphy Model*. Heidelberg: Springer.
Proaño, C., P. Flaschel, and W. Semmler (2007). Currency and financial crises in emerging market economies in the medium run. *The Journal of Economic Asymmetries* 2, 105–30.
Reinhart, C. and K. Rogoff (2009). *This time is different: Eight centuries of financial folly*. Princeton University Press.
Rødseth, A. (2000). *Open Economy Macroeconomics*. Cambridge University Press.
Rogoff, K. (1999). International institutions for reducing global financial instability. NBER working paper no. 7265.
Rose, H. (1966). Unemployment in a theory of growth. *International Economic Review* 7, 260–82.

— (1967). On the nonlinear theory of the employment cycle. *Review of Economic Studies*, 153–73.

— (1990). *Macroeconomic Dynamics. A Marshallian Synthesis*. Cambridge, MA: Basil Blackwell.

Rosen, K. T. and L. B. Smith (1983). The price-adjustment process for rental housing and the natural vacancy rate. *The American Economic Review* 73(4), 779–86.

Rosser, J. B. (2000). *From Catastrophe to Chaos: A General Theory of Economic Discontinuities* (2nd edn.), Volume 1 of *Mathematics, Microeconomics, Macroeconomics, and Finance*. Boston: Kluwer Academic.

Röthig, A., W. Semmler, and P. Flaschel (2007). Corporate currency hedging and currency crises. *Australian Economic Papers* 2, 224–33.

Rowthorn, R. (1977). Conflict, inflation and money. *Cambridge Journal of Economics* 1(3), 215–39.

Sargent, T. (1987). *Macroeconomic Theory*. New York: Academic Press.

Schneider, M. and A. Tornell (2004). Balance sheet effects, bailout guarantees and financial crisis. *Review of Economic Studies* 71, 883–913.

Semmler, W. (2011). *Asset Prices, Booms and Recessions: Financial Economics from a Dynamic Perspective* (3rd ed). Heidelberg/New York: Springer (forthcoming).

Semmler, W. and Bernard, L. (2009). Banking, complex securities, and the credit crisis. *Economic & Political Weekly*, 44(13), 28 March–7 April.

Sethi, R. (1996). Endogenous regime switching in speculative markets. *Structural Change and Economic Dynamics* 7, 99–118.

Sgard, J. (2002). *L'Économie de la panique. Faire face aux crises financiéres*. Paris: La Découverte.

Shiller, R. J. (1991). *Market Volatility*. Cambridge, MA: MIT Press.

— (2001). *Irrational Exuberance*. New York: Random House.

Shilling, G. (1999). *Deflation. How to Survive and Thrive in the Coming Wave of Deflation*. New York: McGraw Hill.

Shilling, J. D., C. F. Sirmans, and J. B. Corgel (1987). Price adjustment process for rental office space. *Journal of Urban Economics* 22, 90–100.

Stiglitz, J., J. Ocampo, S. Siegel, R. French Davis, and D. Nayyar (2006). *Stability with Growth, Macroeconomics, Liberalization, and Development*. Oxford University Press.

Stock, J. and M. Watson (1999). Business cycle fluctuations in U.S. macroeconometric time series. *Handbook of Macroeconomics* 1(1), 3–64.

Tadeu Lima, G. and A. Meirelles (2003). Endogenous banking markup, distributional conflict and capacity utilization. *Metroeconomica* 54, 366–84.

Taylor, J. (1993). Discretion versus policy rules in practice. *Carnegie-Rochester Conference Series on Public Policy* 39, 195–214.

Tobin, J. (1969). A general equilibrium approach to monetary theory. *Journal of Money, Credit, and Banking* 1(1), 15–29.

— (1975). Keynesian models of recession and depression. *American Economic Review* 65(2), 195–202.

Van den Heuvel, S. (2002). Does bank capital matter for monetary transmission? *Federal Reserve Bank of New York Economic Policy Review* (May), 259–65.

Wilson, D. (2000). Japan's slow-down: monetary versus real explanations. *Oxford Review of Economic Policy* 16(2), 18–32.

Index